INVADING
MEXICO

INVADING MEXICO

AMERICA'S CONTINENTAL DREAM AND THE MEXICAN WAR,

1846–1848

JOSEPH WHEELAN

CARROLL & GRAF PUBLISHERS
NEW YORK

INVADING MEXICO
America's Continental Dream and the Mexican War, 1846–1848

Carroll & Graf Publishers
An Imprint of Avalon Publishing Group, Inc.
245 West 17th Street
11th Floor
New York, NY 10011

AVALON
publishing group incorporated

Library of Congress Cataloging-in-Publication Data is available.

ISBN-13: 978-0-78671-719-4
ISBN-10: 0-7867-1719-X

9 8 7 6 5 4 3 2 1

Interior design by Maria E. Torres

Printed in the United States of America
Distributed by Publishers Group West

*To my mother, Joan Barron, dean of Wyoming journalists,
who encouraged me to write*

CONTENTS

CAST OF CHARACTERS

UNITED STATES

Lieutenant Pierre G. T. Beauregard: The Louisianan's reconnaissance of Cerro Gordo would prove as consequential as his arguments shaping the plan of attack on Mexico City.

Senator Thomas Hart Benton: Variously a Polk adversary and ally, he urged taking the war into Mexico's heartland. When his beautiful daughter Jessie became John C. Frémont's teenaged bride, Benton aggressively promoted his son-in-law's endeavors.

Major Jacob Brown: He supervised the construction of a fort for General Zachary Taylor's army on the Rio Grande and then gave his name to it by becoming the war's first fallen hero.

Secretary of State James Buchanan: The ambitious Buchanan's shadowy political maneuverings caused Polk to distrust his key adviser's judgment and motives. But Buchanan would one day see his dreams become reality.

Colonel Jefferson Davis: The future president of the Confederacy led the Mexican War's best-known volunteer regiment, the Mississippi Rifles, in two of the biggest battles of the war, turning the tide in one of them.

Colonel Alexander W. Doniphan: The towering red-haired lawyer-militiaman's mounted troops would perform astounding feats of courage and endurance that would evoke comparisons to "Xenophon's Ten Thousand."

Captain John C. Frémont: The Byronesque "Pathfinder," married to the influential Senator Thomas Hart Benton's beautiful daughter, was the era's most celebrated explorer. Frémont figured prominently in California's transformation from Mexican province to U.S. state.

Lieutenant Archibald Gillespie: His secret mission at the behest of the president would change John Frémont's plans, and possibly California's future.

Lieutenant Ulysses S. Grant: Unhappy as a minder of mules, young Grant found a way to get into battle and proved his resourcefulness on the battlefield at Mexico City.

Lieutenant Thomas Jackson: Quiet, intense, and misanthropic, the young artillery officer's reckless courage would amaze everyone. The future "Stonewall" could as easily have won his nickname at Chapultepec as later at Manassas.

Colonel Stephen Watts Kearny: The intrepid Indian fighter would have arguably the most arduous mission of all, once the fighting began, taking him across the Great Plains to two war zones and a climactic showdown at Los Angeles.

George W. Kendall: The resourceful editor of the New Orleans *Picayune* was the best-known of the syndicated newspaper correspondents covering the war, enjoying unmatched access to the battlefront. As the correspondents' unofficial leader, Kendall organized an efficient system of speeding battlefield dispatches to publication in the United States.

Captain Robert E. Lee: The Army would discover that the son of the famed "Light Horse Harry" Lee was a gifted reconnaissance officer and a tremendous battlefield asset.

The Mormons: Hounded from Missouri and Illinois, murdered prophet Joseph Smith's followers were broke and in trouble. President James Polk's proposition would result in the creation of a unique military unit, the Mormon Battalion.

General Gideon Pillow: President Polk's former law partner was never much of a military leader, but he was a ruthless politician who had the president's ear, as Winfield Scott would discover to his misfortune.

President James K. Polk: A disciple of Andrew Jackson, the Tennessee Democrat was the first "dark horse" president. The eleventh president, arguably the hardest-working chief executive in U.S. history, so coveted California that he was ready to force Mexico into a war to obtain it.

General of the Army Winfield Scott: His daring expedition into Mexico's heartland would demonstrate why Scott was the best American general between the Revolutionary and Civil wars. But vanity and tactlessness would damage his career and his presidential hopes.

John Slidell: A leading Louisiana attorney and deft political operative, he helped get James Polk to the White House. His diplomatic mission to Mexico City set the course for war.

Commodore Robert F. Stockton: The swashbuckling expansionist, engineer, businessman, and scion of one of New Jersey's wealthiest families was willing to do whatever was needed to help the United States obtain Texas and California.

General Zachary Taylor: Beloved by his men, plainspoken "Old Rough and Ready" led them to the war's first victories. President James Polk only belatedly recognized that his Whig general was a greater threat than Scott to the Democrats' plans to retain control of the White House.

Henry David Thoreau: As President James Polk was settling into the White House, Thoreau was preparing to move to Walden Pond. Because he did not pay his poll tax, he would go to jail and later write a famous essay.

Nicholas Trist: The chief clerk of the Department of State would become arguably the most consequential U.S. diplomat since James Monroe went to France. While his stubborn willfulness would serve America well, Trist would pay a steep price for his great achievement.

Captain Sam Walker: Slouching, slender, and blue-eyed, he didn't look like a leathery Texas Ranger, but he was one of the most famous of the breed.

David Wilmot: The freshman Pennsylvania congressman's stunning amendment would reopen the debate over slavery and forever link his name to it.

General William J. Worth: A hero of the Battle of Monterrey, the much-respected Worth anguished over his losses at Molino del Rey and grew to hate Scott by the war's end.

MEXICO

General Jose Castro: After attempting to drive Captain John Frémont from Northern California and subdue the American settlers, Castro and his Southern California counterpart would reach an important understanding.

Jose Fernando Ramirez: The Mexico City lawyer's faith in Mexico's army would crumble with his nation's military fortunes.

The San Patricios: The Irish-American deserters became Santa Anna's best artillery unit, fighting under their own green banner. But they paid dearly for their treachery.

General Antonio Lopez de Santa Anna: Brave, devious, and power-hungry, the exiled Mexican president had an irresistible proposition for President Polk that would restore him to Mexico's leadership, but not in the capacity that Polk had envisioned.

General Romulo Diaz de la Vega: Captured after fierce resistance at Resaca de la Palma, the artillery commander so charmed Lieutenant George Meade that Meade invited him to his Pittsburgh home. La Vega would be paroled to fight again—and to become a prisoner again.

PROLOGUE

*"Time, with his scythe and hourglass, had brought another and a newer race.
. . . Nothing could exceed the beauty of this spectacle. . . ."*

—Lieutenant Raphael Semmes, with the U.S. invasion fleet off Vera Cruz

MARCH 9, 1847: D-DAY, VERA CRUZ, MEXICO

Like an actor taking center stage, General of the Army Winfield Scott appeared
on the quarterdeck of the USS *Massachusetts,* evoking a thunderous roar from the
men of the vast American invasion fleet. Scarcely acknowledging the loud acclaim
of the thousands of troops, Scott peered through a spyglass at the tropical coastal
plain two miles away. The climactic moment of invasion was nearly at hand.

The Mexican shore lay in deceptive repose beneath eighteen-thousand-foot
Mt. Orizaba, whose snowy summit glistened in the late-afternoon sunshine.
Upholstered in yards of tailored blue cloth that glinted with gilt and braid, the six-
foot-four Scott, who had the figure of the gourmand and gourmet that he was,
might have been a human counterpart to the immense peak.

The cheering for the Army commander crested and ebbed as the *Massachusetts*
threaded its way through the largest-ever assembly of U.S. warships—eighty vessels, their decks jammed with sailors and six thousand soldiers. Scott's shock
troops were to conduct the first major American amphibious assault, thereby
opening a second front in the ten-month-old Mexican War.

Scott and the Army regulars and volunteers aboard the ships anxiously watched
the sixty-seven shallow-draft, flat-bottomed surfboats two miles away, arrayed in
parallel rows 450 yards from Collado Beach. The specially designed thirty-five-foot

boats bobbing in the light chop were filled with the twenty-five hundred blue-clad regulars of General William J. Worth's First Division. They would land first. Besides weapons and ammunition, each man carried a haversack with two days' provisions, canteens, and a greatcoat or a blanket.

No one knew what terrors awaited them on the beach—perhaps thousands of enemy troops, or hidden artillery batteries, or lancers poised to gallop from hiding places behind the sand dunes to cut down the invaders in the surf. Scott himself secretly dreaded "meeting at our landing the most formidable struggle of the war."

In the thin-hulled craft, coxswains, oarsmen, and Worth's troops nervously awaited the signal to commence the invasion. Lieutenant George P. McClellan and his men, hunched down in one of the surfboats with eight Navy crewmen, silently contemplated the manifold perils before them. The strains of "Yankee Doodle," "Hail Columbia," and the "Star-Spangled Banner" reaching them from the regimental bands aboard Scott's armada did not wholly steady their nerves.

"Everyone expected to hear and feel their [Mexican] batteries open every instant," wrote McClellan. Lieutenant Gustavius W. Smith, busy attending to his troops and to his mortally ill captain, who had insisted on accompanying his men, grimly observed: "A single cannon-shot striking one of the closely packed surfboats would probably have sent it, and all on board, to the bottom."

Far more ebullient were the six thousand soldiers who would go ashore next, after the surfboats finished landing Worth's division. Private George Ballentine avouched that he and his comrades would have instantly traded places with Worth's first wave and "gladly incurred the hazard of the enterprise, for the shadow of glory with the distinction conferred."

Anchored at Sacrificios Island were three European warships, tarrying during a routine deployment to watch the riveting spectacle. Their sailors hung in their ships' rigging like "so many robins or black birds on a wild cherry tree, or crows on trees watching the dead carcass lying beneath," morbidly noted Jacob J. Oswandel of the Pennsylvania Volunteers.

A pair of third-class U.S. steamers with double-shotted guns, the *Vixen* and *Spitfire*, and five schooner-gunboats hovered ninety yards offshore as the figures of Mexican horsemen phantasmagorially appeared and vanished among the fifty-foot-high sand dunes behind the beach.

• • •

Three miles beyond Collado Beach, the invaders' objective rose in a jumble of domes and spires: the port city of Vera Cruz, gateway to Mexico City, the enemy capital 280 miles distant. Nearly five thousand Mexican troops had spent weeks readying Vera Cruz's strong fortifications.

Six days earlier, Vera Cruz's military governor had spurned Scott's surrender ultimatum, overruling civil authorities who wanted to hand over the city without a fight. Scott and his staff speculated about whether Antonio Lopez de Santa Anna, Mexico's president and army commander, would march to Vera Cruz's aid from Mexico City. But Mexico City was once again convulsed by civil war, and Santa Anna would not be sending reinforcements.

• • •

Aboard Commodore David Conner's flagship *Raritan,* Navy Lieutenant Raphael Semmes had the odd sensation that he was seeing history repeat itself. "Every step of our progress was fraught with the associations of three hundred years; and the mind, as it recognized object after object, famous in the history of the [Spanish] conquest, became tinctured with the romance of that remote period, and emulous of the deeds which had characterized its actors. Time, with his scythe and hourglass, had brought another and a newer race. . . . Nothing could exceed the beauty of this spectacle. . . ."

Indeed, a surprisingly large number of the American troops knew that Hernando Cortes and his conquistadors had landed on this very shore on Good Friday in 1519. Planting their black velvet flag emblazoned with a red cross surrounded by blue and white flames, the Spanish invaders had proclaimed New Spain's first colony Villa Rica de Vera Cruz, "Rich Town of the True Cross"—the first of three Vera Cruzes on this coast. From here, the Spaniards had begun their famous march to the Valley of Mexico, seat of the mighty Aztec empire.

However, Scott had selected Collado Beach, not because of its umbilical connection to Cortes, but because of his wish to avoid the enemy's formidable defenses. A military scholar who brought a five-foot shelf of military manuals, histories, and biographies on his campaigns, General Winfield Scott was a devotee of Napoleonic tactics and strategy, which eschewed frontal assaults. Collado Beach was not only beyond the range of Vera Cruz's 250 guns, it was eight miles from San Juan de Ulua, regarded as the most impregnable fort in North America. Defended by 1,030 Mexican troops, Ulua lay a thousand yards offshore from Vera Cruz. Its batteries bristled with 135 guns, and its thick walls of soft coral were said to be impervious to cannon fire. Scott intended to slip behind Vera Cruz and attack it from the rear, avoiding Ulua altogether.

This day was personally auspicious for Scott, known by the nickname "Old Fuss and Feathers" because of his devotion to martial discipline and sartorial splendor. It was the thirty-third anniversary of Scott's promotion to general. Following the early disasters of the War of 1812, President James Madison and War Secretary John Armstrong had rooted out all of their dilatory, timid, incompetent generals, whose average age was sixty, and replaced them with aggressive, younger officers whose average age was thirty-six. Besides twenty-seven-year-old Scott, the new generals had included Andrew Jackson, Alexander Macomb, William Henry Harrison, Edmund Pendleton Gaines, and Jacob Brown. Upon Macomb's death in 1841, Scott succeeded him as General of the Army and held that rank when the Mexican War began.

• • •

With General Zachary Taylor's army fighting in northern Mexico, and Mexican leaders evincing no interest in U.S. peace overtures, President James K. Polk had sent Scott to invade central Mexico and end the war. After rendezvousing at Lobos Island, 120 miles north of Vera Cruz, Scott's invasion fleet had lumbered down Mexico's Gulf Coast, reaching Anton Lizardo, the Navy anchorage south of Vera Cruz, on March 2, 1847. Observed one awed soldier, "The whole eastern horizon looked like a wall of canvas." There were so many masts, noted Oswandel of the Pennsylvania Volunteers, that the staging area looked "more like a wilderness of dead pine trees than so many spars and riggings of ships."

Singing "We Are Bound for the Shores of Mexico," eighty-six hundred of Scott's twelve thousand troops—the others remaining on forty-five ships at Anton Lizardo—boarded transport vessels to the staging site, Sacrificios Island, so named by the Spanish for the human sacrifices once performed there. After nearly a month on board ship, many troops, including Lieutenant Ulysses S. Grant, longed to get off the cramped ships and tread solid ground again. "The transports used were built for carrying freight and possessed but limited accommodations for passengers," Grant understatedly observed.

• • •

Four days before the planned landing, Scott, his staff, and Commodore Conner had conducted a harrowing, nearly disastrous reconnaissance of Vera Cruz and San Juan de Ulua. Boarding the small steamer *Petrita,* a prize from an aborted raid on Tabasco in October, the scouting party first examined Collado Beach and then followed the shoreline to Vera Cruz. While studying the formidable Ulua fortress through spyglasses from a mile away, the American officers watched as gunners raced to their batteries. Then the castle's big cannons began firing at the steamer. The first round was long, a second round fell short, and a third burst overhead. The *Petrita*'s pilot hastily raised a head of steam and carried the officers out of range as more errant shells splashed down nearby.

Had the gunners been better marksmen, they might have wiped out the American leadership and scuttled the landing. Besides Scott and Conner, the invasion's land and sea marshals, the steamer also carried Scott's three division commanders, Generals Worth, Robert Patterson, and Gideon Pillow; Scott's chief of staff, Lieutenant Colonel Ethan Allen Hitchcock; Captains Robert E. Lee and Joseph E. Johnston; and Lieutenants Pierre G. T. Beauregard and George G. Meade.

• • •

Along the departure line marked by the first-class steamer *Princeton*'s anchorage a quarter mile from Collado Beach, the twenty-five hundred soldiers crouching behind the gunwales of their frail landing craft silently prayed that they would reach dry land alive. They hyperalertly scanned the sand dunes and watched the sun dip toward Mt. Orizaba. They waited for the "go" signal.

• • •

At 5:30 P.M., a cannon boomed on the *Massachusetts,* and everyone's pulse quickened. It was the signal. The regimental bands launched into their repertoire of patriotic songs, beginning with the thrilling "Yankee Doodle." The surfboat crewmen pulled for shore, the coxswains counting cadence. "With each stroke of our oars . . . [we] expected a withering fire," wrote Frederick Zeh, a German immigrant in the first wave. Mexican cavalrymen appeared and vanished among the dunes like smoke. Shells and cannonballs suddenly whistled over the Americans' heads, causing a momentary fright. Was it the dreaded enemy artillery? No, it was American gunboats aiming at Mexican sentinels on shore.

From the line of advancing surfboats, one pulled sharply ahead of the others into the shallows. A figure leaped into water up to his armpits, the sun glinting off his gold braid. General William Worth, the division commander and a hero of Monterrey six months earlier, claimed the distinction of being the first U.S. soldier to reach Collado Beach. The other boats grounded on a small sandbar, and soldiers jumped into water reaching to their knees, and sometimes their necks, holding their muskets and ammunition boxes aloft.

The Mexicans didn't fire a shot. The first U.S. troops splashed ashore, formed up on the beach, unfurled their regimental colors, and dashed to the top of the sand hills. There wasn't an enemy soldier in sight. At 5:40 P.M., a mere ten minutes into the invasion, the invaders planted the American flag on a high dune. The roar that went up from the jubilant troops on the beach traveled to the fleet, and three cheers rolled back to shore, along with the strains of "The Star Spangled Banner."

Sentries were posted, fires appeared up and down the beach, and the troops washed down their cold supper of fat pork and biscuits with hot coffee.

The surfboats, meanwhile, returned to the transport ships to shuttle more soldiers ashore. Five hours after the first landing, the entire assault force of eighty-six hundred men was on the beach without a single casualty, "to the astonishment of all," as Scott observed.

During the night, two hundred Mexican lancers harassed the Americans with musket fire. These were the first shots fired in anger that most of the volunteers had ever heard, including Zeh, who confessed "that the hissing of bullets right next to me for the first time stirred in my breast very unpleasant, melancholy feelings." The skirmishing subsided after ten minutes.

• • •

From behind Vera Cruz's twelve-foot-high walls, citizens and soldiers stolidly watched the Americans secure their beachhead. General Jose Juan de Landero declined to risk his small force of five thousand men in a gamble to drive the Americans into the sea. He kept them at work preparing the fortifications, knowing that no reinforcements would be coming to Vera Cruz's aid.

While the Mexican government had abandoned Vera Cruz to its fate, the city's defenders were full of fight. Five days earlier, soldiers and citizens had celebrated their determination to defend their city with a rally, procession, and music. Few really believed, though, that they would be able to withstand the attack that was coming.

• • •

The war had begun nearly a year earlier when Mexican cavalry ambushed General Zachary Taylor's dragoons along the Rio Grande. By March 1847, Taylor's army had waged four major battles in northern Mexico; fighting had also occurred in New Mexico and California. Yet, despite the United States' insuperable technological advantages in firepower, its superbly trained regular Army, and a population nearly three times Mexico's 7.5 million people, Mexico was far from beaten. President James K. Polk and General Winfield Scott believed that only the conquest of Mexico City would compel Mexico to negotiate peace.

The precipitating attack on the dragoons, which occurred in April 1846 in disputed territory (although Polk insisted that Mexico had "shed American blood on American soil"), had climaxed a year of spiking tensions. The ambush enabled Polk, who was already planning to go to war, to ask Congress to declare that a "state of war exists," to appropriate $10 million, and to authorize him to raise fifty thousand troops.

On May 13, 1846, Congress approved all these measures, cutting off the protests of a handful of war opponents who would become the nucleus for the first important U.S. antiwar movement. It marked the first time, but it would not be the last—witness the sinking of the *Maine,* the purported Gulf of Tonkin attacks, and Iraq's weapons of mass destruction—that an arguable pretext would plunge the United States into war.

But "Mr. Polk's War," as its opponents called it—and James Polk did indeed supervise its every aspect—was not so much due to the dispute over Texas's putative border as to the president's eagerness to divest Mexico of California and the New Mexico territory. Polk envisioned an America stretching from "sea to shining sea," thereby fulfilling her "Manifest Destiny," a catchphrase for an expansionist eighteenth-century political philosophy dating to Thomas Jefferson. But he did not foresee that expansionism would kindle a bitter debate over slavery, resulting in the catastrophic American Civil War.

In invading Mexico, the United States was upholding an American Revolution–era doctrine whose last avatar would be James K. Polk.

1

"THE MOLE"

"So far as principle & measures are concerned, my path is plainly marked before me & I shall pursue it without turning to the right or to the left. My opinions & political doctrines are not of yesterday."

—President James K. Polk

MARCH 4, 1845: WASHINGTON

President-elect James K. Polk and President John Tyler drew their heads together in their open carriage so that they could converse over the rain drumming loudly on their umbrellas. The rain had fallen without letup for nearly a day and now drenched the long parade to the Capitol, where at noon Polk would be sworn in as the nation's eleventh chief executive. Ahead of the presidential carriage marched ten companies of cavalry and light infantry troops. Polk and Tyler nodded to the dense crowds that lined the street despite the rain; a record thirty thousand people had come to Washington for the inauguration.

Save for the throngs of parade-watchers, Washington, D.C., on this dreary day, appeared much as it had forty-four years earlier when Thomas Jefferson had walked from his rooming house to the unfinished Capitol during the city's first presidential inauguration. Charles Dickens described mid-nineteenth-century Washington in *American Notes* as a place of "spacious avenues, that begin in nothing, and lead nowhere; streets, mile-long, that only want houses, roads, and inhabitants. . . ."

Neither the capital's lack of grandeur nor the rain could dampen Polk's high spirits; this was a day that he could have never imagined except for the singular events of the past year. His stunning Democratic presidential nomination, a bolt from heaven, was aptly summed up by the opposition Whigs' campaign slogan, "Who is James K. Polk?" Polk had then further shocked the experts by winning the election. Polk's carriage companion, whose road to the presidency had been equally serendipitous, could understand the rather pleasant cognitive dissonance that Polk was experiencing. Exactly four years earlier, John Tyler, then vice president-elect, had watched the frail, weary president-elect, William Henry Harrison—the "Tippecanoe" of the popular campaign slogan, "Tippecanoe and Tyler Too"— deliver a two-hour oration on a cold, windy day. A month later, Harrison was dead of pneumonia, jaundice, and overwhelming septicemia. The matter of presidential succession, never questioned before and unaddressed in the Constitution, was resolved by Tyler's determined claim on the office, thereby earning him the bitter-sweet sobriquet, "His Accidency."

Earlier on the morning of Polk's inauguration, Tyler had joined James and Sarah Polk in their room at Coleman's Hotel and had held private discussions with the president-elect before setting out for the Capitol. Outside the hotel, Polk supporters greeted the presidential party with hickory branches to show their solidarity with "Young Hickory." The nickname, a needed antidote to Polk's colorless image, played on the nickname of his mentor—Andrew Jackson, "Old Hickory," still the Democrats' patriarch, although his scarred, seventy-seven-year-old body was shutting down. Without Jackson's political acumen and influence, Polk's nomination and election would have been impossible.

Polk and Tyler arrived at the Capitol as Vice President-elect George M. Dallas, a former senator, minister to Russia, and Philadelphia mayor, was concluding his inaugural address in the Senate chamber. Dallas joined Polk and Tyler on a temporary platform over the east portico, where the president-elect began delivering his own inaugural address to "a large assemblage of umbrellas."

• • •

The twenty-minute speech was a conflation of Jeffersonian ideology—Polk's campaign biography had not exaggerated in depicting him as a Jeffersonian republican of the "straitest sect"—and Jacksonian action.

"Without solicitation on my part, I have been chosen by the free and voluntary suffrages of my countrymen to the most honorable and most responsible office on earth," he began. He made a pledge, which he would not honor, to eschew party politics and "not be the President of a part only, but of the whole people of the United States."

His fiscal philosophy could have been written by Thomas Jefferson himself: "Ours was intended to be a plain and frugal government, and I shall regard it to be my duty . . . to enforce by all the means within my power the strictest economy in the expenditure of the public money. . . ."

As for the rest, it might just as well have been Old Hickory speaking—and, in fact, Jackson's former speechwriter, Amos Kendall, had helped Polk write the address. The new president vowed to block any effort to reestablish a national bank; and he promised to reduce tariffs, to obtain the Oregon Territory, and to annex Texas. "We need no national banks," Polk said; indeed, as a congressman in the 1830s, he had played an indispensable role in Jackson's successful campaign to thwart the charter renewal for the Second Bank of the United States. Polk instead favored an independent treasury.

Imports should be taxed to produce revenue, with "reasonable incidental protection to our home industry," but not for protection alone, declared Polk, to the delight of fellow Southerners who wanted low tariffs for their cotton, and to the consternation of Northerners who favored higher tariffs to protect their manufactured goods from foreign competition.

However, the people hadn't come to Washington to hear Polk expound on banking and tariffs, but on Oregon and Texas. And now they heard what they had hoped that they would hear.

Regarding Oregon—a vast territory stretching from the northern border of Mexico's Upper California province (present-day California) at 42° latitude, to the southern border of Russian Alaska, at 54°40'—Polk said the United States' title was "clear and unquestionable," the very words of a Democratic National Convention resolution adopted the previous May. Great Britain and the United States, who both claimed the remote territory, had consented in 1818 to joint occupancy. The arrangement was extended indefinitely in 1827 while negotiations were held. But years of intermittent talks had yielded no treaty, and Polk planned to invoke the joint agreement's one-year notice of cancellation. In his inauguration speech, however, Polk only promised to "assert and maintain by all constitutional means" America's right to the territory.

• • •

But Polk's position on Texas annexation was the reason for his nomination and election. After General Antonio Lopez de Santa Anna's Mexican army was annihilated in eighteen minutes at San Jacinto on April 21, 1836, the Lone Star flag had flown over the sovereign Republic of Texas for nine years, despite halfhearted attempts by Mexico to reclaim her province.

Polk, whose political aspirations in 1844 only compassed becoming former President Martin Van Buren's running mate, had emerged from the party's fractious national convention in Baltimore with the presidential nomination because of one assertion, made on April 23, 1844: "I am in favour of the immediate re-annexation of Texas to the territory and Government of the United States." This position placed him at odds with Van Buren and the Whig nominee, Henry Clay, but in stride with popular sentiment. Before there were polls, there was intuition, and the shrewd Democratic Party demigod, Andrew Jackson, intuitively knew that the people wanted to annex Texas. Jackson pushed Polk's candidacy over Van Buren's.

President John Tyler in 1844 tried to make Texas annexation his legacy issue but failed. Then, on February 28, 1845, four days before Polk's inauguration, Congress, at the behest of both Tyler and Polk, approved a joint resolution to invite Texas to join the United States. Ignoring Mexico's warnings, Tyler signed the resolution, leaving to Polk the tricky job of carrying it out.

• • •

Looking out over the soggy assemblage on the Capitol lawn, Polk pledged to "consummate the expressed will" of the American people and annex Texas. It was a question that involved only Texas and the United States, he asserted. "Foreign nations have no right to interfere with them or to take exception to their reunion." Specifically, Polk was referring to Britain and France, who preferred an independent Texas as a trading partner, and to Mexico, who wanted Texas back. The congressional resolution had caused Mexico's minister plenipotentiary, General Juan Nepomuceno Almonte, to angrily start packing his bags; never having recognized Texas's independence, Mexico regarded its annexation as sufficient reason for breaking off relations. Polk's uncompromising words assured Almonte's imminent departure.

For those who might mistake praiseworthy expansionism for brazen territorial aggrandizement, Polk offered soothing double-talk: "Our union is a confederation of independent States, whose policy is peace with each other and all the world. To enlarge its limits is to extend the dominions of peace over additional territories and increasing millions."

When Polk finished speaking, Chief Justice Roger B. Taney administered the oath of office, and James K. Polk at age forty-nine became the youngest president in the United States' fifty-six-year history. The rain continued to pour down. Cannons belched smoke, and a cheering crowd accompanied Polk to the White House. In keeping with the inauguration's Jacksonian themes, the doors were opened to the mighty and humble—and, evidently, to even the criminal class: at the reception, a man had his pocket picked while talking to the new president.

That night at the two inaugural balls—at Carusi's Saloon and the National Theater—there was a general consensus of approval for Polk's address. Some Whigs even praised the speech. Diarist and former New York City Mayor Philip Hone pronounced it "a plain, sensible document, not very elegantly written, but apparently honest, and creditable on the whole to its author."

• • •

The year 1845 was pregnant with auguries and the anticipatory air of a great adventure about to begin. Nearly a million Americans held manufacturing jobs. Railroad tracks were being laid at a feverish pace, although steamboats remained ascendant and, in fact, were just entering their golden age, with a traveler able to reach Louisville from New Orleans in less than five days. The telegraph, invented in 1832 by Samuel F. B. Morse (his namesake telegraphic code followed in 1838), was slowly transforming communications. The telegraph line connecting Baltimore and Washington now extended nearly to Richmond.

Dr. Crawford Long's anesthetic gas was beginning to ease the pain of surgery, as Charles Goodyear's vulcanized rubber was easing the pain of travel. Matthew Brady operated a chain of studios employing Louis Daguerre's photography precursor, the daguerreotype; Polk would become the first U.S. president whose image was captured on one. Cyrus McCormick's reaper was introducing efficient, larger-scale farming techniques to the prairies, while Samuel Colt's revolving-cylinder pistol brought greater efficiency to the crimson science of slaughter.

The population was growing rapidly because of a high birth rate and a wave of immigrants from potato-blighted Ireland, quickening the characteristic American urge to pull up stakes and move west. In 1789, three million people lived in thirteen states. In 1840, there were 17.1 million Americans living in twenty-six states, and the population increased by 36 percent during the 1840s, to 23.2 million people living in thirty-one states in 1850. These numbers did not include the 2.5 million black slaves living on Southern farms and plantations, whose soaring production of cotton made it America's leading export; 1836–1840 cotton exports of $321 million would increase to $744.6 million in 1856–1860. In

American Notes, Dickens described the migratory Americans as "descendants of Cain proper to this continent, who seem destined from their birth to serve as pioneers in the great human army."

• • •

The man now at the throttle of this sprawling dynamo, President James Polk, possessed many attributes, but patience was not one of them. At least in one important respect, this was understandable; no president before or since had promised, as Polk did, to serve just one term. As the compromise candidate of a divided Democratic party, he rightly concluded that only a one-term pledge would unite his party's factions long enough for him to be elected. Although, as future events would reveal, Polk sometimes reneged on his promises, he never considered seeking reelection, even when beseeched by Democrats.

With just four years to accomplish his stated goals, Polk drove himself harder than any president before or since. He intended to take possession of Oregon, annex Texas, reduce the tariff, and establish an independent treasury. "The path of duty lies plain before me," he told New York Governor Silas Wright on July 8, 1845, and he would "pursue it whatever may be the consequences to myself without turning to the right or to the left."

• • •

The new president had omitted from his inaugural speech what he desired above all: California, and possibly Mexico's other immense northernmost province, New Mexico, which included all or part of the future Arizona, Colorado, Nevada, and Utah.

With Mexico accusing the United States of trying to steal Texas, it would have been impolitic for Polk to evince interest in California and New Mexico. Yet the president had confided this express design soon after his inauguration to his new Secretary of the Navy, the historian George Bancroft—slapping his thigh for emphasis, as Bancroft would recall years later.

Polk would launch several covert operations in California before publicly professing any interest in the province. By then, the president's secretiveness and obsessive planning would be well known to Washingtonians, who would not disagree with the nickname that Polk's friends had bestowed upon him, "The Mole."

• • •

Portraits and daguerreotypes of James Polk are windows to his character. The high forehead, prominent cheekbones, and hard, penetrating steel-gray eyes set in deep sockets convey his chilly intensity, stubbornness, and unbreachable reserve. Even the shadowy, tight-lipped smile suggests a man who habitually conceals his thoughts and feelings behind a mask of stiff amiability.

Polk was born in 1795 in Mecklenburg County, North Carolina, where his father, Sam Polk, raised cotton on a four-hundred-acre farm in the rich bottom-land along Sugar Creek, south of present-day Charlotte. His mother, the former Jane Knox, was the great-grandniece of John Knox, the father of Presbyterianism.

In 1806, the Sam Polk family left North Carolina. After traveling through five hundred miles of wilderness and over the Appalachian Mountains, the Polks settled on the Duck River, near Columbia, Tennessee, in an area of canebrakes more than ten feet high. Sam Polk cleared the land, built a home, went into the land business, and prospered. His influential friends included Tennessee's first congressman, Andrew Jackson, a frequent visitor to the Polk home. The forty-year-old Revolutionary War veteran's acquaintance with Sam Polk's sickly son would evolve into an enduring political and personal friendship.

• • •

A thin, undersized, studious boy, James was fifteen when he was afflicted with severe, chronic abdominal pain that prevented him from attending school regularly or forming close friendships with peers. His parents took him to a succession of doctors who tried every known nostrum. None provided relief. By James's seventeenth birthday, his family was certain that he had a bladder stone, and the only remedy, besides the stone's natural passage through the body in its own good time, was a lithotomy, at that time a rare surgical procedure.

Seeking relief from the stabbing pains that doubled him up without warning, James in 1812 embarked with an uncle on the eight-hundred-mile trip through the western wilderness to Philadelphia, where the renowned surgeon Dr. Philip Physick had agreed to perform the operation. But in Kentucky, when James was felled by his worst attack yet, his uncle found a Danville physician, Dr. Ephraim McDowell, who agreed to operate immediately. McDowell prepped the teenager for surgery according to the medical protocol of the day: he strapped Polk to a table, gave him brandy, and began to cut.

Amazingly, when considering the little that was then known about the causes of infection, or the deadly threat posed by sepsis, Polk completely recovered. However, the operation that cured him probably left him sterile; Polk never fathered children. His long apprenticeship in pain and semi-invalidism also kindled a blazing ambition and an urgent desire to make up for lost time.

At an age when most young men had completed their schooling, eighteen-year-old James began his in earnest. He asked his father to enroll him in Bradley Academy in Murfreesboro, Tennessee. There he obtained the classical education that his invalidism had made impossible. Two years later, the intense scholar entered the University of North Carolina where, as a member of the university debating team, James once argued the portentous question: "Would an extension of territory be an advantage to the U.S.?" In 1818, he graduated with "first honors," or class valedictorian, in the classics and mathematics.

Polk studied law in Nashville, Tennessee, with Felix Grundy, the ex-congressman and former Jeffersonian radical; after being admitted to the bar in 1820, Polk returned to Columbia, opened a law practice, and speculated in land with his father. He was a smart, capable lawyer who won cases by addressing juries in plain language. In 1819, he was elected clerk of the Tennessee State Senate and was re-elected in 1820. When the Senate was in session in Murfreesboro, the state capital from 1819 to 1826, Polk kept a record of its proceedings, earning $6 a day. So began his apprenticeship in politics.

• • •

In Murfreesboro, Polk also made the acquaintance of his lifelong companion, Sarah Childress, a local belle. Her father, Joel, a farmer and tavern owner, had achieved an odd celebrity for having purchased, for the princely sum of $500, a dress uniform that had belonged to Andrew Jackson at the time of his great 1815 New Orleans victory.

James Polk and Sarah Childress married on New Year's Day, 1824. Theirs was a happy match of soulmates; Sarah was as much a devotee of politics as James. Later, when James represented Tennessee in Congress, Sarah was a daily visitor to the House gallery. Stylish, charming, intelligent, and vivacious, she was an accomplished hostess as well as a savvy political confidante to her husband.

Politics was the Polks' vocation and avocation, the source of their friendships, and the sum of their intellectual pursuits. James Polk labored with intensity to succeed as a politician and, later, as president. His single-mindedness, however, caused the famed explorer Charles Wilkes to observe that when Polk wasn't talking about politics, he resembled a "penny postman" with little to say.

• • •

It is a testament to Polk's determination that he could rise above his inherent reserve, lack of natural charisma, and pessimistic view of mankind to become one of the leading congressmen of his era. As befitted a descendant of John Knox, he was raised as a Presbyterian, although never baptized. Presbyterianism, Polk once acknowledged, had imparted to him the bleak certainty that "from the fall of our first great parent until the present hour, man has been depraved, frail, and impure." The Polks' intrinsic Calvinism compelled them both to shun cards, horse races, and dancing—Washington's socially acceptable pleasures.

Polk's sober outlook, drive, and fanatical work habits could cause him to be unreasonable, impatient, demanding, and self-righteous. But Polk knew that these weren't winning qualities in a politician, so he willed himself to develop a courteous but formal conversational style and a vigorous handshake. This public persona, described by his biographer, Charles Sellers, as "controlled affability," masked Polk's natural shyness and stiffness. He did possess one attribute that any politician would envy—a remarkable memory that, he claimed, enabled him to recall even a decade later the name of any man with whom he had conversed for ten minutes.

When addressing an audience, Polk assiduously practiced a popular oratorical style that early in his career earned him the nickname "the Napoleon of the Stump." Polk's political foes rated him only a fair orator but recognized the effort that went into his speeches. John Quincy Adams assayed him to be "just qualified for an eminent County Court lawyer. . . . He has no wit, no literature, no point of argument, no gracefulness of delivery, no elegance of language, no philosophy, no pathos, no felicitous impromptus; nothing that can constitute an orator, but confidence, fluency and labor."

• • •

Polk never wavered in his faith in limited government, low taxes, low tariffs, and "republican economy and simplicity." His Jeffersonian orthodoxy became his ideological lodestar, his avowals of which were numbingly mantralike. Months after he had reassured Silas Wright that his views were unchanged, he told another correspondent, in nearly the same words, that his philosophy "is not of yesterday. . . . My opinions remain unchanged and on measures of policy, my path is plainly marked before me. I shall pursue this path without turning to the right or to the left."

In a House speech years before his presidency, Polk, sounding very much like Thomas Jefferson, described how he would ideally govern: "I would sell out the public lands at low prices—at much lower prices than they have ever been sold. I would have them speedily settled by a hardy race of enterprising freemen, who would feel that they had a stake in the government. I would impose no unnecessary taxation upon them, to support any particular interest. I would relieve the burdens of the whole community, as far as possible, by reducing the taxes. I would keep as much money in the treasury as the safety of the government required, and no more. I would keep no surplus revenue there to scramble for, either for internal improvements, or for anything else. I would bring the government back to what it was intended to be—a plain economical government."

•••

Polk's Jeffersonianism was in his blood, passed down from his iconoclast grandfather Ezekiel Polk, a Deist who greeted Jefferson's election in 1800 with jubilation. The Polks had always been on the Jeffersonian side of the great subterranean ideological struggle that had raged since the founding of the republic, a disputation that can be traced to the colonial-era tensions between the "yeoman farmers" of the American interior and the aristocratic landowners of the coastal plain. Soon after the Revolutionary War, like daggers of lightning, it flared into Shays's Rebellion in western Massachusetts and the Whiskey Rebellion of western Pennsylvania. This nascent ideological struggle memorably surfaced in George Washington's first cabinet, before there were political parties, when the competing visions of Secretary of State Jefferson and Treasury Secretary Alexander Hamilton collided. With Washington's approval and to Jefferson's dismay, Hamilton established the Bank of the United States, with a twenty-year charter. Modeled on the Bank of England, the national bank financed the foreign and domestic debt, created a sinking fund to stabilize government securities prices, and established branches around the country. Jefferson believed that the bank portended the dreaded concentration of wealth and power in the hands of an "entrepreneurial elite," as had happened in Europe, where the unprivileged had been condemned to servile "wage dependency." The adversaries and their allies gravitated into rival camps: Hamilton's Federalist Party, and the Republican Party led by Jefferson and James Madison. They clashed over banks, tariffs, internal improvements, a standing military, and relations with France and England.

•••

However, these battles signified a deeper ideological chasm between Hamiltonians and Jeffersonians—and, until the Civil War, between their philosophical descendants. Would the United States, as Hamilton had hoped, become an urban industrial nation of factories, harbors, shops, and smokestacks, or would she become Jefferson's "Arcadian State" of independent farmers and mechanics, living in "republican simplicity"? These opposing versions of America apprehended contrasting types of Americans: Hamilton's wealthy businessmen and urban wage earners, and Jefferson's independent "yeoman farmers." Deeply suspicious of Hamilton's market economy, Jefferson believed that only an agrarian-based system could preserve the republic and "republican virtue," which would be smothered by the coalescing economic and political power of a rising market economy.

Passages from Jefferson's 1781 *Notes on the State of Virginia*, an encyclopedic monograph whose topics included geography, geology, farming, climate, laws, religion, and manufactures, supplied the philosophical underpinnings for what became known as the "moral economy." *Notes* sometimes reads like the pronouncements of an Old Testament prophet: "Those who labour in the earth are the chosen people of God, if he ever had a chosen people, whose breasts he had made his peculiar deposit for substantial and genuine virtue."

But wage "dependance [*sic*] begets subservience and venality, suffocates the germ of virtue, and prepares fit tools for the designs of ambition. . . . The proportion which the aggregate of the other classes of citizens bears in any state to that of its husbandmen, is the proportion of its unsound to its healthy parts, and is a good-enough barometer whereby to measure its degree of corruption. *While we have land to labour then* [author's italics], let us never wish to see our citizens occupied at a work-bench, or twirling a distaff. . . . The mobs of great cities add just so much to the support of pure government, as sores do to the strength of the human body."

But after the War of 1812, market forces inexorably pulled the United States toward Hamilton's ideal. Henry Clay's business-friendly "American System" promoted rechartering the Bank of the United States, imposing protective tariffs, and building a network of federally financed roads, bridges, canals, and seaports that would facilitate commerce. And just as easy prosperity was causing memories of the ideological divide to blur and fade, the financial Panic of 1819 revived the old antipathies.

• • •

In 1823, Polk, newly elected to the Tennessee legislature, joined the front lines of the backlash against the market economy's excesses with his bill permitting western Tennessee tenant farmers to buy land they had cultivated before speculators could purchase it. The modest land reform measure was in step with the "democratic revolution" of the 1820s that was raising the curtain on the Jacksonian age, and that took aim at banks, paper currency, shrinking credit, and toll roads—virtually anything believed to profit the rich. The revolution's last avatar would be James K. Polk.

• • •

In seven congressional terms, from 1825 to 1839, including two years as House Speaker, Polk helped to reverse some of the Hamiltonian inroads made after the War of 1812. His political adversaries understandably derided him as Andrew Jackson's "puppet." Polk aided the president in restricting tariffs and government-financed harbor and river improvements—the latter seen by Jackson, Polk, and their allies as abetting industrialization and federal power.

Polk's greatest service, however, was helping Jackson crush the "hydra-headed monster," Nicholas Biddle's 2nd Bank of the United States. To Jeffersonians, the bank was evil incarnate: its liberality with credit encouraged a greater concentration of economic power and, consequently, political power. Biddle, who was the bank's president, in 1832 tried to win an early extension of its twenty-year charter, which was due to expire in 1836. In vetoing the charter extension, Jackson wrote that it would "make the rich richer and the potent more powerful," at the expense of "the humble members of society, the farmers, mechanics, and laborers. . . ." With Congressman Polk's assistance, Jackson's veto was sustained, and the bank's charter expired in 1836.

• • •

Jefferson's surpassing remedy for checking the rise of urban manufactures had been providing virgin lands for one and all—just as it was for James Madison, James Monroe, Andrew Jackson, and finally James Polk. Thus, the most potent weapon available to Jefferson's ideological descendants, as it had been for Jefferson himself, remained territorial expansion. By obtaining land for hundreds of thousands of small-acreage farmers, the market economy and all the evils ascribed to it by the Jeffersonians could be prevented from destroying the revolutionary ideal of individual freedom. It is no coincidence that under Jefferson, Monroe, Jackson, and Polk, the United States more than doubled in size.

Unsurprisingly, territorial expansion fanned the fires of the slavery debate. The

Constitution's framers had tiptoed around the explosive issue of slavery in the greater interest of drafting an instrument that met the approval of both slave-holding and free states. Their one stipulation was that no more slaves be imported after 1808. But as states began to be carved from the former Louisiana Territory, the issue flared again. The 1820 Missouri Compromise and its 36°30' latitude demarcation between future slave and free states temporarily put it to rest. Then, in December 1835, Northern congressmen flooded the House of Representatives with petitions to abolish slavery in the District of Columbia, over which Congress exercised direct authority. Abolitionists had been heartened by Great Britain's eman-cipation of the slaves in her West Indies possessions two years earlier. But the British action had also given Southern cotton growers a reason to cling all the tighter to slavery: the West Indies' emancipation meant that Southern slaveholders could now raise cotton more cheaply than England's colonies.

Contending that abolition was an unconstitutional interference with the states' regulation of slavery, Southern congressmen met the petitions with a "Gag Rule" that squelched all congressional debate of slavery. For six weeks, con-tention over the proposed ban aroused such virulent passion in the House of Representatives that some congressmen armed themselves with knives.

House Speaker James Polk, slaveholder and believer in the states' absolute right to regulate slavery, appointed eight Democrats and a border-state Whig to the committee that took up the Gag Rule. On the House floor, Polk peremptorily cut off John Quincy Adams before he could challenge the favorable committee report. The Gag Rule was adopted and was renewed each year until 1844.

• • •

Polk was elected Tennessee governor in 1839, but his nearly two decades of unbroken political successes was ending, just as Jacksonian democracy appeared to be waning. In 1840, he failed to win the second spot on President Martin Van Buren's reelection ticket; Van Buren inadvisably ran without a running mate and was defeated. In 1841, Polk was unseated as governor by James Jones.

When Polk lost to Jones a second time in August 1843, he became uncharac-teristically downhearted, and for a week he met with no one, wrote nothing, and said little. It seemed unimaginable that in just ten months James Polk would become the Democratic nominee for president.

THE DYNAMO

"The locomotive and the steamboat, like enormous shuttles, shoot every day across the thousand various threads of national descent and employment, and bind them fast in one web."

—Ralph Waldo Emerson, "The Young American"

As James Polk began his presidency, Henry David Thoreau was beginning his hermitic sabbatical at Walden Pond, just outside Concord, Massachusetts. The politician and the philosopher seemed impossibly dissimilar in character and temperament, and in their views on most consequential questions: commerce, slavery, materialism, war and peace, and pragmatism and idealism. Yet in one important respect, they and nearly every American were in accord: in their belief in the individual and his limitless capacity for improvement. This American article of faith made possible the inventions that were the engines of the "Roaring Forties," as well as an emerging American counterculture, which in 1845 was questioning whether commerce was killing man's soul. Twenty years of Jacksonian democracy had abetted the ascendancy of the American "common man" and universal white male suffrage; in most states, property ownership was no longer a prerequisite to voting. And a staggering 80 percent of eligible voters cast ballots in 1844.

• • •

A Harvard alumnus, ex-schoolteacher, handyman, poet, and essayist, Henry David Thoreau was, by the day's calculus of 1845, a thirty-eight-year-old failure. However, he did not regard himself as a ne'er-do-well, nor did his best friend,

Ralph Waldo Emerson, who in fact believed that Thoreau was a great talent. Emerson was a leading light of a New England philosophical and literary movement, "Transcendentalism," whose adherents sought knowledge through Nature and "spiritual intuition." Emerson had generously given Thoreau carte-blanche use of some undeveloped property that he had recently purchased at Walden.

While Thoreau was certainly irascible and misanthropic, he sought more than solitude for its own sake; he was taking Transcendentalism to its radical extreme in the belief that he would be rewarded with a new understanding of himself and the world. He bought an Irish shanty for $4.25, pulled it apart, and carted the boards to his building site. With a borrowed ax, Thoreau felled young white pines near Walden Pond for a cabin. He cut and hewed the pine into boards, beams, and posts and built a cabin at a total cost of $28.12.

On the Fourth of July, 1845, Thoreau walked the mile and a half from Concord to his completed cabin and took up full-time residence. He meant to live simply, observe Nature, meditate on society, and finally write a long-contemplated book about a thirteen-day trip he and his brother John had made down the Concord River and up the Merrimack six years earlier. In *A Week on the Concord and Merrimack Rivers,* the rowboat trip would serve as a narrative thread for Thoreau's ruminations on fishing and Perseus, Chaucer and friendship, and Christianity and the Concord Cattle Show.

Thoreau employed the same narrative structure in his later *Walden, or Life in the Woods,* as well as rhetorical devices such as aphorisms, puns, and allegories to jolt readers into fresh insights about society, government, and materialism. Under the heading of Economy, for example, he lamented how men, to earn their bread, must make concessions that rob them of their capacity for enjoying life: "Most men, even in this comparatively free country, through mere ignorance and mistake, are so occupied with the factitious cares and superfluously coarse labors of life that its finer fruits cannot be plucked by them. Their fingers, from excessive toil, are too clumsy and tremble too much for that. . . . He has no time to be anything but a machine." The creative mind, Thoreau believed, was of incomparable value.

Thoreau's *Walden* touches upon the closest-held tenets of Transcendentalism— a broad, active movement whose putative leaders were the Unitarian ministers Ralph Waldo Emerson and Theodore Parker, along with Margaret Fuller. The Walden experiment was being tried out in self-sufficient Utopian agricultural communes known as "phalansteries," based on the socialist system sketched a decade earlier by Francois Marie Charles Fourier in his *The Theory of the Four*

Movements. One such cooperative was Brook Farm, established in 1841 nine miles from Boston. Its members aimed for "right development"—harmony with the earth and mankind—and shared the farmwork and profits. Emerson, Fuller, Parker, and Bronson Alcott frequently visited Brook Farm until its disbandment in 1846, and it appeared in Nathaniel Hawthorne's novel *Blithedale Romance.* More successful Utopian communes were Oneida Community in New York state, and New Harmony, Indiana, where Robert Owen organized the astonishingly idealistic "World Convention to Emancipate the Human Race from Ignorance, Poverty, Division, Sin and Misery."

• • •

Belief in mankind's perfectability inspired the first campaigns to reform prisons and asylums, and to abolish drinking, slavery, and discrimination against women. "The trumpet of reform is sounding throughout the world for a revolution of all human affairs," proclaimed Bronson Alcott in *The Dial* in January 1841. From the Unitarian Church pulpit and in the lecture hall, Theodore Parker urged prison reform, equal rights for women, and the abolition of slavery (abolition societies were taking root in most major Northern cities). Dorothea Dix crusaded for better treatment of the mentally ill, "treatment" that at the time typically included being chained naked and beaten with rods. Elizabeth C. Stanton and Lucretia Mott organized the women's suffrage movement in Seneca Falls, New York. By 1840, there were five thousand temperance societies, claiming membership of more than a million Americans.

• • •

The revolutionary Hoe rotary steam press, which could print eight thousand newspapers per hour, launched the "penny press" and the first "paperback revolution," which flooded shops with new books costing as little as 12 cents each. Even people of modest means could now afford to buy and read Charles Dickens's novels, Sir Walter Scott's romances, and homegrown authors such as Washington Irving, James Fenimore Cooper, and Edgar Allan Poe. Surpassing these literary authors in popularity, however, were vivid, often crudely written potboilers, manufactured by the bushel.

The penny press abetted the expansion of public education from its humble beginnings in Massachusetts, Philadelphia, and New York City. Employing Horace Mann's popular system, schoolteachers drilled children in rote memorization and recitation.

Their lesson books were Webster's "Blue-Backed" *Speller, Ray's Arithmetic,* the *King James Bible,* and *McGuffey's Eclectic Readers* and *Peerless Pioneer Readers.* By 1850, literacy had soared to 90 percent among white men in New England and 70 percent among white males in the South and on the Western frontier.

• • •

New, precisely calibrated machine tools permitted factories to make goods from components that were exactly the same in each finished product, and were in fact interchangeable. It was a manufacturing revolution. Beneficiaries of this new process included Samuel Colt's six-shooter and Cyrus McCormick's reaper, along with John Deere's steel plow, Thomas J. Sloan's wood screw, and Elias Howe's sewing machine. The manufacturing workforce increased from 500,000 to 1.2 million during the 1840s.

The 1846 National Fair, a manufacturers' exposition rather than a public entertainment, displayed the latest factory technology alongside quotidian innovations such as coffee mills, ice cream freezers, hot-air furnaces, refrigerators, clothing, and bullet molds. Weeks before it opened, Democratic newspapers pronounced the Fair a ploy by New England industrialists to advance their interests, such as discouraging tariff reductions. After strolling through the exhibit hall, Polk reached the same conclusion.

• • •

The era's enduring icons, however, were the steamship, the railroad, and the telegraph, all of which quickened America's pulse. In his lecture "The Young American," Emerson wrote: "The locomotive and the steamboat, like enormous shuttles, shoot every day across the thousand various threads of national descent and employment, and bind them fast in one web."

Paddle- and side-wheel steamboats plied the rivers and canals. While the elegant clipper ships continued to dominate oceangoing travel and trade, in 1846 two transatlantic U.S. steamship lines received charters: the Collins Line and the Ocean Steam Navigation Co.

Travelers now preferred the comparative comfort of rail travel to the bone-jarring misery of stage travel and thrilled to its then breathtaking speed of fifteen miles per hour. In 1846–1847, charters were issued to the Pennsylvania Railroad, the Hannibal and St. Joseph Railroad, the future Chicago and Rock Island Railroad, the Mobile and Ohio Railroad, and the Hudson River Railroad. With its capital tied up in land and slaves, the South lacked the money for large-scale railroad construction. Businessmen discussed a transcontinental railroad that would link the Mississippi Valley and the Pacific Coast, but it would not be completed for a quarter of a century. Nearly everyone agreed with the *Democratic Review* that a national railroad was needed to bind "in its iron clasp our fast settling Pacific regions with that of the Mississippi Valley."

• • •

Thoreau and the Transcendentalists believed that the age's "commercial spirit" would one day corrupt republican principles, institutions, and virtue. The early effects of unbridled capitalism were readily apparent to Alexis de Tocqueville, that shrewd observer of American character: "One usually finds that love of money is either the chief or a secondary motive at the bottom of everything the Americans do. This gives a family likeness to all their passions and soon makes them wearisome to contemplate." During his rambles along the East Coast and to Detroit and St. Louis, Tocqueville noted: "It's odd to watch with what feverish ardor the Americans pursue prosperity and how they are ever tormented by the shadowy suspicion that they may not have chosen the shortest route to get it. . . . Death steps in in the end and stops him before he has grown tired of this futile pursuit of that complete felicity which always escapes him."

• • •

But there was more to the American character than merely the pursuit of wealth observed by Tocqueville. In 1845 America, powerful forces—the craving for adventure, chivalry, romance, and land—affected hearts and minds. Sir Walter Scott's historical novels especially appealed to the Southern aristocratic planters' chivalric self-image (Mark Twain half-jokingly blamed Scott for causing the Civil War). But equally influential, and without regard to geography, were books about the Levant, and William H. Prescott's *History of the Conquest of Mexico;* Robert Montgomery Bird's novel *Calavar; or, The Knight of the Conquest: A Romance of Mexico;* and Edward Maturin's *Montezuma: The Last of the Aztecs*. Rather than satisfy the longing for exotic lands, the books merely contributed to the restlessness peculiar to Americans.

In the pages of his New York *Tribune,* Horace Greeley spurred on the restlessness that Tocqueville found so compelling by exhorting, "Go West, young man, go West!" Greeley and other advocates of Jefferson's "yeoman's republic" believed that men had as much right to land as they did to air and sunshine. "The nervous, rocky West is intruding a new and continental element into the national mind, and we shall yet have an American genius," wrote Emerson.

• • •

Polk was decidedly in step with this expansionist sentiment in the spring of 1844, as he positioned himself to become former President Martin Van Buren's running mate. He had shaken off the ennui of the previous August and regained his old relish for politics. Van Buren's nomination, however, was not foreordained. The "Little Magician" faced several challengers, and the Democrats were in disarray over the issue of annexing Texas. And even if Van Buren's New York "Holy Alliance" of the Albany Regency and Tammany Hall helped him obtain the nomination, Polk was not assured of becoming his running mate; Senator Robert J. Walker of Mississippi and former Senator William R. King of Alabama were lobbying Van Buren to pick them.

All three major political parties held their 1844 national conventions in Baltimore, to be within telegraph's reach of the seat of power, Washington, while distancing themselves from the capital's intrigues. The Whigs had met May 1 at Baltimore's Universalist Church, nominating Henry Clay. President John Tyler's Democratic-Republicans gathered at Calvert Hall to nominate Tyler, of course, on May 27, the same day that the Democrats convened at the Odd Fellows Hall.

Because of the simmering controversy over Texas annexation, Democrats gaveled their national convention into session without any certainty as to who would emerge as the nominee. Cigar smoke and mystery cloaked the proceedings in the Baltimore hotel rooms where deals were being made.

• • •

When Van Buren succeeded John C. Calhoun as Andrew Jackson's vice president at the beginning of Jackson's second term in 1833, the savvy New York politician began the journey that ended in the White House four years later. The Panic of 1837—caused by state banks overextending credit, and worse than any previous depression —ruined his hopes for a second term, opening the door to the backwoods war hero, William Henry Harrison. His log-cabin, hard-cider campaign slogan, "Tippecanoe and Tyler Too," reminded voters of his military victory over Tecumseh's Native-American Confederacy thirty years earlier. At sixty-eight the oldest man to become president, Harrison also became the first president to die in office.

Tyler was a lifelong Virginia Democrat who, as a U.S. senator, had switched sides to vote in favor of censuring President Jackson for withdrawing funds from the Bank of the United States. He abandoned his party to become the 1840 Whig vice presidential candidate. Upon becoming president, he reverted to his Democratic sensibilities and vetoed two successive bills to establish a new national bank. His cabinet resigned in protest, and the Whig Party expelled him.

In 1844, Tyler established the Democratic-Republican Party and campaigned to be elected president in his own right, espousing the annexation of Texas. To discourage contenders from co-opting his platform, Tyler sowed the idea that Texas's annexation would extend slavery—the "Texas bombshell," as Senator Thomas Hart Benton called it—and the strategy initially worked. Fearful of alienating Northern voters by appearing to support slavery, frontrunners Clay and Van Buren stated their opposition to annexation on the same day, April 27. Clay's letter appeared in the *National Intelligencer,* while Van Buren wrote, in the Washington *Globe,* "We have a character among the nations of the earth to maintain."

To Tyler's delight, Van Buren's letter touched off a tempest within the Democratic Party. Northern Democrats lined up behind Van Buren, and Democrats from the South and West condemned him. Tyler's Secretary of State, John Calhoun, declared that "any man who takes ground against Texas will be set down with those who opposed the last war with Great Britain," a reminder that the Federalists' opposition to the War of 1812 had assured their party's extinction.

With far less fanfare, James Polk had also stated his position on Texas annexation, in an April 22 letter to Salmon Chase and the citizens of Cincinnati. "I am in favor of the *immediate re-annexation* of Texas," he had written, for "Texas once constituted a part . . . of the United States. . . ."

Polk was only following the lead of his revered mentor, Andrew Jackson. In a just-published letter from 1843, Jackson had asserted that Texas was "the key to our safety in the South and the West. She offers this key to us on fair and honorable terms. Let us take it and lock the door against future danger."

• • •

At the Hermitage, Jackson, who despite failing health continued to exert a planet-like gravitational pull on the Democratic Party, read Van Buren's letter with a sinking feeling, certain that the South and West would now elect Clay. "I am quite sick really, [and] have been ever since I read V.B. letter," he wrote. To beat Clay, Jackson and other Democratic leaders believed, they must nominate a candidate from west of the Alleghenies and south of the Mason-Dixon Line who would support annexation.

After party leaders dismissed Van Buren's leading rivals—Calhoun, Michigan's Lewis Cass, and James Buchanan of Pennsylvania—Senator Silas Wright of New York suggested James Polk. Jackson, who had also thought of Polk, summoned him to the Hermitage for a private talk two weeks before the national convention. Afterward, Polk wrote to his friend, Tennessee Congressman Cave Johnson, "He [Jackson] openly expresses (what I assure you I had never for a moment contemplated) the opinion that I would be the most available man. . . ."

• • •

In Baltimore, Southern delegates who supported Texas annexation preempted Van Buren's nomination by adopting a rule requiring a two-thirds majority vote to nominate. On the first ballot on May 27, Van Buren fell 31 votes short of the necessary 177. In subsequent balloting, he lost ground steadily to Lewis Cass. After seven ballots, Van Buren trailed Cass, 123–77.

That night in the convention's back rooms was born the candidacy of James Polk, a lifelong Democrat without powerful enemies. Delegates began switching from Van Buren to Polk under intensive lobbying by George Bancroft of Massachusetts and Polk's law partner, Gideon Pillow, both of whom later took sole credit. When the Democrats reconvened on May 28, Polk got forty-four votes on the eighth ballot. On the ninth ballot, he was swept to the nomination on a dizzying updraft of pent-up emotion that ended in unanimity. The result was so unexpected that when Philadelphia lawyer George M. Dallas, chosen to be Polk's running mate, was awakened in the middle of the night to be given the news, he initially believed that someone had died.

Washington politicians were just as flabbergasted as Dallas when the news clattered over the new telegraph machine inside the U.S. Capitol—the most consequential news yet transmitted over Morse's invention. The bulletin was printed on a placard and stuck in a window of the Capitol. Soon, a large, excited crowd gathered outside the Washington *Globe* office to obtain more details.

The Democrats adopted a radical pro-expansion platform that advocated annexing Texas and settling the Oregon question with Great Britain. The platform also endorsed a reduction in tariffs, and limiting the federal government's reach. In an inspired attempt to unite his fractured party and provide Van Buren's disappointed supporters with an anodyne, Polk made his one-term pledge.

• • •

"Who is James K. Polk?" Whigs scornfully asked, and it became their campaign slogan. Henry Clay condescendingly remarked that it was a pity "that a person more worthy of a contest with us had not been selected." But Polk made other Whigs uneasy, for the same reason that he made Jackson hopeful; they knew that Polk was a more formidable candidate than Van Buren or Cass would have been.

Adam Huntsman, a former Tennessee congressman who had aided Polk early in his political career, gently jibed him with the observation "that such a Possum looking fellow as you were twenty five years ago, would ever have [been] nominated for President of the United States would have been deemed quixotism. But so it is, and we must make the best we can out of you."

From the Hermitage, Jackson threw all of his declining powers into his protégé's campaign, promising Sarah Polk: "I will put you in the White House you can so adorn it if it costs me my life!"

• • •

"We have had one old hickory tree. . . . And now, to take its place, is springing up at its very side a tall and noble sapling. . . . It springs from the same staunch old democratic stock. It is heart of oak and sound to the core," wrote Gansevoort Melville, diplomat and older brother of Herman Melville. Polk was known thereafter as "Young Hickory."

Of course, he welcomed the connection to the most popular president since George Washington; in fact, most voters knew nothing more than that about him. Conversely, Clay's every utterance over thirty years could be found in the public record.

The old way of campaigning still held in 1844; the candidates did not tour, attend rallies, or make speeches. Occasionally they would write a letter to a newspaper. Their parties did the work of promoting the platforms and candidates.

Voters in 1844 had a clear choice. Clay's "American System" appealed to businessmen and manufacturers, mainly in the Northeast and upper Midwest. It meant national banks, federally financed internal improvements, and higher tariffs to protect U.S. industry. To maintain a large, cheap reservoir of labor in the East and bolster Eastern land prices, Whigs opposed territorial expansion, except in the case of Oregon, which would give New England merchants a trading window on the Pacific. The Democrats' platform of low tariffs, smaller govern-ment, and territorial expansion found abundant support west of the Appalachians and south of the Mason-Dixon line. President Tyler remained a quixotic third-party candidate until Jackson, concerned that Tyler would siphon off Democratic support, persuaded him to withdraw on August 20.

Out on a limb for opposing Texas annexation, Clay claimed in letters to Southern newspaper readers that he in fact supported annexation, while in Northern publications he continued to oppose it. His desperate flip-flopping cost him votes everywhere.

• • •

Everyone tiptoed around the slavery question. Both candidates were slaveholders who opposed abolition, and half of the twenty-six states permitted slavery. Clay believed that slavery would eventually disappear of its own volition; when it did, he would sell his slaves. Polk had pronounced the institution "evil" but a matter for each state to decide. Abolitionist Whigs occasionally broached the slavery issue, while taking care not to unmask Clay as an unrepentant slave owner. More often, slavery surfaced in simplistic partisan slogans, such as the Whigs' "On one side, Polk, slavery, and Texas, and on the other, Clay, Union, and liberty."

The one exception was an ill-advised attempt by a Whig newspaper to inflame abolitionists against Polk. The Ithaca (N.Y.) *Chronicle* reprinted an excerpt from an anonymous travel journal titled *Roorback's Tour through the Southern and Western States in the Year 1836,* in which the author claimed to have visited Polk's plantation, where he allegedly observed Polk's forty slaves bearing "the mark of the branding iron, with the initials of his name on their shoulder[s]. . . ."

But the shocking travelogue was a fake, and the article had to be retracted, harming rather than helping Clay and the Whigs.

Polk defeated Clay by the close popular vote of 1,338,464 to 1,300,097, win-ning 170 electoral votes to Clay's 105.

• • •

Indebted to no special interests, "my object will be to do my duty to my country," Polk wrote to his friend Cave Johnson. He would name cabinet members who would place the nation's interests ahead of their own. And, Polk declared, "I intend to be myself President of the U.S."

Andrew Jackson was exultant. "Polk and Dallas are elected, and the Republic is safe. I am now like Simeon of old having seen my country safe, I am prepared to depart in peace."

The *Times* of London pronounced Polk's election "the triumph of everything that is worst over everything that is best in the United States of America." This was unfairly condemnatory, considering that Polk had not served a day as president, but John Quincy Adams and other Northeastern Whigs agreed. Polk, wrote Adams, "is sold soul and body to that grim idol, half albino, half negro, the compound of Democracy and slavery. . . ." Sounding like a doom-ridden Old Testament prophet, Adams predicted that Polk's election augured no good for America, "which nothing less than the interposition of Omnipotence can save."

Polk and the fading Jackson, suffering from a host of ailments, met for the last time at the Hermitage in January 1845. Afterward, Jackson assured W. B. Lewis, in much the same language as Polk's later avowal to Silas Wright, that the president-elect would "fearlessly carry out all his principles heretofore acted upon, neither turning to the right or to the left."

Jackson knew his man. Polk would never waver.

3

THE PACIFIC DREAM

"If California ever becomes a prosperous country, this bay will be the center of its prosperity. . . . In the hands of an enterprising people, what a country this might be, we are ready to say."

—Richard Henry Dana Jr., describing San Francisco Bay and
California in *Two Years Before the Mast*

"Westward! The Star of Empire Takes Its Way."

—New York *Sun*

Until the 1830s, North America's vast uncharted regions supplied challenge enough for American explorers. In Europe, where every valley and stream bore a name, there was a millennium-old tradition of world exploration. Except for the Lewis and Clark Expedition, such ventures were unknown to the United States until the U.S. Exploring Expedition sailed from Norfolk, Virginia, on August 18, 1838. Scientists, artists, sailors, and Marines crowded six vessels, led by Lt. Charles Wilkes—a "stormy petrel" with a vindictive bent—aboard his sloop-of-war flagship *Vincennes*. Wilkes's Ex-Ex, as it was called, navigated gale-lashed Cape Horn, entered the Pacific, and explored its islands. The expeditioners drew the first complete chart of the Fiji Group, cruised along fifteen hundred miles of Antarctica's coastline, and measured, mapped, and studied areas along the North American West Coast.

The Ex-Ex returned to the United States in 1842 with tens of thousands of artifacts—fifty thousand plant specimens alone—and more than a thousand living plants that became the first exhibits displayed at the U.S. Botanic Garden at the foot of Capitol Hill. The expedition's dried plant specimens launched the National Herbarium. There were 2,150 bird specimens, 134 mammals, 588 fish species, 490 coral species, and a thousand crustacean species. The Ex-Ex's geographers made 241 charts that mapped 280 Pacific islands. The nonplant artifacts, temporarily housed in the U.S. Patent Office Building, later found a place in philanthropist James Smithson's gift to the United States, the Smithsonian Institution, whose Norman-style "Castle on the Mall" would be designed by Lieutenant Wilkes's nephew, architect James Renwick Jr.

But the Ex-Ex's mission wasn't exclusively scientific; geopolitics brought it to the Columbia River and San Francisco Bay in 1841. The enormous Oregon Territory, extending from the present-day California–Oregon border to Alaska's southern tip, was jointly occupied by the United States and Great Britain under the Anglo-American Convention of 1818. Spain and Russia had also made claims on the territory but had later relinquished them and left America and Britain to their rivalry.

Britain declared ownership of everything north of the Columbia River, which divides present-day Washington and Oregon, while the United States claimed the land between the forty-second and forty-ninth parallels—in other words, the area compassing both states. Many Americans, however, wanted all of the Oregon Territory, clear to Alaska.

• • •

Both nations took credit for having "discovered" Oregon. George Vancouver, a junior officer serving under British Captain James Cook, had sailed into Puget Sound in early 1792. Months later, Robert Gray, a Boston trader of otter pelts, boldly entered the churning mouth of the Columbia River, so named by Gray because 1792 was the tricentennial of Christopher Columbus's American landfall and Gray's sloop was the *Columbia Rediva*. While traveling fifteen miles up the river, Gray observed five-foot-long salmon and trees three hundred feet tall. From the local Indians, he obtained hundreds of otter and beaver pelts. Thus commenced a fierce U.S.–British competition for the Northwest fur trade, with the British Hudson's Bay Company initially achieving dominance by building chains of forts on Frazier's River and the Columbia. John Jacob Astor's American Fur Company erected a trading post at Astoria in 1811; but after the war with Britain cut into his profits, he sold Astoria to the Hudson's Bay Company. American missionaries settled the Willamette Valley in the 1830s, and, a decade later, thousands of settlers were pouring into Oregon each year, tipping the demographics in America's favor.

• • •

Wilkes, whose Byronic appearance concealed an iron will and a streak of mean-ness, reached the mouth of the Columbia River in April 1841. Sailing north to Puget Sound, he and his men then trekked overland south to Astoria, along the way salting the region with three hundred place names. Wilkes's party surveyed the Willamette River, and, before sailing to San Francisco Bay, it surveyed the Columbia River and met the Hudson's Bay Company's managers.

When Wilkes returned to Washington, D.C., in June 1842, four years after set-ting sail for the Pacific islands, he learned that President John Tyler's administra-tion had decided to suppress the Ex-Ex's findings. The administration did not want to jeopardize promising negotiations with England regarding the Maine–Canada border and Oregon. Wilkes channeled his gnawing frustration into writing a massive report of the Ex-Ex.

• • •

When James Polk made his strident assertion of America's "clear and unquestion-able" title to "the Oregon country" in his March 1845 inaugural address, his critics, through ignorance or malice, condemned it as needlessly provocative and bellicose. But it was actually a deliberate strategy of "graduated pressure"—one that he would also employ, to less effect, with Mexico—to prod Great Britain to resume negotiations that had broken down. "Great Britain was never known to do justice to any country with which she had a controversy, when that country was in an attitude of supplication or on her knees before her," the new president wrote to Alfred Nicholson, editor of the *Nashville Union*. In a letter to former law partner Gideon Pillow, Polk observed: "The only way to treat John Bull is to look him straight in the eye, and let him see, that we are resolved to maintain all our just rights. . . . On the other hand, if we faulter [*sic*] or hesitate in our course, he will become arrogant, and war may follow."

It was vintage Andrew Jackson. Old Hickory, in fact, had encouraged Polk to adopt "a bold & undaunted front" toward Britain because "England with all her boast dare not go to war." Polk reassured Jackson, "You need have no uneasiness about the course of the administration on the Oregon question. . . . We stand firmly and boldly on our rights. . . . We are resolved to maintain our rights, at any hazard." John Quincy Adams understood what the president was up to. "Mr. Polk will finish by accepting" a compromise, he predicted.

• • •

On June 8, 1845, Andrew Jackson died at seventy-eight at the Hermitage, and Polk mourned the passing of his beloved mentor, whom he had known and admired for forty years.

• • •

In July, Polk extended an olive branch to Britain, proposing that they divide the Oregon Territory at the forty-ninth parallel, the present U.S.–Canada boundary. Polk also professed a willingness to cede all of Vancouver Island.

Britain spurned the overture, and Polk tersely announced that the United States was withdrawing from the negotiations. He asked Congress to place Britain on one year's notice that the United States planned to terminate the Oregon joint occupation agreement.

England's rebuff and Congress's resolution in April 1846 caused a powerful upwelling of nationalism whose equal had not been seen since 1812—and whose rallying cry became "54°40' or Fight!" In its cryptic form of "P.P.P.P." (Phifty-Phour-Phorty or Phight), the slogan was inscribed on seals and chalked on public buildings, on fences and walls, and on windows and doors.

After Polk twice rejected English overtures proposing arbitration, England made a show of preparing for war. The Royal Navy began readying thirty warships for an expedition to Oregon. "We are perfectly determined to yield nothing to force or menace and are fully prepared to maintain our rights," England's Foreign Secretary, Sir George Hamilton-Gordon, the fourth Earl of Aberdeen, wrote to the British minister in Washington. The Hudson's Bay Company dispatched two engineer officers to make blueprints for fortifications on the Columbia River.

But with famine ravaging Ireland, and England in an uproar over farm policy, there was little enthusiasm, despite Aberdeen's tough-sounding rhetoric for the benefit of opposition party members, for a distant war in Oregon. English diplomats in Washington privately conceded that their government was willing to settle the Oregon dispute on practically any terms. Polk and his advisers consented to new negotiations, and England made a proposal to divide the Oregon Territory at the forty-ninth parallel—the very boundary previously recommended by Polk and rejected by England. The Oregon Treaty was signed on June 15, 1846.

• • •

While Lieutenant Wilkes's three-thousand-page *Narrative of the United States Exploring Expedition* filled five volumes, and the pedantic prose left much to be desired, it was an unexpected commercial success; it would undergo fourteen printings before the Civil War. The *Narrative* was a testament, plain and simple, to Americans' insatiable interest in the Far West, whetted by Richard Henry Dana Jr.'s tantalizing descriptions in *Two Years Before the Mast.* Illustrated by engravings and woodcuts, the *Narrative* influenced Herman Melville in the composition of *Moby Dick* and inspired a pair of sea novels by James Fenimore Cooper. Wilkes's literary fame was brief; his *Narrative* was soon eclipsed by another expeditionary account by another Far West sojourner, John C. Frémont.

In portraying the Far West as an unspoiled Eden of unsurpassed beauty— which it in fact was—the books of Wilkes, Dana, and Frémont planted in their congenitally restless readers the desire to see the Pacific country. The trickle of immigrants to Oregon and California increased to a stream.

• • •

Nowhere was the quickening westward migration more evident than in Benton's home state, and especially in St. Louis, Missouri's "gateway to the West," at the confluence of the Mississippi and Missouri rivers. On St. Louis's streets and sidewalks, French explorers, missionaries, trappers, and hunters mingled with dapper businessmen, boatmen, and immigrant families that had just arrived by boat. Along the five-mile Mississippi River waterfront, docks and warehouses brimmed with flour barrels, tobacco, and corn. Merchants supplied everything settlers needed for a long, dangerous passage by "prairie schooner" to Oregon or California. The immigrants followed the Santa Fe Trail from St. Louis's western precincts to Independence, Missouri, where the Oregon Trail began. The eruption of riotous spring colors signaled a commensurate eruption of wagon trains from Independence into the Great American Desert. This would be the lifetime adventure for most settler families. In 1845, three thousand immigrants descended into the lush Oregon valleys in the shadow of the Cascade Mountains. Four hundred others left the Oregon Trail at Fort Hall in present-day southeastern Idaho to follow the California Trail to San Francisco Bay.

• • •

That California belonged to Mexico, and that Oregon was claimed by England, deterred neither the settlers, their countrymen, Congress, nor President Polk; they all believed it was America's "Manifest Destiny" to one day occupy the continent from Atlantic to Pacific. The singular catchphrase at once gave expansionism a cachet of entitlement, geographical predestination, and divine sanction.

Since the Republic's early days, Americans had believed they had the *right* to spread over the entire continent and display their republican system for the rest of the world to admire. John Quincy Adams in 1819 predicted that in the future everyone, everywhere, would "be familiarized with the idea of considering our proper dominion to be the continent of North America," and would "find it a settled geographical element that the United States and North America are identical." This belief gained ascendance until Manifest Destiny and U.S. nationalism became synonymous and axiomatic.

John O'Sullivan, the editor of the New York *Morning News,* had coined the incandescent slogan in 1845 when he wrote that America "had a manifest destiny to overspread the continent, allotted by Providence for the free development of our yearly multiplying millions." Months later, in the July 1845 *United States Magazine and Democratic Review,* O'Sullivan had warned that Europe's purported designs on Oregon and California had the sinister purpose of "limiting our greatness and checking the fulfillment of our manifest destiny"—when the United States was fated to become a nation whose "floor shall be a hemisphere, its roof the firmament of the star-studded heavens." Charles H. Nelson, a Georgian who was a major general during the Seminole Indian War, informed Polk in a letter: "The hand of Destiny . . . points with unerring finger the path to pursue."

• • •

In 1823, when the European Holy Alliance had promised to help Spain recover Mexico and her other former colonies in the Western Hemisphere, Great Britain had proposed that she and the United States jointly oppose any encroachment. But Secretary of State John Quincy Adams wasn't inclined to—in his amusing turn of phrase—"come in as a cockboat in the wake of the British man-of-war." He instead proposed that the United States declare the Americas off-limits to *all* European intervention, England included. President James Monroe proclaimed the "Doctrine" in his 2nd Annual Message to Congress on December 2, 1823.

Twenty-two years later, in his first Message to Congress, President James Polk invoked the Monroe Doctrine to discourage the rumored maneuvering by Britain and France to acquire California from Mexico.

"We must ever maintain the principle that the people of this continent alone have the right to decide their own destiny," he wrote, in words that John O'Sullivan might have penned. It was the United States' "settled policy that no future European colony or dominion shall with our consent be planted or established on any part of the North American continent." Should a foreign power attempt to interfere in American affairs, the United States "will be ready to resist it at any and all hazards." Polk's resistance to European meddling in North America was later christened the "Polk Doctrine."

The London *Times* of January 1, 1846 soberly observed: "To assert a prospective dominion over territories beyond [a nation's] frontiers, is to confuse and overthrow all the barriers of power, and to hasten the return of universal war and confusion."

But Polk's words resonated with most Americans, particularly those living in the Ohio and Mississippi river valleys, and also in Pennsylvania, New York, and even parts of New England. While some Eastern merchants believed expansionism would drive up labor costs by siphoning off part of their labor force and prevent Eastern land prices from appreciating, others recognized that Puget Sound, San Diego, and San Francisco, as Polk had observed, would place within their grasp "the rich commerce of the East, and . . . new and increased markets." Daniel Webster of Massachusetts pronounced San Francisco Bay to be "twenty times as valuable to us as all Texas."

However, other New England Whigs feared that new territories might bring more slave states into the Union. Even South Carolina Senator John C. Calhoun was uneasy. Expansion, he believed, might reopen the bitter debate over slavery, with catastrophic results. The Democrats' cunning "gag rule" had stoppered the dreaded doppelgänger for years, but additional territories—and the prospect of new slave states—would undoubtedly lead to a rending congressional debate that no one really wanted, but which would suck one and all into its vortex, and to what end?

• • •

The national infatuation with California, whose very name evoked romance, mystery, and limitless potential, was chiefly due to the vivid prose of John C. Frémont and Richard Henry Dana Jr. From divergent perspectives—Dana as a deckhand on the Boston merchant brig *Pilgrim,* and Frémont as leader of a celebrated expedition—they had reached identical conclusions about California's beauty and vast, untapped natural resources.

"If California ever becomes a prosperous country, this bay will be the center of its prosperity," Dana wrote in 1835 of San Francisco Bay. Charles Wilkes, too, had foreseen the bay at Buena Yerba—the incipient settlement was named for an abundant vine bearing a small white flower—someday becoming one of the "finest ports in the world" and the crossroads of a rich commerce with Asia.

The "magnificent bay," wrote Dana in *Two Years Before the Mast,* abutted the high cliff of the Presidio, and encompassed a "large and beautifully wooded island and the mouths of several small rivers. . . . The abundance of wood and water; the extreme fertility of its shores, the excellence of its climate, which is as near to being perfect as any in the world; and its facilities for navigation, affording the best anchoring grounds in the whole western coast of America—all fit it for a place of great importance."

Dana was a poet's son who had once studied under Ralph Waldo Emerson. Compelled to leave Harvard after measles weakened his vision, he had gone to sea in hopes that "hard work, plain food and open air" would cure him. His two-year voyage (1834–1836) to California on the *Pilgrim,* to gather cowhides for Massachusetts's booming shoe-manufacturing industry, not only restored his eyesight, but gave him material for a book that was an instant best-seller when published in 1840. Today, *Two Years Before the Mast* is regarded as a classic. It was Dana's only literary work; a lawyer, Dana later helped prosecute Jefferson Davis after the Civil War.

Dana assayed the native Spanish Californians to be "an idle, thriftless people, and can make nothing for themselves." John Bidwell, an early California settler and author, agreed. "It is a proverb here . . . that a Spaniard will not do anything which he cannot do on horseback." The country, Dana astutely noted, abounded in grapes, yet the Californians made no wine: they imported expensive, low-quality wine from Boston. The Boston traders bought cowhides, known as "California banknotes," for $2 apiece, and shipped them to Massachusetts, where they were sold for $4 each to manufacturers who made them into shoes—and shipped them back to California. In 1838, as the Northwestern fur trade was going into decline, the cowhide trade peaked with two hundred thousand hides exported to Boston. Dana's trading ship, *Pilgrim,* brought a cargo of Massachusetts finished goods to California and returned to Boston with fifteen thousand cowhides. "In the hands of an enterprising people, what a country this might be, we are ready to say."

• • •

Frémont's richly detailed account of his 1843–1844 expedition into Mexican California—after traveling from Kansas to Fort Vancouver and then to Oregon— extolled the "surpassingly beautiful country, entirely unequalled for the pasturage of stock by anything we had ever seen." A river bottom where his party stopped was "broad, rich and extremely fertile; and the uplands are shaded with oak groves. A showy lupinus (foxglove?) of extraordinary beauty, growing four to five feet in height, and covered with spikes in bloom, adorned the banks of the river, and filled the air with a light and grateful perfume."

Sensitive to beauty, Frémont at times becomes so rapturous that an inattentive reader might think he was describing Eden: "The air was filled with perfume, as if we were entering a highly cultivated garden; and, instead of green, our pathway and the mountain sides were covered with fields of yellow flowers." Southern California was "so beautiful that it is considered a paradise, and the name of its principal town (Puebla de los Angeles) would make it angelic."

Frémont and his thirty-nine men, armed with Hall's carbines and a howitzer, gathered fourteen hundred plant species, many from areas never visited by botanists (later, a Kansas flash flood ruined most of them—"the hard labor of many months destroyed in a moment.") His party collected fossils and geological specimens, and, with sextants and chronometers, noted the latitude and longitude where each was found. Every day, aided by a barometer and six thermometers, Frémont meticulously recorded the barometric pressure, wind direction, temperature, elevation, sunrise, and sunset, as well as the number of miles traveled, and the expedition's accumulated mileage—6,475 when it disbanded in Kansas on August 1, 1844.

Frémont's report to Colonel J. J. Abert, chief of the Corps of Topographical Engineers, was rushed into print by Congress and went through several large press runs in 1845 alone after reviewers favorably compared it to the reports of the Lewis and Clark Expedition.

• • •

Spain had been the first European nation to reach Upper California, in 1542, just fifty years after Columbus's epic voyage. Navigator Juan Rodrigues Cabrillo sailed up the West Coast as far north as the forty-fourth parallel, making landfall somewhere on the Oregon coast. In 1578, Sir Francis Drake briefly visited California and cruised along the Oregon and Washington coasts, naming the region "New Albion" in honor of his beloved England. Spanish mariners Francisco Gali and Sebastian Viscayana carefully surveyed the California shoreline in 1578 and 1603, respectively. It was not until 1787 that the first detailed account of California was written—fittingly, considering the arc of California's early history—by a Spanish-Catholic missionary priest, Father Francesco Palou.

The Spanish viceroy of Mexico, the Marquis de Croix, in 1768 had instructed the Franciscan Friars to establish Catholic missions in Upper California. A year earlier, Spain had replaced the Society of Jesus with the Franciscans as its sanctioned missionary order; the Jesuits' loyalty to the papacy was interfering with Spain's nationalistic goals. The Jesuits, who had begun more than a dozen Lower California (present-day Baja California, Mexico) missions, were expelled from Spain's dominions.

Father Francis Junipero Serra was named the expedition leader and Missionary Presidento of Upper California. Sixteen friars from the convent of San Fernando joined him. The Franciscans planned to establish three missions initially: in San Diego, in Monterey, and at a place between, San Buenaventura. The friars trekked north from Lower California in the spring of 1769, bringing with them seed, agricultural implements, and cattle. On May 14, they reached San Diego, where they laid the foundation for their first mission. Later that year, they continued on foot to Monterey, where they hoped to build a second mission, but instead reached the shores of a mighty bay. The intrepid friars gave it the name of their religious order's patron saint, San Francisco.

In 1770, the Franciscans reached Monterey; they concluded their first Mass there by firing cannons and muskets. During the construction of their fourth mission, at San Gabriel near Los Angeles, the friars unfurled a banner of the Madonna to calm the hostile Indians. San Juan Capistrano was the fifth mission, built in 1775–1776, as Americans and British troops fought on the other side of the continent. When Father Junipero Serra died in 1782 at the age of seventy, there were nine California missions. Eventually, twenty-one were built.

• • •

The missions lay in the protected valleys of California's coastal mountain ranges, about a day's ride apart. Not only did the red-and-white missions with the serrated roofs complement the lush greenness of the mountain valleys, they were also hubs of economic, social, and religious life; each mission fulfilled the spiritual and temporal needs of hundreds of Indian parishioners, who tilled the fields and tended the large herds of cattle raised by the friars for the hide industry. Thomas O. Larkin, the future U.S. Consul at Monterey, estimated that the mission herds contained sixty thousand to one hundred thousand cattle.

By 1821, when Mexico overthrew Spain's colonial rule and became a sovereign nation, the Franciscans' careful stewardship had elevated the California missions to their zenith of material and spiritual prosperity. The missions' halcyon era of abundant harvests and profitable animal husbandry lasted another decade while Mexico was preoccupied with its unceasing revolutions. Then, in 1835, Mexican dictator Antonio Lopez de Santa Anna stripped the clergy of their missions and gave them to secular authorities, in the hope that they would bring tax revenues into the empty national treasury.

Within months of the clergy's departure, Dana was describing the Santa Barbara mission's "decayed grandeur." The new administrators, wrote Larkin, "managed to completely ruin the establishments without, in general, benefiting themselves—even taking the tiles off the roofs of the houses." The Indians and the friars' cattle dispersed, and the rich mission lands were subdivided and then neglected. The Mexico City government lost interest in California, which after 1841 lacked a coherent government. "It would be a sound policy to pension some of those high in office and influence, or give them a sinecure," observed Larkin. Visitors to the missions found deserted, crumbling buildings, rotting grapevines, and weedy fields. The lone friar remaining at San Luis Obispo slept on a cowhide on the ground and drank water from a cow horn.

• • •

As decay beset the formerly productive Spanish colony and it became increasingly dysfunctional under Mexican dominion, the California government, hoping to stimulate immigration, began giving away land to anyone who signed citizenship papers—a policy similar to the fateful one adopted in Texas that brought a flood of American immigrants and then a revolution. California's rate of settlement, however, was comparatively slow, because of its relative inaccessibility. It could be reached by land only by first crossing the forbidding Sierra Nevada mountains, or traveling to Oregon on the Oregon Trail, and then turning southward. An early passage through the Sierra Nevada, mapped in the 1830s by Joseph Walker and challenging even by mountain-man standards, ended in the San Joaquin Valley. Frémont and the famous scout Kit Carson discovered a better route south of Lake Tahoe, over Carson Pass, but it, too, was not for the fainthearted. In 1844 Elisha Stevens found the "Truckee route," which became the immigrant highway into the Sacramento Valley.

Even the Truckee route was arduous, and just 250 American immigrants reached California in 1845. Predominantly Spanish and Mexican in the mid-1840s, California had sixteen thousand inhabitants, with just eight hundred of them Americans, living mainly in the Sacramento Valley near Sutter's Fort. The trading post and settlement was owned and operated by John A. Sutter, a Swiss-German who had immigrated to California to escape creditors.

• • •

Thomas O. Larkin arrived in Monterey in broken health in 1832, but the salubrious climate reinvigorated him. The swarthy New Englander went into business, got rich, and extolled California's virtues in a torrent of letters and articles appearing in Eastern newspapers and journals. In a letter signed "Paisano" in the *New York Herald,* he described how officers on a vessel anchored at Monterey spent their leisure time ashore "hunting wild Deer and dancing with tame Dear, both being plenty in and about Monterey." More seriously, he reported in 1845 that Hudson's Bay Company agents were snooping around California and warned that, at Britain's instigation, Mexican troops were outfitting an expedition to California to restore Mexico's authority.

In fact, England, France, and the United States were all covetously eyeing the neglected province and had all appointed consuls in Monterey. Britain's minister to Mexico, Richard Pakenham, emphasized that California, if it slipped from Mexico's grasp, must "not fall into the hands of any Power but England." M. Gasquet, the French consul at Monterey, wrote, "His Majesty . . . would forever honor the ministers" who obtained California, and would "wreathe for them immortal crowns, and our descendants would glorify and bless their names."

In 1844, Larkin became the first U.S. consul to California—and, as it turned out, the only one ever. The following year, Polk and Secretary of State James Buchanan also made him a "confidential agent," earning an additional $6 per day, after Larkin wrote that Californians would prefer U.S. troops to the Mexican soldiers supposedly being sent to govern them.

As an American secret agent, Larkin would continue to inform the government of developments, but he now was also authorized to take action on the United States' behalf. Buchanan's instructions to Larkin stated: "The interests of our commerce and whale industries on the Pacific ocean demand that you should exert the greatest vigilance in discovering and defeating any attempts which may be made by foreign governments to acquire a control over that country." Larkin was instructed to disrupt foreign plots while inspiring Californians "with a jealousy of European dominion, and . . . arouse in their bosoms that love of liberty and independence so natural to the American Continent." And if the people wished to "unite their destiny with ours, they would be received as brethren." Buchanan knew that he was asking Larkin to take risks, for he warned him to never give Mexico "just cause of complaint."

Larkin began quietly encouraging Californians to revolt and distributed copies of the Texas Constitution, translated into Spanish. In his reports to Buchanan, Larkin tantalized him with descriptions of California's potential: its "wheat, beans, peas, flour, fat, tallow, butter, cheese, pork, bacon, salmon, horses, mules, spars, boards, shingles, staves and vessels," enough to supply all of Polynesia, western Mexico, and the Northwest, and mines producing gold, silver, lead, sulfur, coal, and slate. Guided by the "Anglo-Saxon race," California would become the "stopping-place from New Orleans and New York to the China ports, now open to all the world."

• • •

Dana was a seaman on the California coast, and Wilkes and Frémont had not yet traveled there, when President Andrew Jackson attempted to buy part of California. Aware that San Francisco Bay, one of the world's finest natural harbors, would establish the United States as a commercial power in the Far East, Jackson in 1835 offered Mexico $5 million for Texas and a land corridor extending to San Francisco and then north to the forty-second parallel. Mexico was uninterested. The next year, Jackson suggested to the Republic of Texas's representative in Washington that Texas claim California; the president believed that New Englanders who opposed Texas annexation would warm to the idea if they also got California's whaling ports.

The idea went nowhere, as did President John Tyler's overture to Mexico in 1842 through the U.S. Minister to Mexico, Waddy Thompson. "The acquisition of California is a thing uppermost in the public mind. Do you think that it is possible to bring it about?" It was not, nor was a three-way exchange proposed the following year by Secretary of State Daniel Webster to divide Oregon with England on the Columbia River, if England persuaded Mexico to sell San Francisco to the United States. England may have later regretted turning down Webster's offer. In 1844, Secretary of State John C. Calhoun and his kinsman Duff Green tendered a $10 million offer, but Mexico replied that California was not for sale at any price.

• • •

In the fall of 1842, Commodore Thomas ap Catesby Jones nearly caused an international incident over California. A friend of Andrew Jackson, Catesby Jones had suffered a disabling shoulder wound at the Battle of New Orleans in 1815, and had commanded the Ex-Ex before it sailed with Wilkes in charge. Rumors suggesting that Mexico was secretly dealing with Britain or France for California were reaching the Pacific Squadron commander at his moorage in Mazatlán. Then the commodore received an unsubstantiated report that the United States and Mexico were in fact at war, and that Mexico had ceded California to England. Catesby Jones took decisive action. On October 19, he sailed into Monterey harbor with two warships and demanded the provincial capital's surrender.

Startled Monterey authorities complied the next day. Catesby Jones and 150 sailors and Marines rowed ashore and marched six abreast into Monterey's fort as a naval band played "Yankee Doodle" and the "Star-Spangled Banner." The frigate *United States* fired a thirty-six-gun salute that was echoed by Monterey's shore guns.

But the commodore's jubilation over his instant conquest lasted only until the next day, when he received dispatches informing him that America and Mexico were *not* at war, and that California remained a Mexican province.

Catesby Jones sheepishly lowered the Stars and Stripes, apologized to Monterey officials, returned to his warships with his landing party, and fired an honorary salute to the Mexican flag. Hoping to mitigate the enormity of his error, the commodore threw a series of gala balls and banquets, with musical accompaniment by his flagship band.

• • •

Wilson Shannon, the U.S. minister to Mexico, reported in January 1845 that documents belonging to recently exiled President Santa Anna showed that he had held discussions with the English about selling both Upper and Lower California to England.

Some British leaders believed California was one of the keystones, with Hawaii and Tahiti, to commercial success in the Pacific. British creditors lobbied for a mortgage on California, hoping to recover some of the $26 million owed them by the bankrupt Mexican government. But Britain never bid for California. While British diplomats in Mexico urged their government to make an offer, the British government never evinced real interest in acquiring California, rather being content to see it remain a Mexican province. Nor did England encourage a scheme by an Irish Catholic priest, the Rev. Eugene McNamara, to establish a California colony of two thousand Irish families as a bulwark against the encroachment of the "irreligious" United States. McNamara's plan was never acted upon.

Unaware of the British government's position, U.S. officials read with alarm strident British newspaper articles urging England to take possession of California's ports. The London *Times* wrote in 1845 that Britain must "prevent those noble ports from becoming ports of exportation for brother Jonathan for the Chinese market." When those words were written, more than five thousand New England vessels were trading annually with Southeast Asia and in China's five open ports, a threefold increase from a decade earlier. Honolulu was beginning to exhibit a decidedly New England influence, with Yankee rum and dry goods for sale, and Sunday services held in a coral chapel.

• • •

While the United States, France, and England were maneuvering to catch California should it suddenly ripen and break free from Mexican authority, the province erupted in civil war in November 1844 for the third time in seven years. In 1837, native Californians led by Don Juan B. Alvarado, Don Jose Castro, and others had overthrown Mexican provincial authorities and established an autonomous government. Six years later, upon the orders of President Santa Anna, General Manuel Micheltorena and more than three hundred troops marched into California and restored Mexican authority. In 1844, Castro and Alvarado led another uprising.

On February 21, 1845, Castro's forces defeated Micheltorena's army outside Los Angeles, and Micheltorena returned to Mexico. Chubby, cheerful Don Pio Pico became California's governor, presiding over civil affairs from Los Angeles, while Castro returned to Monterey as commandant general, controlling the army, the Monterey customs house, and the treasury.

Pico and Castro agreed on nothing. Their bickering and petty jealousies escalated to their sending emissaries to Mexico City to complain about one another. After a summit meeting in March 1846 failed to produce a rapprochement, Pico and Castro began raising troops. "The people hardly care what Flag is exchanged for their own," Larkin reported.

• • •

California was a Mexican province in name only, and only nominally governed by Pico, Castro, and their Spanish-Californian ranchero friends. Its rich farmlands were uncultivated, its world-class harbors undeveloped, and its fabulous mineral wealth untouched. (In 1842, a ranch hand had found $8,000 worth of gold in the dirt outside Los Angeles, but no one bothered to look for more.) Mexico had even permitted the Franciscan missions and the other vestiges of California's genteel, colonial Spanish heritage to go to ruin; the San Francisco presidio lay beneath a patina of gnawed cattle bones, overrun by wild dogs and vultures.

California, larger than the British Isles, was yet waiting to be born.

Small wonder that American newspapers exhorted, as did the New York *Sun*: "Westward! The Star of Empire Takes Its Way."

4

THE LONE STAR REPUBLIC

"You cannot have peace with Mexico without a war."

—Duff Green, U.S. emissary to Mexico

The amazing career of Antonio Lopez de Santa Anna is so entwined with the early years of Texas and Mexico that it is impossible to relate their history without telling his. Born in 1794 in upland Jalapa into a venerable Spanish Castillian family, Antonio was a quarrelsome boy who matured into a fractious, luxury-loving man. Unquestionably courageous, he was also elegant and charming. His favorite amusements were soldierly ones—gambling, cockfighting, and dancing. He was ambitious, opportunistic, crafty, and egotistical.

Sketchily educated, he became an army cadet at sixteen, and as a seventeen-year-old cavalryman pursuing raiding Indians, he took an arrow in his left arm. As a young officer fighting Texas-Mexican rebels at the Battle of the Medina, Santa Anna formed two misconceptions about Texans: that they were inferior warriors, and that they could be terrorized into submission.

Early on, Santa Anna's intelligence and political acumen set him apart from the other young officers of aristocratic breeding, as did his large ambitions. Named governor of the Yucatan at the age of thirty, he was dismissed after just one year, in 1825, after he proposed the conquest of Spanish Cuba. During a brief, forced retirement as a country gentleman at Jalapa, he married Doña Ines Garcia, who in time bore him five children.

But by 1828, he was again in the middle of national affairs, helping lead a successful rebellion, whose reward was the governorship of Vera Cruz. In 1829, Spain, in an attempt to exploit Mexico's discord and reclaim its colony, landed twenty-six hundred troops in Tampico. Santa Anna raised an army, repelled the invaders, and became a national hero. For the next twenty-five years, he would dominate Mexican politics.

Santa Anna's principles were flexible, yoked as they were to the more urgent matter of advancing his own interests. Elected president in 1833 as a liberal, he abandoned the liberals in 1834 and became a conservative. Supported by the Catholic Church and the aristocracy, he assumed dictatorial powers and tightened control over Mexico's twenty-nine states. After brutally crushing a rebellion in Zacatecas in 1835, Santa Anna's regime became known as the "Supreme Government." Within months, Santa Anna's government would clash with its fractious province north of the Rio Grande—Texas.

• • •

In 1536, exactly three hundred years before the birth of the Republic of Texas, Spanish colonialist Alvar Nuñez Cabeza de Vaca was shipwrecked with three companions on the Texas Gulf Coast. Captured by Indians, de Vaca and his fellow travelers were held prisoner for six years before escaping. In a spectacular feat of endurance and courage, they walked all the way to the Pacific Ocean. De Vaca's colorful account of his exploits appeared in 1542, fifty years after Christopher Columbus's voyage, and as Francisco Vasquez de Coronado was leading an expedition north from Mexico into present-day New Mexico, north Texas, Oklahoma, Kansas, and Colorado. De Vaca was the first known European to set foot in what became known as Texas.

While seeking the mouth of the Mississippi River, French explorer Rene Robert Cavalier LaSalle established the first European Texas colony at Matagordo Bay in 1684. An Indian attack, the predominant danger in the seventeenth-century New World, obliterated the colony five years later. In the meantime, Spain clung to de Vaca's claim to the largely unknown province, and later Spanish explorers made peace with the Hasinai Indian confederation. Possibly in relief at finally being received with friendship, they named the new territory "Tejas," an archaic colloquialism meaning "friends" or "allies." To spread Christianity and commerce, they built El Camino Real (King's Highway) from the Rio Grande into east Texas. One of the new missions established along the highway in 1718 by Franciscan friars was named San Antonio. It later became the Texas provincial capital.

• • •

In 1820, when only several thousand people inhabited all of Texas, Moses Austin and Felipe Neri, the Baron de Bastrop, proposed a three-hundred-family colony in south Texas. Spain gave its blessing and granted Austin land. But Moses died before he could lead his pioneers to the promised colony, and his son Stephen became its impresario. Then, in 1821, when new laws jeopardized the privileges of the clergy and army, Mexico overthrew Spain's colonial viceroy. After a year of hard diplomacy, Stephen Austin finally convinced the newly independent Mexican government that he should be permitted to carry out his father's plan.

The first American colonists arrived in boats in 1823 and began tilling the rich earth between the Brazos and Colorado rivers near Matagordo Bay. Their first settlement was San Felipe de Austin. It was a difficult year: The colony's very survival was imperiled by drought, famine, and the cannibalistic Karankawa Indians, upset that the Americans had invaded their hunting grounds. The hardy colonists prevailed; by 1824, they were several hundred strong.

To expedite settlement of the vast, virtually uninhabited province, Mexico distributed more land grants to other American colony companies. The Texas Company, founded by Robert Leftwich, had among its investors Sam Houston, a former Indian fighter, lawyer, and Tennessee governor, coming off a year of hard drinking at the Cherokee Agency in Arkansas. Another land grant-seeker was James Wilkinson, who, as General of the U.S. Army, had conspired with Aaron Burr in 1806 to seize Texas and Mexico from Spain. Wilkinson died in 1825 in Mexico City while awaiting permission to start a Texas colony.

• • •

South Texas became a thriving enclave of American colonists—all welcome so long as they became Roman Catholics and renounced slavery. The Mexicans modified the latter stricture so that settlers could bring adult slaves, but not sell them. Ignoring every rule, Protestant Americans poured into the province, buying and selling slaves of all ages. As their settlements spread north and east and more lands came under cultivation each year, the Americans, accustomed to freedom and low taxes, grew weary of being in the middle of the tug-of-war between government centrists and federalists who favored local autonomy.

Mexican tariffs and restrictive laws targeting Americans were enacted after Manuel de Mier y Teran of the Mexican Boundary Commission warned that if

American immigration were not curtailed, Texas "is lost forever." In 1830, the Mexican Congress banned all further U.S. immigration to Texas and the importation of additional slaves. Colonization of the Trinity River area by immigrant Swiss, Germans, and Mexicans was encouraged. Military forts were built.

In 1833, the resentful American settlers held their first convention and discovered that they wanted more from Mexico than removal of the tariff and the immigration ban; they wanted autonomy. Teran was certain that "the revolution is about to break forth, and Texas is lost," he wrote in his journal, shortly before committing suicide.

In 1824, Texas and neighboring Coahuila Province together had become Coahuila y Texas State, with Coahuila controlling their joint legislature until such time as Texas's population became large enough to justify establishing a separate government. Once the Texas delegates saw that their many grievances would disappear if Texas became autonomous, they drafted a petition to the Mexican government requesting separation from Coahuila, self-government, and full statehood within the Mexican confederation.

Mexican authorities coldly received the Texans' emissary, Stephen Austin, and rejected his petition. They arrested Austin on his trip home upon learning that he had urged Texans to proclaim their autonomy from Coahuila, regardless of the Mexican government's action on the petition.

• • •

As Austin was being led away to prison in Mexico City, Sam Houston and other Texas leaders reached the momentous conclusion that even Mexican statehood would not be enough; nothing less than independence would satisfy them. Houston rode to Washington to discuss Texas's situation with his one-time military commander and friend, President Andrew Jackson. Houston had been badly wounded in 1814 at Horseshoe Bend, Alabama, where Jackson smashed the Creek Indian nation's war-making capacity, killing nine hundred Indians. Jackson was sympathetic to Houston and the Texans but was unable to promise them assistance.

• • •

In 1825, President John Quincy Adams had instructed Minister to Mexico Joel R. Poinsett to try to buy Texas. To cultivate the goodwill of influential Mexicans and counter the influence of the pro–British Scottish Rite Masons, Poinsett helped members of Mexico's York Rite Mason lodges obtain charters from the mother organization. But he failed to convince the government to part with Texas. In 1829, President Jackson quietly revived the overtures through Minister Anthony Butler, while publicly disavowing knowledge of Butler's efforts—the same plausible-deniability strategy that Polk later employed. Jackson instructed Butler to suggest to Mexican officials that the discussions were Butler's idea, unsanctioned by the U.S. government. Jackson authorized him to spend up to $5 million. Until 1835, Butler diligently tried to bribe and otherwise persuade Mexican leaders to sell Texas but only managed to arouse their resentment; they steadfastly believed that giving up Texas would signify the failure of their revolution.

• • •

Santa Anna's heavy-handed measures in 1835 evoked comparisons by the American settlers to the British "Coercive Acts" that had precipitated the American Revolution. The Supreme Government ordered all state militias and legislatures disbanded. When it resumed the collection of tariffs, William Travis, a twenty-six-year-old lawyer and schoolteacher who had abandoned his wife and children in Alabama, led an insurgent force against the port authority at Anahuac, driving out the Mexican officials. Texas militia led by Jim Bowie seized the Mexican armory at Nacogdoches. Bowie was a fifty-nine-year-old land speculator and storyteller known for his capacity for violence; in a massive brawl outside Natchez in 1827, he had been shot twice and stabbed seven times yet had still managed to kill a man with the long-bladed knife that bore his name. A famed bear hunter named David Crockett, another veteran of Jackson's 1814 Creek campaign, drifted to Texas after losing his Tennessee congressional reelection bid.

Released from prison in Mexico City, Stephen Austin returned home in August 1835 to find Texans arming for insurrection. Austin embraced the revolutionary movement. "We must rely on our own selves, and prepare for the worst," he wrote.

• • •

A Mexican army led by General Martin Perfecto de Cos sailed to Texas to crush the rebellion. Armed with flintlock rifles and Bowie knives, Americans under Austin's command clashed with Cos's troops in October 1835 at Gonzales on the Guadalupe River. After Mexican Texans under Juan Seguin joined Austin's rebels, the combined force captured Goliad. On October 28, rebels led by Bowie defeated four hundred Mexicans outside San Antonio at the Battle of Concepcion, and on December 5, after a four-day battle, the insurgents entered San Antonio.

Texas leaders met at San Felipe de Austin to decide whether to seek independence or Mexican statehood. Flinching from a bold course that would lead inevitably to all-out war, they chose the milder option of statehood, deluding themselves that Mexico would negotiate and not retaliate. Sam Houston became the new military commander, replacing Austin, who was appointed envoy to the United States.

• • •

When he was informed of Cos's defeat, Santa Anna took personal command of a new, five-thousand-man army of conscripts and prison inmates, the "Army of Operations." He led his ill-equipped men across the Chihuahuan Desert in freezing winter weather to deal with the "pirates and outlaws. . . . No quarter will be given them." Indeed, Santa Anna planned to impose draconian measures after subduing Texas: executing all captured leaders; banishing and confiscating the property of anyone who had participated in the uprising; relocating the remaining Americans away from the Gulf Coast and U.S. borders; freeing all black slaves; nullifying land grants to nonresidents; and barring any more Americans from settling in Texas.

Houston ordered Bowie to evacuate San Antonio before Santa Anna got there, after first destroying its fortifications and blowing up the old Franciscan Mission San Antonio de Valero, also known as the Alamo. Bowie, however, disregarded Houston's order, instead resolving to defend the Alamo. He requested reinforcements. Travis, with thirty men paid from his own pocketbook, joined Bowie, and they split the command.

Crockett arrived as Santa Anna's army, through forced marches, reached San Antonio on February 23, 1836, a month before the Texans had expected it. Just as Bowie had ignored Houston's evacuation order, Santa Anna had disregarded his generals' requests that he march directly to San Felipe de Austin. The self-styled "Napoleon of the West" wished to first avenge Cos's defeat.

MARCH 1836: THE ALAMO

Santa Anna's cannons pounded the Alamo as a blood-red flag denoting a war of vengeance against rebels fluttered over the Mexican trenches that nearly encircled the Texans' redoubt. During Santa Anna's first two days in San Antonio, Bowie and Travis could have withdrawn from the Alamo, but they did not. The Mexican army then sealed all escape routes and began its siege. Santa Anna's men intercepted a Texan raiding party headed for Matamoros and killed or captured eighty men.

Texas volunteers at Goliad started for the Alamo but turned back for lack of supplies and transport. Thirty-two reinforcements from Gonzales managed to slip through the Mexican encirclement, bringing the defenders' numbers to about two hundred, against five thousand Mexican troops. Bowie fell ill with pneumonia or tuberculosis, and Travis now habitually closed his correspondence with the apocalyptic words, "God and Texas—Victory or Death."

As the siege continued, Texas leaders at Washington-on-the-Brazos reconsidered their decision to remain part of Mexico—and now declared independence in a document modeled upon the American Declaration of Independence.

• • •

At daybreak on March 6, Mexican soldiers killed the Texan pickets before they could fire warning shots. As a Mexican army band played "Deguello" ("No Quarter"), blue-jacketed Mexican troops swarmed the Alamo. Travis was the first defender killed, shot in the head while leaning over the wall to fire down on enemy troops climbing scaling ladders. During the short, savage battle, most of the two hundred defenders were killed. The surviving defenders, including possibly Crockett, were put to the sword. Some women, children, and slaves were spared; Santa Anna gave each woman a blanket and $2 in silver. Upon Santa Anna's orders, the remains of 182 Texans were stacked in a pyre and burned. The Mexican dead, numbering between six hundred and sixteen hundred, were buried in a cemetery; when it became full, the remaining bodies were dumped in the river.

Santa Anna won the battle, but he had given Texas a pantheon of new heroes that included Bowie, Travis, and Crockett, as well as a rallying cry, "Remember the Alamo!"

• • •

After failing to reinforce the Alamo with his 420 men, which would have given the defenders a fighting chance, Colonel James Fannin, the commander at Goliad, now unaccountably failed to obey Houston's evacuation order. He dallied for a week, and when he finally began his plodding withdrawal, the Mexicans caught him at Coletto Creek, surrounded his force, and compelled its surrender. Then Santa Anna ordered Colonel Nicholas de la Portilla to kill the prisoners.

Fannin and four hundred of his men were marched out and massacred, with only Fannin's medical personnel spared.

• • •

It was the nadir of the Texas revolution, which hindsight has endowed with inevitability, when in fact it was on the brink of failure in 1836. Hastening to wind up the campaign so he could return to Mexico and reclaim his presidency, Santa Anna marched east to bring the curtain down on the insurgency. The Texans fled at his approach, burning their homes, towns, crops, and supplies—as the Russians had done in 1812 when Napoleon Bonaparte marched on Moscow. Evidently not expecting their scorched-earth retreat to end as well as the Russians' did, the Texans nicknamed it the "Runaway-Scrape."

Austin implored the Jackson administration to send troops. U.S. Army units marched to the Sabine River on the Louisiana–Texas border to protect American interests but did not advance farther.

APRIL 21, 1836: SAN JACINTO

Texans had harshly criticized Sam Houston for avoiding battle with Santa Anna, but some historians believe that he wished to lure the Mexicans to the Sabine and a clash with Major General Edmund Gaines's U.S. troops. Even if that were the case, Houston was inadvisably permitting the enemy to penetrate the colony's heartland without resistance. Santa Anna captured Harrisburg, nearly bagging the Texas government; the officials escaped and rowed a boat to Galveston Island. When Santa Anna led 750 troops in pursuit, Houston decided to follow.

Acting initially on their own but finally with Houston's reluctant assent, too, six hundred Texas volunteers crept through the woods at San Jacinto to within a quarter mile of the exhausted Mexicans, who were taking siestas in their tents. At 3:30 P.M., the Texans charged, shouting "Remember the Alamo! Remember Goliad!" The panicked Mexicans tried to flee, but Houston's men killed them in their tents, in the fields, and in the bayou, and rounded up six hundred prisoners. Santa Anna ignominiously fled the battlefield but was captured the next day, dressed in civilian clothing.

• • •

Hoping that the Texans would treat him with the clemency that he had denied them, Santa Anna consented to every condition in what became known as the Treaty of Velasco. He ordered his subordinate commanders to withdraw to

Mexico, and he, in his capacity as Mexico's president, recognized Texas as a sovereign nation, with its southwestern border resting on the Rio Grande. Within the larger framework of Santa Anna's shattering defeat and Mexico's impending forfeiture of Texas, the border might have appeared to be a secondary issue to the Mexican president, who was mainly interested in staying alive. But it was a consequential matter to Texans, as it soon would be for the United States and Mexico.

Santa Anna's ready acquiescence to the dictated treaty, whose final terms were to be negotiated by Mexican and Texan commissioners, did not satisfy the Texans' vengefulness. They called for his speedy removal to Goliad, there to be put to death at the site of the massacre that he had ordered. But Austin convinced his countrymen that Santa Anna might better serve their purposes alive; he proposed sending the Mexican leader to Washington as a prisoner, to meet with President Jackson, and perhaps to then take to Mexico an American offer to buy Texas. Austin intended for Santa Anna to serve, in effect, as Texas's representative and Mexico's titular head. It was very strange indeed.

Willing to go along with anything that preserved his life, Santa Anna cheerfully mounted a horse, and, under heavy guard, rode to Washington for his appointment with Jackson. At every stopover, he charmed the Americans whom he met with his graceful manners and pleasant demeanor, turning what should have been a disgraced captive's mean passage through the enemy heartland into a celebrity tour.

• • •

When they met in Washington, Jackson and Santa Anna might have recognized in each other an imperfect reflection of himself. With little formal education, they had risen to power by virtue of personal magnetism, sound political instincts, and proven leadership on the battlefield—Jackson at New Orleans, Santa Anna at Tampico. The battle-scarred warriors had ruthlessly crushed insurgencies: Jackson putting down the Creek uprising, and Santa Anna the Zacatecas rebellion. Their meeting was undoubtedly cordial, for their nations were officially at peace with one another.

But whatever his personal feelings, Jackson could neither recognize Santa Anna as a representative of a rebellious Mexican province, nor as Mexico's president—for he had learned that Santa Anna had been deposed and his treaty with Texas repudiated by the Mexican government. The United States would consider buying Texas, Jackson told Santa Anna, if California were part of the deal, for a total of $3.5 million, but Santa Anna must first persuade Mexico to end its war against Texas. The former Mexican leader allowed that Mexico could probably never defeat Texas, and that its occupation would require at least twenty thousand troops that Mexico did not have. The exchange of views ended inconclusively; the same unresolved issues would lead to war a decade later. Jackson sent Santa Anna to Vera Cruz on a U.S. Navy frigate.

• • •

An ailing Stephen Austin had returned to Texas from Washington to discover that his home had been destroyed during the Runaway Scrape. He moved into an unheated rented room, contracted pneumonia, and died on December 27, 1836, at the age of forty-three. "The Father of Texas is no more!" lamented Sam Houston. Texas officials wore black armbands for thirty days, and military garrisons fired twenty-three-gun salutes, one for each Texas county.

• • •

Jackson wished to annex Texas but dared not risk a debate over the admission of a slave state into the Union. Jackson cautiously waited until March 3, 1837, the day before he left office, before even officially recognizing Texas as a sovereign nation.

Five months later, Texas formally applied to the United States for annexation. Like Jackson, President Martin Van Buren was unwilling to risk political capital on a contentious debate over slavery. A joint congressional resolution proposing Texas annexation was filibustered by former President John Quincy Adams in 1838, and Texas withdrew the application. France and Belgium recognized the Republic of Texas, respectively, in 1839 and 1840, and Great Britain added its recognition in 1842.

• • •

The new republic led a precarious existence. It was always just a short step from financial collapse. The settlements, rife with crime, violence, and vice, were magnets for lawless adventurers and organized gangs. Meanwhile, a surge in immigration pushed the population of 50,000 in 1836 to more than 125,000 by 1845. So many immigrants passed through Arkansas on their way to Texas that the river ferry at Little Rock was upgraded to a steamboat, and Arkansas corn prices soared from 25 cents to $2 a bushel.

Two dangers loomed. Of course, Mexico could, and did, renew military operations aimed at reoccupying Texas, although the Texans resumed hostilities first. In 1841, Texas President Mirabeau B. Lamar, an expansionist from Georgia, sent militia and volunteers to capture Santa Fe, in the current state of New Mexico, hoping to cement Texas's arguable claim to the Rio Grande's eastern bank, all the way to its source. The poorly planned expedition, part military and part commercial, was captured by Mexican troops without a shot fired, and marched into captivity in Mexico City. Santa Anna, once more Mexico's president, freed the prisoners on his saint's day, June 13, 1842. He then resumed the Texas war. Mexican troops captured San Antonio, withdrew, and then recaptured it.

Texan troops drove the Mexicans from San Antonio, killing a hundred of them. While pursuing the retreating army, the Texans impulsively paused to loot Mier, Mexico, and three hundred of them were captured after a battle in the streets with Mexican troops. The Texans escaped during their long march to Mexico City but were hunted down and recaptured. Santa Anna ordered every eleventh man shot. A diabolically random method was devised for deciding who would die: Each Texan drew one bean from an earthen jar containing black and white beans—ten white beans for every black one. Seventeen men who drew black beans were executed.

• • •

A graver threat to Texas's security than the Mexican Army were the Comanche Indians. "Comanche" was a rough Spanish translation of the Ute expression for "anyone who wants to fight me all the time." Superb horsemen, horse thieves, and warriors, the Comanches were so powerful during the eighteenth century that Spain agreed to pay them tribute and to respect their southern border along El Camino Real.

Texas's 1840s population explosion shattered this equipoise forever. The Comanches butchered immigrant settlers who strayed onto their lands, bringing bloody retaliatory raids from the Texas Rangers, leathery mounted troops who fought the Indians on their own brutal terms. In 1840, a dozen chiefs, twenty-five other Comanches, and seven Texans were killed in a wild shootout at a San Antonio peace conference. The "Council House Fight" triggered reprisals that killed scores of Texans and Comanches.

• • •

In 1844, Secretary of State John C. Calhoun again tried to buy Texas, California, and New Mexico and drafted an annexation proposal for Congress. Calhoun chose as his emissary to Mexico Duff Green, a prominent Democrat whose *United States Telegraph* published congressional documents, and who had been a member of Andrew Jackson's "Kitchen Cabinet." Green's daughter was married to

Calhoun's son. Named U.S. consul at Galveston, Green immediately sailed to Mexico with Calhoun's purchase proposal. When it was summarily rejected, Green ominously predicted, "You cannot have peace with Mexico without a war."

In fact, Green had grandiose plans to prosecute such a war himself, with a private army of sixty thousand Plains Indians that would invade northern Mexico under the auspices of Green's Del Norte Company. Indignant Texas officials protested to the U.S. government when they learned of Green's delusional scheme. Changing tactics, Green founded The Texas Land Company and bribed Texas President Anson Jones with company shares in an attempt to win him over to the invasion plot. When Jones rejected the overture, Green allegedly threatened to overthrow Jones's government. This was too much for the Tyler administration, which disassociated itself with Green, ended its efforts to buy Texas, and redoubled its annexation efforts.

• • •

In Congress, Texas annexation fell short of the two-thirds majority needed, although thousands of people were streaming into Texas in anticipation of state-hood. But Polk's election on a Texas annexation platform inspired Tyler, with Polk's behind-the-scenes assistance, to a last attempt to make it his legacy issue. On February 28, 1845, Congress approved a joint resolution to invite Texas to join the United States. With great satisfaction, Tyler signed the resolution March 2, two days before leaving the presidency.

• • •

Mexico's minister in Washington, General Juan Nepomuceno Almonte, denounced the annexation resolution as "an act of aggression the most unjust which can be found recorded in the annals of modern history—namely, that of despoiling a friendly nation . . . of a considerable portion of her territory. . . ." Almonte requested his passport, preparatory to breaking off relations and sailing home.

In Mexico, Foreign Minister Luis G. Cuevas informed U.S. Minister Wilson Shannon that "diplomatic relations between the two countries cannot be con-tinued." Relations would not be restored, wrote Cuevas, until "complete repara-tion has been made for the wrong. . . ."

James Buchanan, the new Secretary of State, brushed aside Mexico's objections and pronounced the Texas question settled. "Texas has long since achieved her independence of Mexico. . . . Neither Mexico nor any other nation will have just cause of complaint against the United States for admitting her into this Union."

TO MANUFACTURE A WAR

" 'So, gentlemen, the Commodore, on the part of the United States, wishes me
to manufacture a war for them!' . . . to which they replied affirmatively."
—Anson Jones, president of the Republic of Texas,
recounting an 1845 meeting with U.S. envoys

MARCH 1845: WASHINGTON

James Polk had learned from Andrew Jackson the importance of acting decisively,
and March 10—six days after Polk's inauguration and four days after Mexico's
diplomatic break with the United States—was a day for decisive action. On this
day, Secretary of State James Buchanan penned his curt rejoinder to Mexico's minister, General Juan Almonte, spurning further discussion of the Texas annexation
question, and Polk and his cabinet agreed on a far-reaching secret operation.

Polk was already displaying the secretiveness and vigilant preservation of executive prerogatives that would become hallmarks of his administration. In rejecting
a Senate request for all Tyler administration correspondence regarding the February 28, 1845, congressional resolution to annex Texas, Polk argued that its
release would cause "injury to the public interest." In other words, Texas annexation might be jeopardized or delayed.

Another likely reason for Polk's refusal, however, was to conceal his own
shadowy role in the resolution's enactment. Before it approved the annexation
offer, Congress had been divided between competing proposals for effecting it:
Senator Thomas Hart Benton's plan to send five commissioners to Texas to negotiate a treaty; and an offer of immediate statehood that skipped the usual interim

territorial status and that deliberately left Texas's borders undefined. To break the stalemate, Benton suggested that Polk, after his inauguration, would choose one of the options. Congress accepted this compromise after Polk privately assured senators that he would adopt Benton's plan.

However, Tyler ignored the compromise and sent Andrew Jackson's nephew, Andrew Jackson Donelson, to Texas to offer immediate statehood, after first consulting Polk, who offered no opinion. After his inauguration, Polk could have recalled Donelson and implemented Benton's plan to send commissioners to negotiate a treaty, as he had promised. But he did not, believing that Texas must be quickly annexed to circumvent any foreign interference.

Benton's Senate allies angrily threatened to delay approval of Polk's cabinet selections unless he honored his pledge and sent commissioners to Texas. Polk readily consented to nominate five commissioners, and the Senate approved his cabinet. But Polk then never nominated the commissioners. When senators accused the president of tricking them, he claimed that he had been misunderstood—that he had agreed to name the commissioners only if Congress adopted Benton's annexation plan, and it had not. This would not be the last time that congressmen would accuse Polk of deceiving them. They bestowed a new nickname on "The Mole": "Polk the Mendacious."

• • •

Polk and his advisers had not only shelved the Benton plan, they had acted to ensure the success of the Tyler annexation offer by dispatching three secret agents to Texas in Donelson's wake. Their mission was to arouse enthusiasm for annexation, to thwart England's and France's efforts to preserve Texas as a sovereign nation, and much more.

The highest-profile of the three emissaries, Commodore Robert F. Stockton, reported to Navy Secretary George Bancroft, Polk's closest friend in the cabinet. (On the rare occasions that the president and First Lady left the White House to pay a social call, their destination often was the Bancroft home.) On April 2, Bancroft countermanded orders sending Stockton to the Mediterranean, issuing new orders for him to sail with the *USS Princeton, Saratoga, St. Mary's,* and *Porpoise* to the Gulf of Mexico and join Commodore David Conner's Home Squadron. On April 22, a second Bancroft order instructed Stockton to land at Galveston and "make yourself acquainted with the dispositions of the people of Texas, and their relations with Mexico." Stockton reached Galveston on May 13.

•••

The commodore's grandfather, Richard Stockton, a lawyer and judge, had been a signer of the Declaration of Independence—and the only signer to later pledge his loyalty to England, to keep his mansion, Morven, outside Princeton, New Jersey. Morven later served as the summer residence for New Jersey governors, and Richard Stockton's descendants became one of New Jersey's wealthiest families.

Robert F. Stockton, a bright, dashing naval officer, successful businessman, and gifted engineer, in 1821, selected and purchased, on behalf of the American Colonization Society, the site for what became the free black African colony of Liberia. He also helped design the first U.S. warship driven by a screw propeller, the *Princeton,* and its two twelve-inch guns, one of which exploded during a demonstration on the Potomac River for President John Tyler, his cabinet, and guests in 1844. The explosion killed Secretary of State Abel Upshur, Naval Secretary Thomas Gilmer, and five other men.

•••

In Galveston, Stockton rendezvoused with another Polk administration agent, Charles A. Wickliffe, a former Postmaster General and Kentucky governor. The third agent, Congressman and former Arkansas Governor Archibald Yell, a Polk confidant, reached Texas about the same time. The men were to foil any attempts by Great Britain or France to delay or block Texas's annexation; to inspire Texans to support statehood; and to pledge the United States' support of Texas's putative claim to the Rio Grande as its western boundary.

Polk disingenuously informed his official Texas envoy, Donelson, that Wickliffe and Yell were in Texas on their own initiative, not under his sanction. In deceiving Donelson and cloaking himself in plausible deniability in case accusations of meddling arose, Polk was deftly employing the same artifice that his mentor, Andrew Jackson, had used when attempting to buy Texas. "The Mole" had a spy's instincts.

MAY 1845: WASHINGTON-ON-THE-BRAZOS

While Yell and Wickliffe made pro-annexation speeches all over Texas, Stockton conferred with Texas's militia commander, Major General Sidney Sherman, at the Republic of Texas's raw capital, Washington-on-the-Brazos, population six thousand. The House of Representatives met in an unfinished loft above a barroom;

when the House was in recess, the Treasury Department did its business there. The Senate convened in $3-a-week rooms above a grocery. The rest of the national government, such as it was, was scattered about town in rude buildings: the War Department in a log cabin, the State Department in a clapboard edifice.

Stockton enlisted Sherman in an audacious plot to raise a Texas militia to attack Mexico. In a private letter to Bancroft on May 27, Stockton described "how I propose to settle the matter without committing the U. States—The Major General [Sidney Sherman] will call out three thousand men & 'R.F. Stockton Esq' will supply them in a private way with provisions & ammunition." By no stretch did Stockton plan to arm, feed, and equip the volunteers exclusively from his own pocket; he had requisitioned government supplies and ammunition from Pensacola, Florida. "War now exists," wrote Stockton, "and . . . the Texians [*sic*] ought therefore in my opinion to take possession and drive the Mexicans over the other side of the [Rio Grande] river before the meeting of [Texas's] Congress."

Just whose plan this was has never been satisfactorily explained, although, as later events showed, it compassed Polk's most optimistic hopes. Some historians have attributed the entire scheme to Stockton, who, they say, far exceeded his authority. It is true that Bancroft's written instructions only stipulated that Stockton was to gather intelligence, and that the wealthy naval officer–businessman was undoubtedly an aggressive, freewheeling expansionist. Yet it is difficult to believe that even the self-assured Stockton would brazenly send an emissary to Texas President Anson Jones to propose starting a war with Mexico, while claiming to act with the Polk administration's support—if he did not, in fact, *have* that support. Yet that is just what Stockton did.

Stockton's emissary was Dr. J. H. Wright, the *Princeton*'s surgeon. At a meeting with Jones on May 28, Wright recommended that Sherman raise two to three thousand volunteers. With Stockton's fleet providing support, said Dr. Wright, the volunteers would capture Matamoros, on the southwestern bank of the Rio Grande.

The skeptical President Jones, a physician who had fought at San Jacinto, asked Wright to give him a written proposal. That was impossible, Wright said, but Stockton could speak to him if he wished. Captain Jack Coffee Hays of the Texas Rangers interrupted the meeting at one point to report that Mexican troops were preparing for battle on the Nueces River. The false report was calculated to pressure Jones to call out the militia.

Hays's report, however, only heightened Jones's suspicions. Wright then played his last card. "The President of the United States," Jones later recalled Wright saying, "wished Texas to place herself in an attitude of active hostility towards Mexico, so that, when Texas was finally brought into the Union, *she might bring a war with her* [Wright's italics]; and this was the object of the expedition to Matamoros, as now proposed."

This was not exactly a surprise to Jones, who knew from Texas's ambassador in Washington of "the anxiety of Mr. Polk for a pretext for a war with Mexico." Jones now learned that, not only had General Sherman approved Stockton's plan, so had practically everyone "from Galveston to Washington," according to Wright—except the U.S. envoy to Texas, Donelson, who was unaware of it. Wright told Jones, "All that was now wanting was the sanction of the Texas Government to the scheme."

"I then said, smiling," recalled Jones, " 'So, gentlemen, the Commodore, on the part of the United States, wishes me to *manufacture a war* for them!' . . . to which they replied affirmatively." While Wright's acknowledgment filled Jones with "disgust and abhorrence," Jones gave no reply to Wright's proposition. Ashbel Smith, Texas's Secretary of State, noted that while the conspirators wanted a war with Mexico, they possessed "neither military plan, nor means, nor capable head, nor reasonable object. . . . Its [the amorphous plan's] purpose was by exasperating Mexico to destroy the prospects of peace."

A week after Wright met with Jones, Wickliffe tried his hand at persuading the Texas president. Just as Hays had burst into Jones's meeting with Wright, a courier interrupted the Wickliffe meeting with news that up to eight thousand Mexican soldiers were massing along the Rio Grande, Wickliffe reported in a leter to Polk. General Sherman, who was present, urged immediate military action, but Jones, having been through this before, was noncommittal.

Jones's Attorney General, Ebenezer Allen, believed that Polk's agents wished "to hurry us into hostilities with Mexico. I hope they may be disappointed, and that in spite of their efforts we shall be able to preserve the peace *at present,* if not the Republic."

General Edwin Morehouse, who was stationed on Texas's frontier throughout this period, later informed Jones, "It is all humbug as to the Mexicans concentrating on the frontier."

• • •

Better than anyone else in Texas, Jones knew why the Polk administration appeared eager for Texas to start a war with Mexico. It was to spoil an intrigue in which Jones was at that moment engaged—permitting Britain to secretly lobby Mexico to make peace with Texas and officially recognize her sovereignty, thereby wrecking Polk's annexation plan. To buy time for Britain, Jones and former Texas President Sam Houston had managed to delay until June the Texas Congress's consideration of the American annexation offer. By then, they hoped to also be able to offer Congress the option of continued Texas independence, with the fillip of Mexican recognition.

The British charge d'affaires in Texas, Charles Elliot, had volunteered to travel secretly to Mexico City and attempt to effect a reconciliation between Texas and Mexico. He hoped to return to Texas with an agreement. The French charge d'affaires, Alphonse de Saligny, had signaled his government's support for Elliot's mission. Britain and France not only wished to preserve their commercial treaties with Texas; they hoped that a sovereign Texas would become their chief cotton supplier and break the U.S. South's domination of the cotton market.

The Mexican Congress grudgingly concluded that it preferred sharing a border with a Texas republic, rather than with a U.S. state. Elliott triumphantly hastened back to Texas with Mexico's recognition of Texas sovereignty. Upon receiving the news, Jones announced that Mexico had proposed peace—he omitted Britain's intermediary role—and that he had accepted the offer. At the same time, he informed Wright that he would not participate in Stockton's proposed war scheme.

But it would not be that simple. Elliot, supposedly traveling incognito but wearing a hat so blindingly white that it turned heads, had been spotted while returning to Texas with the Mexican-approved proposal. When all the details emerged, the affair of the "Man in the White Hat" blew up in the faces of Jones and Elliot. Britain and Jones were condemned throughout the United States, and fierce pro-annexation sentiment welled up in reaction to the perception of European meddling. "The interference of the Governments of England and France has not only reconciled nearly the whole country to annexation, but even to the manner of accomplishing it," wrote the New York *Courier and Enquirer*. The quasi-official Washington *Union* and other Democrat-leaning newspapers denounced Jones for having even considered a treaty with Mexico. As Jones wryly noted, the *Union* decried his actions as "Treason! in tones of thunder."

At the same time, Polk was plying Houston with the honeyed promise that the United States would defend Texas's arguable Rio Grande border claim, come what may. "You may have no apprehensions in regard to your boundary," he wrote, reiterating his dubious assertion that Texas had once belonged to the United States.

"We will maintain all your rights of territory, and will not suffer them to be sacrificed." Andrew Jackson Donelson was similarly reassuring Ebenezer Allen, now Texas's acting Secretary of State: "You may look with confidence to Mr. Polk as ready to maintain the claim to the Rio Grande; and that no expression from Texas is necessary to stimulate his exertions."

Jones and Houston now resigned themselves to the fact that Texas overwhelmingly favored statehood and possibly war. With Houston muttering that Stockton and Wickliffe were "scoundrels," the Texas leaders distanced themselves from Elliot's plan, unconvincingly claiming that they had gone along with it to inspire stronger support for annexation. Earnest, conscientious Anson Jones would be the Republic of Texas's last president.

While neither Polk's diary nor his papers contain proof that Stockton, in urging Texas to attack Mexico, was carrying out the president's orders, it is almost a certainty that he was. If Stockton were conducting *unsanctioned* foreign policy to embroil America in a war with Mexico, he would probably have been court-martialed. But Stockton was promoted to commander of the Navy's Pacific Squadron—in charge of covert U.S. efforts to seize California.

• • •

On June 18, 1845, the Texas Congress accepted the U.S. annexation proposal and scheduled a ratification convention in Austin on the Fourth of July. Almost as an afterthought, the Congress rejected Mexico's peace proposal recognizing Texas's sovereignty.

Her pride deeply wounded, Mexico declared that she could never be reconciled to the United States' annexation of a Mexican province.

The Washington *Union* mocked Mexico's "gasconading about her pretended rights and pretended wrongs," and sneered: "If she [Mexico] now persists in carrying into effect her absurd threats of war . . . she will exhaust what remains of disposition on our part to deal generously with her."

• • •

"Texas may now be regarded as part of the Country," Polk declared upon receiving the ratification convention's official acceptance of the annexation offer. U.S. congressional approval in December would complete the process of Texas becoming a state. "In anticipation of the consummation of the great event," Polk added, "our land and Naval forces are in a position ready to protect and defend her. I do not however anticipate that Mexico will be mad enough to declare war." To ensure that Mexico did not, the president smoothly added, a three-thousand-man U.S. force would begin moving toward Texas's frontier with Mexico.

• • •

Mexico angrily pronounced Texas's annexation and the planned U.S. troop deployment to be "a grave injury," adding that "the Supreme Government has resolved upon a declaration of war against that Power. . . ." Four days later, the Mexican government began raising troops.

Annexation opponents such as John Quincy Adams squinted sourly into the future and saw nothing good resulting from Texas statehood. "I have opposed it for ten long years, firmly believing it tainted with two great crimes: one, the leprous contamination of slavery; and two, robbery of Mexico. . . . Fraud and rapine are at its foundation. They have sown the wind. . . ."

6

THE ARMY AND THE BORDER

"These energetic & ample preparations will I think probably prevent war."
—President James K. Polk, August 1845

"Our people ought to be damned for their impudent arrogance and domineering presumption!"
—Lieutenant Colonel Ethan Allen Hitchcock

LATE JUNE 1845: LOUISIANA

Fort Jesup's sultry air trembled with electric excitement, the shouts of officers and noncoms, and red dust. General Zachary Taylor's "Army of Observation" was finally on the move. For more than a year, Taylor and his fifteen hundred regulars had been in perpetual readiness at their camp east of the Sabine River, the Texas-Louisiana border. Officially, the Army of Observation's mission was to deter Indian attacks, but its unstated purpose was to defend Texas if necessary. The corps was now deploying to western Texas, to a place of Taylor's choosing, "best adapted to repel invasion."

Taylor, sixty-one, blunt and homely, had been an Army officer for thirty-seven years. Commissioned in 1808 when the Army added eight regiments after the British attack on the USS *Chesapeake* off the Virginia Capes, Taylor had defended Fort Harrison, Indiana, against attacks by the great Shawnee chief, Tecumseh, during the War of 1812. During the Black Hawk War of 1832, where a young militiaman named Abraham Lincoln also saw action, Taylor had personally accepted the surrender of Chief Black Hawk after winning the Battle of Bad Axe. He was promoted to brevet brigadier general during the Seminole War after his victory on Christmas Day 1837 at Lake Okeechobee. Three years later, when named commander of the Army's Southern Division, Taylor and his corncob pipe-smoking wife Peggy had settled into a Baton Rouge plantation.

The son of a Louisville, Kentucky, farmer and land speculator, Taylor, like many Westerners of his generation, had received little formal education and was "unused to the pen." With this in mind, General of the Army Winfield Scott had assigned a bright junior officer, Captain William W. S. Bliss, to be Taylor's adjutant general and chief of staff. Bliss perfectly complemented Taylor: he was well educated; he wrote clearly; and, as matters developed, he made a fine Taylor son-in-law. The reports and letters that flowed from Taylor's tent under Taylor's name but in Bliss's hand redounded to the general's credit. Scott declared "the whole intent . . . a success, the combination of the general and the chief of his staff working like a charm."

While Taylor's West Point–trained subordinates sometimes snickered at his homespun speech and attire and disparaged his simple tactics, the common soldiers embraced him as one of them. He was "Old Rough and Ready," who shared their hardships and displayed an iron calm under fire. Scott described his contemporary as "kind-hearted, sincere, and hospitable in a plain way . . . and [who] left behind him not an enemy in the world."

Taylor dressed like an old farmer, in a large straw sombrero or other nonmilitary headgear, loose frock coat, enlisted man's trousers, and "soldier's shoes." Taylor's unpretentiousness puzzled U.S. soldiers who had recently emigrated from Europe, where military pomp was de rigueur, as it would later baffle the Mexican people, also accustomed to seeing their leaders in dazzling uniforms. A soldier from Germany, Adolph Englemann, said Taylor was "short and very heavy, with pronounced face lines and gray hair, wears an old oil cloth cap, a dusty green coat, a frightful pair of trousers and on horseback looks like a toad."

There was an oft-told story of a Virginia militia lieutenant who mistook Taylor for an enlisted man when he saw the general seated outside a tent in his plain clothes, cleaning a sword. The lieutenant promised Taylor a dollar if he would clean his sword, and Taylor accepted it without comment. The next day, when Taylor handed over the gleaming sword to the lieutenant, the Virginian playfully poked Taylor in the ribs and said, "Come, old fatty, show me General Taylor and the dollar is yours." Taylor turned around. "Lieutenant!" he said. "I am General Taylor, and I will take that dollar!"

In letters, Taylor habitually displayed concern for his men's well-being, devotion to his mission, profound patriotism, and deep solicitude for his family. Sometimes he longed to simply retire to his plantation. Taylor struggled with pessimism, and possibly depression, confiding to his son-in-law, Dr. R. C. Wood, "I consider it a great misfortune to be always looking at the dark side of the picture of life or to be anticipating evils or misfortunes."

• • •

Ordered on June 29 to join Taylor's command with two companies of the Army's 3rd Infantry Regiment, Colonel Ethan Allen Hitchcock glumly noted in his journal: "Violence leads to violence, and if this movement of ours does not lead to others and to bloodshed, I am much mistaken." Such sentiments appear incongruous coming from a professional soldier whose life was supposedly one long preparation for war, but not from Hitchcock, a highly educated, intelligent career Army man known as "The Pen of the Army" because of his elegant, forceful writing. His facility with words and strong opinions sometimes put him at odds with his superiors, which might explain why Revolutionary War hero Ethan Allen's grandson did not hold higher rank.

While some officers shared Hitchcock's forebodings about the deployment as they sailed to Texas in July 1845—for example, Captain George Deas disdained "sustaining the pretensions of Texas" for a Rio Grande border—the majority believed they were being sent to defend Texas against Mexican aggression, not to incite a war.

On August 1, the task force reached the small village of Corpus Christi, situated at the head of a bay protected by a barrier island. It did not concern the Americans that in occupying Corpus Christi, on the *southwestern* side of the Nueces, they were technically trespassing upon territory claimed by Mexico. Taylor's small army began making a permanent camp there.

• • •

The Washington *Union,* along with other Democratic newspapers and pro-expansionists nationwide, wrote approvingly of the deployment. "Our Government is prepared for any issue. Our squadron is off the coast. Three thousand troops will be on the borders of Texas to preserve our just rights and protect her from invasion."

But the Whig *American Review* called it "a taunting aggression, calculated to arouse into activity resentments which otherwise might have remained inert, though smouldering." The *National Intelligencer* accused the Polk administration of cynically invoking the Monroe Doctrine—whereby America swore to safeguard the Western Hemisphere from European interference—to play "just the part which we would not let the Holy Alliance play between Spain and the South American states. . . . We cannot set up for protectors, after we have become plunderers."

• • •

While Taylor's army settled in at Corpus Christi, Polk and his cabinet were making even more ambitious plans. In mid-August 1845, Taylor received ambiguous orders from War Secretary William Marcy that, in effect, directed Taylor to march to the Rio Grande, yet made Taylor solely responsible for such a movement. "It is expected that you will approach as near the boundary line—the Rio Grande—as prudence will dictate. . . . The President desires that your position . . . should be near the river Nueces." The instructions reflected the U.S. government's uncertainty about Mexico's intentions; Polk's agent in Mexico City, William S. Parrott, believed that Mexico was going to declare war because of Texas's July 4 decision to accept annexation. But the Mexican Congress did nothing.

Taylor prudently chose to remain on the Nueces; but the Polk administration, after receiving reports that the Mexican army was approaching the Texas frontier, acted as though Taylor were on his way to the Rio Grande. "Attack her army first" if Mexican troops crossed the Rio Grande, Taylor was advised. In the event of a river crossing, which "shall be regarded as an act of War on her [Mexico's] part," Commodore David Conner's squadron was authorized to blockade Mexico's principal Gulf ports and "attack and take them if deemed practicable."

• • •

More Army units reached Corpus Christi in a trickle, then a flood. Taylor's fifteen-hundred-man Army of Observation grew to nearly four thousand men—comprising nearly half of the regular Army's fourteen regiments. It was the largest concentration of U.S. troops in thirty years. Before the American deployment, Corpus Christi, with its score of wind-blown buildings strung along a riverbank abutting a hundred-foot-high bluff, was best known for its flourishing black-market trade with Mexican border towns. With the arrival of camp followers, entrepreneurs, and adventurers, the civilian population exploded to a thousand in November and then doubled over the next month.

While remaining for the time being at Corpus Christi, Taylor consulted his subordinates about marching 120 miles southwest to the Rio Grande to stand guard on Texas's putative border. A handful of officers opposed the movement without comment, while the others either supported the plan, had no opinion, or merely relished the prospect of battlefield glory.

Hitchcock believed Texas's assertion that its border lay on the Rio Grande was preposterous. "Her original limit was the Nueces and the hills ranging north from its sources, and she has never conquered, possessed, or exercised dominion west of the Nueces," he wrote. He incorrectly inferred that Taylor was chafing to start a war. "I think the Gen. wants an additional brevet, and would strain a point to get it."

• • •

In his practice of foreign policy, James Polk was an adept of the black diplomatic art of graduated pressure—partnering the threat of military action with aggressive negotiations. As a fellow practitioner, England recognized Polk's saber-rattling over the Oregon Territory for what it was. Like a veteran poker player who weighs whether to call an opponent's bluff, England did not take Polk's rhetoric seriously; it was part of the game.

But graduated pressure was an unsuitable strategy to pursue with a diplomatic neophyte such as Mexico—also proud, nationalistic, and sensitive to insults. Annexing Texas, which Mexico still passionately believed to be her northern province, was provocation enough. By sending Taylor to the Nueces and suggesting a further movement to the Rio Grande, Polk and Secretary of State James Buchanan were playing with fire; yet, in their view, they were only applying pressure that they expected to result in negotiations, a border settlement, and the purchase of California. They did not expect Mexico to actually go to war. "These energetic & ample preparations will I think probably prevent war," the president predicted in late August 1845 to Tennessee Governor Aaron Brown.

But if, contrary to Polk's expectations, Mexico did fight, the president was certain that the conflict would be short and virtually bloodless. "We are prepared to drive her back to the [Rio Grande] and take her ports, and in a word, to conduct the war with the greatest possible energy, so as to make its continuance very short," Polk told his former law partner and confidant Gideon Pillow.

Whigs either deliberately misrepresented Polk's strategy to be a calculated provocation or believed it so. Yet in deploring Taylor's maneuvering in southwest Texas, the Whig *National Intelligencer* accurately described Mexico's view of the Army deployment as "nothing short (as everybody knows) of an invasion of Mexico. It is *offensive war,* and *not* the necessary defense of Texas."

• • •

The first known reference to the Rio Grande as Texas's southwest border was in 1803, when the United States asserted that the newly purchased Louisiana Territory, in fact, included Texas, "to the Del Norte [Rio Grande]." France had expropriated the Louisiana Territory from Spain when Spain failed to contribute money or troops to their military alliance during the Napoleonic Wars. But the Louisiana Territory's boundaries were undefined then, and still just as vague when France quickly sold it in 1803 to the United States for $15 million.

Spain rejected the U.S. claim to Texas, asserting that it had never been part of Louisiana. The 1819 Adams-Onis treaty, in which Spain ceded the Floridas to the United States, established the Sabine River as the Texas–Louisiana border and settled the dispute over Texas's ownership.

On early nineteenth-century Mexican maps, the Nueces River is clearly Texas's border with adjacent Coahuila Province. Spain drew this boundary in 1816, and over the next two decades, in atlases and maps—including Stephen Austin's when he was colonizing southeast Texas—the Nueces was the Texas–Coahuila border. When he was attempting to buy Texas, Andrew Jackson had accepted the Nueces as Texas's boundary.

In 1836, twenty years after Spain drew the Nueces boundary between Texas and Coahuila Province, the newly triumphant Texan-American insurgents compelled General Santa Anna to sign a treaty—which Mexico repudiated—placing the Texas–Mexico boundary on the Rio Grande. The Texans did not so much covet the 120 miles of mostly arid, snaky wasteland between the Nueces and Rio Grande rivers as they did the territory upriver in New Mexico. If the Rio Grande became Texas's boundary, Texans could conceivably claim eastern New Mexico and Santa Fe. The Texas Congress on December 19, 1836, declared the Rio Grande to be the Republic of Texas's boundary with Mexico. But until Texas's annexation by the United States in 1845, Mexico did not bother to quibble about the border, regarding all of Texas as rightfully hers.

Nor had Presidents Jackson, Van Buren, or Tyler given much thought to the location of the Texas–Mexican border. When Secretary of State John C. Calhoun sent Duff Green to Mexico in 1844 to buy Mexico's northern territories, Green had suggested a boundary somewhere between the Nueces and Rio Grande rivers. Congress's 1845 annexation offer to Texas did not specify a border. Only when persuading Texas to accept annexation did Polk resurrect the hoary Louisiana Purchase argument, thereby becoming the first president to recognize Texas's spurious claim to the Rio Grande border. This fiction became part of expansionist dogma, as did the myth that John Quincy Adams—the Secretary of State Adams of the Adams-Onis treaty of 1819—had traitorously signed away the United States' rightful claim to Texas. Adams and other Congressional Whigs who opposed annexing Texas expressed incredulity over the border claim; those not rejecting it outright judged the Nueces–Rio Grande area to be "disputed territory."

Robert Greenhow, the State Department's librarian and a respected historian, in 1845 completed *History of Florida, Louisiana, Texas and California, and of the Adjoining Countries.* The book purportedly demonstrated that Texas had remained a Spanish possession from 1763 until Mexican independence in 1821—and never was part of the Louisiana Purchase. Greenhow's work, which could have embarrassed his government's plans, was never published. While there is no evidence suggesting that the Polk administration suppressed it, Greenhow might well have imposed a self-censorship, in the belief that the book's publication would jeopardize his career.

General Zachary Taylor had ordered a new Texas map drawn with the most up-to-date information. After the map was completed, Taylor, Colonel Hitchcock, and other staff officers critiqued it and then forwarded it to the Quartermaster General's Office in Washington for printing.

When the printed map was delivered to Taylor's camp in late August, Taylor and his staff observed that someone in Washington had made a slight change; a boundary line had been added, tracing the Rio Grande. Hitchcock angrily wrote, "Our people ought to be damned for their impudent arrogance and domineering presumption! It is enough to make atheists of us all to see such wickedness in the world, whether punished or unpunished."

• • •

During the first days of Polk's presidency, when he sent Commodore Robert Stockton, Charles Wickliffe, and Archibald Yell to Texas, a fourth agent was dispatched to Mexico. He was a dentist, Dr. William S. Parrott. Polk had confidence in Parrott, although some of his advisers had reservations about Parrott's ability to accurately assess Mexico's political situation. Parrott certainly was familiar with Mexico's language, politics, and leading men; he had practiced dentistry in Mexico City for several years. But he had also memorably misread the political situation, with the result that Mexican officials had seized a large shipment of bottled port that Parrott had purchased. Parrott's estimated, and probably inflated, $690,000 loss had forced him into bankruptcy.

Strangely, Parrott's business debacle made him an ideal choice for the mission that he was given in Mexico City. His task was to settle what had been, until the Texas annexation question, the most fractious issue between the United States and Mexico—namely, the money Mexico owed U.S. citizens for financial losses incurred during Mexico's numerous regime changes. Parrott, in fact, owned the unhappy distinction of being America's top claimant.

Under an 1843 claims settlement, Mexico had agreed to pay the United States $2 million in quarterly payments of gold or silver over five years. But the payments stopped in July 1844, with Mexico announcing bankruptcy, and only $500,000 paid on the principal. Mexico also was in debt to England and France, which had threatened military reprisals if they were not paid. (In 1838, France had made a punitive raid on Vera Cruz.) The U.S. claims, Polk believed, were an excellent lever for pressuring Mexico to sell her northern provinces.

Parrott hoped to reestablish diplomatic relations with Mexico and to gather intelligence when he sailed from New York in April 1845 on the same vessel, the *Anahuas,* as Mexico's departing U.S. minister, General Juan Almonte.

• • •

Parrott's June 10 report to Secretary of State Buchanan said that Mexico would not resume normal relations with the United States unless she was compensated for the loss of Texas. An emissary, Don Juan de Dios Canedo, was on his way to Washington, Parrott wrote, "to sound the American administration, and to ascertain, what round sum, would be given, in compensation, for the loss of Texas." But compensation was a dead issue. While previous U.S. administrations had been willing to buy Texas when it was a Mexican province, Polk never would; since 1837, the United States had recognized Texas as a sovereign republic.

Through October 18, Parrott sent Buchanan thirty-two reports from Mexico City, about Texas's annexation and independence; Mexico's chaotic politics, financial problems, and military capabilities and movements; and the possibility of Mexico resuming relations with America. Not altogether trusting Parrott, Buchanan quietly asked the U.S. consuls in Mexico to evaluate his information. It was almost always accurate.

By late summer, Parrott was confident that Mexico would negotiate. "I have good reasons to believe that, an Envoy from the United States would not only be well received; but that his arrival would be hailed with joy," he wrote, ebulliently predicting that the Texas question might even be settled *"over a breakfast."*

However, Parrott warned, Mexico still expected compensation for Texas, although he had tried to throw cold water on that idea, telling Mexican authorities: "The United States could never recognize in Mexico the right to claim indemnity for the annexation of Texas. . . ."

The Mexican government's condescending attitude grated on him. In exasperation, he wrote: "I am fully persuaded, they can never love or respect us, as we should be loved and respected by them, until after we shall have given them a positive proof of our superiority."

The president and his advisers were also growing frustrated. In an editorial bearing the Polk administration's imprimatur, the Washington *Union* struck a belligerent tone on October 2: "Does Mexico prefer war? We are ready to wage it. Does she desire peace? She must be the first to seek it."

Then, Mexico City consul John Black corroborated Parrott's earlier report about Mexico's evident willingness to negotiate. But, he said, Mexico's foreign minister, Manuel de la Peña y Peña, would not accept Parrott as the U.S. negotiator. "The prejudices existing against him cannot easily be removed," wrote Black.

• • •

Polk and Buchanan chose Louisiana Congressman John Slidell, a Polk political ally, and authorized him to not only resolve the Texas and claims questions but to also purchase New Mexico and California.

Before Mexico would accept a U.S. peace commissioner, Peña y Peña demanded that Commodore David Conner withdraw the Gulf Squadron from Vera Cruz's waters, so the commissioner "might not have the appearance of being forced on them, by threat. . . ." Mexico pledged to abjure "any act of hostility against the United States" during negotiations.

On October 29, Conner's squadron disappeared from Vera Cruz's waters into the Gulf of Mexico.

Polk and Buchanan, hopeful that they might now sign a treaty with Mexico, overlooked a seemingly minor matter: Slidell's diplomatic powers. They had given Slidell broad authority, while the Mexicans' conception of the U.S. commissioner's title and authority was far more restrictive: "The commissioner [should have] full powers from his Government, to settle the *present dispute* [author's italics], in a peaceful, reasonable and honourable manner." This issue would prove to be thornier than anyone imagined.

THE NEGOTIATIONS THAT NEVER WERE

*The United States professed a desire for peace while "causing their squadrons
& their troops to advance upon the ports & the frontiers of Mexico; exacting
an humiliation, impossible to be submitted to. . . ."*

—Mexico Foreign Minister Joaquin M. de Castillo y Lanzas

In early November 1845, President Polk informed John Slidell that he was the new
Minister to Mexico, endowed with the complete array of diplomatic powers that
went with the title. Tall and square-jawed, with glossy black hair, dark eyes, and a
Roman nose, fifty-two-year-old John Slidell was one of Louisiana's leading citizens
in 1845. After growing up in New York City and graduating from Columbia College in 1810, Slidell moved to New Orleans and began practicing maritime law. He
married a French Creole woman, Mathilde Deslonde and soon became a political
power in his adopted state, where he served as U.S. Attorney and a state legislator
before going to Congress in 1843. During the 1844 election, Slidell's vote manipu-
lations ensured Louisiana's support of Polk. Slidell would later become a confidant
of Secretary of State James Buchanan, his campaign manager in 1856, and President Buchanan's most trusted adviser, until regional loyalties divided them.

• • •

Polk instructed Slidell to be ready at a moment's notice to go to Pensacola, Florida.
From there, he would sail to Vera Cruz, but without tipping off the French or English, whom the president believed would try to wreck the negotiations if they knew
about them. The president's letter does credit to his nickname, The Mole. "So

important do I consider the secrecy, with which the matter is kept, that I cannot charge you too strongly on that point. It will not be safe for you to communicate it to a human being." Slidell's response on September 25 shrewdly anticipated the major contretemps that would arise over his title and duties. Mexico's President Jose Joaquin Herrera, he said, "may not feel prepared to encounter the force of public opinion . . . by receiving from us an accredited agent. But of this, of course, you have much better means of judging, than anyone here possesses."

• • •

But diplomatic nuances were not uppermost in the minds of Polk and Buchanan, consumed as they were by their anticipation of obtaining California. "I am exceedingly desirous to acquire *California,*" Polk wrote Slidell on November 10, "and am ready to take the whole responsibility, if it cannot be had for less, of paying the whole amount authorized by your instructions. If you can acquire both *New Mexico* and *California,* for the sum authorized, the nation I have no doubt will approve the act."

The Polk administration's craving for California arcs kinetically across Buchanan's eleven pages of instructions to the new "Envoy Extraordinary and Minister Plenipotentiary of the United States." Obtaining San Francisco Bay was "all important to the United States," Buchanan emphasized, and Slidell could spend up to $25 million for California. "Money would be no object when compared with the value of the acquisition."

Buchanan summarily pronounced New Mexico of slight importance to Mexico and, in fact, a burden because of its distance and hostile Indian tribes. If Mexico, as was hoped, recognized the Rio Grande as the Texas–Mexico border, disputes over New Mexico could not be far behind; here, Buchanan was alluding to the delusory assertions by Sam Houston and other militant Texas expansionists that Texas was entitled to all of the territory east of the Rio Grande, including Santa Fe, clear to the river's source. Buchanan believed that Slidell might reasonably expect to acquire New Mexico for $5 million.

But he was to first press the issue of the $2 million (the sum included accrued interest) in outstanding U.S. citizen claims—described by Buchanan as "the injuries and outrages committed by the authorities of Mexico on American citizens." In this, the secretary was merely following the Polk formula of first applying diplomatic pressure, then offering to deal—for Slidell was to then profess the United States' willingness to pay off those claims if Mexico accepted Texas's annexation and the Rio Grande as the border. Under no circumstances, cautioned Buchanan, must Slidell permit Mexican officials to challenge Texas's status. "The independence of Texas," he wrote, "must be considered a settled fact."

If Slidell reached concord on any of the four objectives—the claims, the border, New Mexico, or California—he should conclude a treaty, instructed Buchanan. "Your mission is one of the most delicate and important which has ever been confided to a citizen of the United States."

A letter from Polk appended to Slidell's instructions more ominously stated: "If unfortunately, you shall fail to effect a satisfactory adjustment of the pending differences between the two countries (which I will not anticipate), we must take redress for the wrongs and injuries we have suffered into our own hands, and I will call on Congress to provide the proper remedies."

If Slidell's mission did not succeed, Polk intended to take military steps.

• • •

The president's inclusion of a letter with Buchanan's instructions exemplified the personal oversight he brought to all administration matters. Through relentless hard work, Polk had become remarkably knowledgeable about every executive department during his short time in office. Yet his pride in having mastered the details of governance was the bait for his own trap. Perfectionist that he was, Polk increasingly resisted delegating tasks and steadily took on more work himself. Soon, he was toiling every day except the Sabbath—and occasionally on Sundays, too—from morning until late at night. His only leisure was a walk around the grounds early in the morning. "No President who performs his duty faithfully and conscientiously can have any leisure," Polk wrote. "If he entrusts the details and smaller matters to subordinates, constant errors will occur. I prefer to supervise the whole operations of the Government myself . . . and this makes my duties very great."

The president paid his one secretary, nephew Joseph Knox Walker, from his own pocket (Walker, his wife, and their children lived in the White House for four years). When Walker took a vacation, the president found himself "having to perform the duties of secretary as well as President." Polk revered hard work, as had his Presbyterian forefather, John Knox, and he seemed to best like working alone in his office, or with his unpaid assistant—First Lady Sarah Polk, the first and possibly only presidential wife to serve as her husband's secretary. Mrs. Polk was politically astute and well-educated for a woman of her era, having studied at the Moravian Female Academy in Salem, North Carolina after attending elementary and secondary schools. She and Polk often worked side by side at their desks late into the night.

During the first year of his presidency, Polk left the White House just five times and dined out once. "My time has been wholly occupied in my office, in the discharge of my public duties," Polk wrote in his diary on April 1, 1846, a little more than a year after his inauguration. Months later, he would add, "In truth, though I occupy a very high position, I am the hardest working man in this country."

Besides immersing himself in the details of running the nation, Polk closely monitored the quasi-official Washington *Union* to ensure that it accurately represented his views. Upon his election, he had dismayed Andrew Jackson by exercising his prerogative as head of the Democratic Party to unceremoniously remove Jackson's old confidant, Francis Blair, as editor of the party newspaper, the Washington *Globe*. Polk replaced Blair with Thomas Ritchie, the editor of the Richmond *Enquirer* since Thomas Jefferson's presidency. Ritchie renamed the newspaper the *Union*. As Polk explained to the unhappy Jackson, "The *Globe*, it is manifest, does not look to the success or the glory of my administration so much as it does the interests and views of certain prominent men of the party who are looking to succeed me in 1848." Polk often used the sixty-eight-year-old Ritchie as a sounding board for his speeches and policy statements, and he sometimes clarified his administration's position in anonymous columns.

• • •

The president kept a rigid schedule of regular meetings with his cabinet, which he consulted on absolutely every matter, on Tuesdays and Saturdays. Over four years, the cabinet met 364 times. Polk was such a demanding manager that his six department heads were compelled to work full-time, year-round, a departure from the previous practice of cabinet members taking long vacations when Congress was in recess.

Like Jackson, Polk believed the White House belonged to the people. He opened his doors four mornings a week to anyone who wished to call—and was badgered by petitioners for government jobs and money. At the twice-weekly White House public receptions, ordinary people mingled with congressmen and diplomats. "Everyone feels at home, and they sometimes stalk into our bedroom and say they are looking at the house," wrote Johanna Rucker, Sarah Polk's niece and a longtime houseguest. When Polk entered the reception room, the Marine Band was instructed by the First Lady to play "Hail to the Chief," because the somewhat short-statured president's arrival often went unnoticed otherwise. The playing of the stirring march became a tradition.

Besides serving as her husband's amanuensis and political adviser, Sarah Polk supervised the White House domestic staff, oversaw the White House social calendar and dinner guest lists, and, when necessary, served as a lubricant between her stiff husband and the outside world. She permitted wine, but not hard liquor, at White House functions and forbade dancing, which she thought "indecorous." Mrs. Polk chose the carpeting, wallpaper, and new furniture when Congress appropriated $14,900 to give the rundown White House a facelift. Central heating, gas lighting, and a kitchen icebox were installed during the Polks' tenancy.

DECEMBER 1845: MEXICO CITY

When Slidell arrived in Mexico City, President Herrera would not meet with him. Herrera's envoys said the Mexican president could not receive a fully accredited U.S. minister, because it would be a de facto acknowledgment of Texas annexation and completely unacceptable to the Mexican people, poised to erupt again in revolution. Peña y Peña's earlier nuanced words, that "the commissioner [should have] full powers from his Government, to settle the present dispute"—in other words, Texas annexation—now loomed in importance. But Slidell was empowered to discuss everything *except* annexation—"a settled fact," in Buchanan's words.

Peña y Peña reminded Slidell that he had told William Parrott "that the Commissioner should be *ad hoc*—that is to say—commissioned to settle in a peaceful and honourable manner, the questions relative to Texas." But Slidell had come with "the absolute and general functions of an Envoy Extraordinary and Minister Plenipotentiary." The latter title presumed a normality of relations between the two countries that did not exist, said Peña y Peña. The Mexicans would only receive Slidell if his credentials were restricted to "the questions which have disturbed the harmony and good understanding between the two Republics, and which will bring on war between them, unless such settlement be effected." The question, of course, was Texas. Mexico, which had no illusions about ever getting Texas back, would have settled for cash.

• • •

Polk knew that he could neither permit Slidell to discuss an indemnity for Texas, nor change his credentials. Except for a few Northeastern Whigs, Americans believed they owed Mexico nothing for Texas; before agreeing to annexation, the Republic of Texas had been a sovereign nation for nine years and had repelled two Mexican invasions. The president had hoped that paying a generous sum for California and New Mexico—which the Polk and Herrera administrations both recognized were ordained to one day become U.S. territories—would serve as reparations for Texas without appearing so. This would also accomplish the important work of depositing cash in the bare Mexican treasury, enabling Herrera's government to buy enough loyalty to survive.

In point of fact, the United States need not have paid a cent either to keep Texas, or to obtain New Mexico and California, which were Mexican provinces in name only. But Polk understood that without a treaty, Mexican leaders would continue to exploit the Texas annexation issue for political purposes, and the border would become a running sore. He preferred all-out war to a dirty conflict that might well smolder for years.

• • •

Refusing to acknowledge that his credentials were the issue, Slidell contended in his blistering response to Peña y Peña that the titles "Commissioner" and "Minister Plenipotentiary" were "convertible terms." He demanded payment of the United States' $2 million in claims. "Mexico rejects the olive branch which has been so frankly extended to her," he wrote, hinting at "the consequences to which it may lead."

In a letter to Secretary of State Buchanan, Slidell disparaged Mexican statesmanship as rife with "chicanery and Ignorance," her leaders interested only in looking "with complacency upon any corruption or abuse of power," and her people willing to "submit with the most stupid indifference to any masters that might be imposed upon them." Only "hostile demonstrations" would convince Mexico to negotiate, and his job, wrote Slidell, was to "throw all the responsibility & odium of the failure of negotiations on the Mexican Government."

• • •

It appeared that Polk and Buchanan had either terribly misjudged Mexico's receptiveness to broader negotiations, or that they had, in fact, *wanted* Mexico to reject Slidell.

There is no evidence that Slidell's rejection was the Polk administration's aim, as some historians maintain. Undermining this cynical interpretation is evidence that

Polk believed Slidell's mission would succeed. In a letter to his brother William, Polk asserted, "There will be no war with Mexico." On December 17, he told Slidell that if tendering a larger sum would buy New Mexico and California, he should do so. In the same letter, Polk offered naval transport for Slidell's family to join him in Mexico. Had failure and war been the mission's objectives, the president would have suggested neither expedient. Ignorance of Mexico and her politics and people better explains the missteps that doomed Slidell's mission.

• • •

During twenty-five years of independence, the Republic of Mexico had made little progress toward stability or true democracy. The nation of 7 million people—4 million Indians, 1 million whites, 2 million mixed-bloods, and six thousand blacks—had careered from dictatorship to dictatorship, each a quicksilver coalescence of the military, wealthy landowners, clergy, or liberal intellectuals, and each dissolving as rapidly as it had formed, with the leaders carting off all the loot they could carry. Since 1836, Mexico's manipulative leaders, whenever they needed public support, had found it useful to arouse the people's anger over losing Texas and to direct it at the United States. Had Polk looked beyond Mexico's financial embarrassments and her chaos and poverty, he might have seen that her people, despite everything, remained fiercely proud and would not readily give up an acre of land to their powerful northern neighbor and her 20 million people.

JANUARY 1846: HAVANA

Charismatic, courageous, and devious, Antonio Lopez de Santa Anna, Mexico's best-known leader, was once again in exile after having been deposed from his third presidency in December 1844. Three years was his longest tenure, his first having been from 1833 to 1836, his second in 1839 as interim president, and finally from 1841 to his latest removal. The price of his return to power in 1839 was his left leg, lost during a skirmish with French troops at Vera Cruz as France sought payment of its unpaid claims during the "Pastry War" (so named because drunken Mexican army officers sacked a French pastry shop in Mexico City). His celebrated battle wound notwithstanding, Santa Anna had to promise to pay France 600,000 pesos before she would lift her blockade of Vera Cruz. When he was ousted in 1844, Santa Anna's amputated leg was dug up and dragged ignominiously through the streets.

As millions of people around the world gazed at the night sky hoping to glimpse Biela's Comet during its brilliant septennial passage within sight of Earth, Santa Anna was quietly plotting another lightning foray on Mexico's presidency. Incredibly, the man whose aid he planned to enlist was none other than President James K. Polk.

• • •

In February 1846, Colonel Alejandro J. Atocha, exiled to Cuba with Santa Anna, visited the White House. During three secret meetings, Atocha laid before Polk an intriguing proposition: if Polk did not block Santa Anna's return to Mexico, he would negotiate a treaty with the United States. "He said that Santa Anna was in favour of a Treaty with the U.S. and that in adjusting a boundary between the two countries the Del Norte [Rio Grande] should be the Western Texas line," the president noted in his diary after the first meeting, on Friday, February 13. While Atocha never said outright that Santa Anna had sent him, Polk assumed that he had. Atocha whetted Polk's interest for more details when he said that Santa Anna was willing to transfer most of New Mexico and California to the United States for $30 million.

On Monday, Atocha met with Polk for an hour in the morning, and again in the afternoon. The president stated that Mexico must still pay the more than $2 million in outstanding claims made against Mexico by U.S. citizens, to which Atocha replied that any Mexican government would be overthrown if it accepted that condition. "He said they must appear to be forced to agree to such a proposition," Polk wrote afterward. How? The U.S. Army must make a demonstration along the Rio Grande, Atocha said, and the Navy must threaten Vera Cruz. Then came the catch: Santa Anna needed a $500,000 down payment to bribe Mexican officials when he returned from exile.

Polk made no promises to Atocha, and when he consulted his cabinet about dispatching an envoy to Havana to meet with Santa Anna, it could not reach a decision; the cabinet members distrusted the oleaginous Atocha, a Spanish-born former New Orleans resident with a Mexican military title. Just six months before meeting with the president, Atocha had introduced himself to Polk at the White House as a U.S. citizen pressing a claim against Mexico.

• • •

John Slidell's diplomatic mission was stalled. "A war would probably be the best mode of settling our affairs with Mexico, but the failure of the negotiation will be very disagreeable & mortifying to me," wrote the lugubrious diplomat. On December 29, 1845, Congress accepted Texas into the Union as the twenty-eighth state, prompting Tennessee lawyer Adam Huntsman to crow in a letter to the president: "Texas is in, Oregon & California follows [sic] as natural as the apple falls from the tree at its maturity."

Would that it had been that easy. The next day, December 30, Herrera's government succumbed to a peaceful coup, darkening Slidell's prospects for negotiations.

Herrera's successor was General Mariano Paredes y Arrillaga, forty-nine, former commander of the Army of the Reserve at San Luis Potosi. Herrera had dismissed Paredes for refusing to march to the Texas frontier to reinforce General Mariano Arista; Paredes complained that he lacked resources. A veteran troublemaker who had overthrown Santa Anna in the fall of 1844, resulting in his exile to Cuba, Paredes got even with Herrera by accusing him of agreeing to meet with Slidell to "dismember" Mexico. The army transferred its loyalty to Paredes, who led troops into Mexico City, overthrowing Herrera. In his inaugural address, Paredes pledged to uphold Mexico's suzerainty over all of Texas. "The tone of Gen'l Paredes' proclamation breathes war against the U. States, though that was probably to enable himself to obtain power," Polk observed to his brother William on January 29.

• • •

Polk's assessment of Paredes was correct; he was a moderate who had become president by acting as a war hawk. His rise to power was part of a complex scheme by landowners, clergy, and conservatives to bring in a Spanish nobleman to rule Mexico. If this monarchist plot appeared outrageously self-serving, it was; yet at the same time, it was understandable. The conspirators longed for a respite from revolutions. A ringleader was Spain's Minister to Mexico, Salvador Bermudez de Castro, who had identified the would-be monarch as twenty-two-year-old Don Enrique, a cousin of Queen Isabella II. Buchanan had confidentially briefed Slidell on the conspiracy, declaring that the United States would never countenance European interference in Mexico. To maintain his power so that the secret plan could unfold, Paredes feigned a reverence for republican institutions and maintained a defiant posture toward the United States.

• • •

During the first months of 1846, even before knowing the outcome of Slidell's attempt to negotiate with Paredes, Polk reverted to graduated pressure. On January

13, he ordered General Taylor to march to the east bank of the Rio Grande and directed the Gulf Squadron to hover off Vera Cruz. "If our minister shall be ordered home, or be compelled to demand his passports, we will take the redress of our grievances into our own hands," the president declared.

Increasingly, Polk and his advisers spoke of war. After a February 17 cabinet meeting, Polk noted: "I expressed the opinion that it would be necessary to take strong measures toward Mexico before our difficulties with that Government could be settled."

The prospect of war disconcerted neither the president nor his cabinet. Just as they had disdained Mexico's diplomatic capabilities—believing she could be bullied, manipulated, and bribed—so they had a low opinion of Mexico's military capabilities. They believed that Mexico's army would shatter at the first blow, her leaders would sue for peace, and the United States could then take possession of California and New Mexico.

• • •

On March 12, Buchanan instructed Slidell to make a last attempt to obtain an audience with General Paredes. If, as expected, he were again rebuffed, wrote Buchanan, the president could state that he had tried every means to settle America's differences with Mexico before having to resort to force. Buchanan asked Slidell to extend to Paredes an offer to "relieve his administration from pecuniary embarrassment, if he would do us justice and settle the question of the boundary between the two Republics." Polk asked Democratic congressmen C. J. Ingersoll of Pennsylvania and Alvin Cullom of Tennessee to seek a House appropriation of $1 million for the negotiations.

But even as Buchanan was composing these instructions to Slidell, the Paredes administration's new Foreign Minister, Joaquin M. de Castillo y Lanzas, was informing Slidell that the government would not grant him an audience. The United States, said Castillo y Lanzas, professed a desire for peace while "causing their squadrons & their troops to advance upon the ports & the frontiers of Mexico; exacting an humiliation, impossible to be submitted to, in order to find a pretext, if no reason can be found, which may occasion the breaking out of hostilities."

As Slidell prepared to return to Washington, he sent Castillo y Lanzas a letter that ended with the words: "the question has now reached a point where words must give place to acts." To Buchanan, Slidell wrote: "Be assured that nothing is to be done with these people, until they have been chastised."

• • •

When the first report of Slidell's rejection reached Washington on April 7, it set in motion a series of consultations that led inexorably to war with Mexico. Congress's 1845 Texas annexation resolution had required the Polk administration to attempt to negotiate a boundary settlement with Mexico—and it had, only to be twice rebuffed by the Mexican government. Polk and his advisers agreed that if Slidell came home empty-handed, they would "take the remedy for the injuries and wrongs we had suffered into our own hands." On April 21, when it was evident that Slidell was returning without a treaty, the president recommended to his cabinet that Congress be asked to take "strong measures." Four days later, on April 25, Polk polled his advisers about the measures Congress should be urged to adopt. Surprisingly, Secretary of State James Buchanan, previously dovish about Mexico, now hawkishly favored urging Congress to declare war.

Buchanan had always been the most troublesome of the president's advisers. When Polk had required his six cabinet members to pledge to forgo politicking for the presidency in 1848, and to resign if they did decide to run, only Buchanan balked. While he did finally promise to not actively seek office, Buchanan was not above seeking allies outside the administration when his colleagues acted contrary to his views. He had secretly solicited support in Congress for his position on Oregon when the administration rejected it. He had allegedly masterminded the Senate's rejection of the U.S. Supreme Court nomination of George Woodward, a district judge from Buchanan's home state of Pennsylvania, and then had secretly persuaded friends in Congress to advance his own name. When Polk found out, he asked Buchanan pointblank whether he wanted to go to the Supreme Court. Abashed at being discovered, Buchanan said that he could not abandon the president in a time of need.

Thus, Buchanan's new, aggressive stance on Mexico revived the president's old suspicion that his Secretary of State had his eye on the presidency in 1848. "I cannot rely upon his honest and disinterested advice," Polk wrote in his diary.

None of it mattered at the moment, for Polk didn't need Buchanan's advice; he knew what he wanted. The president directed Buchanan to draft a statement asking Congress to authorize strong measures against Mexico.

8

THE WAR BEGINS

"General Taylor would regard in a hostile light any armed body of men who might cross . . . the Rio Grande, and that he would pursue them and treat them as enemies."

—General William Worth's warning to Mexican army officers

APRIL 10, 1846: THE RIO GRANDE

At daybreak, Colonel Trueman Cross, the middle-aged Quartermaster General of the Army of Observation, mounted his horse and rode out of Fort Texas, the American fortification rising on the eastern riverbank within cannon range of Matamoros. For recreation and exercise, Cross and other staff officers often rode in the countryside, even though bandits roamed the area.

Cross, who had three grown children (a son acted as his clerk), evidently was not worried about bandits, and he might have been preoccupied by his impending premature retirement from the Army. In just a few weeks, he would be back in Washington with his wife and daughter.

Like another of General Zachary Taylor's senior officers, Colonel William Worth, Cross was leaving the Army because of a controversy raging in the officer corps over brevet rank—temporary ranks awarded for merit but without commensurate pay. Army officers spoke of little else.

With the U.S. Army's size limited to 8,613 officers and men, there was room for only three generals; each of the fourteen regiments was allotted a colonel, a lieutenant colonel, and a major. Officers were few enough as it was, but the situation was exacerbated by the refusal of many disabled or aged senior officers to give up their commissions. Rather than resign, they took leave or went on inactive status, blocking the advancement of meritorious active officers, yet compelling them to take on the inactive officers' greater responsibilities. As a stopgap measure, the Army had created brevet rank. A major might be promoted to brevet lieutenant colonel, or, in Taylor's case, from colonel to brevet brigadier general, and be given greater responsibilities, but without more authority or pay—in other words, a paper rank.

Now that war loomed and new commands were being assigned to ranking officers, the question had arisen: Was brevet rank equal to ordinary, or "lineal," rank? The issue had come to a head when Taylor had asked the War Department to determine whether Colonel David Twiggs or Colonel William Worth should be his second-in-command. Twiggs had held lineal colonel rank longer than Worth, but Worth had recently been promoted to brevet brigadier general.

General of the Army Winfield Scott assayed Worth's higher brevet rank superior to Twiggs's more senior lineal rank, and the officer corps erupted. Lieutenant Colonel Ethan Allen Hitchcock wrote a protest petition that 158 officers signed, and he forwarded it to the president of the U.S. Senate. The petition melodramatically accused Scott of having embraced "a wrong principle—one of the most erroneous and dangerous that has ever been discussed among men." The angry officers suggested that because Scott had essentially declared the Army's rules null and void, his subordinates might justifiably emulate Scott's example "until his own orders and letters may be pronounced illegal, null, and void." This contretemps with Scott would not prevent Hitchcock from later serving as Scott's chief of staff, and becoming his most loyal defender.

When the petition reached the Senate, Missouri Senator Thomas Hart Benton called on President Polk, reminding him that in 1829 President Andrew Jackson had pronounced lineal rank superior to brevet rank. As Benton had calculated, Young Hickory invoked Old Hickory's seventeen-year-old ruling, reversing Scott.

Learning that he would not be Taylor's second-in-command after all, Worth angrily wrote out his resignation, as did Cross and other officers.

• • •

Because murderous bandits roamed the Rio Grande area, Army officers had been urged to travel in groups and under arms, but Colonel Cross left the Army encampment alone and unarmed. He did not return. The next day, April 11, search parties tried to find Cross; they were unsuccessful. Day after day, the troops searched the tall grass, chaparral, and swamps. "All of us felt very badly about Colonel Cross, and every effort has been made in vain to ascertain his fate," Lieutenant George Meade wrote on April 19.

General Taylor sent a letter to Major General Pedro de Ampudia, who had just taken command of the Mexican troops across the river, inquiring whether Cross was in his custody. Ampudia, who by then was wearing Cross's watch, solemnly professed to know nothing of the missing colonel's whereabouts.

On April 21, eleven days after Cross was last seen alive, his decomposing body was found four miles from camp, stripped of clothing, with "nothing left but the skeleton, the flesh having been torn off by wolves and vultures," reported Captain Philip Norbourne Barbour. After interviewing Mexican witnesses, officers reconstructed Cross's last minutes: ambushed by Mexican militia who robbed him of his gold epaulets and watch, Cross was led into the woods by a Mexican army officer, who then bludgeoned Cross to death with a pistol butt.

His remains were returned to Fort Texas, where his comrades had last seen him alive. A dragoon squadron and eight infantry companies escorted Cross's casket, borne by a hearse drawn by six horses, as a band played the "Dead March." A soldier led Cross's horse, covered entirely in black cloth, with the dead officer's boots and spurs backwards in the stirrups. An honor guard fired three volleys as Cross's remains were lowered into the ground at the foot of the flagpole. Cross was the first casualty of an undeclared war.

• • •

Anger permeated the Army of Observation after the murder of its venerated quartermaster general. The officer corps was like a tight-knit clan that sometimes squabbled, but that closed ranks when a common enemy threatened. Many regular officers were acquaintances from West Point or previous service, and the assembly of virtually the entire U.S. field Army on the Rio Grande—the largest gathering since the War of 1812—resembled a family reunion. Cross's death and Ampudia's prevarication "have inspired us all with a burning desire to avenge the Colonel's murder, and have destroyed all the sympathy that some few did still entertain for a people whom they deem unjustly treated," grimly noted Lieutenant Meade.

Lieutenants Stephen D. Dobbins and Theodoric H. Porter—a popular officer whose father was Commodore David Porter—volunteered to hunt down the killers. With ten men each, they set out on separate search-and-destroy missions.

Porter and his men overran an encampment of Mexican soldiers and galloped away on Mexican horses. Then they were caught in a downpour. Porter insisted on pressing on through the rain, despite his men's concerns about keeping their powder dry. Porter's men were right to be worried: when up to a hundred Mexican soldiers suddenly fired on the patrol from behind a thicket, the Americans' wet weapons misfired. In the melee, an American soldier was shot dead, and Porter was hit in the leg and abandoned by the nine survivors. Before he died, Porter made a last stand, killing a Mexican soldier and wounding two others.

Porter's death, coming so soon after Cross's, had a profound effect on the Army of Observation, which now clearly understood, as Lieutenant Meade observed, that "such acts as these, if continued, must bring on a general collision."

• • •

The orders from Washington that had brought General Taylor and his army to the Rio Grande for once were plain and authoritative—"directed by the president"— yet granted Taylor latitude in responding to circumstances. "It is not designed, in our present relations with Mexico, that you should treat her as an enemy," wrote War Secretary William Marcy on January 13, "but should she assume that character by a declaration of war, or any open act of hostility towards us, you will not act merely on the defensive, if your relative means enable you to do otherwise."

The orders reached the general's headquarters in Corpus Christi in February. Communications between Washington and the far-flung army would always be problematic; in the best of circumstances, a full month would elapse between the sending of a communiqué, and receiving a reply.

"I shall lose no time in making the necessary preparations," Taylor wrote. By March 11, all was in readiness, and a long, serpentine column of horses, men, and wagons—nearly four thousand men and their provisions, weapons, and ammunition —marched south from Corpus Christi. The weather was sultry-warm when the wind came from the south but cut like a knife when it shifted to the north. When the weather was dry, the roads were thick with dust; when wet, they were morasses. The soldiers, unaccustomed to marching in rain and alternating cold and heat, contracted a host of ailments, dysentery being chief among them.

Most of the officers and men were relieved to finally be under way after seven months of waiting. "I hope for a war and a speedy battle," Lieutenant Meade wrote to his wife, "and I think a good fight will settle the business, and, really, after coming so far and staying so long, it would hardly be the thing to come back without some laurels."

Lieutenant Ulysses S. Grant and a few others, however, disliked the role they believed they were being asked to play—in Grant's words, serving as bait "to provoke hostilities." "Mexico showing no willingness to come to the Nueces to drive the invaders from her soil, it became necessary for the 'invaders' to approach to within a convenient distance to be struck," he would later write. Lieutenant Colonel Ethan Allen Hitchcock, commanding the 3rd Infantry Regiment despite scarcely being able to sit up because of acute diarrhea (in April he would receive a sixty-day leave in St. Louis to recover), astutely observed, "It looks as if the government sent a small force on purpose to bring on a war, so as to have a pretext for taking California and as much of this country as it chooses."

• • •

When the Americans reached the Arroyo Colorado, a Mexican officer appeared and handed Taylor a message that warned if he "attempted to cross the river, it would be regarded as a declaration of war." The army crossed it and pressed on to the Rio Grande.

In Matamoros, General Francisco Mejia announced that "the degenerate sons of Washington" had crossed the Nueces River, "the line separating Tamaulipas from [Texas]," and exhorted Mexicans to defend their homeland. A delegation of Matamoros civil authorities hand-delivered to Taylor a formal protest written by the prefect of Tamaulipas's northern district warning that if Taylor did not withdraw, there would be war.

As the Army of Observation neared the Rio Grande, it tramped over springtime fields of bluebonnets, splashed through swampy grassland, and tried to avoid becoming tangled up in the impenetrable thickets of chaparral that were everywhere. On March 28, four columns of troops marched into a plowed field just yards from the river. Hundreds of Mexicans across the river in Matamoros watched the Americans stack arms and draw water from the river. A flagstaff was erected, and the Stars and Stripes were run up it, as a band played "The Star Spangled Banner." The martial ceremony evoked murmurs from the Mexican spectators.

• • •

Taylor tried to arrange a meeting between the Mexican commander and General William Worth, acting as Taylor's second-in-command (Polk's reversal of Scott's decision favoring brevet rank had not yet reached the army). But after crossing the river, Worth learned that General Mejia, soon to be replaced by General Ampudia, would meet only with Taylor, and that Worth was forbidden to enter Matamoros. Instead, General Romulo Diaz de la Vega, Mejia's artillery commander, met Worth beside the river. When Worth asked la Vega to personally deliver a letter written by Taylor to Mejia, la Vega refused. Worth then reluctantly *read* the letter in French to a la Vega aide, who translated it into Spanish.

Taylor's letter stated that the U.S. president had ordered the army to take possession of all the territory to the Rio Grande, but that the army's intentions were not hostile.

La Vega was not swayed. "His people regarded it as an act of war and . . . viewed with great indignation our flag planted on Mexican soil," noted Major Philip Norbourne Barbour, a member of Worth's party.

Worth demanded to see John Peter Schatzell, the U.S. consul at Matamoros. An aide conveyed the request to Mejia and returned with his refusal. Was the consul under arrest? Worth asked. No Americans were under arrest, replied la Vega.

Worth declared that Mejia's refusal to permit him to see the consul was a "belligerent act" and warned that "General Taylor would regard in a hostile light any armed body of men who might cross . . . the Rio Grande, and that he would pursue them and treat them as enemies."

Three days later, a note to Taylor from Mejia pronounced the Americans' occupation of the Rio Grande's east bank to be a "positive declaration of war on the part of the United States."

• • •

Although a stranger to any warfare more nuanced than fighting Indians, Taylor now tried his hand at propaganda. In an announcement to Matamoros leaders, he assured them that the American army had marched to the Rio Grande with peaceful intentions and promised to honor citizens' civil and religious rights, and to pay for any provisions his men obtained.

The Americans' highly conspicuous actions, however, belied Taylor's conciliatory words. Rapidly taking shape on the east riverbank, Fort Texas would provide American gunners with firing positions from which they could hit most of Matamoros. Captain James Duncan sighted his battery on Mejia's headquarters after the Americans' Mexican guide, Chipita, pointed it out to him. Mexican engineers began throwing up fieldworks.

Recognizing the warning signs, the English, French, and Spanish consuls raised the flags of their nations over their homes so they would not be bombarded.

While Taylor exuded calm confidence, he was understandably uneasy. His small army faced a hostile force three times its size. His Gulf of Mexico supply depot, Port Isabel, was 27 miles away on the Gulf of Mexico; he was more than 120 miles from Corpus Christi; and reinforcements were hundreds of miles away in New Orleans. While Taylor had the authority to mobilize militias from nearby states, it would take weeks for them to reach him.

Worst of all, without a war declaration, he could not take the offensive but had to wait to be attacked and hope that his regulars would respond quickly and decisively, for a defeat on the Rio Grande at the war's outset would be an enormous setback. While a few officers, as well as some American newspapers, wondered whether Taylor had brought too small a force to the Rio Grande, most of his officers and men were supremely confident that they could defeat the Mexican army, despite its numerical advantage. They simply believed that the American army was superior. "No one seems to think a disaster to our Army a thing possible," noted Major Barbour.

• • •

The Rio Grande Valley's riotous springtime colors and fragrances were a diversion from the execrable food, endless patrols, and enervating boredom that were the Army of Observation's daily fare. "The country immediately on the banks of the river is beautiful, and fully equal in fertility to the banks of the Mississippi," wrote Lieutenant Meade. But there were swarms of mosquitoes and flies, and snakes. While water and wood for fires were plentiful, the troops' daily ration too often was rancid beef and bacon, moldy hardtack, and coffee dosed with vinegar to disguise its vile taste.

Dozens of deserters swam the river to Matamoros, where the Mexicans welcomed them. Many were recent Irish and German immigrants who could no longer abide the abuse of "nativist" officers who despised foreigners and Catholics. Xenophobia was growing in Antebellum America as ever-larger waves of immigrants arrived in New York and Boston, and anti-immigrant sentiment was strong in the officer corps. Immigrant soldiers were three times more likely than native-born Americans to be severely punished for minor infractions. A favorite punishment was "bucking and gagging." The soldier sat on the ground, "feet drawn up to his hams, and his wrists tied firmly in front of his legs: a long stick or broom handle is then inserted between his legs and arms, going over his arms and under his bent knees, a gag is then placed in his mouth and tied firmly behind his head." He might be left in this agonizing position for hours, even days.

The Mexicans in Matamoros smuggled pamphlets into Taylor's camp that urged immigrant soldiers to join their Catholic brethren in Matamoros. Deserters were promised Mexican citizenship, 320 acres of land, and a welcome as "true friends and Christians."

Every day, deserters tried to swim the Rio Grande to Matamoros. Some drowned, but others reached the west riverbank. So many Irishmen deserted—forty on April 11 alone—that they were mustered into a Mexican artillery battalion, "The Legion of St. Patrick," under Lieutenant John Riley, also a deserter. The "San Patricios" would later distinguish themselves in battle against their former American comrades, sometimes targeting officers who had tormented them.

U.S. officers added more guards on the riverbank and ordered them to shoot to kill. In one night, guards shot four deserters in the water; three were killed, one wounded. "Those who were killed called loudly for mercy," wrote Lieutenant Napoleon Jackson Tecumseh Dana, who witnessed the shootings, "but the more they cried, the more the pickets fired. They were said to be shot all to pieces."

• • •

The Mexicans celebrated the completion of the Matamoros fieldworks on April 3 with a religious ceremony. Robed priests sprinkled holy water on the guns as laborers and troops bowed their heads and knelt in the dirt. Protestant American soldiers viewed the proceedings with wry amusement. "Two priests threw waters by the pailfull [sic] upon [the guns]," Lieutenant John P. Hatch wrote to his sister. "I rather think this must have been done because they had nothing but nine pounders in them." Major Barbour observed: "It is very well for them to invoke protection of their feeble defenses from a higher Power, for if they provoke a fire from our eighteen-pound battery it will not be in the power of their guns to prevent the destruction of everything they have done."

• • •

When finally completed, Fort Texas, nestled in a bend of the Rio Grande and a mere half-mile from Matamoros, was equipped to repel attacks and withstand bombardments. The fort's walls were nine feet thick—fifteen feet at the base—and surrounded by a twelve-foot-deep ditch spanned by a drawbridge. The fort's rear was protected by a large pond, bordered by woods and the road to Port Isabel. Fort Texas's commander, Major Jacob Brown, a grizzled fifty-eight-year-old, knew what he was doing when he made the blueprint for the fort. He had begun his Army career as a private and had advanced through the ranks during thirty years at a succession of frontier posts with the 7th Infantry Regiment, known as the "Cotton Balers" for its valor at the Battle of New Orleans in 1815. Brown had delegated to his second-in-command, Captain Joseph Mansfield, an 1822 West Point graduate, the supervision of the fort's construction.

The fort's defenses included more than four hundred troops, four heavy 18-pounder guns (such designations refer to the weight of the cannon balls), and four 6-pounder field guns under the command of Lieutenant Braxton Bragg. The 18-pounders' two-mile range enabled them to hit any spot in Matamoros; Bragg's battery had a one-mile range. "At the first gun we shall rattle them about their ears in such a manner as will soon silence their fire," predicted Lieutenant Meade.

Meade's confidence was justified. The American artillery units of 1846 were the best in the world, led by professional officers trained at West Point and the Artillery School at Fortress Monroe, Virginia. The artillery would be the Americans' best ally in the months ahead.

• • •

General Mejia's successor, Major General Pedro de Ampudia, inspected the Matamoros artillery positions on April 11. A military decoration conspicuously displayed on his left breast piqued the curiosity of the Americans across the river. Their mood darkened when they learned that Ampudia had earned it for his role in capturing three hundred Texas militiamen at Mier in 1842. The Mier disaster, in which one of every eleven captives was randomly selected for execution, was indelibly etched in Texas's institutional memory; seventeen Texans had been shot. In 1844, after crushing a revolt in Tabasco, Ampudia had ordered fifteen Mexican rebels shot and had their heads cut off, boiled in oil, and hung in iron cages on the town walls. While conceding that Ampudia was courageous, Major Philip Norbourne Barbour also rated him "a blood-thirsty fiend. . . . Ampudia had the sick of his army shot on his march to this frontier to get rid of transporting them. . . ."

Ampudia ordered U.S. Consul J. P. Schatzell and all other Americans to leave Matamoros within twenty-four hours; they were sent 170 miles south to Victoria, the capital of Tamaulipas. The following day, April 12, the Mexican general gave Taylor an ultimatum: "I require you in all form, and at latest in the peremptory term of twenty-four hours, to break up your camp and retire to the other bank of the Nueces River, while our governments are regulating the pending question in relation to Texas." If Taylor refused, "it will clearly result that arms, and arms alone, must decide the question."

Taylor replied that the United States had attempted diplomacy, but that the Mexican government had refused to receive the U.S. minister. His orders were to occupy the Rio Grande's east bank until the U.S.–Mexican boundary question was settled. "I regret the alternative that you offer . . . leaving the responsibility with those who rashly commence hostilities."

• • •

Taylor ordered the Navy to blockade the mouth of the Rio Grande. While his instructions from the War Department did not expressly authorize this action, Taylor believed that Ampudia's peremptory banishment of Americans from Matamoros and other Rio Grande towns to the Mexican interior demanded a sharp response, even if it led to hostilities. On April 17, the schooner *Alert*, commanded by Navy Lieutenant Francis Renshaw, turned back two merchant vessels, the *Equity* and *Floridian*, carrying flour from New Orleans to Ampudia's army in Matamoros.

Ampudia demanded that Taylor permit the vessels to deliver the flour to his army. Taylor replied, "I am certainly surprised that you would complain of a measure which is no other than a natural result of the state of war so much insisted upon by the Mexican authorities." He would lift the blockade, Taylor said, if Ampudia consented to an armistice, with both armies remaining on the Rio Grande, while their governments discussed the boundary question.

Taylor knew that the blockade would push the Mexicans to the breaking point. "It will . . . *compel* the Mexicans either to withdraw their army from Matamoros, where it cannot be subsisted, or to *assume the offensive* on this side of the river."

• • •

On April 23, Mexican President Mariano Paredes y Arrillaga proclaimed the commencement of "a defensive war, and those points of our territory which are invaded or attacked will be energetically defended." In Mexican history books, the coming conflict would be known variously as the "Guerra de la Defensa" and "War of 1847." Enumerating the "ancient injuries and attacks" by the United States on Mexico since 1836, Paredes alleged that America was now embarked upon "new conquests upon the frontier communities of the departments of Tamaulipas and New León, and progressing at such a rate that troops of the same United States threaten Monterey in Upper California." The latter was untrue, but explorer John C. Frémont's activities in California had indeed alarmed Mexican authorities.

Major General Mariano Arista, commander of the Army of the North, marched into Matamoros on April 15 with thousands of reinforcements from the army headquarters at San Luis Potosi. President Paredes had ordered him to drive the Americans from the Rio Grande Valley. Arista took command at Matamoros and made Ampudia his deputy.

• • •

Brigadier General Anastasio Torrejón was to lead sixteen hundred cavalry, sappers, and light infantrymen across the Rio Grande above Matamoros. After cutting the road between Fort Texas and Port Isabel, the Mexican troops would secure a river ford below Matamoros so that Arista and the rest of the army could cross to the east side. Late in the day on April 24, Torrejón's fast-moving troops reached the American side of the Rio Grande, about twenty miles upriver from Fort Texas.

Within hours, Taylor had learned that a Mexican force of unknown size was on his side of the river. He dispatched Captain Seth B. Thornton and sixty-three dragoons to determine the enemy's strength and location.

• • •

Gaunt and hard-bitten, Thornton had fought in the Florida Indian wars, and by chance had been aboard the side-wheeler steam packet SS *Pulaski* in 1838 when its boiler exploded. Thornton had the presence of mind to help push several women and children into lifeboats before the steamer went down off the North Carolina coast with a hundred passengers and crewmen. Cast adrift on his own, Thornton was found three days later, lashed to a chicken coop and raving.

Now, at the head of a troop of dusty, bearded, cigar-smoking dragoons, Thornton pushed upriver as darkness fell on April 24. The next morning, the troopers' guide, Chipita, reported enemy troops ahead and refused to advance further. Thornton and the dragoons proceeded without Chipita.

Twenty miles north of Fort Texas, the Americans rode into a Mexican ranch, Rancho de Carricitos, and entered a field bordered by chaparral. As Thornton and some of his officers questioned a Mexican civilian, gunfire suddenly erupted from the chaparral, where hundreds of Torrejón's men lay concealed in ambush. The dragoons wheeled around, firing blindly at the invisible enemy and looking for an escape route. Amid the gunfire, gunsmoke, men's shouts, and the piercing screams of wounded horses, Thornton bolted for the passageway that had admitted the dragoons to the field, with his men right behind him. Mexican soldiers suddenly blocked the way and loosed a volley of musket fire into the dragoons galloping toward them. Thornton's horse—a roan that had carried him through the Florida Indian wars—was wounded, and it fell, pinning the captain. His men recoiled into the center of the field, where they milled as the Mexicans hidden in the chaparral riddled them. Facing annihilation, they surrendered. Eleven dragoons lay dead, and six were wounded.

• • •

Chipita reached Fort Texas at reveille the next morning with the news of the ambush and surrender. At noon, a horse-pulled cart creaked into the American camp with one of Thornton's wounded dragoons and a note from General Torrejón stating that he was handing over the soldier for medical treatment. The other troopers were prisoners, Torrejón wrote.

Expecting an attack at any time, American soldiers slept in their clothing with their weapons by their sides—as Hernando Cortes's men had done nearly 350 years earlier during their march on Mexico City. But Torrejón's troops marched around Fort Texas without molesting it and secured a crossing downriver for General Arista's army.

Taylor fired off letters to the governors of Texas and Louisiana, requesting four regiments of volunteers from each state—five thousand men in all.

In his report on the Thornton attack to Adjutant General Roger James, Taylor wrote: "Hostilities may now be considered as commenced."

9

"A STATE OF WAR EXISTS"

"They wanted a small war, just large enough to require a treaty of peace, and not large enough to make military reputations, dangerous for the presidency."

—Senator Thomas Hart Benton of Missouri

SATURDAY, MAY 9, 1846: WASHINGTON

Dry and unsentimental though he was, President James Polk surely sensed the portentousness of this day. The *National Intelligencer* had reported the murder of Colonel Trueman Cross and that two thousand Mexican troops had crossed the Rio Grande "evidently to cut off American troops from their supplies." Only one president, James Madison in 1812, had ever sought and obtained a congressional war declaration.

Polk and his advisers had placed the Mexico question in abeyance since deciding on April 25 to recommend that Congress take unspecified "strong measures" against Mexico. The cabinet knew about John Slidell's second rebuff and his departure from Vera Cruz, but Polk wanted to speak with Slidell in person before actually going to Congress—as asking for "strong measures" would clearly mean war.

On Friday, May 8, Polk's Minister Plenipotentiary had officially reported his mission's failure to the president. The United States, declared Slidell, must avenge his humiliating rejection and "take the redress of the wrongs and injuries which we had so long borne from Mexico into our own hands, and to act with promptness and energy," Polk recorded in his diary that night.

• • •

At noon sharp on Saturday, Polk convened his cabinet. Dismissed as mediocrities by the Whigs, they were, if not the nation's most gifted men, undoubtedly men of talent: Secretary of State Buchanan, the former Minister to Russia, Pennsylvania senator, and future president; War Secretary William Marcy, the former New York governor and member of Martin Van Buren's "Albany Regency," who had memorably said, "To the victors belong the spoils," coining the shorthand term for political patronage, the "spoils system"; and Navy Secretary George Bancroft, the gifted Massachusetts poet and historian (his *History of the United States* would span ten volumes), who, with the help of Gideon Pillow and Treasury Secretary Robert J. Walker of Mississippi, had secured Polk's nomination at the 1844 Democratic National Convention. In his brief tenure as Navy Secretary, Bancroft had already accomplished what his predecessors had unsuccessfully attempted for thirty years—to establish an academy for naval officers. The Navy School (renamed the Naval Academy in 1850, with its first graduating class in 1854) had opened its doors on October 10, 1845, after Bancroft, bypassing Congress, transferred Fort Severn, at Annapolis, Maryland, from Army to Navy jurisdiction. Rounding out the cabinet were two Polk confidants, Postmaster General Cave Johnson of Tennessee, and Attorney General John Y. Mason, a former Polk classmate at the University of North Carolina who had served as President John Tyler's Navy Secretary after Thomas Gilmer perished in the USS *Princeton* explosion.

Polk wanted to ask Congress to declare war on Mexico. Buchanan, Marcy, Walker, Johnson, and Mason concurred, while Bancroft did not see how the United States could declare war when Mexico had not committed a hostile act. Polk impatiently replied that there were abundant reasons for declaring war—the unpaid claims, the U.S.–Mexico border question, the Mexican troops at Matamoros, the snubbing of Slidell—and "it was impossible that we could stand *in statu quo,* or that I could remain silent any longer." The president proposed to deliver the war message to Congress in three days, on Tuesday. Before the cabinet adjourned at 2 P.M., it agreed, with Bancroft dissenting, to prepare the message for Congressional consideration.

• • •

Four hours later, Army Adjutant General Roger Jones hand-delivered General Zachary Taylor's April 26 report on the Thornton attack and a copy of his urgent request to Louisiana and Texas for five thousand volunteers. With mounting excitement, Polk summoned his cabinet to a meeting at 7:30 P.M.

• • •

Polk read Taylor's dispatch aloud to his reassembled advisers, who now unanimously concurred that Congress must be asked to authorize "vigorous & prompt measure(s) to enable the Executive to prosecute the War." Through the late hours of Saturday, the cabinet discussed how the war message should be worded.

The president broke his rule of not working on Sunday and, except for church services and dinner, he labored over the message from early morning until 10 P.M., with Buchanan and Bancroft coming and going with drafts and revisions. "It was a day of great anxiety to me," Polk wrote before retiring for the night, "and I regretted the necessity, which had existed to make it necessary for me to spend the Sabbath in the manner I have."

• • •

By Monday morning, the Thornton ambush was the sensation of Washington, with the news having percolated all day Sunday through the congressmen's boarding houses. Monday's *National Intelligencer* carried a report of the attack, along with further information from a Colonel R. Fitzpatrick, stationed with Taylor's army. Having consumed these sketchy details, congressmen were now eager to hear what the president had to say.

Polk's message, read at noon to the House and Senate, assailed Mexico's intransigence on the U.S. claims and Texas border issues, and her "threatened invasion of Texas . . . threatened solely because Texas had determined, in accordance with a solemn resolution of the Congress of the United States, to annex herself to our Union."

Polk declared that because America had recognized Texas's claim to all land east of the Rio Grande, that land was now part of the United States. Mexico's refusal to receive John Slidell was a provocation, as was her sending an army to the Rio Grande. He acknowledged that he had been ready to recommend war even before learning of the Thornton ambush. "The cup of forbearance had been exhausted even before the recent information from the frontier. . . .

"But now, after reiterated menaces, Mexico has passed the boundary of the United States, has invaded our territory and shed American blood on American soil. She has proclaimed that hostilities have commenced, and that the two nations are now at war.

"As war exists, . . . we are called upon . . . to vindicate with decision the honor, the rights, and interests of our country." Polk asked Congress "to recognize the existence of war, and to place at the disposition [*sic*] of the Executive the means of prosecuting the war with vigor." The president expressed his "anxious desire" to end the war swiftly, and to reach a negotiated settlement with Mexico.

Before the day ended, the House Committee on Military Affairs drafted and sent to the full House a bill appropriating $10 million and authorizing the president to call up fifty thousand volunteers.

• • •

To quash dissent, House Democrats, on Ohio Congressman Jacob Brinkerhoff's motion, limited debate of the war bill to just two hours, declaring that any delay would place Taylor's army in grave danger. Whigs angrily protested that hasty action would not bring Taylor succor any quicker. Democrats shifted ground, arguing the war should be accepted on faith. "For myself, I hold it to be no part of my duty to inquire *how* this war originated, nor *wherefore*," said Brinkerhoff. "It is enough for me, as a man professing an ordinary share of patriotism, and representing a patriotic constituency, to know that it exists."

South Carolina Congressman I. E. Holmes scoffed, "We know nothing more than that the two armies have come into collision in the disputed territory, and I deny that war is absolutely, necessarily the result of it." In 1807, he pointed out, war was not declared when the British warship *Leopard* attacked the USS *Chesapeake* off the Virginia Capes; why should it be now? Kentucky Congressman Garrett Davis, who represented Henry Clay's home district, said such a momentous matter should be debated for a full day at the least. Yet he was forced to concede that "the haughty and dominating majority will not allow now this much."

Democrats drowned out the Whig protests by reading, for the next hour and a half, excerpts from the documents submitted with Polk's war message.

Then, Democrat Linn Boyd of Kentucky administered the coup de grace, proposing that the appropriations bill be given a preamble that read: "By the act of the Republic of Mexico, a state of war exists between that government and the United States." Whigs indignantly protested, but the language was adopted, 123–67. The minority party had been slickly outmaneuvered. Now, anyone voting against the preamble could be accused of voting to deny materiel to the troops. When the roll call vote was taken on the appropriations bill, only fourteen congressmen dared oppose it; the final vote was 174–14.

Ohio Congressman Joshua R. Giddings, one of the fourteen who voted against the war bill, in a letter to his wife described what happened next: "As was expected, a shower of abuses was let loose upon us, and my friends who voted with me appeared somewhat alarmed at our position." Giddings believed that the president had unlawfully invaded Mexico, violating "every principle of international law and of moral justice," to procure "the conquest of Mexico and California" and "render slavery secure in Texas."

Davis, who did not stand with "The Fourteen," as they were called, reproached Polk for "carrying [the war] on for months in a series of acts. . . . The river Nueces is the true western boundary of Texas. The country between that stream and the Del Norte [Rio Grande] is part of Mexico; and that power had people and establishments in it."

Even the few squeaks of protest that were heard in the House were too much for the Washington *Union,* which accused Whigs of being "willing to tie up the hands of the president in such a manner as must ultimately bring disgrace upon the nation." The *Union*'s editor, Thomas Ritchie, continued: "The fiery-eyed head of party spirit is up, and hissing with forked tongue in our high places, even at the moment when patriotism stretches out its arm to save our soldiers from threatened slaughter, and to chastise the invaders on our soil."

• • •

In the Senate, John Calhoun of South Carolina and Thomas Hart Benton pulled every parliamentary trick to slow down the war bill's passage. Significantly, both men represented slave states. Calhoun, as did many Southern congressmen, feared that a consequence of a war with Mexico would be the wholesale admission of new slave-free states, thereby tipping the political balance—after Texas's admission, there were fifteen slave and thirteen free states—against the Southern slave states.

Calhoun challenged the preamble's assertion, "a state of war exists," on the ground that under the Constitution, there could be no war unless Congress declared it, although "there may be invasion without war, and the President is authorized to repel invasion without war." Before the Senate voted, it should spend a full day examining the documents accompanying Polk's war message, said Calhoun, so that senators with doubts "have some short time allowed for reflection."

Benton recommended that the war declaration be uncoupled from the appropriations bill and be assigned to the Committee on Foreign Affairs. Calhoun and Senator Willie Person Mangum of North Carolina both liked this plan. What if

Mexican troops had acted contrary to their government's orders? Mangum asked. Calhoun favored sending supplies to Taylor's army; but as for adopting the preamble, he would as soon "plunge a dagger into my own heart."

Senate hawks drowned out Calhoun, Benton, and their allies with passionate speeches. The Mexicans, said Texas Senator Sam Houston, had crossed the Rio Grande "in military array—they had entered upon American soil with a hostile design." Michigan Senator Lewis Cass declared, with high drama: "A hostile army is in our country; our frontier has been penetrated; a foreign banner floats over the soil of the republic; our citizens have been killed, while defending their country. A great blow has been aimed at us; and while we were talking and asking for evidence, it may have been struck, and our army annihilated." Added William Allen of Ohio: "A delay of 48 hours might produce events which would become the occasion of a lasting war."

Pressured by Allen, Vice President George Dallas, and Polk himself, Benton reluctantly shepherded the war bill through his Military Affairs committee to the Senate floor. Polk reassured Benton that he would not be prodigal with men and money in prosecuting the war; with "a large force on land and sea . . . it could be speedily terminated." Benton wrote later that "they wanted a small war, just large enough to require a treaty of peace, and not large enough to make military reputations, dangerous for the presidency."

On a 25–20 vote, senators refused to separate the preamble from the appropriations bill, and the war bill and preamble were approved, 40–2. Only Senators Thomas Clayton of Delaware and John Davis of Mississippi voted against it. "It was as much an act of aggression on our part as pointing a pistol at another's breast," Clayton said disgustedly. "Never was so momentous a measure adopted, with so much precipitancy; so little thought; or forced through by such objectionable means," complained Calhoun, who did not vote. He wrote with remarkable prescience to Commodore David Conner: "It sets the example which will enable all future Presidents to bring about a state of things, in which Congress shall be forced, without deliberation, or reflection, to declare war, however opposed to its convictions of justice or expediency."

• • •

Polk signed the war bill into law on May 13, and in a public proclamation announced "the existence of the war." In short order, Congress granted the president authority to increase the regular Army to 15,540 men, by raising the number of privates per company from 64 to 100; creating a company of sappers, miners, and "pontooners"; and adding a dragoon regiment to protect emigrants and traders on the Oregon Trail.

• • •

Newspapers applauded Congress's swift decisiveness, and thousands of young men heeded the recruiting broadsides that appeared overnight, seemingly by magic. "MEN OF OLD ESSEX! MEN OF NEWBURYPORT! Rally round the bold, gallant and lion-hearted Cushing! He will lead you to victory and to glory!" exhorted a solicitation for volunteers for Colonel Caleb Cushing's Massachusetts regiment. Herman Melville, busy completing his South Seas novel, *Typee,* described the war fever to his diplomat brother Gansevoort: "People here are all in a state of delirium. . . . A military ardor pervades all ranks. . . . Nothing is talked of but the 'Halls of the Montezumas.' " At City Hall in New York City, twenty thousand people attended an outdoor rally conducted from three stages. Everywhere there were placards bearing the ringing slogan: "Ho, for the Halls of the Montezumas."

• • •

The seeds of dissent were also being quietly sown. Northern critics were murmuring that the war's secret purpose was to extend slavery—a conspiracy theory scorned by the Washington *Union* as "utterly and absolutely false" and that revealed the "abolitionist tendencies of the Whig party throughout New England . . . [that] can no longer be doubted." The *United States Gazette* blamed the war on "the unskillful course of the Administration—unless, indeed, its skill has been manifested in the means to bring about the war." The New York *Tribune* wrote that Mexico, not the United States, had displayed the greater forbearance during the preceding months, and warned: "No true honor, no national benefit, can possibly accrue from an unjust war." Anson Jones, the last president of the Republic of Texas, observed: "The war was sought to be made everywhere except under the Constitution, and by every means known to human ingenuity." General Taylor's march to the Rio Grande, Jones noted, was "the consummation of [these] hopes and purposes. . . . General Taylor thereby sprung one of the numerous *traps* which had been set by the Government, and *caught the war. . . .*" Recovering from severe diarrhea in St. Louis, Lieutenant Colonel Ethan Allen Hitchcock read Polk's war message in the newspaper and angrily observed: "We ought to be scourged for this!"

• • •

Britain and France were incredulous. The London *Times* wrote that the U.S. Congress had "legislated a lie" by adopting the war bill preamble blaming Mexico. "We cannot suppose that Mr. Polk is so blind as not to have foreseen these events. He must not only have foreseen them, but intended to bring them to pass." Citing provocations such as Taylor's marching to the Rio Grande and the Gulf Squadron's menacing Vera Cruz, the *Times* speculated—accurately, as it turned out—that the Navy probably also had orders to seize California. "The head of the American Government has, with as much deliberation as he is capable of, plunged this country into this most flagitious war."

• • •

Secretary of State Buchanan apprised American ministers abroad of the war, in a circular intended to be shared with foreign governments. His letter was a primer on the administration's public war policy, blending the oft-heard jeremiads against Mexico with buttery assurances of America's peaceful intentions. "We go to war with Mexico solely for the purpose of conquering an honorable and permanent peace," Buchanan wrote. "We shall bear the olive branch in one hand, and the sword in the other; and whenever she will accept the former, we shall sheath the latter."

As an announcement of open warfare, the circular was blandness incarnate, but it would have been even milder had not Polk rejected Buchanan's first draft on May 13; amazingly, it had disavowed any U.S. territorial ambitions. In going to war, Buchanan's draft read, the United States "did not do so with a view to acquire either California or New Mexico or any other portion of the Mexican territory."

In his diary that night, Polk explained with lawyerly precision why Buchanan's disavowal had to be excised: "We had not gone to war for conquest, yet it was clear that in making peace we would if practicable obtain California and such other portion of the Mexican territory" to satisfy the U.S. claims against Mexico and to compensate the United States for the expense of prosecuting the war.

Buchanan had not readily consented to the revision. If the United States did not disclaim all designs on Mexico's territory, he argued, then England and France would come to Mexico's aid.

Let them, Polk shot back. Better that than to "tie up my hands or make any pledge to any Foreign powers" that had no right to make any demands.

England and France wouldn't stand for it, insisted Buchanan.

Since learning of the Thornton ambush four days earlier, Polk had been under great pressure and had been working intensely during every waking hour. Losing his customary self-possession, the president launched an angry tirade: Before he would ever attempt to mollify England and France by repudiating any attempt to "honorably" acquire California "or any other part of the Mexican Territory which we desired," he would fight them both, Polk tigerishly declared. For that matter, he would battle "all the Powers of Christendom . . . and I would stand and fight until the last man among us fell in the conflict."

After Polk uttered those words, there was nothing more to say. The five cabinet members who had witnessed the donnybrook sided with the president, and Buchanan was instructed to redraft the circular.

• • •

Before the end of May, Polk and his advisers were quietly plotting the permanent acquisition of all of Mexico's provinces north of the thirty-second parallel—today's U.S.–Mexican boundary. "I declared my purpose to be to acquire for the U.S. California, New Mexico, and perhaps some others of the Northern Provinces of Mexico whenever a peace was made," Polk wrote in his diary on May 30. Confident that it would not only seize these territories but win the war with ease, the administration even sketched a peace treaty. "For a suitable cession of territory," Polk wrote, "we are willing to assume the debts [the $2 million in claims] to our own citizens & to pay an additional consideration."

The president began quietly discussing the peace proposal with select congressional leaders. His aim "was not conquest," he assured South Carolina Senator George McDuffie on July 30, "but that in concluding a peace I desired in consideration of a fair equivalent to acquire California and otherwise adjust a suitable boundary." The next day, he was telling Senator Lewis Cass of Michigan that besides obtaining California and New Mexico, he might even look "further south if practicable."

The man on whom Polk was relying to carry out this "not conquest" in the Southwest and California was Colonel Stephen Watts Kearny, fifty-two, one of the Army's ablest officers. At Fort Leavenworth, Kansas, Kearny was readying 1,660 expeditionary troops—the First U.S. Dragoons and ten companies of Missouri mounted volunteers and light artillery—and was beginning to send them in groups onto the Santa Fe Trail. Nearly eight hundred fifty miles of parched, dusty prairie lay between Fort Leavenworth and Santa Fe. If all went well in New Mexico, Kearny was to continue to San Diego, about eight hundred miles beyond Santa Fe, while sending another detachment south into Chihuahua Province. If the New Mexicans resisted, the California expedition would be postponed until the following spring.

Until Kearny reached San Diego, American interests in California would have to be safeguarded by the government agents already on the scene, Captain John C. Frémont and Consul Thomas O. Larkin, and by the commander of the Pacific Squadron, Commodore John Sloat.

10

THE EXPLORER AND THE MARINE

"Flee this day, and the longest life cannot wear out your disgrace! Choose ye this day what you will be! We are robbers, or we must be conquerors!"

—Exhortation by Bear Flag Republic leader William B. Ide to
insurgent American settlers in California

"There is yet time for us to rise en masse, irresistible and just."

—General Jose Castro, commander of Mexican-Californian forces

MAY 9, 1846: KLAMATH LAKE, OREGON

While President Polk and his advisers were discussing the Thornton attack and their congressional war message, Captain John C. Frémont, Kit Carson, and nine heavily armed men were camped in a streamside meadow near Klamath Lake, waiting for a mysterious messenger with dispatches. The previous evening, companions of the dispatch-bearer had overtaken Frémont's sixty-man exploring party. Eager for news after eleven months without any, Frémont and ten picked men had ridden to this glade where they hoped to encounter the messenger. As the daylight faded, the snow-mantled Cascade Mountains that crowded Klamath Lake's opposite shore exhaled a chill breeze among the black firs adjoining the meadow.

At twilight, horsemen emerged from the forest, and Frémont and his men warmly welcomed Marine First Lieutenant Archibald Gillespie and three companions.

In just one week, Gillespie's party had ridden all the way to Oregon from the Sacramento Valley, a distance of six hundred miles—the route taken by Frémont and his men weeks earlier. Unable to ford the Klamath Lake outlet, Gillespie had given two of his men the last of the food and sent them after Frémont. But that morning, a band of Indians had shared their salmon with Gillespie and his men, and had ferried them across the inlet in canoes. They had traveled thirty miles that day before meeting Frémont.

• • •

Gillespie had sailed from the East Coast to Vera Cruz bearing instructions written on October 17 by Secretary of State James Buchanan for Monterey Consul Thomas O. Larkin and Frémont. Before reaching Vera Cruz, he had memorized and then destroyed Buchanan's letter, lest it fall into Mexican hands. Crossing Mexico on foot and horseback and by stagecoach, he had boarded the USS *Cyane* at Mazatlán and sailed to Monterey, by way of the Hawaiian Islands. Gillespie had conveyed Buchanan's orders to Larkin, either orally or by written reconstruction on the *Cyane*.

Before a campfire at Klamath Lake, the Marine lieutenant now recited the letter for Frémont's benefit. "The interests of our commerce and our whale industries on the Pacific Ocean demand that you should exert the greatest vigilance in discovering and defeating any attempts which may be made by foreign governments to acquire a control over that country," Buchanan's letter said. "On all proper occasions, you should not fail prudently to warn the Government and people of California of the danger of such an interference to their peace and prosperity; to inspire them with a jealousy of European dominion, and to arouse in their bosoms that love of liberty and independence so natural to the American Continent."

While Frémont and Larkin were not to overtly solicit Californians to abandon Mexico and join the Union, "if the people should desire to unite their destiny with ours, they would be received as brethren, whenever this can be done without affording Mexico just cause of complaint."

Gillespie handed Frémont a packet of letters from his wife, Jessie; his father-in-law, Senator Thomas Hart Benton; and others. A Benton letter, Frémont later reported, contained "passages and suggestions" that were "enigmatical and obscure," but suggested a larger role for Frémont in California.

According to Frémont's *Memoirs,* Gillespie now delivered his piece de resistance: verbal instructions from the president and Navy Secretary George Bancroft. "The information through Gillespie . . . absolved me from any duty as an explorer, and I was left to my duty as an officer of the American Army with the further authoritative knowledge that the Government intended to take California. . . . To obtain possession of California was the chief object of the president. . . . Under his [Bancroft's] confidential instructions I had my warrant. Mr. Gillespie was directed to act in concert with me."

Gillespie also told Frémont that U.S.–Mexican relations were rapidly deteriorating.

Captain John B. Montgomery of the USS *Portsmouth* had informed Larkin that the Navy was poised to blockade Mexico, and that Mexican officials were evacuating Mazatlán. The consul had sent a courier after Gillespie with that information. Commodore John Sloat would soon appear off California "to take the Country!" Larkin had buoyantly predicted.

Frémont, who had intended to leave southern Oregon for home, now decided to turn back to California with Gillespie.

• • •

To this day, the substance of the verbal instructions from the White House to Frémont remains a mystery. The subject has stimulated endless conjecture by historians. Depending on their orientation on the Mexican War, they either believe that the instructions evidence a Polk administration conspiracy to overthrow California's Mexican government, or to only place an Army officer on the scene in case American intervention was required. The Polk administration's *written* instructions to Larkin and Frémont neither told them to start a revolution nor to commence military action. However, the belief persists that Gillespie gave Frémont secret instructions to incite an American settlers uprising, even though there is no evidence to support this, other than Frémont's own account of arguable veracity. This fact and Frémont's restrained actions over the ensuing months have persuaded most historians that Gillespie did no more than recite Buchanan's letter to Larkin, and that Frémont improvised. Even the historian Hubert Howe Bancroft, a severe critic of America's conduct during the Mexican War, believes it would have been "stupidly inconsistent" for the president to send one messenger with "two radically different and utterly irreconcilable sets of secret instructions" to two agents in California.

Yet, the Polk administration had shown previously that it was capable of just such actions, especially when one of the parties was a secret agent and the other was a highly visible American diplomat. When the United States extended its annexation offer to Texas, Commodore Robert F. Stockton, evidently with the Navy Department's approval, tried to persuade Texas to send its militia to fight Mexican troops. However, U.S. Consul Andrew Jackson Donelson knew nothing of the scheme.

In 1848, a House committee investigating a California claims case was unable to satisfactorily explain Frémont's actions. "What the purpose was in sending an officer of the United States in search of Colonel Frémont [by that time, he had

been promoted from captain], with a simple letter of instruction . . . is left to conjecture . . . but the effect was to turn Colonel Frémont with the men under his
command from their exploring expedition to Oregon back into California. . . . It
is very manifest that much yet remains to be told of this as yet dark and mysterious proceeding."

FALL 1845: WASHINGTON

An explosive letter from Consul Thomas Larkin began the chain of actions that
resulted in the rendezvous of Gillespie and Frémont in southern Oregon several
months later. Larkin's letter, dated July 10, 1845, warned Secretary of State
Buchanan that Mexico, at England's prompting, was sending troops to California.
This letter revived the virulent fear, which had haunted Jacksonians throughout
Texas's nine years of independence, that England wished to curtail American
expansion, and perhaps even one day reconquer its former colony.

Mexican troops, wrote Larkin, were being equipped in Acapulco for an expedition to California for the purpose of suppressing the squabbling factions of Governor Don Pio Pico and General Jose Castro, and reestablishing central
government authority. It was the result of "the instigation of the English Government under the plea, that the American settlers in California want to revolutionize
the Country. . . ." If the military operation succeeded, Larkin warned, it would
smother the Californians' nascent "wish to govern themselves . . . [they would]
prefer to see the United States troops, to those from Mexico, to govern the
country."

After taking the usual three months to travel by ship from California down the
length of South America, around Cape Horn, and then up the eastern coasts of
the Americas to the Potomac River, Larkin's letter reached the State Department
on October 11. That same day, Buchanan received a similar alarm about British
meddling from his secret agent in Mexico City, William Parrott. "Everything
coming from California excites great interest here in the English circle," reported
Parrott. "The British delegation is all alive on such occasions."

Until October 11, the Polk administration's policy toward California had been
essentially passive, grounded on the conviction that so many Americans would
emigrate to California that it would eventually slip from Mexico's grasp and into
that of the United States—either by Texas's path of revolution, independence, and
annexation, or by a purchase agreement.

Larkin and Parrott, however, had raised the wholly unacceptable possibility that England, and not the United States, might obtain California.

• • •

James K. Polk, one of the most proactive of U.S. presidents, could never countenance this. He and his advisers immersed themselves in intensive consultations from October 11 to 14, emerging with a set of interlocking countermeasures whose details became crystallized in confidential letters: Larkin to be named a "special agent"; Gillespie, who had returned only a month earlier from a two-year cruise on the USS *Brandywine,* to be assigned to duty as a secret courier; Commodores Stockton and Sloat, and diplomats John Slidell and Larkin, to monitor British and French actions and baffle any attempts by them to take control of California. Finally, War Secretary William Marcy asked General Zachary Taylor to advance from Corpus Christi nearer to the Rio Grande, if he thought it advisable. As has been seen, Taylor elected to remain on the Nueces River until he received specific orders.

Stockton was to operate as a roving naval agent, counteracting any English or French schemes in California. If war broke out between Mexico and the United States, he was to assist Commodore Sloat in seizing San Francisco Bay, Monterey, and San Diego. Sloat, commander of the Pacific Squadron in Mazatlán, had already received similar orders, written in June by Navy Secretary Bancroft. Stockton was to also deliver to Larkin and Sloat duplicate orders to those that Gillespie carried to Vera Cruz and across Mexico to Mazatlán. Stockton, sailing around Cape Horn, would reach California weeks after Gillespie; he was insurance against misfortune befalling Gillespie.

Gillespie was also given a second assignment, later amended, to deliver to Larkin a packet of family letters for Captain John Frémont. The consul could give the letters to the explorer whenever he reached California.

• • •

Gillespie's mission evolved further after Polk invited Benton, the chairman of the Senate Committee on Military Affairs, to the White House on October 24, to brief him on Larkin's and Parrott's alarming letters. Benton had opposed Texas annexation and other Polk policies; but on this day, the men for once were in accord, agreeing that the United States could never permit a European power to possess Oregon or California, even if preventing that made it necessary to use military force. This represented a seismic policy shift for Benton, who previously had advocated only diplomacy.

The conversation then evidently turned to the countermeasures Polk and his advisers had been planning, because the subject of Benton's son-in-law, Frémont, came up. "Some conversation occurred concerning Captain Frémont's expedition, and his intention to visit California before his return," Polk elliptically noted in his journal afterward. "Col. B. expressed the opinion that Americans would settle on the Sacraminto [sic] River and ultimately hold the country."

It is probable, although Polk's diary does not reflect it, that Polk and Benton also decided to include Frémont in the administration's countermeasures. A few days later, Gillespie received new instructions to personally deliver the Frémont family letters to the explorer, rather than leave them with Larkin.

• • •

On the evening of October 30, Archibald H. Gillespie was summoned to the White House for a private conversation with the president. The tall, red-haired thirty-three-year-old Marine first lieutenant, classically educated and fluent in Spanish, had enlisted in the Marines as a teenager and had served on four Pacific warships and as a station commander. He had just returned from a two-year cruise on the USS *Brandywine,* where he was in charge of the Marine detachment.

Gillespie had already received his orders from Navy Secretary Bancroft and had arranged passage from New York to Vera Cruz on the *Petersburg.* More importantly, from the standpoint of operational secrecy, he had been given a letter from a longtime Bancroft friend, Samuel Hooper of the Marblehead, Massachusetts, mercantile house William Appleton & Company, identifying Gillespie as a Hooper representative who was traveling to California on business. If Mexican officials questioned Gillespie, Bancroft believed the letter would protect his identity and mission. Henry Mellus, William Appleton's agent in California, was instructed to give Gillespie cash from the company account, to be reimbursed by the U.S. government.

In his journal entry for October 30, Polk cryptically described meeting with "Lieutenant Gillespie of the Marine Corps, about 8 o'clock P.M., on the subject of a secret mission on which he was about to go to California. His secret instructions & the letter to Mr. Larkin, U.S. Consul at Monterey, in the Department of State, will explain the object of the mission." No copy of Gillespie's secret instructions survives; he probably destroyed them before reaching Vera Cruz, as he did the duplicate orders for Larkin and Sloat—after memorizing them. Gillespie later told a Senate committee that his instructions were broad, and harmonious with Larkin's and Frémont's: "to watch over the interests of the United States and to counteract the influence of any foreign agents who might be in the country with objects prejudicial to the United States."

Whatever Gillespie's instructions were, Polk undoubtedly reviewed them in detail with the Marine. Judging by Gillespie's future behavior in California, his orders included informing Frémont of the California situation and the Polk administration's countermeasures; apprising Frémont of Buchanan's instructions to Larkin; aiding Frémont in his future operations, whatever they might be; and most importantly, concealing his mission from Mexican authorities.

• • •

On the last day of the *Petersburg*'s stormy twenty-four-day voyage down the Atlantic Seaboard and across the Gulf of Mexico to Vera Cruz, Gillespie finished committing to memory Larkin's and Sloat's instructions and destroyed them. "The Despatch was destroyed and thrown overboard the night before we came into port, in accordance with my instructions," he informed Bancroft on December 13, three days after reaching Vera Cruz, "and it was well I did so, for my luggage underwent the very closest search."

While traveling through the heart of Mexico, Gillespie filled his letters to Bancroft with his observations. He noted that Mexican troops were on the march to the Texas border, and that in their ranks were "Indians forced into service, having a musket in their hands for the first time." Interestingly, the Mexican government's intention—to win a favorable treaty with the United States by "having arms in our hands"—was Polk's strategy, too. Moreover, Mexico's leaders, it turned out, were as scornful of the American troops as the Americans were of Mexican soldiers, wrote Gillespie. They derogated Taylor as "a mere farmer, noted for cowardice," whose predominantly foreign-born soldiers were "treated with very great tyranny by young American officers." The Marine lieutenant concluded that the credulous Mexican people "require a terrible shock to awaken them to the truth of their arrogance and entire ignorance."

On February 10, Gillespie joined the Pacific Squadron at Mazatlán. Twelve days later, he boarded Captain William M. Mervine's sloop *Cyane* and embarked for Monterey—via the Hawaiian Islands. Gillespie chafed at the long delay in reaching Larkin: "My anxiety to hand him at an early day the instructions of the Government is very great."

But he, as did everyone in the eight-ship squadron at Mazatlán, understood the need for misdirection. An equally powerful British naval squadron under Admiral Sir George F. Seymour was also anchored at Mazatlán, and because of tensions over Oregon rather than California, the two fleets were shadowing one another's every movement.

• • •

Because of the detour to Hawaii and a week's layover there, Gillespie did not reach Monterey until April 17, after "one of the most disagreeable and stormy passages I have ever experienced—Constant headwind, blowing a gale from the East hard for fourteen days. . . ."

Within hours of the *Cyane*'s arrival in Monterey, Gillespie and Larkin were in deep discussions on the ship. Larkin emerged from the meeting as a newly commissioned "special agent." He ebulliently wrote to friends that if war broke out with Mexico, "I believe the stars would shine over California before the Fourth of July! blessing those who see them and their posterity after them."

Gillespie began his pursuit of Frémont, keeping notes for Bancroft on what he observed. General Jose Castro's twenty-five regulars were predominantly "degenerated Indians," he wrote, and the two to three hundred Californians of Spanish descent that Castro might enlist "have a holy horror of the American rifle, and will never expose themselves to make an attack."

MAY 9, 1846: KLAMATH LAKE, OREGON

Beside the campfire at Klamath Lake, Gillespie related to Frémont his journey to the Sacramento Valley, where the American settlers were "very much incensed against the officers of the [California] Government, who were treating them with the greatest tyranny and breaking every promise made when they were invited to this Country."

Unknown to Gillespie, he had been identified at Sutter's Fort by a Mr. Loker, who had seen him previously at the Washington Navy Yard. Moreover, John Sutter remembered Gillespie's name from a register of the USS *Brandywine*'s officers published in a Sandwich Islands (Hawaiian) newspaper that he had read. The news spread swiftly that a mysterious U.S. naval agent was seeking John Frémont.

Preoccupied with the sudden bounty of information from the East after eleven months without any news, Frémont retired for the night without taking his usual precaution of posting a guard.

• • •

Around midnight, Kit Carson's shouts of "What's the matter over there?" awakened everyone. Carson's light slumber had been disturbed by the sickening sound of an Indian ax being driven into the skull of one of Frémont's men, Basil Lajeunesse. "Indians!" Carson cried. Upwards of fifteen Klamath Indians had crept into the camp, killing Lajeunesse and riddling one of Frémont's Delaware Indians with arrows as they slept.

The explorers snatched up their weapons as another Delaware went down fighting and died, his body bristling with five arrows. The attackers charged across the open ground, and Frémont's men opened fire, killing their leader, whom Gillespie recognized as one of the Indians who that morning had shared their salmon and boated him across the lake outlet. He had evidently followed Gillespie to Frémont's camp. An English half-ax dangled from a thong attached to the Indian leader's wrist. A Delaware Indian scalped him.

The expeditioners' months of shared privations had forged strong bonds of trust and friendship, and the three savage murders upset and angered them, especially the Delawares, whose dead comrades had traveled across the continent with them. "We kill some," promised Frémont, and their moods brightened.

The explorers attended to their weapons, tracked the Klamaths around the lake, and fought them in a series of sharp engagements; in one clash, fourteen Klamaths were killed. Frémont's men burned down a hastily evacuated Indian fishing village. Gillespie, who had never witnessed so much violent death at such close quarters, confessed to Frémont: "By heaven, this is rough work."

• • •

A pale, slender man of five feet two, John Charles Frémont more resembled a clerk than the extraordinary backwoodsman and explorer that he was. Frémont's fiercely loyal men deeply respected his calm, decisive leadership and his remarkable capacity to endure heat, cold, hunger, and fatigue while buoying his companion's spirits.

John Charles Frémont was born out of wedlock in Savannah on January 21, 1813, soon after Jean Charles Frémon, a refugee of the French Revolution, eloped with Anne Beverly Whiting, who left her elderly Tidewater husband, Major John Pryor.

Frémont's father died in 1817, and his mother Anne, with two sons and a daughter, moved to Charleston, South Carolina, and became a clerk for a prominent lawyer. The lawyer paid Frémont's tuition at a preparatory school and helped him gain admission to the College of Charleston. But three months before graduation, Frémont was expelled for missing classes.

After teaching mathematics to midshipmen aboard the USS *Natchez* on a cruise to South America, Frémont got a job surveying Cherokee lands in the southern Appalachians. That led to two expeditions with Joseph Nicollet to the northern territories between the Mississippi and Missouri rivers. From Nicollet, Frémont learned the business of exploration: setting up camp; making maps; navigating by the stars; observing and recording topography, soils, and minerals; and collecting botanical specimens.

Through Nicollet's expeditions, Frémont met Senator Thomas Hart Benton and Benton's teenage daughter, Jessie. The instant attraction between Frémont and their daughter alarmed Jessie's parents. Senator Benton tried to break up the romance by dispatching Frémont to explore the Des Moines River in 1841, but the couple secretly married in Washington that year, when Frémont was twenty-eight and Jessie seventeen. The senator graciously invited them to move into the Benton home.

Benton had plans for Frémont. In 1842, he sponsored Frémont's first Western expedition. With Kit Carson guiding him, Frémont, a lieutenant in the U.S. Army Topographical Corps, explored the South Pass of the Wind River Mountains in present-day Wyoming. In 1843, he led a new expedition across the Rocky Mountains, and after striking the Columbia River, traveled through Oregon and California (a last-minute destination), returning by way of the Great Salt Lake.

• • •

As she did after the South Pass expedition, Jessie helped her husband write the report for his second expedition. Time was short; Frémont planned to leave Washington in the spring of 1845 to begin his third Western expedition, ostensibly to find better crossings through the Sierra Nevada to California. The Frémonts outfitted a small two-story house near the Benton home as a "workshop." Each day, from 9 A.M. to dusk, with a break for lunch, Frémont would give Jessie "dictation," with Jessie possibly editing his words as she took them down. Many historians credit Jessie for the report's readability; its popularity made Frémont famous as "The Pathfinder."

A paean to California's beauty and its unlimited potential for farming, fishing, and trade, Frémont's report regretfully noted that under Mexico's governance, these endowments "were all unused, lying waste like an Indian country.

. . . Its fertile sea-board was one great stock-farm and its whole population only a few thousands; so far distant from the Central Government that it was ready at any moment to break off."

1845–1846: FRÉMONT'S THIRD EXPEDITION

Days after James Polk's inauguration, Frémont and Senator Benton met with the new president at the White House. According to Frémont's *Memoirs,* they discussed Western geography, not geopolitics. Frémont pointed out errors in a Library of Congress map that showed three great rivers flowing from the Great Salt Lake to the Pacific. Even though Frémont had just returned from exploring the Great Salt Lake and had not found any westward-flowing rivers, the president could not be convinced of the map's inaccuracy. "He found me 'young,' and said something of the 'impulsiveness of young men," Frémont wryly noted.

A few weeks later, Frémont, newly promoted to brevet captain, finished preparations for his new expedition to California and submitted to the printer the report of his second expedition. Benton and Polk administration officials briefed him on California, Britain's supposed designs on it, the possibility of war with Mexico, and "the contingencies anticipated and weighed," including Commodore Sloat's June 24 instructions to seize California's ports if there were war.

"For me," Frémont wrote, "no distinct course or definite instruction could be laid down, but the probabilities were made known to me as well as what to do when they became facts." Frémont left the meetings with the understanding that "the President and Mr. Bancroft held it impossible for Mexico, situated as things then were, to retain possession of California. . . ." Should the administration need to send him new orders, Benton would conceal them in a letter about Frémont's future California home that "would convey no meaning to others while to me they would be clear."

• • •

On June 23, 1845, Frémont and sixty hardy, experienced, well-armed men embarked for California from their camp near present-day Kansas City. The party included twelve Delaware Indians, all excellent hunters, and many veterans of Frémont's previous expeditions, including Kit Carson, who, when contacted by Frémont, had sold his ranch and livestock to become Frémont's adjutant.

By January 1846, Frémont was in Monterey, meeting with Larkin and arousing the suspicions of California authorities. To official queries about his expedition, Frémont replied that he was surveying a route from the United States to the Pacific Ocean, and that he and his men only sought scientific and commercial information. The provincial government granted Frémont permission to spend the winter in California, so long as he and his men remained on the eastern frontier near the Sierra Nevada, away from the coastal settlements and Monterey. But Frémont ignored the Mexicans' injunction against approaching the California coast and led his men toward Santa Cruz.

• • •

Rather than leading a reconnaissance in force, as Mexican authorities suspected, Frémont was scouting real estate for a future home. The quest drew him inexorably to the seashore: "I had before my mind the home I wished to make in this country, and first one place and then another charmed me. But none seemed perfect where the sea was wanting. . . . The piny [*sic*] fragrance was grateful, but it was not the invigorating sea breeze which brings with it renewed strength. This I wanted for my mother. . . . All this I found reason to believe I would find somewhere on the Santa Cruz shore."

Traveling at a leisurely pace, Frémont and his men descended from the coastal mountains to the shore of Monterey Bay, then followed it southward, finally camping twenty miles from Monterey at a ranch owned by William E. P. Harnell.

Monterey's commandant, General Don Jose Castro, and his brother, Prefect Manuel de Jesus Castro, had previously been troubled by the presence of sixty heavily armed Americans in Mexican California at a time of high tension between their nations. Their concern now turned into alarm.

• • •

On March 5, a Lieutenant Chavez rode into Frémont's camp to deliver warning letters from the Castros. "The prefecture orders you as soon as you receive this communication, without any excuse, to retire with your men beyond the limits of this department." If Frémont did not, the Monterey government would take "necessary measures" to remove him. Provoked by the letters' peremptory tone and Chavez's "abrupt" manner, Frémont refused to leave California and instructed the haughty messenger to apprise his superiors of "my astonishment at General Castro's breach of good faith, and the rudeness with which he committed it." Expecting the Castros to carry out their threat of force, the explorers left Harnell's ranch and climbed nearby Gavilan Peak, atop which they defiantly began constructing a log fort. "While this was being built, a tall sapling was prepared, and on it, when all was ready, the American flag was raised amidst the cheers of the men," wrote Frémont. Larkin, who was anxiously monitoring the situation, observed that Frémont's men were "remarkably well-armed," possessing three to six guns apiece.

Hundreds of mounted Californians assembled at the Mission of San Juan. "The natives are firm in the belief that they will break you up, and that you can be entirely destroyed by their power," Larkin warned Frémont. Frémont scrawled a response in pencil: "I am making myself as strong as possible, in the intention that if we are unjustly attacked we will fight to extremity and refuse quarter, trusting to our country to avenge us. . . . We will die every man of us under the flag of our country." Larkin sent an urgent request to Commodore Sloat in Mazatlán for a warship at Monterey.

From their aerie, Frémont's men watched Castro's cavalrymen riding up the road toward them, and the Americans swiftly laid an ambush in a thicket near a creek, waiting in absolute silence with cocked guns. At the last minute, the cavalry halted and turned back.

• • •

On March 10, the third day of the standoff, the flagpole unexpectedly crashed to the ground. Frémont took it as a sign for his men to retire. "Thinking I had remained as long as the occasion required, I took advantage of the accident to say to the men that this was an indication for us to move camp." Frémont described to Jessie how "we retired slowly and growlingly, before a force of three or four hundred men and three pieces of artillery."

Learning that Frémont's party had been spotted fording a river three miles away, Castro sent a man in pursuit, but he found only a deserted campsite, with fires still burning and castoff gear littering the ground. Frémont and his men were on their way to Oregon. Castro announced that, with the help of "200 patriots," he had driven out Frémont's "bandeleros."

Whether it was true, or whether he wished to maintain good relations with Larkin, Castro told the consul that he had acted under orders. While Frémont was roaming the shore of Monterey Bay, Castro said, he had received "direct and specific" orders from Mexico City "to drive Captain Freemont [sic] from the country." But Larkin, aware that Castro needed no orders to remove Frémont, doubted that he had received any.

LATE MAY 1846: SACRAMENTO VALLEY

The American settlements in the Sacramento Valley were in an uproar when Fré-mont and Gillespie returned from Klamath Lake. Monterey Prefect Don Manuel Castro had announced a draconian plan to expel all foreigners from California. It was partly reaction to Frémont's defiance at Gavilan Peak, and a response to reports of imminent war between Mexico and the United States. At an April 11 meeting in Monterey of northern California's army commanders and civilian leaders—the "junta," as they called themselves—Castro warned of the "imminent risk of an invasion founded on the extravagant design of an American Captain of the United States Army." He proposed suspending the civil war with Governor Pio Pico and joining forces with him against the Americans. Castro issued a proclamation stating that settlers who had not become California citizens—in other words, most American settlers—were subject to expulsion, and their lands to confiscation, "whenever the Government may find it convenient."

Thus, the settlers welcomed the appearance of sixty heavily armed Americans led by an Army captain and a Marine lieutenant. Gillespie and Frémont exhorted them to "be prepared to resist [expulsion] as one man and with stout hearts"; if they did so, Frémont promised a "happy period" in the future. To throw the Castros off their trail, Frémont and Gillespie, in conversations and letters that they hoped would find their way to the Castros, stated that they would soon leave California.

Of course, Frémont had no plans to leave. Always sensitive about his reputa-tion, he privately acknowledged feeling "humiliated and humbled" as a result of his withdrawal from Gavilan Peak and was "determined to take such active and anticipatory measures as should seem to me most expedient to protect my party and justify my own character."

Amid the rising anxiety in the settlements arrived further disturbing reports. Castro had reportedly incited the Indians living in the Sacramento and San Joaquin valleys to burn the settlers' wheat crops. Provincial authorities had also allegedly given a rifle to an Indian for the express purpose of murdering colonist-businessman John Sutter, whose trading post was the settlers' meeting place. And Mexican-California cavalry were said to be riding to the Sacramento Valley to wreak their own kind of havoc.

Frémont sent Gillespie to the USS *Portsmouth* in San Francisco Bay for ammu-nition and provisions. Commodore Sloat had dispatched Captain John B. Mont-gomery's twenty-four-gun sloop-of-war after receiving Larkin's summons during

Frémont's Gavilan Peak standoff in early March. Gillespie returned with three hundred pounds of American rifle lead, enough to make nine thousand bullets; a keg of powder; eight thousand percussion caps; medicine, flour, sugar, pork, salt, and three hundred pounds of tobacco; and $1,500 in cash for buying fresh horses.

Frémont led a preemptive attack against the upper Sacramento Valley Indians that Castro had supposedly enlisted to attack the settlers. The raid caught the warriors in the act of blackening their faces and donning feathers—their usual preparations for battle. "We rode directly upon them," reported Frémont, "and at this place several Indians were killed in the dispersion."

• • •

Frémont then began coordinating his operations with the settlers' and invited them to a meeting at his camp at the foot of "the Buttes of Sacramento." The settlers were disappointed to hear that while Frémont would freely give advice and support, he and his men would not take up arms against the Mexicans unless Castro first attacked. "Several persons, among whom was Kit Carson, begged of Frémont their discharge from the service of the exploration expedition that they might be at liberty to join us," wrote William B. Ide, the fifty-nine-year-old New Englander whom the settlers elected as their leader. "This was peremptorily refused."

While killing Indians had no geopolitical consequences, taking up arms against the Mexican-Californian government did. Thus, Frémont proceeded cautiously until such time as America and Mexico went to war, or the settlers rebelled. "He preferred to see for himself how far the settlers of Napa and Sonoma were ready to go in shaking off the Mexican yoke," noted William Hargrove, another settler attending the Buttes meeting. Frémont's instructions had been to foil any attempted European interference, and to win over the settlers. Gillespie had learned that Larkin now had "perfect confidence that the English Vice Consul [James Forbes] was quite indifferent under which flag California might choose to be governed." And the settlers did not need wooing so much as tangible support in the present emergency.

Informed that two hundred Mexican-Californian cavalrymen were riding toward the settlements, a dozen settlers led by Ezekiel Merritt went to meet them. Instead of a cavalry force, they encountered ten wranglers and 170 horses. Lieutenant Jose Maria Alviso, Castro's secretary Francisco Arce, and eight men were driving the horses to Santa Clara, where General Castro and his militia planned to use them in their operations against the American settlements. After overpowering the Mexicans, Merritt's men left them a few mounts and took the rest to a pasture near Frémont's camp.

• • •

By seizing Castro's remuda, the settlers had now committed a flagrant, irrevocable act of rebellion. Frémont appointed Merritt, "my Field-Lieutenant among the settlers," to lead a raid on Sonoma. Early on Sunday, June 14, thirty-four settlers invaded the sleepy outpost. There was no resistance and no garrison, only old, stockpiled weapons. The three Mexican army officers on the scene cooperated fully; Colonel Don M. Guadalupe Vallejo and Merritt drew up capitulation terms over morning brandy.

Merritt and two other settlers escorted Colonel Vallejo, Lieutenant Colonel Don Victor Prudon, Captain Don Salvador Vallejo, and a civilian, Jacob B. Leese, to Frémont. He prudently refused to take custody of "prisoners of the people," and they were locked up at Sutter's Fort.

After the excitement had died down, the settlers began to worry and to lose heart; they feared that Frémont would not support them, and that Castro would crush them. William B. Ide gave a rousing speech that put the fight back into them. "Flee this day, and the longest life cannot wear out your disgrace! Choose ye this day what you will be! We are robbers, or we must be conquerors!"

So inspired, the settlers raised a flag designed by William L. Todd, a twenty-six-year-old settler who was a cousin of Mrs. Abraham Lincoln. On light-brown cloth, he had drawn a red star in the upper left corner; a 4-inch red stripe across the bottom; the words "California Republic," in black ink; and a painted bear (some snidely remarked that it looked more like a hog). The insurgents proclaimed their dominion the Bear Flag Republic; California natives called them "Osos." Ide penned an impromptu proclamation: "This day we proclaim California a Republic, and our pledge of honor that private property shall be protected. . . . It is our object and earnest desire to embrace the first opportunity to unite our adopted and rescued country, to the country of our early home."

• • •

Until now, Frémont had advised the settlers and shared his munitions with them, but he had scrupulously avoided participating in any direct action against the Mexican authorities. He had stood by as Merritt, Ide, and the settlers captured Sonoma. But Frémont believed that Castro now would send an army against the settlers, resulting in "inevitable disaster." He could no longer sit on the fence, believing as he did that he was destined "to govern events [rather] than to be governed by them." But he still did not know whether the United States and Mexico were at war; if they were not, he did not wish to start one by his actions as a U.S. Army captain.

For those reasons, Frémont sent a letter to Senator Benton resigning his Army commission, instructing him to submit the letter to the War Department if it became necessary to deny responsibility for his future actions. Frémont, Benton, and administration officials a year earlier had very likely discussed such a contingency plan, giving the U.S. government "plausible deniability," a hallmark of Polk's covert operations.

Coincidentally, at about this time Polk decided to advance Frémont by two grades to lieutenant colonel, breaking his rule of never directly promoting regular Army officers. The president planned to assign Frémont command of a new Western Regiment that would escort immigrants to Oregon. "He has made several explorations to Oregon and California," Polk noted, "and his reports show that he is an officer of high merit and peculiarly fitted for this Regiment."

Rapid developments, however, overtook Polk's well-intended plans for Frémont.

• • •

General Jose Castro increased his force to 160 men and divided them into three divisions, commanded by J. A. Carrillo; Joaquin de la Torre; and Castro's brother, Prefect Don Manuel Castro. The general penned a fiery public condemnation of "the contemptible policy of the agents of the government of the U.S. of the north" for their "invasion" of Sonoma. "There is yet time for us to rise en masse, irresistible and just." From Los Angeles, Governor Pio Pico called the uprising "the darkest treason that could be invented," committed by "North American adventurers." In a letter to Larkin, Pico said he suspected American government involvement.

Torre's division of fifty to sixty men marched north and crossed the mouth of San Francisco Bay in boats to confront the Bear Flag insurgents. The Sonoma settlers appealed to Frémont for help. On June 23, Frémont led his sixty men and two dozen armed settlers from the Sacramento Valley on a relief mission to Sonoma. It was a remarkably polyglot force. "They were Americans, French, English, Swiss, Poles, Russians, Chilians [sic], Germans, Greeks, Austrians, Pawnees, native Indians, etc.," wrote James W. Marshall.

• • •

Seventeen insurgents led by Henry L. Ford left Sonoma to rescue a pair of men reportedly taken prisoner while traveling to Bodega to obtain cannons. Ford's men stumbled upon Torre's force at a ranch at Olompali, midway between San Rafael and Petaluma. Ford and his men dismounted, took cover behind some trees, and fired on Torre's men when they attacked, killing one of them and wounding another. The Mexicans broke off their assault and, after exchanging rifle fire at long range with the settlers, they withdrew to the other side of the bay.

The captives' bodies were found in a ditch. The victims had been lashed to trees and tortured and mutilated with knives until they died—"proceedings," disgustedly wrote one of Frémont's men, E. M. Kern, "that would disgrace even a Pi-Eute [*sic;* Paiute]. . . ."

Frémont reached Sonoma the next day, June 25. Outraged by the mutilation-murders, he issued a harsh new order: no more prisoners. The order was carried out a few days later when Kit Carson and two other Frémont men killed a pair of unarmed men and their elderly uncle as they alighted from a boat.

With 130 men, Frémont marched to San Rafael but encountered no enemy soldiers. Then, he and twelve picked men crossed the mouth of the bay in a borrowed boat to a fort opposite Sausalito, where they scattered several Mexican horsemen and spiked fourteen "long brass Spanish pieces." Whether because of the angle of the sun, or euphoria over the easy victory, Frémont was inspired to pronounce the southern "gate" of the bay the "Golden Gate."

• • •

The rebellious settlers officially proclaimed California's independence at Sonoma on July 4, just as the brief life of the Bear Flag Republic was about to end, and as a broader conflict was commencing. They and Frémont's men formed the "California Battalion," composed of 250 men in three companies. Frémont was elected battalion commander, and Gillespie became his adjutant. Ide, the Bear Flag revolt leader, entered the ranks as a private. The battalion returned to Sutter's Mill, where Frémont hoped to learn what had become of Castro and his three divisions.

But Castro's three divisions were marching south to San Luis Obispo, where they planned to join Governor Pio Pico's forces and make common cause against the Americans.

JULY 1846: MONTEREY BAY

Commodore John Sloat's six warships lay at anchor in Monterey Bay within sight of the provincial capital. His orders were clear: he was to seize California's principal ports if hostilities commenced with Mexico. Sloat was well aware that fighting had begun along the Rio Grande, and that Commodore David Conner was blockading Mexico's Gulf ports.

Yet the Pacific Squadron commander hesitated. His reluctance to act is a mystery. Perhaps age had made him overly cautious; he was sixty-five and had served in the Navy since 1800. During the War of 1812, he was an officer aboard Captain Stephen Decatur's *United States* when her crack gunners pounded the HMS *Macedonia* into submission. With his first command, the schooner *Grampus,* Sloat cruised against pirates in the West Indies in 1823. He had led the Pacific Squadron since 1844 and was one of the Navy's most experienced officers, which made his irresolution all the more puzzling.

On May 17, William Parrott's news of the Thornton ambush had reached Sloat at Mazatlán. The commodore had promptly sent the *Cyane* to Monterey, with a letter to Larkin that read: "It appears certain that hostilities have commenced on the north bank of the Rio Grande." Sloat planned to sail immediately to Monterey to consult with Larkin about "the course of operations I may be disposed to make on the coast of California."

Inexplicably, Sloat was still in Mazatlán two weeks later when he learned that General Taylor had fought two major battles on the Rio Grande. On June 6, while continuing to linger at the Mazatlán anchorage, the commodore wrote a letter informing Navy Secretary Bancroft that he had reached the bizarre conclusion that his instructions "will not justify my taking possession of any part of California, or any hostile measures against Mexico . . . as neither party have declared war." But two days later, after apparently finding out that Commodore David Conner was blockading Vera Cruz, Sloat and his squadron were under sail to Monterey, although to what purpose was unclear, given his stated refusal to capture any California ports.

• • •

Consul Larkin came aboard the *Savannah,* Sloat's flagship, on July 2 and briefed the commodore on the Sonoma uprising, Frémont's movements, and Castro's march to San Luis Obispo to rendezvous with Governor Pico. Sloat also learned from Larkin that the instructions Gillespie had given both of them were virtually identical. The indecisive commodore was so beset by misgivings about his mission that rather than occupy Monterey, he sent an officer ashore with greetings and "an offer to salute the Mexican flag." The surprising offer was declined on the ground that the Mexicans had no powder with which to return a salute.

And then, on July 5, dispatches from Captain Montgomery of the *Portsmouth* reached the *Savannah* with more details about Frémont and the settlers' revolt. Sloat scratched out a peremptory order to Montgomery to refuse Frémont further assistance. However, the *Cyane*'s purser, Rodman M. Price, a future New Jersey governor, persuaded the commodore to reconsider. Sloat countermanded the order to Montgomery.

Perhaps Price's arguments had done it; or maybe Sloat merely reread Montgomery's accounts of Frémont's march to Sonoma, his pursuit of Torre's men, and the spiking of the guns. But the commodore convinced himself that Frémont had received confirmation that the United States and Mexico were at war. Sloat's fears of repeating Commodore Thomas ap Catesby Jones's blundering occupation of 1842 receded. "I have determined to hoist the flag of the United States at this place to-morrow," he informed Montgomery on July 6, "as I would prefer being sacrificed for doing too much than too little." He also ordered Montgomery to raise the American flag at Yerba Buena "and take possession of the fort and that portion of the country."

• • •

July 7 dawned bright and clear on Monterey Bay. At 7 A.M., Captain William Mervine of the *Cyane* and two other officers were rowed ashore to present a formal surrender demand. An elderly Mexican artillery officer, Captain Mariano Silva, informed them that Monterey had neither troops nor arms, and that he was not authorized to surrender the city.

At 9:30 A.M., the harbor and Monterey's waterfront resounded with creaking oarlocks and the sharp commands of coxswains. Boats bristling with 250 armed Marines and sailors approached the shore. Before the troops had embarked, officers read aloud Sloat's general order, which bid them to be on their good behavior when they entered Monterey: "It is not only our duty to take California, but to preserve it afterward as a part of the United States at all hazards."

Met by only the sound of waves lapping at the shore, the assault troops marched to the customs house and ran the American flag up the bare flagpole

(General Castro's departing troops had taken the Mexican flag with them). Marines paraded through Monterey's streets, and later in the day, their patrols uncovered weapons caches.

At the customs house, Purser Price read a proclamation, written by Sloat, asserting that with the United States and Mexico now at war, America was justified in seizing California. "I declare to the inhabitants of California that, although I come in arms with a powerful force, I do not come among them as an enemy to California; on the contrary, I come as their best friend, as henceforward California will be a portion of the United States, and its peaceful inhabitants will enjoy the same rights and privileges as the citizens of any other portion of that territory."

• • •

News of the Navy's occupation of Monterey reached Frémont and the California Battalion at Sutter's Mill on July 11, and they excitedly raised the American flag over the settlement. Two days later, the Stars and Stripes replaced the Bear Flag at Sonoma, and it now also snapped in the Pacific breeze over Yerba Buena and Bodega. The Bear Flag revolt was over. Frémont and two hundred men from the California Battalion prepared to march to Monterey.

• • •

When the eighty-gun HMS *Collingwood*, flagship of British Rear Admiral Sir George Seymour, majestically sailed into Monterey Bay nine days after Sloat's occupation, American crews raced to general quarters. The USS *Plymouth*'s crew at Yerba Buena also cleared for action when the HMS *Juno* appeared off Sausalito. But the British did not contest the American occupation.

Perhaps Purser Price was only reporting legend, but perhaps not, when he wrote years later that Seymour remarked to Sloat after the British reached Monterey: "Sloat, if your flag was not flying on shore I should have hoisted mine there."

• • •

U.S. and British sailors and Marines, American settlers, and Mexican Californians stopped what they were doing when they saw the California Battalion nearing Monterey amid "a vast cloud of dust." Lieutenant Fred Walpole of the *Collingwood* and his shipmates were especially eager to glimpse Frémont and his "true trappers." They were not disappointed. "Thence in long file emerged the wildest wild party. Frémont rode ahead, a spare, active-looking man," amid a bodyguard of five

Delaware Indians. "The rest, many of them blacker than the Indians, rode two and two, the rifle held by one hand across the pommel of the saddle." They wore long deerskin coats tied with thongs and trousers "of their own manufacture."

• • •

Sloat reacted with dismay when Frémont told him that he had not acted on any written orders, but on his own authority, when he and his men had fought beside the Bear Flag insurgents. Perhaps still fearful that he might have repeated Commodore Catesby Jones's famous blunder, the commodore blurted out that he had expected "*written* authority as would support [my] action in raising the flag [at Monterey]." Before Frémont could explain, "the interview terminated abruptly," and Sloat did not ask to see Frémont again. Frémont regretted that Sloat's "mind closed against anything short of the written paper; the full information that I might have given should, in my judgment, have been sufficient to satisfy him." In relating his misbegotten meeting with Sloat in his *Memoirs,* Frémont noted that he had left Washington "with full knowledge of their [government officials'] wishes . . . and I was relied upon to do what should be in my power in the event of opportunity to further their designs."

Sloat was being disingenuous when he claimed that he had captured Monterey only after learning that Frémont was operating in concert with the American insurgents. Even before sailing from Mazatlán, the commodore knew about the Thornton ambush, General Taylor's battles on the Rio Grande, and Commodore Conner's blockade of Vera Cruz. It defies credulity that if Sloat were unpersuaded by these official reports to obey his orders to seize California's ports, that he would act upon learning that American irregulars had clashed with Mexican-California militia.

Sloat now reverted to his previous overcautiousness. He rejected Frémont's proposal to conduct joint operations against Castro, in fact forswearing all offensive operations, and refused to recognize the California Battalion.

Commodore Robert Stockton and his frigate *Congress* anchored off Monterey after a long passage around Cape Horn, and he handed Sloat and Larkin copies of the outdated written orders that they had already received from Gillespie. Stockton awaited Sloat's orders. None came.

• • •

Sloat's June 6 letter announcing his refusal to seize California's ports without a declaration of war reached Navy Secretary Bancroft after Bancroft had just written to an ally: "The object of the United States is, under its right as a belligerent nation, to possess itself entirely of Upper California." Unsurprisingly, the expansionist-minded Navy Secretary sternly rebuked his timid commodore. His June 24, 1845, instructions to Sloat to seize California's ports, Bancroft wrote, were "framed to be executed even in the event of the mere declaration of war, much more in the event of actual hostilities." While the Navy Secretary believed in "the purity of your intentions . . . your anxiety not to do wrong has led you into a most unfortunate and unwarranted inactivity."

Sloat had lost his nerve, and he recognized that he should relinquish his command to an officer who would vigorously prosecute the war. He quietly informed Stockton that, due to ill health, he would transfer his Pacific Squadron command to him.

In the interim, before taking over the squadron, Stockton was given command of land operations. He immediately accepted Frémont's California Battalion as a U.S. volunteer force and made Frémont a major, and Gillespie a captain. On July 29, Sloat transferred his pennant from the *Savannah* to the *Levant* and cast off for home.

• • •

The new Pacific Squadron commander issued a proclamation strikingly different in tone from Sloat's conciliatory declaration of July 7. The capture of Monterey and Yerba Buena were retaliation for Mexican "outrages" on the Rio Grande, it said, and he demanded that California officials recognize U.S. authority. He pledged to crush "these boasting and abusive chiefs . . . who unless driven out, will with the aid of the hostile Indians, keep this beautiful country in a constant state of revolution and blood."

Only a year earlier, the dashing engineer, entrepreneur, and secret agent had attempted to embroil Texas in a war with Mexico. Stockton now commanded a vast theater of operations in the war that he had so avidly sought.

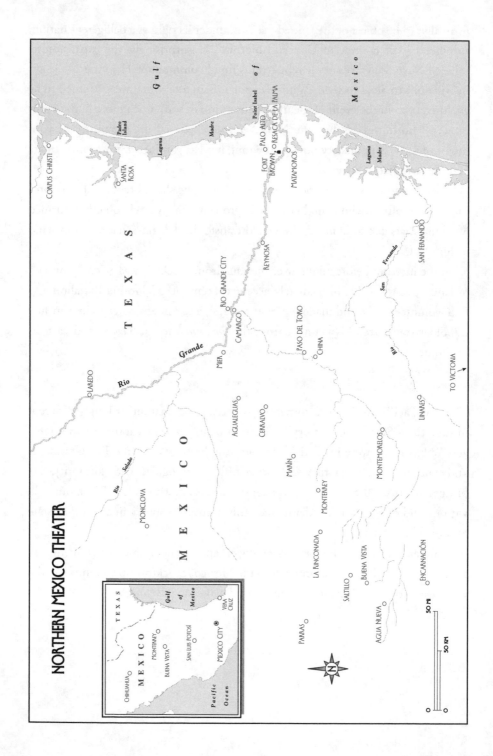

NORTHERN MEXICO THEATER

Gulf of Mexico

TEXAS

MEXICO

CORPUS CHRISTI
Padre Island
SANTA ROSA
Laguna Madre
Point Isabel
PALO ALTO
FORT BROWN
RESACA DE LA PALMA
MATAMOROS
Laguna Madre
SAN FERNANDO
RIO GRANDE CITY
REYNOSA
CAMARGO
MIER
Río Grande
PASO DEL TORO
CHINA
Río San Fernando
TO VICTORIA
OLAREDO
Río
AGUALEGUAS
CERRALVO
LINARES
Río Salado
MARÍN
MONTEMORELOS
MONCLOVA
MONTERREY
LA RINCONADA
BUENA VISTA
ENCARNACIÓN
SALTILLO
PARRAS
AGUA NUEVA

50 MI
50 KM

N

TEXAS
Gulf of Mexico
MEXICO
CHIHUAHUA
MONTERREY
BUENA VISTA
SAN LUIS POTOSÍ
MEXICO CITY
VERA CRUZ
Pacific Ocean

TESTING THE ENEMY

"Let us ride a little nearer. The balls will fall behind us."

—General Zachary Taylor's rejoinder to a suggestion
that he withdraw from enemy musket range

MAY 1, 1846: RIO GRANDE

General Zachary Taylor knew that he must secure the vulnerable twenty-seven-mile supply line to Port Isabel without delay. Inaction could cost him Port Isabel and leave him adrift in hostile territory, amid enemy forces three times his army's size.

But before Taylor could act, Brigadier General Anastasio Torrejón and his sixteen hundred men, following the annihilation of Captain Seth Thornton's dragoon force, bypassed Fort Texas and on April 28 overran a Texas Ranger camp on the Port Isabel road, killing five Texans and capturing four others. Torrejón temporarily cut Taylor off from his supply depot. Nearby, the main body of General Mariano Arista's army, more than forty-five hundred men, began crossing the Rio Grande, prefatory to isolating Fort Texas altogether.

Torrejón's men should have remained on the Port Isabel road and kept the Americans bottled up at Fort Texas until Arista's army was across the river. But rumors had reached Arista that Taylor was sending snipers to kill him at the river ford, and the red-haired general with the booming voice lost his nerve. He withdrew Torrejón and his men from their strong position on the Port Isabel road and placed them on the eastern riverbank below Matamoros to protect the crossing approaches from the phantom American snipers.

Learning that most of Arista's army had crossed the river, Taylor hastened toward Port Isabel on May 1 with twenty-three hundred troops, leaving 550 men at Fort Texas. The army was on high alert, and dragoons rode miles ahead, expecting to encounter Mexican forces that would contest the army's passage. To their amazement, the road to Port Isabel was wide open.

After sleeping on the ground without benefit of blankets or fires, the troops marched into Port Isabel at midday on May 2. Work parties immediately began building a new fort—Fort Polk. Taylor asked naval commanders in the area to send Marines and sailors to complete the fort and garrison it. He soon had five hundred men. His quartermasters began loading 270 wagons with provisions to take with them on the trip back to Fort Texas.

• • •

Taylor's men were awakened at 5 A.M. on May 3 by the sound of distant artillery fire, coming from the direction of Fort Texas and Matamoros. The camp buzzed with rumors that Fort Texas was under attack.

Anxious to obtain information, Taylor dispatched Captain Charles May with a detachment of dragoons and Captain Sam Walker of the Texas Rangers. He scrawled a note to Major Jacob Brown, Fort Texas's commander: hold out to the last man. May's men, however, discovered that large numbers of Mexican troops now blocked the Fort Texas–Port Isabel road.

Sam Walker, one of the most celebrated of the legendary Texas Rangers, volunteered to lead a small party through the Mexican lines. With four volunteers, he set out on a circuitous journey toward the beleaguered fort with Taylor's message to Brown. May and the dragoons awaited their return. Walker did not return that night, or the next day.

• • •

If anyone could get through to Fort Texas, it was Walker. Slightly built, slouching, and blue-eyed, Walker did not look the part of the merciless, hard-riding Ranger that he was. A Maryland native, Walker was a veteran of the Seminole War, where he had distinguished himself during a reconnaissance mission sent by Colonel William S. Harney deep into the Florida swamps. After the war, Walker joined Captain Jack Coffee Hays's Rangers.

Captured with three hundred other Texans during the disastrous 1842 Mier expedition, Walker had helped lead the breakout from the prison at Salado by seizing weapons and horses and crashing through massed Mexican troops, only to get lost in the mountains. Nearly dead from starvation, the Rangers were recaptured, but Walker escaped a second time with eight other men, this time reaching Texas.

In 1844, Walker was one of fifteen Rangers who, armed with the new Samuel Colt six-shooters, attacked eighty Comanche, killing half of them. (Colt's six-shooter for mounted troops would one day be known as the "Walker Colt.") In 1845, Taylor authorized Walker to form a company of Rangers to serve with the Army of Observation.

• • •

Walker returned to Port Isabel during the night of May 4, weather-beaten and dusty, with news that Fort Texas was holding its own, and in fact had silenced the Mexican batteries in Matamoros. Walker's already high standing among the regular Army officers rose a notch for the "fearless manner" in which he had completed the dangerous mission.

Scouting ahead for the enemy on May 6, Walker found Mexican troops near the Fort Texas road "in great force." Arista's and Torrejón's roughly thirty-seven hundred men were camped near potable water three miles from the Palo Alto crossroad. But when Walker returned the following morning, the Mexicans were gone.

Taylor's army bivouacked seven miles from Port Isabel on May 7, planning to advance the next day toward Fort Texas. "If the enemy oppose my march, in whatever force, I shall fight him," Taylor informed the War Department in a letter. In his journal, Major Philip Barbour wrote: "We expect a hard fight on our return. God be with us."

FORT TEXAS

Taylor's departure from Fort Texas on May 1 had occasioned a spurt of activity across the river in Matamoros. Major Brown's 550 men uneasily watched the preparations; the stockpiling of ammunition at the enemy batteries told them what they needed to know. Thus, it was almost a relief for the Americans, who had been sleeping for days in their boots, swords, and belts, with arms at hand, "ready to spring up," when at 5 A.M. on May 3, General Arista's batteries erupted with a roar that awakened Taylor's men twenty-seven miles away.

While the initial bombardment of Fort Texas was loud, the Mexicans' small-caliber brass shells had no effect other than shredding the Americans' tents. Then

Brown's battery of 18-pounders went into action, dismounting two Mexican guns within thirty minutes. While the targets were beyond the range of Braxton Bragg's four 6-pounder field guns, the superbly crewed 18-pounders methodically, if temporarily, knocked out every Mexican gun, except for a sunken mortar that defied their marksmanship. The American gunners tried to ignite blazes in the city by firing superheated cannonballs, or "hot shot," but the stone buildings would not burn. Yet the Mexican army was beginning to discover that it faced arguably the world's best-trained and -equipped artillerymen. Lieutenant George Meade's confident promise to his wife, to "rattle them about their ears in such a manner as will soon silence their fire," was becoming actuality.

Over the next two days, the uneven artillery duel flared and subsided. A Mexican shell struck at a man's feet, rolled over another man's back, and passed between the legs of a third man, without causing any injury. But their good fortune was balanced by the misfortunes of a Sergeant Weigart. Hit in the chin by grapeshot, he was carried to a hospital tent—where an enemy shell then took off his head, "as if they had a special spite against that particular man," observed Lieutenant Napoleon Jackson Dana.

On the fourth day of the siege, the Mexicans set up a mortar battery on the American side of the river north of Fort Texas, where General Mariano Arista had also positioned more than two thousand troops. They never attacked, possibly because they would have had to charge across a drawbridge spanning a twelve-foot-deep ditch. But even if the Mexicans had somehow managed to break into the fort, they would have met Brown's efficient gun crews, amply supplied with round shot, explosive shell, grapeshot, and case shot—the latter soon to be better known by the name of its inventor, Henry Shrapnel. The Seventh Infantry troops attached to Brown had plenty of cartridges for their .69-caliber Springfield flintlock muskets, and the fort was stocked with a month's provisions. As Mexican infantrymen harmlessly peppered the fort with small-arms fire, Bragg's gun crews discovered that the enemy infantry was now within the killing zone of their four 6-pounders and fired on them. Instead of attacking, Arista's troops withdrew beyond the gunners' range.

On May 6, a Mexican shell blew off one of Major Brown's legs. Captain Edgar S. Hawkins assumed command of the beleaguered fort. Mexican officers demanded that the Americans surrender. Hawkins refused. The desultory Mexican bombardment resumed, with a shell hitting a tent that contained the Seventh Infantry's band instruments, destroying most of them.

The enemy infantrymen who had skulked outside the fort to no good result, trying to stay outside the range of Bragg's guns, now marched away. The miserably ineffective shelling finally stopped, and the siege, such as it was, ended, although the Americans had not yet seen evidence of Taylor returning.

Over six days, the enemy had fired twelve hundred rounds of shot and sixty shells, yet caused only fifteen casualties, including two deaths—Sergeant Weigart and Major Brown, who died on May 9, just before his men began to hear in the distance the loud rumble of a major battle.

Brown's men honored their fallen commander by renaming their fortress Fort Brown.

• • •

Most Americans regarded the Army's "regulars" as misfits and felons, suited only for fighting Indians and forcibly removing them from the path of American expansion. It was true that the regular Army's enlisted ranks were not filled with America's best and brightest, and for good reason: the pay was low, the hours were long, the duty was hard and thankless, and there were few opportunities for advancement. So the public perception was partly correct, that drifters, former ne'er-do-wells, and penniless immigrants tended to gravitate to the Army. Enlisting on average at age twenty-five, most were from the northern Atlantic Coast. Forty percent were foreign-born men who often did not grasp the difference, noted a frustrated captain, between charging their muskets, charging the enemy, and charging the government for their services.

In Mexico, the U.S. troops were perceived as being soft, and the Mexican soldiers as "better disciplined, more inured to hardships." The Americans, the Mexicans believed, would break in battle. "Those adventurers cannot withstand the bayonet charge of our foot," declared General Francisco Mejia, one of the generals sent packing before hostilities erupted on the Rio Grande.

But it would have been a huge mistake to judge the regulars' fighting qualities by their humble, sometimes mean origins. While the Army of Observation might not have had the best raw human material to work with, long enlistments and ceaseless drill and discipline effected by dedicated, West Point-trained junior officers, had molded it into a confident, efficient fighting force. Shockingly underrated by Mexicans and by their own countrymen, Taylor's troops were easily the match of any force of comparable size in the world.

Most of the regulars were devoted to the institution that gave them a home, fed them, and clothed them in handsome uniforms of white cotton in the summer and blue wool in the wintertime; in gold buttons and belt buckles adorned with raised American eagles; and in plumed shakos, or forage caps. They carried the world's best firearms and could efficiently fire and care for them. Their officers, more likely than not West Point graduates versed in modern tactics and training techniques, knew how to drill and discipline their men so that in combat they would obey orders under fire. Yet the logjam of aged and disabled officers in the billets left a shortage of field officers, with the result that captains, who ordinarily commanded companies, were asked to lead regiments, and lieutenants took charge of companies.

Congress neither expanded the officer corps nor increased soldiers' pay. A private made $7 a month; a bugler, $2 more. An infantry lieutenant received only $25 per month; a captain, $40; a colonel, $75; and a brigadier general, $104. (An 1846 dollar was worth about $23.60 in 2006 dollars, so the brigadier was earning roughly $2,400 a month, the private about $165, in today's currency.) And the Army was undoubtedly undersized. Force reductions had whittled the Army's authorized strength to eight thousand officers and men, and at least a fourth of them were ill or disabled.

Although woefully understrength with fewer than five hundred men each, the Army's fourteen regiments were armed with the world's best smoothbore flintlock muskets, mass-produced with interchangeable parts at the Springfield Arsenal and at factories in the Connecticut River Valley. The flintlock musket was essentially the same weapon used by George Washington's army seventy years earlier. When the trigger was pulled, flint struck steel, shooting sparks into a small pan of gunpowder that then ignited, sending a spark through a hole in the barrel into the main chamber, and discharging the weapon. Newer muskets that substituted a percussion cap for the flint and steel were crowding out the flintlocks on production lines but were not reaching frontline troops in 1846, mainly because of concerns about the soldiers' unfamiliarity with them.

War Secretaries John C. Calhoun and Joel Poinsett had instituted two changes to the Army that would have enormous consequences during the coming war. During Calhoun's 1817–1825 tenure, the United States Military Academy at West Point, founded in 1802, became the preeminent school for U.S. Army officers. It adopted a standardized curriculum, ordnance, and equipment. In 1821, the regular Army began awarding officers' commissions only to West Point graduates. While the populist Andrew Jackson struck down this rule after he became president in 1829, by the time the Civil War began in 1861, three-fourths of all Army officers would be West Point graduates.

Poinsett's horticultural legacy, the poinsettia, often overshadows his dominant role in establishing the artillery as a separate branch of the Army. The former Minister to Mexico elevated the soot-faced cannoneer into perhaps the most important soldier on the mid-nineteenth-century battlefield. Insisting that the Army have the best available gunnery technology, Poinsett sent officers to Europe to investigate. They returned with copious notes on English, French, and German artillery designs and tactics. The result was a new generation of American smoothbore artillery pieces cast in foundries employing the most up-to-date metallurgical techniques.

Foremost among them were light 6- and 12-pounder guns mounted on gun carriages that teams of horses swiftly moved around the battlefield. Quickly loaded and fired, the new "field artillery" was versatile. Its guns, weighing sixteen hundred pounds, could batter forts with solid shot; shred men with grapeshot, which were clumps of one-inch balls that flew apart when fired; and fire fused canister rounds that exploded into clouds of lethal balls, or shrapnel, at 350 to 500 yards.

In each of the Army's four artillery regiments was one field artillery company, consisting of two 6-pounder guns and two 12-pounder howitzers, each crewed by five to eight gunners. A well-drilled 6-pounder team could load and fire three rounds a minute in combat. In a profession whose tactics had changed little since the Napoleonic wars thirty-five years earlier, the "light artillery," or "flying artillery," as it was sometimes called, was a major innovation. The U.S. Army's field artillery was the best in the world.

Field artillery officers were trained at West Point and at the new Army artillery school at Fortress Monroe, Virginia, another Poinsett-inspired innovation. They were active, colorful men who stamped their units with their personalities to the extent that they became known by their commanders' names rather than their official unit designations—for example, "Ringgold's Battery" (named for Major Samuel Ringgold) instead of Light Battery C, Third Artillery. General Taylor had the good fortune to have with him three of the Army's top field artillery commanders: Braxton Bragg, Captain James Duncan, and, arguably the best of all, Ringgold.

After graduating first in the West Point Class of 1818, Ringgold, a Maryland physician's son, had studied at Europe's finest professional military institutes, including the Polytechnique and Woolwich, where he discovered his lifelong passion for the artillery. He became its leading exponent in the United States and organized and equipped the first field artillery company, at Carlisle, Pennsylvania.

It was after Ringgold, in 1838, demonstrated to Poinsett that his mobile gunners could keep up with and support infantry and dragoon units that the Army authorized the creation of one field artillery company for each artillery regiment. The light artillerymen rode horses, not gun limbers, and were known as "red legs," because of the red stripe down their uniform trouser seams.

• • •

In addition to the Army's four artillery regiments, there were eight infantry and two dragoon regiments. The blue-uniformed infantryman was trained to load and fire his flintlock three times a minute, and to hit targets up to 220 yards away. Weighing ten pounds, the flintlock was five feet long without the bayonet; with it, a soldier wielded a six-foot lance whose cruelly honed blade, glittering in the sunlight, was designed to strike terror into the enemy. Dragoons, armed with shorter-barreled, breech-loading Hall's carbines and six-shot pistols, were horse infantrymen who dismounted to fight; before the Texas Rangers were mustered into federal service, they were the regular Army's only mounted troops.

In camp, officers relentlessly drilled the enlisted men in the manual of arms and close-order marching, and there was target practice, although it was not conducted as faithfully as it would later be. The soldiers' uniforms, persons, and gear were regularly inspected. The Army's encampments, with tents all pitched and aligned with mathematical precision, were models of order.

When Ulysses S. Grant looked back on his Mexican War service nearly four decades later, he made a remarkable observation about Taylor's little army: "A better army, man for man, probably never faced an enemy than the one commanded by General Taylor."

MAY 8, 1846: PALO ALTO

After breaking their overnight encampment seven miles from Port Isabel, Taylor's twenty-three hundred men and 270 wagons resumed the march to Fort Texas in the early morning. By late morning, the sun was blazing and the air was heavy and close. Chest-high, sharp-tipped "cord grass" grew from the spongy swampland flanking the road. The hum of mosquitoes rose from the thick grass and from the standing water left by recent heavy rains.

About noon, dragoons that had scouted ahead for signs of Arista's army galloped back to Taylor, who was dressed in a cloth coat and straw hat and riding Old

Whitey. The Mexican army, in battle array, blocked the road ahead, reported the scouts. Anticipating a long engagement under the broiling sun, Taylor ordered his men to bring plenty of water. Half a regiment at a time, the troops hiked to a nearby pond, knelt on the muddy bank, and filled their canteens.

• • •

In his glittering dress uniform, General Mariano Arista might have been Taylor's antipode. Tall, bewhiskered, and gaunt, his bushy red hair poking out from beneath his hat, Arista, reputed to be one of the best cavalry officers in the world, reviewed his army before its first test against the Americans. Drawn into a line at least a mile long, his nearly four thousand infantry and two thousand mounted troops made an impressive sight, standing tall in their chin-strapped, plumed shakos, with their bayonet-tipped muskets and nine-foot-long lances at the ready, beneath colorful banners that rustled in the hot breeze. The place where Arista had chosen to bar Taylor's passage was known as Palo Alto, meaning "tall timber." But there was no timber—perhaps encroaching salt water had killed it; only thickets, the chest-high grass, and marshes remained.

As they waited for the Americans, the artillerymen stood in readiness beside their cannons, while the lancers and cavalrymen calmed their horses. Regimental bands played martial music. In a loud voice, Arista exhorted his men to fight bravely in defense of their country. His battlefield eloquence evoked loud cries of "Viva!"

It was remarkable that Arista's army exhibited any spirit at all. Its enlisted ranks were filled largely with vagrants and the poor who had been impressed into service, and convicts who had been sentenced to the army for their crimes. Few enlisted men became commissioned officers—usually sons of old, wealthy families, military cadets, or other young men of good breeding and privilege.

Arista's men were armed with assorted castoff flintlocks from the Napoleonic wars that had been dumped by the European powers onto the international arms market, where Mexico had bought them cheaply. While American smoothbore muskets were reasonably accurate up to 220 yards, the Mexican flintlocks, mostly British India Pattern muskets, were effective to just 100 yards. Many of the Mexican artillery officers were professional soldiers—some were even European-born and -trained—but their cannons, gunpowder, and unwieldy gun carriages were old and unreliable, the result being a wide variance in accuracy.

• • •

Taylor's twenty-three hundred men now saw the mile-long enemy line blocking the road at the Palo Alto waterhole. Its two flanks and rear were protected by dense chaparral. In front of the Mexicans lay a two-mile field of cord grass cratered with watery depressions. Arista had placed his cavalry on the left and his infantry on the right.

The Mexican artillery began firing on the advancing American columns. The first cannon shot killed an American caisson driver, and the Mexicans shouted "Viva Mexico!" Taylor's men quickly formed a battle line that was scarcely half the length of Arista's. The Americans unfurled their battle flags and cheered loudly.

Both armies practiced the same European tactics of concentrating men in formations to fire deadly musket volleys. When anticipating a cavalry attack, troops deployed into squares, bayoneted muskets facing outward, just as the Duke of Wellington's troops had done at Waterloo thirty-one years earlier. Assaults were carried out at bayonet point. Taylor expected to strike Arista's army with just such a telling blow of "cold steel." This day, however, would prove unpropitious for bayonet attacks.

• • •

Major Samuel Ringgold's field artillery battery of four 6-pounders dashed into position in front of the American right flank and opened fire. Then Captain James Duncan's four field guns and the two 18-pounders under Lieutenant Colonel Thomas Childs began firing from the left. The concentrated gunnery prevented General Torrejón's cavalry from massing for an attack. When Arista's lancers attempted to loop around the Americans' right flank and swoop down on the 270 supply wagons in the rear, Captain Sam Walker's Rangers, Ringgold's lethal flying battery, and the Fifth Infantry Regiment soldiers who were guarding the supply train repelled them with heavy losses.

The combatants then settled into a "terrible cannonading" of one another that lasted an hour. The infantry and mounted troops stood their ground, gritting their teeth as flying metal shards pinged off sword blades and bayonets, and shot and shell whistled around them and overhead. The skilled, efficient American gun crews wreaked bloody havoc on the Mexican ranks. The enemy gunners, firing eight 4-pounders and a pair of 9-pounders, did not exact a commensurate toll. Ringgold's battery moved and fired at seven hundred yards, hitting a number of targets, including a Mexican regimental band as it was launching into "Los Zapadores del Jalisco" ["The Sappers of Jalisco"].

The artillery duel ignited a crackling prairie fire. There was a forty-five-minute lull in the fighting when dense smoke hid the armies from one another. When the smoke lifted, the Americans saw that Arista's army had pivoted counterclockwise, and no longer blocked the road. Taylor's troops secured the now-open road and rearranged their ranks as the general prowled among his men, dispensing words of encouragement. Everyone tried to ignore the piercing screams of wounded Mexicans burning to death in the tall grass.

Captain Duncan's flying artillery, which had moved to a better position under cover of the smoke, suddenly opened fire with "terrific effect" on the Mexican infantry, "whose ranks were broken and hundreds of them mowed down." The Mexican right flank buckled but did not collapse, evoking murmurs of admiration from Taylor's men. However, Lieutenant George Meade learned later from a prisoner that desertions were endemic, and a wholesale panicked flight was avoided only because Mexican officers shot some of their men.

Mexican gunners cut down several men in Lieutenant Colonel Childs's battery and then shifted their fire, mortally wounding Major Ringgold as he was directing fire, and killing the mount of Colonel David Twiggs, who commanded the right flank.

Torrejón's cavalry now attacked Twiggs's flank. An American infantry battalion formed square to meet the onslaught. As the horsemen bore down on the infantrymen, Childs arrived with his two 18-pounders and poured body-shredding canister into the dense mass of men and horses, sending them crashing to the ground in a writhing heap. The failed attack was the closest this day's combatants would come to one another.

Mexican troops thrust at Taylor's left flank, but Duncan alertly maneuvered his battery into range, and his 6-pounders, aided by the Eighth Infantry and a dragoon squadron, broke up several enemy attempts to flank the Americans.

• • •

In the late afternoon, Arista's army withdrew into the chaparral. Technically, the battle was a draw; but in actuality, Palo Alto was a supreme triumph of the now battle-tested American field artillery. Over five hours, Arista had launched several attacks on Taylor's army, each failing largely because of the agile, accurate "flying artillery," which seemed to be everywhere at once, as befitted its nickname. The artillery's grisly handiwork was in abundant evidence; mutilated bodies strewn and heaped everywhere. "It was truly a shocking sight; our Artillery had literally *mowed* them down," wrote a stunned Captain William S. Henry of the Fourth U.S. Infantry. For most American soldiers, this was their first exposure to war's horrors. "There were heaps of dead lying hither and yon, with the most ghastly wounds I ever saw," Henry continued; "some had died with a smile on their countenance; others, in the agony of death, with a fierce convulsive struggle had caught at the rank grass, and died with their hands clinched firmly in it, looking defiance at the enemy."

Palo Alto's marshy grasses were littered and stained with more than a hundred of Arista's dead. The Mexicans admitted to fewer than three hundred killed and wounded, but their casualty total was closer to eight hundred. The Army of Observation lost nine dead and forty-five wounded. "We fired at their masses; they at our batteries," noted Captain Henry. Taylor's army camped that night on the torn battlefield.

Still a cohesive force, Arista's battered army yet blocked Taylor's troops from reaching their 550 comrades at Fort Texas.

MAY 9, 1846: RESACA DE LA PALMA

General Arista adopted a new strategy. His army had withdrawn five miles down the road to a dried-up river oxbow that was less than ten miles from Fort Texas. Out of respect for the U.S. artillery's lethality, Arista and his staff decided not to fight again on open ground; the Mexicans, who had repeatedly attacked at Palo Alto, would wage the next battle from prepared positions, letting the Americans come to them.

Resaca de la Palma, whose proper name was Resaca de Guerrero, appeared to be ideal for this purpose. The muddy, meandering ravine was three to four feet deep on average, and up to several hundred feet wide. It straddled the Fort Texas–Port Isabel road in an arc whose apex pointed toward the advancing Americans. Thick chaparral and trees grew all around the ravine, providing excellent cover for Arista's men, who had not recovered from the previous day's battle and, in fact, had not eaten in twenty-four hours. But two thousand fresh infantrymen and a cavalry unit had crossed the river during the night, increasing the Mexicans' troop strength to about seven thousand.

• • •

While Arista had received reinforcements to replace his dead and wounded, Taylor had fifty-four fewer men, and he had to divert troops to protect the 270 wagons filled with food, clothing, and arms. At a war council early on May 9, most of

Taylor's officers favored digging defensive positions, or even retreating to Port Isabel to await reinforcements. Old Rough and Ready had not attended West Point, but he had fought Indians for thirty years and had never lost a battle. Supported by Captains James Duncan and Lewis Morris, and by brigade commander Lieutenant Colonel James McIntosh, Taylor rejected the timid counsel and ordered his army to resume its march to Fort Texas.

Scouts reported that Mexican troops blocked the road ahead. Taylor left his supply train at Palo Alto, guarded by three hundred armed wagon drivers, fifty troops, and Lieutenant Colonel Childs's two 18-pounders. With about seventeen hundred men, he resolutely advanced toward the Mexican lines.

• • •

Nearing the enemy positions at 3 P.M., the hot, dust-covered Americans could see bayonets glinting behind the mesquite and chaparral. Taylor sent forward a light infantry detachment and a flying battery to probe the Mexican lines. When the enemy batteries loosed a volley of grapeshot, Taylor deployed infantrymen on the Mexicans' two flanks and on the road. With gunfire blazing from the thickets concealing the Mexican positions, the Americans stepped out in a ragged skirmish line, supported by the peripatetic field artillery. Lieutenant Thomas P. Ridgely's light battery began firing from four hundred yards at targets pointed out by Captain Sam Walker, darting to and fro on his horse. Ridgely's gunners advanced and fired on an enemy battery, until they were dueling with canister at one hundred yards.

Taylor grasped his drawn sword, musket balls clattering around him and Old Whitey. The Fourth Infantry's sutler, watching the fighting with Taylor, grew nervous as the enemy musket fire crept uncomfortably closer. The sutler proposed that they move out of range. "Let us ride a little nearer," Taylor replied; "the balls will fall behind us."

As the skirmish line neared the mesquite and chaparral cloaking the Mexican lines and the firing rose to a crescendo, Taylor released Captain Charles May's two hundred dragoons in a mad charge on the Mexican batteries. The dragoons galloped through the ravine, driving enemy gunners away from seven artillery pieces.

• • •

The American infantrymen became separated from one another in the dense thickets, and the battle devolved into brawling gunfights between gangs of soldiers. The Mexicans stood their ground and fought hard in the scratchy tangle.

Colonel James McIntosh suddenly found himself alone in the chaparral. Six Mexicans pulled him off his horse and pinned him to the ground by crossing two bayonets in his mouth. One bayonet he managed to force out, but the Mexican wielding the other pressed down. "I felt my teeth go, and the exit of the bayonet at the back of my neck," McIntosh later wrote. He survived by "playing possum," and watched as his assailants shot a soldier ten yards away and "beat his brains out with a musket."

Two dozen men under Captain Robert C. Buchanan of the Fourth Infantry discovered a path through the labyrinthine thickets on their right flank and captured a gun emplacement. Mexican lancers and infantry launched a desperate counterattack. Major Philip Barbour and twenty-five men from the Third Infantry repelled the lancers, and then the accurate gunnery of Ridgley's flying artillery broke up the lancers before they could reform for another attack. The hodgepodge American unit shattered the Mexican attack and seized the enemy flank, bellowing "a deafening shout of triumph." Arista's army collapsed and bolted for the river.

"The pursuit now commenced and on we went," wrote Major Barbour. "Dragoons, Artillery and Infantry in one mass at full run, yelling at every stop, which kept up for three miles, until we reached the Rio Grande."

• • •

General Arista was in his tent writing letters when he saw his troops sprint past the doorway. He had not expected the Americans to attack so soon after Palo Alto; he had heard shooting but had mistakenly believed that it was a clash of skirmishers, not a battle. Arista joined his defeated army's pell-mell flight to the river, abandoning his baggage, writing desk, silver service, and papers, all seized by U.S. soldiers. Among the documents was a government order for Arista to send General Taylor to Mexico City as a prisoner.

• • •

Throwing away their weapons, the Mexicans reached the river with the Americans close behind them. Some swam and paddled boats across; others continued their wild flight upriver, attempting to cross closer to Matamoros and drowning in great numbers.

Taylor's men seized all of the Mexican supplies, personal baggage, eight artillery pieces, 393 small arms, 155,600 musket ball cartridges, the Tampico Battalion colors, five hundred mules, and twenty horses. They also captured a general, two colonels, several captains and subalterns, and 150 enlisted men.

General Romulo Diaz de la Vega, the Mexican artillery commander who had parleyed with General William Worth on the riverbank, was taken prisoner after a fierce struggle. In their headlong attack early in the battle, Captain May's dragoons had driven off Vega's gunners and captured his cannons, only to lose them to the general and his men after a determined counterattack. May and six dragoons attacked again, and they commanded Vega, "gallantly fighting in person at his battery," to surrender. Recognizing May as an officer, Vega handed him his sword. Lieutenant George Meade and the prisoner general later became such good friends that Meade invited Vega to visit his home in Pittsburgh. Meade wrote to his wife, "You will find him a most gentlemanly man and will be pleased, I am sure, with him."

• • •

There was no question that this day belonged to the Americans. In his report, Taylor wrote with evident pride that "a small force has overcome immense odds of the best troops that Mexico can furnish—veteran regiments, perfectly equipped and appointed."

Arista and Taylor had both failed to capitalize on opportunities. Arista, who had crossed the Rio Grande only when higher-ups insisted, had permitted Taylor to march unmolested to Port Isabel when his army could have blocked the road. After besieging Fort Texas, Arista did not make a serious attempt to wrest it from the Americans. And at Palo Alto, he might have turned the tide of battle had he ordered his entire force to attack, utilizing its numerical superiority, rather than passively enduring the U.S. artillery barrage and launching piecemeal assaults.

Taylor might have crushed Arista's army at Palo Alto—obviating the need for a second battle and, some say, perhaps even ending the war—if he had launched a full-scale attack after his artillery barrage had buckled the Mexican ranks. But Taylor had been unwilling to commit the two regiments and dragoon squadron guarding his wagon train and risk losing the 270 wagons filled with provisions. Even so, although outnumbered more than two to one, the Americans had mauled Arista's army in the war's first major battle.

Some officers criticized Taylor for making only a general battle plan and not adapting it to changing circumstances when the fighting began. Meade called it a "perfect inability to make any use of the information" given him. Another officer declared that Taylor was "*utterly, absurdly* incompetent to wield a large army." Yet, by giving his talented, West Point-trained junior officers autonomy on the battlefield, Taylor had found another way to win. Battlefield improvisations might not have worked against a first-rate European army, but they did against Arista.

• • •

The Americans devoted May 10 and 11 to clearing the enemy dead clogging the road and thickets around Resaca de la Palma. Mexican authorities reported 154 killed and 156 missing, many of the latter probably drowned; Taylor said the Mexican dead exceeded two hundred. They were buried with the thirty-three Americans killed during the battle.

• • •

Taylor rode to Port Isabel on May 11 to confer with Commodore David Conner about ferrying the army across the Rio Grande. The men's desire to put one another at ease during their first meeting created an amusing mixup. Knowing that Conner was reputed to be a dapper dresser, Taylor uncharacteristically wore his uniform for the occasion. Conner, aware of Taylor's dislike of uniforms, dressed in civilian clothes. After sharing a laugh over their misbegotten good intentions, the general and the commodore went to work planning the river crossing.

Taylor's subordinates fumed at the delay in occupying Matamoros. Even while facing Arista's army at Palo Alto and Resaca de la Palma, they had urged Taylor to order pontoon bridges built and scows brought up from Port Isabel, but the general had done nothing.

As Conner's light river craft began arriving, and Taylor's engineers looked for suitable river crossings, Arista sent a General Requeña to Taylor to propose an armistice until their governments could settle the boundary question. Taylor turned down the proposal.

• • •

On May 18, Taylor's army crossed to the western bank of the Rio Grande, where it was met by Matamoros civil authorities dressed entirely in white and riding horses of the same color, so the American could not possibly mistake their intentions. Arista's army had withdrawn into the interior. The civilians requested fair terms in exchange for surrendering their city. Relieved that he would not have to take the city by force, Taylor generously pledged to protect the city's property and inhabitants.

For the first time since Andrew Jackson's invasion of Spanish Florida in 1818, U.S. troops occupied territory belonging to a foreign power. Captain Ker of the dragoons raised the American flag over one of the former Mexican fortifications, and the U.S. soldiers gave "three deafening cheers," which echoed through the ranks until "the air was fairly rent with the glorious shout."

• • •

True to Taylor's promise, the Americans camped outside Matamoros, and only a few of them at a time were permitted to go into town. Restrictions notwithstanding, some of them managed to find an enormous cache of cigars. "Tell Joel just to imagine his store packed full of cigar boxes from the floor to the sealing [*sic*] and he will have some idea of the quantity of cigars we found in one house," wrote Lieutenant Jenks Beaman. Soon, it seemed that everyone in Taylor's army was smoking a cigar.

Taylor sent a squadron of dragoons in pursuit of Arista's army. Twenty-seven miles from Matamoros, the dragoons pounced on the Mexican rearguard, but the main army—about four thousand men and fourteen artillery pieces—marched on to Monterrey, 250 miles away.

• • •

At Sunday services on June 1, Captain R. A. Stewart, who, in addition to being a soldier and a Methodist minister, was a fervent believer in Manifest Destiny, devoted his first sermon at Matamoros to reminding U.S. soldiers that they were carrying out the "order of Providence." The American invasion, he said, was the natural extension of law, enlightenment, and "the blessing of freedom" into "the dark borders of Tamaulipas." God not only intended for the Anglo-Saxon race to possess all of North America but to "influence and modify" mankind's character. The American people were God's "children of destiny." Stewart was mainly preaching to the choir on this Sunday, but not everyone was willing to go so far as one avid expansionist, who observed that Taylor's army was embarked on "The Crusade of the Nineteenth Century."

Zachary Taylor saw nothing divine about the war. In his view, it was a calculated land grab and an attempt to enrich well-connected claim-holders. While he carefully concealed his political opinions from his men, Taylor was candid with his son-in-law (Ann Taylor's husband) Dr. Robert C. Wood, to whom he expressed the hope that negotiations would begin soon, while adding, "I apprehend our government will require vast amounts of territory to indemnify us on account of the expenditures of the war, as well as for spoliations for real & pretended robberies [*sic*] on our commerce; which will no doubt be double & triple awarded to certain claimants over & above what they ever lost by the commissioners who will be appointed for that purpose."

MAY 1846: WASHINGTON

At a time when President Polk should have been absorbed by the prosecution of the war, he was instead questioning the conduct of his two most senior generals, Winfield Scott and Edmund Pendleton Gaines.

After learning of Captain Seth Thornton's ambush, and without authority or consultation, the sixty-nine-year-old Gaines—the fiery, outspoken commander of the Army's Western Division, the Army's senior general, and a War of 1812 hero—had called out eleven thousand militiamen, volunteers, and regulars from Louisiana, Alabama, Kentucky, Mississippi, and Missouri. The call-ups were completely unnecessary; Taylor had already requested five thousand volunteers from Louisiana and Texas. Alarmed War Department officials ordered Gaines to cancel the order, but it was too late.

"Gen'l Gaines has greatly embarrassed the Government," wrote Polk, "and the danger is that a very large body of 3 & 6 months men may be assembled on the Rio Grande for which there is no use, and who will consume Gen'l Taylor's provisions and otherwise greatly embarrass him."

Indeed, throughout the summer of 1846, thousands of unwanted troops overwhelmed Taylor's encampment outside Matamoras. The first six companies reached Port Isabel as Taylor was marching toward Palo Alto. Taylor was not only unprepared to feed, shelter, and train such a massive force, he lacked even the money to pay them. The volunteers, Taylor observed, were arriving "faster than they can be landed, what are [*sic*] to be done with them when they arrive . . . or become of them, I am unable to say." And as the volunteers' enlistments lapsed after three, six, or twelve months, the men would be going home just as they were becoming useful.

It was not the first time that Gaines had summoned volunteers without first checking with Taylor, or the War Department. In August 1845, after reading in the New Orleans newspapers that three thousand Mexican soldiers were marching on the Rio Grande, with another ten thousand troops behind them, Gaines had asked the Louisiana governor to send four infantry regiments and two artillery companies to reinforce Taylor in Texas. When the report proved false, the order was countermanded before the infantry regiments had formed, but the artillery companies reached Corpus Christi on August 25. They served until November 4, and then were mustered out. On that occasion, War Secretary William Marcy had rebuked Gaines for not consulting him first.

This time, Gaines was sacked from the Western Division command and ordered to report to Washington. On June 20, after Gaines had met with Marcy, the Army took steps to convene a Court of Inquiry, and the Senate began an investigation, too, requesting all correspondence regarding Gaines's panicked troop callups. Whig senators drafted a resolution asking Marcy to explain whether "any individual" besides Polk and Marcy had authority to call up volunteers for the war.

Polk gathered all of the requested documents on the subject and invited the Senate resolution's chief sponsor, Reverdy Johnson of Maryland, to the White House. While reading the documents to Johnson, Polk inadvertently revealed to him the administration's heretofore-secret instructions for seizing California. Remarkably, until that moment few people outside of the cabinet and a handful of military officers were aware of the administration's "projected campaign by land and sea into Upper California."

Conjuring up all of the persuasiveness learned over twenty-five years in politics, the president urged Johnson to drop the investigation. The administration had broken no laws in planning to occupy California, but broadcasting its intentions "would probably defeat our object & . . . excite the jealousy of England and France, who might interfere to prevent the accomplishment of our objects. . . ." Senator Johnson agreed to terminate the inquiry, and he left the White House empty-handed.

The Court of Inquiry, meeting in August at Fortress Monroe, found Gaines guilty of violating orders and acting illegally but recommended no punitive action because of Gaines's patriotic motives and his forty-nine years as an Army officer. While concurring with the court's leniency, Polk insisted that Gaines be reassigned to a command where he "cannot repeat the mischief." Gaines was appointed commander of the Army's Eastern Division.

• • •

When he signed the war declaration, Polk had also placed Taylor's forces on the Rio Grande under the command of sixty-year-old General of the Army Winfield Scott. Scott was to sail to Texas to personally lead operations against northern Mexico.

But Old Fuss and Feathers could be as tactless and arrogant as he was gifted in the military arts. Already working against him was the fact that he was a Whig—an ambitious one, and therefore suspect, in Polk's view—who had sought his party's presidential nomination in 1840. It went without saying that Scott was not part of the president's inner circle, but his egotism and indiscretion quickly made matters worse. Scott managed to so antagonize both the president and War Secretary Marcy that they reversed the decision to send Scott to the Rio Grande and grounded him in Washington instead.

The precipitating incident was an ill-considered letter of complaint by Scott to War Secretary Marcy after a week of working on war plans with Polk. Scott and the president were politically and constitutionally mismatched. Polk, preternaturally attuned to politics as he was, was well aware that Scott was positioning himself for the 1848 presidential campaign (a Scott campaign biography had just been published). Probably of greater consequence, however, Scott's pomposity and pretentiousness grated on the ascetic president, just as Polk's presumption in planning military operations—with a ticket-punching militia stint in 1821 his only military experience—offended Scott, an Army officer for twenty-eight years.

In March, Polk had weighed whether to punish Scott for signing a letter protesting Polk's reversal of the general's decision to make brevet rank equal to "lineal" rank. Senator Thomas Hart Benton had suggested that Polk reassign Scott for insubordination to the northern frontier, an early manifestation of Benton's evolving ambition to become the Army's highest-ranking general. Polk, however, did nothing.

A day after the president signed the war declaration, he was already grumbling about Scott's methodical, deliberate methods in a diary entry: "Gen'l Scott did not impress me favourably as a military man. He has had experience in his profession, but I thought was rather scientific and visionary in his views." During their four-hour war council that day, Polk said nothing, even though he disagreed with Scott's insistence that he would need twenty thousand men and that it was necessary to first build up supplies and troops before invading northern Mexico.

The fact was that Polk, accustomed to working on projects with a sense of urgency until completion, did not understand why Scott was not already on a ship to Port Isabel, prefatory to leading an expedition into Mexico's interior. Polk's patience, such as it was, evaporated when Scott announced that he did not plan to travel to the Rio Grande until September, and would spend the summer supervising logistics from Washington.

The president directed Marcy to "take the matter into your own hands" and send Scott to the Rio Grande immediately. "Issue his [Scott's] orders and cause them to be obeyed."

When Marcy relayed the president's peremptory order to Scott, the general penned an intemperate protest. He noted peevishly that he had been working fourteen hours a day for several days, and now had learned that "much impatience is already felt, perhaps in high quarters," because he was not already en route to the Rio Grande. "I find myself compelled to stop that necessary work to guard myself against, perhaps, utter condemnation in the quarters alluded to.

"I am too old a soldier, and have had too much special experience, not to feel the infinite importance of securing myself against danger (ill-will or pre-condemnation) in my rear, before advancing upon the public enemy. My explicit meaning is, that I do not desire to place myself in the most perilous of all positions—*a fire upon my rear from Washington, the fire in front from the Mexicans.*"

The very day that Scott was writing these words that would be used to condemn him, Polk was reading a copy of another Scott letter, which the general had written to Senator William S. Archer of Virginia. If Scott's letter to Marcy did not harden Polk's resolve to act against Scott, the Archer letter, which revealed Scott's bitter antipathy toward Polk's Democratic administration, surely would.

Scott explained to Archer why a Captain Hutter, dismissed from the Army during the Tyler administration, would not be reinstated. "With the officering of a new corps I am sure I should not be allowed the least possible agency except in favour of a democrat. . . . Not an eastern man, not a graduate of the Military Academy and certainly not a Whig would obtain a place under such proscriptive circumstances or prospects. You may be certain I shall not dishonor myself by recommending any individual whatever, and so I have already replied to hundreds of applicants, most of them democrats."

The Archer letter, Polk coldly noted in his diary, was "highly exceptional in its tenor and language toward the President. It proved to me that Gen'l Scott was not only hostile, but recklessly vindictive in his feelings towards my administration."

Thus, when the president read Scott's Marcy letter to his cabinet on Saturday, May 23, there was little doubt what this portended for Scott. Closely vetted by Polk and the cabinet, Marcy's reply rebuked Scott for his insinuations about the president: "How could you, under these circumstances, arrest your labors of preparation, and suffer your energies to be crippled, for the purpose of indulging in illiberal imputations against the man who has just bestowed upon you the highest mark of his confidence?" The letter informed Scott that he was "excused" from his twelve-day-old field command of the Rio Grande army, and was to remain on duty in Washington.

• • •

Scott's effusively apologetic reply contained an unfortunate, self-pitying allusion to having just "sat down to a hasty plate of soup" for supper—implying that his workload scarcely permitted him time for even this—when Marcy's letter had arrived. (Scott's "hasty plate of soup" became a standing joke among Democrats and Scott critics.) Scott denied that the term "high quarters" was an allusion to the president; it had meant members of Congress. He praised the president's "magnanimity" in not having him court-martialed.

Scott's letter reached Marcy on May 26. It came too late. News had just arrived of Taylor's victories at Palo Alto and Resaca de la Palma. Polk had already drafted a message to the Senate nominating Taylor for the rank of brevet major general "for his gallant victories obtained over the Mexican forces on the Del Norte on the 8th & 9th days of this month."

Because of his "brilliant victories" on the Rio Grande, Zachary Taylor, and not Winfield Scott, would lead the expedition into northern Mexico, Polk announced. Congress awarded Taylor a gold medal. It was a terrible punishment for Scott, who yearned for a field command.

Nor was the decision welcomed by Taylor, who resignedly observed, "The honor [was] greatly overbalanced by the . . . duties which have been assigned me, which I neither wished or expected, & which I would have avoided had I been consulted in the matter."

• • •

Scott's severe punishment perfectly illustrated the blurring of politics, personal loyalty, and policy that was becoming a hallmark of the Polk administration. Scott's *"fire upon my rear"* letter to Marcy, interpreted as insubordinate and potentially embarrassing to the president, might just as easily have been read by Marcy as a plea to mediate the differences of opinion between Polk and Scott over how the war should be prosecuted.

It was not unusual that strongly opinionated men from divergent backgrounds, working together for the first time, would disagree. Marcy might have interceded and helped Polk and Scott build a working relationship. Instead, he took Scott's letter straight to the president, and, casting it in the worst possible light, evoked a predictably condemnatory reaction from Polk.

In his superb *Memoirs,* Ulysses S. Grant recalled his service during the Mexican War, the defining event of his young manhood. Conceding that Scott could be insufferably vain, and being as conversant as Polk with politics, ambition, and the presidency, Grant concluded that Polk sought to "kill off" Scott politically.

But in seeking to damage Scott's prospects, Polk underestimated Taylor's.

12

A QUESTION OF "PECULIAR DELICACY"

"What connection slavery had with making peace with Mexico it is difficult to conceive."

—President James K. Polk's reaction to the Wilmot Proviso

The day that war was declared, May 13, the Polk administration displayed fresh interest in Santa Anna's three-month-old proposition to return to Mexico and negotiate a treaty. Navy Secretary George Bancroft instructed Commodore David Conner in a confidential memo, "If Santa Anna endeavors to enter the Mexican ports, you will allow him to pass freely."

At the same time, Polk dispatched William Linn Brown, a private citizen from Pennsylvania, on a secret mission to Havana to further divine Santa Anna's intentions. But Brown, it turned out, had too many scruples for the president. In his report, he advised against giving any aid to the banished ex-president. Santa Anna, he wrote, was motivated solely by self-interest and only wished to "twist [Mexico's] chains tighter." Brown boldly recommended that rather than parley with Santa Anna, the United States should instead *kidnap* him and imprison him on Key West, where he could do no more harm to the Mexican people. Polk and his advisers, who were unconcerned about Mexico's welfare but only about whether Santa Anna could advance their purposes, sought a new agent to send to Cuba.

They looked no further than John Slidell's brother, Alexander Slidell Mackenzie, a forty-three-year-old travel writer, naval biographer, and former naval officer. Mackenzie, who had adopted his mother's maiden name to continue her

Scottish clan's royal lineage, had been acquitted in 1843 of murder in a sensational naval discipline case. While commanding the USS *Somers*, he had hanged the son of War Secretary John Canfield Spencer for mutiny, along with two sailors.

Mackenzie reached Havana on July 5 on the U.S. brig *Truxtun* in the guise of a naval observer assigned to watch Cuba's ports for Mexican-commissioned privateers. However, his real assignment had already been leaked to the press. No sooner had the *Truxtun* departed Norfolk than the *New York Journal of Commerce* was reporting that Mackenzie had been entrusted with "a mission to Santa Anna."

If the newspapers had not already exposed Mackenzie's secret mission, his own comportment almost surely would have. He arrived at Santa Anna's residence in an open carriage, wearing his full-dress Navy uniform. "Why has the President sent me that fool?" Santa Anna is said to have exclaimed.

Polk's emissary promised the scheming exile that the United States would suspend hostilities when Santa Anna returned to power if he would pledge to hold negotiations to transfer California and resolve the Texas–Mexico boundary question. Santa Anna seemed more than willing, ridiculously asserting that after a treaty was concluded, he planned to move to Texas and become a U.S. citizen. He coached Mackenzie on how the United States could best appear to force him into peace talks: General Taylor should march from the Rio Grande to San Luis Potosi, and U.S. forces should capture Tampico and Vera Cruz, the latter best approached from beyond cannon range of the Castle of San Juan del Ulua's guns. But while Santa Anna was cultivating Polk's secret complicity in his return to Mexico, his letters to the "puro" archliberals in Mexico who supported his political restoration were full of patriotic defiance of the United States.

Santa Anna's Mephistophelean intrigues worked to perfection. On August 8, he left Havana aboard the British steamer *Arab*. The U.S. blockading fleet permitted the *Arab* to proceed to Vera Cruz. "I have allowed him to enter without molestation, or even speaking to the vessel," Commodore Conner reported.

AUGUST 16, 1846: VERA CRUZ

Thousands of people watched in silence as the *Arab* glided into its moorage in steamy Vera Cruz. Accompanying the "Immortal Three-Fourths," as some Mexicans sardonically called the fifty-two-year-old Santa Anna because of his missing left leg, were three fellow exiles—General Juan Nepomuceno Almonte, the former minister who had broken off relations with the United States in March 1845; and

Manuel Crescencio Rejon and Jose Ignacio Basadre, members of the exiled dictator's inner circle.

The gunners at the Castle of San Juan de Ulua fired a thunderous salute as Santa Anna, wearing a dazzling, tailored blue uniform, strode among the troops standing at attention. He was officially welcomed home by three sons of Valentin Gomez Farias, the Santa Anna ally who, with Jose Mariano Salas, had ten days earlier overthrown President Mariano Paredes, restored freedom of the press, and called for congressional elections. Farias and Salas staged the coup after obtaining from Santa Anna both his support and his promise to lead Mexican forces against the United States. Salas was now provisional president, Farias the head of the Council of State. Salas, however, intended to remain president only until Congress met in December and elevated Santa Anna to the position. As Salas had declared in his "pronunciamiento": "Santa Anna is invited to return and take command of the Army as General in Chief, & until the Sovereign Congress meet, and decree what may be necessary for the war. . . ."

Significantly, few ordinary citizens attended the elaborately staged homecoming celebration; they were weary of Santa Anna. The former president and his entourage left Vera Cruz for the cooler precincts of his four-thousand-foot-elevation hacienda at El Encerro, near Jalapa. In Mexico City, officials restored Santa Anna's name to street signs and repaired and re-erected statues that had been dragged through the streets when he was deposed two years earlier.

Santa Anna published a long-winded manifesto, the aim of which was to help him rise again to the presidency. As a sop to his archliberal puro supporters, the former dictator applauded Mexican republicanism and advocated a return to the 1824 Constitution. He denounced the deposed Paredes for plotting to install a Spanish monarch—the so-called "monarchist scheme" secretly backed by the Catholic Church, rich landowners, and conservatives. Santa Anna derogated former President Jose Joaquin Herrera's willingness to negotiate with the United States and reminded everyone that he had once been saluted with "the enviable title of soldier of the people.

"Allow me again to take it," his manifesto continued, "never more to be given up, and to devote myself until death, to the defense of the liberty and independence of the republic."

• • •

He lingered for weeks at his hacienda, claiming that the ship's journey had inflamed the stump of his left leg, but really waiting to see how his repatriation was received. When Salas and Farias urged him—although the idea evidently was Santa Anna's—to come to Mexico City to claim the presidency, Santa Anna declined. It would be "most degrading," he said, to serve as president when he was needed to fight Mexico's enemies: "Neither my honor nor my loyalty demand that I abandon interests that are so dear." In actuality, he was trying to distance himself from Salas, Farias, and the puros—in anticipation of the day when he swept them all from power. Santa Anna had already begun to play the puros against the moderados, to gain ascendancy over both.

General Santa Anna, who liked to think of himself as a "Napoleon of the West," spent two weeks in Mexico City in September, raising money to support an army that could take the offensive against the invading Americans. With twenty-five hundred men, he marched 320 miles north from Mexico City to the crossroads city of San Luis Potosi, where he established his headquarters and took charge of the four thousand troops already there.

Without public funds for weapons, uniforms, or provisions, Santa Anna patriotically put up "the sum total of the property I owned, worth half a million pesos," as collateral for one hundred silver bars that he ordered from the Mint. The bars paid for the army's needs. As his army marched and drilled, Santa Anna, who often began projects that he failed to see through, grew bored with the duties of actively commanding an army. He began devoting most of his time to his first love, politics, and seldom watched his soldiers training.

After observing the army, Mexican artillery officer Manuel Balbontín wrote: "These troops were in general badly armed; there were corps in which were seen arms of all sizes, and a large part without bayonets . . . many guns held together with leather straps or with cords instead of braces." Moreover, there was no powder for target practice.

SUMMER 1846: WASHINGTON

James Polk confidently believed that with Santa Anna's return to Mexico, the war would soon end. Senator Thomas Hart Benton later insisted that Polk's plan from the very beginning was "to put him [Santa Anna] back in Mexico, and he to make peace with us," thereby realizing the president's aim of a war "fixed for its term" of 90 to 120 days. Polk certainly thought this was possible in July 1846, when he predicted to his brother William that the war would be "of short duration. I doubt whether there will be much more fighting unless it be in a guerrilla warfare."

Mackenzie's secret trip to Havana was soon known everywhere. His boasting about the mission's success, Benton wrote, "put the report on the winds and sent it flying over the country." There were so many published reports linking the Polk administration to Santa Anna's repatriation that the Washington *Union* was compelled to issue a haughty demurral: "This country declines all such intrigues or bargains."

While the *Union* was denying the truth, Polk was proceeding with his plan for ending the war, settling the Texas boundary at the Rio Grande, and annexing California and New Mexico. In a July 27 letter to the Mexican government, Secretary of State James Buchanan proposed peace negotiations, while callously observing that it would be "useless . . . to discuss the causes of the existing war. This might tend to delay or defeat the restoration of peace. The past is already consigned to history. . . ."

Polk informed Congress of the proposal on August 4, the day after he received Mackenzie's secret report detailing his free-passage-for-negotiations agreement with Santa Anna in Havana. Polk made no mention of the report in his diary, nor did he suggest in his message to Congress that the peace overture was motivated by anything other than duty and a desire for peace: "Considering the relative power of the two countries, the glorious events which have already signalized our arms, and the distracted condition of Mexico, I did not conceive that any point of national honor could exist which ought to prevent me from making this overture. . . . I have deemed it my duty to extend the olive branch to Mexico."

The president informed Congress that he would request an unspecified amount of "ready money" to be used as a down payment on a peace treaty, just as Thomas Jefferson in 1806 had gotten Congress's approval to spend $2 million as a down payment on the Floridas (the purchase fell through).

While Polk's congressional allies, such as Senator Benton, were aware that "the war was made to get the peace," they did not see how the president could predict with any certainty that the mercurial Mexican government would agree to a parley—until they learned that Santa Anna was returning, with Polk's secret help. This heretofore-missing puzzle piece clarified for Benton "the reliance which was placed on the termination of the war in ninety to one hundred and twenty days. It was the arrangement with Santa Anna! . . . It was known at what time Santa Anna was to leave Havana for Mexico, and the overture was made, and the appropriations asked."

In fact, a week before Polk's message to Congress, he and Benton had already settled on $2 million as the amount needed for a down payment on a treaty. "I had but little doubt that by paying that sum in hand at the signature of a Treaty we might procure California and such a boundary as we wished," Polk wrote in his diary on July 26.

• • •

Polk tried to persuade Congress to secretly appropriate the money. It began well enough. Presented in a confidential message to the Senate on August 4, the $2 million appropriation was approved 33–19 in executive session two days later.

But it was one thing to obtain the cooperation of the Senate's fifty-six members, and quite another thing to expect the House's 216 representatives to do likewise. Polk tried presenting the proposal to a handful of trusted House leaders, hoping they would quickly push it through "without attracting much public attention." The plan fell apart when Whig congressmen began demanding more information.

Resigned now to his $2 million request being made public, Polk sent a message to both houses, to be read in open session. It explained why the money was needed and acknowledged publicly for the first time the president's design to acquire Mexican provinces.

• • •

Polk, his advisers, and nearly everyone in Congress were all caught off guard by the bolt of lightning that struck the so-called "Two Million Dollar Bill" after it was introduced in the House on Saturday, August 8. The House appeared to have plenty of time to act before recessing Saturday, and the Senate would then have all of Monday morning to vote on the bill before the Twenty-ninth Congress adjourned its First Session at noon.

When the bill was introduced in the House on Saturday afternoon, however, a murmur arose among the representatives as Polk's avouched intention to annex Mexican territory registered with them. Congressman Charles H. Carroll of New York grumbled that it appeared that "the money was wanted to purchase California, and a large part of Mexico to boot." Antislavery Whigs saw that they had just been handed a juicy campaign issue three months before the crucial midterm congressional elections. Polk's floor managers limited debate to two hours, restricted individual speakers to ten minutes each, and called a recess.

As congressmen were leaving the stuffy House chamber in search of fresh air, David Wilmot readied the amendment that he and a group of young Northern antislavery Democrats had contemplated for just such an occasion as this. The thirty-two-year-old Democratic lawyer from northeastern Pennsylvania was serving the first of what would become three House terms. He supported Polk and the war, and he believed that the United States should obtain Mexican territory as compensation for her war expenses. He had endorsed Texas annexation and its admission into the Union as a slave state, because slavery was a preexisting condition in Texas. But Wilmot and other Northern antislavery Democrats adamantly opposed permitting slavery in any new Western territories.

When the House reconvened, one of the antislavery Whigs, Hugh White of New York, mischievously suggested that Democrats should demonstrate their good intentions by proposing an amendment abjuring slavery in any territories obtained from Mexico. It is possible that White did not know that Wilmot was ready to do just that, but it is more likely that he did. The Pennsylvanian proceeded to read his amendment:

"Provided, That as an express and fundamental condition to the acquisition of any territory from the Republic of Mexico by the United States, by virtue of any treaty which may be negotiated between them, and to the use by the Executive of the moneys herein appropriated, *neither slavery nor involuntary servitude shall ever exist in any part of said territory* [author's italics], except for crime, whereof the party shall first be duly convicted."

The amendment to the Two Million Dollar Bill became known as the Wilmot Proviso; David Wilmot's name would be forever entwined with the revival of the dormant debate of the "peculiar institution," slavery. For the next fifteen years, the same arguments would boil up with ever-greater fury whenever new territories were formed, poisoning politics and steadily pushing the nation toward the precipice of civil war.

• • •

Illuminated by candles and lamps, the House floor on Saturday evening resembled a theater stage. About a hundred spectators, including General of the Army Winfield Scott, watched from the gallery. It was a sultry night, and faces glistened with perspiration. Men fanned themselves with newspapers and drank ice water.

The voting on the Two Million Dollar Bill and its explosive amendment followed sectional and not political lines; still a novel phenomenon in 1846, the sectional orientation would become accepted fact during the turbulent years ahead. Northern Whigs voted with Northern and Western Democrats for the measure. Southern Whigs and Democrats opposed it on the ground that it purportedly violated the Tenth Amendment, which reserved for states those powers not assigned to the federal government; it became the South's bulwark against abolition. But the bill and its incendiary amendment passed the House, 87–64.

While many Northern congressmen saw this as their chance to finally retaliate against the "slave oligarchy" for degrading white labor with black slaves, and for its affront to free speech (the notorious "Gag Rules"), not every "yes" vote meant opposition to slavery. Some Western Democrats were registering their displeasure with the Polk administration—for agreeing with England two months earlier to divide the Oregon Territory at 49 degrees latitude instead of 54-40; for the failure of a bill to sell public lands at graduated prices to different classes of buyers; and for Polk's veto of government-funded river and harbor improvements. Polk disgustedly observed that some congressmen were drunk when they voted, "noisy and troublesome . . . a most disreputable scene."

The "mischievous & foolish amendment," as Polk described it, may have been responsible for confining him to his sickbed on Sunday, August 9. He was so ill that he neither attended church nor prepared any countermeasures for Monday, when the Senate would take up the Wilmot Proviso. Instead, he brooded over why the slavery issue should resurface at this of all times: "What connection slavery had with making peace with Mexico it is difficult to conceive."

• • •

As a lifelong Southern slaveholder reared in a society of slaveholders, Polk had difficulty grasping the moral imperative behind the Wilmot Proviso. He did not understand why David Wilmot, an otherwise loyal Democrat, would jeopardize a bill that was vital to the national interest. For much the same reason, the president would not have grasped the import of Charles Dickens's bleak description of 1842 Virginia, "where slavery sits brooding. . . . There is an air of ruin and decay abroad, which is inseparable from the system. . . . There is no look of decent comfort anywhere."

There were three million slaves in the South, compared with about five million whites. The Southern white population was just a third that of the North, where waves of immigrants, mainly Irish and German, had effected a stunning 33 percent population increase during the Roaring '40s. In Congress, a political balance remained between North and South, but only because the Founders had conceded to the "Slave Power" the privilege of counting their slaves for census purposes, each slave as three fifths of a white person. Virginia had the most slaves, 470,000, followed by South Carolina, 380,000; Georgia, 360,000; and Alabama, 340,000.

Polk, the penultimate president to own slaves (Zachary Taylor, Polk's successor, would be the last), had once called the institution an evil "entailed upon us by our ancestors." It was a question of "peculiar delicacy" and an "unfortunate subject," but in his view a situation that must be accepted. Yet Mexico had abolished slavery in 1829, and England in 1833, while France would do so in 1848. The United States was the only nation where slaveholders would take up arms; even Spain's eventual abolition of slavery in Cuba during the years 1870–1886 would be peaceful.

An unrepentant slaveholder, Polk as a congressman had consistently sided with Southern interests in blocking attempts to interfere with slavery. As president, he did not act as if he believed slavery was inherently evil, nor did he, as did George Washington, arrange for his slaves to be freed upon his death. His policy was avoidance, as it was for most public officials, abolitionists excepted.

During the 1844 campaign, when Whigs attempted to turn abolitionist Democrats against Polk, his law partner and political ally Gideon Pillow publicly soft-pedaled Polk's slave holdings. According to Pillow, Polk had inherited nearly all of his two dozen slaves, and had purchased only six more, to prevent families from being broken up. Most of them worked on a Mississippi cotton plantation, thirty-five miles south of Oxford, owned by Polk and his brother-in-law John Childress.

But Polk actually had purchased fifteen slaves by 1844, according to historian William Dusinberre; just two were bought to keep a family intact. Polk visited his 920-acre plantation once or twice a year, leaving its daily management to his competent overseer. Unlike some slaveholders, Polk believed slaves should be treated well and not overworked, but he did not educate them or give them religious instruction. When disciplining his slaves, he preferred corporal punishment to imprisonment, because "a slave dreads the punishment of stripes more than he does imprisonment, and that description of punishment has, besides, a beneficial effect on his fellow-slaves."

While he was president, Polk would buy nineteen more slaves. He purchased a female slave, Caroline, for $450 in August 1845, and in June 1846 he bought three slaves from Gideon Pillow for $1,450, through his brother-in-law, Childress. To conceal the president's role in the transactions, Childress or another person would usually buy the slaves in their names and then transfer ownership to Polk. "You can take the title in your own name and make quit-claim conveyance without warranty to me," Polk once instructed Childress. Polk noted the Pillow slave transaction in the same letter in which he offered Pillow an Army generalship.

The new slaves were probably replacements for those that First Lady Sarah Polk brought to the White House after dismissing ten paid domestics to save money.

Like her husband, Mrs. Polk had been raised amid slaveholders and slaves. And, as a devout Presbyterian, she believed some people were preordained to be slaves.

When Childress informed Polk that he had hired the president's cousin, Robert Campbell, as their agent, the president reminded Childress that no one else should know of Polk's involvement in any slave purchases. "There is nothing wrong [in] it, but still the public have no interest in knowing it, and in my situation it is better they should not." Polk wrote this letter several days after the Wilmot Proviso debate.

• • •

The Two Million Dollar Bill with its Wilmot Proviso reached the Senate floor on Monday, August 10, an hour before the Twenty-ninth Congress's scheduled noon adjournment. The president's Senate allies were poised to strike the amendment and send the bill back to the House, where Polk had been assured that a Proviso-less appropriations bill would be approved. Alabama Senator Dixon H. Lewis moved to strike the Proviso.

But Senator John Davis, a Massachusetts Whig, rose to ask Lewis to explain his proposed action. "No time now for giving reasons or making explanations," Lewis curtly replied.

Davis embarked on a rambling discourse of the bill, refusing to yield the floor and ignoring warnings that time was running out. He later claimed that he had intended to leave just enough time for the Senate to cast an up-or-down vote on the bill, with the Proviso still attached. He did not know that the Senate clock was eight minutes slower than the House's. By the time Lewis was finally able to interrupt Davis, it was to inform him that the House had adjourned, and that the bill was dead.

In his journal that night, Polk railed, "Should the war be now protracted, the responsibility will fall more heavily upon the head of Senator Davis than upon any other man, and he will deserve the execrations of the country."

In the same long journal entry, Polk reiterated his determination to possess Mexico's distant provinces. He reasoned that with Mexico already indebted to the United States and unable to pay what she owed, "when peace is made the only indemnity which the U.S. can have is a cession of territory. The U.S. desires to acquire Upper California, New Mexico, and perhaps some territory South of these Provinces. For a suitable cession of territory we are willing to assume the debts to our own citizens & to pay an additional consideration." But "no Government . . . is strong enough to make a treaty ceding territory and long maintain power unless they could receive, at the time of making the treaty, money enough to support the army."

• • •

The Two Million Dollar Bill's failure proved inconsequential. Replying to Secretary of State Buchanan's July 27 peace overture, Foreign Minister Manuel Crescencio Rejon wrote that only Mexico's Congress, which would not convene until December, could decide such an important question. "For the executive to accept such a proposition, when dealing with a subject which concerns the honour of the country, and the integrity of its territory . . . would be to waive the question of its justice, and to complete the irritation of Public opinion already highly alarmed."

When Rejon's letter reached Washington on September 19, Polk recognized it for what it was, a rejection. "Our overture for peace having been in effect declined, my strong impression was that the character of the war which we were waging in Mexico should be in some respects changed."

War Secretary William Marcy ordered the Army to henceforth seize rather than buy supplies from the Mexican people. "Make them [the Mexican people] feel the evils of the war more strongly, in order that they may appeal to their own Government for peace," exhorted the Washington *Union*. Polk began planning military operations at Tampico "and all the principal places in the Province of Tamaulipas."

Buchanan's reply to Rejon said that Mexico's attitude demonstrated to "the whole world that no alternative remains for [the United States] but to prosecute the war with vigor," until the U.S. overture was met by "a corresponding sentiment" from Mexico.

While the president was publicly avowing war without mercy, he confided to his brother William his belief that Santa Anna still intended to participate in peace negotiations, after he established his authority.

England volunteered to mediate peace talks between the United States and Mexico, but both governments declined. Wary of England's motives, Polk noted that the United States had just made a peace overture, and mediation "might rather tend to protract the War." The equally suspicious Santa Anna and Rejon also demurred, believing that England was only interested in preserving her commerce with Mexico, at the expense of Mexican honor and territory.

Neither side was yet willing to lay down its arms.

13

ZACHARY TAYLOR'S ARMY

"The truth is our troops, regulars & volunteers, will obtain victories wherever they meet the enemy. This [they] would do if they were without officers to command them higher in ranks than Lieutenants. . . . Our forces are the best troops in the world. . . ."

—President James K. Polk

SUMMER 1846: CAMARGO

Camargo was the new headquarters and supply depot for the Army of Invasion, as Taylor's force was now called, and the staging area for the highly anticipated march into northern Mexico. On a map, Camargo appeared ideally situated strategically and logistically. Four miles from the San Juan River's confluence with the Rio Grande, Camargo's waterfront received steamships crammed with fresh volunteers and supplies from Matamoros, 150 miles to the southeast. The soldiers lived in camps that stretched for miles along the San Juan. General Zachary Taylor's next objective, Monterrey, a stone city guarding the approaches to the soaring Sierra Madre Mountains, lay 130 miles to the southwest. On paper, Camargo was perfect.

The reality was far different. With the exception of a few respectable homes in the middle of town, mud-plastered "miserable hovels" with dirt floors comprised most of Camargo's habitations. In June, the San Juan River had flooded every part of town except the main plaza and a church. One fourth of the city's residents had moved away, and fewer than three thousand remained. By July, when the army marched into Camargo, many of the flood-damaged buildings had been abandoned to snakes, tarantulas, and scorpions, and some of the city squares had been fenced in and were being used as vegetable gardens and orchards. "It is one of the most miserable places I ever saw, dirty and dilapidated and but little better than a Seminole village," observed Lieutenant Colonel Ethan Allen Hitchcock.

Nestled amid nearly bare limestone hills that reflected heat like a kiln, Camargo baked in August temperatures that routinely surpassed 100 degrees and sometimes reached 112. The fiery city was choked with dust stirred by wagons and marching men, and the water was wretched; the San Juan was used for drinking water, washing, and bathing. Flies and mosquitoes swarmed the tent cities, and famished wolves skulked outside town.

Throughout July and August, fifteen thousand troops assembled in Camargo for the coming offensive. Because there were not enough tents at first, volunteers slept on the ground, often in the rain and wrapped in wet blankets.

• • •

The camps were ecosystems for dysentery, pneumonia, yellow fever, and malaria. Privies were usually indescribably filthy, and men drank river water even as dead cows and horses floated past them. Rations were often eaten half-cooked. The Army and greater American society did not yet understand the mosquito's elemental role as a disease carrier. As a consequence, U.S. cities were often ravaged by yellow fever; a recent outbreak in New Orleans had forced General Zachary Taylor's family to flee to East Pascagoula, Mississippi, where refugees occupied every bed in town.

The troops began to die as amoebic dysentery and diarrhea (nicknamed "the blues") roared through the encampments, followed by yellow fever ("vomito"), malaria, cholera, measles, mumps, and smallpox. Disease would kill seven times more soldiers during the Mexican War than would battle wounds, a ratio comparable to the Napoleonic Wars forty years earlier. During the Civil War, the ratio would be 2:1, but more as a consequence of the huge number of combat deaths than of medical advances.

Building one's immunity to these diseases was called "seasoning," and the process usually lasted a year. Not as diligent about field sanitation as the regulars, the volunteers succumbed to disease in disproportionately larger numbers. And volunteers from farms and villages were more vulnerable than city-bred soldiers, who had acquired some immunity from living in tenement houses.

The volunteers died in such great numbers that a coffin shortage developed. As a result, the deceased were often wrapped in blankets and laid in a "soldier's grave," without "the decencies of Scripture." In noting the deaths of two Illinois volunteers in early September, Thomas D. Tennery wrote: "Calvin Payne . . . died at daybreak this morning; he was a good man; the other was [Private Alonzo A. Yan] of Co. K. They were buried within a few minutes of each other. We have to lay the dead in the vault without coffin or box, for the boards or planks cannot be found in this place."

So frequently did regimental bands play "The Dead March" that the Camargo mockingbirds whistled the dirge. About fifteen hundred graves would eventually line the banks of the San Juan River. "Oh, what a horror I have for Camargo," wrote a general. "It is a Yawning Grave Yard."

The ubiquity of illness and death disheartened new arrivals. Captain William P. Rogers, the Mississippi Rifles' quartermaster, complained of being "low in spirits" after a wretched steamship trip to Camargo on the *Col. Cross* [named for the unfortunate Colonel Trueman Cross], whose decks were covered with troops suffering from diarrhea. "The sick strewed about, some delirious & crying out for their friends. I became so weak that I could scarcely walk." The Rifles' commander, Colonel Jefferson Davis, observed that disease depleted his regiment to such an extent that even the healthy volunteers were no longer "full of zeal, and vigor."

The myriad illnesses went by grimly colorful nicknames: There was the "cold plague," a flu that hit the Mississippi Rifles especially hard (diseases claimed the lives of 186 of Davis's 1,037 men and resulted in the discharges of another 178); the vile "black tongue," which afflicted the 1st North Carolina Regiment; the "bloody flux," or dysentery.

The well-intended treatments were usually ineffectual. Cold plague patients were bled; subjected to "cupping," a technique for drawing the patient's blood to the skin's surface; and administered opium, brandy, and mustard. For dysentery, the treatment was copper, opium sulfates and acetates, and lead. Yellow fever patients, who had a 25 percent death rate, were dosed with quinine, calomel, and enemas. Leeches were usually administered at some point during every illness.

One of the worst things that could happen to an ill soldier was to be taken to a field hospital. There, he was not only liable to contract another illness, but to be berated by doctors accusing him of malingering; to be compelled to subsist on crackers and coffee; to be neglected, abused, and robbed by orderlies; and, if he survived, to be pronounced fit for duty when he was not, and discharged to his unit.

• • •

Amid the dirt, flies, heat, bad food, and illness, the soldiers discovered an unexpected diversion and morale-booster: the fondness of Mexican peasant women for bathing nude in the San Juan River. The soldiers lined the riverbank to watch. One day while riding horseback near the river, a Captain Electus Backus encountered a "perfectly naked" woman who conversed with him without the slightest embarrassment.

Nudity aside, the Americans regarded the Mexican women as superior to Mexican men, who foisted most physical labor onto the women and forced them to carry heavy loads. To the Mexicans' amusement, the soldiers sometimes gallantly shouldered the women's burdens. The troops picnicked and danced with the native women, who, to the Americans' amazement, chain-smoked hand-rolled cornhusk cigarettes, even on the dance floor. Inevitably, some of the soldiers married them and settled down in Mexico.

· · ·

Monterrey was the sanctuary to which General Mariano Arista had retreated after Palo Alto and Resaca de la Palma. General Francisco Mejia had replaced Arista, and General-in-Chief Pedro de Ampudia had then reportedly taken personal charge of the eighteen hundred remaining veterans of the two battles. The soldiers disliked this arrangement, remembering how Ampudia had boiled decapitated heads in oil. Reinforcements streamed into Monterrey from the south.

At Monterrey, Taylor hoped to fight "a great battle" which "would do more to bring about a peace, than anything else." While waiting for men and materiel to arrive, Old Rough and Ready sat outside his tent on a blanket-covered box. During the heat of the day, he remained inside his tent, eating his meals and composing letters on a makeshift desk made of two rough blue chests.

Peace was Taylor's most cherished wish, because then he could go home to Louisiana, perhaps even before his sixty-second birthday in November. His worst fear was that the Mexican army would avoid a decisive battle and dissolve into guerrilla bands that would "attack our trains, attempting to cut off our supplies at favorable positions, destroy the corn, & drive away the stock," compelling his army to pull back to the Rio Grande and the Gulf coast.

Taylor truly cared about his men; they knew it and repaid him with undying devotion. Vowing to spare "neither expense or anything else" to give comfort to the sick, Taylor wrote: "Humanity as well as duty ought to prompt us to do all in our power to alleviate their sufferings as much as possible."

Taylor's growing irritation with the Polk administration had supplanted his brief glow of pride from being promoted to major general and placed in charge of the invading army. A year earlier, the administration had left to him, a rough soldier of the frontier, the sticky decision of whether to advance to the Rio Grande. Paradoxically, now that the fighting had begun, Polk and his cabinet, civilians all, were burying him under their instructions.

Elated that one of their own was now a bona fide war hero, the Whigs had begun to excitedly tout Taylor as a presidential candidate in 1848. Taylor professed no interest in the presidency. "I would not be a candidate for the presidency if certain of reaching it," he told his son-in-law, Dr. R. C. Wood, on July 25. He wished the Whigs would choose General Winfield Scott, not him. Yet, for all his protestations of disinterest, Taylor left the door slightly ajar. "Even if I had [an interest in it] this is not a proper time to discuss the subject; let this war at any rate be first brought to a close."

• • •

Upon conquering a province, Taylor was instructed to sow dissatisfaction with the Mexican government among the people, and to inspire their allegiance toward the United States—the nineteenth-century equivalent of "winning hearts and minds." The president and his cabinet had even sent Taylor a proclamation to distribute: "We come to overthrow the tyrants who have destroyed your liberties, but we come to make no war upon the people of Mexico. . . . Your religion, your altars and churches, the property of your churches and citizens, the emblems of your faith and its ministers, shall be protected and remain inviolate."

Ostensibly to reassure Mexico's Catholics that the war was not a crusade against their religion, which was despised by many American Protestants, but probably to stanch the soaring desertions of Irish Catholic soldiers, Polk resolved to send Catholic priests to Taylor's army. He summoned three bishops to the White House from a national conference in Baltimore and told them: "The false idea had been industrious[ly] circulated by interested partisans [sic] in Mexico that our object was to overthrow their religion & rob their churches."

Acting with his usual decisiveness, the president asked the bishops to recommend two priests for commissioning as the Army's first de facto Catholic chaplains. Bishop John Hughes of New York went to Georgetown College and found two able Jesuits, Father John McElroy, pastor of Washington's Trinity Church; and Father Anthony Rey, a Georgetown College administrator. Neither priest knew

Spanish, but McElroy, a native of Ireland, was fluent in Gaelic, while Rey spoke German—lending credence to the likelihood that Polk's real purpose was to curb the high desertion rate among immigrant Irish and German soldiers. War Secretary William Marcy gave each priest $1,200 in gold for expenses, and they joined Zachary Taylor's army in the fall of 1846. Months later, Mexican bandits murdered Rey; his body was never recovered.

• • •

A greater irritant to Taylor than Polk's tips for pacification, his proclamation, or his Catholic chaplains, was the detailed plan for conquering northern Mexico drafted by Scott, Polk, and Marcy—without Taylor's participation. Taylor's reaction was sullen acquiescence, what might be called "passive-aggression" in an era more conversant in the terminology of psychoanalysis.

"Although I did not approve the plan of said campaign, nor was I consulted in regard to it," Taylor informed Secretary of State James Buchanan on August 29, "yet I hazard nothing when I say that no one ever entered on the performance of any duty than I did in this, with greater zeal, better spirit and determination to carry it out to the very letter. . . ."

While Taylor marched on Monterrey in northeastern Mexico, General John E. Wool, a sixty-two-year-old War of 1812 veteran, would lead the new two-thousand-man Army of the Center from San Antonio, Texas, over more than a thousand miles of mountains and deserts to Chihuahua, establishing an operational base in northwestern Mexico. Meanwhile, Colonel Stephen Kearny was already on his way with sixteen hundred volunteers across the dusty prairies of southern Kansas and Colorado to seize New Mexico and its three-hundred-year-old capital, Santa Fe. Further orders were on their way to Kearny: to lead a few hundred troops from Santa Fe to southern California and a rendezvous with Commodore Robert Stockton's naval forces; together, they were to take control of all of California.

• • •

This was America's first foreign expeditionary campaign, and no one had foreseen the unprecedented demands for men and materiel. But with the telegraph helping speed orders to Northern manufacturing plants, American industry quickened its pace to supply the Army's needs. The Schuylkill Arsenal in Philadelphia expanded its workforce of tailors and seamstresses from four hundred to four thousand to make shoes, tents, and uniforms. By the war's end, the arsenal and the twenty or more like it around the country would produce twelve thousand pairs of shoes a month. Quartermasters in Pittsburgh and Cincinnati supplied knapsacks, mess gear, and canteens; E. I. duPont and Samuel Colt made artillery pieces and shells.

Before Taylor could begin his campaign against Monterrey, where Generals Ampudia and Mejia were busily constructing redoubts, fortresses, and ambuscades to shatter the anticipated American attack on the provincial capital of ten thousand, he had to first grapple with daunting logistical problems. A bottleneck had developed at New Orleans, from where everything—men, uniforms, horses, mules, camp gear, wagons, food, arms, and ammunition—had to be transported by boat to Point Isabel, and then put on steamships for the two-hundred-mile journey up the Rio Grande to Camargo. Scarce shipping was the surpassing problem; supplies stacked up on the New Orleans docks for lack of ships. At Port Isabel, another mountain of supplies accumulated on the docks, because no more than ten steamships were available to ferry troops and provisions. "I consider there is an entire breakdown in the Q'Master department everywhere," Taylor concluded.

Thus, thousands of troops had to wait in the Rio Grande camps for more than a month until steamships could ferry them to Camargo, "time enough to have sent to Liverpool for them," grumbled Taylor. At Port Isabel, men waiting for transport killed enormous rattlesnakes, ate "hard bread, broken by an axe; mess pork, with fat four inches thick," wrote Mississippi volunteer Rufus K. Arthur, who said the sand got in their hair, whiskers, noses, and mouths "and mixes with our victuals, so that I am afraid we should wear out our teeth."

Some regiments marched to Camargo rather than wait for steamships. The crushing daytime heat persuaded the more flexible commanders to turn their marching routine upside down, blowing reveille at midnight and compelling their men to march from 1 A.M. until 9 A.M. Regiments that traveled in the heat of the day paid a severe price. John R. Kenly described the Maryland Volunteers' ordeal of traveling under the searing sun, led by incompetent guides who missed the waterholes. "I saw men fall down in convulsions on this march, frothing at their mouths, clutching the sand with their hands."

• • •

Polk, too, was exasperated with the Army Quartermaster and Commissary Departments, expressing "astonishment" to Quartermaster General Thomas Sydney Jesup when a New York volunteer regiment had to wait six weeks for a ship to transport it to California. Even though Jesup replied that there was indeed a ship shortage—and that more ships were being built—Polk was convinced that Army laxness was the root problem. "Some of them [are] required to have a coal of fire put on their backs to make them move promptly. . . . There is entirely too much delay and too much want of energy & promptness in execution on the part of many of the subordinate officers, which must be corrected." The president even suspected some Whig officers of deliberately dragging their feet to embarrass his administration. He would reprise this complaint many times during the war as his distrust of Whig officers grew.

When Taylor reported that he did not have enough wagons to make up a baggage train for an army of fifteen thousand, Polk reminded Jesup that mules had been used in previous wars in Mexico. "I then asked of him and the Secretary of War why a similar means of transportation had not been provided in this instance," Polk noted after meeting with Jesup and War Secretary Marcy. Jesup began canvassing the Southwest for mules. Polk was outraged when he learned that the Army was buying horses and mules in the United States and shipping them to Mexico. Why couldn't they be bought in Mexico, where they were plentiful and cheaper? He railed at "the extravagance & stupidity of purchasing these animals in the U.S. and transporting them at vast expense to Mexico."

About nineteen hundred mules were eventually shipped to Mexico, and regimental quartermasters such as Lieutenant Ulysses S. Grant were given the thankless job of caring for and loading the temperamental beasts. "It took several hours to get ready to start each morning, and by the time we were ready some of the mules first loaded would be tired of standing so long with their loads on their backs. Sometimes one would start to run, bowing his back and kicking up until he scattered his load; others would lie down and try to disarrange their loads . . . by rolling on them. . . . I am not aware of ever having used a profane expletive in my life; but I would have the charity to excuse those who may have done so, if they were in charge of a train of Mexican pack mules at the time."

• • •

Already working longer hours than any president before or since, Polk, dissatisfied with the War Department's performance, now willed himself to work even harder. He dug into the minutiae of logistics and supply. He appointed the commanders of the proliferating militia regiments, choosing men from both political parties, and satisfying neither. Because Marcy was "overwhelmed" and some of Marcy's subordinates "cared but little what disasters happened, provided they could avoid censure or responsibility," Polk was "compelled to give some attention to these details, or the movements of the army will be delayed and embarrassed."

The administration's staunchest champion of the American fighting man was

Polk, which explains his quickness to anger when he believed that they were not getting all that they needed. "The truth is our troops, regulars & volunteers, will obtain victories wherever they meet the enemy. This [they] would do if they were without officers to command them higher in ranks than Lieutenants. . . . Our forces are the best troops in the world. . . ."

The more the president applied himself to the details of the war and the Army's materiel needs, the more attention these matters seemed to require, the snare of micromanagers. Army officers began complaining directly to Polk about equipment shortages and mismanagement, and the president responded by upbraiding the logistics officials who were responsible and prodding them to move faster.

• • •

The president believed that the citizen-soldiers whose needs now occupied so much of his time would perform in battle as well as veteran regulars. As had his ideological ancestor, Thomas Jefferson, Polk frowned on large standing armies, thinking that, "contrary to the genius of our free institutions, [they] would impose heavy burdens on the people and be dangerous to public liberty." Volunteers levied on weeks' notice, he believed, were adequate for national crises. Of course, this was largely untrue, but to Polk and his advisers—none having served a day in the regular Army—it was an article of faith, as it was to the American public. It was a hoary Revolutionary War myth that American citizen soldiers had beaten the world's best professional army, when in reality a multitude of other factors were arguably just as consequential: France's timely intervention, England's divided mind, and the war's sheer length. And by the war's end, the Continental Army in fact was a battle-hardened army. For all of their faults, the Mexican War volunteers, with a few notable exceptions, would be hard fighters, too, when the chips were down.

The first volunteers were the best: "Young men of firm futures, families and education are privats [sic] in the companys [sic] and seem delighted to have an opportunity to serve their country," wrote Congressman and former Arkansas Governor Archibald Yell, who raised a cavalry regiment. The sons of Henry Clay and Daniel Webster volunteered, as did Congressman Jefferson Davis, who led the Mississippi Rifles. The volunteers of the first days of the war were much as Alexis de Tocqueville had described them a decade earlier. After a long peace, he observed, a democracy's armies attracted volunteers who were "almost children," who craved glory because it was "brilliant and sudden, won without hard work, by risking nothing but one's life."

Indeed, young patriots swamped the new volunteer units. Baltimore filled its quota in less than thirty-six hours, Ohio in two weeks; in Tennessee, thirty thousand men had to draw lots for the three thousand available billets. There were "Yale College Regulars," a company of New Orleans clerks, and one consisting exclusively of Nashville law students. Sailors, fire companies, and fishing clubs volunteered. They endowed their regiments with nicknames appropriate to such a grand adventure: the "Wabash Invincibles," "Hickory Blues," "Black Hussars," "Louisville Legion," and "Irish Jasper Greens." If there were no places for them in their home states, they would join a unit in another state. In the supercharged atmosphere of the war's early days, they volunteered without regard for political affiliation, or ethnicity; besides the many German and Irish immigrant volunteers, there were even American Indians, and a Polish exile commanded an Illinois company.

Later levies would attract a more calculating sort of volunteer, sometimes motivated by a desire to escape problems at home, or to get money and land (they were promised 160 acres or $100 in land script if they completed twelve months' service).

Before the war ended, 73,260 men would volunteer.

• • •

The first volunteers set out for the Rio Grande amid patriotic orations, rousing band music, and the tender ministrations of the town women, who made them quilts and ice cream cake for their sendoffs. Often after a special church service and with friends and relatives cheering, they boarded boats and sailed away with steam whistles blowing. Intoxicated by the chivalry and romance of Sir Walter Scott's Waverley novels and the glorified histories, biographies, and novels about the Revolution, the citizen-soldier merchants, farmers, lawyers, doctors, teachers, and mechanics saw themselves as the reincarnation of "the boys of '76," beginning the adventure of their lives in the distant mountains, jungles, and deserts of Mexico.

The volunteers only glimpsed New Orleans—a metropolis of more than one hundred thousand in 1846—from a distance while marching to Camp Jackson, located at the place where Andrew Jackson's troops had crushed Sir Edward Pakenham's army in 1815. The soldiers toured the battlefield as though it were a religious shrine. But Camp Jackson was a wretched place, flooding when it rained and humming with mosquitoes, the bearers of yellow fever and malaria. With relief, the volunteers boarded ships for the Rio Grande, but the sluggish hulks were scarcely an improvement; the seasick troops lived under the constant threat of the cook stoves setting the vessels on fire.

• • •

When the regular officers first beheld the volunteers, they despaired of ever making soldiers of them. Many did not know how to salute or address an officer, or care for a weapon, or maintain an orderly, sanitary encampment.

They were undisciplined, rowdy, and sometimes mutinous. "One who has never commanded a company of volunteers can form no idea of the unpleasantness of the life," grumbled Captain William Rogers. "They are perfectly ignorant of discipline and most restive under restraint," noted Meade.

Lieutenant Abner Doubleday, the putative inventor of baseball [his role was later disproven] and future Union general at Gettysburg, wrote that the regulars were shocked "by the gross familiarity with which they addressed our officers." They were "more like organized mobs than military forces."

The volunteers' pillaging prompted the regulars to call them "Mohawks." Lieutenant A. P. Hill toured a village sacked by volunteers and pronounced them "perfectly unmanageable." Lieutenant Daniel Hill noted in his journal, "The Volunteers have murdered about twenty persons in Matamoros, have committed rape, robbery etc., etc." He reported that the Louisville Legion camped near his unit "and our Camp was disturbed with their yells and shouts at night. This morning the 15th, they set fire to the Quartermaster's inclosure [*sic*] and shouted like maniacs as the fire progressed." Taylor ordered all arriving vessels searched for liquor, and confiscations sent to New Orleans to be sold; informers received half the proceeds, with the rest going to the "Hospital Funds."

Winfield Scott illustrated the differences between regulars and volunteers by describing how they set up their respective encampments:

"A regiment of regulars, in 15 minutes from the evening halt, will have tents pitched & trenched around, besides straw, leaves or bushes for dry sleeping; arms & ammunition well secured & in order for any night attack; fires made, kettles boiling, in order to [have] wholesome cooking; all the men dried, or warmed, & at their comfortable supper, merry as crickets, before the end of the first hour. . . . Volunteers neglect all these points; eat their *salt* meat raw (if they have saved any at all) or, worse than raw, *fried*—death to any Christian man the fifth day; lose or waste their clothing; lie down wet, or on wet ground—fatal to health, &, in a short time to life; leave arms & ammunition exposed to rain, mud & dews; hence both generally useless & soon lost, & certainly hardly ever worth a cent in battle, &c., &c., &c. In a short time the ranks are thinned, the baggage wagons & hospitals filled with the sick, & acres of ground with the graves of the dead! . . . *In the field* [their deficiency in drilling is seen in] the want of the touch of the *elbow* (which cannot be acquired with the best instructors in many months); the want of the sure step in advancing, falling back & wheeling; . . . the want of military confidence in each other, & above all, the want of reciprocal confidence between officers & men."

• • •

The regulars were appalled by the volunteers' unsoldierly appearance. Lieutenant George P. McClellan described one group as resembling "Falstaff's company. . . . Most of them were without coats; some without any pants [other] than the parts of pants they wore; all had torn and dirty shirts—uncombed heads—unwashed faces—they were dirt and filth from top to toe." Some Mexicans thought they resembled "clowns at a carnival." A letter to the Charleston *Mercury* described the South Carolina Palmetto Regiment: "each company with the exception of the Charleston and Richland, adorned with red, blue, green, check, and white, shirts over their unmentionables, Kilmarnock caps, or white cotton skull hats, of the old Grimes cut, protecting their seats of knowledge . . . while their lower extremities are encased in every variety of boot, shoe and stocking."

Not every volunteer unit was ragged and unkempt; the Mississippi Rifles, for example, wore red flannel shirts and carried state-of-the-art rifles. But even when they were bedraggled-looking, it wasn't always the volunteers' fault. Among Taylor's criticisms of the Quartermaster Department's inefficiencies was that not enough new clothing was reaching his men. When uniforms wore out, often there were no replacements. Some volunteers were later forced to wear captured Mexican uniforms.

• • •

After the War of 1812 and the Florida Indian wars, Taylor had recommended that volunteers be required to remain in service for at least one year—time enough to learn the soldiering trade and give back useful service. But his proposal was ignored. Each state remained in absolute control of its militia, which elected its own officers, who consequently were often reluctant to discipline their men, fearing "their popularity would be endangered," observed Lieutenant McClellan. "I have repeatedly seen a Second Lieutenant of the regular army exercise more authority over the Volunteers—officers and privates—than a Mustang General."

Some of the regular officers' animus was due to their resentment over the politically connected volunteer officers' rapid rise through the ranks. Regular officers were predominantly Whigs, while volunteer officers, and especially those holding high rank, were mainly Democrats (of the thirteen volunteer generals appointed by Polk, all were Democrats). "I find that every confounded Voluntario in the

'Continental Army' ranked me," complained McClellan. "[T]o be ranked and put aside for a soldier of yesterday, a miserable thing with buttons on it, that knows nothing whatever, is indeed too hard a case." Class-consciousness was another factor: the first volunteers represented the best families in their states, while the regulars, particularly the enlisted men, came from humbler origins.

From the volunteers' perspective, the regular officers treated them unfairly and favored the regular troops. Even Colonel Samuel Ryan Curtis of the 1st Ohio Infantry, a West Point graduate who had served five years in the Army, resented how regular officers "put the regulars forward and make them certain to be the authors of every acceptable movement." But other volunteer officers admired the regulars and, after the war, sought Army commissions. After watching a regular unit execute a precision parade-ground maneuver, Captain Franklin Smith, a volunteer quartermaster, "felt what it was like to be a warrior."

• • •

The touring companies that brought mass entertainment to American cities and towns during the Roaring '40s followed Taylor's army to the grimy camps at Camargo and Matamoros. Theatrical troupes performed Stephen Foster's enormously popular songs and other music that the soldiers had enjoyed back home. The Texas Chaparral Serenaders staged the "Ethiopian Concert," with Austin D. Look dancing the "celebrated grapevine twist and other popular Extravaganzas." Army officers sometimes entertained themselves by staging Shakespearian productions. Not all of them were triumphs: *Othello*'s Desdemona, played by bearded Ulysses S. Grant, elicited loud grumbling.

Printing presses that were laboriously shipped to Matamoros and Camargo published camp newspapers read by nearly everyone. Daguerreotypists captured the troops' likenesses, and recorded the first images of warfare, although few would survive. Far and away, lithography remained the most popular illustration medium; demand soared after U.S. newspapers reproduced dramatic lithographs of Mexican War battles. Americans would remember the war as thirty-three-year-old lithographer Nathaniel Currier portrayed it in his eighty-five prints. In 1850, Currier would unite his fortunes with James Merritt Ives in a famous partnership.

• • •

Around their campfires, the soldiers sang popular songs, such as "The Girl I Left Behind Me" and "Home Sweet Home," and assayed the enemy's shortcomings. Except for the graceful Mexican women, the soldiers regarded the Mexicans as a "mongrel race" inferior even to American slaves. The Americans' comparable good fortune suffused them with an inflated sense of mission. "The finger of Fate points," wrote Captain William S. Henry, "if not to their [Mexicans'] eventual extinction, to the time when they will cease to be owners, and when the Anglo-American race will rule with republican simplicity and justice, a land literally 'flowing with milk and honey.' " Mexican Catholicism, Taylor's men believed with some justification, was a decadent institution that cynically conspired with the Mexican army to oppress the people. "They wink at the tyranny and excesses of each other," observed Sergeant Thomas Barclay of Pennsylvania.

They read aloud to one another passages from George Lippard's *Washington and His Generals,* which made strained analogies between the Revolutionary and Mexican wars. William Hickling Prescott's *History of the Conquest of Mexico* served as a historical travel guide. (Prescott, busy writing *History of the Conquest of Peru,* refused to recognize any parallels between Hernando Cortes's 1519 expedition and the Mexican War, which he condemned.) So highly regarded was Prescott's book that Navy Secretary George Bancroft ordered it added to every U.S. ship's library. Also popular were Walter Scott's *Ivanhoe,* a trope on chivalry and courage, and Herman Melville's *Typee,* the prototype of travel books. Through these touchstone books, read and heard around crackling campfires, the Americans imagined themselves as patriots or knights errant, and they reached for their omnipresent notebooks to jot down their observations, impressions, and thoughts.

It was an army of amateur travel writers, historians, and tourists. Gazing for the first time upon Cerralvo in northern Mexico, Captain William Rogers of the Mississippi Rifles wrote that it "bears the impress of an antiquated fortress, and reminds one of the dilapidated castles we read of in romances." The soldiers enclosed seeds and flowers in their letters to loved ones. In central Mexico, a colonel once awakened his troops early to view a spectacular sunrise.

The American flag, the eagle, and national music—*Yankee Doodle* was by far the most popular—inspired the impressionable American soldiers. They professed a singular eagerness to "see the elephant," their nickname for combat, not knowing that its horrors would rip to shreds their gauzy daydreams. Dizzy with patriotic fervor, Chatham Roberdeau Wheat, a Tennessee infantryman and former law student, wrote to his friend George Mancy, "I would like to die with you George and be wrapped in the same Star Spangled banner and be borne triumphantly by victorious troops to burial."

AUGUST 1846: CAMARGO

When the wagons and pack mules promised by the War Department did not arrive, General Taylor decided to march to Monterrey without them. "The country expects us to do or attempt something," he wrote. But the transport shortage meant that just six thousand of his fifteen thousand troops could be fed and supplied on an extended march; Taylor would have to leave the rest behind at Camargo to guard his supply line.

Taylor's letters to Dr. Wood suggest that the mule and wagon shortage might have been a convenient excuse for him to leave most of the volunteers at Camargo: "The whole system of volunteers at best is defective, but [made] much worse than it might be, by the mismanagement of the same." Taylor privately believed that volunteers were never meant to fight outside the United States, but to quell insurrections and defend the nation from attack.

For the Monterrey expedition, Taylor chose his regulars, all veterans of Palo Alto and Resaca de la Palma, and five volunteer regiments, from Tennessee, Kentucky, Ohio, Mississippi, and Texas—as much because of the men's longer enlistment terms, twelve months or the war's duration, as for their fighting qualities. The uselessness of the "three-month men" was manifest when Colonel Albert Sidney Johnston, after attempting to persuade his 1st Texas Foot Riflemen to reenlist for a year or more, had to disband the unit because too few of his men extended their service. Captain William S. Henry deplored the men's eagerness to go home when they were just a week's march from a decisive battle at Monterrey, writing, "Experience has proved their patriotism not equal to their self-interest."

Generals David Twiggs and William Worth commanded, respectively, the all-regulars First and Second divisions. General William O. Butler's Third Division consisted of the Mississippi Rifles, and regiments from Tennessee, Kentucky, and Ohio. The Texas Volunteer Regiment comprised most of the Fourth Division, commanded by Governor James Pinckney Henderson.

• • •

Taylor's selection of the Mississippi Rifles was a personal triumph for Jefferson Davis, Taylor's former son-in-law. Davis had accepted command of the 1st Mississippi Regiment on the condition that his men carry rifles, not muskets. His rationale was that "There would probably be no other body of men so armed, and it would be known and referred to as the Mississippi Rifles and, consequently, would be more conspicuous." Davis obtained a thousand Whitney Rifles, muzzle-loaded .54-caliber weapons of 1841 vintage that were accurate up to four hundred yards. The thirty-eight-year-old first-term congressman, planter, and 1828 West Point graduate had further burnished his regiment's unique identity with rigorous training.

He also had finally assuaged Taylor's ancient resentment over Davis's brief marriage to his late daughter. Davis had met Knox Taylor during the Black Hawk War, and they married in June 1835, contrary to Taylor's wishes. Taylor objected to his daughter marrying an Army officer—he did not want her following a husband to a succession of dreary Army posts. Davis had obligingly resigned his commission before the wedding, but Taylor had not been completely mollified. The newlyweds settled in at the Davis family plantation in Natchez, and they both immediately contracted malaria. Knox died in September in a delirium. Although Davis had remarried in 1845 (Varina Howell), the men's relationship had recently thawed; they were both Delta landowners, and they shared memories of Knox.

• • •

The Taylor expedition's scouting and reconnaissance unit was the colorful Texas Rangers, whose bloody wars with the Comanches had shaped their flinty, take-no-prisoners battle ethos. They were expert horsemen whose fine mounts were known for their strength and agility and for their superiority to the Mexican cavalry horses. The Rangers were crack shots and traveled heavily armed with long rifles, pistols, and Bowie knives. Strikingly unmilitary in bearing, they were typically bearded, lean, sunburned, and savage-looking, wearing greasy buckskin shirts and leggings, caps, and dusty trousers tucked into high boots. They bore hardship stoically. While reconnoitering routes to Monterrey, Captain Sam Walker's company rode all day in the August heat without "one drop of water," a regular Army officer noted admiringly. During an extended reconnaissance to Linares, Walker's men lived off the land for days, intercepted enemy correspondence, and gathered intelligence. "As a mounted soldier he has had no counterpart in any age or country," Major Luther Giddings of the 1st Ohio Volunteers wrote of the Texas Rangers. "Neither Cavalier nor Cossack, Mamaluke nor Mosstrooper are like him; and yet, in some respects, he resembles them all."

Walker's Rangers were the first to be federalized when the war began, initially as a company in the U.S. Regiment of Mounted Riflemen. After the Rio Grande battles, a second Ranger company, under Captain John T. Price, joined the regiment. Then when Taylor requested four Texas regiments, Walker's and Price's companies were transferred into the new 1st Regiment of Texas Mounted Rifles, commanded by arguably the best-known Ranger of all, Colonel Jack Coffee Hays; Walker became Hays's second-in-command; Price, one of the regiment's six company commanders. A Second Regiment of Texas Mounted Rifles was organized later under Colonel George Wood.

The Rangers' competence and utility to the Army persuaded regular officers to overlook their indifference to military discipline and courtesy and even their occasional bacchanalias. In Reynosa, Army Lieutenant Rankin Dilworth, hearing a racket at the cotton gin where the Rangers were quartered, "looked out in that direction and saw them on top of it dancing a war dance to the infinite amusement of the natives who were collected below." On the Fourth of July, the Rangers drank two horse buckets of whiskey and dined on pigs and chickens "accidentally killed while firing in honor of the day."

Taylor privately professed to be "appalled" by the Rangers' behavior, but because he had no other scouts as skilled as them, he tolerated their idiosyncrasies.

• • •

On August 17, the eight regular Army regiments at Camargo paraded in a dress review in immaculate blue uniforms. The sun glinted on their gleaming weapons and brass. The review impressed both volunteers and regulars, who had never before witnessed a dress parade.

Two days later, the first units of the Army of Invasion marched out of Camargo on the road to Monterrey. The scarcity of mules and wagons was felt. Just three artillery pieces suitable for siege warfare—two 24-pounder howitzers and a ten-inch mortar—accompanied the army, but there were also four field batteries of four 6-pounder guns each to support mobile operations.

The soldiers left their tents behind and carried their provisions and ammunition. "We were nearly covered from neck to waist" with gear, noted Z. K. Judd of the Mississippi Rifles. A large cartridge box was strapped to a belt over the left shoulder; a bayonet and scabbard were clipped to a similar belt over the right shoulder; and a three-pint canteen rode on their white leather waistbelts. The soldiers' knapsacks bulged with clothing and personal items, and a rolled-up blanket and a haversack with food were slung over one shoulder.

In the stone city of Monterrey, 130 miles away, seven thousand Mexican regulars and three thousand volunteers, armed with forty-five artillery pieces, awaited the Americans behind their new fortifications.

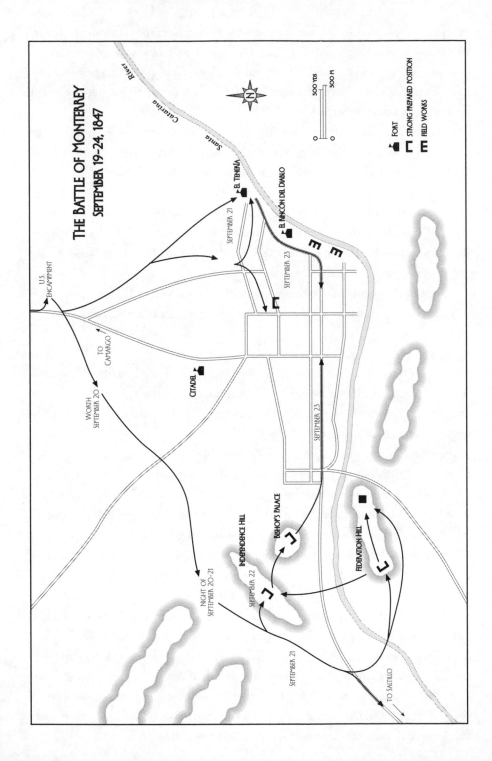

THE BATTLE OF MONTERREY
SEPTEMBER 19–24, 1847

Santa Catarina River

N

500 YDS
500 M

FORT
STRONG PREPARED POSITION
FIELD WORKS

U.S. ENCAMPMENT

EL TENERÍA
September 21

EL RINCÓN DEL DIABLO
September 23

TO CAMARGO

CITADEL

WORTH
SEPTEMBER 20

September 23

NIGHT OF
SEPTEMBER 20–21

INDEPENDENCE HILL
BISHOP'S PALACE
September 22

FEDERATION HILL
September 21

TO SALTILLO

14

MONTERREY

"Lacking the moral courage to return to camp—where I had been ordered to stay—I charged with the regiment."

—Lieutenant Ulysses S. Grant at Monterrey

SEPTEMBER 19, 1846

General Taylor and his staff glimpsed the city for the first time that morning. There wasn't much to see. The heavy mist hugging the Santa Catarina River concealed even the church spires and the steep spurs of the Sierra Madre mountains that spiked up west and south of Monterrey. As the sun climbed higher into the sky, the mist parted like a curtain to reveal the city's white stone buildings, framed by the foothills.

Through their field glasses, the Americans studied the fortified Bishop's Palace on a hill dominating the city's west side and recognized that it might hold the key to the city. Immediately in front of them, commanding the two roads entering the northern suburbs, was a twenty-five-foot-high earthwork erected where construction of a cathedral had been abandoned. Its masonry blackened by years of exposure to the elements, it was called the Citadel by Taylor's staff; four hundred men and thirty-two cannons guarded it from behind a twelve-foot ditch and an eleven-foot-thick parapet. Taylor's soldiers gave it a more evocative nickname, the Black Fort, because of its sinister aura of impregnability.

The Santa Catarina descended from the mountains and described Monterrey's southern limits before flowing east along the base of the Sierra Madre to the San

Juan River. Most of Monterrey's ten thousand residents lived in a densely populated area twelve blocks long east to west and eight blocks deep. Around the main plaza were a cathedral and the city's principal buildings; smaller plazas, too, were scattered throughout the city.

Taylor and his officers rode closer for a better look, to a hill less than three miles from the Black Fort. Suddenly, the fort swarmed with activity, and cannons boomed. The first round plowed into the ground ten feet from Taylor. The reconnaissance party scattered as subsequent shots whistled past the Texas Rangers riding with Taylor. The close call persuaded the Americans to withdraw a half mile.

The Army of Invasion camped at a spring-fed oak-pecan grove known as the Bosque de San Domingo, a handsome park where Monterrey's elite picnicked. Evidently mistaking pecans for walnuts, the soldiers called it Walnut Grove. Taylor and his top officers began preparing their plan of attack.

• • •

Earlier, on the road to Monterrey, the Americans had been as thrilled as tourists by the change in the land features and the flora as they marched south, and by their first glimpse of the blue Sierra Madre, which appeared to rise straight out of the level plain into the pale sky.

But the dust on the road was a foot thick, ground to the finest consistency by thousands of pairs of feet. It coated the heavily laden soldiers and their gear with a gray patina. The men seldom saw any natives, but "upon almost every hill, and in every valley" there were crosses inscribed with requests for prayers for people who had died, or who had been murdered by bandits. The mountains, taller than anything most of them had ever seen, helped them bear the dust, the late summer heat, and the memento moira crosses. They drank from the streams that flowed north from the Sierra Madre and foraged among groves of apples, oranges, figs, lemons, and pomegranates.

As the jagged, treeless mountain peaks came into clearer view, the Americans, weaned on romances and fanciful medieval history, saw castles, fortresses, towers, and battlements and imagined themselves as knights on their way to a climactic battle. At Cerralvo, Captain William Rogers remarked in his journal on the "beautiful clear stream, spanned by bridges and arches" that passed through the center of town, which reminded him of an ancient city; its cathedral, he noted, was 166 years old. A rainbow over the Sierra Madre foothills at sunset moved Lieutenant Daniel H. Hill to confess that the "hues gave the hills a loveliness which I never saw surpassed."

The Americans' heightened sensitivity to Mexico's natural beauty might be partly explained by their awareness that they might soon die in battle. They prepared themselves by penning long letters, or lingering over their journals, or burning the candle at both ends. Lieutenant Rankin Dilworth and some officers attended a fandango at Puntiagudo and danced until 2 A.M. with the fifty women who were there. The next night, Dilworth and his fellow officers went to another fandango. The following day, Dilworth, unable to march with his men, reported sick and rode on the baggage train.

On the last leg of the journey from Cerralvo, the troops noted that the Mexican civilians no longer vanished when the Americans appeared, but watched from their doorways as the invaders passed by, confident that they would not be harmed. They made an edged joke about the officers' fondness for fandangos, which the officers asked about at every stop. "Mucho fandango in Monterrey," they cheerfully told the Americans again and again. Lieutenant Abner Doubleday recognized the remark for the veiled warning that it was meant to be: "They are getting up a dance for [us] in Monterey [*sic*]. They evidently looked forward to our discomfiture there for they knew great military preparations had been made to receive us."

• • •

General Pedro de Ampudia had sent a thousand mounted irregulars led by General Antonio Canales to harass Taylor's advancing army. But Canales did not attack the Americans; he dragged his feet and made excuses. More than once, his cavalrymen appeared before Taylor's mounted troops like apparitions, but they always galloped away before there was any fighting.

Canales's irregulars devoted themselves instead to the less risky activity of driving unarmed Mexicans from their homes. This scorched-earth policy, ordered by General Antonio Lopez de Santa Anna and Ampudia, was the reason that the Americans had seen so few people; Canales's marauders had forced them out, scattered their cattle, destroyed foodstuffs, and disabled water systems. Looting, however, was often the irregulars' paramount interest. It became so prevalent that Reynosa officials sought the protection of the Texas Rangers, their ostensible enemies. Santa Anna's policy, however, did have an effect. American soldiers returned from foraging with little to show for their long hike. At Agua Fria, the Americans found dry ditches, because the Mexicans had shut the irrigation headgates.

On the outskirts of Monterrey, as dragoons passed Lieutenant Dilworth and the 1st Infantry, an officer leaned down from his saddle to ask Dilworth "if I heard the 'Elephant' groan in Monterey [*sic*]."

• • •

Ten thousand Mexican regulars and volunteers manned fortifications and breast-works at strategic locations throughout the city. Several thousand other citizens had volunteered to bear arms if needed. Enough food and ammunition had been stockpiled during the weeks of preparation to withstand a long siege.

Yet disagreements and indecisiveness at the highest leadership levels had eroded the defenders' natural advantages. Foremost were Santa Anna's deep misgivings about Monterrey's defensibility by the troops now in the city. After taking com-mand of all Mexican forces, he had strongly urged Ampudia *not* to make a stand at Monterrey unless he had complete confidence in General Francisco Mejia's for-tifications. Then, evidently after assaying the condition of the Mexican army in the wake of Taylor's Rio Grande victories, Santa Anna had bluntly ordered Ampudia to withdraw Mejia and his soldiers to Saltillo.

• • •

Santa Anna had taken over an unraveling army that had too little money, a surfeit of politics, and a ridiculously large number of officers: about twenty-four thousand, many of them inactive, compared with twenty thousand enlisted men. While the officers were trained in European-style warfare—fighting at long range with mus-kets and cannons—and many were brave and intelligent, their uncoordinated lead-ership structure was apt to disintegrate in the heat of combat. Their soldiers were either draftees, or men caught in dragnets at dance halls and on the street, or con-victs sent to the army straight from prison. They were poorly fed and paid. Because of the Mexicans' proud equestrian tradition, the cavalry and lancers were regarded as the cream of the army, and therefore figured prominently in its tactical planning, even though the American field artillery had proven to be an effective deterrent.

The best infantry units were the elite cazadores and grenaderos—veteran light infantrymen and grenadiers—but they were usually held in reserve while the con-script fusileros, or line companies, did most of the fighting. On the battlefield, the infantrymen were impressive-looking, attired in white trousers and blue tailcoats with cloth facings in their regimental colors, and red collars embroidered with their company initials. Fringed, embroidered epaulets, colored sashes, and gilded buttons distinguished the officers. The infantryman's headgear was a visored

shako, while cavalrymen wore a "combed helmet" made of brass or leather, sometimes adorned with a silver shield decorated with a large Mexican eagle.

Marksmen they were not; some fired their muskets for the first time in battle,
using copious amounts of gunpowder because of its poor quality, and then
shooting from the hip because of the ferocious recoil. Consequently, the Mexicans
often fired high, over the heads of the enemy.

• • •

It often seemed that Mexico's top generals were more interested in obtaining political power and the keys to a treasury that repeatedly got picked clean, than in
fighting the Americans. Within the past year, General Jose Joaquin Herrera had
been ousted as president by General Mariano Paredes, in turn forced out on August
4 by Valentin Gomez Farias and General Jose Mariano Salas, the men who had welcomed Santa Anna when he returned from exile. All of them, Santa Anna included,
had had to address the nation's pitiable finances; revenues totaled just $200,000 per
month, while the army and its pensioners cost three times that amount.

Paredes attempted to raise money at the war's outset by making the astonishing
proposition to Charles Bankhead, Britain's minister to Mexico, that Mexico would
mortgage California to Great Britain in exchange for a loan. Bankhead's noncommittal response reflected Britain's wariness of any involvement in California. In
1845, William S. Parrott had observed that Mexico lacked "the physical means
necessary to carry on a war. . . . *Money*, they have none. . . ." Even when the government managed to obtain $2 million by persuading the clergy to mortgage
some property, it squandered most of the money on bribes and graft.

• • •

While most Mexicans appeared indifferent to the war's outcome or even to who
ruled them, the nation's elite kept Mexico in the war, despite losing two battles
and having to beg for money to defend the homeland. Political power and patriotism were the reasons. The ruling "puro" nationalists did not dare admit defeat
with the invader on Mexican soil; its credibility with the army and clergy, whose
support made the Salas–Farias regime possible, would have evaporated. While
Salas, Farias, and Manuel Crescencio Rejon wore their national pride on their
sleeves, it was more than cynical political posturing; there was genuine patriotic
feeling, and a stubborn determination not to yield to the American invaders.

As Taylor marched on Monterrey, the Mexican newspapers, at the instigation of Salas and Farias, tried to whip up nationalistic fervor by publishing Secretary of State James Buchanan's July 27 peace overture and Foreign Secretary Rejon's dismissive response. Then came a flood of war decrees from President Salas's government. Hoping to raise thirty thousand troops, the government ordered all Mexican men between the ages of sixteen and fifty to report to the army and lifted all duties on the importation of muskets, carbines, cannons, and ammunition. Salas's administration also announced that Santa Anna intended to withdraw troops from Monterrey to San Luis Potosi and fight the Americans there. "Not one Yankee should return to tell the tale," Santa Anna blustered.

• • •

General Ampudia, however, refused to give up Monterrey to Taylor without a fight. He and General Mejia had been readying Monterrey's forts and breastworks since Ampudia's arrival with three infantry brigades on August 29. But Ampudia and Mejia knew that ten thousand troops were not enough to adequately man all of the prepared defenses; they improvised by planning for cavalry and lancers to dash to the aid of positions under heavy attack. The generals believed it would be dishonorable and shortsighted to abandon the city and the strategically important Saltillo road over Rinconada Pass. They would only have to recover Monterrey later, after the Americans had had an opportunity to fortify it.

Mejia had begun building the fortifications in June, after straggling into Monterrey with the ragged, hungry, dispirited survivors from Palo Alto and Resaca de la Palma. Described by historian Justin Smith as "a pockmarked man in blue glasses," Mejia was part of the Army of the North's oft-confusing ensemble of rotating commanders—he, Ampudia, and Mariano Arista chief among them. Mejia had attempted to see Monterrey with an invader's eyes, and, until Ampudia replaced him, he had fortified those points that he believed an invader would attack.

• • •

The Black Fort, formidable as it was with two thirds of the defenders' forty-five cannons, was only Mejia's first line of defense. Trusting to the Santa Catarina River and the Sierra Madre's steeply rising foothills to protect the city's southern flank, Mejia devoted his efforts to protecting Monterrey's east and west approaches.

He had fortified five-hundred-foot Federation and Independence hills, which flanked the crucial Saltillo road on the city's west side. On the smaller of the two, Federation Hill, on the south side of the road, there was a redoubt for eighty men and a 9-pounder on the western crest. On the eastern crest six hundred yards away was a masonry fort, Fort Soldado, defended by three hundred men and a second 9-pounder.

Across the Santa Catarina River and north of the Saltillo road was Independence Hill and its two strongpoints: on the west side, Fort Libertad, with fifty to sixty men and two light guns; and on the east side, overlooking Monterrey's western neighborhoods, the ruined Bishop's Palace, one of the keystones to the city's defense. Mejia and Ampudia had painstakingly built up the ruins and assigned two hundred men with four guns to defend them.

Mejia and Ampudia had built a chain of fortifications in east Monterrey, each able to join in a mutual defense with its neighbor fort. On the northeast side was La Teneria, a former tannery with earthen works manned by 350 troops and two 8-pounders, a 4-pounder, and a mountain howitzer. Nearby, soldiers in a two-story stone distillery with a sandbagged flat roof and firing holes in the walls could rake troops assaulting La Teneria. Behind the distillery was a deep ravine, whose south bank was a complex of breastworks and yet another earthen fortification, El Rincon del Diablo—"Devil's Corner." (Taylor's men would call it Fort Diablo.) Farther up the ravine toward the city stood La Purisima bridge, and its namesake, a statue of the Virgin Mary. Nearby was Mejia's headquarters, a series of breastworks filled with three hundred troops reinforced by three cannons.

East Monterrey's thoroughfares bristled with breastworks and barricades, whose purpose was to turn the streets into killing zones if the invaders broke into the center of the city. Many of the sturdy stone houses had been converted into sandbagged fortresses with loopholes drilled through the walls. The Mexican army had even found a use in the Main Plaza for the city's massive cathedral, whose twin towers contained a clock and chimes. The cathedral was now the army's magazine.

• • •

Ampudia, powerfully built and mustachioed, with an erect martial bearing, appeared to be the perfect parade-ground general. In actuality, he was a political opportunist and a cruel bully who was feared and disliked by his men. But, worst of all in the present situation, Ampudia was indecisive. At the last minute, he changed some of Mejia's carefully prepared defenses, throwing everything into confusion just as Taylor's army reached Monterrey's outskirts.

Ampudia had one other weakness that would matter during the imminent battle: beneath the fierce scowl, the bristling moustache, and the fearsome reputation, Ampudia lacked courage.

• • •

After nightfall on September 19, Major Joseph Mansfield, the versatile Army engineer who had supervised the construction of Fort Texas and helped defend it during its investment, returned to Taylor's headquarters at Walnut Grove from a day-long reconnaissance of the Mexican positions. Mansfield had made an important observation: By marching in a wide arc around the west side of Monterrey, he told Taylor and his staff, the army could cut the road to Saltillo and then attack Federation and Independence hills. The Mexican defenses there would crumble, he predicted.

The craggy-faced Taylor and his division commanders and aides adopted a bold but risky plan of attack. General William Worth, his Second Division of regulars, with two field artillery batteries and Colonel Jack Coffee Hays's Texas Rangers, would loop around the west side of Monterrey to the Saltillo highway where it emerged from between Federation and Independence hills. The Second Division would seize the two heights as General David Twiggs's First Division and volunteer regiments from the Third and Fourth Divisions made a "strong demonstration" on the east side of the city. Taylor and his staff believed that these simultaneous movements would prevent the Mexicans from mounting a massive counterattack against Worth.

Even junior officers such as Abner Doubleday recognized that it was "somewhat audacious to attack 11,000 men in a fortified position with less than 6,000 men." But Taylor was now going to also violate a cardinal tactical rule by dividing his force in the face of the numerically superior enemy. Taylor's officers also understood that if the Saltillo road remained an open pipeline for Mexican supplies and reinforcements, Ampudia could resist American attacks indefinitely. And it would be foolhardy for the entire Army of Invasion to seize the highway, thereby exposing its own supply line. The double envelopment, conceded Doubleday, "seemed the only feasible way to take the town."

• • •

Darkness swiftly descended on the regimental camps scattered throughout Walnut Grove. Beyond the range of Ampudia's forward guns, Taylor's soldiers huddled around campfires, pondering their fate on the eve of battle. Major Philip Norbourne Barbour pronounced himself as calm as if he were at "Astor House, having long since made up my mind that, during a time of war, my life is the rightful property of my country, and cannot be taken from me, or preserved, except by the fiat of the great God who gave it. And to His will, whatever it be, I am perfectly resigned." Two days later, a musket ball would end Barbour's life in the streets of east Monterrey.

· SEPTEMBER 20, 1846

Lieutenant Doubleday trained his spyglass on the old Bishop's Palace looming above him to the east and saw "the last rays of the setting sun . . . reflected back from a forest of bayonets." Earlier in the day, Doubleday and his men had been hastily mustered— for what, they were not told. With General Worth and his two thousand men, they had marched around the northwestern part of the city, seven miles in all.

The soldiers heard gunfire ahead; a reconnaissance by Texas Rangers had encountered enemy troops. The Second Division stopped for the night. Camp-fires were forbidden. Throughout the night, the Mexican fortifications sporadi-cally erupted in ragged musket fire and shouts of "Viva Ampudia!" Many of the Americans, including Doubleday's company, had no food or blankets, because Worth had given them no time to collect their gear. When a drenching rain began falling, the hungry men huddled together on the wet ground for warmth.

The unnecessarily hard use of his men was an unfortunate characteristic of the otherwise talented Worth, who had held an officer's commission for thirty-three years, and was now fifty-two years old. His subordinate officers resented the suf-fering that he needlessly inflicted on his men. Lieutenant Ulysses S. Grant grum-bled that Worth was "nervous, impatient and restless on the march," pushing his men as though they were "going to the relief of a beleaguered garrison." On the march from Camargo to Monterrey, thirty to forty men collapsed during one afternoon while struggling in the heat to keep up with Worth's fast pace. Grant observed, "Some commanders can move troops as to get the maximum distance out of them without fatigue, while others can wear them out in a few days without accomplishing so much. General Worth belonged to the latter class."

But no one disputed Worth's "fighting qualities," which secured him his men's respect and loyalty. He had first distinguished himself in 1814 at the battles of Chippewa and Niagara, where he was seriously wounded and promoted to major. He won the Battle of Palaklaklaha in 1838 and ended his service in the Florida Indian wars as a brevet brigadier general.

Worth had angrily left the Army when President Polk declared lineal rank superior to brevet rank, with the consequence that David Twiggs, and not Worth, became

Taylor's second-in-command. But when the fighting began, Worth hastily rejoined Taylor's army, although not in time for Palo Alto or Resaca de la Palma. Now eager for laurels, he had vowed to win either "a grade or a grave" at Monterrey.

SEPTEMBER 21, 1846: FEDERATION HILL

The shivering troops stiffly rose from the wet ground, relieved that nighttime was over. As the San Juan Valley filled with light and the scraps of fog lifted off the spongy ground, the Americans fell in without a warming fire or breakfast. Led by three companies of Texas Rangers, the thick blue column of Worth's Second Division traced the footings of Independence Hill to the Saltillo road.

A squadron of splendidly uniformed Mexican lancers on silver-trimmed saddles, the Guanajuato Regiment, suddenly materialized to block the Americans' way. The lancers' green and red pennants rustled in the breeze as they steadily advanced upon a Texas Ranger company commanded by Captain Ben McCulloch, a San Jacinto and Mier veteran. Captain C. F. Smith's light infantry company ducked behind a fence as the lancers attacked. "A galling fire was opened upon them by the Texans at the fence while McCulloch's men [still mounted] at the same time poured in a perfect storm of lead from their rifles, double-barreled guns and pistols," wrote New Orleans *Picayune* correspondent George Kendall, who witnessed the attack. "The lancers tumbled from their saddles by the dozens; yet with uncommon daring the survivors dashed onward, engaging, hand to hand, with the Rangers still mounted." The lancers withdrew, were joined by cavalry and infantry reinforcements, and attacked again. Field artillery joined the Texas riflemen and shattered the lancers' attack, leaving the field strewn with 150 Mexicans dead and wounded. The Americans swarmed the Saltillo road, effectually cutting off Ampudia from retreat or reinforcements.

About 650 U.S. infantrymen and a hundred Rangers quick-timed to the foot of Federation Hill. Worth had decided to assault it first, because it was not as heavily defended as Independence Hill. As the troops splashed across the Santa Catarina River, the Mexicans blazed away at them from both hills with muskets and artillery.

Without pausing, the storming party began climbing the "almost perpendicular height" of Federation Hill's western crest, stopping to shoot at the Mexicans who crowded the hillcrest and fired down on them. The extremely accurate American fire dispersed the defenders. "The dreaded Texans, who had unnumbered wrongs to avenge, were picking off each his victim at every shot," reported news-paperman Kendall.

Gaining the summit, the Americans captured a Mexican 9-pounder, and Lieu-tenant Edward Deas aimed it at El Soldado on the hill's eastern side, where Mexican gunners were taking pot shots with another 9-pounder. "By one lucky shot [we] upset the cannon in the work, upon which the enemy fled precipitately leaving his piece in our hands," reported Lieutenant Daniel Hill. By 3 P.M., Federation Hill was secured. The American flag was run up amid loud cheers, echoed by the troops below.

• • •

At the height of Worth's attack, with round and grapeshot falling around them, several Mexican women made tortillas and sold them to hungry U.S. soldiers bowed down under the storm of lead and iron. "It was a singular scene," wrote Kendall. "Mexican females cooking for the enemies of their country, while very likely their husbands or brothers were busy on the height above pouring death and destruction into their very midst."

SEPTEMBER 21, 1846: EAST MONTERREY

The First Division regulars and the Third and Fourth Division volunteer regi-ments were poised to make their diversionary attack against east Monterrey. For the past hour, since 7 A.M., the Americans' two 24-pounders and ten-inch mortar, concealed in a nearby fold in the terrain, had been bombarding the Black Fort.

Before the shooting started, General Twiggs, the splenetic, red-faced, bull-necked commander of the First Division, had become a casualty of sorts. During the previous night, the fifty-six-year-old Georgian, who had been an Army officer since the War of 1812, had fought in the Indian wars, and had ably served at Palo Alto and Resaca de la Palma, had dosed himself liberally—too liberally, it turned out—with a purgative, in the belief that if he had "loose bowels" and was shot in the abdomen, the bullet would not penetrate his intestine. In one respect, the purgative did prove to be an amulet for Twiggs; he was so incapacitated that he had to relinquish his command to Lieutenant Colonel John Garland.

Taylor ordered the advance of the First Division, consisting of the U.S. First, Third, and Fourth Infantry Regiments and the Baltimore Battalion. The Third and Fourth Divisions, and their regiments from Tennessee, Mississippi, Kentucky, Ohio, and Texas, were held in reserve.

The gunners in the Black Fort and Teneria opened fire when they spotted the First Division marching toward the city. But the Americans disappeared into a field of tall sugar cane that concealed them from the Mexicans' guns. The respite was temporary, and, as it turned out, costly. While the cane hid the Americans, it also disoriented them and broke up their formations. When finally, many found themselves in an open field two hundred yards west of where they were supposed to be—and in the middle of a murderous artillery crossfire from the Black Fort, the Teneria, and Fort Diablo. "Shot after shot crashed through our ranks or enfiladed our line, strewed its pathway with mangled bodies, shattered limbs, and headless trunks," wrote a survivor. A twelve-pound cannonball tore off one of Lieutenant Rankin Dilworth's legs. The eloquent diarist would linger for six days before dying at age twenty-four.

• • •

Lieutenant Grant, the restless quartermaster and minder of mules, ached to be with the assault regiments and not in the rear. When the shooting began, he borrowed a horse and rode to the front, where he discovered that he was the only mounted officer in a frontal assault on the Teneria by the Fourth Infantry Regiment. "Lacking the moral courage to return to camp—where I had been ordered to stay—I charged with the regiment." In minutes, a third of the attackers fell dead or wounded. The regiment pulled back and regrouped. Grant gave his mount to an adjutant, Lieutenant Charles Hoskins, appropriated another horse and returned in time for a second attack that ended in the cane field, with Hoskins among those killed. Grant became the new adjutant.

• • •

The First and Third Infantry Regiments raced across the open field and into northeastern Monterrey's narrow streets, a maze of crooked thoroughfares that sometimes led to dead ends, or worse, ended abruptly at fortified barricades. The Americans ran into grapeshot and canister from La Purisima Bridge and a hailstorm of bullets delivered by hundreds of Mexican troops firing through loopholes and from behind sandbagged breastworks. "Showers of balls were hurled on us," wrote Lieutenant Robert Henry. "Being in utter ignorance of our locality, we had to stand and take it . . . concealed fire, which appeared to come from every direction. On every side we were shot down."

Captain Electus Backus's company from the First Infantry ran south down a long street and, after routing some Mexicans, scrambled into a building. The soldiers raced up the stairs to the roof. To their surprise, they were 150 yards behind the Teneria, from where two hundred Mexican infantrymen and a battery of five guns were shooting in the other direction, their rear completely exposed.

• • •

After the bloodied Fourth Infantry broke off its attack on the Teneria with a third of its men dead or wounded, Taylor, whose diversionary attack had turned into a desperate battle, sent General William O. Butler's Third Division of volunteers to support the regulars. The First Tennessee led the way, followed by the Mississippi Rifles. An eighteen-pound round of solid shot from the Black Fort tore through the Tennesseans' ranks. Mississippian Rufus K. Arthur had regarded the battle as just "a frolic," until he and his fellow volunteers came upon the mangled Tennesseans, "uttering the most distressing groans and shrieks—some with their legs or arms off, and others crawling on the ground and dragging their entrails after them." Thereafter, the First Tennessee was known as the "Bloody First."

Three hundred yards from the Teneria, Mexican cannon fire and musketry rained down on the volunteers as they deployed into lines and loosed a crashing volley of their own. From the nearby cane field, the dazed survivors of the Fourth Infantry's failed attacks added their fire to the volunteers'. The din became a roar, the air dense with flying lead. To Private Edward M. Cohea, it seemed that "I could hold up my cap, and catch it full of bullets in a minute."

"Damn it, why do not the men get nearer to the fort?" barked Davis. "Why waste ammunition at such distance?" The volunteers quick-stepped 120 yards closer to Teneria and fired another volley.

Expecting a reciprocal storm of lead and copper shot, the volunteers were surprised when Teneria's guns instead fell silent. Their volley had drowned out a nearly simultaneous discharge by Captain Backus's company, crouched on the roof of the building behind the Teneria. Backus had chosen that instant to rake the Mexican positions exposed to his men's muskets. "The effect was visible in a moment of time," observed Backus. "The roof was cleared in a few shots, and the enemy retreated across the creek to Fort Diablo." A Mexican light infantry officer might have been as responsible as Backus's muskets for the precipitate flight; the lieutenant colonel had exhorted his men to follow him in a sally from the fort, and the Mexicans had abandoned their positions but had then fled ignominiously across the creek. The colonel joined the flight. "By the desertion of the chief of the Light, the enemy took the Teneria," wrote Mexican historian Ramon Alcarez.

Astride his charger Tartar, Davis instantly recognized this fleeting opportunity to grasp the prize and chafed as the seconds leaked away and no order came from the Mississippi brigade commander, Brigadier General John A. Quitman, to storm the fort. "Now is the time!" he sputtered. "Great God, if I had thirty men with knives I could take that fort." A Davis subordinate, Lieutenant Colonel Alexander Keith McClung, a swashbuckling duelist who lacked Davis's reverence for military hierarchy, drew his saber and shouted, "Charge! Charge!" As McClung's men surged toward the fort, Davis and the First Tennessee's commander also released their men. The Americans raced through the Teneria's embrasures as the last of the Mexicans ran out the other side. Unaware that Teneria had changed hands, volunteers outside the fort continued to fire at Teneria until the Tennesseeans ran up their regimental flag, blue with stars and an eagle. The Mexicans fired a last volley as they retreated to Fort Diablo, and a ball tore away part of Colonel McClung's left hand as it rested on his sword scabbard.

• • •

American soldiers crouching beside the gunfire-swept streets watched in amazement as a Mexican woman, ignoring the lead and iron whizzing around her, brought food and water to wounded Americans and Mexicans, wherever they lay.

"I saw her lift the head of one poor fellow, give him water, and take her handkerchief from her own head and bind up his wounds; attending one or two others in the same way, she went back for more food and water," wrote a soldier eyewitness. "As she was returning I heard the crack of one or two guns, and she, poor creature, fell."

The Americans later buried her "amid showers of grape and round shot . . . expecting every moment to have another grave to dig for ourselves."

• • •

Lieutenant Grant's temporary regiment, the Fourth Infantry, was one of the units fighting in east Monterrey's labyrinthian streets, and it was running out of ammunition. Grant, rated as West Point's best horseman when he graduated in 1843, volunteered to ride for more powder and lead, and to report the regiment's position to Colonel Garland. Before galloping off, he daringly slid down the side of his horse to keep it between him and the enemy's bullets, exposing only "one foot holding the cantle of the saddle, and an arm over the neck of the horse." At nearly every street crossing, the Mexicans fired at him, but Grant managed to slip out of the combat zone "without a scratch." On his way to division headquarters, he saw an American sentry guarding a house filled with wounded officers, including an acquaintance, First Lieutenant J. C. Territt, his "bowels protruding." After obtaining the needed ammunition, Grant started back but encountered American regiments withdrawing from the city.

• • •

Taylor had remained at his headquarters miles away to better coordinate the simultaneous attacks on east Monterrey and Federation Hill. Too far away from east Monterrey to effectively direct the fighting there, he tried to anyway, issuing orders on the basis of outdated field reports. The result was confusion.

Upon receiving Colonel Garland's report of the Fourth Infantry's initial failure to capture the Teneria, Taylor had granted Garland's request to break off the attack. But in the meantime, the volunteers had not only taken possession of the Teneria, they were poised to attack Fort Diablo, and Garland's First Division was inching toward La Purisima under intensive fire. The withdrawal order, reaching Garland after the Teneria had fallen, was followed by a countermanding order, issued by Taylor after he learned of Teneria's capture, to General Butler to capture Fort Diablo with his all-volunteer Third Division volunteers. But Butler had been wounded, and his command was in disarray.

As night approached, Taylor withdrew all of his troops from east Monterrey, except for a small force occupying the Teneria, won at such great cost, and nearby buildings.

• • •

Taylor's grimy, exhausted soldiers were streaming out of east Monterrey toward their camp at Walnut Grove, when the gates of the Black Fort flew open. Out galloped General Garcia Conde's Third and Seventh Lancers, the razor-sharp tips of their nine-foot spears glittering in the sunlight. Leading one of the lancer companies was a woman wearing a captain's epaulets. Before the day's fighting began, Dos Amades, as Taylor's troops later called her, had been "paraded before the troops," like a latter-day Joan of Arc, proclaiming her "desire to be posted at that spot where the first shot would fall and where the thickest of the battle should rage." She was rumored to be the daughter of a former Nuevo León governor.

At a shouted command, the lancers formed a line, lowered their lances so that they were at about the height of a dismounted man's torso, and charged. The sight sent a thrill of fear through the volunteers, who had heard reports that the Mexican lance tips were dipped in poison. Their nerves already frayed by their harrowing baptism by fire, some volunteers bolted for the cane fields. The lancers overtook some of them and impaled them, and then entered the cane field, where they butchered the wounded and attacked the medical personnel treating them.

The lancers split into two wings and made ready to swoop down on the disorganized Americans. At this critical moment, there came forward Colonel Albert Sidney Johnston, the erstwhile commander of the former First Texas Foot Riflemen whose three-month volunteers had refused to reenlist. Now serving as an aide-de-camp, Johnston rode among the frightened volunteers and formed them into a battle line, with their backs to a dense chaparral thicket. Colonel Davis quickly threw his Mississippi Rifles into a second defensive line, just as the Mexicans began their assault. "They came up gallantly, their fiery little chargers prancing & rearing," but the volunteers' volleys shattered the attack. Re-forming into tight formations, the Americans completed their withdrawal.

SEPTEMBER 22, 1846: INDEPENDENCE HILL

In the 3 A.M. darkness, Independence Hill rose like a sheer cliff above the five hundred wet, tired American soldiers. Rain continued to fall, as it had much of the night, sluicing off the hill's upper reaches, which were enveloped in a velvet fog. The soldiers waited in tense silence. At nightfall, they had reached the base of Independence Hill, as the Mexican cannoneers on its summit dueled with the American artillerymen atop Federation Hill. Newspaperman George Kendall found the artillery fireworks to be "full of grandeur and sublimity." But the gunners had long since stopped wasting their ammunition, except for the occasional hiss of a rocket climbing into the sky, where with a loud *pop!* it would throw a sickly yellow-white light over the Americans.

Two hundred Texans, six companies from the Artillery Battalion, and the Eighth Infantry began to climb the slippery, nearly perpendicular western slope of Independence Hill. By finding handholds in crags, fissures, and bushes, they inched their way into the dense fog, where the rattle of their canteens informed the Mexicans of their presence, if the illuminating rockets had not already done so. Fifty yards from the summit, the Americans could just discern the shape of sixty Mexican soldiers manning breastworks, at the very instant that the enemy saw the Americans and began firing at them. Captain Robert A. Gillespie of the Texas Rangers fell dead (General Worth later honored him by renaming the hill Mount Gillespie). The attackers kept coming, holding their fire until they were almost at the breastworks. They charged, firing at the same time. The Mexicans sprinted madly 350 yards down the sloping hilltop to Bishop's Palace on the east side, as the Americans stormed into their breastworks, unfurling the Stars and Stripes in the steel-gray dawn. Loud cheers erupted from the Americans watching anxiously from the valley below. In their camp north of the city, Taylor's men, guessing the meaning of the cheering, threw their caps in the air.

Worth's shock troops fell into a skirmish line and marched on Bishop's Palace. Mexican infantrymen suddenly sallied out of the fort and stopped the U.S. attack, before withdrawing back into the fortress. Then, all morning long, the gunners inside the palace raked the hilltop with shot and shell while the Americans hugged the ground.

Meanwhile, U.S. artillerymen used slings to haul a dismantled 12-pounder howitzer up the cliff. There the gun was reassembled, and Worth's men launched another attack. Trumpets sounded inside Bishop's Palace, and lancers and infantrymen poured out of the fort. They closed ranks to meet the Americans.

The five hundred Americans fired successive volleys that, with the howitzer's added destructive power, smashed the Mexican counterattack, and then stormed into Bishop's Palace. Lieutenant George Washington Ayers of the Third Artillery lowered the Mexican standard, as Americans and scattered groups of Mexicans blasted one another at close range. The battle ended when gunners dragged the howitzer into the palace and scattered the defenders with grapeshot. Unspiking the enemy cannons, the American artillerymen fired on the Mexicans fleeing down the hill into the city.

SEPTEMBER 22, 1846: EAST MONTERREY

The Mississippi Rifles and the First Tennessee relieved the small force that had occupied the Teneria throughout the night. Except for sporadic firing on the Teneria, east Monterrey had been quiet since the lancer attack the previous afternoon. The volunteers could hear the distant thud of cannons and the crackle of musketry coming from Federation and Independence hills, wreathed in gunsmoke.

Inexplicably, Taylor did not resume the attack on east Monterrey, for the moment suspending his plan for a double envelopment of the city. While Taylor's men rested from the previous day's battle, so did Ampudia's army. In the afternoon, a storm blew in from the north, heavy rain fell, and it suddenly felt like autumn.

That night, the shivering volunteers, without blankets or hot food, stood in the cold rainwater that had pooled in their breastworks, watching signal rockets arc from the city into the black sky. They could hear movement inside the enemy lines at Fort Diablo. The Americans braced for an attack. None came.

SEPTEMBER 23, 1846: EAST MONTERREY

In the damp, cool early morning, Jefferson Davis led a patrol from the Teneria toward Fort Diablo, hyperalert for Mexican patrols and snipers. There was only silence. The Mississippians cautiously entered Diablo and found it deserted, its guns gone. The nearby streets and houses were empty. The patrol edged deeper into the city. La Purísima bridge had also been abandoned. As they neared the Main Plaza, the Americans ran into street barricades and heavy gunfire. Davis informed Taylor that Ampudia had withdrawn his forces into the heart of the city.

Davis brought up the rest of the Mississippi and Tennessee Regiments. Then Taylor arrived on Old Whitey with a composite force consisting of the Third Infantry of the First Division; the Second Texas Regiment; and Braxton Bragg's field artillery battery. Lieutenant Grant discovered that the wounded U.S. officers that he had seen two days earlier had been captured by the Mexicans, and were now dead.

Taylor's scratch force penetrated deep into the eastern city as Mexican soldiers shot at them from houses, rooftops, and behind street barricades. "Brave boys, Americans are never afraid!" former Texas Governor Mirabeau B. Lamar shouted to the Second Texas. Bragg's artillerymen methodically blasted away the barricades thrown up by the Mexicans and steadily pushed the enemy toward the Main Plaza.

Wherever the fighting was heaviest, Taylor and his staff were there to direct operations, having learned the folly of commanding at too great a distance. At times, Taylor got too close to the action. "He was very imprudent in the exposure of his person. He crossed the street in which there was such a terrible fire in a walk, and by every chance should have been shot," wrote Captain William S. Henry, who dashed up to Taylor with some of his men and mildly rebuked the general for risking his life. Taylor curtly replied, "Take that ax and knock in that door."

Under a flag of truce, the governor of Nuevo León requested that the city's inhabitants be permitted to leave; Taylor refused the request.

Late in the day, the Mississippi Rifles captured a two-story stone house one block from the Main Plaza. Then Taylor, uneasy about leaving his men in the unsecured city, pulled all of his troops out of east Monterrey for a second time.

Major John Munroe set up the ten-inch mortar in a cemetery on the north edge of the city and began lobbing rounds into the Main Plaza, where Ampudia's troops were congregated. Besides killing a number of Mexican soldiers, the slow, steady mortar fire operated on the Mexicans' nerves like the drip of a faucet; they were terrified that a round would hit the Cathedral, their ammunition depot. The resulting explosion would kill hundreds of people and obliterate buildings around the Main Plaza.

SEPTEMBER 23, 1846: WEST MONTERREY

Not content to rest on his laurels after capturing Federation and Independence hills, General Worth led two columns down into the city from Bishop's Palace. His men advanced swiftly and without losses, breaking the doors of every house they passed so that they could enter them quickly should they need ready sanctuaries.

The Mexicans awaited them at a barricade about a mile from the western edge of the city, and four blocks from the Main Plaza. As the Americans approached the barricade, a hailstorm of grapeshot and musket fire erupted from the streets and rooftops. The Spanish consul's flag was riddled with holes "in a hundred places," and the projecting bay windows of the houses were splintered and torn by round shot. Worth's men instantly shot any hand showing above a parapet or loophole.

Lieutenant Abner Doubleday quickly learned to distinguish between "the roaring rushing sound of the cannonball, the *'whiff! Whir!'* of the grape and the *'tsing'* of the musket balls." Amid the deafening gunfire, Doubleday encountered a boy who was "wild with terror. His knees were shaking, his eyes rolling and his tongue making inarticulate sounds." Yet women stood in some doorways, calmly handing oranges to the Americans.

Texas Rangers who had fought at Mier showed their fellow soldiers how to advance without exposing themselves to the killing fire in the streets. With crowbars and picks, they knocked holes in the two-foot-thick soft adobe walls separating the stone homes from one another. Crashing through the interior walls—the loud noise could be heard above the cannon and musket fire—they slowly progressed from one house to another, securing the roof of each house that they entered. In this manner, they were able to cover an entire block without exposing themselves to enemy gunfire.

Captain Sam Walker's Rangers burst through a wall into one home and startled a Mexican infantry company. When the infantrymen tried to scramble away, the Rangers shot and killed half of them. In another house, Lieutenant Doubleday and his men encountered a family that expected to be massacred by the Americans. "One little boy took down a picture of Christ from the walls . . . and held it up to me, as if to implore my compassion, exclaiming, 'It is our Lord, sir.' "

Taylor's withdrawal from east Monterrey permitted some of Ampudia's men to join the fight against Worth's troops. However, the Second Division's tactic of advancing from house to house through the interior walls negated the Mexicans' numerical advantage. By late in the day, the division was just a block away from the Main Plaza. With nightfall, Worth did not withdraw his men but held his position while his gunners—including Major Munroe and his ten-inch mortar crew, debouched from the cemetery—wrestled four guns onto rooftops and pounded the center of the city throughout the night.

SEPTEMBER 24, 1846: MONTERREY

Dawn revealed a wrecked city. Streets were strewn with the bodies of Mexican soldiers and smashed adobe and masonry. Blue-uniformed American troops swarmed into positions for a final assault on the Main Plaza, as the U.S. gunners, now able to distinguish targets in the daylight, intensified their bombardment of the city center. Then, a white flag appeared over the Main Plaza. During the lull that followed, Worth brought more troops into the city from Independence Hill and placed a 32-pounder carronade on a rooftop a block from the Main Plaza.

To the great disappointment of many American officers, the armies agreed to a ceasefire. "After one hour's fighting, the Cathedral would have been blown up and the Mexican Army captured," complained Lieutenant Daniel Hill. Others were just relieved that the bitter street fighting had ended. "Monterey [sic] is ours!" Lieutenant Lucien Webster crowed to his brother Francis.

Ampudia offered to withdraw, and Taylor rejected the proposal. They then named commissioners to negotiate the city's surrender. Taylor selected Worth, Colonel Jefferson Davis, and General James Pinckney Henderson of the Texas Volunteers; Ampudia chose Don Manuel M. Llano, the Nuevo León governor; and Generals Ortega and Requeña.

Taylor granted surprisingly generous terms: After Ampudia surrendered Monterrey, his army would be permitted to leave the city and march over Rinconada Pass with its muskets, sidearms, and six cannons. Both armies agreed to observe an eight-week armistice.

• • •

Taylor's subordinate officers grumbled about the armistice, but Taylor misguidedly believed that the U.S. government would welcome it. "As the president of the U. States had offered to settle all differences between the two countries by negotiation . . . the gallant defence of the town, and the fact of a recent change of government in Mexico, believed to be favorable to the interests of peace, induced me to concur with the commission in these terms, which will, I trust, receive the approval of the government."

In his defense, Taylor did not know that Mexican President Salas had refused to act on Secretary of State James Buchanan's July 27 peace overture. Yet Taylor, while commander of the American army, did not have the authority to suspend the war. It would not be the last time that a U.S. general would prematurely order a ceasefire.

Taylor's professed wish to expedite the peace process aside, military considerations, too, compelled him to act as he did. When his conduct of the battle was later criticized, Taylor observed in a letter to the New York *Express* that his army, outnumbered nearly two to one, was unable to block every avenue of escape, and, moreover, if he had stormed the city, scores more Americans would have died. "I also wished to avoid the destruction of women and children, which must have been very great, had the storming process been resorted to."

On the other hand, if Taylor had been bolder, he would have won a decisive victory at Monterrey that might have toppled the puro government, or at least forced it into peace talks. His leniency with Ampudia, however, permitted the Mexican government to outrageously proclaim Monterrey a victory.

And by allowing Ampudia's troops to depart with their weapons, Taylor had practically assured that, if negotiations failed and the war continued, he would meet them again on the battlefield.

• • •

Taylor had squandered early opportunities to quickly crush Monterrey's defenders. When the First Division's "demonstration" against east Monterrey became a pitched battle against prepared defenses among a warren of narrow streets and passageways, Taylor reflexively threw the volunteer regiments of the Third and Fourth Divisions against the Teneria. If he had instead regrouped and deliberately concentrated his three divisions' considerable firepower against a single objective and then afterward focused on another one, his diversionary attack could have delivered a knockout blow.

But as he did at Palo Alto and Resaca de la Palma, Taylor made a general plan and stuck with it, even when circumstances changed. While this leadership style might work when both armies were fighting in the open—and, it goes without saying, with smart, well-trained junior officers who could quickly change their tactics—in a city bristling with fortifications, a detailed attack plan was needed. The September 21 attack on east Monterrey could easily have become a debacle, had not Taylor's field commanders improvised and the volunteers and regulars exhibited the raw courage that they did. Yet when his supervision from a distance sowed confusion, Taylor did move to the front during the later fighting in east Monterrey.

Taylor's cautious withdrawal of his troops from east Monterrey on September 21 and 23, negating their hard-fought gains, may have also cost him a resounding victory. Had he pressed on, the battle might have ended in hours, instead of days, with Ampudia's unconditional surrender. His hesitancy prolonged the suffering by soldiers and citizens that he professed to deplore.

• • •

Fortunately for Taylor, Ampudia's irresolution neutralized his many advantages—numerical superiority, strong defenses, ample provisions and ammunition, and more than a two-to-one edge in artillery. Ampudia's failure to counterattack following Taylor's two withdrawals from east Monterrey cost him opportunities to recapture the Teneria and other strongholds and to damage American morale. And he never launched a coherent counteroffensive, although he retained possession throughout the battle of the Black Fort, from which he might have easily disrupted Taylor's lines of communications.

Perhaps Ampudia's tentativeness stemmed from his puzzling decision to establish his headquarters in the Cathedral, which was also his army's ammunition dump. Throughout the fighting, he lived in terror of the American artillery. After the battle, Lieutenant Doubleday encountered a Mexican army surgeon, a Scotsman, who said derisively, "Do you believe that d[rule] scoundrel Ampudia never once left the church to see what was going on?"

• • •

Ampudia's army marched out of Monterrey beginning September 26, appearing anything but defeated. "They went out sullenly, defiantly, and their attitude was such as to create a well-founded apprehension that a collision would occur between them and our troops who lined the roadside," wrote John R. Kenly, a Maryland volunteer, who believed "they only lacked one daring leader to have made their escape or a successful attempt." But Lieutenant Grant observed that many of them were "mounted on little half-starved horses that did not look as if they could carry their riders out of town." The Mexicans left behind their sick and wounded. At least seven hundred Mexican soldiers were killed in the battle.

The Americans recognized among the retreating Mexicans former comrades who, in the war's early days, had deserted to the enemy camp. Among them was John Riley, now captain of the San Patricio Brigade, the Mexican artillery unit composed exclusively of American deserters, most of them Irish-Americans. "He was recognized by his old mess-mates, and passed them amid hisses and a broad-side of reproaches," recounted Captain William S. Henry, who witnessed the exchange. "The dastard's cheek blanched, and it was with difficulty [that] he retained his position on his gun."

• • •

Monterrey residents returned to their rubble-strewn neighborhoods, where some of the houses, observed Lieutenant Benjamin S. Roberts, had been "literally torn to pieces with the balls, canister and grape from the Mexican batteries—the trees in the streets cut down with balls—the sides of the houses down the streets, commanded by the Mexican batteries, appear as though iron harrows had been dragged over them."

The Americans requisitioned a mansion belonging to General Mariano Arista and converted it to a hospital for the 368 U.S. wounded. Taylor remained in his tent with the army at Walnut Grove. There, the Americans buried their 120 dead.

• • •

An American circus came to Monterrey to entertain the troops. "We Americans are a great nation!" wrote Captain Henry. "Whip the Mexicans one day, and offer them the amusements of the circus the next."

But it wasn't long before some volunteers, having imbibed "the foul spirit of mischief and depravity," were perpetrating atrocities. "Murder, rape and robbery were committed by the Volunteers in the broad light of day," Lieutenant Daniel Hill noted disgustedly. "They would have burned the City but nine-tenths of the houses were fireproof. They, however, burned the thatched huts of the miserable peasants." Hill and Taylor blamed most of the outrages on Colonel Hays's First Mounted Texas Regiment, the only unit quartered in the city. In his battle report, Taylor had praised the Texans' conduct at Independence and Federation hills, but he expressed relief when they left Monterrey.

While returning to Texas, one of Hays's men was killed by Mexican rancheros. His friends "in revenge laid waste some three or four ranches," after which five or six Texans were waylaid and attacked, "their brains knocked out and their bodies mutilated." This "war within a war" between the Texans and the Mexican irregulars smoldered and flared over the next year.

• • •

On October 11, Polk read with dismay Taylor's dispatches from Monterrey. The president pronounced the eight-week armistice "a great mistake, & I regret that I cannot approve his course. He had the enemy in his power & should have taken them prisoners, deprived them of their arms, discharged them on their parole of honour, and preserved the advantage which he had obtained by pushing on without delay further into the country. . . ." Meeting the next day, Polk's cabinet agreed that Taylor "had committed a great error" in not capturing Ampudia's army, which "would have probably ended the war."

The administration did not rebuke Taylor, though. War Secretary William Marcy's letter congratulated the general on his victory and merely instructed him to terminate the armistice and resume offensive operations; the letter graciously allowed that the armistice might have been dictated by "circumstances." The quasi-official Washington *Union* said Monterrey was "a triumph every way memorable in military annals," while adding noncommittally that Taylor would be ordered to end the armistice.

Taylor complained that Marcy's letter was a "very cold one"—and suspected that he was being ordered to return to the offensive so that he would fail, because his name had been linked to the 1848 presidential election.

• • •

Upon reconsideration, however, the Polk administration decided that Taylor should *not* advance beyond Monterrey. The populace was hostile, and Ampudia's army, which had been permitted to retain "arms in their hands," might join Santa Anna at San Luis Potosi in a counteroffensive. Marcy suggested that Taylor cancel General John E. Wool's expedition to Chihuahua and summon him to Monterrey.

In the diary entry in which Polk enumerated these reasons for keeping Taylor at Monterrey, the president noted yet another, of which Taylor had not yet been informed: General of the Army Winfield Scott planned to strip Taylor of two thousand regulars for future expeditions against Tampico and Vera Cruz.

15

THE WAR IN THE WEST

"None but ourselves will ever know how much we suffer."
—Mormon Battalion volunteer Henry G. Boyle, of the Mormons'
journey through the Southwestern deserts

*"They were mounted on elegant horses, and are without exception the best
horsemen in the world."*
—Marine Lieutenant Henry Bulls Watson, describing the
Mexican cavalry before battle outside Los Angeles

JUNE 1846: FORT LEAVENWORTH, KANSAS

On a bluff overlooking the Missouri River where it formed Missouri's northwest
border stood Fort Leavenworth, the Army's oldest outpost west of the Mississippi
River. It was the home of the Army of the West. Three hundred miles west of St.
Louis, Leavenworth was the true gateway to the West. Through Leavenworth
passed settlers bound for the Oregon Trail and the Pacific Northwest; traders on
their way to the desert Southwest on the Santa Fe Trail; and mounted soldiers on
their forays against hostile Indians—Leavenworth's reason d'etat.

Ordered in 1827 to build a fort to serve as an operations base against the Plains
tribes, Colonel Henry H. Leavenworth had chosen this site on the Missouri
River's sloping western bank, where steamboats could unload their cargoes with
ease. Malaria, spread by the plentiful mosquitoes inhabiting the dense riverside
vegetation, initially delayed site preparation by the Third Infantry Regiment from
Jefferson Barracks in St. Louis, but the fort got built. A dozen years later, Colonel
Stephen W. Kearny led ten dragoon companies from Leavenworth to assist General Winfield Scott in the forcible relocation of fourteen thousand Cherokee
Indians from the Southeast to the Western territory—the "Trail of Tears."

• • •

From the porch of "The Rookery," the command headquarters facing Leavenworth's parade grounds, the same Colonel Kearny presided over the Army of the West's feverish preparations for its march to Santa Fe. Not a man to dither, Kearny was in a hurry to carry out his broad mandate from the Polk administration, and Fort Leavenworth had never seen anything like it. The unprepossessing Indian fighter calmly watched the spectacle of uniformed Army dragoons mingling with carelessly dressed volunteers, traders, mule-drivers, and half-naked Indian scouts, their shouts and the noise from thousands of mules, horses, oxen, and cattle blending in a cacophony of sound.

Kearny had entered the Army during the War of 1812 at age eighteen, after attending Princeton College. While serving under Scott at Queenston Heights, he was captured and exchanged. For many years Kearny was an officer of the frontier, acquiring a reputation as a tactician and disciplinarian. At Jefferson Barracks, Missouri, during the 1840s, he had organized the First U.S. Dragoons, a body of well-armed horse soldiers that, unlike cavalrymen, dismounted to fight. Missouri Senator Thomas Hart Benton had helped secure Kearny's appointment as leader of the expedition that was to seize the immense Mexican province of New Mexico, sprawling over more than two hundred thousand square miles (all or parts of the future states of New Mexico, Arizona, Colorado, Utah, and Nevada).

Kearny was to capture its capital, Santa Fe, and crush insurgent threats to U.S. commerce and government. The Army of the West, wrote Benton, would protect the Santa Fe trade and advise the people of New Mexico, Chihuahua, and Mexico's other northern provinces "that they remain quiet and continue trading with us as usual," to be "treated as friends." Traders who traveled the Santa Fe Trail between Independence, Missouri, and Chihuahua reported that few New Mexicans felt a strong allegiance to the Mexican government, which appeared to them remote and indifferent to their interests.

This was fortunate for Kearny, who commanded just 1,660 men. They included 300 regulars from Kearny's own First U.S. Dragoons; 250 regular St. Louis artillerymen commanded by Major Meriwether Lewis Clark, the son of the famous explorer and a West Point graduate; the 860 men of the First Regiment of Missouri Mounted Volunteers, led by their elected commander, Colonel Alexander W. Doniphan, a lawyer by profession and a red-haired giant at six feet four; two small companies of volunteer infantrymen; a hundred mounted St. Louis volunteers known as the Laclede Rangers; and fifty Delaware and Shawnee Indian scouts. The expedition's guide, Thomas Fitzpatrick, was one of the era's best-known mountain men and had crossed the Great Plains with John C. Frémont in 1845.

Under their protection was a caravan of 414 wagons belonging to hundreds of dry-goods tradesmen who were traveling to Santa Fe and Chihuahua. Nearly twenty thousand oxen, cattle, mules, and horses, along with their herders and drivers, lent the expedition the appearance of a Biblical migration.

• • •

Traveling nearly eight hundred fifty miles from Leavenworth to Santa Fe, roughly the same distance as Napoleon Bonaparte's march from Poland to Moscow in 1812, might take up to two months. Hoping to deprive New Mexico Governor Manuel Armijo of extra time to prepare his defenses, Kearny intended to send units from Leavenworth piecemeal as they reached readiness. Before crossing the Arkansas River into New Mexico and beginning the last leg of the journey, the expedition would reassemble at Bent's Fort.

On June 23, the eve of the first departures, a delegation of women stepped off the steamboat *Missouri Mail* and presented a hand-made American flag to Captain Oliver Perry Moss, commander of a volunteer unit from Clay County. A Mrs. Cunningham made a speech, which included a spine-stiffening exhortation to Clay County's volunteers: "We would rather hear of your failing in honorable warfare than to see you return sullied with crime or disgraced by cowardice."

By early July, soldiers, scouts, baggage trains, livestock herds, and a caravan of traders dotted the scorching-hot Kansas plains for many miles.

• • •

But even as the Army of the West tramped the prairie into a boiling dust cloud, new orders were on their way to Kearny. On May 30, two weeks after the start of the war, President Polk and his advisers had decided that they could leave nothing to chance in California; it was risky to expect the Navy and Frémont's small force alone to secure the province. The new orders directed Kearny to march to San Diego from Santa Fe once New Mexico was subdued. "You should establish a temporary civil Government in each of these Provinces," read the new orders, drafted by the president and issued by War Secretary William Marcy. "A large discretionary power is invested in you in regard to these matters. . . ." The administration had also instructed the state of Missouri to send a thousand additional mounted troops in

Kearny's train to Santa Fe, either to join Kearny's California expedition, or to serve as a New Mexico occupation force. And the War Department was raising a regiment in New York that would make the six-month sea voyage to California.

• • •

Finally, Polk was inspired by his abhorrence of religious intolerance to raise yet another force to follow the well-trod Santa Fe Trail to New Mexico and thence to California. This third army would be composed exclusively of Mormons, members of the much-maligned Church of Jesus Christ of Latter-day Saints. The "Saints" were pariahs everywhere. Recently, they had been expelled from Illinois, where a mob had murdered their prophet, Joseph Smith, and his brother Hyrum in the Carthage jail. Kearny was to recruit up to five hundred Mormon soldier-settlers from the Mormons' enormous encampment at Council Bluffs, Iowa, to accompany his California invasion force. Since the Mormons planned to remove themselves from the United States anyway, Polk believed they could serve American interests in California, much as religious castoffs had helped England secure her claim to America. The Mormon Battalion might become the vanguard for up to twenty thousand Mormon settlers. It was important that Kearny, in his dealings with the Mormon recruits, "conciliate them, attach them to our country, & prevent them from taking part against us," counseled Marcy.

• • •

The Army of the West marched southwest through green rolling hills, where water was plentiful. But this first part of their journey tested the patience and endurance of man and beast. Because no major trail connected the fort to the Santa Fe Trail, the long column necessarily had to travel cross-country, where every ravine taxed the ingenuity and muscles of men, oxen, and mules. The army struck the Santa Fe Trail at the Narrows of the Kansas River, about sixty-five miles west of Independence. Steady marching of twenty-five to thirty miles per day carried the expeditioners out of eastern Kansas's humidity and onto the baking-hot southern Great Plains, where, noted Private John T. Hughes, "the earth was literally parched to a crust and the grass in many cases crisped by the heat of the sun." The men were tormented by mirages of "ephemeral rivers and lakes." There being a scarcity of trees, the soldiers made their cookfires with buffalo chips, whose pungent odor killed appetites, perhaps making it easier to bear the short rations resulting from the quartermasters' failures.

Men wilted in the 95-degree heat, and livestock grew thin on the sparse vegetation—mainly short grass, brush, and sage—and began to die. Mules and horses that faltered were left behind. Day after day, the sun blazed out of the vaulting sky. "How discouraging the first sight of these immense plains is to one who has read the numerous glowing accounts of them!" wrote Frank S. Edwards, a soldier in Colonel Alexander Doniphan's Missouri regiment. Of course, the march was hardest on the infantrymen. "Their feet were often blistered. . . . The ground was often marked with blood in their foot-prints." Soldiers who succumbed to illness were buried beside the trail beneath simple markers that sometimes bore only their initials.

• • •

In southern Kansas, men and horses were plunging thirstily into the highly anticipated Arkansas River when they flushed about four hundred bison that bolted through the Army column. They were the first buffalo many of the men had ever seen. In the maelstrom of men, horses, and buffalo, the soldiers killed several bison with pistols, rifles, and sabers. The men quickly learned that the best way to hunt a buffalo was on horseback with a pistol, galloping "close enough to almost touch the side of the buffalo" and then killing it with a "well-directed shot behind the shoulder blade."

As they followed the Arkansas River upstream, Kearny's men supplemented their subsistence flour-and-meat rations with buffalo, deer, and antelope meat; pheasant; and fish. They studied the vast prairie dog villages with interest, and the plentiful scorpions, tarantulas, lizards, and snakes with great circumspection. Frank Edwards observed that after a heavy morning dew, one might kill more than twenty rattlesnakes within a quarter mile of camp.

• • •

Across the Arkansas River from New Mexico, Bent's Fort lay in unincorporated U.S. territory acquired in the Louisiana Purchase. Built in 1833 by the four Bent brothers—Charles, William, Robert, and George—in partnership with Ceran St. Vrain, it was a trading post for fur trappers and Indian robe hunters, a way station for Santa Fe Trail traders, and occasionally a temporary base for U.S. military operations against hostile Indians. It was made of adobe, with fifteen-foot-high walls and towers at two corners. A huge American flag flowed in the steady western breeze. As Kearny's army neared Bent's Fort, trader caravans that had congregated there stirred. Their long wait for a military escort to Santa Fe and Chihuahua was ended.

The Army of the West camped outside Bent's Fort after having traveled nearly 650 miles in one month. Two hundred miles further lay Santa Fe, the New Mexico provincial capital.

Kearny's men captured three Mexican spies who, by displaying fake letters addressed to Kearny, had slipped into the American camp. Rather than imprison them, Kearny showed the spies the army's artillery, troops, and weapons, then released them, knowing they would race to Santa Fe to give exaggerated accounts of what they had seen. Kearny sent with them a proclamation declaring that Kearny was "seeking union" with New Mexicans, and warning that "all who take up arms . . . will be regarded as enemies."

• • •

On August 2, the Army of the West forded the Arkansas River and entered enemy territory. The snow-flecked Spanish Peaks rose tantalizingly in the distance, as Kearny's men drank "nauseating" water and trekked across a parched land scoured by wind-blown sand that felt like "pelting hail." "We suffered much with the heat and thirst," recalled Private John T. Hughes, "and the driven sand—which filled our eyes and nostrils and mouths almost to suffocation." Conditions improved on the other side of seventy-eight-hundred-foot Ratón Pass, where the Americans enjoyed the cool pine and cedar forests, and where their horses found good grass.

Near Las Vegas, New Mexico, a courier delivered the letters from War Secretary Marcy apprising Kearny of his new expedition to California, of the second Missouri mounted regiment that Colonel Sterling Price was raising, and of the formation of the Mormon Battalion. Another letter informed Kearny that he had been promoted to brevet brigadier general.

Kearny, however, had no time to savor his promotion or to be gratified that 1,500 men were joining his command; he had just learned that thousands of New Mexican troops planned to waylay him in a canyon a few miles ahead. The regulars and volunteers prepared for battle. But when they reached the canyon, no one was there. "We are disappointed in not meeting the enemy today," noted a Kearny aide, "as all appeared eager for the fray." Reaching Las Vegas on August 15, Kearny climbed onto a roof to announce to the townspeople that they were now U.S. citizens; public officials were required to pledge allegiance to the United States.

A new alarm swept through Kearny's army: three thousand artillery-supported

New Mexican troops and their Indian allies had built fortifications in Apache Canyon outside Santa Fe. Kearny's advance parties warily entered the canyon and found partially completed defensive positions, but no one in them. As the troops passed through the forty-foot-wide canyon, they counted themselves fortunate that the enemy had decided not to fight there. "It was thought by us, that their position was equal to 5,000 men," an unidentified Kearny officer wrote in *Niles' National Register.*

• • •

On August 18, fifty-two days after marching out of Fort Leavenworth, the Army of the West entered Santa Fe with drawn sabers, as white-shirted Mexican men in sombreros silently watched. When the American flag was raised over the governor's palace, Kearny's artillerymen, positioned on the eastern heights to bombard the city if necessary, fired an artillery salute instead. From homes near the main plaza, Lt. Richard Elliott thought he heard "a wail of grief," ascribing it to humiliation over the city having fallen "without a gun having been fired in its defence."

Santa Fe's surprising capitulation was the handiwork of the wealthy cigar- and wine-loving trader, James Magoffin. Two months earlier, Magoffin had briefed President Polk and War Secretary Marcy on the New Mexico situation. Then, evidently with their blessing as well as Kearny's, Magoffin had opened secret negotiations with Governor Manuel Armijo, persuading him—probably with a substantial bribe—to withdraw his troops from Apache Canyon and not oppose the Americans' entry into Santa Fe. Armijo and the remnants of his army were now on their way to Chihuahua.

• • •

In his proclamation to New Mexicans, Kearny bluntly declared New Mexico to be "a part of the United States," demonstrating why he was a soldier and not a diplomat. "You are no longer Mexican subjects; you are now become American citizens," he wrote, evidently unaware that the president and Congress ordinarily made such decisions. Kearny also vouchsafed public safety, private property, and freedom of worship, and instructed Colonel Doniphan to write a New Mexico constitution and territorial laws. Later, when Congress investigated the general's actions, even Polk had to concede that Kearny had "exceeded the power of a military commander over a conquered territory," but forgave him because he had "acted from patriotic motives."

In three weeks, the efficient lawyer Doniphan composed and printed a state constitution, territorial laws, and a bill of rights that guaranteed trial by jury, habeas corpus, and free elections; the one-hundred-page booklet, which did not mention slavery, became known as the Kearny Code and was the foundation for a New Mexico territorial government. Charles Bent, one of the Bent's Fort brothers, became provisional governor.

Santa Fe dashed the soldiers' grandiose expectations of a Spanish Valhalla in the mountains. They contemptuously nicknamed it "Mud Town" and described it as "an immense brickyard," because nearly every structure was made of adobe brick. The streets were "narrow and dirty," and the citizens "meanly clad, dirty and indolent." As had Taylor's troops, Kearny's men resented the New Mexican practice of women doing all the work, while the men loafed. At a ball a week after Santa Fe's occupation, Henry Smith Turner, a captain of the U.S. First Dragoons and a Kearny adjutant, was not only annoyed by the "execrable" music, but by "everybody smoking—women and men, clouds of smoke all the time. General goes to bed sick in consequence."

• • •

Kearny and his staff officers, however, had formed a different impression of the New Mexicans; the provincial leaders, at least superficially, welcomed Armijo's departure and the American occupation. The upper classes appeared especially eager to cooperate with Kearny and share power with the Americans.

Learning that Mexican dragoons were streaming north from Chihuahua to fight, Kearny led a detachment one hundred miles down the Rio Grande to watch for them, while assaying the people's temper in the outlying districts. At Valencia, Kearny's men, who had not yet been paid, sold the buttons off their Army coats for twelve cents apiece to buy fruit. In Tomé, Kearny and his staff carried lighted candles in a procession honoring the Virgin Mary. The general paid his respects to ex-Governor Armijo's wife in Albuquerque.

For the most part, the New Mexicans were happy to have seen the last of the Mexican provincial government. Mexican troops were not in evidence anywhere; the army that had been sent north from Chihuahua had stopped in El Paso upon learning of Santa Fe's capitulation. Satisfied that New Mexico would not revolt, Kearny returned to Santa Fe to plan the next phase of his expedition.

• • •

Kearny split his command. With the First U.S. Dragoons, he would cross the New Mexico desert to California. Colonel Doniphan, after signing treaties with New Mexico's restive Indian tribes, would lead the Missouri mounted troops south into Chihuahua, where they would rendezvous with General John E. Wool's two-thousand-man Army of the Center. Colonel Sterling Price, the lawyer-politician who commanded the Second Missouri Mounted Volunteers regiment that was on its way from Leavenworth, would take over in Santa Fe. The Mormon Battalion would follow Kearny to southern California.

With a small wagon train and a pair of howitzers, Kearny and his three hundred dragoons rode out of Santa Fe on September 25. Price's more than a thousand dragoons and their long train rumbled into Santa Fe a few days later and assumed routine occupational duties. Two weeks after Price's arrival, the Mormons reached Santa Fe.

• • •

The Mormons' large numbers, insularity, and sharp business practices had aroused the hatred of their Gentile neighbors in Ohio, compelling them to move westward. In western Missouri, the situation was even worse: spiraling mob violence, murders, arson, and armed clashes between Mormons and Gentiles prompted Missouri Governor Lillburn Boggs to call out ten thousand militiamen to either drive the Mormons from the state or "exterminate" them. In 1838, the militia massacred eighteen Mormons at Haun's Mill and rounded up Smith and six other church leaders. Convicted of treason, they were sentenced to death. Militia Colonel Alexander Doniphan, who had previously defended Mormons in the courtroom, was ordered to carry out the sentence. Doniphan refused, declaring that it was illegal to court-martial civilians, and executing them would be "cold-blooded murder." The Mormon leaders were eventually released.

In 1839, the Mormon prophet Joseph Smith led his followers to Nauvoo, Illinois, where the cycle began again of Mormon prosperity followed by smoldering Gentile hatred—and, this time, too, outrage over Smith's not-so-secret polygamist practices. A mob murdered Smith and his brother Hyrum in the jail in Carthage, Illinois, in June 1844. The Twelve Apostles and Brigham Young, who had assumed Smith's mantle of authority as well as responsibility for five of his twenty-seven widows, decided that it was time for the Mormons to seek a new Canaan. But the Missouri and Illinois expulsions had exhausted the Mormons' carefully husbanded capital, and without money, draft animals, or supplies, a migration to the Far West was impossible.

• • •

As more than ten thousand Mormons streamed across Iowa in the early spring of 1846 to Council Bluffs on the Missouri River, Young and his advisers sent an emissary to Washington in the hope that President James Polk would treat them fairly. The portents were good; when congressmen had tried to block the Mormons from traveling to the West, Polk had defended their right to migrate: "If I could interfere with the Mormons, I could with the Baptists or any other religious sect."

The Mormon emissary, Jesse C. Little, met with Polk on June 3, 1846, and proposed that the Mormons haul supplies and build Army posts for the U.S. government, in return for money to migrate to the Far West and the government's pledge not to interfere with them. Polk made a counterproposal: five hundred Mormons would enlist as volunteers in the Army and spearhead a migration of Mormons and other American settlers to California, helping secure the Mexican province as a U.S. territory. Army wages would finance the Mormons' journey across the plains. Little quickly acquiesced.

After years of receiving "little save neglect or persecution" from the U.S. government, the Mormons had finally found a friend in Washington, President James Polk. Brigham Young expressed his gratitude in a letter to Polk on August 9: "Your Excellency's kind feelings have kindled up a spark in our hearts, which had been well nigh extinguished." His people, Young wrote, planned to settle "within the bason [sic] of the Great Salt Lake or Bear River Valley, as soon as circumstances shall permit."

In late June, Army Colonel James Allen began signing up recruits at Mount Pisgah, the Mormon encampment at Council Bluffs. A month later, he led 496 officers and men of the new Mormon Battalion, along with thirty-five women and forty-four children, to Fort Leavenworth. The recruits drew government arms and equipment, but no Army-issue clothing other than heavy white waistbelts. Army officers drilled them in the oppressive August heat for two weeks in the basics of marching and maneuver.

• • •

With Colonel Allen unable to travel due to illness, Lieutenant Andrew Smith was placed in charge of the Mormon Brigade when it left Fort Leavenworth on August 13. Smith and the volunteers clashed immediately over medical treatment, with the Mormons preferring prayer and the "laying on of hands" to the treatments prescribed by the expedition's Dr. Sanderson, who cursed heartily as he forced them to swallow calomel, arsenic, bayberry bark, and chamomile flowers.

The volunteers' prayers for the return of the popular Colonel Allen were met by the news that he had died on August 23. The loss of the only Army officer who had treated the Mormons respectfully inspired William Coray to write, "Suffice it to say that it caused more lamentation from us than the loss of a Gentile ever did before."

The battalion entered Santa Fe on October 9 with fixed bayonets and drawn swords. When the Mormons assembled for inspection in the main square, Doniphan ordered his Missouri troops to fire a salute from the rooftops.

In southern Kansas, most of the more than seventy Mormon women and children who had joined the battalion in Council Bluffs had been escorted to Pueblo, in present-day southeastern Colorado; the desert country ahead was deemed too harsh and dangerous for them. In Santa Fe, all the rest except five women and a child were sent to Pueblo with eighty-six men whom Dr. Sanderson judged unfit for duty.

After sending $2,447.32 of the Army pay they received in Santa Fe to Brigham Young in Council Bluffs, the Mormon expeditioners embarked on October 20 for California.

• • •

Weeks earlier, Kearny's dragoons had followed the Rio Grande south from Santa Fe for 225 miles before turning west toward the Gila River. With detours and zig-zags due to rough terrain, the journey to San Diego would cover more than a thousand miles, most of it through desert country.

The expedition encountered Kit Carson, traveling from California to Washington with a fifteen-man escort, and a pouch full of dispatches from Commodore Robert F. Stockton. California's pacification was complete, Stockton reported—prematurely, as events would show. The dispatches and Carson convinced Kearny that he would not need three hundred troops; he sent two hundred of them back to Santa Fe. The general pressured Carson to guide him through the desert that he had just crossed. With reluctance, Carson assented, handing over his dispatches to mountain man Tom Fitzpatrick to carry the rest of the way to Washington. Carson suggested that Kearny use pack mules and ditch his wagons, which would slow him down in the rugged country ahead. Kearny took the advice.

The dragoons passed copper-mining areas abandoned because of Indian attacks. One day, the powerful Apache chief Mangas Colorado and some of his warriors visited the soldiers' camp. After carefully examining the dragoons' arms and horses, the Apaches decided to leave the Americans alone.

For a couple of weeks, the expeditioners enjoyed their novel surroundings. Along the Gila River, they caught dozens of ten-inch trout, dined on deer, bear, partridges, and turkeys, and gazed in amazement at the ruins of an ancient city where up to twelve thousand people had once lived. They savored a "remarkably fine" view from the Continental Divide, as well as the pure, dry air that would one day lure the ailing and tubercular to the Southwest. Everywhere they saw evidence of ancient volcanic eruptions. Near the Gila, they met the hospitable Maricopa and Pima Indians.

The rough country, however, wore down men and animals. "It is *labor, labor* from morning until night, up hill and down, over rocks and gullies," groaned Captain Turner of the 1st Dragoons. The howitzers, he noted, "have broken down most of the mules."

• • •

When he learned of Colonel Allen's death, Kearny had sent Colonel Philip St. George Cooke back to Santa Fe to take charge of the Mormon Battalion, an assignment that Cooke described as "turning a very sharp corner indeed." Cooke, a regular Army officer, found the Mormons obedient but undisciplined: "They exhibit great heedlessness and ignorance—and some obstinacy." The Mormons were determined to bring their wagons to California and so would travel farther south than Kearny, into Mexico's Sonora Province, to avoid the mountains. Cooke hoped this wagon road to the Pacific would be useful to future sojourners, and so it was; during the gold rush two years later, Cooke's Wagon Road became a thoroughfare to California.

Hardship stalked the Mormons. Daytime brought intensive heat, while hard frosts came with nighttime. As the Mormons' provisions dwindled, Cooke reduced the daily ration to nine ounces of flour and ten ounces of pork, down from a pound each. The hungry travelers tried to corner a small herd of wild cattle; the dangerous, quick-footed livestock nearly got the best of them, goring some of the men and killing a pack mule before the troops killed nine bulls, one of them requiring twenty gunshots to bring down. At a Pima village, the Mormons traded buttons from their clothes for corn cakes, and old clothing for corn, beans, and molasses. Some men, having traded their only shirts, wrapped themselves in blankets. A private named Allen who went missing for five days was found alive, stripped by Indians of everything, including his knife, and reduced to eating a dead horse "in the fashion of a wolf."

Since the only enemy that might have contested their march, a two-hundred-man Mexican garrison at Tucson, evacuated the city as they approached it, the Mormons' sole remaining worry was about persevering in the harsh desert country. To reduce the burden on mules and wagons, Cooke discarded all the tent poles and some of the tents, assigning nine men to each remaining tent, now supported by muskets.

The Mormons were consumed by the quest for the scarce water; they once dug ten feet into the sand to get it. They marched sixty miles in two days without any water at all, as their mules fell dead around them. "We were all weary & fatigued, hungry, nearly naked & barefoot but our burning thirst drowned every other suffering," wrote a volunteer. "None but ourselves will ever know how much we suffer," dolefully observed Henry G. Boyle. Yet, even though hungry and thirsty, the men at nighttime danced to fiddle music.

• • •

Because Kit Carson knew where to find water, Kearny's dragoons did not suffer from thirst, but they faced a more immediate threat in early December, after crossing California's coastal mountains in the snow: the threat of combat. At Warner's Ranch on the night of December 5, the expeditioners met an American reconnaissance party sent from San Diego by Commodore Robert Stockton—thirty-five Marines and sailors commanded by Captain Archibald Gillespie, President Polk's former emissary. Gillespie informed Kearny that 160 Mexican-Californian soldiers were camped several miles away near San Pasqual ranch.

DECEMBER 6, 1846: SAN PASQUAL

Kearny impetuously threw his weary little army into motion. By 2 A.M., his one hundred dragoons, reinforced by Gillespie's thirty-five men and their brass 4-pounder, were on the march in a cold rain. Then the storm ended, the sky cleared, and a bright moon lighted their way. From the snow-covered mountains, a freezing wind swept down on the drenched men, whose hands became so numb that only with difficulty could they grasp their bridle reins.

They reached the enemy camp at dawn. The Mexican-Californians, led by Andre Pico, the brother of former Governor Pio Pico, were mounted, armed, and waiting.

Strategy and tactics went by the board in the Americans' excitement, after marching all the way from Kansas, at finally meeting the enemy. Captain

Abraham Johnston and the advance guard recklessly charged. Kearny and the others set off after them. The Mexican-Californians stood their ground long enough to get off several volleys, killing Johnston with a bullet to the head, and then galloped away, with Johnston's next-in-command, Captain Benjamin Moore, and forty dragoons in hot pursuit.

Borrowing a favorite tactic of Indian war parties, 150 of Pico's lancers suddenly stopped, whirled around, and charged Moore's men, who, the lancers had observed, had ridden far ahead of the rest of Kearny's force. The Mexican-Californians wielded their nine-foot lances with terrible effect. Moore fell mortally wounded. Gillespie was struck from behind, knocked off his horse, and lanced through his upper back. When he turned toward his assailant, another lancer struck him in the mouth, cutting his lip and breaking a front tooth. Somehow, Gillespie managed to "cut my way out of the crowd" to the howitzer that had arrived with the rest of Kearny's men. After a brief brawl between Pico's men and the main American force with pistols, rifles, swords, and lances, the howitzer went into action, and the enemy withdrew. Eighteen dragoons lay dead, and fifteen were wounded, including Kearny. Pico's lancers suffered just twelve casualties, none fatal.

• • •

It was a rare Mexican victory in a war in which Americans had won every battle. Kearny had plunged shivering, exhausted men into a battle against an enemy of unknown strength. Kearny later claimed that he attacked because Kit Carson had assured him that the Mexican-Californians would flee when they saw his advance guard. But Johnston's vanguard, ordered to advance at a trot, had instead charged at a gallop. Justin Smith, the preeminent Mexican War historian of the early twentieth century, believed that Kearny could have marched into San Diego without any losses if he had used his howitzers to keep the enemy at bay.

The dragoons limped off the battlefield with six ambulances full of wounded men, many of them bleeding from multiple lance wounds. As Dr. John S. Griffin treated the men's wounds, he was struck by how the lancers had systematically aimed for the Americans' kidneys. After driving the Mexican-Californians from a hill, the Americans buried their dead there in a mass grave.

• • •

Pico had received fresh troops, and his men now blocked all of the roads between Kearny and San Diego, twenty-nine miles away. Kit Carson, a Lieutenant Beale of the Navy, and an Indian scout volunteered to go to San Diego for help. "We took our shoes off and fastened them under our belts" to move silently, wrote Carson, and they then crawled for two miles, sometimes a mere twenty yards from Mexican sentinels. While they avoided detection, they lost their shoes, and "had to travel barefooted over a country covered with prickly pear and rocks."

Wary of the American howitzers, the Mexican-Californians didn't risk an attack. They drove horses through Kearny's camp in an attempt to run off the dragoons' mounts; the Americans shot several of Pico's horses and made a "gravy soup."

• • •

Two days after Carson's party slipped into the hills, no relief force had yet arrived from San Diego, and Kearny concluded that Carson and his companions had been captured. He resolved to fight his way to San Diego with the wounded. Everything unessential was burned in preparation for the breakout.

Like an answered prayer, two hundred Marines and sailors from the USS *Portsmouth* in San Diego that night marched into Kearny's camp; Carson had gotten through after all. The relief troops were shocked by the "pitiable condition" of Kearny's troops, "nearly naked, and without tents, living on mule meat and parched wheat."

Pico's soldiers melted away. The battered Kearny expedition and its Marine–Navy escort reached San Diego on December 12.

• • •

Nearly shoeless, half-starved, and suffering greatly from thirst, the Mormons reached Palm Springs, California, on January 17. To alleviate their hunger pangs, they gnawed on their leather belts; to relieve their thirst, they sucked on small stones. For footwear, they had been compelled to adopt "every expedient, such as rawhide moccasins and sandals, and even wrapping their feet in pieces of woolen and cotton cloth," reported Colonel Cooke. Just five wagons remained. When the flour ran out, there was only beef left to eat. As they neared San Diego, heavy rains and winds lashed them and blew down their tents at night. Soaked and miserable, they continued on. On January 27, their sagging spirits were suddenly buoyed by their first glimpse of the Pacific Ocean. "It was so calm," wrote Cooke, "that it shone as a mirror." Two days later, the Mormon Battalion marched into San Diego.

The 317 members of the Mormon Battalion that reached California disbanded in July 1847 without ever having seen combat. The Mormon Battalion's wages—at their final mustering-out, each received $31.50—helped finance the great

Mormon migration whose destination was the valley of the Great Salt Lake, and not California, as President Polk had initially hoped. Many Mormon Battalion veterans left California to join Brigham Young there, while seventy-nine reenlisted. Others joined 238 Mormons who had debarked at Yerba Buena from the USS *Brooklyn,* the first settlers to land in California after it became a U.S. possession.

• • •

After discussions with Captain Gillespie and Commodore Stockton, Kearny surely regretted having sent two hundred of his dragoons back to Santa Fe. California was anything but secured; in fact, Los Angeles was occupied by defiant Mexican-Californians.

When Stockton had taken command in July 1846, Colonel John Frémont, Gillespie, and the California Battalion had sailed to San Diego on the *Cyane,* intending to interdict rumored attempts by Mexico to resupply the Mexican-Californians. But they learned that Mexico was sending no aid. Leaving Gillespie and a small force at San Diego, Frémont marched north with 120 men, as Stockton sailed to Santa Barbara on the *Congress.*

In mid-August, Stockton and Frémont had seized Los Angeles, after its evacuation by Comandante General Jose Castro and Governor Pio Pico, who had suspended their civil war without yet sending troops against the Americans. Believing resistance was at an end, Stockton appointed Gillespie commander of the Southern Department of California and sent him to Los Angeles with fifty men. Frémont, placed in charge of the Northern Department, returned to Monterey with Stockton and the rest of the California Battalion.

But Stockton had misread the mood of the Los Angelinos who, unlike most other Californians, were not reconciled to the American occupation. Gillespie was understandably nervous about governing a restive city of fifteen hundred with just fifty troops, and the Los Angelinos were insulted by his force's diminutive size. Gillespie adopted stern measures to maintain control—a strict curfew, a crackdown on disorder, and exiling troublemakers caught arousing the populace against him.

The repressive measures backfired, and on September 23, Lieutenant Colonel Jose Maria Flores led a city-wide revolt. Besieged at Government House and Fort Hill, Gillespie and his tiny force fought the six hundred insurgents to a standstill. On September 29, he consented to an armistice that permitted the Americans to leave the city with their muskets and pistols. They marched out of Los Angeles with their flags flying.

Stockton dispatched Captain William M. Mervine and the *Savannah* to recapture

Los Angeles, but Flores's men and their single artillery piece repelled Mervine and Gillespie's combined landing force, which had neither cannons nor cavalry. A second attempt to recapture the city also failed. Stockton transferred his headquarters to San Diego, where he and Kearny began planning a campaign to reoccupy Los Angeles and end the California war.

JANUARY 1847: SANTA FE

A grim Colonel Sterling Price led a contingent of Second Mounted Missourians, a field artillery battery, and a clattering cavalcade of supply wagons and mules through Santa Fe's narrow streets. Exiting town, they rode north into the Sangre de Cristo Mountains, buried in deep midwinter snows, to Taos, which had exploded in a bloody rebellion.

Insurgent New Mexicans and Pueblo Indians had killed Governor Charles Bent and five other government officials and had seized the city. On the same day, January 19, seven Americans were murdered at Arroyo Hondo, and two more on the Colorado River. "It appeared to be the object of the insurrectionists to put to death every American and every Mexican who had accepted office under the American government," noted Price.

Hundreds of insurgents were on the move. Price and his 350 men were determined to put down the rebellion.

Suffering from the cold and even from frostbite, the dragoons broke trail through the deep mountain snow for the cannons and wagons. At Cañada, insurgents held the heights until Captain Felix St. Vrain's cavalry and four howitzers drove them off, leaving thirty-six enemy dead on the field. The timely arrival of Captain James Burgwin and 130 men from the U.S. First Dragoons—some of the troops sent back to Santa Fe by Kearny—increased Price's force to 480 men, just as seven hundred insurgents pounced on the column at a mountain pass near Embudo. Burgwin's dragoons counterattacked, killing 20 men.

Hundreds of insurgents made a stand at Taos, a walled town that they had also fortified. Price launched a full-scale infantry and artillery attack against a heavily defended church that, if captured, would give the Americans access to the entire town. For four hours, the insurgents fiercely repelled all assaults. Captain Burgwin fell mortally wounded. In frustration, American gunners placed a 6-pounder gun sixty yards from the church and blew the door apart. The Americans stormed inside and fanned out through the town. Dragoons pursued the fleeing insurgents into the mountains, killing fifty-one of them.

Price's campaign, which cost the lives of seven Americans and at least 150 insurgents, broke the back of the rebellion. Of the enemy ringleaders, two were killed in action, one was hanged, and one was shot dead while in custody. The insurgency continued fitfully until July, when the arrival of more Missouri volunteers increased the size of Price's force to three thousand men.

JANUARY 8, 1847, 2:30 P.M.: OUTSIDE LOS ANGELES

On the San Gabriel River's northern bank, the Mexican-Californian scouts had formed a line of battle with which to meet the Americans. On the high ground behind them were massed another six hundred mounted enemy troops, armed with carbines, pistols, and lances. Two days earlier, Lieutenant Colonel Jose Flores's representatives, under a white flag, had proposed a peace treaty, but Commodore John Stockton had peremptorily rejected the overture. Flores was a paroled prisoner of war who had broken his parole and was now "a rebel in arms," declared Stockton, adding: "If I caught him I would have him shot."

Now, pausing only to fire a few artillery rounds across the river—Stockton himself manned one gun—six hundred U.S. soldiers, Marines, and sailors plunged into the San Gabriel's knee-deep water. As the Americans struggled across the fifty yards of soft river bottom that sucked at their boots, the Mexican-Californians "made the water fly" with grapeshot and round shot.

Gaining the northern riverbank, the Americans threw themselves into a square just in time to repel an enemy cavalry charge. Then, with Stockton's gunners blazing away and the Americans shouting "New Orleans!"—an invocation of Andrew Jackson's incandescent victory over the British on this same day in 1815—they charged the hill. "We . . . topped it & ran our friends the Mexicans clearly out of the field," wrote Dr. John Griffin.

Flores's cavalry again counterattacked, but the Americans fired a volley at seventy yards that stopped the attack cold. The Mexican-Californians carried away their casualties and withdrew toward Los Angeles. During the ninety-minute fight, one American was killed and eight wounded. The Americans camped that night on the heights they had captured. Momentarily forgotten in the glow of victory was the command crisis that had surfaced ten days earlier in San Diego.

• • •

Kearny believed that his orders to take charge of land operations and form a civil government made him the senior commander. But Stockton insisted that his claim was stronger, pointing to his six-month tenure as military commander and his year-old instructions from the Navy Secretary to establish a civil government. New naval orders written November 5 would have clarified matters: they placed Kearny in charge of land operations and civil affairs. But the orders had not yet reached Stockton.

With neither man willing to cede authority to the other, Stockton, whose men comprised 85 percent of the mixed force, became its presumptive commander. But the dispute was unresolved, and soon it would erupt again, causing lasting hard feelings and tarnishing reputations.

JANUARY 9, 1847: OUTSIDE LOS ANGELES

Colonel Flores's force, reduced to just three hundred effectives by casualties and desertions, anxiously watched the cloud of dust that signaled the approach of Stockton's army. The Mexican-Californians harried the Americans with their "long guns" and deployed into a horseshoe-shaped defensive position on a mesa. Their cavalrymen, wearing white bands on their hats so they could identify one another, flung themselves against the American left flank and rear. "They were mounted on elegant horses," observed Marine Lieutenant Henry Bulls Watson, "and are without exception the best horsemen in the world." The Americans met them with sheets of musket fire and grapeshot that emptied many of the Californians' saddles. Without dismounting, Flores's horsemen stripped the dead horses of saddles and bridles, and then rode off with them and their dead and wounded, as Stockton's men watched in grudging admiration.

Among the five Americans wounded that day was Captain Gillespie, shot in the right hip. He had commanded the rearguard, even though he was still recovering from the wounds he had suffered at San Pasqual. In spite of his injuries, Gillespie on January 10 performed the honor of raising the U.S. flag over Los Angeles's Government House, the building that he had been compelled to evacuate three months earlier.

The Americans had fought and won the last battle of the California campaign.

• • •

But where was John Frémont, commander of California's Northern Department? Ordered in October to lead his men south to a rendezvous with Stockton, Frémont had spent weeks in Monterey raising troops. Then he had unaccountably *marched,* rather than sailed, to Los Angeles, even though Stockton had dispatched the *Savannah* to Monterey for the express purpose of transporting Frémont's four hundred men and three guns. Reaching Mission San Fernando two days after Los Angeles's reoccupation, Frémont encountered the remnants of Flores's broken army. Flores's men requested a surrender parley.

Without the authority to do so, Frémont signed a generous treaty granting the insurgents the amnesty and protection Stockton had refused them a week earlier. The Cahuenga Capitulation of January 13 permitted the enemy combatants to return home if they surrendered their arms and agreed to obey American laws.

When Frémont sent the treaty to Stockton in Los Angeles, with instructions to the courier to find out who was in charge there (Stockton, the courier reported), the displeased commodore dryly remarked: "It seems that not being able to negotiate with me, and having lost the battles of the 8th and 9th, they met Colonel Frémont . . . who[,] not knowing what had occurred, he [*sic*] entered into capitulation with them."

Stockton did not hold it against Frémont; in fact, he named Frémont governor of California, and Gillespie secretary of state, believing them "eminently qualified to perform the duties." Kearny promptly challenged Stockton's authority to organize a civil government, and the dispute that had simmered during the Los Angeles battles boiled over.

Stockton suspended Kearny from all commands except for his hundred dragoons. Kearny's officers, who witnessed the power struggle in mute rage, derogated Stockton as "a low, trifling, truckling politician, regarded with as much contempt by the officers of the Navy, as by those of the Army."

Outmaneuvered, Kearny returned to San Diego to await the arrival in California of the new Pacific Squadron commander, fifty-six-year-old Commodore William Branford Shubrick. Kearny hoped that Shubrick would recognize the authority invested in him that Stockton and Frémont had chosen to ignore.

• • •

The First New York Volunteers sailed into San Francisco Bay, only to discover that the California fighting was over. The regiment's 760 officers and men were dispersed among garrisons and units from Sonoma to Los Angeles. They impatiently awaited the war's end so that they could settle down in California to civilian pursuits. Colonization, of course, was the reason why the New Yorkers had made the six-month voyage around Cape Horn, just as it had been the real purpose of the Mormon Battalion.

Colonel Jonathan D. Stevenson, the regiment's commander, had been beset by crises at every turn. Unlike the Mormon Battalion, which marched into the Southwest without attracting attention, the New York volunteers were raised in the summer of 1846 in the middle of the nation's fastest-growing city. The fact that the volunteers' mechanical skills seemed to be prized above their physical soundness aroused suspicions about the regiment's real object, although President Polk had not yet said anything publicly about obtaining California. Some New Yorkers, disgruntled at not obtaining places in the regiment, filed a lawsuit to strip Stevenson of his commission and stop the regiment from sailing. But the three ships carrying the First New York cast off from their moorages before the sheriff, racing to the dock, was able to serve the papers.

At sea, the rowdy volunteers aboard the *Susan Drew* threatened mutiny. To keep order on the *Thomas H. Perkins,* Stevenson punched a soldier, and in desperation threatened to blow up the powder magazine. In Rio de Janeiro, Stevenson became the troublemaker, nearly causing a diplomatic breach with Brazil when he threatened military action if Brazil did not release from custody some U.S. sailors who were under arrest. At Valparaiso, Chile, the troops again threatened mutiny until their officers granted them one day ashore. Stevenson must have been relieved to reach California in March 1847, and to watch his regiment being parceled out to other units.

Arriving in California six weeks ahead of the New York regiment was its artillery detachment, the U.S. Third Artillery, which included Lieutenant William Tecumseh Sherman. During their voyage, the Army regulars had dismayed the superstitious sailors by baiting fishing lines with pork to reel in albatrosses off Cape Horn. The sailors believed that harming an albatross would bring a curse.

• • •

Stockton's self-proclaimed suzerainty over California's civil and military affairs ended with Commodore Shubrick's arrival at Monterey. Shubrick had received his sailing orders the previous August, four days after Navy Secretary Bancroft had rebuked Commodore Sloat for not quickly seizing California's ports. After meeting with Kearny, Shubrick officially recognized the brigadier general's authority ashore, while retaining naval authority over California's ports and customs. Stockton sailed home.

Left in the lurch was John C. Frémont. Kearny ordered Frémont to muster the California Battalion into federal service, and he replaced him as governor with

Colonel Richard B. Mason. Frémont dragged his feet and only agreed to cooperate after an interview with Kearny. Then he quarreled with Mason and challenged him to a duel, never consummated. Kearny turned down Frémont's requests to join an American regiment in Mexico, or to return home.

• • •

War Secretary William Marcy summoned Kearny and Frémont to Washington, where the Kearny-Stockton-Frémont contretemps was contributing to the growing criticism of Polk's prosecution of the war. On May 31, the adversaries and the much-traveled dragoons began the long ride from California to Fort Leavenworth.

In the Sierra Nevada, the soldiers discovered cannibalized human remains at Lake Truckee—some of the thirty-five Donner party members who had perished in the recent deep winter snows. They buried the bodies.

On August 22, 1847, the weather-beaten travelers reached Fort Leavenworth, where Kearny obtained a measure of revenge by promptly placing the famous explorer under arrest. Kearny charged Frémont with mutiny, disobeying orders, and conduct prejudicial to good order.

Senator Thomas Hart Benton demanded a court martial to clear his son-in-law's name. Frémont "was brought home a prisoner . . . to expiate the offence of having entered the army without passing through the gate of the Military Academy," Benton outrageously asserted. The senator would never forgive Kearny, carrying on a vendetta to blacken the general's name until Kearny's untimely death in 1848.

The imbroglio prompted the Whig *National Intelligencer* to question whether the Polk administration was up to the job of administering conquered Mexican provinces. "If the Administration has so much trouble with California, what will it do when it comes to have a dozen Mexican provinces to look after?"

16

AMERICA'S XENOPHON

*"To the astonishment of the world . . . volunteer troops can be depended upon
. . . private citizens can be transformed [by training] into good soldiers."*
—Missouri Senator Thomas Hart Benton

OCTOBER 1846: SANTA FE

Pacifying New Mexico's Indian tribes proved to be the thorniest of the tasks that
Brigadier General Stephen Kearny had set for Colonel Alexander Doniphan. In just a
few weeks, Doniphan had finished the one-hundred-page Kearny Code, and construction of Fort Marcy was nearly completed; cast in the shape of an uneven, eight-
sided star, the fortress made Santa Fe eminently defensible if attacked. And soon,
when Colonel Sterling Price reached Santa Fe with the Second Missouri Mounted
Volunteers, Doniphan would lead the thousand men of the First Missouri Mounted
Regiment to Chihuahua, there joining General John E. Wool's Army of the Center.

Although Price would arrive in a matter of days, Doniphan was postponing his
expedition because the Navajo tribe, the largest in New Mexico with seven thousand members, had failed to come to Santa Fe for a peace council. He had signed
treaties with the Utes, Apaches, and Zunis, and the Pueblos had pledged their
cooperation. But the Navajos continued their bloody raids on the New Mexican
ranchers and traders. In a recent attack on a ranchero, Navajo raiders had killed
seven men, spirited away women and children, and driven off ten thousand livestock. Learning of the Navajos' refusal to parley, Kearny, on his way to California, sent orders to Doniphan to subdue the tribe.

Unlike their settled agrarian descendants, the Navajos of 1846 were nomadic shepherds. Whenever they needed new horses, or additional livestock, they took them from the New Mexican rancheros and then vanished like smoke into the northern New Mexico mountains. The Navajos were understandably reluctant to sign a treaty that would require them to stop their raids and upset their entire way of life.

To bring the Navajos to heel, Doniphan sent companies under Major William Gilpin and Lieutenant Colonel Congreve Jackson by different routes into the rugged mountains to request that tribal leaders meet him at Ojo del Oso—Bear Springs. Doniphan, leading a third column to the rendezvous, intended to compel the Navajos to stop their depredations.

• • •

The Missouri frontier lawyer who would be lionized as "the Xenophon of the age" embodied the best qualities of the Mexican War volunteers: Alexander Doniphan was brave, energetic, cheerfully independent, stoical, and supremely confident that he would triumph over daunting odds. Born in Kentucky in 1808 and the youngest of ten children, he graduated with honors in 1826 from Augusta College, studied law, and in 1833 moved to Liberty, Missouri, to practice criminal law. He defended the so-called Mormon "Destroying Angel," Orrin Rockwell, accused of attempting to assassinate retired Governor Lillburn Boggs, who had driven the Mormons from Missouri (the jury convicted Rockwell but sentenced him to just five minutes in jail). As a militia leader during Missouri's war against the Mormons, Doniphan had won the Mormons' respect by refusing an order to execute Joseph Smith and several Disciples. Much like his men, Doniphan had no regular Army training—fifty-one of the Mexican War's other sixty-two volunteer colonels had none, either.

Doniphan stood out in a crowd with his striking orange-red hair, matching beard, and imposing height. When Doniphan met Abraham Lincoln, who, like Doniphan, stood six-foot-four when the average for men was five-five, the two stood back-to-back to determine who was taller. Doniphan reportedly topped Lincoln by a half inch, prompting Lincoln to quip that Doniphan was "the only man connected with any great military enterprise who ever came up in his looks to my expectations."

Doniphan's mounted volunteers came from ten counties spanning mid-Missouri from St. Louis to Fort Leavenworth, and they represented some of the state's most prominent families. They were armed with .52-caliber breech-loading Hall's Rifles, which were accurate to 250 yards; and the longer-range, lever-action, muzzle-loading U.S. Model 1841 Whitney Rifle, nicknamed the "Mississippi Rifle" because it was the adopted weapon of Colonel Jefferson Davis's regiment.

• • •

Navajo scouts shadowed Doniphan's three columns as they rode deep into the mountains. The November snows tested the hardiness of the Missourians who, still wearing their summer cotton clothing, often preferred to sit up all night beside a campfire than to lie on the frozen ground. They broke trail for their horses and mules through the waist-deep snow that blanketed the soaring mountains, hiked through dense pine forests, and followed the courses of icy streams that had scoured canyons through the tilted bedrock. When their rations ran low, they ate pumpkins and parched corn left behind by the Indians.

Finally, they encountered the Navajos, who welcomed them to their villages. The Missourians traded their thin cotton clothing for buckskin and discovered that the surprisingly egalitarian Navajo women bartered like the men (but would not part with their hand-spun blankets, for any sum), saddled their own horses, and played a dicelike game with bones. The Americans' estimation of the generous Navajos rose steadily.

A volunteer captain described the Navajos as "a warlike people . . . celebrated for their intelligence and good order . . . a highly civilized people, being, as a nation, of a higher order of beings than the mass of their neighbors, the Mexicans." Private Jacob Robinson had never seen such superb horsemen. "The Arab cannot excel the Nebajo [*sic*] in horsemanship. . . . They are undoubtedly the most enlightened tribe of wild Indians inhabiting this continent."

The Missourians broadcast Doniphan's summons to parley at Ojo del Oso throughout the Navajo nation, with Major Gilpin even riding into the future state of Colorado to notify tribal leaders.

• • •

With some trepidation, the volunteers approached Ojo del Oso deep in the mountains on November 21. Would the Navajos fight, or talk? The Missourians found five hundred Navajos and their tribal leaders waiting peaceably.

Doniphan explained to them that America always "first offered the olive branch, and, if that were rejected, then powder, bullet, and the steel." A Navajo headman, Zarcillos Largos, professed puzzlement at Doniphan's bellicosity; the

Navajos, just like the Americans, were at war with the Mexicans. "You now turn upon us for attempting to do what you have done yourselves." America was "interfering in *our* war, begun long before you got here."

Using lawyerly persuasion, and letting the presence of 330 well-armed volunteers have its effect, Doniphan convinced the Navajos that they should sign the Treaty of Ojo del Oso and consent to U.S. territorial rule.

The Missourians returned to Santa Fe to complete their preparations for the expedition to Chihuahua.

DECEMBER 1846: SOUTHERN NEW MEXICO

In the vanguard of the Doniphan expedition, which was strung out over a great distance because separate companies embarked from Santa Fe whenever they reached readiness, were the so-called Chihuahua Rangers. Lieutenant Colonel David D. Mitchell of the Second Missouri Mounted Volunteers led this new reconnaissance force, which included ten volunteers from each company under Doniphan, as well as some of the Laclede Rangers.

Mitchell sighted Mexican troops north of El Paso. Among them were the four hundred Chihuahua dragoons sent, too late, to aid New Mexico Governor Manuel Armijo. The Mexicans were not marching on Doniphan, but they were not withdrawing, either.

Still worried about the volunteers having just two weeks of formal military training when he was sending them eight hundred miles into enemy territory, Kearny had assigned three regular Army officers, all West Point graduates, to advise Doniphan: Captain Philip Thompson of the U.S. First Dragoons; First Lieutenant Charles F. Wooster, an artillery officer; and Second Lieutenant Bezaleel W. Armstrong, of the U.S. Second Dragoons. George Ruxton, a former British Army officer who was accompanying the Doniphan expedition, undoubtedly applauded Kearny's prudence. He thought highly of West Point's graduates and thoroughly disapproved of the "ragged and dirty" volunteers, whose "almost total want of discipline was apparent in everything," and who, he was certain, would never be the equal of regular Army troops.

The volunteers knew that they must march through the dreaded Jornado del Muerto ("Dead Man's Journey"), a waterless, sixty-mile passage between two bends of the Rio Grande. Here the unlucky Texans of the disastrous Santa Fe expedition of 1841 had been force-marched by their Mexican captors, and had been summarily executed if they did not keep up. Some of the Missourians filled their canteens with whiskey in the hope of making the punishing march as painless as possible. The whiskey worked fine until it was gone; then the imbibers were racked by thirst and hangovers. The expeditioners crossed the high desert in two days.

On Christmas Eve, the Missourians were just fifty miles from El Paso.

CHRISTMAS DAY, 1846: BRAZITO

The volunteers awoke in a celebratory mood, firing their rifles into the air and singing. They saddled up and rode eighteen miles to Brazito, the "little arm," an oxbow of the Rio Grande. Brazito had potable water, and, it being Christmas Day, Doniphan ended the day's march there about 1 P.M.

The colonel and some officers were playing the card game "three-trick loo" when a reconnaissance party galloped into camp to report approaching Mexican troops. Doniphan joined a group of volunteers watching "an immense cloud of dust" in the distance. He flung down his cards, grasped his saber and said, "Boys, I had an invincible hand, but I'll be d—d if I don't have to play it out in steel now."

Because the Missourians had fanned out in search of firewood and water, and forage for their mounts, in the present emergency Doniphan was able to muster only five hundred men. They had no cannons, although a battery was supposed to be coming from Santa Fe. Doniphan threw his small force into a crescent blocking the road, and awaited the Mexicans.

• • •

Confident of victory, Major Antonio Ponce de Leon advanced with a howitzer and eleven hundred men—five hundred Mexican Army lancers and dragoons, one hundred infantrymen, and five hundred militiamen. The Americans ruefully compared their motley appearance with the dragoons' scarlet-trimmed green jackets, blue trousers, and tall, plumed, brass-plated hats.

A mounted Mexican officer emerged from the long enemy line of glittering swords and lances, riding toward the Americans with a black flag. Two skulls and crossbones were painted on one side of the flag, and on the other were the words "Libertad o Muerte" ("Liberty or Death"). Lieutenant Manuel Lara demanded that the Missourians surrender and that Doniphan come with him to parley. Through Thomas Caldwell, an American merchant who acted as interpreter, Doniphan refused. Lara replied that his soldiers would then make Doniphan a prisoner. "Charge and be damned!" Caldwell shot back.

Ponce de Leon's cavalry, lancers, infantry, and militiamen now advanced on the Missourians. Doniphan walked among his men, shouting encouragement.

The Mexicans fired one volley, and then another. After each, Doniphan ordered his men to lie or kneel in the grass and hold their fire. Believing they had inflicted heavy casualties, the enemy surged forward, crying "Bueno! Bueno!" The enemy horse soldiers, now one hundred yards from Doniphan's men, got off a ragged pistol volley that wounded several Americans. "Fire," Doniphan shouted. As one, his men rose and poured two volleys into the Mexicans, tearing gaping holes in their line. Simultaneously, the traders crouching behind their wagons loosed a "sheeting fire" that scattered the attacking lancers. Captain John Reid and fourteen mounted troops rushed an enemy 6-pounder gun and captured it. The Mexicans ran away "as fast as possible." The battle was over thirty minutes after it began.

• • •

Wounded in his left side, Ponce de Leon futilely tried to rally his men and then joined the retreat, stunned by what had happened. His troops had responded enthusiastically when he had exhorted them before the battle to dedicate the certain victory to General Antonio Lopez de Santa Anna and Mexico. But as they advanced on the Americans, some soldiers began slipping away. The Missourians' volleys threw his army into a panic; even the dragoons had "turned tail." Ponce de Leon officially reported eleven killed and seventeen wounded, but American estimates placed the number of enemy dead alone at more than thirty.

The Americans' seven minor casualties failed to mar what had become a "merry Christmas frolic." In their precipitate flight, the Mexicans had left food and skins of wine strewn about the battlefield. "We ate their bread, drank their wine, and went to bed as comfortable as if no Mexicans were near."

American mounted troops pursued some Mexican dragoons into the mountains. A band of Navajos that had watched the battle killed the Mexicans, coveting their bright uniforms and weapons.

Two days later, El Paso's leading citizens surrendered the city to Doniphan.

FALL 1846: THE ARMY OF THE CENTER

General John E. Wool's fourteen-hundred-man Army of the Center, which Doniphan anticipated joining in the city of Chihuahua, had gotten sidetracked.

Wool had marched south from San Antonio on September 26, with the objective of capturing the city and its province. With General Zachary Taylor occupying Monterrey and Saltillo, the possession of Chihuahua would secure a large swath of northern Mexico. Moreover, traders who did business in the city of Chihuahua, northern Mexico's principal commercial crossroad, reported that residents were unhappy with the Mexican government and would welcome American occupation.

• • •

Only Gaines, Scott, and Taylor were senior to Wool, whose Army service, as did theirs, dated to the War of 1812. As a young captain, Wool had been severely wounded while fighting beside Scott at Queenston Heights. After he recovered from his wounds, Wool had led a small force that delayed twelve thousand British troops from reaching Plattsburgh, New York, until the main American army arrived and won a great victory.

Now sixty-two years old, Wool was an active, demanding officer—some called him a high-strung martinet—who slept little while campaigning and was apt to inspect his outposts at any hour. A spare man of medium height, Wool was deeply religious and hated profanity. "He was always in uniform, with a leather stock about his neck and epaulets on his shoulders," observed Lew Wallace, a volunteer officer from Indiana who would later write *Ben Hur.* It was widely accepted as fact that Wool "received visitors capped, booted, and spurred; that he began business at daybreak and ate with his sword on; some believed he even slept with his sword," noted Wallace. "In short, there was no limit to the general's unpopularity."

• • •

Captain Robert E. Lee, a thirty-nine-year-old Army engineer whose father was the "Light Horse Harry" Lee of Revolutionary War fame, welcomed his reassignment to Wool's expedition. Lee was one of the Army's best engineers. At Fort Hamilton in Brooklyn, New York, he had supervised repairs and renovations to the facilities lining the four-mile-long Narrows between Upper and Lower New York bays. He now commanded a company of pioneers but was also expected to lead reconnaissance missions—a calling for which Lee would display astonishing proficiency.

• • •

Wool marched to the Rio Grande with regulars from Colonel William Harney's Second U.S. Dragoons, the Fourth U.S. Artillery, and the Sixth U.S. Infantry, and volunteers from Kentucky, Arkansas, and Illinois. Because of reports that Mexican troops were massing along the Rio Grande, the Army of the Center was on high alert when it approached the area on October 9. There were no enemy troops, but the men were eager for a fight. "There has been a great whetting of knives, grinding of swords, and sharpening of bayonets ever since we reached the river," Captain Lee wryly noted.

As it was for Kearny's expeditioners and Doniphan's troops in the Jornada del Muerte, finding water became surpassingly important to Wool's men as they advanced into Mexico. "The suffering for want of water in crossing these plains is beyond all conception of the mind," observed Jonathan Buhoup of the Arkansas Cavalry. The army "marched in the sulphur heat through brush of all the different thorns in the world," noted Second Lieutenant Adolph Engelmann of the Second Illinois, and paraphrasing a popular saying about Mexico, he added: "All plants here have thorns, all animals sting or [have] horns, and all men carry weapons and deceive each other and themselves."

Wool enacted strict rules of conduct for the Army of the Center. He would not abide looting, foraging, vandalism, or needless bloodshed. Before new orders came from Washington announcing a harsher policy of expropriation, his men were required to pay for anything procured from Mexican civilians, although Wool fussily preferred that they rely on what they carried with them. He drilled the troops almost daily, demanded regular uniform inspections, and made no secret of his belief that the volunteer officers were "not worth a damn." The volunteer officers, resenting his attitude toward them and his pettiness, nicknamed him "the big Corporal."

At San Rosa, 105 miles from the Rio Grande, welcoming citizens handed out cakes and fruit to the Americans. Reports reached them that Mexican forces had left Chihuahua and were marching south to join Santa Anna at San Luis Potosi. Wool asked General Taylor to permit him to abandon the seemingly pointless expedition, then marched the Army of the Center into Monclova.

Taylor instructed Wool to remain in the city of eight thousand residents until the Monterrey armistice expired. Brigadier General James Shields arrived with Illinois volunteers that had been left behind in San Antonio for lack of wagons, increasing the army's size to more than two thousand men. The soldiers drilled, mended their gear, and scouted for Mexican troops. The only enemy unit in the area, twenty-five hundred irregulars commanded by a Colonel Blanco, disbanded without encountering Wool's army.

• • •

After three weeks in Monclova, the Army of the Center resumed its march. At the crossroads town of Parras 180 miles away, the troops paused again while Wool awaited orders from General Taylor. From Parras, Wool either could march 200 miles to Chihuahua by a northwest road, or join Taylor's army at Agua Nueva, 110 miles to the southeast.

• • •

On December 17, the grinding uncertainty ended. In an urgent dispatch from Agua Nueva, General William Worth reported that Santa Anna's army was marching north. Within two hours, Wool's army of two thousand had packed its wagons and broken camp and was on the road to Agua Nueva. Each day for the next three days, the army was rousted at 1:00 A.M. to resume its urgent journey, covering thirty-one miles on the first day and thirty-seven miles on the second. The dragoons began calling the infantrymen "the sleepwalkers," and complained that they were killing their horses. Captain Robert E. Lee seemed to be always in the saddle, scouting far ahead; he changed horses every fifty miles, the distance that he rode in a night. So as not to signal his approach to the enemy, Wool banned the beating of drums at reveille and retreat.

Four days after Worth's cryptic message had reached Wool, the Army of the Center completed its 110-mile march to Agua Nueva. Wool and Worth moved their combined force to a more defensible position in Saltillo, 21 miles to the north. There they learned that Santa Anna's army was not advancing on them after all.

The Army of the Center had marched seven hundred miles without firing a shot in anger. "They have marched farther than any other American troops, but have not seen any enemy," Lieutenant Adolph Engelmann wrote home in a letter also containing exotic plant seeds.

But the forced marches across deserts, prairies, mountains, and rivers had transformed the volunteers and regulars into a tough fighting army, disciplined and inured to hardship. In the weeks ahead, it would be tested as never before.

FEBRUARY 1847: WITH DONIPHAN

Dispatches from Santa Fe arrived on February 15 informing Colonel Doniphan of General Wool's lightning march to Saltillo and the abandonment of his expedition to Chihuahua. With his orders to join Wool in Chihuahua now irrelevant, Doniphan was free to return to El Paso or Santa Fe to await the expiration of his regiment's one-year enlistment, and then to go home. But having traveled two thirds of the way to Chihuahua with seven thousand livestock and hundreds of traders, wagoners, and mule skinners carrying $1 million worth of merchandise in four hundred wagons, Doniphan and his officers preferred to complete their mission, Wool or no Wool. The long-awaited artillery batteries commanded by Major Meriwether Lewis Clark and Captain Richard H. Weightman had finally caught up with Doniphan in El Paso on February 1, adding 130 artillerymen, four 6-pounder cannons, and two 12-pounder howitzers. Doniphan's 1,100-man Army of the West was less than two weeks away from Chihuahua. There would be no turning back.

The Chihuahua Trail was dry and dangerous. While scouts ranged ahead to watch for Mexican troops, Apaches raided laggard traders, one time driving away 250 mules and sixty oxen, later recovered by a patrol. Watering holes were maddeningly scarce. After forty-eight hours without fresh water, soldiers greedily drank from a sulfurous spring ringed by mule and horse carcasses. The respite from thirst was temporary, though; soon, the troops were despairing in their great thirst, and the mules and horses were "crying piteously for water." With the situation looking hopeless, a storm suddenly drenched the mountains, sending fresh water rushing down the arroyos to the thirsty soldiers and their mounts. Closer to Chihuahua, the army found good water at Laguno de los Patos (Lagoon of the Ducks).

Winds sandblasted the Missourians almost daily, at Carrizal flattening their tents, and on February 25 nearly wiping out the expedition. After embers from a noon cookfire ignited the dry grass, the booming winds fanned the small blaze into "a perfect sea of flames," reaching up to twenty feet in height. The soldiers tried to outrun the prairie fire, but they might as well have tried to outrun the wind. It "came raging and sweeping like a wave," and after a two-mile race, the soldiers could see that the fire was gaining on them. In desperation, the troops parked the cannons and some of the wagons in a lake. Then, forming a long line, they scratched out a thirty-foot firebreak with swords, knives, and broken branches and set a backfire that stopped the flames from burning over them. Whipped by the wind in another direction, the conflagration roared over the mountains.

The next day, Mexican ranchers informed Doniphan's scouts that fifteen hundred enemy troops were dug in at the estate of Angel Trías Álvarez, the governor of Chihuahua Province and a brigadier general of volunteers. But when they reached the Trías ranch, Doniphan's men found only abandoned fortifications. Then news reached them that thousands of Mexican troops had prepared defenses on the heights overlooking the Rio Sacramento, outside the provincial capital, Chihuahua.

FEBRUARY 28, 1847: RIO SACRAMENTO

Hundreds of Chihuahua's citizens, in a festive holiday spirit, had come straight from Sunday Mass to witness the defeat of the Americans. Major General Jose Antonio Heredia's troops had stockpiled handcuffs and rope for the coffle of prisoners they expected to drive to Mexico City. The Mexicans had good reasons to be so confident: Heredia held a four-to-one numerical advantage with his four thousand troops—1,200 cavalrymen, 1,200 infantrymen, 119 artillerymen with ten cannons, and 1,420 local militiamen—and he had carefully chosen the battleground and prepared its defenses. Brigadier General Pedro Garcia Conde, a former Minister of War and one of Mexico's most knowledgeable military men, had known for weeks that Doniphan's army was on its way to Chihuahua and had personally supervised construction of the works, built with the assistance of French engineers.

On the sixty-foot-high plateau that dominated the mile-and-a-half-wide valley and the main river ford, the Mexicans had erected twenty-seven redoubts—five of them large and circular, connected by trenches. Supported by artillery, the redoubts were arrayed in an inverted "U" with the open end facing the advancing Americans. On Heredia's right, his troops were dug in on a ridge that, together with the plateau's bristling defenses, choked off the Chihuahua road where it crossed the river. A fifty-foot-wide, thirty-foot-deep ravine protected the Mexicans' left flank, where Conde had also stationed cavalry to instantly parry any attempted flanking movement.

• • •

Through their field glasses, Colonel Doniphan, his staff officers, and their three regular Army advisers could see for themselves what their reconnaissance patrols had described the night before. But while Garcia Conde had chosen and prepared the ground well, the Americans saw a possible chink in his defenses.

• • •

A Mexican chaplain celebrated Mass for Garcia Conde's soldiers and gave them his blessing. Then the Mexican troops moved into their positions below the plateau and faced the Missourians. The major battle long anticipated by Doniphan and Garcia Conde was about to begin.

Recognizing that mounted troops alone would not win this battle, Doniphan assigned a hundred men to hold hundreds of horses so they would not run away. That left him with 924 troops and six cannons with which to fight the four thousand Mexicans.

(RIGHT) President James K. Polk and First Lady Sarah Childress Polk. (James K. Polk Memorial Association, Columbia, Tennessee)

(BELOW) This daguerreotype of President James K. Polk and his cabinet is the first known photograph taken inside the White House. Standing: Postmaster General Cave Johnson and Navy Secretary George Bancroft. Seated, from left: Attorney General John Y. Mason, War Secretary William Marcy, Polk, and Treasury Secretary Robert J. Walker. Not present is Secretary of State James Buchanan. (James K. Polk Memorial Association, Columbia, Tennessee)

Mexican President and General Antonio Lopez de Santa Anna. (Mexican War Graphics Collection, Special Collections, The University of Texas at Arlington Library, Arlington, Texas [Hereafter MWGC])

General Zachary Taylor. (MWGC)

(RIGHT) General of the Army Winfield Scott. (MWGC)

(BELOW) Major Samuel Ringgold, the field artillery pioneer, lies mortally wounded at Palo Alto. (MWGC)

American troops fight in Monterrey's streets. (MWGC)

Lieutenant Ulysses S. Grant (left), shown with Lieutenant Alexander Hays in 1845. (MWGC)

A rare surviving daguerreotype of U.S. troops in Mexico. General John Wool (foreground, in cape) and his staff ride through Saltillo in 1847. (The Beinecke Rare Book and Manuscript Library, Yale University)

Battle of Buena Vista. (MWGC)

Captain John C. Frémont. (MWGC)

General Stephen W. Kearny.
(MWGC)

Colonel Alexander W. Doniphan. (Kansas State Historical Society)

The amphibious landing at Vera Cruz. (MWGC)

(LEFT) Captain Robert E. Lee. (Cook Collection, Valentine Richmond History Center)

(BELOW) U.S. troops storm Chapultepec. (MWGC)

Before launching his attack, Doniphan made a speech to his men that ended with the confident prediction that they would make their camp that night in the enemy positions now bristling with cannons and bayonets. The Missourians lustily cheered Doniphan's sanguinity.

Then a murmur ran through the ranks: "An omen, an omen." The men gazed into the blue sky, where "slowly and majestically above our heads, sails America's bird, a large bald eagle."

• • •

The Mexicans frowned in puzzlement as the Americans marched toward them in a battle formation that they had never seen before: Doniphan had commandeered 315 traders' wagons and arranged them in the shape of a narrow, rectangular box; amid the wagons and screened by them, the Missourians kept pace on foot, while two hundred horsemen rode around the edges to further block the enemy's view. The clattering, three-mile-long fort on wheels deliberately advanced on the Mexicans' prepared positions.

It abruptly veered off the road to the right—toward the ravine that Garcia Conde believed would safeguard his left flank. Here was the weakness that Doniphan and his subordinates had seen in the enemy defenses. When the caravan reached the long hollow, hundreds of Missouri men with picks and shovels suddenly poured out of the mobile fort; working with incredible speed, they began filling in the ravine. In short order, they built a ramp of dirt and rocks. The Mexicans watched in amazement as Doniphan's men prodded their draft animals and wagons across the earthen bridge.

Too late, General Garcia Conde sent a thousand cavalrymen to stop the attack on his left, while his artillerymen repositioned their batteries. The Missourians reached the high ground first, and Captain Weightman's gunners quickly unlimbered their two twelve-pound howitzers and began firing rapidly into the Mexican horsemen's ranks, "emptying saddles and bowling them over like so many ten pins." The deadly artillery fire forced the enemy cavalry to take cover behind breastworks as the Mexican gunners fired on the Missourians.

Captain Weightman raced ahead with two howitzers, and, it turned out, with only Captain John Reid's mounted troops and virtually no one else—Captain James DeCourcy, Doniphan's adjutant, had galloped down the line shouting incoherent orders, and many men thought he had halted the attack. Weightman's gunners opened fire on the Mexican artillery from fifty yards away. The enemy gunners fired back, and one of their shots took off the head of a horse, spattering the gun crews with blood.

Doniphan, who had been watching the action from his chestnut charger while whittling on a piece of wood, gazed in horror as Captain Reid's men dismounted and began to advance on the redoubts. The Mexicans, unwilling to expose themselves, fired their muskets by holding them over their heads and blindly pulling the triggers. Doniphan covered his face with his hands and groaned, "My God! They're gone! The boys will all be killed!" Then, regaining his composure, Doniphan spurred his horse, rallied the rest of the Missourians, and joined the attack.

The Mexican gunners overshot the advancing Missourians with their plunging fire and instead slaughtered mules and horses in the American rear, nearly ending the life of Private William H. Richardson as he held the reins of eight mules. Seeing a cannon ball coming at him, Richardson leaped from his mount, and the round "passed just over my saddle without injury."

The Missourians overran the Mexicans' central redoubts, shooting, clubbing, and bayoneting the defenders. Weightman's field artillery, firing grapeshot and canister with chain shot, "cut roads" through the fleeing enemy. Two hundred Mexicans who reformed to attempt a counterattack were scattered by Lieutenant Colonel David D. Mitchell's dismounted volunteers.

Mexican lancers attacked the wagons and were beaten back by Major Meriwether Lewis Clark's gunners, and by teamsters and a dozen slaves firing muskets. During this melee, Private Richardson watched an American who was about to be impaled by a Mexican lancer snatch up and hurl a rock, hitting the horseman in the head and dismounting him. The volunteer then "knocked his brains out with a butt of his gun."

An enemy battery on a hill twelve hundred yards away shelled the Missourians in the captured redoubts until Clark's gunners knocked it out. American mounted troops cleared the battery of its gunners and five hundred enemy troops that had rallied around it.

After three hours of fighting, the Mexicans withdrew, leaving behind at least three hundred dead and hundreds of wounded soldiers, many of whom bled to death while awaiting medical treatment. A captured Mexican surgeon refused to attend to his own men.

The traders' unofficial leader, Samuel Owens, who perished while leading a foolhardy frontal assault against the Mexican guns, was the only American killed on the battlefield. Of the eight Missourians wounded in the fighting, three later died.

In their headlong flight, the Mexicans discarded everything except personal effects and the weapons they carried. The Missourians captured all of Heredia's cannons; his ammunition and baggage; thirteen thousand pounds of hard bread; sixteen thousand pounds of dried meat; seven hundred thousand cigarettes; several thousand head of cattle; and thousands of sheep. Major Clark took charge of the black skull-and-crossbones flag displayed by Ponce de Leon's troops at Brazito.

• • •

On March 2, the Army of the West entered Chihuahua with flags flying, as a band played "Yankee Doodle" and "Hail, Columbia." The artillery fired a twenty-eight-gun salute in the main public square. The Missourians attended services for Samuel Owens in the city's massive Gothic cathedral.

Chihuahua's fourteen thousand citizens lived in well-appointed homes on straight, clean, tree-lined streets. Water reached the city through an impressive stone aqueduct. The simple explanation for Chihuahua's obvious prosperity lay just a few miles away—a profusion of silver mines. But the city's wealth attracted not only traders from the north but marauding Apaches from the outlands; in the provincial Secretary of State's office, a wall full of shelves was crammed with letters complaining about Apache attacks and thefts. Soon enough, the Missourians learned for themselves about the Indian depredations. For days, Lieutenant Jack Hinton's patrol pursued Apaches who had rustled oxen and mules before retrieving the livestock and killing one of the Indians.

Initially hospitable, the Chihuahuans grew noticeably cooler toward the Americans after the soldiers expropriated homes for use as their personal quarters and stables for their horses, set up outdoor kitchens on rooftops, and bathed in the public drinking fountain. Susan Magoffin, the wife of trader James Magoffin, disapprovingly observed that the volunteers, "who[,] though good to fight[,] are not careful at how they soil the property of a friend much less an enemy." Undoubtedly contributing to the Missourians' careless behavior was the ready availability of the maguey plant's popular intoxicants—the beerlike fermented pulque, and mescal, the acrid-tasting colorless liquor distilled from pulque.

• • •

While the Missourians rested from their arduous marches, Doniphan and his officers pondered their next move. They had captured Chihuahua. Wool was not
there. Should they join Generals Taylor and Wool, or begin the long journey
home? Doniphan banged his fist on the table and thundered, "I'm for going home
to Sarah and the children!"

But orders arrived on April 23 directing Doniphan to join Wool at Buena
Vista, where Taylor's army had won a great victory the week before Doniphan's triumph at Rio Sacramento. Doniphan's heartfelt declaration, which amused the
tough Missourians and deepened their fondness for him, would have to wait.

The Army of the West returned to the dusty Mexican roads, marching and
riding 535 miles in the springtime heat before reaching Saltillo on May 21.

Wool's troops, who had been eager to see Doniphan's renowned army, were aston-
ished by the Missourians' ragged, wild appearance. They "looked as though they had
not only seen the elephant but the kangaroo, too," observed Jonathan Buhoup of the
Arkansas Cavalry. Frank Edwards conceded that his comrades' beards, matted hair,
and buckskin clothing would have made "Falstaff . . . ashamed of us."

When the regiment passed in review before General John E. Wool, the notorious disciplinarian, the Missourians were dressed more like Mexicans and Indians
than American soldiers, but it couldn't be helped; their own clothing had disinte-
grated months earlier. They presented "a ludicrous sight," ruefully acknowledged
Edwards. Predictably, Wool was affronted by their tatterdemalion appearance, but
he quickly warmed to them and generously praised their feats. Wool's officers led
the Missourians on a tour of the Buena Vista battlefield.

The Missourians had marched across two thousand miles of New Mexico and
Mexico and had fought and won two major battles, accomplishing their mission
of occupying Chihuahua. Their exploits had been extolled in nearly every U.S.
newspaper. Even the antiwar New York *Tribune*'s attempt to diminish Doniphan's
feat—arguing that it would have been "the height of madness and folly" to send
such a small force against a worthier foe—read like a backhanded compliment.

• • •

The Missourians' one-year enlistments were due to expire in a month, and so
General Taylor sent them home, meaning another journey of 350 miles to
Brazos Santiago, where they would board steamships to New Orleans. The
march across the hot, dry Mexican plain in late spring became yet another ordeal.
With mules and cattle collapsing from thirst, the expedition was forced to halt.

Suddenly, rain and hail poured down without warning "in torrents," instantly flooding the plain. The prostrated cattle drank the water as they lay on the ground and were revived. Awed Mexicans who witnessed the deluge explained it as an act of divine intervention. "God is for you," they told the volunteers.

Near Parras, Doniphan learned that Lipan Apaches had recently killed ten Mexicans, kidnapped nineteen women and children, and stolen two hundred horses and three hundred mules. Sent by Doniphan to chase down the raiders, Captain John Reid and thirty men caught up with them at a hacienda on May 13.

For two hours, the Missourians and Apaches fought on horseback with pistols, rifles, bows, arrows, and knives. As the battle reached its climax, Reid unexpectedly received reinforcements—Missouri volunteers escorting traders through the area. The Indians broke off the fight, leaving behind seventeen dead warriors and all of the abductees and stolen livestock. Reid was wounded in the face and shoulder by arrows. While volunteers stripped the Indians' bodies of souvenir blankets, bows, arrows, shields, and headdresses, Dr. Frederick Wiszlenus, a medical doctor attached to Doniphan, was claiming a more gruesome trophy—a medicine man's skull, collected "for scientific purposes."

Reid's rescue of the kidnapped women and children persuaded Mexican citizens in the area to cooperate with the Americans.

• • •

New Orleans's residents pronounced the returning Missourians to be "lions," gawking at them as though they in fact belonged to that species. A worshipful spectator described Doniphan as a rawboned 240-pounder with nine-inch fingers, "and his men say that he is not afraid of the Devil or the God that made him." Like their commander, the Missourians "look more like giants than men." The regiment was decommissioned, the volunteers received their back pay, and they booked steamboat passages to Missouri.

At St. Louis's grand celebration on July 2 to commemorate the return of Colonel Doniphan and three hundred volunteers, the Missourians displayed the ten cannons seized at Rio Sacramento, and five captured enemy flags, including Ponce de Leon's infamous skull-and-crossbones banner. Seven thousand people cheered, church bells tolled, and cannons added their noisy tribute.

Addressing a crowd at the Planter's House Hotel, Senator Thomas Hart Benton declared the regiment's exploits equal to "Xenophon's Ten Thousand," the Greek army whose epic thousand-mile fighting withdrawal from Persia is related in the

Anabasis. The pro-war press seized on the analogy to pronounce Doniphan to be "the Xenophon of the age." Fortunately for Doniphan and his men, their expedition did not parallel Xenophon's in every respect; fully half of the Greek mercenaries died from wounds, illness, and hunger.

Benton was attempting to make a broader point—with which President Polk concurred—about the fighting qualities of America's citizen-soldiers: "To the astonishment of the world . . . volunteer troops can be depended upon . . . private citizens can be transformed [by training] into good soldiers."

PLANNING A SECOND FRONT

"He is evidently a weak man and has been made giddy with the idea of the Presidency. . . . I am now satisfied that he is a narrow-minded, bigoted partisan, without resources and wholly unqualified for the command he holds."

—President James Polk on General Zachary Taylor, after passing over Taylor for command of the Vera Cruz expedition

"I would as soon have heard of his death if true, as that of any other individual in the whole Union."

—General Taylor on President Polk

FALL 1846: WASHINGTON

If James Polk were a man to rest on his laurels, he might have taken a self-congratulatory bow after his first eighteen months in office. The American flag now snapped in the breeze over Monterrey in Mexico, and in Oregon, California, and New Mexico. It was a stunning achievement. Before Britain and America had agreed in June to divide Oregon at the forty-ninth parallel, the English press routinely disparaged Polk. But now the London *Examiner* described him as "the greatest of American conquerors, the most successful of American diplomatists."

On domestic issues, Polk had been just as effective, although in June he had had to apply the whip to Congress when it contemplated adjournment without acting on his ambitious agenda. He had threatened to take his case to the people, just as his mentor Jackson had done, and to deny patronage to foot-dragging congressmen. Congress fell into line, approving what Polk regarded as "the most important domestic measure of my administration." On a razor-thin 28–27 vote, the Senate agreed to reduce import tariffs, despite strong opposition by manufacturers. Of arguably greater importance was the reestablishment of an independent treasury; the institution would serve as the repository for government funds until the advent of the Federal Reserve in 1913. In keeping with his Jacksonian aversion to federally financed internal improvements, Polk had vetoed a rivers-and-harbors improvement bill. With the settlement of the Oregon question, Polk and his Democrat-majority Congress had accomplished every goal outlined in his inaugural address.

In a journal entry one night, Polk permitted himself to bask in Virginia Governor Littleton Waller Tazewell's dinnertime salute to him. In eighteen months, said Tazewell, Polk had achieved more than "any of [his] predecessors had done in eight years." Polk's remarkable legislative successes in 1846, a testament to his superb political skills, surpassed those of nearly every other nineteenth-century president.

• • •

Yet Polk never revisited his decision to serve just one term, resisting the blandishments of some Democrats to seek reelection in 1848. Polk seemingly took little pleasure in the presidency but instead grimly drove himself to his limits. "I will do my duty to the country and rejoice that with my own voluntary free will & consent I am not to be again a candidate. This determination is irrevocable," he wrote.

Every day, office-seekers and congressmen badgered him for appointments, a practice that Polk sarcastically called "the patriotic business of seeking office." He heard them all out, although he was admittedly curt with the most persistent ones. He had little patience with congressmen who tricked him into appointing unqualified men, or who sought to "create offices by their own votes and then seek to fill them themselves." Polk made it a policy to never appoint congressmen to self-created jobs: "I will not countenance such selfishness."

He also disliked the ceremonial duties that took him away from "the business of the country," as well as the "annoyance" of having to chat with official visitors. He complained about the long hours sitting for portraitist George P. A. Healy and could scarcely conceal his impatience whenever a foreign ambassador arrived in full ministerial regalia to announce the birth or death of a royal family member. When the Russian ambassador announced the death of one of Czar Nicholas's nieces, the president "simply remarked that such occurrences would take place." A juggler and magician performed at the White House, with Polk conceding that while the innocent performance was amusing to the forty people watching, it was "not much to their edification . . . I thought the time unprofitably spent." Writing on his fifty-first birthday, the president tersely noted, "The last year has been one of great anxiety and labour to me."

Yet he relished playing "The Great Father," as he put it, to Indian tribal representatives: a Winnebago delegation in September 1846 presented him with a four-foot pipe, lighting it with flint and steel and passing it around the room. He also enjoyed the White House public receptions on Tuesday and Friday nights. Out of his own pocket, he helped needy friends. In September 1846, he gave $100 in gold to Congressman Felix G. McConnell of Alabama, who had spent all his money during a drunken spree. Two days later, Polk was shocked to learn that McConnell had committed suicide. "It was a melancholy instance of the effects of intemperance." A newspaper story about the suicide mentioned Polk's generosity, and he was besieged by money-seekers.

• • •

On September 9, the president strolled around the Washington Mall for an hour with the city's mayor and the regents of the new Smithsonian Institution created by Congress a month earlier. British scientist James Smithson's 1838 bequest of $500,000 (the equivalent of $11 million today) to the United States was to finally become bricks and mortar. One of the first collections in "America's attic" would be the data, charts, notes, and specimens from the U.S. Exploration Expedition of 1838–1842 led by the "stormy petrel," Lieutenant Charles Wilkes. The regents and the mayor, whom Polk suspected of having land investments in the area, proposed a hundred-acre site. Secretary of State James Buchanan vetoed the "extravagant" plan. The regents returned with a more modest design for a sixteen-acre site between 9th and 12th streets on the south half of the Mall. The following May, the cornerstone was laid for the "Castle on the Mall."

• • •

After Foreign Secretary Manuel Crescencio Rejon had set aside Buchanan's July 27 peace overture until the Mexican Congress met in December, Commodore David Conner was ordered to capture Tampico. Major General Robert Patterson and four thousand troops were to seize Victoria and the rest of Tamaulipas Province. But now Polk was pondering an even grander strategy: opening an entire second front. Because of his ill-considered Monterrey armistice, Taylor would have no role in this expedition. "Gen'l Taylor, I fear, is not the man for the command of the army," Polk concluded. "He is brave but he does not seem to have resources or grasp of mind to conduct such a campaign." And while Taylor readily obeyed orders, he was unwilling to "express an opinion or take any responsibility on himself." The president had also been listening to his former law partner, General

Gideon Pillow, and to Quartermaster R. B. Reynolds, who both served with Taylor. They "gave an account of great dissatisfaction in the army [with] Gen'l Taylor, for having granted the terms of capitulation he did to the enemy at Monterey [*sic*], and for some other acts indicating partiality among his officers."

Polk suspected Taylor and other Whig officers of being "violent partisans" who were "disposed to throw every obstacle in the way of prosecuting the Mexican War successfully"—exactly what Taylor suspected of Polk and his advisers. Taylor's presidential ambitions, Polk believed, had made him a political pawn of Whigs on General Worth's staff, and of George W. Kendall, the New Orleans *Picayune* editor who was traveling with Taylor's army as a correspondent.

Ironically, as he planned the war's next phase, the president complained about all of the unsolicited advice and criticism that *he* was receiving. Sounding much like Taylor, he grumped, "I hoped my friends in Congress and elsewhere would suffer me to conduct the war with Mexico as I thought proper, and not plan the campaign for me." But it was Polk who initiated or approved every major war decision, and kept track of the costs, never doubting that the United States would win.

• • •

On October 17, Polk, Buchanan, and War Secretary William Marcy questioned F. M. Dimond, the U.S. consul in Vera Cruz, about "the topography of the country around the City of Vera Cruz, and the practicability of landing a force near that City, so as to invest it in the rear." They asked Dimond to draw a map of the Vera Cruz area and to bring it to a meeting that evening. The War and Navy secretaries attended this session, as did a General Thompson and a Navy Commander Warrington, but General of the Army Winfield Scott was not invited. The war council decided to attack Vera Cruz, estimating that no more than four thousand troops would be needed.

Marcy informed Scott of this momentous decision a couple of days later, also apprising him that Taylor had been ordered to remain at Monterrey and that General Wool's expedition to Chihuahua had been canceled. Polk and Marcy had a host of reasons for keeping Taylor at Monterrey: to not further antagonize the already hostile people of northern Mexico; because General Pedro de Ampudia still had more than seven thousand armed troops, and Santa Anna was bringing more men to San Luis Potosi; Taylor's vulnerable supply line; and because advancing beyond Monterrey would not lead to peace negotiations.

While Scott's opinion clearly was unimportant to Polk and his advisers, Scott voiced his objection anyway to the four-thousand-man invasion force; at least twenty-five thousand troops were needed to capture Vera Cruz, he said. And Scott requested that he be named the expedition's commander.

Polk did not want to give the command to Scott, whom he suspected was arguing for a larger landing force to discomfit his administration. In fact, the president was considering transferring Scott to an outpost where he would not be "constantly embarrassing to the Secretary of War."

• • •

Polk's full cabinet was more skeptical than his military advisers about the merits of invading Vera Cruz and could not reach a consensus; the advisers also considered simply holding the territory that Taylor now controlled. On November 10, the president candidly discussed the impasse, as well as his disapproval of Scott and Taylor, with Missouri Senator Thomas Hart Benton.

Benton urged Polk to "press the war boldly," because Americans were a "go-ahead people" who would not support a defensive policy. He agreed that neither Taylor nor Scott should command the Vera Cruz expedition, and then stunned Polk by suggesting that perhaps *he* might be given the command—if Congress agreed to his appointment as lieutenant general, thereby outranking Major Generals Scott, Gaines, Taylor, William Orlando Butler, and Robert Patterson. Only "a man of talents and resources as well as a military man" should be considered, said the immodest Benton, whose brief service as a militia colonel during the War of 1812 did not include combat experience.

Dizzy with the prospect of the influential Benton, who only recently had relented in his opposition to Polk's war policies, now becoming a staunch political ally, Polk said he "would be pleased to see him at the head of the army in such an expedition." Benton warmly pledged to support Polk's war measures.

But after weighing Benton's proposition overnight, and sounding out cabinet members and others, Polk reluctantly informed Benton the next day that Congress probably would not consent to give him command of the Army. The president gamely made the attempt anyway, wanting a Democrat General of the Army who would "sympathize" with his administration. Rightly viewed as partisan, the lieutenant-general bill was tabled in the Senate, and Congress instead added two major-general positions. Polk offered Benton one of them; the senator declined.

• • •

During cabinet meetings on November 14 and 17, the president and his advisers debated whether to invade Vera Cruz, and who would lead the expedition. It was risky to attack a densely populated region surrounded by jungles where guerrillas could hide, and only Attorney General Nathan Clifford favored marching from Vera Cruz on Mexico City. But the cabinet finally decided to open the second front, while delaying a decision on a Mexico City expedition until Mexico was afforded a chance to negotiate—Polk's "graduated pressure."

The question of who would lead the attack proved more problematic. Polk's advisers agreed that Taylor was "unfit" to command the expedition, even though he had won three major battles in four months. "He had not mind enough for the station," insisted Polk, an arguable position that nonetheless echoed Winfield Scott's assessment of Taylor as honest and courageous, with "a good store of common sense," but uneducated and unread, "slow of thought," and contemptuous of "learning of every kind." "Rigidity of ideas was the consequence," Scott concluded. While there was truth in all of this, Polk's political animus and a tincture of professional jealousy on Scott's part certainly influenced this harsh judgment of the war's great hero. So, who would lead the expedition?

It pained Polk and his inner circle to concede the inescapable conclusion, first ventured by Marcy, that Scott must be given command of the Vera Cruz invasion. Whenever they discussed appointing someone else, they were compelled to face the ineluctable fact that Scott was, after all, General of the Army. On November 17, Polk unhappily resigned himself to Scott's appointment: "Nothing but the stern necessity and a sense of public duty could induce me to place him at the head of so important an expedition. I do not well see how it can be avoided."

If there was ever one moment when James Polk and Winfield Scott were able to see past their mutual enmity and regard one another with fellowship, it was when Polk informed Scott that he was "willing that by-gones should be by-gones" and was naming Scott commander of the Vera Cruz expedition. Miserably confined to a desk while Taylor racked up victory after victory, Scott became emotional. "He expressed himself as being deeply grateful to me & said he would show me his gratitude by his conduct when he got to the field," noted Polk. "He was so grateful & so much affected that he almost shed tears."

• • •

Taylor complained to War Secretary Marcy when Marcy peremptorily ordered Taylor to send troops to assist the Navy in capturing Tampico. The Polk administration's

habit of trampling on his authority as field commander, and the orders, direc-
tives, and instructions issuing from Washington, had pushed Taylor beyond the
limits of his patience. After reading Taylor's letter, Polk indignantly instructed
Marcy to send a sharp rebuke. "He is evidently a weak man and has been made
giddy with the idea of the Presidency. . . . I am now satisfied that he is a narrow-
minded, bigoted partisan, without resources and wholly unqualified for the
command he holds."

Taylor, in turn, detested his commander-in-chief. When a rumor reached him
that Polk had died, Taylor confided to his son-in-law, Dr. R. C. Wood, that while
he regretted learning of anyone's death, "I would as soon have heard of his death
if true, as that of any other individual in the whole Union."

The general was neither the calculating politician nor the opportunist that Polk
made him out to be. While understandably intrigued by the speculation swirling
around himself regarding the 1848 presidential race, Taylor had ostensibly
renounced all presidential ambitions until after the war. He often wished that his
friends would find another candidate: "If some good honest man can be elected I
will acquiesce in such an arrangement with great pleasure."

• • •

In November, Commodore David Conner's Gulf Squadron easily captured
Tampico, a key to Polk's plan to take control of Tamaulipas Province and
Mexico's northern Gulf coast. Much of the operation's success was due to the
efforts of Irish-born Ann Chase, the wife of the U.S. consul at Tampico, Franklin
Chase. When the Mexican government expelled her husband, Mrs. Chase invoked
her British citizenship and remained in Tampico. In the months following, she sent
Conner detailed plans of the city and the river, noting the locations of enemy troops
and guns. A week before the American invasion, Mrs. Chase erected a flagstaff outside
her home. When the one thousand Mexican Army defenders abandoned Tampico
without a fight, she notified Conner and then ran the national colors up her new
flagstaff in anticipation of the invasion. Indignant Tampico civil authorities ordered
Mrs. Chase to lower the flag, but she defiantly refused and stood guard over the flagpole until Conner's Marines and sailors landed. The Americans placed three field
pieces around the U.S. consulate. "I am willing to stand by my husband at a gun until
we both die or are victors," Mrs. Chase declared in a letter to the Washington *Union*.

Santa Anna withdrew the Tampico garrison all the way to San Luis Potosi,
having concluded that only with great difficulty could he reinforce Tampico.

• • •

On December 14, Taylor set out from Monterrey with two brigades to occupy Tamaulipas's principal towns, as Marcy had ordered him to do. He planned to rendezvous in Victoria with General Robert Patterson, who was marching south from Matamoros. But three days after leaving Monterrey, Taylor received the alarming report that Santa Anna and twenty thousand troops were advancing on Saltillo, where General William Worth commanded a force one tenth the size of Santa Anna's.

The news posed a dilemma for Taylor, who wanted to go to Worth's aid but did not wish to leave Patterson unprotected in Victoria. He reluctantly split his three-thousand-man force, sending the U.S. Second Brigade under General John Quitman ahead to Victoria, while turning back toward Saltillo with the Mississippi Rifles and Colonel Charles May's dragoons. When the news about Santa Anna's army reached General William Orlando Butler in Camargo, he dispatched the Second and Third Indiana infantry regiments and Colonel Humphrey Marshall's Kentucky cavalry regiment, relieving it of the tedium of convoying wagons and mule trains.

Taylor hadn't traveled far when he received new information that Santa Anna's army had returned to San Luis Potosi. He resumed his march to Victoria.

While traveling through Montemorelos for the third time on December 24, Taylor received a letter from Scott asking, but not ordering, Taylor to meet him in Camargo to discuss strategy. There was more to it than that, however; Scott wanted to personally inform Taylor that he was going to appropriate Taylor's Monterrey veterans for the upcoming Vera Cruz campaign. Taylor declined Scott's invitation. He needed to join Patterson and Quitman in Victoria to complete the conquest of Tamaulipas, and Camargo was too far out of the way.

Quitman's Second Brigade reached Victoria before Patterson and accepted the city's surrender on December 30. U.S. troops now controlled all of northeastern Mexico.

Taylor's men slogged through 96-degree heat and thick dust, sampling the local bananas, oranges, and figs and marveling at the fact that they were sweltering in December. They celebrated Christmas Day with mescal eggnog toasts. On January 4, Taylor and Patterson joined Quitman.

In Victoria, someone stole Taylor's horse, Old Whitey, and the angry general arrested Victoria's alcade and held him hostage. Old Whitey was returned the next day.

• • •

When Taylor did not join him in Camargo, Scott sent written orders to Butler—technically senior in rank to Taylor—with two copies for Taylor, one sent via Monterrey, and the other through Matamoros. Scott ordered Butler to send him forty-five hundred of Taylor's regulars and forty-five hundred volunteers from the encampments at Camargo and Matamoros. As Scott knew they would be, Taylor's feelings were bruised by the "outrage," as he bitterly described it, of first being passed over for command of the Vera Cruz assault and then having to part with his best troops.

Taylor obediently dispatched Patterson to Tampico with most of the five thousand troops in Victoria, retaining only an artillery battery, May's dragoons, and the Mississippi Rifles.

• • •

To his son-in-law, Dr. R. C. Wood, Taylor complained of being "stripped of nearly the whole of the regular force & more than one half of the Volunteers, & ordered here to act on the defensive." He concluded that the Polk administration's purpose was to force him to resign his command, thereby furnishing the Democrats with ammunition to use against him politically. "But in this I shall disappoint them, as I have determined to remain & do my duty no matter under what circumstances."

Taylor, in fact, was ready to do more than merely persevere in his command—he had reached the momentous decision to accept the presidential nomination if it were offered to him. By coincidence, a group of Taylor supporters had just organized a club, the "Young Indians," to promote his candidacy. Among the charter members were Georgia Congressmen Alexander H. Stephens and Robert Tombs, and Illinois congressman-elect Abraham Lincoln.

• • •

Taylor suspected something was wrong when he received the *second* copy of Scott's orders, the one routed through Matamoros, but never got the first copy, sent by way of Monterrey. Then news reached Taylor of the murder of the courier, Lieutenant John A. Richey, and the theft of the orders, which contained details of the coming attack on Vera Cruz.

After discovering that Taylor was not in Monterrey, Richey and ten dragoons had started for Victoria. In the town of Villa Gran on January 13, 1847, Richey was out for a nighttime stroll when guerrillas lassoed him, dragging him through the prickly pear and chaparral until he died. Rifling through Richey's courier pouch, the Mexicans found Scott's orders; realizing their importance, they left for San Luis Potosi to place them in Santa Anna's hands.

With his several hundred remaining troops, Taylor began the journey back to Monterrey. At Villa Gran, he marched the dragoons and the artillery battery into the town's main plaza and demanded that the alcade turn over Richey's killers. When the alcade professed to not know their identities, Taylor threatened to hang him. But when the official persisted in his disavowals, Taylor let him off with a warning: if he did not produce the killers in three weeks, Taylor would impose a $50,000 fine on the town.

• • •

Scott's actions confirmed Taylor's delusional suspicions that the General of the Army had allied himself with War Secretary Marcy and Polk with "the view of breaking me down . . . to make a little capital for themselves disregarding the interest of the country." He wrote to Scott on January 15 that his treatment was "unprecedented in our history. . . . I cannot misunderstand the objects of the arrangements. . . . I have lost the confidence of the government." Indeed he had, because of an imprudent old friend, General Edmund P. Gaines.

In November, Taylor had written Gaines a letter that condemned the Polk administration's prosecution of the war and its insulting treatment of him, while alluding to the coming Vera Cruz campaign. The impulsive, fiery Gaines, no friend of Polk, Marcy, or Scott after they had court-martialed him for calling out volunteer regiments without authority, sent the letter to the New York *Express* without Taylor's knowledge. It was published on January 22.

Polk erupted when he read the "highly exceptionable letter, assailing as it does the administration, uttering unfounded complaints, and giving publicity to the world of the plans of campaign contemplated by the Government, which it had been desired by the Government to keep concealed from the enemy until they were consummated."

When Marcy rebuked him for the letter, Taylor replied in a wounded tone that he had not intended that it be made public and objected to his loyal service to his country being repaid by his government's disfavor. Taylor then composed an "open letter" to Senator John Crittenden of Kentucky announcing that he would accept the Whig presidential nomination if it were offered to him.

• • •

Scott's rapprochement with the president did not even survive 1846 before devolving into the same mordant accusations and recriminations that now characterized Polk's relationship with Taylor. The first crack appeared before Scott had even left New Orleans for the Rio Grande. A New Orleans newspaper published a story detailing the Vera Cruz invasion plan, and Polk jumped to the conclusion that Scott had leaked the information. "His vanity is such that he could not keep the most important secrets of the Government," Polk fumed, although no evidence suggested the newspaper's source was "Old Fuss and Feathers." Scott, in fact, had not leaked the plan, but a subordinate probably did.

Scott was stung by the accusation, just as he had been upset by his recent discovery that Polk planned to create the rank of lieutenant general and name Benton to it. "A grosser abuse of human confidence is nowhere recorded," Scott sputtered. The president was "an enemy more to be dreaded than Santa Anna and all his hosts."

A few weeks later, the president overturned Scott's decision to remove Colonel William S. Harney from command of the U.S. Second Dragoons. Scott had punished Harney for leading an unauthorized, reckless raid into Mexico before the commencement of General Wool's expedition. Harney's improvident actions had directly resulted in the panicked destruction of U.S. supplies stockpiled near the Rio Grande. Stripped of his command, Harney left Taylor's army to join Scott's expedition; Scott ordered him to return to Taylor. When Harney refused, Scott court-martialed him for insubordination.

Polk, who at times suspiciously regarded both Scott and Taylor as little more than uniformed political operatives, was certain that Scott, a Whig, was persecuting Harney because he was a Democrat. "He [Scott] has availed himself as [of] his power as chief in command, has seized his victim, & is resolved to satiate his vengeance by destroying [Harney]. This I will not permit."

In countermanding Scott's disciplinary action, Polk was unaware that after Harney was found guilty of insubordination, Scott, in a conciliatory gesture, had absolved him of the charges and permitted him to join his campaign. The president's intervention spoiled Scott's generous gesture, left bad feelings all around, and exposed the administration's dysfunctional relationship with its generals. The House of Representatives requested all of the government's correspondence with Taylor and Scott.

Scott now despised Polk as much as Taylor did and began contemptuously referring to the president as "Little Jimmy Polk of Duck River." Polk's "little strength," Scott wrote, "lay in the most odious elements of the human character—

cunning and hypocrisy. . . . It might be added that a man of meaner presence is not often seen."

Amazingly, Polk claimed to abjure politics when he was prosecuting the war. He proudly declared to his cabinet "that I had never suffered politics to mingle with the conduct of this war."

DECEMBER 1846: WASHINGTON

Growing dissatisfaction with the war was just one of the factors that caused dozens of Democrats to be swept from the House of Representatives during the 1846 midterm elections. Others included discontent with the Oregon settlement's boundaries; and Polk's veto of the Rivers and Harbors Bill, depriving constituents west of the Appalachians of needed roads, canals, and bridges. The tariff reductions were unpopular in the Northeast, and the reconstituted independent treasury had been coldly received by banking interests. When the Thirtieth Congress was sworn in the next year, the Democrats' sixty-six-seat advantage in the House would be transformed into a seven-seat Whig majority. Among the many Whigs elected in the backlash against Democrats was thirty-seven-year-old Abraham Lincoln of Illinois.

But Polk knew that the fallout from the midterm election results would be felt long before the Thirtieth Congress went into formal session in December 1847. (Unlike today, a Congress, while officially "in session" as of early March, often did not actually meet until December.) Whigs and dissident Democrats would now be emboldened to challenge his policies. Thus, Polk composed his Second Annual Message to Congress with the surpassing purpose of justifying the Mexican War.

• • •

As was his method, Polk began working on the message weeks in advance, sharing early drafts with advisers. Polk did not govern by committee, but he habitually consulted others, including the First Lady, when faced with a major decision or composing a speech as important as this Annual Message. Always the pragmatist, Polk reined in his ego when it served a greater object.

Polk intended to recommend establishing permanent civil governments in the occupied Mexican provinces—in effect, seizing the provinces to recoup the expense of conquering them. In expounding this "line of boundary" policy, Polk believed he would be preparing Americans for the eventual annexation of New Mexico and California, his never-acknowledged reason for having gone to war in the first place.

But the "line of boundary" plan implied a great strategic shift from offensive to defensive operations, although Scott would proceed with the Vera Cruz invasion. While Secretary of State James Buchanan and Treasury Secretary Robert Walker supported the plan, Navy Secretary John Y. Mason and Senator Thomas Hart Benton believed it would fail if carried out to the letter. Even if a chain of heavily garrisoned forts were built around the conquered territory, they argued, mobile guerrilla forces could wreak havoc at will, and Mexico would remain largely intact and defiant.

Take the language out, urged Benton, forget the boundaries, and destroy Mexico's will to fight by carrying the war into her heartland. The cabinet members, even those who supported the "line of boundary" proposal, were in unanimity on one point: If Benton opposed the plan, Congress would also reject it. Polk instructed Buchanan to rewrite the controversial paragraphs.

• • •

The Mexican Congress finally convened on December 6, two days before the opening of the Twenty-ninth U.S. Congress's Second Session—a lame-duck session, taking place after the elections but prior to the installation of the newly elected congress. As expected, the Mexican Congress never debated Buchanan's July 27 proposal for peace talks. Instead, the moderados and puros named, as Mexico's new president, the phoenix-like General Antonio Lopez de Santa Anna—his fourth time as Mexico's leader—but for the duration of the war designated Valentin Gomez Farias, the new vice president, to serve as acting president while Santa Anna led the army from San Luis Potosi.

• • •

Polk devoted fully two-thirds of his thirty-five-page Annual Message to Congress to refuting the Whigs' "erroneous views" that he, and not Mexico, had started the war, and that the Nueces River, and not the Rio Grande, was the true Texas–Mexico border. The war critics had mischaracterized the war as "unjust and unnecessary" against "a weakened and injured enemy," he said, when it was Mexico that had "by her own act forced the war upon us." Even before the attack on Captain Seth Thornton's dragoons, "we had an ample cause of war against Mexico." He launched into a recitation of these grievances: American property had been unlawfully expropriated during twenty years of chaotic Mexican rule, with Mexico yet owing more than $2 million in claims adjudicated by Mexican and U.S. commissioners; and there had been "insults" committed against the U.S. flag.

American forbearance, Polk hyperbolically asserted, had been "without parallel in the history of modern civilized nations." The annexation of Texas was "no just cause of offense to Mexico," he said, reiterating the fiction that Texas was joined to the United States in 1803 by the Louisiana Purchase, and its boundary established on the Rio Grande. Polk then related a fanciful history of Texas independence and annexation.

"Every honorable effort has been used by me to avoid the war . . . but all have proved vain," he said and then tested Congress's credulity by declaring, "The war has not been waged with a view to conquest." But now that the United States had made "extraordinary expenditures" in prosecuting the war, "justice to our own people will make it proper that Mexico should be held responsible for these expenditures." An honorable peace must include "indemnity for the past, and security for the future."

This was the extent of Polk's willingness to level with Congress about his plan to annex California and New Mexico, which in his mind was already accomplished fact. (He had been far more candid with his brother William two months earlier: "I think that California & New Mexico—being our possessions by our forces—will not be given up, but will be retained—to indemnify our claimants upon Mexico & to defray the expenses of the war.")

Embedded in the message was his ambitious legislative agenda: $3 million for peace diplomacy (fifty percent more than his request in August), the lieutenant generalcy, ten new regiments, a $23 million loan to bridge the rising wartime deficit, and increased duties on coffee and tea to help pay for the war.

Polk also indulged himself in the timeless political tactic of smearing war critics by suggesting that a "more effectual means could not have been devised to encourage the enemy and protract the war than to advocate and adhere to their cause, and thus give them 'aid and comfort' "—a pointed allusion to the Constitution's treason clause.

Polk's earlier proposal for a defensive perimeter around the conquered Mexican provinces had, under Buchanan's red pen, been completely altered to instead emphasize the *perils* of pursuing such a strategy. "It would encourage Mexico to persevere, and tend to protract [the war] indefinitely. . . . A border warfare of the most savage character, extending over a long line, would be unceasingly waged. It would require a large army to be kept constantly in the field, stationed at posts and garrisons along such a line, to protect and defend it."

Finally, the president acknowledged that he had indeed ordered Commodore David Conner, on the very day that he had signed the war bill and authorized the blockade of Mexico, to permit Santa Anna to reenter Mexico. It would have been impossible to stop Santa Anna's repatriation, Polk said, and it might yet produce peace; the former dictator had reportedly stated that he wished to end the war. He did not say how he knew this, nor did he mention Alejandro J. Atocha's embassy to Washington on Santa Anna's behalf, or Alexander Slidell Mackenzie's secret mission to Havana.

• • •

Polk's Second Annual Message neither reassured his Democratic allies nor swayed the Whig war critics, who had become more intractable since the fall elections. Instead, the address, acting like a magnifying glass, amplified and concentrated the Whigs' diffused discontent with the administration's war policies. Whig congressmen boycotted the president's White House receptions. They ridiculed Polk's adoption of Texas's grandiose claim that the Rio Grande was the historical Mexican–Texan border. Mexico had never recognized such a line, they said, even after Santa Anna's defeat at San Jacinto. It was "a low demagogical attempt to deceive the nation—to tell just enough of the truth to cause the people to believe a lie," remarked Congressman Meredith Gentry, a Tennessee Whig. "Was any government through its chief magistrate ever more vilely prostituted?" asked Garrett Davis of Kentucky. Some Whigs, disliking Polk's incessant carping about Generals Taylor and Scott, suggested that the president was more intent on "waging war on a certain political party" than on fighting Mexico.

Above all, the Whigs resented Polk's assertion that by questioning his conduct, Whigs were aiding and abetting the enemy. Gentry bitterly observed: "Because we will not crouch, with spaniel-like humility, at his feet, and whine an approval of all his acts, we are met . . . with the grateful compliment from the President that we are traitors to our country."

When the Washington *Union* chastised Whigs who questioned the war's rationale as purveyors of "the coarsest, the most false, and the most unmeasured invective," the *National Intelligencer* launched into the *Union* for having "striven to stifle all inquiry into the justifying causes, to hector the press into silence . . . by denouncing as no better than 'moral treason' all examination into the conduct of the Executive, and by stigmatizing all questions about the inception of the war. . . ."

Polk's invocation of the Constitution's treason clause to cow the war's critics had backfired. And he had not only furnished the Whigs with a rallying point, he had nudged the nascent antiwar movement to full wakefulness.

18

DISSENT, PATRIOTISM, AND THE PRESS

"My friend Mr. Thoreau has gone to jail rather than pay his tax. On him they could not calculate."

—Ralph Waldo Emerson

Henry David Thoreau, an avowed individualist who objected on principle to all government, was now paying the price for his apostasy. From his cell in the Middlesex County jail in Concord, Thoreau pondered his decision to not pay his poll tax for the past six years and found no cause for regret. The town constable had arrested Thoreau when he hiked from his shack on Walden Pond into Concord to have a shoe mended. The recluse shared a cell with a man accused of burning a barn. "It was like traveling into a far country, such as I had never expected to behold, to lie there for one night," he wrote.

It was morally wrong, he concluded, to support a government that sanctioned slavery and invaded weaker nations, such as Mexico.

"When a sixth of the population of a nation which has undertaken to be the refuge of liberty are slaves, and a whole country [Mexico] is unjustly overrun and conquered by a foreign army, and subjected to military law, I think that it is not too soon for honest men to rebel and revolutionize. . . . If a thousand men were not to pay their tax-bills this year, that would not be a violent and bloody measure, as it would be to pay them, and enable the State to commit violence and shed innocent blood."

Except for his Aunt Maria, who quietly paid her nephew's delinquent poll tax, enabling Thoreau to collect his mended shoe and join a "huckleberry party" the next day, and a small circle of friends that included Ralph Waldo Emerson and James Russell Lowell, Thoreau's gesture went unnoticed. Emerson, who shared his friend's views on the war and slavery, observed, "My friend Mr. Thoreau has gone to jail rather than pay his tax. On him they could not calculate."

Individuals of conscience would one day hail as a "declaration of independence" Thoreau's ostensible explanation to his neighbors of just why he went to jail, "Resistance to Civil Government" (later shortened to "Civil Disobedience"). "This people must cease to hold slaves, and to make war on Mexico, though it cost them their existence as a people," Thoreau wrote. Thoreau's essay, and its themes of freedom and individuality, would in the future lend inspiration to independence and civil rights movements and leaders around the world, including, more than a hundred years later, Mahatma Gandhi and Martin Luther King, and would inform the Vietnam War protesters of the 1960s.

Few others of his era stated their beliefs with Thoreau's Manichaean clarity, or went to jail to uphold them, but Thoreau was far from being alone in opposing the Mexican War and slavery, now inextricably connected under the rubric of expansionism.

An antiwar movement, the first in America since Federalists protested the decision to fight England in 1812, had stirred to life. Strongest in the Northeast and among the literati and the Whigs, it also increasingly included merchants, immigrants, and even soldiers, who prudently confined their dissent to diaries and journals.

• • •

If there was a public face to New England's moral opposition to the war, it belonged to John Quincy Adams and his son, Charles Francis Adams. During the congressional debate in May 1846, the elder Adams was the most prominent of "the 14" House members who voted against the war bill. The scholarly, deeply religious ex-president candidly described himself as "a man of reserved, cold, austere and forbidding manners: my political adversaries say, a gloomy misanthropist, and my personal enemies, an unsocial savage." While Adams acknowledged this "defect" in his manner, as well as not having "the pliability to reform it," Massachusetts embraced him. Unbidden, Adams's friends had elected him in 1830 to Congress—he was the only former president to serve in the House—after Andrew Jackson thwarted his bid for presidential reelection.

Few congressmen were as grateful to their supporters as Adams after his election to the House: "No election or appointment ever gave me so much pleasure." He repaid his home state's regard by becoming one of Congress's most outspoken opponents of slavery, rolling back the "gag rule" prohibiting discussion of anti-slave petitions in the House, and successfully arguing before the U.S. Supreme Court the case of the slaves who commandeered the *Armistad* in 1839.

As did many of their fellow New Englanders, the Adamses believed that the war's secret, immoral purpose was to seize a weak neighbor's territories and introduce slavery into them. Charles Francis Adams, a lawyer, editor, and Whig politician, editorialized in the *Boston Daily Whig* following Polk's Second Annual Message to Congress that it was strange that Polk, waging war on Mexico with such manifest confidence, would yet devote two-thirds of his message to attempting "to remove the scruples of a small minority of dissentients." The president apparently now believed that his initial justification for the war, "American blood shed on American soil," was insufficient, and that new explanations were required, the younger Adams wrote.

The Massachusetts Legislature registered its objection to the war by rejecting a bill to equip Caleb Cushing's volunteer regiment. And then Governor James N. Briggs refused to issue officer commissions, citing technical problems. (Cushing, a Whig statesman and politician, eventually embarked for Mexico with his regiment.) The Legislature condemned the war as "a war of conquest, so hateful in its objects, so wanton, unjust and unconstitutional in its origin and character, [that it] must be regarded as a war against humanity, against justice, against the Union . . . and against the free states."

The New England town-meeting tradition fathered new advocacy groups that displayed their opposition to the Mexican War in a rich stream of resolutions and manifestos. The New England Anti-Slavery Convention, dismayed that "the Constitution of the United States has been trampled underfoot by the Slave Power," pronounced the Polk administration to be an illegal entity of "usurpers" who "have plunged this nation into a most atrocious War—a War of endless aggression for the unlimited establishment of Slavery." Four hundred New York merchants, fearful that the war would ruin business, signed a petition denouncing it. Without the antislavery movement's stridency, the American Peace Society, as befit its name, urged Mexico and the United States to mediate their differences.

Other Transcendentalists besides Thoreau and Emerson believed that America was descending into a barbaric materialism and was despoiling a weak nation for the benefit of slaveholders and businessmen. Of course, this was the antithesis of the Transcendentalists' close-held beliefs in democracy, individualism, and the regeneration of the human spirit through nature. Margaret Fuller, the feminist leader and former editor of *The Dial,* lamented that the United States had forsaken her "high calling" to become "a robber and a jailer; the scourge hid behind her banner; her eyes fixed not on the stars, but on the possessions of other men. . . . The spirit of our fathers flames no more, but lies hid beneath the ashes."

Theodore Parker, the minister of the Twenty-eighth Congregational Society of Boston, said the war was "a sin; that it is a national infidelity, a denial of Christianity and of God. . . . Treason against the people, against mankind, against God, is a great sin. . . ." He ridiculed "the appeals to our 'patriotism' and 'humanity' as arguments for butchering the Mexicans." In the *Massachusetts Quarterly Review,* Emerson wrote, "The country needs to be extricated from its delirium at once."

As American casualties increased, observed Herman Melville, enjoying the celebrity from his sensational first novel, *Typee,* "The day is at hand when we will be able to talk of our killed & wounded like some of the old Eastern conquerors reckoning up the thousands. . . ." William Lloyd Garrison, the firebrand abolitionist who in later years would burn a copy of the Constitution [coincidentally, with Thoreau in the audience] because it sanctioned slavery and therefore was "a covenant with death," penned these treasonous words in the *Liberator:* "We only hope that, if blood has had to flow, that it has been that of the American, and that the next news we shall hear will be that General Scott and his army are in the hands of the Mexicans." (Upon James Polk's death, Garrison wrote, "Neither humanity, nor justice, nor liberty has any cause to deplore the event. . . . His administration has been a curse to the country.")

Indeed, among New England's intellectuals, there reigned the belief, as unshakable as it was erroneous, that the war's nefarious purpose was to spread the "peculiar institution" throughout the Southwest to the Pacific shore. In verses accusatory and snidely humorous, John Greenleaf Whittier and James Russell Lowell dogmatically expounded upon this theme.

In "Yorktown," Whittier moralized against waging a war to extend slavery under the same banner that flowed above the famed Revolutionary War battlefield.

Where's now the flag of that old war
Where flows its stripe? Where burns its star?
Bear witness, Palo Alto's day,

Dark Vale of Palms, red Monterey,
Where Mexic Freedom, young and weak,
Fleshes the Northern eagle's beak;
Symbol of terror and despair,
Of chains and slaves, go seek it there!

• • •

James Russell Lowell's satire, *The Biglow Papers,* a compendium of the fictional letters and musings of a New England rustic named Hosea Biglow, mocked the Polk administration's assertion that America was bringing democracy to Mexico. "It's all to make 'em free that we air pullin' trigger."

They just want this Californy
So's to lug new slave-states in
To abuse ye, an' to scorn ye,
An' to plunder ye like sin.

• • •

Former government officials and diplomats joined the debate. The octogenarian Albert Gallatin, who was Thomas Jefferson's and James Madison's Treasury Secretary, wrote in "Peace With Mexico" that the annexation of Texas was a "deep and most offensive injury . . . tantamount to a declaration of war," made worse when General Taylor, in "an open act of hostility," marched into territory over which the United States had never exercised jurisdiction. Gallatin pronounced the war "one of iniquitous aggression on our part." Joel R. Poinsett, who in 1825 became the first U.S. minister to Mexico after Mexican independence, advised compassion toward the Mexican people, while continuing to wage war on her "tyrannical military despotism."

• • •

For all that, "Polk's War," as its opponents snidely called it, enjoyed strong public approval throughout 1846. Even as the Twenty-ninth Congress's enthusiasm for the war waned in December 1846, never did the Polk administration consider withdrawal because of slipping public support. U.S. regulars and volunteers had won every major battle and now controlled two-thirds of Mexico. Most Americans supported the war, for reasons ranging from patriotism to a desire to avenge the Alamo and Goliad, to a belief in Manifest Destiny and its beneficence in "spreading democracy" to an oppressed people, to wanting to confer Protestantism's blessings on a Roman Catholic nation, to a craving for excitement because, observed the New York *Journal of Commerce,* "the world has become stale and insipid."

• • •

When Polk asserted that Mexico had started the war by rejecting negotiations and sending troops across the Rio Grande to bushwhack American dragoons, most Americans believed him. And they would have concurred with the Virginia House of Delegates resolution that the war culminated "a long series of acts of injustice and outrage toward the United States." The rumors and half-truths repeated in the press, Congress, and the White House about purported British and French designs on California, Oregon, Cuba, the Yucatan, and even Texas fed the upwelling of proud nationalism. The war released a coiled energy, described metaphorically by Senator John Calhoun as a "young man of 18, full of health and vigour." Military recruiters pitched their inducements accordingly, sometimes in verse: "Come all ye gallant volunteers/Who fear not life to lose,/The martial drum invites ye come/And join the Hickory Blues."

Books, paintings, souvenirs, and theatrical productions celebrated the war as it was being fought. *Tanner's Traveling Map of Mexico* was a best seller, as were books on Mexican history and infantry tactics. Biographies of Zachary Taylor were rushed into print. Merchants advertised Palo Alto hats and Palo Alto root beer, and men drank in the Resaca de la Palma Saloon and the Taylor Tavern. At New York's Chatham theater, "The March of Freedom," featuring "Zachary Taylor and the Goddess of Liberty," enjoyed great success, as did the Bowery theater's "The Campaign on the Rio Grande." Paintings honored the deaths at Palo Alto of Major Samuel Ringgold and his horse, Davy Branch.

The fanciful poetic work "They Wait for Us," which portrayed the American invaders as racially superior democratic reformers, exemplified a popular romantic view of the war:

> *The Spanish maid, with eye of fire,*
> *At balmy evening turns her lyre*
> *And, looking to the Eastern sky,*
> *Awaits our Yankee chivalry*
> *Whose purer blood and valiant arms,*

Are fit to clasp her budding charms.
An army of reformers, we –
March onto glorious victory;
And on the highest peak of Ande,
Unfurl our banners to the wind,
Whose stars shall light the land anew,
And shed rich blessings like the dew.

• • •

In the Brooklyn *Daily Eagle,* Walt Whitman declared during the first days of the war that "Mexico must be thoroughly chastised!" Later, he defended General Zachary Taylor's controversial armistice because "he preferred all the solid reasons of a sure and less bloody triumph, to the more brilliant contingency of storming the citadel, of immense slaughter on both sides, and taking a ponderous army prisoners of war."

Of the legendary Texas Rangers, Whitman wrote:

Matchless with horse, rifle, song, supper, courtship,
Large, turbulent, generous, handsome, proud, and affectionate,
Bearded, sunburnt, drest in the free costume of hunters,
Not a single one over thirty years of age.

• • •

War supporters described it variously as a democratic crusade to bring the torch of freedom to the dark recesses of tyranny, a twilight struggle between civilization and barbarism, and a divinely ordained mission to spread Protestantism to a Catholic land. "The question of extending *constitutional republican institutions* over this whole continent is one of the broadest, noblest and most important that was ever presented to any nation," wrote an officer of the American Union of Association-ists. The Washington *Union* pronounced the war to be "a continuation of the great struggle of the Anglo-Saxon race on this continent for self-government. It is a war of civilization to repress the lawless practices of comparative anarchy and barbarism."

Even *The Harbinger,* the publication of Brook Farm, the Boston-area utopian cooperative, granted that while the war might outwardly appear to be a "monstrous iniquity," it actually served the greater purpose of "completing a more universal design of Providence, of extending the power and intelligence of advanced civilized nations over the whole face of the earth." Conservative Presbyterians, Methodists, and Baptists believed that God had chosen America to introduce the "Redeemer's Kingdom" to benighted, Roman Catholic Mexico. Not all Baptists, Presbyterians, and Methodists agreed, and other Protestant denominations—notably Unitarians, Quakers, and Congregationalists—opposed the war on the moral grounds of pacifism and abolitionism.

• • •

Whether they supported or opposed the war, for the first time Americans read about its progress in timely accounts written by newspaper correspondents, and not from outdated government dispatches. A consequence of improving literacy and the advent of the fast Hoe rotary steam press, the new "penny press" coincided with the rise of a generation of resourceful war correspondents, and a communications revolution driven by steamships, railroads, and the telegraph.

Because they were closest to the action, the nine New Orleans newspapers published the war news first. Their accounts were reprinted in scores of newspapers around the country (a few, like the Baltimore *Sun* and the New York newspapers, carried their own reports), and thus, readers everywhere came to know the bylines of a handful of New Orleans correspondents.

The best known of them was George W. Kendall, or "GWK," co-publisher of the New Orleans *Picayune,* which formed a partnership with the Baltimore *Sun,* resulting in the syndication of Kendall's more than two hundred wartime dispatches to a nationwide readership. Nearly as well known were James Freanor, the "Mustang" of the New Orleans *Daily Delta;* and John N. Peoples, who went by "Chaparral" in the *Daily Delta* and the New Orleans *Crescent.*

Renowned as America's "eyes and ears" in Mexico, Kendall enjoyed unparalleled access to battlefields and commanders, traveled with Captain Ben McCulloch's Texas Rangers company, and even served on General William Worth's staff. Kendall was respected by soldiers and colleagues—by the former for having survived the disastrous Santa Fe expedition of 1841 and its subsequent ordeals and cruelties, and by the latter for his proficiency as a reporter, writer, and editor. As the correspondents' unofficial leader, Kendall established a Mexican courier service, "Mr. Kendall's Express," to carry dispatches from the front to the nearest ports. Fast steamers equipped with typesetting equipment set the stories in type during the trip to New Orleans, where they went straight to publication.

When the editions hit New Orleans's streets, fast riders stuffed copies of the newspapers into their saddlebags and galloped north to the nearest telegraph station to get the news on the wire. The Baltimore *Sun* operated a private "pony express" service of riders and sixty fast horses at post stations that sped dispatches from New Orleans to the telegraph near Richmond. The *Sun* sometimes published bulletins from the battlefront before official dispatches reached the White House.

The newsgathering costs—the pony relay system, telegraphic equipment, and the riders—were so prohibitively high that most newspapers shrank from bearing them alone. The New York *Journal of Commerce* hit upon the novel idea of the large New York dailies forming a cooperative to share costs. Representatives from six newspapers in 1846 established The Associated Press, which later became the world's largest, most respected news organization.

Besides carrying the latest war news, the penny press in 1846 published articles about the discovery of an eighth planet, Neptune, first seen by an "M. Galle, of Berlin" and also sighted in London; and a serialization of Charles Dickens's new novel, *Dombey and Sons.* There were ominous reports from Ireland of a potato blight and an unfolding human tragedy that would have a lasting effect on U.S. demographics.

• • •

Discerning readers gravitated to the newspapers that suited their political tastes. The Washington *Union* was readily identifiable as the voice of the Polk administration and the pro-war lobby: "We shall invade her territory; we shall seize her strongholds; we shall even TAKE HER CAPITAL, if there be no other means of bringing her to a sense of justice." The *United States Magazine and Democratic Review* was just as unfailingly supportive, going so far as to invent an axiom that justified the war as a moral imperative. "It is an acknowledged law of nations that when a country sinks into a state of anarchy, unable to govern itself, and dangerous to its neighbors, it becomes the duty of the most powerful of those neighbors to interfere and settle its affairs." Another pro-war newspaper, the *Federal Union* of Milledgeville, Georgia, reasoned that no sensible Southerner could oppose a war that would "secure to the South the balance of power in the Confederacy [United States], and, for all coming time . . . and give her the control in the operations of the Government." In the Brooklyn *Daily Eagle,* Walt Whitman chided the unpatriotic: "Cold must be the pulse, and throbless to all good thoughts . . . which cannot respond to the valorous enterprise of our soldiers and commanders in Mexico."

• • •

The *Union's* great rival, the *National Intelligencer,* and its fellow war critics were careful to display support for the troops, while relentlessly criticizing the Polk administration. As the *Intelligencer* memorably wrote, "We toast the *men,* but not the cause." Horace Greeley's New York *Daily Tribune,* another indefatigable war opponent, derided Polk's "faultless logic" in portraying Mexico as the aggressor. "Shut your eyes to the whole course of events through the last twelve years . . . and it will become easy to prove that we are a meek, unoffending, ill used people, and that Mexico has kicked, cuffed and grossly imposed upon us." When Polk and others suggested that war critics like Greeley were treasonously giving "aid and comfort" to the enemy, Greeley shot back that if anyone had aided the enemy, it was the president, by facilitating Santa Anna's return "to lead our enemy against us. . . ." Seizing California and New Mexico under the rubric of spreading democracy, wrote the Richmond *Whig,* was like saying: "You must have the same degree of freedom which we enjoy, whether you are fit for it or not. . . . If you refuse, we will ravage your fields, hang you up by the neck until you are dead . . . and leave your towns in smoking ruins."

• • •

When Taylor's victories in northern Mexico failed to force Mexico to negotiate, more Army officers began to grumble about the war's arguable premises and its method of prosecution. Even as he marched to the Rio Grande in March 1846, Lieutenant Colonel Ethan Allen Hitchcock had described the deployment as "a most unholy and unrighteous proceeding," whose purpose was to "bring on a war, so as to have a pretext for taking California and as much of this country as it chooses." He never reconciled himself to the war. Neither did Lieutenant Ulysses S. Grant, known in those days as Sam Grant, who would write in his *Memoirs* that he "had a horror of the Mexican War . . . only I had not moral courage enough to resign." It was "one of the most unjust [wars] ever waged by a stronger against a weaker nation . . . an instance of a republic following the bad example of European monarchies . . . to acquire additional territory." And as battle followed battle, more officers began to agree with Lieutenant George Meade's sardonic appraisal: "Well may we be grateful that we are at war with Mexico! Were it any other power, our gross follies would have been punished severely."

But the regular officers' complaints often were as much due to their political affiliations as to moral qualms about the war. Army officers were predominantly Whigs, while volunteer officers were mainly Democrats. The professional officers, who had instantly resented most of their volunteer counterparts anyway, presuming that the volunteers outranked them because of their Democratic Party affiliations, began to also resent what Captain Robert Anderson described as Polk's "eager desire to secure political influence in his appointees." "At the end of the war every young officer who possibly can will leave it in disgust and contempt," wrote Lieutenant Napoleon Jackson Dana.

Because so many of the disgruntled officers would become generals during the Civil War, their partisan opinions on the Mexican War, stated in diaries and letters, would go far to nurture the censorious attitude toward the war that would predominate among nineteenth-century historians and their readers.

• • •

Taylor's unhappiness with the war increased with each passing month. Before attacking Monterrey, Taylor had confided to his son-in-law, Dr. R. C. Wood, that he "must entirely disapprove" of his government's actions in California. Imperial Britain's conquests were no "more outrageous than our attempt or intention of taking permanent possession of [California]." In another letter to Wood, Taylor wrote, "Our ambitious views of conquest & agrandisement [*sic*] at the expense of a weak power will only be restrained & circumscribed by our inability to carry out our view."

When Democrats lost their House majority in the 1846 election, Taylor ascribed it to disapproval in the Northern states of Polk's policies and obfuscations. "The country has been so misled & mystified in regard to this Mexican war, that they hardly know how to act" when informed of a new development, "no matter how absurd or outrageous it may be."

The pragmatic engineer, Captain Robert E. Lee, conceded that America had "bullied" Mexico, for which he was "ashamed," but believed that dwelling upon it served no good purpose. "If we have been wrong in our Course, we should have discovered it before." Lee was scornful of those who wished to return captured Mexican territory to assuage their guilty consciences, sarcastically noting, "If this retrograde step would restore us our glorious dead, I should be content. It will rather tend to condemn their devotion to their country & the next step will be to convict them of Suicide."

• • •

By early 1847, citizen petitions against the war were arriving in Congress nearly every day. On February 6, Congress received pleas to end the war from fifty-one residents of Milford, Michigan; seventy-one people in Madison County, Illinois; and the citizens of Manlius, New York, reported the *Congressional Globe*. A more explicit statement signed by thirty-two citizens of Chester County, Pennsylvania, asked Congress "to vote no more supplies for the prosecution of offensive operations in Mexico, and that measures be taken for the withdrawal of the army within the acknowledged limits of the United States."

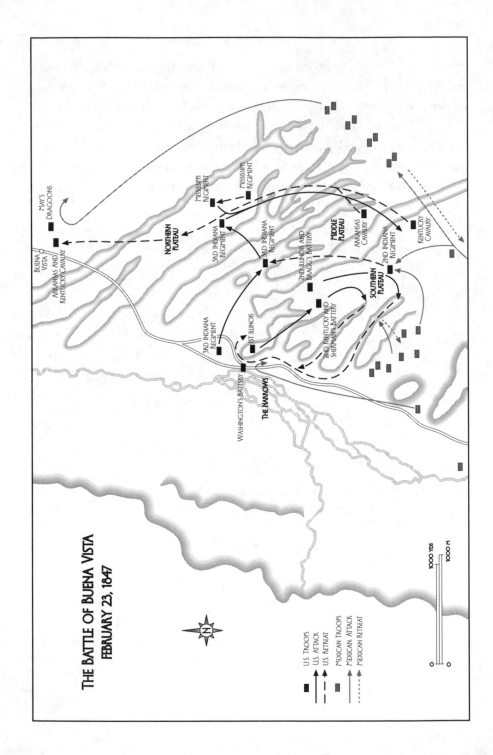

THE BATTLE OF BUENA VISTA
FEBRUARY 23, 1847

MAY'S DRAGOONS

MISSISSIPPI REGIMENT

NORTHERN PLATEAU

3RD INDIANA REGIMENT

3RD INDIANA REGIMENT

MIDDLE PLATEAU

ARKANSAS CAVALRY

KENTUCKY CAVALRY

BUENA VISTA

ARKANSAS AND KENTUCKY CAVALRY

2ND ILLINOIS AND BRAGG'S BATTERY

2ND INDIANA REGIMENT

SOUTHERN PLATEAU

3RD INDIANA REGIMENT

1ST ILLINOIS

2ND KENTUCKY AND SHERMAN'S BATTERY

WASHINGTON'S BATTERY

THE NARROWS

N

U.S. TROOPS
U.S. ATTACK
U.S. RETREAT
MEXICAN TROOPS
MEXICAN ATTACK
MEXICAN RETREAT

1000 YARDS
1000 M
0
0

19

BUENA VISTA

"A bitter curse upon them, poor boy, who led thee forth,
From some gentle, sad-eyed mother, weeping, lonely, in the North!
Spake the mournful Mexic woman, as she laid him with her dead,
And turned to soothe the living, and bind the wounds which bled."

—John Greenleaf Whittier, "The Angels of Buena Vista"

"What are you firing, captain?" General Zachary Taylor asked Captain
Braxton Bragg.
"Canister, sir," Bragg replied.
"Double or single?"
"Single, sir."
"Then double it and give 'em Hell!"

—Overheard by a U.S. officer at height of Buena Vista fighting

1:00 A.M. FEBRUARY 22, 1847: AGUA NUEVA

Arrayed in a long line with swords drawn, Colonel Enoch Steen's First U.S. Dragoons calmed their jittery mounts and watched the fire burn down the hacienda at Agua Nueva. General Zachary Taylor was reluctantly abandoning the forward outpost because a large force led by Santa Anna was less than a day's march from Taylor's small army.

The dragoons shouldn't have been there. But at 10 P.M. they were rousted from their bivouac at Angostura, "the Narrows," twelve miles to the north, and sent by the U.S. command to Agua Nueva. The Arkansas Cavalry Regiment had been ordered to load twenty-two wagons with provisions stockpiled at the hacienda and to destroy the rest. But the unruly "Rackensackers," scarcely ever drilled or disciplined by their commander, Colonel Archibald Yell, had refused, protesting that they had come to fight, not serve as laborers. When the dragoons reached Agua Nueva at midnight, the Rackensackers were sleeping or playing cards, a huge fire was burning, and the wagons were empty. The disgusted dragoons loaded the wagons, and they had just sent them on their way to Angostura when one of the Arkansans shouted, "Run, boys, run! The Mexicans are on us!" The Rackensackers leaped on their horses and fled, nearly stampeding the dragoons' mounts.

Mexican cavalrymen were indeed nearby. Steen ordered his men to throw burning logs into the chapel and all the houses. They then tossed into the fire stacks of barley and sides of bacon and pork, and "the whole place blazed up grandly."

The dragoons rode out of Agua Nueva, turned their mounts around, and watched the hacienda burn. The enormous fire lit up the countryside for miles. Munitions occasionally exploded with concussive force.

Ominously, the flames illuminated more than just the hacienda. "The hill back of the place fairly glittered with the sheen of Mexican lance points," observed Samuel Chamberlain. Then, like a spreading wave, columns of enemy cavalry lapped around the ranch and fanned out over the plain.

The dragoons had seen enough. They turned back to the Narrows, reaching their camp at daybreak, with the Mexicans not far behind.

• • •

For weeks, Taylor's headquarters at Saltillo had been receiving reports about large formations of Mexican cavalry to the south. Old Rough and Ready was willing to meet any enemy attack, even with his reduced force of five thousand volunteers and a few hundred regulars, but he was not convinced that Santa Anna would march north from San Luis Potosi to fight.

Taylor assumed that Santa Anna by now had in his possession the murdered Lieutenant Richey's courier pouch with Scott's instructions and the description of the Vera Cruz expedition. Santa Anna surely would march south to aid Vera Cruz—and not attempt the grueling 240-mile northern journey across the high desert during wintertime, Taylor believed. While this was a logical scenario, it did not excuse Taylor from heeding the growing volume of sightings indicating that Santa Anna was indeed advancing toward his army, or from establishing a viable intelligence network. But Taylor did neither.

In the remote event that Santa Anna did march north from San Luis Potosi,

Taylor intended to force him to fight "before he had time to refresh and organize his troops, whom I knew must be much exhausted by their march." He could not permit the Mexicans to reach Saltillo, a city of eighteen thousand that could easily replenish an army of twenty thousand, the estimated size of Santa Anna's force at San Luis Potosi. Beyond that, Taylor had given little thought to where he would meet Santa Anna if he marched north.

General Winfield Scott had ordered Taylor to pull back seventy miles from Saltillo to Monterrey, whose forts and stone houses, Scott believed, would afford better protection. But Taylor opposed making a stand there for the same reasons that Santa Anna had urged General Pedro de Ampudia to abandon Monterrey in September: it could easily be invested, its supply line cut, and its defenders starved into submission.

Taylor declined to carry out Scott's order and informed the War Department of his intention, if it came to that, to deny Saltillo to Santa Anna. Concerned about Taylor's exposed position, President Polk observed that Scott "has probably reduced General Taylor's forces to too small a number."

• • •

Taylor initially sent forty-five hundred troops led by Brigadier General John Wool to Agua Nueva, twenty miles south of Saltillo, to intercept Santa Anna's army should he choose to march north from San Luis Potosi. Morale was high, noted Taylor: "The greatest enthusiasm appears to pervade the whole of the forces & all express themselves desirous to come in collision with the enemy."

Wool, however, was uneasy about Agua Nueva's vulnerability to flanking and encirclement. While returning one day to the encampment from Saltillo, Wool and Lieutenant James Carleton discovered a more defensible position. It was a two-mile-long, six-thousand-foot-elevation tableland divided by ravines into fingerlike plateaus. The area had sufficient firewood and forage for livestock. Barren peaks abutted the tableland on the east and west. On its south end was the Narrows, where fifty-foot-high bluffs on the east side and a small river and plunging ravines on the west squeezed the San Luis Potosi road to a forty-foot-wide passage. A mile farther south, the last of the three plateaus dropped off. On the tableland's northern extremity was the hacienda whose name would become inextricably linked with the surrounding landscape—Buena Vista.

Wool and Carleton studied the ground carefully. West of the road, a web of gullies, some of them twenty feet deep or more, formed a natural barrier. The east side of the road was more problematic: The ravines were shallower and broader, even ford-able by enemy cavalry that could then flank the American left if the armies met there. But in his enthusiasm for Buena Vista, Wool missed this potential flaw in its natural defenses. "If we have to fight a superior force, this is the place," he declared.

• • •

While Taylor and Major General Robert Patterson were busy securing Victoria in early January, Brigadier General William Worth and Major General William O. Butler had affirmed Wool's assessment of the Buena Vista plateau's defensibility. A new camp was established at La Encantada hacienda on the south side of the Nar-rows, a dozen miles north of Agua Nueva. "The Enchanted," as the hacienda was known, was nothing like its name; the soldiers were miserable there, having to endure cold, windy conditions in flimsy tents without adequate firewood. Butler, the senior officer in Taylor's absence, denied Wool's request to move the camp to the less-exposed north side of the Narrows. But after Taylor's regulars were appro-priated for the Vera Cruz expedition, Butler relented. Agua Nueva, however, remained the army's forward outpost.

• • •

Thirty-five miles south of Agua Nueva, Major Solon Borland's fifty Arkansas Cav-alry troopers were investigating reports of enemy lancers in the high desert. The Rackensackers stopped at the La Encarnacion hacienda on the San Luis Potosi road, and there were joined by thirty Kentucky cavalrymen led by Major John P. Gaines and Captain Cassius Marcellus Clay. Two days later, on January 22, the combined force set out to check a report of enemy lancers seen several miles away, but heavy rains forced the eighty cavalrymen to cancel the mission. They returned to camp and went to sleep without posting a guard.

The Americans awoke the next morning in a thick, clinging fog, from which came the eerie strains of a popular song, "Love Not." To their horror, the caval-rymen discovered that five hundred Mexican lancers and their regimental band had surrounded them during the night. Concluding that resistance was futile, the Americans surrendered to General Jose Vincente Miñon and were marched south toward San Luis Potosi.

A Mexican lancer recognized Daniel Henrie, the patrol's interpreter and scout, as one of the Texans captured at Mier in 1842. Major Gaines, who understood Spanish, overheard the Mexicans discussing how they were going to kill Henrie.

Because he was an officer, Gaines had been permitted to keep his horse and pistols, and he now obtained permission from his captors to allow an ill prisoner to ride in his place. He gave his horse to Henrie, who vaulted into the saddle, shot a pair of lancers with the loaded pistols Gaines had left in a saddlebag, and galloped away, with the other lancers on his heels. Henrie ditched his pursuers in the mountains and got lost. On the fourth day, his horse died. After cutting steaks from the mare's flanks, Henrie walked the last sixty miles back to Saltillo.

Mexican lancers captured seventeen Kentucky cavalrymen sent to look for the overdue Gaines and Borland; the hapless rescuers had stopped at a ranch and got drunk. Due to their officers' carelessness, nearly a hundred volunteer cavalrymen would spend the rest of the war in captivity in Mexico City.

• • •

In retribution for some Arkansas Cavalry volunteers having purportedly molested some of the Agua Nueva women on Christmas Day, an Arkansan was lassoed February 9 and dragged through the prickly pear and rocks until dead. The victim's body was "perfectly black . . . bruised and mangled in a most shocking manner." Without their officers' knowledge, about a hundred Arkansas troopers—two full companies—went hunting for the killers. They found some Mexicans hiding in a cave near Cataña, presumed that they were the guilty parties, and began shooting and scalping them. A detail of regular Army dragoons, hearing screams coming from the cave, arrived to find it "full of our volunteers yelling like fiends, while on the rocky floor lay over twenty Mexicans, dead and dying in pools of blood," one of them recalled. "Women and children were clinging to the knees of the murderers and shrieking for mercy." The dragoons stopped the massacre by threatening to shoot the Arkansans and then arrested them all. An inquiry failed to identify who had killed the civilians, and the two companies were sent back to the camps on the Rio Grande.

The tension would only grow worse. Concerned about the presence of large numbers of enemy lancers, Taylor moved his command from Monterrey to Saltillo, in case Santa Anna sent more troops from San Luis Potosí to reinforce them. If the Mexicans offered battle, "I shall indulge them, be the consequences what they may," he vowed, adding bitterly, "We now begin to see the fruits of the arrangements recently made at Washington, by an intrigue of Marcey [sic], Scott & Worth to take from me nearly the whole of the regular forces under my command, while in the immediate front of the enemy."

Matters were far more serious than Taylor suspected. Santa Anna was not sending reinforcements; he was bringing his entire army north.

• • •

Santa Anna believed that one major victory would transform his and Mexico's fortunes. His own shaky political position—the twenty Mexican states had elected him president by just 11–9—would find surer footing. He would be able to raise a large army of better soldiers. And a victory would magnify the voices of America's growing antiwar movement, whose words reached him via the newspapers. All these developments would improve the prospects for negotiations favorable to Mexico.

Knowing that Winfield Scott had stripped Zachary Taylor's army of nearly all its regulars, Santa Anna now assayed the odds of beating Taylor to be in his favor. The remaining American force was not even a third the size of the twenty-thousand-man army Santa Anna had assembled at San Luis Potosi. And he couldn't afford to wait until spring. His political adversaries were already complaining about him, and the Mexican newspapers were suggesting that he had not yet taken the offensive because he was conspiring with the Americans. It was necessary, too, that he lead his army into battle before it melted away; desertion was a major problem.

Should he defeat Taylor at Saltillo, Santa Anna knew from General Jose Urrea, whose fifteen hundred irregular cavalry he had sent north of Monterrey to harry Taylor's supply line, that there was nothing to stop him from marching clear to the Rio Grande and reclaiming all of the territory lost during the previous ten months. Scott would have to postpone the Vera Cruz invasion and rush to Texas's defense. To silence its critics, the Polk administration would be compelled to wind up the war quickly with a negotiated settlement, possibly less favorable to the United States than Polk wished.

While Taylor simplistically believed that Santa Anna would utilize the information in Scott's intercepted letter to prepare massive defenses at Vera Cruz, Santa Anna had chosen the more daring and potentially more rewarding alternative, attacking Taylor's reduced force.

• • •

When his "desponding letter" seeking cash from the Mexican government netted him a mere $35,000, Santa Anna expropriated ninety-eight bars of silver from mines outside San Luis Potosi. The silver was melted down to buy arms, uniforms, and provisions for his slapdash force, composed of remnants of the army beaten at Monterrey, the units withdrawn from Tampico, and levies and press-ganged "recruits" from the provinces.

The feverish preparations culminated in the Mexican army's majestic departure from San Luis Potosi on January 28, as a band played "Adios." Santa Anna traveled in a carriage pulled by eight mules, while his 19,525 men walked or rode. Hundreds of miles ahead, three thousand cavalrymen and lancers led by Generals Urrea and Jose Vincente Miñon roved the countryside.

It was the largest Mexican offensive in a century. In addition to the infantry and cavalry, the expedition included 450 mules, twenty-one ammunition wagons, and twenty guns ranging from mortars to 24-pounders. The heavy guns were crewed by the San Patricio Brigade; the Irish deserters from Taylor's army marched under a silken-green banner with gilt images of an Irish harp and St. Patrick. The soldiers' new lightweight uniforms were scant protection against the sharp cold of the high desert a hundred miles north of San Luis Potosi, where a "blue whistler" tormented them for a week with wind-driven rain, sleet, and snow, causing hundreds of deaths. Then they sweltered through a sudden spell of hot weather. Many soldiers threw away gear and rations, and the sick were left beside the road. There were so many desertions that Santa Anna ringed the army's nighttime encampments with pickets, with orders to shoot anyone who tried to slip away.

Three weeks and two hundred miles after leaving San Luis Potosi, Santa Anna's army reached La Encarnación with four thousand fewer men than it began with, yet still with nearly sixteen thousand infantrymen and another three thousand mounted troops in the vicinity.

Santa Anna was so certain that he would find a stockpile of American provisions at Saltillo that he had provisioned his army with only enough food for the march. Now, as his army, strung out for miles to the south, streamed into La Encarnación between February 17 and 20, Santa Anna knew that he could not remain there long; for his army to eat, it must continue its march northward and defeat Taylor.

• • •

The capture of a hundred of his cavalrymen deprived Taylor of a reconnaissance force that might have spotted Santa Anna's army at La Encarnación and shadowed Miñon's and Urrea's mounted troops.

Thus, he was delighted when Captain Ben McCulloch and twenty-six Texas

Rangers rode into Saltillo; here were the experienced scouts that Taylor needed. Major William W. S. Bliss, Taylor's chief of staff, signed them on the spot to six-month enlistments, and they officially became "McCulloch's Company, Texas Mounted Volunteers (Spies)."

On February 20, McCulloch's Rangers and three hundred U.S. dragoons commanded by Colonel Charles May embarked on an extended reconnaissance south of Agua Nueva. A large dust cloud drew the dragoons to a campsite, now abandoned, where a large cavalry force had spent the previous night. Then, in the distance, a long column of horsemen could be seen riding north. The strong evidence of a possible enemy offensive sent May and his now skittish men galloping into the American camp at Agua Nueva, rousing everyone from their slumbers early February 21.

Meanwhile, McCulloch and four Rangers had left May's party to ride farther south. At La Encarnación, they found Santa Anna's main army. McCulloch immediately dispatched three Rangers to give Taylor the news, while McCulloch and the fourth Ranger disguised themselves as rancheros and slipped into the enemy camp. Throughout the night, they rode among the sleeping Mexicans, and by the light of the campfires assayed the enemy army's size and capabilities. Before daybreak, February 21, they left the camp undetected and rode to Agua Nueva.

• • •

General Wool sought Taylor's permission to abandon Agua Nueva and concentrate the American forces at the Narrows and on the Buena Vista plateau. But Taylor stubbornly insisted on at least initially meeting Santa Anna at Agua Nueva, even with Wool arguing that the enemy lancers would have maneuvering room there that they would lack at Buena Vista.

The debate continued through the morning of February 21, until Wool at last convinced Taylor of Buena Vista's superior tactical features: difficult terrain for enemy cavalry and artillery, and a relatively small battlefield that would fetter Santa Anna's ability to deploy his multitudinous ground troops. Wool began positioning the army at Buena Vista, while Taylor rode off to Saltillo to secure the army's rear against the cavalrymen spotted by May's dragoons.

• • •

While the Americans were withdrawing from Agua Nueva, leaving behind the Arkansas Cavalry to cart away the stores, Santa Anna's army was marching out of La Encarnación, expecting to meet Taylor in battle the next day. As a goad to his hungry peasant troops, Santa Anna had promised them a feast of American provisions after they defeated the invaders.

At Agua Nueva early February 22, the Mexicans found no enemy army, and no American food stockpiles. The fires lit by Colonel Steen's dragoons still crackled, and a pall of smoke hung over the gutted hacienda.

There was nothing for Santa Anna's lean, weather-beaten troops to do but continue marching northward.

FEBRUARY 22, 1847: BUENA VISTA

At midmorning, the first columns of Santa Anna's army were seen approaching the Narrows. "The whole country in our front was covered with their dense masses," noted the dragoon Samuel Chamberlain. An American regimental band struck up "Hail, Columbia," and General Wool rode up and down the American ranks, reminding the volunteers that it was George Washington's birthday; the day's watchword was "Honor of Washington." Washington's name, recalled a volunteer, "nerved the hearts of our soldiers."

At 11 A.M., Surgeon General Pedro Vanderlinden and two other emissaries rode toward the American lines under a white flag and handed General Taylor a communiqué from Santa Anna. It was a surrender demand:

"You are surrounded by twenty thousand men, and cannot in any human probability avoid suffering a rout, and being cut to pieces with your troops, but as you deserve consideration and particular esteem, I wish to save you from a catastrophe, and for that purpose give you this note, in order that you may surrender at discretion, under the assurance that you will be treated with the consideration belonging to the Mexican character; to which end you will be granted an hour's time to make up your mind, to commence from the moment when my flag of truce arrives in your camp . . . God and liberty!"

• • •

Surely disbelieving that Taylor would meekly lay down his arms, Santa Anna studied the battlefield through his spyglass and consulted with his generals while Taylor and his staff composed a reply. The Mexicans saw three avenues of attack. The most obvious was the one straight up the road through the forty-foot-wide Narrows. The two other routes, however, would permit the Mexicans to bypass the chokepoint at the Narrows and, using the broad ravines to funnel infantry and cavalry, flank the

American left wing—the vulnerable point that Wool had overlooked. A short right hook would take the Mexicans across the Middle Plateau and behind the Narrows, thereby cutting the road to Saltillo. A wider-arcing thrust farther east would send Santa Anna's men down a long ridge, around Taylor's entire left flank to the army's baggage train at the Buena Vista hacienda, and from there to Saltillo.

• • •

Upon reading Santa Anna's surrender demand, Taylor reportedly blurted out profanities, but his formal response, probably written by Major Bliss, his chief of staff, was coolly sardonic:

"In reply to your note of this date, summoning me to surrender my forces at discretion, I beg leave to say that I decline acceding to your request."

• • •

Mexican troops lunged toward the American right flank west of the road—the unpromising ground carved by deep ravines and closely hemmed by the mountains. Taylor quickly shifted to his right Braxton Bragg's battery, Colonel William McKee's Kentucky infantry regiment, and a company of Arkansas Cavalry commanded by Captain Albert Pike.

But it was only a feint by the Mexicans. About a thousand light infantry troops commanded by General Pedro de Ampudia suddenly poured out of a ravine on the south side of the Buena Vista plateau and began struggling up the dominating ridge on the American left. The position's importance was now evident to the lowliest private: From the heights, Mexican artillery could dominate the looping route to the hacienda and Saltillo. Santa Anna had decided on the gambit of seeking a limited tactical advantage without giving away his battle strategy.

Colonel Humphrey Marshall's Kentucky Cavalry and four companies of Indiana infantry raced Ampudia's men to the ridge's summit. Throughout the afternoon, the opposing armies of spectators watched Ampudia's men and the Americans vie to reach the top first. Whenever the Kentuckians and Indianans appeared to gain the edge, Taylor's troops cheered loudly. But when General Wool sent an officer to warn Marshall about a second Mexican climbing party, the message got garbled and Marshall's men hesitated, believing they were being ordered to withdraw. By the time the miscommunication was straightened out, Ampudia's men had taken possession of the upper slopes. There they dug in for the night, and the skirmishing ceased.

• • •

With nightfall, the six-thousand-foot-high Buena Vista plateau was plunged into freezing darkness. Camped so near each other that neither army dared light fires, the men ate their supper cold; for the Mexicans, it was the last of their rations. During the night, a bone-chilling drizzle drenched the thousands of tentless combatants. Huddled in their sodden blankets and clothing, they longed for dawn, even though it would surely usher in a day of bullets, steel, and death.

• • •

Amid reports that more than twelve hundred cavalrymen under General Miñon, "the Lion," were massed near Palomas Adentura, a mountain pass east of Saltillo, Taylor returned to Saltillo with Colonel Jefferson Davis's Mississippi Rifles and a squadron of Colonel Charles May's Second U.S. Dragoons. Taylor inspected the city's defenses. Four companies of the First Illinois Infantry controlled the streets; a pair of twenty-four-pound howitzers guarded the city's main approaches. Two companies from Davis's regiment, supported by a field piece, protected the baggage train and the headquarters camp near the Buena Vista hacienda.

Taylor did not know that he had a secret ally against General Miñon—a small, red-haired American woman who lived near Palomas pass, Caroline Porter. Miss Porter instructed Mexican women at General Mariana Arista's textile factory in Saltillo in the industrial science of cloth weaving, as it was practiced in her native Lowell, Massachusetts. More to the point, Miss Porter was also Miñon's former mistress. Roving the high country east of Saltillo with his lancers, the general diverted himself with a lingering afternoon visit to his former paramour. The "Yankee Delilah," as Miss Porter was later called, was such a distraction to "the Lion" that he neglected to carry out his primary mission of severing Taylor's communication and supply link to Monterrey. Miñon instead returned to Miss Porter's home to spend the night.

FEBRUARY 23, 1847: BUENA VISTA

Santa Anna's army, clad in blue uniforms with red facings, assembled on the open ground below the Buena Vista plateau in long, glittering ranks beneath their silken banners. Regimental bands played sacred music as priests walked down the lines, dispensing blessings. The American army, mustering only four thousand men without the units deployed to its rear, observed the Catholic pageantry of the more than sixteen thousand-strong enemy army with stolid calm, readying their weapons. "The [Mexican] Infantry knelt down, the Cavalry lowered their lances and uncovered, and their colors drooped as the benedictions were bestowed," reported Samuel Chamberlain. The ceremony ended with the Mexican troops roaring "Vivas!"

• • •

General Santiago Blanco's division attacked straight up the road into the Narrows. Captain John M. Washington's artillery battery, supported by the First Illinois and the Third Indiana, held its fire until the enemy troops filled the slim waist of the pass. Then the American guns hurled a storm of canister and grapeshot into the densely packed Mexican columns. Chamberlain saw "fragments of men and horses . . . flying in the air" and Blanco's men falling in "fearful piles of dead and wounded" that clogged the road. The American guns stopped the attack cold.

But Blanco's futile attack was only a diversion for the main event, a massive assault on the American center on the Middle Plateau, the short right hook that, if successful, would place the Mexicans behind the Narrows. General Francisco Pacheco's veteran infantry division and squadrons of cavalry—four thousand men in all—had been working their way eastward through a ravine that traced the plateau's southern edge. Opposite them were about a thousand troops from the Second Illinois and Second Indiana, supported by Colonel Enoch Steen's First U.S. Dragoons, McCulloch's Mounted Texas company, and three guns under Lieutenant John Paul Jones O'Brien, detached from Captain Washington's battery at the Narrows.

Pacheco's troops boiled out of the ravine and onto the plateau with shocking suddenness, and the Americans scrambled to the high ground to meet them. "It was an awful moment to face the thousands of veterans in solid column, with their gaudy uniforms and showy banners," recalled Private B. F. Scribner of the Second Indiana.

It was also a moment of sheer terror for the volunteers, who had never been under fire. A volley of grapeshot from a Mexican battery gusted through the Indiana regiment. The Hoosiers stood their ground and then advanced with O'Brien's battery, unleashing more than a dozen musket volleys at Pacheco's men, who continued to tramp forward steadily, pausing only to load and fire. Some Mexicans worked their way around to the Indianans' left and poured an enfilading fire into them. More enemy troops issued from the ravine. Seemingly from nowhere, a squadron of lancers materialized and bore down on the Indianans.

• • •

Then, in the span of a few minutes, the Second Indiana collapsed, and Taylor's army was in peril of being routed. General Joseph Lane, in overall command of both Indiana regiments, had ordered an advance. As the Second Indiana moved forward, a gap opened between it and the units that were supposed to support it— the Second Illinois and the dragoons and Rangers. In this moment of crisis, Colonel William Bowles, the Second Indiana commander, shouted, "Cease firing and retreat!" Some volunteers advanced, others turned back. Confusion became chaos, and then panic. The Second Indianans "broke and ran like deer."

Their ignominious flight exposed the flank of Colonel William Bissell's Second Illinois to the Mexican attack and murderous enfilading fire, and it, too, now began to crumble.

Left unprotected was O'Brien's battery, which stood its ground and carved great swaths through the oncoming Mexicans even as the enemy assault troops threatened to engulf the three guns. The Americans were on the brink of losing the battle before even an hour had gone by.

Captain George Lincoln, Wool's adjutant general, attempted to rally Bissell's crumbling regiment, shouting, "Come on, my brave Illinoisans, and save this battery!" He was instantly shot in the head and waist, and fell dead. His gallantry, however, inspired the Second Illinois to resolutely advance to protect O'Brien's three guns. The Mexicans were just fifty yards from O'Brien's gunners, who were firing double charges of canister into them, while slowly pulling back toward the advancing Illinoisans.

At that moment, Colonel William McKee's Second Kentucky foot soldiers, jogging from their position to the right of Washington's battery near the Narrows, arrived on the Middle Plateau with two more guns. Pacheco's men, who had been cheering lustily as they rushed O'Brien's battery and the Illinoisans, fell silent as the American gunfire intensified. The San Patricios joined the Mexican attack with their heavy artillery. Then the batteries of Captains Braxton Bragg and Thomas Sherman arrived and added their guns to the din. As Santa Anna watched the attack, his horse was hit by grapeshot; the general was flung to the ground, injuring the stump of his leg.

Pacheco's attack faltered, the Mexicans took cover in the ravines, and the San Patricios pulled back. Four companies of the First Illinois, sent to help plug the breach, attacked the Mexicans in a ravine with bayonets, killing, wounding, and capturing 150 of them, "the most brilliant thing of the day," noted Lew Wallace, the Indiana volunteer officer and future best-selling novelist. Amid the tumult, O'Brien miraculously held onto his 6- and 12-pounders, but was forced to abandon a 4-pounder whose gunners and horses had all been killed or wounded.

• • •

While Pacheco was attacking the Second Indiana and Second Illinois, two Mexican infantry divisions and a squadron of lancers under Generals Pedro de Ampudia and Manuel Lombardini had crushed the Americans' left flank, driving off hundreds of dismounted Arkansas and Kentucky cavalrymen. It was partly the result of Colonel Archibald Yell's having ordered his Arkansas Cavalry to pull back a short distance. "The men . . . understood the word *retreat*, to be an order to make, each man, the best of his way to the rear," observed Captain Albert Pike. Yell's and Colonel Humphrey Marshall's cavalry units did not re-form until they reached the Buena Vista hacienda.

It was only 9 A.M., and Wool was desperately trying to stave off disaster. With his left, or eastern, flank driven back to the hacienda, Wool repositioned his reeling army along a new north–south line to prevent it from being trapped by the marching divisions of Ampudia and General Francisco Perez, who had succeeded the wounded Lombardini. What Pacheco had failed to do on the Middle Plateau, Ampudia and Perez now hoped to achieve on the North Plateau hundreds of yards away: with four thousand infantrymen and lancers, they intended to slice across the plateau to the Saltillo road behind Captain Washington's battery, surrounding the American army.

• • •

At this moment of extreme hazard, General Zachary Taylor arrived on the battlefield with the Mississippi Rifles and Colonel May's Second U.S. Dragoons. Noting the Mexican troops swarming over the east side of the plateau, Taylor quickly grasped the magnitude of the crisis. During a brief command meeting, General John Wool, shaken by the morning's setbacks, blurted to Taylor, "General, we are whipped," to which Taylor snapped back, "That is for me to determine."

Taylor sent Colonel Davis's Mississippi Rifles to round up the Second Indiana, which was scattered all over the plateau, and to then anchor the left flank, now facing eastward and resting on the North Plateau. Wool moved up the Third Indiana to support Davis.

May's dragoons and two guns from Captain Sherman's battery were dispatched to reinforce the Arkansas and Kentucky cavalrymen, who had retreated to the Buena Vista hacienda. About a thousand Mexican lancers led by General Anastasio Torrejón were bearing down on the Arkansans and Kentuckians. May would have to hurry if he was going to intercept them.

Torrejón's lancers reached the edge of the hacienda first. The Mexicans' fusillade of rifle fire panicked the Americans' horses, and the enemy lancers swept the defenders along in a thrashing clot of men and horses. Colonel Yell, at the head of his Arkansans, was killed by lance thrusts to the mouth and chest. Panicked volunteers crowded into the hacienda, where "some seemed mad with terror, and went crying and blaspheming around the streets."

At that instant, May's dragoons struck the lancers' flank, breaking Torrejón's force in two. Some lancers veered into the hacienda's streets, where they unexpectedly encountered a detachment of Mississippi Rifles crouched behind barricades. The Mississippians' sheeting rifle fire killed thirty-five of them, and the survivors turned around and rode away. The rest of Torrejón's men disappeared into the western mountains and were not seen again that day.

• • •

Their crimson shirts, white duck trousers, and "light swinging step peculiar to Indians and hunters" instantly identified the troops advancing across the North Plateau as Jefferson Davis's Mississippi Rifles. Generals Perez and Ampudia planned to roll over Davis's regiment and seize the Saltillo road, thereby surrounding Taylor's army. But rather than wait for the Mexicans to attack, Davis was launching a preemptive assault. As their incredulous countrymen watched, the 370 Mississippians, firing their Whitney rifles, boldly advanced on the four thousand enemy infantrymen and lancers massed on the plateau's east end. An enemy cavalry squadron swept past the Mississippians and then gathered behind them, but Davis's men stopped, pivoted like an oiled machine, and with well-aimed volleys drove the horsemen into a ravine.

As Davis had intended, the Mississippians' audacious advance had purchased time for reinforcements to reach them. The new arrivals included Colonel James Lane's Third Indiana Infantry and hundreds of Hoosiers from the shattered Second Indiana who had either been rounded up by Davis's men, or had been inspired to return to the battlefield by their paymaster, Major Roger Dix. Mounted on a great bay, Dix had held aloft the regimental Stars and Stripes and appealed to their patriotism. Among the flotsam from the Second Indiana was its commander, Colonel Bowles, who fought the rest of the day as a private. The additions gave Davis eight hundred men against the thick wall of lancers, mounted on wiry little mustangs, that was now moving toward them in perfect order.

With no time to form a square, the classic infantry defensive formation against cavalry, Davis threw his men into a shallow V, with the open end facing the nearly two thousand lancers, who advanced at a "graceful gallop, with lines accurately dressed." The silent Americans held their fire as the brilliantly uniformed lancers drew within two hundred yards, then one hundred yards, "chaunting a song." Davis repeatedly called out to his men not to shoot. At eighty yards, the volunteers loosed a deadly crossfire that caused the lancers' front ranks to buckle in a red haze pierced by human and equine shrieks.

As the survivors recoiled and fled, the Mississippians pounced on the wounded with their eighteen-inch Bowie knives. From the Middle Plateau, Sherman's and Bragg's batteries blasted the reeling lancers and Perez's and Ampudia's infantry divisions, which now joined the Mexican exodus from the North Plateau. The broken enemy divisions streamed eastward, to a ravine and box canyon where Santa Anna had placed his reserves. Thousands of men and horses jammed the sanctuaries. The American artillerymen commenced slaughtering them.

• • •

Amid the Mexicans' collapse on the brink of an epochal victory, one unit had stood its ground and performed superbly: the despised San Patricios. Throughout the fight, the Irish deserters had sustained a steady, killing fire on the Americans from a ridge on the southeastern corner of the battleground. Taylor irately ordered the First U.S. Dragoons to take that "d—d battery." Keeping to the ravines until reaching the San Luis Potosi road, the dragoons rode to the Narrows and thence around the heaped Mexican dead killed by Captain Washington's batteries, intending to get behind the San Patricios.

Suddenly the skies opened up, and for fifteen minutes all fighting ceased while a downpour drenched the soldiers of both armies. The rain cleared the thin mountain air of gunsmoke, dust, and the stench of the dead.

• • •

Sherman's and Bragg's batteries then resumed shelling the dense mass of Mexican infantry and lancers wedged into the ravine and box canyon—until a Mexican officer under a white flag approached Taylor's lines. Santa Anna, the officer told Taylor, wished to know "what he wanted." The puzzling message was not exactly an invitation to parley, but General Wool was sent under a white flag to meet with Santa Anna.

As Wool and the Mexican emissary rode toward the Mexican lines, the battlefield was eerily silent, with one exception: the San Patricios' battery continued to fire.

Suddenly, the Mexicans penned up in the ravine and box canyon began streaming back to their lines. The white flag had been a ruse to extricate Pacheco's and Perez's trapped troops, and it had worked.

• • •

General Miñon had finally disengaged himself from Caroline Porter and was leading his horsemen down Palomas Pass toward Saltillo. Refugees excitedly told Miñon that Santa Anna had won the battle. Miñon positioned his fifteen hundred men on the San Luis Potosi road between the Narrows and Saltillo and waited for the retreating American army. It did not appear, but Miñon continued to wait.

Captain William Shover, defending the American baggage train with two companies of Mississippi Rifles, had heard the same dismaying reports of defeat. When no retreating American troops materialized, Shover began shelling Miñon's flank with two field guns. Hearing the shooting, a hastily organized band of a hundred armed American teamsters and civilians poured out of Saltillo with loud whoops.

As their losses mounted, Miñon's officers attempted to organize a defense, but the maze of ravines frustrated their efforts. The cavalry troop returned to Palomas Pass after sixty-three of its men fell dead or wounded. There were no American casualties.

• • •

On the battlefield, there was a lull. The San Patricios' battery had ceased firing and had withdrawn. Pacheco's and Perez's soldiers had emptied out of the box canyon and ravine and had disappeared from sight below the Middle Plateau.

Suspecting—correctly, as matters proved—that Santa Anna was planning another attack, Wool and his officers launched a preemptive assault across the Middle Plateau, thinking it might precipitate a retreat. But in its haste to disrupt a possible Mexican attack, the American command was courting disaster.

• • •

The First and Second Illinois and the Second Kentucky, supported by O'Brien's two guns and a third field piece, moved onto the Middle Plateau, while couriers galloped to the North Plateau and to Bragg's battery with orders to join the attack.

Instead of prompting a full-scale retreat, the American push triggered a full-scale

Mexican counterattack. The San Patricios' guns coughed to life, joined by a battery of 8-pounders that suddenly emerged from the south ravine. Then, thousands
of lancers and Mexican infantrymen—Santa Anna's reserves, plus survivors of the
attack on the Mississippi Rifles—swarmed onto the plateau from the ravine and
swept down from the eastern hills.

The massed enemy troops crushed the left flank of the Illinoisans and Kentuckians
and drove them into the south ravine, where they groped their way toward the Saltillo
road. O'Brien's gunners fired double-shotted canister until they were overrun and had
to abandon their field pieces. Jefferson Davis's near-miraculous triumph on the North
Plateau was in danger of being erased on the Middle Plateau.

Mexican troops lined the lip of the south ravine, firing into the packed Americans making their way toward the road. But remarkably few shots found their
mark. "They are most miserable shots," observed Captain W. H. L. Wallace of the
First Illinois, "or they would have killed every one of us huddled as we were in the
bottom of that narrow ravine." But in hand-to-hand fighting in the ravine, Americans did die, among them the commanders of the First Illinois, Colonel John J.
Hardin, and the Second Kentucky, Colonel William McKee.

A musket ball shattered the thigh of Lieutenant Colonel Henry Clay Jr.,
McKee's second-in-command and the son of the senator and former presidential
candidate. Unable to walk, Clay ordered his men to leave him, handing one of
them a pistol he wanted his father to have. Clay then gripped his saber and fought
to the death.

• • •

Santa Anna's right wing was sweeping across the Middle Plateau toward the
Saltillo road, to close the trapdoor on the three U.S. regiments fighting their way
through the south ravine. In a race to stop the Mexicans, the Mississippi Rifles,
the Third Indiana, the remnants of the Second Indiana, and Captain Braxton
Bragg's battery struggled across the ravines to reach the plateau. Colonels Jefferson
Davis and Joseph Lane were both wounded but remained in the saddle after
receiving field dressings for their injuries. Davis, hit by a musket ball in the right
ankle, was in great pain because the ball had also shattered his riding spur, driving
brass shards into the wound.

Lancers sealed the west end of the ravine but overlooked the silent presence of
Captain Washington's battery in the nearby Narrows. Suddenly, Washington's
gunners blasted the lancers with spherical case shot. The lancers took refuge in the

ravine, where they impaled wounded Americans lying on the ground. But the able-bodied reached the safety of Washington's battery.

• • •

After lashing their tired horses through the labyrinthine ravines, Bragg's gunners reached the Middle Plateau before the other reinforcements got there, joining General Taylor. Alone and unsupported by infantry, Bragg, his battery, and Taylor faced three lines of advancing Mexican infantry. As bullets plucked at his plain clothing and grapeshot pierced his brown coat, Taylor calmly sat on Old Whitey behind Bragg's battery, watching his gunners fire round after round at the oncoming Mexicans. Lieutenant Alfred Pleasonton overheard Taylor say to Bragg:

"What are you firing, captain?"

"Canister, sir," Bragg replied.

"Double or single?"

"Single, sir."

"Then double it and give 'em Hell!" Taylor ordered.

Sherman's and Thomas's batteries joined Bragg's. But no infantrymen took the places of the dispersed Illinoisans and Indianans. The U.S. batteries punched bloody holes in the Mexican lines as they drew nearer.

Just when it seemed that the dense enemy columns, a mere hundred yards from the American batteries, would overrun the U.S. batteries, Jefferson Davis's Mississippi Rifles reached the brow of the plateau.

For the second time this day, the Mississippians were on the critical spot at the pivotal moment. Perfectly positioned to rake all three of the enemy ranks, the Mississippians' sudden volley crushed the Mexican right flank, freezing the enemy attack. In the next instant, the roaring batteries of Bragg, Sherman, and Thomas shredded the enemy front ranks, and the Mexicans turned and ran. The Americans clung to Middle Plateau through repeated Mexican attacks lasting until 5 P.M., when the gunfire began to die away.

Santa Anna's army withdrew to the south ravine, where the fighting had begun ten hours earlier. In a sort of grudge match, the San Patricios continued to duel with Bragg's batteries. Both sides suffered losses, but the American gunners got the best of it, killing twenty-two San Patricios by nightfall, when the shooting finally stopped.

• • •

The exhausted Americans camped on the battlefield without fires, ate their dinner cold, and slept fitfully with their weapons by their sides. The soldiers knew they had fought well, but they were not in a celebratory mood. They expected the battle to resume at daybreak.

• • •

That night, more than seven hundred volunteers who had fled the battlefield jammed the Buena Vista hacienda. Hundreds of other Americans had also abandoned their units that day, many by carrying off wounded comrades and not returning to the battlefield. The regular Army officers were more disgusted than ever with the volunteers, save for the Mississippi Rifles.

When Taylor reached the hacienda, and Lieutenant Samuel French, who had been wounded in the thigh, wished him victory the next day, Taylor eyed the mob of shirkers and ruefully replied, "Yes, yes, if too many of my men do not give me the slip to-night."

• • •

That night, Taylor and his staff discussed whether the American army—with 272 dead, 387 wounded, and more than a thousand men who had run from the enemy—was capable of fighting another day.

Taylor refused to consider withdrawal but conceded that the army needed fresh troops. He drafted orders for General Thomas Marshall, whose command was twenty miles north of Saltillo at Rinconada, to march to Buena Vista with six hundred mounted troops and Captain Benjamin Prentiss's battery of heavy eighteen- and twenty-four-pound guns. Delivering the order to Marshall was going to be difficult, though; a thousand Mexican rancheros blocked the road north. Couriers with dispatches for Rinconada had already been forced to turn back that evening.

Taylor chose Texas Rangers George Washington Trahern and Maurice Simons, reputed to be the best horsemen in the army, for the critical mission. Under cover of darkness, the Rangers slipped through the rancheros' roadblock and reached Rinconada with Taylor's orders. The energetic Marshall swiftly organized a heavily armed convoy that, unchallenged by the rancheros, marched into Saltillo at dawn on February 24, ready for battle.

But Santa Anna's army was gone.

• • •

Loud cheering erupted in the American army when patrols reported that Santa Anna's army had pulled back to Agua Nueva. "I've seen the elephant in every attitude, walking, running, at bay, fighting!" declared a relieved Captain W. H. L. Wallace. The outcome of the previous day's fighting had been inconclusive, but with Santa Anna ceding the battleground to Taylor, the Battle of Buena Vista could now be pronounced an American victory. Generals Taylor and Wool tearfully embraced, knowing what a near thing it had been. Soldiers fanned across the battlefield to look for wounded and dead. Major William Bliss rode to Santa Anna's camp to arrange a prisoner exchange.

• • •

The Mexicans had fought bravely, and they might have won if Santa Anna had attacked multiple points at once and had kept the Americans spread thin. But Santa Anna, a mediocre field marshal, did not exploit his enormous numerical advantage; in fact, he permitted thousands of Mexican reserves to idle away the day without seeing any action. By mounting only single-point attacks, Santa Anna permitted the Americans to race from one trouble spot to another, largely negating his superiority in numbers.

About thirteen thousand Mexican infantry and cavalry remained in the Buena Vista vicinity at nightfall on February 23. On paper at least, this was a formidable army that still enjoyed a nearly three-to-one advantage over Taylor's force, whose reinforcements from Rinconada had only replenished his losses. Fresh Mexican attacks might have overwhelmed the American army and then fulfilled Santa Anna's grand plan by marching to the Rio Grande, compelling Scott to call off the Vera Cruz invasion.

But factors besides Santa Anna's irresolution legislated against this happening—chief among them lack of food. The Mexican troops had not eaten in thirty-six hours, they still had no food, and their reserves of stamina were sapped. The Mexicans had also lost 591 killed and 1,048 wounded, with another 1,894 listed as missing, probably deserters who were on their way home.

Santa Anna had failed to dislodge the smaller American army from the battlefield, and the American field artillery, as in the battles on the Rio Grande, had again played a decisive role. It is doubtful whether the Mexican command knew of the arrival of Captain Benjamin Prentiss's heavy guns, which made Taylor's supporting artillery even more formidable.

Taylor's reasons for not marching on Santa Anna at La Encarnación are more easily apprehended: he had too few men to risk an attack against such a large force, and his horses needed rest.

• • •

As the Americans prowled Buena Vista's plateaus and ravines in search of wounded, they were appalled when they discovered the stripped, mutilated bodies of comrades who had been butchered by the enemy as they lay injured on the ground. Among them was a white-haired soldier who had suffered multiple lance wounds. Seventy-two-year-old Second Lieutenant William Price of the Second Illinois was the oldest man in the U.S. Army.

Scattered everywhere, like the detritus of a cyclone, were dead men and horses, bayonets, hats, cartridge paper, broken muskets, and pieces of clothing. The Americans spread blankets over the dead, keeping a lock of each man's hair. Natives scavenged for anything of utility, even the most commonplace objects. "Groups of swarthy peons, women and men, went about clipping the manes and tails of the dead horses," wrote Lew Wallace.

Dead Mexican soldiers were found all over the battlefield, and even strewn along the Agua Nueva road; it wasn't uncommon to find a dozen bodies in one place.

Scouts reported that Santa Anna was marching south to La Encarnación, after abandoning his wounded without medicine at Agua Nueva. There the Americans found rail-thin Mexicans sprawled in the dirt, with small sacks of parched meal beside them. They gave their enemies bread and water and transported them to the Cathedral of Santiago in Saltillo, now a makeshift hospital. Days later, the Americans collected another two hundred wounded at La Encarnación, along with sixty other Mexicans who were too weak to march back to San Luis Potosi.

• • •

When he reached Agua Nueva, Santa Anna discovered that another three thousand troops had melted away, and that he now had just ten thousand men—half of what he had started with—and that many of the gaunt survivors were ill. Untroubled, the general composed a florid message to the government announcing a great victory and two thousand American battle deaths. Leaving his army on the road, he raced ahead to San Luis Potosi, where he participated in a triumphal procession. The faux victory was celebrated in Mexico City by "the ringing of bells, and displaying to public view two small flags said to have been taken from the enemy," U.S. Consul John Black reported. When Santa Anna's

ragged, starving army reached San Luis Potosi, the Mexican people saw for themselves the fiction of the general's claims. But by then, Santa Anna was in the south,
organizing defenses against the new American threat aimed like a dagger at
Mexico's heart.

• • •

Along the American supply line north of Monterrey, an ugly guerrilla war had
broken out while the armies fought at Buena Vista. General Jose Urrea's cavalry
and General Antonio Canales's "irregulars" struck a 110-wagon American convoy
near Ramos. After the thirty-four U.S. soldiers guarding the train surrendered, the
Mexican cavalrymen massacred forty Mexican teamsters working for the Americans and burned scores of wagons. The Second Ohio Infantry, escorting another
wagon train, repelled an attack near Marin the next day. Ten days later, marauders
swept down on yet another wagon train traveling between Monterrey and
Camargo, guarded by four Kentucky and Ohio volunteer companies. The
attackers hit the middle of the caravan, setting the wagons on fire. A wagon filled
with gunpowder exploded, killing seven guerrillas.

Taylor marched to Monterrey with a relief force. As the losses mounted, he
demanded that the state of Nuevo León, which he believed supported the attacks,
pay $96,000 in restitution—and he sent Texas Rangers to collect the money. On
March 28, the Rangers and some civilian teamsters slaughtered twenty-four civilians at Rancho Guadalupe near Marin in retaliation for the teamsters' massacre.

Taylor's use of the mounted Texas troops, many of whom had been victimized
by Mexican rancheros in Texas years earlier, was questioned even by regular Army
troops. "General Taylor not only collected the money assessed by force of arms, he
let loose on the country packs of human bloodhounds called Texas Rangers,"
wrote the dragoon Samuel Chamberlain.

By June, the Americans and the Mexican guerrillas had so ravaged Nuevo León,
burning towns and haciendas and slaughtering their inhabitants, that Taylor withdrew his demand for the $96,000 payment, and formally condemned the mas-
sacres. But no Americans were ever punished.

• • •

While Santa Anna was taking credit for his "victory," Taylor was crediting the
American fighting men, who "displayed conspicuous steadiness and gallantry in
repulsing, at great odds, a disciplined foe." Victory, he wrote in his official report,

"releases me from the painful necessity of specifying many cases of bad conduct before the enemy," and permitted him instead to extol the performance of the artillery, the dragoons, his former son-in-law Jefferson Davis, and Davis's Mississippi Rifles, who "sustained throughout the engagement the reputation of veteran troops."

And what was Taylor's own contribution? While General Wool chose the battlefield and positioned Taylor's regiments, and Wool and Taylor's junior officers desperately improvised to meet the crises of February 23, Taylor sent the Mississippi Rifles to the North Plateau at the critical moment when Pacheco and Perez were trying to flank his army. Throughout the long battle, Taylor set an example for his men of coolness under fire by conspicuously sitting astride Old Whitey and calmly issuing orders as balls and shells whizzed around him. Taylor's most important contribution, however, was his initial decision to deny Santa Anna access to Saltillo and the provisions the Mexicans needed to continue fighting.

• • •

Zachary Taylor's name was toasted at banquets and celebrated in biographies and coveted engraved portraits. Everyone soon knew that Old Rough and Ready wore homespun clothing that he mended himself, and that he lived by simple values. Taylor's famous dialogue with Braxton Bragg as the Mexicans advanced on them was abbreviated to a single exhortation: "A little more grape, Captain Bragg!"

But at the White House, Polk's reaction upon reading the first reports of the battle was decidedly cooler. Taylor, he complained, had "imprudently" violated his orders to not advance beyond Monterrey. After reading a full account of the battle, and learning that his old friend, Colonel Archibald Yell, had been killed (Polk paid for the education of Yell's son, DeWitt Clinton Yell, at Georgetown College), the president sharply criticized Taylor in a journal entry. "It was great rashness to take the position he did in advance of Saltillo. Having done so he [is] indebted not to his own good generalship, but to the indomitable & intrepid bravery of the officers and men under his command for his success. . . . Gen'l Taylor is a hard fighter, but has none other of the qualities of a great General. From the beginning of the existing War with Mexico he has been constantly blundering into difficulties, but has fought out of them, but with severe loss."

While conceding that the victory was "glorious in itself," General of the Army Winfield Scott, too, believed that Taylor should have remained at Monterrey. He did not credit Taylor and his command for choosing a battlefield that limited Santa Anna's capabilities, or for barring the hungry Mexican army from Saltillo.

Buena Vista, Scott concluded, did not "advance the campaign an inch, nor quicken a treaty of peace an hour."

The Army requested that Polk order a salute fired to honor Taylor for the victory. Polk refused, unconvincingly stating that he did not wish to set a precedent.

• • •

Taylor persisted in his belief that Scott, Polk, and War Secretary William Marcy had calculatingly shortchanged him on troops so that he would fail. Taylor complained to Secretary of State James Buchanan that if he had not been "so weakened by the fire in my rear"—Scott appropriating his regulars—he could have captured Santa Anna and destroyed his army. To his son-in-law, Dr. R. C. Wood, Taylor unreasonably asserted that Marcy and Scott were more interested in damaging his reputation than in defeating Santa Anna. But Providence, he said, had foiled the administration's "nefarious schemes. . . . The battle of Buena Vista I trust is the best reply I can make to them or their slanderous attacks."

THE WAR IN CONGRESS

"The treasury and blood of the North will not be poured out in waging a war for the propagation of slavery over the North American continent."

—Congressman David Wilmot of Pennsylvania

"The day that the balance between the two sections of the country—the slave-holding states and the non-slave-holding states—is destroyed is a day that will not be far removed from political revolution, anarchy, civil war, and wide-spread disaster."

—Senator John C. Calhoun of South Carolina

JANUARY 4, 1847: WASHINGTON

Hoping to stop the Wilmot Proviso from being resurrected during the Twenty-ninth Congress's Second Session, the president had summoned Representative David Wilmot of Pennsylvania to the White House two days before Christmas. James Polk had conjured up all of his impressive persuasive powers to urge Wilmot to not revive his proviso, which would exclude slavery from any new territories acquired from Mexico. Slavery, "purely a domestic question," had no place in foreign policy legislation such as the Two Million Dollar Bill, asserted Polk, disavowing any desire to extend slavery to California or New Mexico. "In these Provinces," said the president, "slavery could probably never exist, . . . [and] would never arise in the future organization of the territory or State Governments in these territories." Wilmot had agreed to not introduce his antislavery amendment but said that if another congressman did, he would support it.

Hours later, the Senate Committee on Foreign Relations knew all about Wilmot's promise, and its members pledged to keep the slavery question out of the

Three Million Dollar Bill, the new, more expensive version of the former Two Million Dollar Bill. Without "a speedy peace," Polk had warned them, "the war with Mexico might be protracted for an indefinite length of time." With support for the war already slipping, the senators did not need to be told that drawing it out would be unpopular with voters.

But a major atmospheric change had occurred as a result of the fall midterm elections, when voters had displayed their dissatisfaction by ending the Democrats' control of both houses of Congress. Democrats had retained their majority in the Senate, but had lost thirty-five House seats to the Whigs; when the thirtieth Congress convened in December 1847, Democrats would become the House's minority party. While these changes were a year distant (this institutional disjointedness continued until the Twentieth Amendment required Congress to begin its sessions on January 3, which also became the swearing-in day for congressmen-elect), the electorate's message still resonated powerfully when the lame-duck Congress's began its work in December 1846. Northern Democrats who had survived the fall housecleaning were listening attentively to their constituencies, particularly regarding slavery.

As a consequence, Polk's countermeasures against the Wilmot Proviso failed. With David Wilmot honor-bound not to revive the resolution, Democratic Congressman Preston King of New York took it upon himself to do so: "There shall be neither slavery nor involuntary servitude in any territory on the continent of America which shall hereafter be acquired by, or annexed to, the United States. . . . "

"The movement of Mr. King to-day, if persevered in, will be attended with terrible consequences to the country, and cannot fail to destroy the Democratic party, if it does not ultimately threaten the Union itself," Polk gloomily predicted. The "wicked" provision "must divide the country by a sectional line & lead to the worst consequences." He railed against Congress, and particularly members of his own party, for "agitating the slavery question" while neglecting the Three Million Dollar Bill and his other war bills: to create a lieutenant generalcy; his war revenue measures; and the Ten Regiment Bill, which would raise ten thousand new troops. "Whilst this is so, the Federalists," as Polk disparagingly referred to the Whigs, "are united, and delighted at the unnecessary and foolish divisions in the Democratic party. I deplore this state of things; I will do all I can to correct it; I will do my duty and leave the rest to God and my country."

• • •

The Whigs' solidarity in opposing the war had served them far better in the fall election than the Democrats' lingering factionalism from 1844. A Democrat splinter led by Senator Thomas Hart Benton had continued to stoke its resentment over Polk's abandonment of Benton's Texas annexation proposal. There was Senator John C. Calhoun's faction, which despised Benton and resented the Polk administration's aggressive policies toward Britain and Mexico over Oregon and Texas. A third splinter, former President Martin Van Buren's "Barnburner" loyalists in New York, Ohio, Pennsylvania, and New England, opposed slavery and believed that Polk preferred their New York rivals, the "Hunkers." In early 1847, as Barnburner leader Preston King was reviving the Wilmot Proviso, his faction was reeling from the loss of fourteen New York congressional seats and the defeat of New York Governor Silas Wright. If unchecked, the willfully destructive infighting foreshadowed grave problems for the Democrats in the 1848 presidential election.

Conversely, the Mexican War had bound Whigs together in common cause as nothing had since "Tippecanoe and Tyler Too" in 1840. Conservative Northern Whigs, led by Daniel Webster and Robert Winthrop, and Southern, or "Cotton," Whigs, whose leaders included Henry Clay and Alexander Stephens, believed the war had been deceitfully launched on the flimsy pretext of Mexican aggression. Kearny's and Stockton's proclamations lent credence to the Whigs' contention that acquiring California and New Mexico was the underlying reason for the war. They denounced the United States's seizure of Mexico's northern provinces, albeit for different reasons: the Northern Whigs on moral grounds, and the Cotton Whigs because it reopened the national contention over slavery that they wished to avoid. The Radical, or "Conscience," Whigs, a third faction composed of abolitionist Northeasterners led by John Quincy Adams, Charles Francis Adams, and Charles Sumner, believed that the government's ulterior motive was to extend slavery into the Southwest. While the Whigs skewered the Polk administration's policies, they were careful to vote for more troops, materiel, and money for the war effort, lest voters, who still overwhelmingly supported the war, view them as unpatriotic.

• • •

Just as Polk's adversaries blamed the war on the secret purposes of "Polk the Mendacious," as they had slyly begun calling the president, so, too, did they believe that the Three Million Dollar Bill was a plot to slip bribe money to Santa Anna, who was in Mexico only because the president had ordered the Navy to let him in. They demanded all government correspondence related to the dictator's return to Mexico.

Representative Garrett Davis of Kentucky requested the Polk administration's instructions to U.S. military commanders about establishing civil governments in New Mexico and California. These actions were a "usurpation of power," declared the combative Davis, also in the midst of an "affair of honor"—never consummated—with Representative Thomas Bayly of Virginia. Georgia Congressman Hugh Haralson protested that the documents' publication would jeopardize national interests. But over Secretary of State James Buchanan's objections, Polk complied with Davis's request, while going through the motions of disapproving of General Kearny's ebullient pronouncement that New Mexico was a new U.S. territory.

Then the House asked for all of the correspondence between the War Department and General Zachary Taylor, its third request in two months. However, Polk had slyly engineered this last request, believing that the War Department–Taylor letters would debunk Taylor's assertion that he had been left in the dark about war strategy: "This is the only mode in which the truth can be set before the public, & the administration fully vindicated."

If Polk believed that by serving just one term he could avoid the pitfalls of a second term, he was wrong; the last half of his single term was beginning to display the hallmarks of a lame-duck administration. The same Congress that had partnered with Polk the previous summer in racking up a stunning list of legislative achievements was now, six months later, putting many of his actions as war president under a microscope: the pretexts for the war, his territorial aims, his not-so-secret role in aiding Santa Anna's return, and his relations with Taylor and Scott.

The workload only increased. While his family attended Christmas church services, Polk remained at home to work on a draft of the Lieutenant General bill and his correspondence. January was even more taxing. And, if one believed in bad omens, there was the "8th of January Ball" at Jackson Hall to commemorate Andrew Jackson's 1815 victory at New Orleans. During the ball, the building caught fire, and Polk and the other celebrants had to evacuate.

• • •

Polk's war bills languished through December and then January, while Congress asked him to explain the need for $3 million (so that Santa Anna could "secure the support of the army and be able to retain power") and the necessity of a Lieutenant General of the Army ("I explained to them . . . the impossibility of conducting the war successfully when the General in Chief of the Army did not sympathize with the government").

Moreover, congressional politics were spinning beyond his control, and he was now witnessing the "sickening" spectacle of "corrupt" Democrats siding with Whigs to block his agenda, and forming a virtual "balance of power" party. The ringleaders were Senators Calhoun and Andrew Butler of South Carolina, and Florida Senators David Yulee and James Westcott Jr. "They had been disappointed in their selfish applications for office for themselves and their friends" and were now opposing his policies. With bitterness, he added, "Many of them are governed by no fixed principles, but are sordid & selfish, if not worse, in all they do."

• • •

The congressional debate of the Three Million Dollar Bill opened the Pandora's box of dangerous questions that Polk had so dreaded. Beginning on February 4, the passionate, freewheeling arguments over the bill's diplomatic justifications, the war's morality, and, most menacingly of all, slavery's extension to new territories, raged for weeks. As he challenged the need for the $3 million appropriation, Kentucky Senator James Morehead snidely inquired whether it really was the "duty of the Government of the United States to dismember the territory of Mexico." America's previous wars, noted Morehead, had been for "human liberty, or in defense of violated rights. Now there was pending a war of conquest." Maryland Senator Reverdy Johnson caustically suggested that by giving Mexico $3 million, the United States would present the "extraordinary spectacle" of supporting both opposing armies, "provided Santa Anna will think proper to cede to the United States at least New Mexico and Upper California." And "what, then is to be the result? One of two things: civil war with all its inconceivable evils, or the disruption of this Union."

The dark genie of slavery was indeed loose in Congress. "The treasury and blood of the North will not be poured out in waging a war for the propagation of slavery over the North American continent," vowed David Wilmot, who had honored his pledge not to revive his Proviso, but was arguing for it now that King had introduced it. New territories, said Wilmot, must be permitted to "religiously preserve [their] character" until statehood, when the people then would "have the right to act for themselves upon this question."

Launching a frontal assault on the institution of slavery itself, Wilmot asserted that slave states were less productive than free states. "How is it? Why, owing to this institution . . . there is always a lack of energy, a want of enterprise in slave labor, which are found in free labor."

If that were true, shot back Georgia Congressman Howell Cobb, the North should be willing to make the territories "a fair and open field of contest, where industry and enterprise shall decide." The North instead wanted to impose its will on the new territories. "Where is that regard, on the part of the North, for the rights of the South?" asked Cobb.

Timothy Jenkins of New York warned that if "slavery is allowed to fasten itself upon the bosom of this new country, the free and enterprising laborer will not go there." Jenkins's New York colleague George Rathbun thundered that "the whirl-wind which is now pervading the North [abolition] . . . will arise and grow in its strength and power, until it becomes a mighty tornado, that will sweep down every man that dares oppose himself to its strong and resistless force."

Southerners knew in their bones that if the Wilmot Proviso won approval, their power would inevitably, intolerably begin to wane, and so they tigerishly fought the amendment, employing every color of argument, some of it fanciful. Maryland Congressman William Giles predicted that if slavery were permitted in California and New Mexico, emancipated blacks would "gradually travel down to the extreme Southwest, where they would mingle with the mixed population of Mexico and meet there a homogenous race." Slavery "was positively ordained of God, under Mosaic dispensation, and was recognized by Christ and his apostles in the New Testament," claimed Georgia Congressman Seaborn Jones. Prohibiting slavery in the territories would be tantamount to "declaring that lands which hereafter may be acquired by the United States shall be occupied by one portion of the country to the exclusion of the other," thereby dooming the South, and "resulting finally in the extermination of the entire white race in that section," apocalyptically pre-dicted Representative William Brockenborough of Florida. Dour, consumptive Representative Alexander Stephens of Georgia, who would become the Confed-eracy's vice president and whose image would adorn its $20 bill, morosely observed that "perhaps Polk in starting one war may find half a dozen on his hands. I tell you the prospect ahead is dark, cloudy, thick, and gloomy."

In the Senate, Calhoun, the former vice president and cabinet member, had long ago joined fellow Southern Democrats in opposing the war. While he agreed with Polk that slavery would probably never exist in the conquered territories, the war, he believed, raised the specter of a congressional prohibition—intolerable because it "would involve a principle." This razor-sharp dagger of a principle was aimed at the heart of the Union, capable of shattering the fragile equipoise between the North and the South. "The day that the balance between the two sections of the country—the slaveholding states and the non-slave-holding states—is destroyed," warned Calhoun, "is a day that will not be far removed from political revolution, anarchy, civil war, and widespread disaster." Yet, more than anyone else, Calhoun was responsible for the hardening of pro-slavery attitudes into a militancy that would embrace secession and war.

Calhoun declared that Southerners had the right to bring their slaves to New Mexico and California. Abolishing slavery in these territories, he said, would "exclude those who are interested in the institutions of the South" from sharing the new lands' bounty. "The war to acquire territory" that he deplored would then not be waged for "the common good, but as a means of . . . ruling us [the South]," Calhoun reasoned. "We are to be made to dig our own grave."

The Wilmot Proviso invited federal infringement on Southern states' rights, cautioned Reverdy Johnson of Maryland, defiantly adding, "This is a question for Southern men exclusively. We will admit no interference with our constitutional rights."

• • •

The nearly thirty major speeches delivered for and against the Wilmot Provision marked Congress's first uninhibited debate of the "peculiar institution" since the imposition of the 1836 Gag Rule. It was in 1836, in fact, that Congressman John Quincy Adams, with remarkable foresight, had warned that annexing Texas would lead to war with Mexico, and "aggression, conquest, and the re-establishment of slavery where it has been abolished [by Mexico] . . . [and the] inevitable consequence of . . . a civil war." Renewed every year until it was rescinded in 1844 on Adams's motion, the Gag Rule permitted the House and Senate to preempt all discussion of slavery by summarily rejecting petitions by abolitionists.

But rather than acting as a safety valve for sectional tensions, open debate of slavery only increased the strains until Southern leaders finally saw secession and war as their last options. Sounding like one of his Old Testament namesake's contemporaries, Vermont Representative Solomon Foot foretold awful consequences: "You are rushing headlong and blindfold upon appalling dangers, before which the stout heart shrinks, and brave men turn pale. You are rekindling the slumbering fires of a volcano, which, whenever they shall burst forth, will consume all the plain." The Augusta (Georgia) *Daily Chronicle and Sentinel* asked rhetorically,

"Can a contest be imagined more frightful and furious than that which this very acquisition of Mexican territory will excite between the North and South?"

• • •

Amid the hot words and chilling warnings flying over slavery in the new territories, there commenced the first substantive debate about the Mexican War. As congressmen shifted their points of attack from the war to slavery and back again, the subjects of the war's justifications, whether to continue offensive operations, and the elements of a just peace were all debated.

Polk's congressional allies reminded the war's critics that just nine months earlier, they had voted to go to war. The war, its supporters said, was never about conquest, but a poor nation such as Mexico could guarantee an "honorable peace" only by ceding territory to the United States. "I do not believe there is a government in Christendom, if it felt itself able, which, under similar circumstances, would not have done as we did," said Senator Lewis Cass of Michigan.

While careful to avouch their support for the troops, Calhoun and other war opponents insisted that the United States, not Mexico, had actually started the war. General Mariano Arista, Calhoun said, had proposed that while their governments negotiated a Texas–Mexican border settlement, Arista would remain west of the Rio Grande if Zachary Taylor stayed at the Nueces. "So then, we have clear evidence that the war was made by the order [to Taylor] to march to the Del Norte [Rio Grande]." When there was disagreement with Britain over the borders of Maine and Michigan, "did any of the presidents ever think of marching troops upon the line?"

Whig Congressman Luther Severance of Maine, one of "The 14" who had opposed the war back in May, called it "an invasion of the Mexican province of Tamaulipas by General Taylor, under express orders from the president of the United States," ostensibly to compel Mexico to pay the claims it owed. Severance added scathingly, "He [Polk] batters down her towns, and murders her people, because her crazy government, with no money in the treasury, has not been punctual in meeting her national engagements."

Until now, the Polk administration had needed only to impugn the patriotism of wavering congressmen to coerce them to vote for its war bills. As this tactic began to lose its potency, war supporters intensified their attacks on their balky colleagues. "America wants no friends, acknowledges the fidelity of no citizen, who, after war is declared, condemns the justice of her cause, or sympathizes with the enemy," declared Congressman Stephen A. Douglas of Illinois. "All such are traitors in their hearts."

Alarmed by Congress's dilatoriness in enacting his war legislation, especially the bill creating ten new regiments, Polk warned, "The worst state of things which could exist in a war with such a power as Mexico, would be a course of indecision and inaction on our part."

• • •

The House crossed a threshold when it voted down Polk's proposed tax on coffee and tea, which he had counted on to bring in millions of dollars to pay for the war. Charles Hudson of Massachusetts said that because the war was unjust, Congress could rightfully withhold war supplies. "To deny [this right] was to assert that we were already under a military despotism, and not a free people." He urged the withdrawal of U.S. troops from Mexico.

Then House Whigs proposed excluding territorial acquisitions from any Mexican treaty that was made. The quasi-official Washington *Union* repudiated the "no territory" resolution as "absurd and extraordinary." The resolution went nowhere, opposed not only by Democrats, but by conservative Whigs led by John Quincy Adams and Charles Sumner, who objected to diverting attention away from the slavery question. Besides, they pointed out, U.S. forces already occupied Mexican provinces.

• • •

Democrats responded to these uprisings with a flood of encomiums reaffirming their enthusiasm for the war. Representative William Giles pledged Maryland's steadfast support. "What, sir, the country engaged in a contest, her arms now upon a foreign soil, the honor of the country at issue, and a representative of Maryland refuse to vote supplies of men and money?" Giles said Congress was duty-bound to fulfill America's "Manifest Destiny." "We must march from Texas straight to the Pacific Ocean, and be bounded by its roaring wave," Giles declaimed. "We must admit no other Government to any partition of this great territory. It is the destiny of the white race; it is the destiny of the Anglo-Saxon race; and if they fail to perform it, they will not come up to that high position which Providence, in his mighty government, has assigned them."

If America did not expand, yet continued to double her population every twenty-two years, Senator Cass of Michigan grimly warned, the neo-Jeffersonian "wage dependency" nightmare would become actuality. Infected with Europe's "social evils," chief among them cities crowded with landless wage-earners, America would soon see, as had Europe, that "minds of the highest order are pressed down by adverse circumstances, without the power of free exertion. There is no starting point for them. Hence the struggles that are ever going on . . . I trust we are far removed from all this; but to remove us further yet, we want almost unlimited power of expansion. That is our safety valve."

But Ohio Senator Thomas Corwin scoffed that the United States's twenty million people already had a billion acres, and did not need more land. "If I were a Mexican, I would tell you, 'Have you not room in your country to bury your dead men? If you come into mine we will greet you with bloody hands, and welcome you to hospitable graves.' "

• • •

The increasingly barbed words reached an apotheosis in February when the Washington *Union* condemned the Senate's rejection of the Ten Regiment Bill in an article signed "Vindicator": "If Santa Anna, Ampudia, or any other Mexican general could snatch from our soldiers a corresponding victory, we should place them upon the same elevation where their compatriots, friends, and fellow-soldiers in the Senate of the United States now stand." The *Union* luridly described the disastrous consequences if the Whigs realized their supposed cherished wish to "abandon California, to tear down the flag of the Union which floats over it, and resurrender it to Mexico, ultimately to fall into the hands of England . . . the disgraceful surrender of California leads to the loss of Oregon, to the loss of the trade of Asia, and the exclusion of our flag from the Pacific Coast."

Senators indignantly banished the *Union*'s editors from the Senate floor for their "public libel." The *Union* protested that it was only voicing the desire of "a patriotic people" for an "honorable peace." Polk denounced the Senate's "foul deed" as "a blow at the liberty of the press."

• • •

There was no congressional consensus, either, on whether to continue to aggressively prosecute the war, or to build a chain of forts along the perimeter of the U.S.-occupied zone. But most congressmen believed it would be a mistake to go exclusively on the defensive; American troops would be sitting ducks for guerrillas. "The proud bird will soon be powerless, and the reptile will coil itself up to strike at its leisure and its pleasure," warned Cass. "How long did the Roman wall keep the North Britons out of England?" A defensive war would become "a never-ending war," predicted Samuel Gordon of New York. "A vigorous war, carried into the heart of the enemy's country . . . will be the shortest, the cheapest, and the least destructive to human life."

Calhoun saw only enormous risks and uncertainty, and soaring human and financial costs, in marching on Mexico City. "If you do not get peace with Mexico in the city of Mexico, can you bring this war to a successful conclusion by subduing the country?" Calhoun evidently didn't think so. "Mexico was to us forbidden fruit; and . . . if we should consume that fruit, it would be almost tantamount to the political death of our own institutions."

Polk's extraordinary streak of legislative triumphs, which had peaked during the summer of 1846, was ended. Whigs and dissident Democrats delayed voting on the president's ambitious agenda for several weeks and then rejected both the proposed coffee-and-tea war duty and the Lieutenant General bill. As Polk's allies had warned, there was no support for creating that rank in order to make Senator Thomas Hart Benton the Army's commanding general.

• • •

After dragging its feet for a month, Congress approved $23 million in new Treasury notes to help pay for the war and resuscitated and ratified the Ten Regiment Bill—but only after Polk threatened to blame Congress for "failing to furnish the means to enable me to prosecute the war with Mexico with vigor." The president was immediately inundated with applicants for officer commissions. "I could soon have an army of officers, such as they would be, if I could appoint all the applicants," he groaned.

The Wilmot Proviso provoked a sharp debate over slavery that adumbrated the next decade's sectarian divisions, but it did not become law. After the House added the Proviso to the Three Million Dollar Bill and approved it, 115–105, on February 15, the Senate on March 1 approved a Proviso-less version by 29–24. Sent to the House, the Senate bill was approved, 115–81, on March 3, after a failed attempt to reinsert the "firebrand thrown into the councils of the nation," as Georgia Senator John Macpherson Berrien characterized the resolution.

The Wilmot Proviso became a Democrat litmus test, with Polk denying patronage to everyone who had supported it. "It should be understood that no man can obtain an office here who is a Proviso man," Senator J. M. Niles, a Connecticut

Democrat, informed Martin Van Buren. The Polk administration also canceled publishing contracts with newspapers that had endorsed the Proviso.

• • •

Polk's presidency had entered a new, contentious phase that he did not gracefully accept. Upset by the unraveling bipartisan support for his policies, and by the Whig newspapers' relentless criticism of the war, he vented his bitterness in his journal: "The articles in the *National Intelligencer* and other federal papers against their own Government and in favour of the enemy, have done more to prevent a peace than all the armies of the enemy. The Mexican papers republish these treasonable articles & make the ignorant population of Mexico believe that the Democratic party will shortly be expelled from power in the U. States, and that their friends (the Federal *alias* Whig party) will come into power. If the war is protracted it is to be attributed to the treasonable course of the federal editors & leading men. These Editors and political leaders are guilty of 'moral treason' to their country. . . ."

Calhoun became the nexus for the president's unhappiness with elements of his own party. "I now entertain a worse opinion of Mr. Calhoun than I have ever done before. He is wholly selfish, & I am satisfied has no patriotism." Calhoun was making "a hobby" of the slavery question and throwing his support behind General Zachary Taylor of the opposition party. "I cannot express the contempt I feel for Mr. Calhoun for such profligate political [in]consistency."

• • •

Santa Anna's emissary, Alejandro J. Atocha, returned to Washington in January 1847, nearly a year after he had helped arrange his patron's repatriation to Mexico. This time, Atocha bore letters written by Santa Anna and General Juan N. Almonte expressing a desire for an honorable peace. Atocha approached Senator Benton with a proposition to designate the disputed region between the Rio Grande and the Nueces as an international buffer; no new settlements could be established there. Mexico would then recognize the Rio Grande as the U.S.–Mexico border and would cede California for $15 million. Negotiations could begin in Havana, Atocha said, whenever the United States lifted its blockade of Vera Cruz.

With the messy congressional donnybrook raging over the administration's war bills, Atocha's overture was indeed welcome. But Polk would not accept a Rio Grande–Nueces buffer, perhaps not realizing its importance as a salve to Mexico's pride. He also insisted that the United States must have New Mexico, too. Polk refused to lift the blockade but expressed a willingness to authorize U.S. peace commissioners to do so, or even to suspend hostilities, if progress were made on negotiations. At the end of January, Atocha boarded a U.S. naval vessel with the Polk administration counterproposal and was escorted through the blockade to Vera Cruz.

Mexico's response arrived in Washington on March 20. To Mexico's demand that the United States suspend its blockade while negotiations were held, it had now added a new condition: withdrawal of all American forces from Mexican territory. "Wholly inadmissible," sniffed Polk. "No alternative was now left but the most energetic crushing movement of our arms upon Mexico."

When Secretary of State James Buchanan expressed misgivings about an expedition to Mexico City, the president declared that he would "not only march to the City of Mexico, but . . . I would pursue Santa Anna's army wherever it was, and capture or destroy it."

21

SCOTT'S EPIC MARCH BEGINS

"The town is crumbling to pieces under this iron rain."

—Lieutenant John James Peck, of the American bombardment of Vera Cruz

"Consternation has spread over the country. The Mexicans are confounded, lost in wonder and despair."

—Lieutenant Colonel Ethan Allen Hitchcock, following the Battle of Cerro Gordo

MARCH 22, 1847, 4 P.M.: VERA CRUZ

The Mexicans would fight, not surrender. General Juan Morales's swift rejection of General Winfield Scott's surrender demand spread through the five miles of American trenches and batteries that, with the seven naval vessels hovering a mile offshore, encircled the walled city like a noose. The crowded four-foot-deep trenches, dug in the sand by soldiers under the broiling sun and in blinding sandstorms while Mexican gunners took potshots at them, held twelve thousand troops. The four roofed U.S. batteries—ten mortars, ranging from 24- to 68-pounders; four twenty-four-pound guns; and two eight-inch howitzers—were marvels of engineering and labor, unprecedented in U.S. military history. The gunners awaited the signal to open fire on the centuries-old city of fifteen thousand, defended by five thousand troops and 250 guns. American troops had never before laid siege to a city.

At precisely 4:15, the signal gun boomed and the battery commanders shouted "Fire!" The new soldiers, including H. Judge Moore of South Carolina's Palmetto Regiment, watched in awe as the gunners bent to their terrible work, "wrapped in sheets of fire and clouds of smoke and sending their death shots thick and fast against the trembling walls of the city." "It was an awful, as well as grand and beautiful, spectacle," wrote Navy Lieutenant Raphael Semmes.

Simultaneously, enemy guns fired back from inside the city and from the massive fortress of San Juan de Ulua. Lieutenant George McClellan, the salutatorian of West Point's Class of '46 who had supervised the construction of one of the American batteries, watched as "a perfect storm of iron burst upon us—every gun and mortar in Vera Cruz and San Juan, that could be brought to bear, hurled its contents around us—the air swarmed with them—and it seemed a miracle that not one of the hundreds they fired fell into the crowded mass that filled the trenches." Even when a massive mortar shell burrowed into the deep sand and exploded thunderously without causing casualties, it was terrifying enough, with the ground "shaken for yards around, as though there had been a miniature earthquake." From a trench five hundred yards from the city walls, Moore heard "the wails of the wounded and dying, together with the shrieks of women and children, rising high above the general din."

• • •

The previous day, Commodore David Conner, the decorated War of 1812 veteran who had led the Gulf Squadron for four years, stepped down from his command, his health broken. "The Navy officers are rejoiced in the change," wrote Army Lieutenant Edmund Bradford. "They say they will now have something to do." Matthew C. Perry, who succeeded Conner, was two years his junior and was the younger brother of the late, famous War of 1812 naval hero Oliver Hazard Perry. Matthew Perry was known for his enthusiastic promotion of steam warships and the education of naval officers. But he would secure his place in U.S. history by negotiating the historic 1854 treaty that opened Japanese ports to American commerce.

Perry's "mosquito fleet"—the gunboats *Bonita, Reefer, Petrel, Falcon,* and *Tampico,* and the steamships *Vixen* and *Spitfire*—formed a line a mile from the city walls, just beyond the range of the enemy guns at Vera Cruz and Ulua. At a signal from the commodore, they added their "well-directed and destructive fire" from 32-pounders and eight-inch Paixhan guns to the Army's bombardment.

Behind the scenes at Collado Beach, where General Winfield Scott's army had landed thirteen days earlier on March 9, the Navy had begun to implement a plan made by Perry and Scott. Six heavy naval guns from Perry's fleet were being trundled ashore to add firepower to the handful of guns that Scott had mustered for the siege. It was the beginning of an unusually amicable working relationship between the Army and Navy.

• • •

Scott needed the Navy's guns, having received just one-fifth of the cannons that he had been promised. Moreover, he had received only fifteen carts and a hundred draft animals, when he was supposed to get thousands of each. As a result, the hundreds of seamen that Perry had assigned to bring ashore and crew the six naval guns would have to drag them to their revetments through three miles of deep sand.

The sailors and Marines who wrestled the heavy guns ashore welcomed the reprieve from the dull routine of blockading Mexico's eight Gulf ports. "No duties could have been more irksome than those which devolved upon the Navy," Lieutenant Semmes wrote of the blockade. "During the whole of the period, we were confined to our ships, and engaged in the most arduous and active cruising. . . . We looked forth from our ship, as from a prison." Semmes was released from this thankless duty when his ship, the USS *Somers,* ran aground and he was assigned to Scott's expedition with orders to protest to the Mexican government, when the opportunity presented itself, the arrest of a midshipman for spying. After the war, Semmes would compile his colorful observations into a best-selling book.

The Mexican Navy's few sailing vessels and two steamships never ventured into the Gulf. American sailors captured Mexican commercial vessels and confiscated contraband from neutral vessels before permitting them to enter the ports. It was laborious duty, interspersed with real danger in the form of the sometimes-capricious Gulf weather. In August, a storm drove the brig USS *Truxtun,* a new ship under Commander Edward W. Carpenter, onto a reef off Tuxpan two days after she began blockade duty. Unable to dislodge their vessel, Carpenter and his crew were forced to surrender to Mexican authorities. The crew of the USS *Princeton* later burned the wreck. Only occasionally, as they had at Tabasco and Tampico and now at Vera Cruz, did the Gulf Squadron sailors and Marines don battle array.

• • •

Scott and Conner had invaded the enemy heartland with half of the 130 surfboats promised, and an understrength, undersupplied army. Lieutenant Ulysses S. Grant later wrote that Scott was promised everything he requested for the campaign, but "the promises were all broken. Only about half the troops were furnished that had been pledged, other war material was withheld. . . ." Quartermaster General Thomas S. Jesup had estimated that when Scott's army reached its projected strength of twenty-five thousand men—it never would be more than half that size—it would require ninety-three hundred wagons, seventeen thousand pack mules, three hundred thousand iron shoes for the horses and mules, five hundred thousand bushels of oats and corn, and one hundred pounds of blister ointment for the soldiers' feet. Jesup also foresaw the need for a half-ton of office tape, made of red cotton or linen, to tie up bundles of official documents —hence the term "red tape."

Receiving nothing approaching Jesup's sanguinary estimates, Scott improvised. He needed mounted troops, but they were either at Tampico, or still on their way to Vera Cruz. "I am much crippled in my operations—particularly in distant reconnoitering by the absence of that portion of the army." So the versatile Army engineers, West Point graduates commanded by Colonel Joseph Totten, became the army's eyes and ears. Soon, Scott was praising them as "exceedingly active and daring."

His greatest fear, however, was to be marooned in Vera Cruz's steamy environs when springtime and the "vomito" season arrived; Scott could not afford to lose men to yellow fever. He appealed to War Secretary William Marcy for three hundred mules, and for more of every kind of transport, knowing that after Vera Cruz was captured, he must quickly move inland to the cooler, more healthful mountain foothills. "March is more than half out, and the return of the black vomit in this region cannot be far distant," Scott told Marcy.

As the American army clung to its toehold in central Mexico, and its guns pounded the great port city, the General of the Army faced many weighty problems indeed.

• • •

Before the siege began, a howling "northerly" had filled the Gulf with whitecaps and sandblasted the troops on shore from March 12 to 15. The winter gales, which sometimes battered the coast for days on end, were reputedly "the most furious periodical winds known anywhere in America." For an entire day, all landing operations were suspended, and the soldiers hunkered down. A transport filled with dragoons ran aground on a reef near Anton Lizardo. When the winds subsided, good news reached Scott's headquarters at "Camp Washington" two miles from the city: General Zachary Taylor's "great and glorious" victory at Buena Vista.

• • •

At Camp Washington, Scott had polled his generals about whether to storm Vera Cruz, or to bombard it into submission. His generals being of two minds, the General in Chief made the decision. A frontal attack, he reasoned, would result in "an immense slaughter on both sides, including non-combatants," because it would have to be made at night. American casualties alone would surely surpass two thousand, leaving fewer than ten thousand men to march on Mexico City. Scott decided to capture the city "by head-work, the slow, scientific process" of laying siege.

"Although I know our countrymen will hardly acknowledge a victory unaccompanied by a long butchers' bill," Scott wrote, revealing his ingrained cynicism, "I am still strongly inclined . . . to 'forego [*sic*] their loud applause and aves vehement' and take the city with the least possible loss of life."

While some of Scott's generals regretted having to forgo the glory of a bayonet assault, the decision made eminent sense to the soldiers. George Ballentine, an enlisted man for five years who had also served in the British Army, recognized the havoc that Vera Cruz's batteries would wreak on American assault columns. "The batteries sweep a perfectly level plain, extending from half a mile to a mile between the walls and the sand-hills, and would have proved very destructive."

When the northerly abated, the army extended its lines around Vera Cruz, all the way to the Gulf on both the city's north and south sides. The engineers built a road through the chaparral and blocked off the underground aqueduct that supplied Vera Cruz's water. Work parties began digging the siege batteries and trenches, taking care to keep a safe distance from the Ulua fortress's formidable firepower. Since the French "Pastry War" of 1838, when French troops had seized Ulua, the Mexican army had steadily fortified it, nearly doubling the number of guns to 130. "The castle had the capacity to sink the entire American navy," noted Scott.

• • •

As the Americans toiled with picks and shovels under the tropical sun, Mexican gunners fired at them from forts embedded in the city walls. But their marksmanship was bad; none of the trench-diggers was injured, and only one man outside the trenches was wounded. Equally ineffective were the Mexican lancers who roved the countryside outside the city, and who vanished at the sight of American units.

American sentries sometimes posed more of a threat than the Mexicans. Lieutenant Pierre G. T. Beauregard—who on April 12, 1861, would order Charleston's batteries to fire on Fort Sumter—was returning from the siege batteries to Camp Washington with Captain Robert E. Lee when a sentry stopped them. "Friends," Lee replied to the sentry's challenge, as Beauregard simultaneously said "Officers." The confused soldier raised his pistol and fired at Lee; the ball passed between Lee's left arm and body, and flames singed his coat. Lee was shaken, but unharmed.

The dense chaparral and cactus, the energy-sapping 250-foot-tall sandhills, and the tarantulas and scorpions and six-foot rattlesnakes dampened the soldiers' initial excitement over being in Mexico. There were also the flies, mosquitoes, ants, chiggers, and sand fleas. "If one were to stand ten minutes in the sand, the fleas would fall upon him in hundreds," observed Lieutenant Dabney Maury. "They don't live very high, for they are ever ready for a change of diet."

Thefts were another aggravation. The regulars blamed the "different hordes of volunteers" for pilfering personal items from their knapsacks. Their already low opinion of the volunteers sank further.

• • •

From behind Vera Cruz's walls, citizens and soldiers observed the industrious Americans' daily progress on the siege trenches. The patriotism so exuberantly displayed during a parade and rally before the American landing had transmogrified into fear and fatalism. The defenders dared not waste lives or ammunition in sorties, because they knew that the National Guard was not marching from Mexico City to their relief.

The Guardsmen, known as the "Polkos" because their "dandified criollo officers" had adopted a polka as their theme song, had revolted against acting President Valentin Gomez Farias. Santa Anna had asked Farias to raise money for his army, and Farias had turned to the wealthy Catholic Church for a loan. When the church refused to lend the money, Farias, an anticleric at heart, had obtained Congress's authorization to seize some of the church's vast land holdings and to sell or use them as collateral for loans. The powerful church induced the National Guard in Mexico City to rebel against Farias.

As had happened so many times before, organized mobs now roamed Mexico City's streets. U.S. Consul John Black disgustedly observed that the Mexicans "cannot under any circumstances refrain from indulging themselves in civil wars, and endeavoring to destroy each other, even while more than half of their country is occupied by a foreign force. . . ."

Besides tying up the National Guard in Mexico City and indirectly aiding Scott's investment of Vera Cruz, the so-called "Rebellion of Polkos" ultimately strengthened Santa Anna's position, even though his army's needs had precipitated the revolt and the mobs' animus had been largely directed at him. After compelling Farias's resignation, the rebels called on Santa Anna to restore order. Relieved to be able to put the Buena Vista debacle behind him, he returned to the capital and named unpretentious General Pedro Maria Anaya as the new interim president.

Amid the turmoil, the Mexican government quietly wrote off Vera Cruz and its defenders.

MARCH 25, 1847: VERA CRUZ

As Scott's gunners angled shot and shell over Vera Cruz's walls to explode in the crowded square mile of streets and buildings, they disappointedly observed that their mortars and 24-pounders were not having the devastating effect that they had hoped for. But "heavy metal" was on the way. "By main strength," sailors were manhandling three 32-pounders and three eight-inch naval guns, weighing sixty-eight hundred pounds each and firing sixty-eight-pound explosive shells, through knee-deep sand. They dragged the massive ordnance through a shallow seventy-yard-wide lagoon, finally reaching the siege trenches three miles from the beach. Captain Lee, who had supervised the building of the gun pits in the Navy's revetment, Battery No. 5, situated on a sandy ridge seven hundred yards from the city walls, oversaw the guns' placement. Early on March 25, their throaty bark joined the bombardment.

The naval guns had an instant impact. "I shall never forget the awful scream, apparently proceeding from several female voices, which came ringing on the night air, as one of those terrible engines of destruction exploded—carrying death and dismay, no doubt, to some family circle," wrote Navy Lieutenant Semmes. Whenever a shot hit its target, the enthusiastic sailors leaped onto their trench parapet, "waving their hats and crowing like roosters." The soldiers in the trenches were thrilled, too, by Battery No. 5's pulverizing basso profundo. "The crash of the eight-inch shells as they broke their way through the houses and burst them was very pretty," observed Lieutenant McClellan.

The 68-pounders blew holes in Vera Cruz's walls, demolished two forts, and flattened enemy strongpoints, homes, hospitals, and businesses. A direct hit on a surgical hospital killed several patients, including one who was "torn in pieces" while on the operating table. Nineteen soldiers were killed in the infirmary at the Santiago fort, as were seventeen patients at the "female hospital."

The crashing American cannon fire, combined with the counterfire from the Mexican batteries embedded in the city walls and at Ulua, was a continuous roar, pierced by the fearful shrieks of American Congreve rockets, which were largely ineffective as projectiles but effective instruments of terror. The din was louder than anything the soldiers had ever heard. The literary-minded George Ballentine compared it to John Milton's description of "the harsh, thunder-grating of the infernal gates."

George Kendall of the New Orleans *Picayune* was riveted by the spectacle's "grandeur and sublimity," while Semmes described five U.S. shells "chasing each other like playful meteors" through the black night sky. At the bombardment's height, the American batteries poured 180 rounds of shot and shell into Vera Cruz every hour.

Mexican gunners hit an Army ten-inch mortar, hurling it thirty feet. Targeting an American battery in a cemetery, enemy shells gouged great craters, spraying the area with fragments of coffins, torn winding sheets, and splintered skulls and bones. The defenders concentrated the fire of three forts on Battery No. 5, killing or wounding ten sailors. A shell took off an arm of a popular thirteen-year-old drummer boy in Ballentine's regiment. "We were all very sorry for him," wrote Ballentine.

• • •

Inside Vera Cruz, weeping orphaned children huddled in the chapel of the Divina Pastora, while "haggard and bloody" people dazedly roamed the streets. American cannon fire three times tore down the Mexican flag flying over the main plaza. After each de-staffing, a brave Mexican color lieutenant and a fifteen-year-old sub-lieutenant raised a new flag; they finally just nailed a flag to the staff. The smoking chimneys of the city's bakeries made inviting targets for the American gunners and, one after another, were systematically knocked out of commission.

• • •

There was a brief lull in the firing when the consuls of Great Britain, France, Spain, and Prussia asked Scott's permission to leave under a flag of truce. Pointing out that they had had ample time to evacuate before the bombardment began, Scott refused the request. The punishing bombardment resumed. "The town is crumbling to pieces under this iron rain," noted Lieutenant John James Peck.

• • •

At 8 A.M. on March 26—eighty-eight hours after the bombardment had begun— the Mexicans raised a white flag. As if nature were responding to the display of human destructiveness with a demonstration of its own primal power, a northerly more powerful than the one two weeks previously struck the area. At Sacrificios Island, where U.S. steamships, schooners, gunboats, and transports were jammed with troops, mules, horses, and provisions, twenty-six vessels ran aground. Two others were stranded north of Ulua, with most of their crews lost. The American soldiers spent "a most uncomfortable night" in the open after the wind blew down half their tents and covered everything with sand.

Two U.S. commissioners, General William Worth and Colonel Joseph Totten, met with Mexican negotiators and settled the terms for the city's unconditional capitulation. Vera Cruz's once-defiant commandant, General Morales, had slipped away in a small boat, leaving General Jose Juan de Landero to carry out the distasteful task of surrendering the city.

MARCH 29, 1847: VERA CRUZ

The day dawned clear and bright; the northerly was spent. At midmorning, more than four thousand Mexican troops marched out of the city and through the gates of San Juan de Ulua "with drums beating, colors flying." On a plain outside the city, the defeated army stacked its arms, and regimental musicians laid down their instruments. They were granted paroles after giving their word not to fight the Americans again—a pledge the U.S. troops expected few to honor after observing the "grief and rage . . . discerned in their features." Refugees laden with personal items, cookware, and "innumerable parrots" joined the exodus of soldiers.

The blue-uniformed conquerors roamed the city and its massive fort, sobered by the sight of the enemy's 250 guns, amazed that with just 23 guns they had triumphed in four days. The Army and Navy batteries and the mosquito fleet had fired nearly a half million pounds of metal—more than sixty-seven hundred rounds. "The God of battles has fought with us," declared Captain George Archibald McCall with awe. "I can scarcely realize the thing."

The soldiers were shocked by the destruction that they saw inside the city; two-thirds of Vera Cruz's homes and buildings were destroyed or damaged. "Hardly a building south of the Plaza Grande but is either burnt, torn in pieces, or much injured, and the streets are filled with rubbish and fragments," wrote George Kendall of the New Orleans *Picayune*. Five shells had crashed into the National Palace, killing a woman and two children sleeping in the kitchen. A daughter of the British consul, whose home was flattened, also perished. The consul and other foreign nationals bitterly criticized Scott for not permitting them to leave when they requested to do so, but Kendall was unsympathetic, noting they had been plainly told in advance that Vera Cruz would be captured.

As Scott had hoped, he had achieved "economy of life, by means of head-work," and the American "butchers' bill" for carrying Vera Cruz by siege was light when compared to the projected cost of storming the city. Of twelve thousand U.S. troops engaged, only thirteen were killed and fifty-five wounded. The enemy defenders and Vera Cruzans paid a far heavier price. While precise figures were never obtained, Mexican sources estimated that four hundred soldiers and at least four hundred citizens were killed, and hundreds more were wounded.

• • •

On April 10, President Polk was handed a telegram from the Baltimore *Sun* announcing the March 27 surrender, proof of the press's dazzlingly swift transmission of major news by fast steamers, couriers, and telegraph. "This was joyful news," Polk happily noted in his journal that night. Hours after the president received the telegram, Colonel Totten arrived at the White House with dispatches from Scott confirming the news.

The signal triumph did not allay Polk's many concerns about the American invasion, nor did it cause him to relent in his obsessive micromanaging of the campaign. Polk and the cabinet advised Scott, who long ago had already thought of it, to remove his troops "from the region of the vomito" during the "unhealthy season." The president brooded over Scott's demands for baggage trains and stockpiles of supplies, wishing for a commander "who would go light and move rapidly" on horses and mules, believing that if he did, "Santa Anna and his whole army could be destroyed or captured in a short time."

The plodding Army bureaucracy in Washington also irritated Polk. "Their movements are entirely too slow, & many of them conducted without judgment." They were too accustomed to "enjoying their ease, sitting in parlours and on carpeted floors . . . and are content to job on in a regular routine without knowing whether they are taking care of the public interest or not." Consequently, "I shall find it to be necessary to give more of my attention to these matters of detail than I have heretofore had it in my power to do."

Adopting a proposal by Senator Thomas Hart Benton, Polk lifted the blockade of Mexico's Gulf ports and began levying a tariff on Mexican imports, intending to use the proceeds to defray war costs. Benton had suggested the idea on March 10. Two days later, acting as though it had been his idea, Polk had proposed it to Benton who, unsurprisingly, approved of it. The president dispatched Customs officials to Mexico to collect the new duties, set low enough, he believed, to encourage the revival of foreign trade there. But European merchants continued to avoid Vera Cruz; during the next six months, just one small shipment from Europe would be unloaded.

Coming so soon after the announcements of Taylor's Buena Vista victory, and of the successful landing at Vera Cruz, the news of the city's capture inspired an upwelling of patriotism throughout the United States. Washingtonians gathered around a huge bonfire. New Yorkers celebrated with candles in the windows of public buildings, a procession, and fireworks and artillery demonstrations. P. T. Barnum presented a special program on the Mexican War, with band accompaniment, at his new American Museum.

• • •

With the "vomito" season nearly upon the coastal plain, Scott and his officers began planning the debouchment from Vera Cruz to the cooler mountain foothills. The "Little Cabinet," as Scott's trusted subordinates were known, gathered at 8:30 nightly around Scott's dinner table and usually discussed Army business until eleven or midnight. If no business pressed, Scott would hold forth, "absorbing the whole conversation," observed Lieutenant Colonel Ethan Allen Hitchcock, whom Scott had named acting Inspector General, and who would become the General of the Army's most trusted aide. The "Little Cabinet" also included Colonel Totten; Lieutenant Henry L. Scott, the general's son-in-law and acting Adjutant General; and Captain Robert E. Lee, who had impressed Scott with his skillful positioning of the siege batteries. Totten had cited Lee in an after-battle citation, along with Lieutenants McClellan and Beauregard.

Lieutenant Sam Grant, who early in his career developed the habit of carefully observing his superiors' qualities, good and bad, sketched a discerning comparison of Scott and Taylor, after serving under both:

> The contrast between the two was very marked. General Taylor never wore uniform, but dressed himself entirely for comfort. He moved about the field in which he was operating to see through his own eyes the situation. Often he would be without staff officers, and when he was accompanied by them, there was no prescribed order in which they followed. He was very much given to sit his horse side-ways—with both feet on one side—particularly on the battlefield.
>
> General Scott was the reverse in all these particulars. He always wore all the uniform prescribed or allowed by law when he inspected his lines; word

would be sent to all divisions and brigade commanders in advance, notifying them of the hour when the commanding general might be expected. This was done so that all the army might be under arms to salute their chief as he passed. On these occasions he wore his dress uniform, cocked hat, aiguillettes, sabre and spurs. His staff proper, besides all officers constructively on his staff—engineers, inspectors, quartermasters, etc., that could be spared—followed, also in uniform and in prescribed order. Orders were prepared with great care and evidently with the view that they should be a history of what followed. . . .

General Scott was precise in language, cultivated a style peculiarly his own; was proud of his rhetoric; not adverse to speaking of himself, often in the third person, and he could bestow praise upon the person he was talking about without the least embarrassment.

• • •

Indeed, Scott's flair for self-promotion and his obvious narcissism were commensurate with his imposing size—six-foot-four and, in his prime, 230 pounds. Scott's boundless faith in his abilities, which were considerable, had driven him to the Army's highest rank and, in the political realm, had impelled him to seek the Whig Party's presidential nomination in 1840. Failing then, he would succeed in 1852, becoming the last Whig candidate for president, only to be beaten by one of his Mexican War generals, Franklin Pierce. His political failures may be laid to his off-putting aristocratic aloofness, while his well-publicized run-ins with civilian superiors can be put down to an unfortunate predilection for sounding off when silence would have better served him.

His faults notwithstanding, "Old Fuss and Feathers" was arguably America's best military leader during the eighty years between George Washington and the Civil War. Like Taylor, he had learned his profession during the War of 1812 and the Indian wars. But unlike Taylor, Scott was also a student of European military science, and especially of the writings of Antoine Henri de Jomini, Napoleon Bonaparte's tactician, whose *Art of War* occupied a place of honor in Scott's portable library.

Scott's experiences during the War of 1812 made him a lifelong disciple of both offensive warfare and the necessity of relentless drill to transform raw enlistees and volunteers into troops that would obey commands amid the noise and confusion of combat. The defining event of Scott's military career was the October 1812 Battle of Queenston Heights, a defensive battle fought by American regulars and volunteers under Stephen van Rensselaer, a politician-cum-general, on the Canadian heights overlooking the Niagara River. American militia refused to cross the river to aid van Rensselaer, claiming that as U.S. militia they could not legally enter Canada. British colonial troops and their Iroquois allies, choosing when and where to attack, overwhelmed van Rensselaer's army and captured eight hundred Americans, among them Scott and Captain John Wool, wounded while making a valiant stand that cost the British one of their best generals, Isaac Brock.

Never forgetting his sense of helplessness as he braced for the British attacks, Scott forever abjured defensive warfare. In May 1813, he led an amphibious assault on Fort George on Lake Ontario that resembled his investment of Vera Cruz, with assault troops in flatboats landing away from the fort and then attacking its rear.

Also as a result of Queenston, Scott in 1814 molded one of the first truly professional U.S. armies, at a training camp in Buffalo. He drilled his men ten hours a day so that they could maneuver and fire in concert, and he taught them military fundamentals such as maintaining outposts and sentinels, camp sanitation, military courtesy, and personal hygiene.

At Chippewa Plain in July 1814, Scott's disciplined brigade outmaneuvered fifteen hundred British veterans of the Napoleonic Wars, broke their line, and defeated them in just half an hour. The English lost 137 killed and 375 wounded, at a cost of 48 American dead and 227 wounded. Henry Adams wrote that the victory "gave to the United States army a character and pride it had never before possessed." Scott never let anyone forget that he was "the hero of Chippewa."

Nineteen days after Chippewa, Scott and a thousand troops attacked eighteen hundred British regulars at Lundy's Lane. It was a draw, with each side losing more than eight hundred men, making it the war's costliest land battle. Scott was wounded in the left shoulder by a musket ball. The war ended with Scott holding the rank of brigadier general.

Because of the success of his training methods, Scott was selected to write the 1821 *General Regulations of the Army*, the first comprehensive U.S. Army manual. A sweeping document that displayed Scott's encyclopedic knowledge of all things military, it laid down rules and procedures for everything from the quotidian—when soldiers should bathe and change their clothes, and what they should eat—to the art and science of combat strategy and tactics. Order, precision, and discipline were the manual's abiding themes, just as they were the governing principles of Scott's life.

Scott later traveled throughout Europe, studying military tactics and adding textbooks to his library. His studies persuaded him to adopt the Napoleonic practice of maneuvering against an enemy's flanks, while avoiding frontal attacks.

None of this prepared Scott for Indian warfare. In 1836, President Andrew Jackson sent him to Florida with four thousand troops to subdue the Seminoles, who had killed U.S. soldiers attempting to carry out a removal policy. To Scott's frustration, the Seminoles would not march out to meet his army in open battle but waged a guerrilla war, materializing unexpectedly to strike and then melting away into the Florida swamps. Scott accomplished so little in Florida that an Army court of inquiry was convened to judge his leadership, but found no fault with him.

• • •

Thus, the specter of an unwinnable guerrilla war remained very real to Scott as he led his army into the enemy heartland. But he believed that he could preempt an insurgency by pacifying the Mexican people in areas under his control. At a distance from Mexico City, this strategy was sound, but its utility would diminish as his army neared the capital, which for many Mexicans was a symbol of their nation's greatness and a source of pride. Scott's innovative linkage of political and military objectives would influence how noncombatants were treated during the Civil War.

Scott began his pacification program in Vera Cruz by promising the Mexicans fair treatment and strictly regulating his soldiers' conduct. Army looters were punished; one was hanged for rape. Scott displayed his personal goodwill by carrying a candle in a procession to the cathedral. The Army opened a soup kitchen to feed the poor and homeless. Scott appointed the efficient General William Worth temporary governor. Mexican laborers were offered $1.50 a day to repair damaged buildings and to clear the rubble that clogged the streets. But the Mexicans, as wary of their own leaders as they were of the invaders, refused to work until the Army gave them papers stating that they had been coerced; when the Americans departed, they did not want to be persecuted for collaboration. After the repairs were well under way, American goods began to pour into the city. Vera Cruz became the army's main supply port in Mexico.

• • •

Santa Anna's new government, which had done nothing to aid Vera Cruz during its investment, now exploited its capture to arouse the capital's resistance to the invaders. In the wake of the Polkos' rebellion, Santa Anna had cemented his authority by naming a new cabinet and abolishing Farias's church land appropriation decree, but for a price—a 1.5 million-peso loan from the Catholic Church.

As the government newspapers clamored for the expulsion of the invaders, Santa Anna raised a new army. Joining the patriotic furor, the Mexican Congress proposed branding as a traitor anyone who espoused peace while American troops occupied any part of Mexico.

In early April, Santa Anna marched out of Mexico City toward Vera Cruz at the head of twelve thousand troops, intending to crush Scott's army in battle. At his Jalapa estate, drovers rounded up cattle bearing Santa Anna's "A.L.S.A" brand to feed the army. The road to Vera Cruz was soon jammed with lowing cattle and singing troops in shakos.

Two hundred miles east of Mexico City, and seventy miles from the American beachhead, Santa Anna deployed his army in a range of imposing hills that dominated the National Highway to the capital. The highlands marked the terminus of the coastal plain and the beginning of eastern Mexico's foothills. Santa Anna had spent most of his life in this region, and his estate was just twenty miles away. He knew that if he could hurl the Americans back to Vera Cruz, "el vomito" would then become a powerful ally.

The largest of the hills where the Mexican army on April 6 began to dig gun pits and a canal to bring it fresh water was one-thousand-foot-high Cerro Gordo, "Fat Hill."

• • •

On April 11, General David Twiggs's Second Division, Scott's spear point, reached the hills' eastern approaches and halted at the Rio del Plan crossing. Ahead, the National Highway curved up into the hills, climbing out of the coastal plain's heat and humidity. Scouts reported that Mexican troops defended all the main approaches. Twiggs began planning a frontal assault on the heavily fortified hill that stood before him.

But before Twiggs could attack, Major General Patterson, arriving with his volunteer division, vetoed the plan because he believed casualties would be unacceptably high. Reaching the area two days later, on April 14, General Winfield Scott sent reconnaissance officers to find other routes through the hills.

APRIL 14, 1847: CERRO GORDO

Captain Robert E. Lee scarcely dared to breathe, much less move a muscle. He lay flat on the ground behind a large log on which sat several Mexican soldiers, their backs toward him, unaware of his presence. The enemy troops had slaked their thirst at the spring and had then gossiped and loafed for hours. Lee was acutely aware that if the soldiers discovered either him or his guide, John Fitzwater, who was concealed nearby, the Mexicans' bayonets would put an end to their critical mission as well as their lives. Being a religious man, Lee must have prayed, when he was not suppressing the natural urge of a man as active as he to move about. The afternoon shadows lengthened, and finally the enemy soldiers rose and drifted away. Lee and Fitzwater waited until the last voice had faded to silence and then raised themselves up to stretch their cramped limbs. They began the long trek back through the maze of deep ravines.

Reaching General Scott's tent after dark, Lee and Fitzwater verified what Lieutenants P. G. T. Beauregard and Zealous B. Tower had reported earlier: Scott indeed might get behind Santa Anna's army by leaving the National Highway and cutting through the tangle of hills and ravines on the Mexican left. Scott had sent Lee, his most trusted junior officer, to investigate further after Beauregard had fallen ill. Lee had found a better route, where a road could be built to support artillery. But it would have to be done without the Mexicans' knowledge.

The next morning, Lee led a work party to clear and grade a road through the jumbled hills and gullies. When it was completed, General Twiggs's regulars could trundle cannons to the top of Atalaya, the steep hill opposite Cerro Gordo, in anticipation of attacking Cerro Gordo and the enemy rear.

Meanwhile, General William Worth's First Division joined Twiggs's and Patterson's divisions at their encampment near the Rio del Plan, giving Scott eighty-five hundred troops to hurl against Santa Anna's twelve thousand men.

• • •

Santa Anna's engineers were less sanguine than their commander about the unassailability of their position. Besides noting the difficulty of obtaining water, they pointed out that the defenses blocking the National Highway were overshadowed by the tall hill behind them, Cerro Gordo; if Cerro Gordo fell, their defensive scheme would be imperiled. But Santa Anna ignored his engineers' concerns, believing that the river on his right and the deep, twisting ravines and rugged hills on his left were sufficient protection for his flanks and rear.

• • •

Throughout April 15 and 16, Captain Lee's detachment of pioneers and Michigan lumberjacks felled trees and bushes, widening and leveling the path that Lee had found through the hogbacks and gulches. It was exhausting, dirty, pickax-and-shovel work. "With infinite labor we made a sort of road turning to the right from the main road in advance of the enemy's works and out of his sight, and, by carrying this road around some two or three miles, we came in view of the rear conical hill," reported Lieutenant Colonel Ethan Allen Hitchcock. This was Atalaya, opposite Cerro Gordo. Here the pioneers stopped, fearing that if they advanced farther they would be discovered.

Not far away was the main enemy camp with Santa Anna's reserves, and, beyond that, the National Highway where it emerged on the west side of the hills to continue to Jalapa. If Scott quickly reached that place on the National Highway, he could seal Santa Anna's avenues of escape and capture or destroy his army.

• • •

Lee led Twiggs's blue-coated regulars down the new road on April 17. Even with all the hard work done by the pioneers, it was still tough going; the cannons had to be manhandled by ropes and brute strength across deep chasms. Lieutenant George McClellan noted that the mule teams "were the worst I ever saw—they had just been lassoed as they swam ashore, and neither they nor their teamsters had ever seen a wagon before." When Twiggs's men reached the end of the road at the foot of Atalaya, Mexican troops entrenched on the steep hill began firing on the column of bluecoats snaking out of the tangle of ravines and hills.

The regulars swarmed up Atalaya's leg-killing slope. "The labor of merely climbing it is alone sufficient to break down any but a tolerably strong man," reported Hitchcock. The enemy fired down on the Americans, but their shots were high, and casualties were light. Spearheaded by a company of the Seventh Infantry Regiment under Lieutenant Franklin Gardner and reinforced by General James Shields's volunteer brigade, Twiggs's Second Division reached Atalaya's summit.

The Mexican defenders ran down Atalaya's far slope toward Cerro Gordo. Some of Twiggs's men impulsively pursued them into the deep valley between the hills. But when they broke off the chase and attempted to return to the top of Atalaya, enemy gunners on Cerro Gordo unleashed a murderous fire, trapping them in the valley. The cannon fire also prevented their comrades from coming to their aid, and the wounded had to lie where they fell in the valley. Some died there during the night.

Under cover of darkness, Captain Lee supervised the placement on Atalaya of a twenty-four-pound gun and two twenty-four-pound howitzers.

APRIL 18, 1847, 7 A.M.: CERRO GORDO

West of Scott's base camp, General Gideon Pillow readied his two assault teams. He intended to storm the fortified hill that Twiggs, until he was overruled, had earlier wanted to attack. But Pillow's assault would be only a diversion; with good reason, Scott had bypassed this strongpoint. Immediately before Pillow's force were three large enemy batteries bristling with cannons and supported by infantry brigades. While Santa Anna knew that Twiggs's capture of Atalaya threatened Cerro Gordo, he still believed that Scott would launch his main attack here, on the National Highway. Scott hoped that Pillow's demonstration would fool Santa Anna for a little longer—long enough for Twiggs and Shields to rampage through the enemy rear.

• • •

The three American 24-pounders on Atalaya began bombarding cone-shaped Cerro Gordo. Colonel William S. Harney's First Brigade of regulars and four artillery companies in attack columns poured into the valley between the two eminences. Shields's brigade tacked westward from Atalaya, intending to pounce on the Mexican camp and then to block the National Highway, the enemy escape route.

Cannon and musket fire bounced, pinged, and zipped through Harney's blue-coated troops as they bayoneted the defenders behind a stone breastwork sixty yards up Cerro Gordo's steep slope. Lieutenant Dabney Maury and his men took potshots at Santa Anna, seen riding among the Cerro Gordo defenders on a gray horse, but no harm came to him.

Maury's left arm suddenly burned with pain; a musket ball had hit him. When Maury reached an aid station, an overworked battlefield surgeon told him that the arm would have to come off. Maury rejected the prognosis, commandeered a horse, and rode five miles to the base camp's field hospital for a second opinion. "I will die before I will lose it, and I assume all responsibility," Maury told the second doctor. The doctor saved the arm. Maury recovered to serve as a Confederate general, and to later found the Southern Historical Society.

Harney's shock troops cleared Cerro Gordo's summit, and Scott, hat in hand, addressed his men. "Brother soldiers, I am proud to call you brothers, and your country will be proud to hear of your conduct this day," he told the cheering men, as tears rolled down his cheeks. Scott "slowly rode off, bowing, and waving his hat."

Shields's brigade, commanded by Colonel Bennet Riley after Shields was shot through the lungs, overran the enemy base camp but reached the National Highway too late to close the net around Santa Anna's army.

• • •

As Harney's men stormed Cerro Gordo, Pillow made a show of preparing to attack the fortified heights on the National Highway. He was supposed to launch his demonstration "the nearer to the river the better." Lieutenant Tower of the engineers had mapped an assault route that would hit the enemy there, on his extreme right, while using the terrain to mask the attackers from the Mexicans' guns. But Pillow, whose pretensions to military command were based on his having been President Polk's law partner, inexplicably decided to attack the middle battery and its seventeen guns. Tower futilely objected that "we would be more apt to be seen" if the attack were launched there.

The American and Mexican positions were so close that Lieutenant George McClellan, attached to Pillow's unit, could clearly hear Mexican officers giving orders. Pillow blunderingly gave away his assault team's position by bellowing a question at the top of his voice. Instantly, a Mexican bugle sounded, "and within three minutes after that their fire opened upon us," wrote McClellan. Just as Tower had warned, the volley scattered the exposed storming party of Tennesseans, Kentuckians, and Pennsylvanians as it was forming. Some of the startled volunteers impulsively rushed the Mexican works, some fled to the rear, and others hid in the rocks.

Pillow was shot in the arm while McClellan was trying to persuade him to cancel a second attack and to authorize McClellan to ask Scott to send regulars. Pillow consented to both suggestions, but by the time McClellan found Scott, Cerro Gordo had fallen and everywhere, even on the heights before Pillow, the Mexicans were fleeing in confusion. While Pillow had bungled his attack, he had still pinned down the main Mexican force.

In just three hours, the Americans had smashed to pieces Santa Anna's new army.

• • •

The mangled Mexican army recoiled westward on the National Highway toward Jalapa, Puebla, and Mexico City, abandoning its dead and wounded, who were found lying "along the roads for miles." On the battleground, dead Mexican soldiers were draped grotesquely over breastworks, and they covered the ground where the fighting had been the fiercest. "Every by-path is strewn with the dead," wrote George Kendall of the *Picayune*. The Americans "could not help pitying the dead & dying as we passed over them," noted Captain James Anderson in a letter to his wife, Ellen. In four months, Anderson would join the ranks of the dead.

This being his first battle, Captain Lee was stunned by "what a horrible sight a battlefield is." He was rounding up enemy wounded when he spotted a Mexican boy drummer or bugler with a shattered arm who was pinned beneath a dying soldier. A distraught Mexican girl, who had tried to roll the soldier off the boy, stood there weeping, "her hands crossed over her breast; her hair in one long plait behind reached her waist, her shoulders and arms bare, without stockings or shoes." Her thanks "lingered in my ear" after Lee helped free the boy and sent him to a hospital.

At a dressing station, Kendall watched Dr. Joseph Wright treat a volunteer who had half his head "carried away by a heavy cannon ball. . . . It was worse than a wound, and a description of it would be too horrible." To Kendall's amazement, the volunteer not only survived, but he returned to active duty, although "without part of his face and jaw and one ear."

• • •

All battlefield wounds were potentially fatal. Wounds to the head, chest, and pelvis were always dangerous, and abdominal wounds usually resulted in death. Amputation, which took eighty seconds on average, was part of the usual treatment for a shattered limb. The surgery was performed under frightfully unhygienic conditions, with the stump sometimes packed in a cornmeal poultice or with "slippery elm bark," mingled with crushed cactus pads. Because of widespread infection and disease, mortality in military hospitals hovered around 15 percent.

Some of the seriously wounded men evacuated to Vera Cruz encountered Dr. E. H. Barton, who was using ether to render his patients insensible before amputating—the first use of anesthetic in treating battle wounds. Anesthetic's earliest surgical use had occurred only six months earlier, during an operation at Massachusetts General Hospital, where Dr. John Collins Warren removed a vascular tumor from Gilbert Abbott while Dr. William Morton, a dentist, administered the ether. Dr. Barton's first anesthetic-aided surgery in Vera Cruz was the amputation of a German teamster's leg. "The limb was removed without the quiver of a muscle," reported the Vera Cruz *American Eagle*.

• • •

The 63 American dead represented less than a fourth of General Zachary Taylor's losses at Buena Vista; another 368 soldiers were wounded. An estimated 1,000 to 1,200 Mexican soldiers were killed or wounded. Scott's troops seized four to five thousand stands of arms and forty-three artillery pieces and captured 2,837 Mexican soldiers and 199 officers, including General Diaz de la Vega, his second time as a U.S. prisoner. Captured at Resaca de la Palma, la Vega had been exchanged in October for forty-three Navy crewmen from the reefed *Truxtun.*

Unable to spare troops to escort the Mexican prisoners to Vera Cruz, Scott paroled them all. They joined the other army refugees who clogged the National Highway.

Santa Anna escaped into the chaparral on a saddle mule that he had unharnessed from his carriage. He left behind his baggage, gamecocks, an immense silver service, papers, $20,000 in cash, and a wooden leg—probably a spare, for Santa Anna usually wore a prosthetic made of cork. Months later, several wooden legs were displayed throughout the United States by enterprising men who claimed that the prostheses had belonged to Santa Anna.

• • •

Santa Anna's dispirited army did not attempt to defend the mountain passes and National Highway towns to the west. "Consternation has spread over the country," observed Lieutenant Colonel Hitchcock. "The Mexicans are confounded, lost in wonder and despair." The easy victory made the Americans contemptuous of the leadership of the Mexican officers, whose own men scorned them for "being the first to run away in battle."

As the American army resumed its march west to the capital, the Mexican government newspaper in Mexico City, *El Monitor Republicano,* was informing its readers that Santa Anna's army had thrown back the Americans, forcing Scott to retreat to Vera Cruz. When *El Monitor* finally did concede the defeat at Cerro Gordo, it exhorted readers to fight to the death rather than make peace on the Americans' terms.

• • •

Twenty-five miles west of Cerro Gordo, General William Worth's First Division entered the infamous mountain fortress of Perote. After the Castle of San Juan de

Ulua, it was Mexico's greatest stronghold; there the unfortunate Texans of the 1842 Mier expedition had been imprisoned. With walls eight feet thick and sixty feet high, and surrounded by a moat, Perote could withstand a large-scale attack with as few as fifteen hundred troops.

But General Pedro de Ampudia and his three thousand cavalrymen had abandoned the fort, leaving behind fifty-four cannons, 1,165 cannon balls, 14,300 bombs and grenades, and five hundred muskets. The Americans were amused by the discovery of a 24-pounder inscribed with the words "The Terror of the North Americans."

Perote was cold, miserably wet, and humid, and wreathed in low, heavy clouds. Many of its inhabitants were poor. "Wrapped in their dingy blankets, looking like specters of famine," they lived in ruined homes, many without roofs. Army doctors set up a hospital for ill soldiers in damp, gloomy Perote castle, where in subsequent months twelve men died every day on average. The soldiers who remained on duty soon resembled "skeletons or mummies" and routinely medicated themselves with pulque, aquadiente, and opium.

• • •

More fortunate than Worth's men was the rest of Scott's army, which settled into Jalapa, on the tableland midway between Cerro Gordo and Perote. A cool, airy city of more than five thousand people—an unusually large number were upper-class Mexicans of mostly Castilian ancestry—Jalapa was four thousand feet in elevation above tropical Vera Cruz, sixty miles away. Mountains rose to the south, west, and north, with eighteen-thousand-foot Orizaba towering over them all. Immense oaks shaded the white adobe buildings, shingled with red tile. The crowded marketplace was the hub of a fertile agricultural region, whose bounty included corn, oranges, bananas, and coffee. After Vera Cruz and Cerro Gordo, the Americans savored the clean air, sunshine, and abundant red and purple bougainvillea, azaleas, dahlias, roses, zinnias, carnations, and orchids. Here, as in Perote, the army established a hospital. It was soon overwhelmed with hundreds of ill men, some "wasted to skeletons by diarrhea."

Named for the medicinal Jalap resin that was extracted from the purple morning glory that grew everywhere, Jalapa also was Santa Anna's birthplace. Scott and his staff toured Santa Anna's hacienda seven miles east of the city before placing it under a guard to discourage looters. It was "a princely place," with "rich prints" hanging everywhere, Hitchcock observed, but "everything is foreign—nothing shows the genius of the Mexicans—no works of art or evidences of science."

In scrupulously following Scott's policy of paying for local provisions, army quartermasters purchased some of Santa Anna's cattle. This irony prompted the *Picayune*'s Kendall to write: "Strange state of affairs, this—Santa Anna making money out of the United States by providing its army with provisions. . . . The 'Napoleon of the South' is ever ready to make an honest (!) penny. . . ."

The American officers encouraged their men to participate in Jalapa's Roman Catholic services, thereby advancing Scott's pacification program. Many volunteers flatly refused to participate in any "papist" ceremony, even when they were excused from kneeling. But the regulars attended Mass, and some officers even carried lighted candles in a procession. Lieutenant Ralph Kirkham, an Episcopalian, was so impressed with the Catholic rites that "I believe I should become a strict Catholic should I live in a Catholic country, for I do like an everyday religion."

• • •

At Puebla, the aptly named "City of Angels" 120 miles from Cerro Gordo and 93 miles from Mexico City, Santa Anna attempted to obtain a 30,000-peso loan. But he was so unpopular among Puebla's eighty thousand residents that he could only raise 10,000 pesos. As a further proof of their lack of confidence in Santa Anna, Puebla authorities distributed instructions on what to do when the Americans occupied the city. Seeing that he could do nothing in Puebla, Santa Anna prepared to move on to the capital.

While Santa Anna was still in Puebla, General Worth's division appeared outside the city. Santa Anna dispatched a large infantry force down the road to confront the Americans and about three thousand cavalry—probably the mounted troops that had abandoned Perote—to harass Worth's rearguard. An American artillery battery dispersed the infantry column, and the cavalrymen vanished.

• • •

On May 15, Worth's division crossed a forbidding landscape of cactus and frozen lava flows, and ascended a tall hill. Catching their breath in the thin air, the soldiers were transfixed by the sight of Puebla spread out at their feet on a 7,000-foot-elevation verdant plain, surrounded by rich farms and soaring, snow-capped mountains, including 17,887-foot, cone-shaped Popocatepetl, and 17,343-foot Iztaccihuatl. "We had a beautiful view of the castles, domes, and spires of that ancient and beautiful city of the angels," South Carolinian H. Judge Moore rapturously observed.

The troops entered Puebla, many times larger than any Mexican city yet occupied by the American armies. They were met by "thousands of men, women and children, ebbing and flowing like the agitated wave of the ocean." Spanish Minister Bermudez de Castro noted that the people had expected "giants" but instead saw columns of ragged, weary men. Touching the Americans' weapons as they passed, the Pueblans found the invaders to be mortal and "received them more like travelers than enemies."

Over the next weeks, Scott and most of his army joined Worth in Puebla. Planning now began for the climactic phase of the American invasion—the conquest of Mexico's ancient capital city.

22

PLANNING THE END GAME

"Scott is lost! He has been carried away by his successes! He can't take the city, and he can't fall back on his bases."

—The Duke of Wellington, when informed of General
Winfield Scott's decision to break free from his supply line

"We are anxious to be moving toward the 'Halls of the Montezumas.'"

—Lieutenant Raphael Semmes

SPRING 1847: PUEBLA

In just two months in central Mexico, the Americans had besieged and captured Mexico's principal port, defeated her army in a pitched battle on ground of the enemy's choosing, and marched 186 miles into Mexico's interior. Their clothes tattered and filthy, their bodies and senses hardened to adversity, the Americans gratefully occupied Mexico's picturesque second-largest city. They welcomed the respite from campaigning and the opportunity to obtain fresh clothing, wash the grime from their bodies, and restore some flesh to their gaunt frames. Lieutenant John Peck was delighted to find himself "on a lovely plain, whose undulations are as gentle as the breezes are balmy. . . . Orange groves and the palaces of the proprietors—you forget you are in Mexico, and fancy you are gazing on the paintings of your favorite novelist."

Winfield Scott, however, never forgot for a moment where he was: deep in enemy territory, at the end of a long supply line that was highly vulnerable to the murderous bandits that prowled the National Highway, their ranks swollen by Mexican army deserters. Travelers were waylaid and butchered almost daily. One of these unfortunates, a dental surgeon named Kingsbury who had been attacked by three Mexicans and robbed of $500, was found "horribly cut to pieces . . . with little life and completely flyblown."

Scott unleashed the Texas Rangers on the bandits. Led by two experts in no-quarter guerrilla warfare, Captain Sam Walker and Colonel Jack Coffee Hays, the Rangers, operating as the First Texas Mounted Regiment, pursued and killed bandits, reducing the depredations along the National Highway. A mounted squadron surprised a large guerrilla force at San Juan de los Llanos, killing forty-three of them, wounding fifty, and capturing two priests suspected of being collaborators. But with so many guerrillas still roaming the area, the National Highway remained dangerous, and the supply trains required escorts by troops who were needed for campaigning.

Another major problem confronting Scott was the looming expiration of the twelve-month enlistments of thousands of volunteers. He could persuade, but not compel, them to extend their enlistments. It could be argued that if Scott had immediately marched on Mexico City after shattering Santa Anna's army at Cerro Gordo, instead of taking twenty-seven days to reach Puebla, he might have captured the capital and then found it relatively easy to persuade the volunteers to extend their enlistments. But Scott's slow, methodical advance, while undoubtedly prudent with his supply line threatened by bandits and with wounded and ill soldiers to care for, had given Santa Anna time to regroup. Thus, faced with a war of indeterminate length, just one in every fifteen of the "twelve-month men" reenlisted. The rest, fifteen hundred or more, embarked for home "in high spirits, and quite satisfied with the amount of 'soldiering' they have done," sardonically observed a Boston *Advertiser* correspondent.

On paper, this left Scott with 7,113 men. But when those too ill to serve also were weeded out, there remained just 5,820 effectives. Scott wisely elected not to march on Mexico City with so small a force. The possible consequences of being trapped or defeated near the capital, 280 miles from Vera Cruz, the nearest resupply point, were too chilling to contemplate. He would await fresh troops in Puebla; about four thousand were en route to Mexico, and Polk and War Secretary Marcy planned to raise six to eight additional regiments to replace the volunteers whose enlistments were now expiring.

• • •

While the Texas Rangers and troop convoys improved security along the 186-mile supply line, too few supplies were reaching Puebla from the Vera Cruz docks, where a mountain of rations, tents, blankets, and clothing sat baking under the tropical sun due to the chronic shortage of wagons and draft animals.

The Quartermaster Department had erroneously assumed that mules and freight teams could be procured in Mexico in large quantities. If Scott's army had been compelled to depend solely on the supply line for its sustenance, it might well have starved.

The unsatisfactory logistical situation impelled Scott to adopt a daring strategy that was at odds with conventional military thinking: The army would largely live off the land, depending on its Vera Cruz supply base only for critical goods unavailable locally. As a consequence, most of the troops tied up with convoy and patrol duties on the National Highway could rejoin the main army.

The decision shocked Marcy and Polk, who were convinced that it was "a great military blunder." Perhaps only a Napoleon or an Alexander could have appreciated its admixture of boldness and flinty logic. The hero of Waterloo, the Duke of Wellington, decidedly did not. An admirer of Scott who had avidly followed the progress of his campaign on a map on his library wall, the duke was said to have exclaimed: "Scott is lost! He has been carried away by his successes! He can't take the city, and he can't fall back on his bases." Alone in U.S. military annals until William Tecumseh Sherman marched through Georgia to the sea, Scott was breaking free from his lifeline while deep in enemy country, with dangers on every side.

• • •

Scott's decision, however, did not obviate the need for a safer National Highway, which yet remained the army's only means of receiving dispatches and reinforcements. The bandits' unremitting outrages compelled Lieutenant Colonel Ethan Allen Hitchcock to adopt one of those desperate measures that in hindsight seem inspired: He hired Mexico's most notorious robber to protect the Americans from the other robbers. The robber-in-chief, Manuel Dominguez, and his cohorts formed the nucleus of what became known as the "Spy Company." Hitchcock initially paid Dominguez $3 a day and five of his men $2 to serve as American couriers on the National Highway. Disguised as merchants, they turned the tables when accosted by other would-be robbers.

The Spy Company sharply reduced the incidence of highway robberies. Impressed, Hitchcock began using Dominguez's men as guides, and to report on enemy troop movements. As Dominguez surely had intended all along, under cover of helping the Americans, he and his men augmented their income by attacking Mexican officers whenever they got the chance, often killing them to avenge past wrongs, and then riding away with the officers' cash, horses, and clothing.

While Dominguez's men were sometimes caught and executed by the Mexicans, the Spy Company expanded to more than a hundred men, including twelve prison inmates freed by Hitchcock upon Dominguez's request. (After the war, certain that they could never safely live in Mexico, Dominguez and sixty men, with thirty dependents, sailed to New Orleans, where Hitchcock tried unsuccessfully to obtain government allowances for them.)

• • •

While waiting for the replacement volunteers, Scott's army prepared for the ninety-three-mile march on the enemy capital, Mexico City. The Commissary and Quartermaster departments stockpiled provisions and animals. Captain Robert E. Lee and Major William Turnbull, the chief topographical engineer, scouted and mapped the countryside between Puebla and Mexico City. Scott adopted the practice of debriefing them separately when they returned from their excursions, incorporating into his plans only those points on which Lee and Turnbull agreed. The army drilled on Puebla's two emerald-green parade grounds in the shadows of the mountain peaks that towered above the city, and the townspeople came to watch the twice-weekly reviews.

In their free time, the soldiers roamed the city, thankful to be there, and not enduring Vera Cruz's suffocating June heat and humidity. Built on a wooded hillside, Puebla, according to a Spanish proverb, was "the first heaven, Mexico [City] the second." The semicircle of snow-capped mountains certainly lent a fairy tale aspect to it, although not always idyllic; during the American occupation, volcanic Popocatepetl rumbled to life, spewing black smoke and melting its snowy crown.

Flagstone sidewalks and two-story stone homes adorned by carvings and painted glazed tiles lined the city's paved streets. In one suburb was a mile-circumference garden filled with trees, shrubs, statues, and fountains. A massive cathedral and its beautifully decorated altars were a lodestar for hundreds of priests and nuns living in rectories and convents scattered throughout the city.

The Americans saw their first bullfights and were disturbed by the Mexicans' obvious enjoyment of the bulls' torments. "It is certainly the most cruel amusement that I ever witnessed," observed Lieutenant Ralph Kirkham. When the bullfights were shut down because the matadors and picadors were jailed for stealing, the soldiers went to the ice cream gardens, coffee houses, billiard rooms, and the Jardin del Tivoli for fandangos. They attended a traveling circus, and the theater, where Kirkham saw a comedy titled *The Mysteries of a Minor* and pronounced the orchestra "excellent." It seemed that everyone, even the poor, owned a pet song-bird and, surprisingly, works of art. "There is not a house or a room occupied by Mexicans in the city of Puebla which has not one to 20 paintings and engravings."

The soldiers overindulged in the alelike pulque and the more potent mescal, and some of them got into trouble. Intolerant of disorderliness, the U.S. command sentenced four soldiers who robbed a Mexican house to thirty-nine lashes each in the Main Plaza. As a band played the "Rogue's March," the miscreants' heads were shaved, and the word "robber" was pasted on their backs.

A leaflet titled "Mexicans to Catholic Irishmen" and signed by Santa Anna appeared in Scott's camp. It promised a $10 bonus and two hundred acres to every American who joined the Mexican army. "Listen to the words of your brother, hear the accents of a Catholic people," the leaflet exhorted. Some American soldiers did listen and did cross the lines, sometimes because they were fed up with the "foolish and tyrannical conduct" of a handful of abusive officers.

In keeping with Scott's pacification program, Lieutenant Colonel Hitchcock drafted two proclamations. The first, written in May, portrayed the Americans as emissaries of freedom, eager to liberate an oppressed people who had been made "the sport of private ambition." "Abandon at once those old colonial habits, and learn to be truly free—truly Republican." In June, Hitchcock penned a second address, which was translated into Spanish and distributed in pamphlets. It astonishingly asserted the *right* of the United States to invade their country—to end the war. "We are here for no earthly purpose except the hope of obtaining a peace."

• • •

The American diplomat chosen to effect that peace was Nicholas Trist. Recently landed at Vera Cruz and on his way to join Scott, Trist was the chief clerk of the State Department but now also carried the title "Minister Plenipotentiary." Polk and Secretary of State James Buchanan had selected Trist on April 10 for this immensely important mission, only hours after learning of Vera Cruz's surrender. Believing that Mexico might now be amenable to peace, the president had first proposed that Buchanan personally go to Mexico to negotiate a treaty. Buchanan, however, had reasonably pointed out that with no immediate prospects for peace, the mission might drag on for months, taking him away from his other duties. Buchanan suggested Trist, and Polk had readily assented, finding him to be "an able man, perfectly familiar with the Spanish character and language, & might go with special and well defined instructions."

Significantly, as events would demonstrate, Polk wanted Trist to carry a peace treaty to Mexico, but to have only limited authority to negotiate its terms. Trist was also sworn to secrecy; Santa Anna must not find out that a peace proposal was on the way to Mexico; he might be encouraged to fight on, believing that the mission signaled a weakening of U.S. resolve.

Indeed, Trist at least superficially appeared to be superbly qualified. Forty-six years old, he was a dependable Democrat who was fluent in Spanish and shared the Polk administration's expansionist views. He was married to Virginia Jefferson Randolph, a granddaughter of Thomas Jefferson, under whose supervision Trist had studied law after he had left West Point without graduating. Upon Jefferson's death in 1826, Trist became coexecutor of his heavily mortgaged estate. Two years later, Secretary of State Henry Clay hired Trist as a State Department clerk. Trist needed the income to help his mother-in-law, Martha Jefferson Randolph, make ends meet. In 1833, Andrew Jackson named Trist consul to Havana, where he served until John Tyler recalled him in 1841. Polk named him chief clerk of the State Department in 1845 after Jackson recommended him as a man of "first-rate talents" whose wife was "the only true representative that great & good man [Jefferson] has left. . . ." Trist had not yet had occasion to display some of his other, less desirable qualities: his sensitivity to criticism, his stubbornness, and his pride.

• • •

Three days after appointing Trist, Polk and his cabinet held their most consequential meeting since deciding to ask Congress to sanction the war with Mexico. As the war had progressed, Polk had often meditated on the terms for an acceptable peace, and the time had now come to spell them out.

The president and his advisers were in agreement on the fundamental conditions: a U.S.–Mexican border on the Rio Grande; the United States getting New Mexico and Upper and Lower California, and in exchange, agreeing to pay the $3 million in claims by U.S. citizens against Mexico. Treasury Secretary Robert Walker and Buchanan advocated seeking free passage for the United States across Mexico's 150-mile-wide Isthmus of Tehuantepec, located between Vera Cruz and the Yucatan Peninsula. The relatively short portage between the Gulf of Mexico and the Pacific would save merchants the time and expense of the months-long sea voyage around Cape Horn. But because the Isthmus "constituted no part of the object for which we had engaged in the War," Polk asserted that it should not be an absolute condition. When Buchanan recommended paying no more than

$15 million for the Mexican provinces, Polk, unwilling to let California get away, argued that Trist should be authorized to spend up to $30 million. Walker and Buchanan yielded on both issues to Polk and the other cabinet members.

• • •

Two days later, on April 15, Buchanan submitted the draft of an eleven-article proposed treaty, along with Trist's written instructions. After making small changes, the cabinet approved the documents.

The instructions clearly directed Trist only to convey the treaty proposal as written, with one exception: he could offer more, if necessary, for Upper and Lower California and New Mexico. If Mexico rejected one of the absolute conditions, yet demonstrated a willingness to continue negotiations, Trist was instructed to contact the State Department, and a more experienced diplomat, possibly Buchanan himself, would take over the mission.

The proposed treaty fixed the U.S.–Mexico border at the Rio Grande, and granted the United States free passage across the Isthmus of Tehuantepec, from "sea to sea"—although this was not an essential prerequisite—as well as possession of the New Mexico territory and Upper and Lower California, for $15 million. Trist's instructions permitted him to bargain for the northern Mexican provinces. He could offer up to $30 million for all the territories; or up to $25 million for Upper California, New Mexico, and the isthmus passage; or $20 million for Upper California and New Mexico, without the passage.

Obtaining Upper California and New Mexico, wrote Buchanan, was to be "a sine qua non of any Treaty. You may modify, change or omit the other terms of the Projet [sic], if needful, but not so as to interfere with this ultimatum."

• • •

The president's attempts at secrecy notwithstanding, the details of Trist's mission found their way into James Gordon Bennett's New York *Herald* just as Trist was preparing to sail from New York. Polk was apoplectic. "I have not been more vexed or excited since I have been president," he wrote in his diary on April 21. He blamed the Whig press and the politicians whose opposition to the war "have been giving 'aid & comfort' to the enemy." Their malevolent purpose, he wrote bitterly, was to prolong the war "in the hope that the Democratic administration might be brought into disrepute by continuing it to a protracted length, and they might gain some political advantage in the next Presidential election." Polk ordered the State Department to find the source of the "treachery." Suspicion fell on William S. Derrick, who in Trist's absence had become acting chief clerk, and who had prepared and copied the proposed treaty and Trist's instructions. But Derrick vehemently denied leaking the information to the *Herald,* and the culprit was never positively identified.

• • •

Polk and Buchanan also were in communication with a secret emissary in Mexico, Moses Y. Beach, the publisher of New York's Democrat-leaning *Sun,* which vied with Bennett's *Herald* for the honor of being the largest-circulation U.S. newspaper. To boost readership, Beach sometimes concocted outrageous hoaxes, such as Edgar Allan Poe's fictitious account of a balloon with eight passengers that had supposedly reached New York from England in just three days.

Before traveling to Mexico City to report on wartime conditions, Beach met privately with the president and the secretary of state and agreed to gather intelligence for the U.S. government. Buchanan bestowed upon him the Polk administration's now well-worn title, "secret agent," with a $6 daily stipend. Beach embarked for Mexico in January 1847 with his daughter Drusilla and Jane McManus Storms, Beach's top reporter and "the other woman" named by Eliza Bowen Jumel when she divorced Aaron Burr in 1833. The only female Mexican War correspondent, Storms would also become the only reporter of either gender to write from behind enemy lines.

Beach initially informed Buchanan that he might be able to secretly negotiate a treaty through the Catholic clergy. But Beach and his daughter were forced to flee for their lives when Santa Anna, suspicious of Beach's activities and hearing rumors of his involvement in the Polko revolt, reached Mexico City in late March after his Buena Vista defeat and while Vera Cruz was under siege. Beach returned to Washington in May. After meeting privately with the editor, Polk reported cryptically, "He gave me valuable information."

It was paradoxical that Polk, who kept such a tight rein on his generals, department heads, and diplomats, gave such latitude to his secret agents—witness his indulgence of Commodore Robert Stockton's freewheeling attempts to incite Texas to start a war with Mexico, and John C. Frémont's mysterious agency in California. So it was with Beach. While Buchanan was writing restrictive instructions for Trist, Polk was remarking that if Beach, who was operating without any written instructions, made a treaty and "it is a good one," he would waive his lack of diplomatic authority and recommend it to the Senate. "It will be a good joke if he should assume the authority and take the whole country by surprise & make a Treaty."

• • •

No sooner had Nicholas Trist reached Vera Cruz on May 6 than he unwittingly instigated a feud with Winfield Scott. Although instructed to personally deliver various letters and instructions to Scott, Trist sent them to the general by military courier. The courier pouch also contained a sealed letter from Buchanan that Scott was to forward to the Mexican Foreign Secretary. The letter formally acknowledged Mexico's rejection of the latest U.S. counterproposal and sketchily described the new peace proposal that Trist wished to present.

If Trist had brought the documents to Scott, explained his mission, and showed him a copy of Buchanan's sealed letter, Scott would not have concluded as he did that Trist, at the behest of the Polk administration, intended to interfere with his military operations. Like Taylor, Scott with good reason distrusted his government's actions, tending to interpret them as unfailingly partisan. But in this instance, partisan politics played no role. However, because Scott and Trist did not meet, Scott's dark suspicions metastasized.

Scott's angry note to Trist established the adversarial relationship that would nearly wreck Trist's mission. "I see that the Secretary of War proposes to degrade me, by requiring that, I, the commander of this army, shall defer to you the chief clerk of the Department of State, the question of continuing or discontinuing the hostilities." Only military commanders, and not civil authorities, could declare an armistice, wrote Scott, and Trist must "refer that question to me, & all the securities belonging to it." Enclosed with Scott's reply was Buchanan's undelivered letter to the Mexican government.

A cooler-tempered diplomat might have yet salved Scott's ruffled pride and rescued their relationship. Trist, however, could not resist penning a sarcastic reply to Scott on May 20:

"The enclosed reply to the tirade against our Government, which you saw fit to put into the shape of a letter to me, (I regret exceedingly that it did not receive a more appropriate form & direction, by being made up, at once, into an 'article,' to adorn the columns of some reckless partizan [sic] press) . . . I passed nearly the whole night in writing; so desirous did I feel to dismiss the unpleasant subject from my mind."

Trist was not sent to Mexico to engage in correspondence with Scott, he wrote, and he condescendingly reminded the general that Scott was supposed to forward the Buchanan letter to Mexico City.

"You will now, sir, I trust, understand, when the communication referred to shall again be placed in your hands, that—greatly deficient in wisdom, as the present (and indeed any democratic) administration of the Government must necessarily be—it has not, in this particular instance fallen into so egregious a blunder as to make the transmission & delivery of that communication dependent upon the amiable affability and gracious condescension of General Winfield Scott."

Scott refused to allow Trist to have the last word:

"My first impulse was to return the farrago of insolence, conceit and arrogance to the author; but on reflection I have determined to preserve the letters as a choice specimen of diplomatic literature and manners. The Jacobin convention of France never sent to one of its armies in the field a more amiable and accomplished instrument. If you were armed with an ambulatory guillotine, you would be the personification of Danton, Marat, and St. Just—all in one.

"You tell me that you are authorized to negotiate a treaty of peace with the enemy—a declaration, which, as it rests upon your own word, I might well question; and you add that it was not intended, at Washington, that I should have any thing to do with the negotiation. This I can well believe, and certainly have cause to be thankful to the President for not degrading me by placing me in any joint communication with you."

Scott instructed Trist to be brief in any future communications with him, "for if you dare to use the style of orders or instructions again, or to indulge yourself in a single discourteous phrase, I shall throw back the communication with the contempt and scorn which you merit at my hands."

• • •

Both men wrote accusatory letters about one another to their respective superiors, War Secretary Marcy and Secretary of State Buchanan, with copies of the wounding letters. Trist complained that Scott had not kept him informed of developments that might aid negotiations. If Scott carried out his plan to occupy Mexico City, he said, there would be "consequences extremely adverse to peace." Scott asked Marcy to recall him because of "the total want of support and sympathy on the part of the War Department which I have so long experienced."

Childish though it might seem, the quarrel threatened to derail both Scott's offensive and Trist's peace initiative. Attuned to this danger, Polk, like the father of squabbling siblings, instructed Buchanan and Marcy to direct Trist and Scott to "act in harmony, each in his respective sphere, in obeying the orders, and carrying out the views of the government." After commiserating with Trist over Scott's rudeness, Buchanan rebuked the Minister Plenipotentiary for not having delivered the dispatches personally to Scott in the first place, and for thus delaying the transmission of the sealed letters. Peace "may have been defeated by a violent and embittered personal quarrel." Find a way to cooperate, Buchanan ordered Trist. Adopting much the same tone, Marcy directed Scott to work in accord with Trist.

Unable to resist the opportunity to reap political advantage from the quarrel, the Polk administration jabbed Scott in a July 22 Washington *Union* article that suggested that it was his fault that the peace proposal had not yet reached the Mexican government. "We undertake to assert, confidentially, that this was not the fault of Mr. Trist. On the contrary, he did everything in his power to have it forwarded through General Scott."

• • •

Before Buchanan's and Marcy's letters reached Puebla, the Trist–Scott feud unexpectedly ended. Trist had fallen ill, having probably contracted a fever, or possibly the diarrhea that nearly every American in Mexico suffered from at one time or another. Either out of remorse or sympathy, Scott sent a jar of guava marmalade to General Persifer F. Smith with this note:

> My Dear Sir:
>   Looking over my stores, I find a box of Guava marmelade [*sic*] which, perhaps, the physician may not consider improper to make part of the diet of your sick companion.
> Yrs very truly
> Winfield Scott

Whether because of the marmalade, Scott's conciliatoriness, or just having a good rest, Trist was in high spirits the next day when he wrote to Buchanan: "With Gen'l Scott's reply to my letter, I received a message from him evincing so much good feeling that it afforded me the sincerest pleasure to meet it as I did, in a way which should at once preclude all constraint & embarrassment between us." Henceforth, the men's relationship was harmonious.

• • •

After Cerro Gordo, Mexicans of all political persuasions longed for a negotiated peace with the United States. Conservatives hoped that a treaty would stop the government's expropriation of church lands. Moderate liberals were willing to hand over northern provinces if U.S. troops would withdraw. A few "puros" wanted the Americans to remain long enough to help Mexico establish a true democracy, one not dominated by the army, wealthy landowners, or the church.

But the budding peace movement withered and died when Santa Anna and his tattered army from Cerro Gordo returned to Mexico City in mid-May. In a published letter to acting President Pedro Maria Anaya, Santa Anna counseled perseverance: "In the name of God, above all, do not allow yourself to conclude with the enemy a disgraceful treaty, which would make our position still worse." The Mexican government took his exhortation to heart, rejecting a British offer to mediate U.S.–Mexican negotiations.

Mexico would fight on, believing that the United States would become disheartened by the war's monetary expense and "butcher's bill," and withdraw its troops. "The Government of the United States have already spent $75 million in the war. The delay is a triumph on our part . . . and if we are only fortunate enough to hinder our enemy a little longer . . . we shall soon see them retire from our country," declared the government newspaper, *El Diario Oficial del Gobierno.*

But as so often was the case with the chameleon-like Santa Anna, peace negotiations were not far from his mind. British intermediaries informed Trist that a bribe might lubricate the peace process; Santa Anna needed to pay off political and military leaders so that his regime would not be overthrown when evincing interest in negotiations.

• • •

Discussing this intriguing development on July 15, Trist and Scott were in agreement "that the only way in which the indefinite protraction of the war can possibly be prevented . . . is by the secret expenditure of money at the city of Mexico." Two days later, Scott explained their plan to his generals and staff. He and Trist proposed to pay Santa Anna $10,000 to advocate peace negotiations, and an additional $1 million when a treaty was ratified, Scott told them. Generals Gideon Pillow and David Twiggs supported the plan (although, five months later, Pillow would denounce it in a letter to Polk). But General John Quitman opposed it, disapproving of bribes on principle and believing that the American people did, too.

General James Shields sided with Quitman but said that if the plan went forward, Trist, and not Scott, should make the payoff.

"We have tempted the integrity of no one," Scott said in defending the bribe. "The overtures we propose to meet, if corrupt[,] come from parties previously corrupted, & we only profit by that corruption to obtain an end (peace) highly advantageous to both the U. States & Mexico. Such transactions have always been considered allowable in war."

Even as Santa Anna was extending peace feelers through the British intermediaries, he was vigorously preparing an all-out defense of the capital. His government drafted into army service all Mexico City men between the ages of sixteen and fifty—more than twenty thousand men. Citizens donated cash, meat, and produce to the army. The government expropriated money from the Academy of Fine Arts and other institutions.

Trist sent the $10,000 to Santa Anna. But there were no peace negotiations. Two explanations reached Scott and Trist: that the Mexican Congress would not grant Santa Anna authority to negotiate, and that the scheme collapsed because of the arrival in the capital of General Gabriel Valencia, a war proponent, with four thousand troops. But it is entirely possible that the self-serving Santa Anna never intended to negotiate at all, and simply pocketed the $10,000.

• • •

Ninety miles away in Puebla, thousands of volunteers had arrived from the United States, strengthening Scott's army to about ten thousand fighting men.

"We are growing somewhat tired of our inactivity," wrote Navy Lieutenant Raphael Semmes. After the escape of the midshipman whose captivity Semmes was supposed to protest to the Mexican government, Semmes had been reassigned to General William Worth's staff.

"We are anxious to be moving toward the 'Halls of the Montezumas,' " wrote Semmes, "that terminus of the campaign which each one has pictured to his imagination in such glowing colors, and which is to repay us for so much tedious delay, and for so much toil and hardship. . . ."

The Americans would be greatly outnumbered and 280 miles from Vera Cruz, living off the land. But Scott's army, which had not lost a battle to the Mexicans, was supremely confident that it would surmount every obstacle and claim the prize, Mexico City.

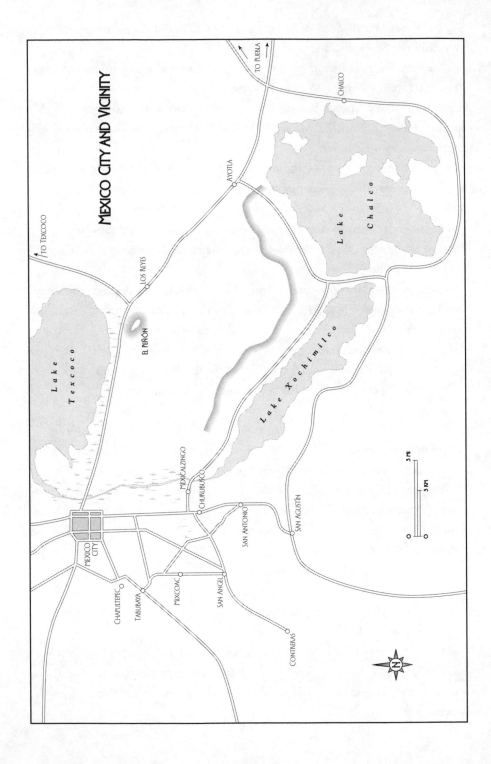

MEXICO CITY AND VICINITY

CLOSING IN ON THE PRIZE

"The greatest feat of physical and moral courage performed by any individual, in my knowledge."

—General Winfield Scott's citation of Captain Robert E. Lee's battlefield exploits

"The men were mowed down in scores . . . [fire] swept over the ground like hail, cutting down men and corn."

—Lieutenant John James Peck, describing the Palmetto Regiment's attack at Churubusco

AUGUST 1847: NEAR MEXICO CITY

After the long climb to the crest of the 10,400-foot Llano Grande plateau, the blue-uniformed column paused to catch its wind. Through the shifting mist and fog of the rainy season, the soldiers glimpsed their destination, the Valley of Mexico. "We seemed to be looking upon an immense . . . sea, surrounded by ranges of stupendous mountains, crested by snow and the clouds," wrote Lieutenant Raphael Semmes. Yet Semmes was disappointed when he could not find a vantage point with a panorama comparable to the paintings of the valley that he had seen; he surmised that the artists had relied on their imaginations to supply details they had not actually observed. As he often did, Semmes fell back on Bernal Diaz, the soldier-scribe who had marched with Cortes on this same road 340 years earlier and whose works Semmes consulted as he would a travel guide. More affecting than the scenery, Semmes concluded, was the sight of the American army, "winding over the same heights, from which had fluttered the pennons of Cortez." The invaders began their descent into the valley.

• • •

From August 7 to 10, a division a day had marched out of Puebla, beginning with General David Twiggs's Second Division regulars. Then General John Quitman's Fourth Division volunteers and Lieutenant Colonel Samuel E. Watson's three hundred Marines began their march. Next came General William Worth's First Division regulars, followed by General Gideon Pillow's Third Division volunteers.

Scott and his staff were aware that their ten thousand troops—and about a thousand of them were on the sick list—constituted a small force indeed for storming a metropolis of two hundred thousand people, defended by at least thirty thousand Mexican soldiers. Even Cortes's several hundred conquistadors had had tens of thousands of Indian allies when they marched on the Aztec capital. But the long odds only hardened the Americans' determination to triumph. "The sentiment of the army is that we cannot afford to be beat, but must enter the capital," noted Lieutenant Colonel Ethan Allen Hitchcock.

Strangely, Santa Anna did not try to stop or harass the invaders, even though the angular, volcanic terrain bordering the National Highway favored ambuscades and fortifications.

On the fourth day of the march, the American soldiers awoke on frost-covered ground high in the mountains and prepared to enter the Valley of Mexico.

• • •

Nestled in the Cordillera of Anahuac, the valley floor rested on an oval-shaped seventy-eight-hundred-foot plateau forty-six miles long and thirty-two miles wide. Mexico City occupied the center of the plateau, and was surrounded by six lakes and by marshes, fields, and villages. As in Cortes's day, causeways only wide enough to accommodate two or three wagons—ideal for defense—provided the best access to the city over the lakes and marshes. But since the conquistadors' era, when Aztec archers in canoes were able to pick off the invaders on the causeways, the waterways had contracted and no longer were a barrier to conquerors.

From a distance, the islets that stippled Lake Chalco southeast of the city reminded Hitchcock of the "floating gardens" of Prescott's *The Conquest of Mexico.* Others were less impressed after they had seen the valley up close. "The lakes became marshes, the fields are not cultivated, the villages are mud, and the inhabitants wretched-looking Indian peons, in rags and splendid misery," observed enlisted man and diarist George Ballentine.

• • •

Mexico City's foundries and gunsmiths, and its bomb and bullet factories, were operating at full throttle to equip the army for the war's climactic battle. Catholic churches, convents, priests, and bishops were cajoled into lending the government $280,000. Despite the crushing defeats at Buena Vista and Cerro Gordo, the surviving Mexican army and National Guard units probably still mustered ten thousand men in all, and Santa Anna had raised twenty thousand more. The new levies joined the Victoria Regiment, made up of young commercial men; the Independencia and Bravo regiments, whose ranks were filled by artisans and mechanics; and other trade-oriented units. The troops were outfitted with muskets, glittering bayonets, and 106 cannons. But one disquieting sign of the desperation that also animated these preliminaries was the establishment of the Hidalgo regiment, consisting of boys, old men, and the heads of families, all previously exempted from military service.

Drums beat Mexico City's defenders to quarters when scouts reported on August 9 that Twiggs's division had marched into Ayotla, just fifteen miles away. Over the next two days, the three other American divisions reached the city's outskirts. Even though Mexico's armies had lost every battle against Scott and Taylor, the capital's citizens were confident that this time the army would win a great victory. "It still seems incredible to me that the Americans can have fallen into the trap set for them without making some daring effort to escape," observed Jose Fernando Ramirez, a lawyer and government official in Mexico City. "The greatest enthusiasm has sprung up among our troops." When a National Guard unit departed Mexico City to take up defensive positions, bands played the polka theme song of the Guard and its once-rebellious "polko" officers.

• • •

The "trap" alluded to by Ramirez was El Peñon. One mile east of Mexico City, the massive fortification stood on a 450-foot-high, 1,000-foot-long hill that dominated the National Highway and the causeway that led to the city's main, northeast gate. Studying the stronghold through their field glasses, Scott and his staff recognized that they must silence El Peñon if they were to attack the city's east side. "The enemy literally swarms at the Peñon," observed Lieutenant Colonel Ethan Allen Hitchcock.

To obtain an accurate picture of El Peñon's defenses, Scott once again called on Captain Robert E. Lee of the engineers to conduct a reconnaissance. With Captain James Mason, Lieutenant Isaac Stevens, and an infantry escort, Lee got close enough to El Peñon to observe its three tiers of artillery batteries, containing thirty to fifty guns capable of raking the National Highway with an enfilading fire at long range. Ringing the hill were breastworks and ditches that could hold several thousand infantry troops, and surrounding these defenses were shallow lakes and marshlands that would impede any flanking maneuvers. To ascertain the depth of the lake water—it was just a couple of feet—Stevens waded to within one thousand yards of the fort, in full view of ten thousand Mexican troops and the American army. Nicholas Trist was impressed by the engineers' daring and élan, a spirit that infused the entire army: "It is indeed a *noble* army: full of confidence in itself & full of confidence in its commander." In his report, Lee coolly observed that while there were "numerous troops both foot & horse on & around the hill . . . I saw nothing that would render an assault *impracticable.*"

Always loath to attack an enemy's strongest position, Scott rejected an assault on El Peñon, and he sent Lee to reconnoiter a route through Mexicaltzingo south of the city. But it, too, was strongly defended, and a key bridge leading to it was unusable. Still, Scott believed it to be more promising than El Peñon, which he resolved to bypass.

• • •

Scott decided to assault Mexicaltzingo. General William Worth, who believed it would cost too many casualties, sent Lieutenant Colonel James Duncan and Captain William Mackall, two artillery officers who had fought at Monterrey, with a three-hundred-man escort to scout the Lake Chalco area. Worth hoped to find a way through the marshes around the lake, so that the army could bypass Mexicaltzingo as well as El Peñon.

A month earlier, an American prisoner in Mexico City had written a letter recommending that the army approach the city's southwestern corner by way of Chapultepec, a hill upon which an old castle was situated next to a military school for teenagers. Near Chapultepec, noted the anonymous U.S. officer, were excellent sites for "throwing shells." The "hill of grasshoppers" guarded two causeways to the city that ended at Belen Gate on the southwest corner and San Cosme Gate on the west side.

Others would later claim credit for suggesting that the army avoid El Peñon by skirting lakes Chalco and Xochimilco to approach the city from the southwest. In fact, Scott himself had studied this route before leaving Puebla—and rejected it because the road south of the lakes was deemed impassable.

Worth's reconnaissance force discovered that the roads and ground south and west of Lake Chalco could support an army. "This report solves all doubts as to the practicability of the southern route," Worth told Scott, suggesting that Tacubaya, southwest of Mexico City and near Chapultepec, could serve as the U.S. operational base.

It made sense to Scott, who abandoned the plan to attack Mexicaltzingo. The army began marching around Lake Chalco. The path was rugged, and at one point, scoria, or "volcanic slag," cut the pack animals' feet until they bled. The Americans climbed a hill, from which they could see San Augustin immediately before them and Tacubaya in the distance.

Lieutenant Semmes, who had accompanied Duncan and Mackall on their scouting expedition, observed: "From the top of the Peñon, now in our rear, still fluttered the Mexican ensign, as if unaware of the great game of strategy that was being played. . . . We were violating one of the exploded rules of European tactics, by leaving a fortified post in our rear; but in the words of General Worth, we were not in a condition to 'entertain the question of the rear.' We had passed the Rubicon. . . ."

• • •

Santa Anna disappointedly watched as the invading army avoided El Peñon, where he had hoped to deal the Americans a ruinous defeat, and then skirted Mexico City's southern suburbs. To meet this new threat, Santa Anna redeployed General D. Gabriel Valencia's seven-thousand-man Army of the North to Contreras south-west of the city and sent another force south to San Antonio to block its access to the capital. Santa Anna himself led twelve thousand men to San Angel, three miles from Contreras. From San Angel, he could support Valencia, or march three miles to Churubusco to meet Scott if he breached San Antonio's defenses.

• • •

The Americans stopped at San Augustin, on the southeast edge of a craggy lava field known as the Pedregal. Scott had two options: marching nine miles directly north through San Antonio and Churubusco to the enemy capital's southern gate; or advancing to the west around the lava field, and then passing through Contr-eras before turning north to San Angel, Tacubaya, and Chapultepec. Scott sent scouting parties in both directions.

A reconnaissance patrol discovered on August 18 that San Antonio was well defended as well as fortified. Firing from long range, enemy gunners with one unlucky shot ended the life of Captain Seth Thornton of the Second Dragoons, whose ambush on the Rio Grande had plunged the United States into the war. Thornton now owned the additional unhappy distinction of becoming the first U.S. soldier to be killed in action in the Valley of Mexico.

A second scouting party rode toward Contreras and was fired on by Mexican troops at the Padierna ranch, nestled in the hills northeast of Contreras. Valencia's Army of the North occupied the ranch's tile-roofed adobe buildings and its cultivated fields.

• • •

At San Augustin, Scott expanded his "Little Cabinet" to include all of his general officers and their aides-de-camp. Every night over dinner, the officers discussed the new intelligence reports and their plans for the following day. The astute Lieutenant Semmes was more impressed by Captain Lee than by any other officer who attended these nightly meetings. Writing a decade before the Civil War, Semmes observed that not only was Lee superior in intelligence, character, and judgment to even Scott's generals and colonels, he was a bona fide genius in one respect: "His talent for topography was peculiar, and he seemed to receive impressions intuitively, which it cost other men much labor to acquire."

As a student of European military strategy who preferred movement to frontal attacks, Scott decided to advance on Contreras instead of San Antonio. Besides giving him more room to maneuver, Contreras possessed the additional advantage of being more distant from Mexico City and enemy reinforcements. And if Contreras could be flanked through the Pedregal, twenty-five square miles of seemingly trackless lava badlands, Scott could attack Valencia's rear.

• • •

If there were a way to cross the Pedregal, Captain Lee would find it, Scott believed. Traveling on foot, Lee found traces in the volcanic frieze of a footpath that could be developed into a road. He climbed a steep hill, Zacatepec, which afforded a good view of the Mexican positions, and drew enemy artillery fire. After being informed for the second time in a week that the seemingly impossible was indeed possible, Scott placed Lee in charge of building a road across the Pedregal.

On August 19, the engineering company and five hundred soldiers from General Gideon Pillow's division began scraping a road through the pumice and obsidian. The Civil War would make the road crew's supervisors household names:

Lee; Lieutenants Pierre G. T. Beauregard, George McClellan, and Thomas Jackson; and Captains Joseph Hooker, J. Bankhead Magruder, and Gustavius W. Smith.

While the engineers dug, Generals Pillow and David Twiggs led a strong force around the southern edge of the Pedregal toward Contreras. Three miles from San Augustin, they ran into enemy skirmishers and artillery fire. All afternoon, the Americans dueled with the enemy hidden behind breastworks and embrasures on the sloping Padierna ranchland. Perhaps Pillow meant only to distract the enemy from Lee's work—which might explain the seemingly pointless exposure of his field artillery to plunging enemy fire from fortified positions. Lieutenant Daniel H. Hill of the Fourth U.S. Artillery, never one to mince words, bitterly remarked: "Human stupidity can go no farther than this, the ordering of six and twelve pounders to batter a Fort furnished with long sixteens, twenty-fours and heavy mortars!! . . . Our light batteries were cut to pieces in a short time and some of our best officers & men killed or mortally wounded." The long-range artillery and musket duel was inconsequential, ending with Pillow's withdrawal to San Augustin. Yet because he hadn't been beaten, General Valencia claimed victory, boasting to Santa Anna: "I have put them to shameful flight," and announcing wholesale promotions of his officers.

Lee's builders completed their rough road by late afternoon. The trickiest part had been fording a stream and deep ravine on the Pedregal's west side. When that problem was solved, Lee's party discovered that it was relatively easy to maneuver behind Contreras, the Padierna ranch, and Valencia's troops. While crossing the Mexico City road, Lee's men saw four dense columns of enemy troops in the distance, marching toward Contreras. Santa Anna was on the move.

• • •

After Lee returned to Scott's headquarters, Scott ordered him to guide General Persifer Smith and his two thousand men through the lava field to a position between Contreras and the capital. Back into the Pedregal went Lee, for the third time that day. By nightfall, Lee was leading Smith's troops into the hamlet of San Geronimo, behind the Padierna ranch and General Valencia's seven thousand men. Scouts reported that Santa Anna and six thousand troops were camped a few miles to the north at San Angel.

Sandwiched between two enemy armies that together totaled thirteen thousand men, Smith was understandably uneasy, but by no means disconcerted—he had led Louisiana volunteer troops during the Florida Indian wars and had recently fought at Monterrey. But there being no point in inviting annihilation by lingering too long, Smith resolved to attack Valencia early the next morning. At 8 P.M., with heavy rain falling, Smith informed his officers that at 3 A.M. they would begin moving to their assault positions.

Smith had to apprise Scott of his attack plan so that Scott would make a demonstration in front of Contreras early the next morning—as Pillow had done at Cerro Gordo. Whom could Smith trust to cross the Pedregal in the rainy, black night and find Scott's headquarters in time to organize the diversionary attack?

Forty-year-old Robert E. Lee volunteered to travel on foot through the Pedregal a fourth time.

In the pouring rain, Lee and his companions dodged enemy pickets and hunted for the ford across the ravine and stream. Guided by lightning that illuminated towering Zacatepec, where Lee had left Scott that afternoon, they finally found the crossing. On the other side, they met a column of General James Shields's men foundering in the rain and darkness; they were on their way to join Smith. Lee detached one of his men to guide them to San Geronimo. Upon reaching Zacapetec, Lee discovered that Scott had decamped and returned to San Augustin, three miles away. He pressed on. It was nearly 11 P.M. when Lee, drenched and exhausted, stumbled into Scott's headquarters at San Augustin.

Scott approved the attack plan, and then asked Lee, now with a mount, to lead General David Twiggs's division to Zacapetec. No sooner had Lee completed his fifth journey into the Pedregal than he was helping guide General Franklin Pierce's men to their diversionary attack positions before Contreras.

In later promoting Lee to brevet lieutenant colonel, Scott would pronounce his exemplary conduct "the greatest feat of physical and moral courage performed by any individual, in my knowledge" during the campaign. As August 20 dawned, Lee, on foot or horseback for twenty-four unbroken hours, faced a new day of strenuous exertion and mortal danger.

• • •

Days earlier, Santa Anna had ordered Valencia to pull back to Coyoacan, four miles northeast of Contreras. "My patriotism will not permit me," replied Valencia. He believed that if he withdrew, Scott would race up the road to San Angelo, and then into the Mexicans' rear, and possibly even enter Mexico City. Recognizing the logic of Valencia's explanation, Santa Anna had not insisted.

But on August 19, Santa Anna grew alarmed when his scouts reported intensified American activity all around the Pedregal. As Lee was setting out for Scott with Smith's attack plan, Santa Anna sent Valencia a second withdrawal order. Spike your cannons, destroy your positions, save what you can, but get out, he instructed Valencia.

Valencia, however, did not evacuate the Padierna ranch, and Santa Anna remained at San Angel three miles away. Valencia's men began to despair when Santa Anna's army did not appear, and some of them slipped away.

AUGUST 20, 1847: CONTRERAS

At 3 A.M., Smith's soldiers stiffly rose from a too-brief sleep beside their weapons in the cold mud. The rain was tapering off, but the predawn was so utterly black that Smith instructed his troops to stay "in *touch* of each other" to avoid becoming separated while negotiating a twisting ravine that led to their assault positions. By daybreak, thousands of U.S. troops were poised to attack Valencia's front and rear.

Leaving the ravine and creeping to the brow of a ridge, Colonel Bennet Riley stood up, drawing a fusillade of musket and cannon fire, and led Smith's men forward with their bayonets and clubbed muskets. Mexican gunners fired on Smith's men with grape and canister, but the gunners were rattled and their aim bad. From the main road, the American diversionary force raked the Mexicans' front with musket fire.

General Anastasio Torrejón's cavalrymen formed a line to make a charge. But when they saw the Americans attacking with bayonets, they bolted, reported Lieutenant Semmes, "trampling under foot the [Mexican] infantry." Then, with the exception of some Buena Vista veterans who stood their ground and gamely fought with bayonets, the enemy infantry also took to its heels, leaving the gunners still at their cannons. Many fleeing Mexicans were intercepted and "shot down in front and rear . . . the helpless Mexicans hid themselves in ravines & gullies, in the cornfields and under the rocks," wrote Lieutenant Daniel Hill. Numerically superior but overwhelmed, Valencia's seven-thousand-man army buckled and collapsed, and the Mexicans ran pell-mell up the road to San Angel.

In a mere seventeen minutes "by the watch," as Lieutenant Colonel Hitchcock put it, Valencia's army had been shattered, at a loss of seven hundred dead, up to a thousand wounded, and 813 captured. A U.S. soldier who surveyed the battleground wrote: "Dying and dead . . . lay thick upon the field. . . . Some had a leg, a foot, an arm or hand mangled to pieces and were lying upon the cold, muddy ground shivering with cold, begging for a bit of bread or a drink of water." Among the twenty-two captured guns were two brass 6-pounders seized by the Fourth Artillery—the same pieces that had been lost by the Fourth Artillery at Buena Vista. It was a "poetic fact," noted Hitchcock. (The cannons today grace the entrance to West Point's administration building.) There were just sixty U.S. casualties. Scott doubted "whether a more brilliant or decisive victory . . . without cavalry or artillery on our side—is to be found on record."

General Valencia vanished into the mountains to the west, avoiding American and Mexican soldiers alike, after learning that Santa Anna, in a towering rage over the debacle, had ordered him shot.

• • •

Scott's army paused at Contreras only long enough to make arrangements for the wounded and to gather prisoners. Late in the morning, the Americans marched three miles north to San Angel. Santa Anna was not there.

Scott sent a courier with orders to General Worth to capture San Antonio. Worth's division had camped just outside the town, listening to the Mexicans celebrate Valencia's "victory" of the previous day. The Mexicans, who were pulling out anyway, hastily retreated to the north without firing a shot.

Scott and Worth advanced separately toward the junction of the San Angel and San Antonio roads less than three miles away, at Churubusco.

AUGUST 20, 1847: CHURUBUSCO

Santa Anna had concentrated his remaining twenty-five thousand troops at Churubusco. It was a logical enough place to make a stand: four miles beyond the village, across a causeway, stood Mexico City, with no intervening towns or intersecting roads. Yet by bringing all of his forces south of the capital to this point, Santa Anna had left open a back door into the city, via Tacubaya and Chapultepec.

But Scott did not take the road to Chapultepec; had he done so, he might have marched into Mexico City that afternoon. The General of the Army, however, believed that if he did not destroy Santa Anna's army in battle, he risked having to fight a lingering guerrilla war.

The Mexican engineers had transformed Churubusco's stone wall–enclosed San Pablo church and convent into a daunting fortress. From the convent, cannons could pour fire onto the San Angel road. The church roof and steeple furnished a good view of the flat terrain for miles around. Eight-foot-thick outer works had been erected for infantrymen. The nearby houses and cross dikes swarmed with soldiers and field artillery.

The San Patricio Battalion, which had fought well at Monterrey and Buena Vista, crewed the guns in the village and at a bridge three hundred yards east of town. The bridge and nearby canal dikes, transformed into mile-long ramparts for thousands of Mexican troops, guarded the causeway to the capital. The enemy positions overlooked fields of tall, tassled corn, the only cover available to the Americans if they attacked here.

• • •

Scott's six thousand men, reaching Churubusco from the west before Worth's division arrived from San Antonio to the south, blindly crashed into Santa Anna's right flank. Neither Scott nor Worth had reconnoitered Churubusco, and so they were ignorant of the enemy's great strength and its defenses. In the village, the Mexican line, anchored at the San Pablo convent and church, extended to the outbuildings, ditches, and fieldworks, terminating at the long, curving canal to the northwest. When Scott's and Santa Anna's armies met, the staccato pop-pop of musketry and the chest-compressing boom of artillery coalesced into a continuous industrial roar, pierced by men's shouts.

Twiggs led Smith's brigade and a field battery in an attack on the church-convent complex, while Captain Lee, thirty-six hours without rest, guided Pierce's and Shields's brigades on a bending, northeasterly path that would take them behind Churubusco.

Intending to cut the Mexico City causeway north of the town and the canal bridge, Shields marched down a secondary road and ran into three thousand enemy cavalrymen and four thousand infantrymen. Intensive enemy gunfire filled the road with dead American horses and mules.

Shields ordered an ill-advised frontal assault. The Palmetto Regiment from South Carolina, occupying the middle and flanked by the New York regiment and the U.S. Ninth, Twelfth, and Fifteenth regiments, lost half of its 272 men. "The men were mowed down in scores . . . [fire] swept over the ground like hail, cutting down men and corn," wrote John James Peck, a Palmetto lieutenant. "I did not expect to live moment to moment." The attack failed.

Twiggs had no better luck at San Pablo church against the well-drilled San

Patricios, fighting under their silken green flag, and a corps of National Guard troops. In one blast of the Patricios' guns, twenty-two U.S. gunners and fifteen horses were cut down. The American turncoats targeted the hated West Point officers, who fell in disproportionate numbers. Cannon and musket fire knocked out Twiggs's field guns and stopped his attack cold. Smoke rose in a dense column over Churubusco.

Quick-stepping past southeast Churubusco's dispersed residences, Worth's division could hear the battle raging at the convent and church and in the cornfields north of town. Without pausing, they proceeded straight up the road toward the canal bridge. Barring the way were the San Patricios's four guns and the Tlapa Battalion, and behind them was the dike protected by thousands of enemy infantry.

• • •

As Worth's dense column passed the road leading to the San Pablo convent and church, Santa Anna, recognizing that the battle's outcome would depend on what happened at the canal bridge, sent four infantry units running to reinforce it. Then the Americans entered the range of the gunners at the bridge and the infantrymen lining the dike, and the enemy unleashed a scorching fire. The Americans veered into the cornfields, which neither provided them cover nor permitted them to see where they were going. "The escopet balls were whistling over our heads . . . and occasionally a cannon ball sang through the corn as it tore its path along in our front," wrote Captain Ephraim Kirby Smith. Emerging from the cornfield, the Americans found themselves in a "dreadful crossfire. . . . The grape, round shot and musketry were sweeping over the ground in a storm which strewed it with the dead and dying." Explosions twice knocked Captain Smith to the ground.

At bayonet-point, Worth's troops stormed and seized the bridge, starting a domino effect. Some regular officers turned the five captured enemy guns to fire on the San Pablo church and convent, and one of Lieutenant Colonel James Duncan's field artillery batteries galloped up and joined the bombardment. "I never witnessed so rapid and destructive a fire," observed Lieutenant Raphael Semmes. Duncan's guns smashed the church tower, filled with Mexican sharpshooters.

• • •

The San Patricios in the church and convent were nearly out of ammunition, and the supporting infantry had used up all of theirs. The incoming cannon salvo from the bridge convinced the Mexicans of the futility of further resistance. As Twiggs's men raced toward the buildings, white flags sprouted everywhere.

Santa Anna's army collapsed. His fleeing troops jammed the causeway to Mexico City. In hot pursuit, Americans captured thousands of Mexican soldiers until Scott halted the chase a mile and a half from the capital. But two squadrons of dragoons led by the impetuous Colonel William S. Harney rode all the way to the city gate. In the hand-to-hand fighting there, Captain Philip Kearny, while slashing the Mexicans with his saber, lost his left arm, and Major F. D. Mills was killed.

• • •

Scott had won, although at a cost of 139 killed and 876 wounded—more American losses than for any other battle of the war. With a thousand sick men left behind at San Augustin, Scott's effective strength was now just eight thousand men.

But the Americans had wrecked yet another of Santa Anna's armies. An estimated four thousand Mexicans were killed or wounded, thirty-seven cannons were lost, and three thousand Mexican soldiers had become prisoners, including eight generals. "On the whole, the events of the day have been—as the phrase is— 'glorious' in the highest degree," Hitchcock noted with great satisfaction.

Among the prisoners were John Riley and more than sixty of his San Patricios, many of them wounded. Their infamous green banner was a battle prize. "These wretches served the guns . . . and with fatal effect upon the persons of their former comrades," wrote General William Worth. The deserters were now in the hands of the military justice system, which prescribed death for traitors.

• • •

An American battle surgeon operated on the wounded continuously until 3 A.M. the next day, when he wearily left his makeshift hospital for some fresh air. "I turned around to look at my amputating table; under it was a perfect heap of arms and legs and, looking at myself, I found I was covered with blood from head to foot."

• • •

After burying the dead and carefully searching the cornfields, dikes, and ditches for wounded men, Scott's army marched west and north to Tacubaya. Scott made his new headquarters in the archbishop's palace, from which he could plainly see the Castle of Chapultepec and, a mile and a half beyond it, Mexico City.

Rather than seize Mexico City that very night, as he knew he could, Scott began drafting a letter to the Mexican government inviting it to peace negotiations, and proposing an armistice. Scott's perplexed officers, believing the sacrifices at

Churubusco might have been in vain, whispered that he was making a mistake. Scott explained to War Secretary William Marcy why he was extending the olive branch:

"Mr. Trist . . . as well as myself, had been admonished by the best friends of peace—intelligent neutrals and some American residents—against precipitation; lest, by wantonly driving away the government and others—dishonored—we might scatter the elements of peace, excite a spirit of national desperation, and thus, indefinitely postpone the hope of accommodation."

He pointedly reminded Marcy that he and the president had urged a policy of combining force with diplomacy. "Remembering our mission—to conquer a peace—the army very cheerfully sacrificed to patriotism—to the great wish and want of our country—the éclat that would have followed an entrance sword in hand into a great capital." Scott's inspector-general, Hitchcock, believed that Scott's plan from the beginning had been "to put the city in jeopardy and then to summon the government to treat for peace or to surrender."

• • •

Before Scott could send his letter to the Mexican government, a "fine carriage" drove up to the army headquarters. General Ignacio Mora y Villamil, the Mexican army's chief engineer, handed Scott two letters. The first, from British Minister Charles Bankhead, requested that the U.S. army not pillage the city. The second letter, from Jose Ramon Pacheco, Mexico's Minister of Foreign Relations, announced that his government was now ready to consider Nicholas Trist's peace proposal and to negotiate a treaty. The government newspaper, *Diario Oficial del Gobierno,* reported: "Such was the panic created by their defeat that the Minister of Foreign Relations immediately convoked the Congress to take into consideration Mr. Trist's proposition."

• • •

Despair had gripped Mexico City after Santa Anna's army, reduced to a dazed mob, had streamed through the city gate after Churubusco. People filled the city's churches, praying to God to lift the "curse of Heaven" that had been laid upon them. One downcast resident observed: "God seems to have written against us the words of the feast of Balshsazzar"—the Biblical "writing on the wall" dooming the Babylonian ruler. "Everything, everything has been lost, except our honor. That was lost a long time ago," wrote Jose Fernando Ramirez, the Mexico City lawyer who only ten days earlier was convinced that the U.S. army was poised to fall into "the trap" of El Peñon. "It is my firm conviction that the whole affair can be explained clearly as being the result of the incompetence and cowardice of our generals and our leaders," especially Santa Anna's dereliction in failing to aid Valencia at Contreras. A Churubusco veteran told Ramirez that soldiers had abandoned one position after their officers simply disappeared.

• • •

Generals John Quitman, Franklin Pierce, and Persifer Smith met with Generals Mora and Benito Quijano to establish the armistice conditions: no troop reinforcements or new fortifications; except for American sutlers buying provisions, only Mexico City residents were permitted to enter the capital; and forty-eight hours' notice must be given before resuming hostilities. The armistice went into effect August 24.

George Kendall of the New Orleans *Picayune* pronounced it "a mistake" made in the pursuit of a "vain or delusive hope" of peace. While he commended Scott and Trist for wishing to end the bloodshed and recognized that capturing the capital might drive away the leaders with authority to negotiate, Kendall believed that Scott and Trist were "entirely mistaking the character of the Mexican people . . . one of the most haughty and arrogant races of the earth. . . ."

A packet of forty-five letters seized outside Mexico City by U.S. officers added to the growing suspicion that the Mexicans planned to regroup while the armistice was in place. The letters, wrote Lieutenant Colonel Ethan Allen Hitchcock, contained disturbing "allusions to the proposed armistice, showing that the Mexicans hope by means of it to gain time to collect their scattered forces and still defend the city; though they say that we could now be in the city if we pleased."

On August 27, Nicholas Trist began peace negotiations with Generals Herrera and Mora, Miguel Atristain, and Jose Bernardo Couto in a private home in the town of Atzcapotzaleo.

THE HALLS OF MONTEZUMA

"History will no doubt speak of our achievement as more glorious than that of Cortéz."

—Lieutenant Daniel Hill four days after entering Mexico City

"He is the greatest living soldier."

—The Duke of Wellington, referring to General Winfield Scott, whom he had previously pronounced "lost"

Nicholas Trist's great hopes for the peace negotiations evaporated when he learned of the unrealistic conditions insisted upon by Mexico. Mexico had lost every major battle of the war, much of her territory was in American hands, and Winfield Scott's army was just a few miles from the gates of Mexico City. Yet the Mexican commissioners had been instructed by Santa Anna's government to negotiate as if Mexico occupied a strong bargaining position and might even yet win the war.

Before the negotiations could go forward, Mexico required the United States to withdraw its army and lift the blockade. Second, Mexico would recognize Texas's independence only if the United States paid an indemnity and accepted the Nueces River as the border. Third, California would remain part of Mexico, but the United States would be permitted to build a trading post at San Francisco with a connecting road to Oregon, if it paid Mexico's war expenses, assumed the outstanding $3 million in U.S. claims, and recognized Mexican land grants made in Texas before 1836. Finally, slavery, outlawed in Mexico, was forbidden in any territories that America obtained from Mexico.

If Mexico's intention was to propose terms that would surely be rejected, it had succeeded admirably.

In presenting the U.S. proposal, Trist had suggested that the Rio Grande border, a Polk administration sine qua non, might in fact be negotiable—although Trist would need to first obtain his government's approval. In his avidness for peace, Trist was taking a huge risk; he was violating his instructions, opening himself to criticism, and potentially undermining his bargaining position. But when the Mexican commissioners forwarded the proposal to their government, its leaders evinced little interest either in the proposal or in Trist's evident willingness to compromise.

• • •

On August 27, American wagons rumbled into Mexico City for food and supplies, as the armistice had stipulated. Initially turned back at the city gate, the hundred-wagon convoy was then permitted to enter the city with Santa Anna's apologies. The sutlers planned to draw cash on U.S. government drafts from local financiers and then buy provisions for the troops. Instead, they became the targets of the Mexicans' virulent hatred of the American invaders.

In the Grand Plaza, where the Americans planned to load the wagons, a surly crowd gathered while Santa Anna placidly watched from a palace balcony, guarded by a thousand troops. The mob suddenly attacked the sutlers and wagoners with clubs, as other rioters on rooftops hurled stones down on them. Santa Anna and his bodyguard did nothing to stop them. Three Americans died in the melee. Somehow, the caravan extricated itself from the mob and fled the city.

"When was anything of the sort ever before known in the history of war?" the U.S. command protested, to which Santa Anna perfunctorily expressed his regrets over the American deaths and assured the safety of future resupply parties. Observing that "the rabble of Mexico" comprised nine tenths of its populace, George Kendall of the New Orleans *Picayune* dryly noted after the attack: "With this . . . we have to make peace."

Another wagon train ventured into the city, but this time at night and with a Mexican army escort. The Americans returned with full wagons and $151,000 in cash.

• • •

The U.S. soldiers enjoyed the respite from the war, brief though it appeared destined to be. In Tacubaya, a pleasant village of fifteen hundred with grand villas, gardens, and baths was an enclave of English diplomats and businessmen. Officially, they were neutral; unofficially, they felt more of a kinship with the Americans than with the Mexicans. They opened their homes to the Army officers, who comfortably passed their leisure hours playing billiards. Scott and his staff enjoyed the archbishop's palace amenities, which included fresh fruit and vegetables. "What a country to dream in," enthused Lieutenant Colonel Hitchcock, who liked "the magnificence of the morning" as much as the glorious sunsets "over the city of Montezuma. The city seems full of spires and domes and very white."

Looming like a storm cloud a mere half-mile from Tacubaya was the prominence known as Chapultepec, the "hill of grasshoppers." It rose, wrote Hitchcock, to "an isolated elevation of 150 feet, crowned with white, neat-looking buildings which constitute a military college"—the National Military School, a Mexican West Point with walls four feet thick and twelve feet high. Adjacent was an ancient imperial summer palace. Hitchcock observed that ditches and artillery guarded Chapultepec.

• • •

When they marched into Tacubaya, the soldiers could not help but notice that alongside the hard macadam road was a marker with the inscription: "This road was constructed by the Texan prisoners under General Santa Anna," or, rather, by the unfortunate Texans captured at Mier in 1842. It wasn't long before the marker was mysteriously smashed to pieces. "Some, perhaps, of the very men who worked on the road, turned out in the night and destroyed it," surmised Lieutenant Ralph Kirkham. Serving under Scott's command in the U.S. Mounted Rifles were Texas Rangers who had fought at Mier.

• • •

Trist and the Mexican commissioners made negligible progress during two weeks of meetings in Atzcapotzaleo. There were too many seemingly insoluble issues: where the U.S.–Mexican border would lie; New Mexico; and how much of California would be ceded. Trist's imprudent assurance that the border was negotiable, when it was not, failed to melt the Mexicans' iron insistence that the United States must recognize the Nueces as the boundary line; Mexico must have a buffer between the Nueces and Rio Grande. "It is with them a *sine qua non*," Trist wrote to Secretary of State James Buchanan, "which they *cannot* abandon, however disposed they might be to do so; and no treaty is to be hoped for, except upon this basis."

And just as New Mexico was an absolute condition for Polk and Buchanan, so it proved to be for the Mexican government, which refused to part with it. Mexico's attachment to New Mexico was such that "in New Mexico, and in the few leagues which intervene between the right of the Nueces and the left of the Bravo [Rio Grande], is peace or war." New Mexico seemed to magically expand north and west before Trist's eyes. The Mexican commissioners asserted that New Mexico extended north to the thirty-seventh parallel and west to the Pacific Ocean, near San Francisco Bay, swallowing up all of California south of Monterey. The United States, they allowed, might obtain a corridor from San Francisco to the Oregon border, but carte blanche to cross the Isthmus of Tehuantepec was out of the question, because England already owned that privilege.

Mexican war hawks still believed that the Americans could be beaten at Mexico City's gates, and that peace could then be secured on Mexico's terms.

• • •

Santa Anna's regrets and promises notwithstanding, the Mexicans continued to harass the sutlers whenever they entered the city, even when halfheartedly protected by Mexican soldiers. And it was becoming apparent that the Mexicans were building new fortifications, in anticipation of a resumption of the war, and that Santa Anna had only been playing for time. Indeed, Santa Anna admitted as much in a letter August 31 to Don Manuel Rejon. In agreeing to hear the U.S. peace proposal, he said, Mexico had eliminated America's chief justification for continuing the war—namely, Mexico's refusal to negotiate. The armistice also "would give my troops rest, re-establish their morale, and enable me to collect the dispersed. . . ."

On September 6, Scott complained to Santa Anna about the obvious military preparations and the continued obstruction of the American supply wagons. These were armistice violations, Scott said. He demanded an explanation by noon the next day.

That same day, the Mexican commissioners informed Trist that the Nueces boundary and the relinquishment of San Francisco and the country north of it were "the utmost possible extent to which they could go, in the way of sacrifices to the cause of peace."

Resigned to the collapse of peace talks and the resumption of fighting, Scott and Trist awaited Santa Anna's reply.

Santa Anna's "explanation" blamed the Americans for the negotiations' failure, while denying that his soldiers were building new works; they were only making "one or two repairs." If the Americans were having difficulty in obtaining food and supplies in Mexico City, it was "owing to the imprudence of the American agents." He accused Scott's troops of turning away millers who tried to bring flour into the city. And U.S. occupation forces, Santa Anna alleged, had sacked villages, violated the inhabitants' wives and daughters, and profaned their churches.

• • •

Scott and Trist decided to end the charade. On September 7, Trist handed the Mexican commissioners a letter acknowledging "the painful necessity of recognizing the absolute irreconcilableness" of the American and Mexican positions, and "putting an end to the negotiation which he has had the honour to conduct with them. . . ." Scott simultaneously declared that because Mexico had violated the armistice, he was not obligated to give forty-eight hours' notice before resuming offensive operations.

• • •

The Americans had broken through Mexico City's outer defenses, but Chapultepec still shimmered in the late-summer heat like a castle keep in a Sir Walter Scott novel. Besides fortifying Chapultepec with breastworks and batteries, the Mexicans had placed batteries near the causeways leading to the San Cosme and Belen gates, and at the gates themselves, to exact a toll in blood if the invaders got that far.

At the foot of Chapultepec was a complex known as Molino del Rey—"King's Mill," a former grain mill and outbuildings. American patrols reported a large number of Mexican troops near Molino del Rey, lending credence to rumors that the mill had been converted to a foundry where church bells were being melted down and recast into cannons. Scott ordered General William Worth to attack the old mill at night, "brush away" the defenders, and wreck the foundry's machinery before returning to Tacubaya.

But Worth opposed a night attack and instead urged using the cover of darkness to move his First Division into position for an early morning attack on September 8. Scott reluctantly approved the change, conceding that the artillery would be more effective in daylight.

SEPTEMBER 8, 1847: MOLINO DEL REY

Santa Anna had personally selected his troops' defensive positions. On the left flank, two brigades led by Generals Antonio León and Joaquin Rangel occupied the stone buildings known as El Molino. A third of a mile to the right, a third brigade occupied another stone building, Casa Mata. Between the two wings lay a dry, shallow ditch filled with soldiers from Colonel Miguel Echagaray's Third Light Regiment, supported by six guns concealed in a stand of maguey. Worth and his officers were aware of the Mexicans' positions, but they did not have a good estimate of how many enemy troops Worth's 3,251 men and eight guns faced. The numbers, if known, might have given them pause—up to twelve thousand Mexican infantrymen, plus four thousand cavalry lurking near Casa Mata.

Just before dawn, Worth's division and General George Cadwalader's brigade were in readiness. The bark of an American battery shattered the silence, and shot and shell rained down on the buildings at Molino del Rey. But the artillery barrage ended quickly, because not all of the guns were yet in place.

Worth began the attack anyway. Five hundred picked men under Major George Wright swung down a slope without a stick of cover, toward the ditch full of Echagaray's men. Suddenly, "a most appalling fire" of grape, canister, and musketry tore through Wright's shock troops, the first terrible indication of the large numbers they faced. At great loss, they overran the Mexicans' center, capturing the enemy guns at bayonet point. But before the Americans could turn them on the enemy, a murderous blaze of musket fire erupted from El Molino, just a pistol shot away, cutting down more than half of Wright's men and eleven of his fourteen officers, including Wright himself. The survivors fell back as a wave of Mexican infantry swarmed the battery, bayoneting and lancing the American wounded where they lay.

Unwilling to give up the position that Wright had captured and lost, Worth ordered a much larger second attack, this time by Cadwalader's brigade and a light infantry battalion under Captain Kirby Smith. The Americans recaptured the enemy battery, driving the Mexicans back into the mill.

Worth now committed the rest of his men to the raging battle. It was not yet 5:30 A.M.

• • •

Fighting with the same fierce obstinacy that Scott's men had encountered at Churubusco, the Mexicans clung to their positions at the mill and Casa Mata. H. Judge Moore, whose Palmetto Regiment had lost half its men at Churubusco, was again impressed by the Mexicans' courage: "Those who are disposed to think that Mexican soldiers cannot, or will not, fight, need only to have been at Molino del Rey."

Once again, the U.S. field artillery—when it caught up with Worth's attack—more than compensated for the Mexicans' overwhelming numerical superiority.

Captain Simon Drum's battery helped Lieutenant Colonel John Garland's brigade drive the enemy from El Molino, while Colonel James Duncan's guns battered Casa Mata during the assault by Lieutenant Colonel James McIntosh's brigade.

Casa Mata turned out to be a citadel, not just a stone house as Worth's staff had mistakenly believed after reviewing reconnaissance reports. It was surrounded by ditches and entrenchments filled with Mexican infantrymen. As McIntosh's men inched toward it under withering fire, four thousand cavalrymen commanded by General Juan Alvarez suddenly appeared and began approaching the American left flank. With a flurry of canister fire, Duncan's artillerymen drove the Mexican cavalrymen away in confusion, never to rejoin the fight.

McIntosh's attack stalled, and his men fell back to Duncan's guns, leaving behind them the bodies of McIntosh, who had survived bayonet wounds at Resaca de la Palma, and Major Martin Scott, his second-in-command, as well as many other casualties. Having dispersed Alvarez's cavalry, Duncan was now free to train all his guns on Casa Mata. His batteries fired "with a furor . . . inspired by the bloody repulse of McIntosh." In minutes, the defenders abandoned their positions and could be seen sprinting across the fields toward Mexico City. The Mexicans were then driven from every point of their line.

By 7:30 A.M., Worth's men occupied El Molino del Rey.

• • •

There was no cannon foundry, although some of Worth's men stumbled onto a powder magazine and accidentally set it off; the explosion killed twelve of them. "No vestige could be found of furnace, tools, or any other apparatus for the casting of cannon; as for the church-bells, these rang forth, that same night, merry peals, in the city of Mexico, in honor of Santa Anna's triumph"—the "triumph" consisting of Scott deciding not to follow up Worth's bloody victory with an immediate assault on Chapultepec.

Scott's hollow congratulations were of little consolation to Worth, who was painfully aware that his heavy losses—117 killed and 660 wounded, about a fourth of his force—were to no apparent purpose. Mexican losses were estimated at two thousand killed and wounded and another 680 captured. In his official report, Worth described El Molino del Rey as "a dear-bought victory." "A sad mistake," was how Lieutenant Colonel Hitchcock characterized the battle. "Many more such victories would ruin our army," observed an unnamed general.

As Worth's exhausted men trudged back to Tacubaya, medics in marked ambulances prowled the killing ground, looking for the wounded and drawing gunfire from the enemy battlements at nearby Chapultepec—"an instance of barbarism but seldom recorded in civilized armies," irately noted Lieutenant Raphael Semmes.

At Tacubaya, the American dead were "carefully and affectionately placed by the messmates of the deceased" in a large trench, wrote Semmes, "side by side in a field on the side hill in [the] rear of the bishop's palace—and in sight of the battlefield."

• • •

The battle had reduced Scott's army to fewer than eight thousand effectives, while scarcely denting the Mexicans' military strength. Yet El Molino del Rey had yielded an intangible benefit of great value: It had damaged Mexican morale, which had soared during the seventeen-day armistice that was mistakenly interpreted as a sign of American weakness. Jose Fernando Ramirez, the Mexico City lawyer, blamed the defeat on Alvarez's timid cavalrymen: "If the cavalry had charged as it was commanded to," the Americans could not have captured Casa Mata. "But the cowardly officers did not obey any of the five orders given them." Ramirez and his compatriots feared what lay ahead. "I cannot even guess what will become of us," he wrote a friend. "Tell the members of my family that I am safe and in good health. But my heart is broken."

• • •

Scott was in an unmistakably foul mood in the days following El Molino del Rey, as he brooded over his losses and pondered his options. Scott's subordinates suffered from his snappishness. "When prosperous, he is pleasant and good-humored, extremely kind and civil," observed Hitchcock, "but when his affairs seem unpromising, he is rather harsh upon those around him. . . . Indeed, his uncomfortability diffuses itself all around him." This purgatory lasted until September 11, when Scott summoned his officers and engineers to a meeting at the Convent and Church of Piedad near Tacubaya.

Should they attack Mexico City's southern or western gates? Scott wanted to know. The southern route, over the causeway north of Churubusco, led to the Candelaria Garita, where Captain Philip Kearny had lost his left arm in hand-to-hand fighting. General Gideon Pillow and Captain Robert E. Lee and the other engineers favored attacking Candelaria, and their arguments convinced most of the general officers. However, Lieutenant Pierre G. T. Beauregard's unusual silence during the freewheeling discussion prompted Hitchcock and Nicholas Trist to pointedly solicit his opinion.

The Louisianan might have been in a classroom at West Point as he outlined the strategy that Scott would adopt for conquering the enemy capital. Beauregard said that attacking from Churubusco would mean marching over a four-mile-long causeway, where U.S. troops would present inviting targets and where it would be impossible to maneuver; casualties would be worse than the battle at Churubusco, he predicted. Better to make only a demonstration toward Candelaria, while launching the primary attack on the western gates. This would mean first capturing Chapultepec, and then using it as a pivot on which to strike at either the San Cosme or Belen gates, over causeways just a mile or two in length.

While Santa Anna could concentrate his forces if Scott attacked along the Churubusco causeway, he would have to diffuse his troops to protect three city gates if the Americans feinted toward the Churubusco causeway and attacked Chapultepec. Being in the rare position of giving a lecture to generals, Beauregard could not resist quoting to them the maxim that it was best "never to do what your enemy expects or wishes you to do." Having discharged his dense cargo of opinions and homilies, Beauregard sat down.

Scott liked the logic of Beauregard's arguments; much of his campaign's success was due to just such gambits. At the same time, he made it known during the debate that followed Beauregard's presentation that he believed the Mexican army must be crushed, not dispersed. For this reason, Scott knew that he must capture Chapultepec, even if the attack were costly. Chapultepec, with its National Military School, ancient castle, and four-foot-thick walls, must not survive as a conspicuous symbol of Mexican military power.

Scott announced that the army would seize Chapultepec and attack the western gates.

• • •

A prolonged artillery barrage would soften up Chapultepec's defenses before the assault. Ammunition for his guns no longer was a problem for Scott, who had earlier worried that he might run out of it. With the enemy ordnance seized from Contreras and Churubusco, Scott's gunners could bombard Chapultepec for two days. And captured enemy cannons had tripled the number of American siege guns.

The instant the bombardment ceased, five hundred volunteers from Generals Worth's and Twiggs's divisions, equipped with scaling ladders, would spearhead two simultaneous assaults. The Worth volunteers, operating under General Gideon Pillow's command, would attack from the west through El Molino del Rey; Twiggs's men, led by General John Quitman, would strike from the southeast, up the road from Tacubaya. Behind Pillow's shock troops would come the rest of his division and Worth's depleted division, while Quitman's division would support the volunteers attacking from Tacubaya.

Once again, Captain Lee's intuitive reading of topography was indispensable in positioning the American guns. Aided by Captain Benjamin Huger, who would be a general under Lee during the Civil War, Lee spent the night of September 11 supervising the construction of four heavy batteries within easy range of Chapultepec.

Along the Candelaria causeway, Twiggs's two batteries and Colonel Bennet Riley's brigade fired and maneuvered in hopes of distracting the Mexicans from Chapultepec. But the noisy demonstration convinced no one. Lieutenant Daniel Hill said it was because Twiggs, who was in charge of the diversion, was unwilling to expose his infantry, essential to creating the illusion of an imminent attack. When the bombardment of Chapultepec began, Santa Anna instantly knew that that was where Scott would launch the main attack. He shifted thousands of troops from the Candelaria Garita to help defend Chapultepec and the two causeways behind it.

From morning until nightfall September 12, the American heavy guns blasted Chapultepec, making "a good impression" on the castle and its outworks by killing or wounding many Mexicans and driving others from the hilltop to safer positions below. Pleased with the results, Scott decided to attack the next morning.

After all the careful planning, maneuvering, and stratagems, the American high command was tense and anxious on the eve of what they expected to be the war's climactic battle. "We shall be defeated," Worth glumly told Hitchcock, who observed: "Even General Scott, when all others had left the room, said to me, 'I have my misgivings.' "

SEPTEMBER 13, 1847: CHAPULTEPEC

In the gray dawn, Captain Huger's guns, just as they had the previous day, belched fire and steel at the twelve-foot-high stone walls surrounding the old castle and National Military College. Captains Samuel McKenzie and Silas Casey commanded the two columns of volunteer shock troops, known as "The Forlorn Hope." One of the volunteers was Lieutenant Hill, leading "thirty as gallant spirits as ever breathed."

About a thousand troops under General Nicolas Bravo Rueda had initially occupied the buildings atop Chapultepec, along with fifty cadets from the military college who had refused to obey orders to leave. But the bombardment, coupled with desertions during the night, had pared the defenders' strength to eight hundred men or fewer. Bravo Rueda sent about half of them to breastworks on Chapultepec's lower slopes, which had also been mined with explosives to be detonated by canvas powder trains. Around the base of Chapultepec, and predominantly on its west side, were fourteen thousand troops under Santa Anna's command.

Surprisingly, for all of the Mexican soldiers around Chapultepec, and the hill's essential role in Mexico City's defense, just thirteen guns defended it.

• • •

At 8 A.M., Huger's batteries, in action now for two hours, abruptly fell silent. McKenzie's blue-clad troops darted through the ruins of El Molino del Rey and started up the southwest slope of the steep hill with pickaxes, ladders, muskets, and bayonets. Behind them came Pillow and his Voltigeurs, the Ninth and Sixteenth Infantry regiments, Captain John Magruder's field batteries, and Major Jesse Reno's mountain howitzers. Advancing under "a shower of balls," the Americans scaled a six-foot wall to enter the wooded military academy grounds and then crossed an open stretch of rocky terrain beneath the academy's twelve-foot inner walls.

Through his field glasses, Hitchcock "saw the colors advance—saw the bearer shot down," and then observed someone else snatching them up. The wounded flag bearer, Lieutenant James Longstreet, would serve at Gettysburg with the man who took the colors from him, Lieutenant George Pickett. Mexican soldiers attempted to light the powder train to the mines they had laid but were shot down before they could do so.

Pillow was wounded in the leg, and the attackers paused under the wall until Worth's reserve division could join the assault.

The brief lull gave American sharpshooters an opportunity to identify enemy firing positions among the rocks, bushes, and "dead angles," and to destroy them.

• • •

Besides the 250 volunteers supplied by Twiggs and commanded by Casey, Quitman's spearhead included 120 picked Marines and soldiers led by Marine Major Levi Twiggs, a brother of General David Twiggs, and forty Marine and Army volunteers under Marine Captain John G. Reynolds. As they neared the southeast corner of Chapultepec on the main road from Tacubaya, they ran into an enemy battery blocking the road. Gunfire also erupted from Mexican batteries around the causeway angling toward the city, and from infantrymen sprawled behind dikes.

Major Twiggs was shot dead in the road, and Casey and General James Shields, still recovering from being shot through the lungs at Cerro Gordo, were wounded. Quitman's attack stalled until an infantry regiment under General Persifer Smith, advancing on the right, overran the battery blocking the road and seized the causeway to Belen Gate, cutting off Chapultepec from any relief from the city.

• • •

When they resumed their attack up the western slopes, Pillow's and Worth's men had an easier time than did Quitman's troops on the Tacubaya road—and they reached the top of Chapultepec. A New York regiment stormed the fortress and raised the Stars and Stripes amid desperate hand-to-hand combat. From below, Lieutenant Hill could see men fighting on the parapets, as well as Mexican soldiers clinging to the walls and trying to squeeze into an aqueduct that led to the city. The searing memory of Mexicans bayoneting wounded Americans at El Molino del Rey brought cries of "Give no quarter to the treacherous scoundrels," and many Mexicans were bayoneted in reprisal. Rather than surrender, six teenage Mexican cadets, one day honored by their countrymen as "Los Niños Heroes," fought to the death, one of them leaping from a parapet while wrapped in the Mexican flag. At 10 A.M., Chapultepec belonged to Scott's army, but the day's fighting was far from finished.

• • •

The Marine Corps on this day was in the biggest fight of its seventy-two-year history. Marines had fought in every U.S. war, especially distinguishing themselves in Tripoli in 1805 and recently in California, but never in great numbers or in a major battle. Chapultepec was everything that Commandant Archibald Henderson had hoped for when, during a meeting with President Polk and War Secretary William Marcy earlier in the year, he had proposed recruiting Marines to replace some of Scott's time-elapsed volunteers. He promised to do it faster, better, and cheaper than the Army. The Corps would find this to be a clinching argument whenever its existence was jeopardized by zealous government budget-cutters.

The days when superfluous volunteers were turned away had long since passed, and only with difficulty did Henderson raise a battalion of twenty-two officers and 324 men, commanded by Lieutenant Colonel Samuel E. Watson and Major Twiggs, both War of 1812 veterans. Three days after its formation, the battalion sailed to Vera Cruz, where it was joined by a small detachment of Marines from the Gulf Squadron. In Puebla, the Marines were attached to Quitman's division and did not participate in the battles of Contreras, Churubusco, or Molino del Rey. Chapultepec was the battalion's first action, but its baptism by fire was not yet ended.

After Twiggs's death, Colonel Watson took charge of Quitman's Marines during the attack up Chapultepec's southern slopes, while Captain George H. Terrett skirted the hill with thirty-six Marines, including Lieutenant Charles Henderson, the commandant's son. Reaching Chapultepec's northern side, Terrett's detachment headed for the mile-long causeway that led to Mexico's western gate, San Cosme, joining forward elements of General Worth's division, which was under orders to storm the gate.

In possession of the south end of the other Chapultepec causeway, Quitman decided to march to Belen Gate on the city's southwest corner. Although he was supposed to only appear before Belen Gate to draw defenders away from the main attack on San Cosme Gate, Quitman, who had missed out on Contreras and Churubusco, had other ideas. It would become a contest between Worth and Quitman to be the first to enter the city.

• • •

On a hill near the battlefield, thirty condemned men stood on wagons with nooses around their necks, watching the American bluecoats storm Chapultepec. As intended, this was to be the last terrestrial sight witnessed by the San Patricios before they went to meet their maker. The order was given, the wagons lurched forward, and the sentence was duly fulfilled. The San Patricios—captured at Churubusco, where the Irishmen had fought so magnificently, but wrong-headedly, against their former comrades—were hanged as deserters and traitors to the United States. A few days earlier, at San Angel and Mixcoac, the army had hanged twenty of their confederates.

The U.S. command had spared the lives of their leader, John Riley, and fourteen others who had deserted before war was declared; it was a capital offense to desert during wartime, but not during peacetime. Yet their punishment was severe: As pipers played "The Rogue's March," the prisoners' heads were shaved bloody, and they were given up to fifty lashes and branded with a "D" on the right cheekbone, just beneath the eye. The hated Riley was initially branded with an upside-down D. To correct the "mistake," General Twiggs ordered him rebranded under the other eye, this time with the D properly positioned.

Of the more than nine thousand Americans who deserted during the war, nearly one thousand were Irish-born regulars, many of them leaving because of Nativist prejudice toward foreigners and Catholics. They did not all join the enemy's ranks; those who did incurred the justifiable hatred of their former comrades.

The San Patricios' adopted Mexican countrymen, however, warmly welcomed "Los Colorados," so called because many had red hair and ruddy complexions. Impressed by their gunnery skills, Santa Anna entrusted the Irishmen with his heaviest ordnance, the 16- and 24-pounders. He once boasted that with a few hundred more men like the San Patricios, he would whip the Americans. The Mexican government later erected a plaque honoring the Irish deserters at the San Angel execution ground, where Saint Patrick's Day is still celebrated annually.

• • •

The Stars and Stripes flowed over Chapultepec castle and the National Military Academy. Dead Mexican soldiers lay in bloody heaps in the smashed buildings and strewn across the lacerated grounds. General Bravo Rueda, Chapultepec's commander, was a prisoner of war.

But the battle was not over. In the dikes and ditches at the base of Chapultepec, and on the causeways leading into the enemy capital, thousands of Mexican soldiers continued to fight.

• • •

Behind Chapultepec, on the road to San Cosme Gate, enemy musket fire sent Lieutenant Thomas Jackson's gunners scurrying for cover behind an embankment. But the twenty-three-year-old Virginian with the burning, pale blue eyes did not seek concealment—no surprise to fellow officers who were familiar with Jackson's utter fearlessness. The determined lieutenant, who had gotten in front of Worth's division, dragged a 6-pounder across a ditch and into the road. Without assistance, he began firing it. "See, there is no danger," he shouted to his men and walked up and down the road to prove it, as enemy balls clattered around him and a cannonball passed between his legs. Worth and his division gaped as Jackson calmly conducted his private duel with the Mexican guns.

Genuinely concerned about Jackson's safety, Worth urged him to take cover.

Jackson's response was a request for a company of infantry to help him capture the Mexican position. Captain John Magruder, possibly the only other artillery officer in Scott's army with Jackson's mad courage, galloped up to his subordinate, just as his horse was shot from under him, and helped Jackson drag a second gun across the ditch. With the two guns, Magruder and Jackson, soon joined by Jackson's men, battled the Mexican batteries, which killed or wounded most of Jackson's horses and men before they were finally silenced.

Jackson hitched his guns to limbers and raced up the San Cosme causeway, joining Lieutenants Daniel Hill and Barnard Bee, and Captain Terrett and his thirty-six Marines, who had ranged ahead of the army. General Pedro de Ampudia suddenly appeared before them with fifteen hundred cavalrymen. On the narrow causeway, the Mexicans' surpassing numbers presented a dense target that Jackson's guns sent reeling backward. But the Americans prudently elected to wait for Worth's infantrymen to catch up to them before advancing upon Ampudia's large squadron.

• • •

The battle shifted to the two causeways ending at San Cosme and Belen gates. Each was a double road straddling an aqueduct "of great height" that rested on enormous pillars and open arches. The causeways were ideally suited for defense, but they might also protect attackers who used the pillars and arches for concealment. The Belen causeway traveled on a straight line for a mile to its gate at the city's southwestern corner. The San Cosme causeway, over which Cortes had retreated from Mexico City in 1520 amid a blizzard of Aztec arrows, was nearly twice as long; it angled north before bending to the east, to its gate on the city's west side. Flat-roofed stone houses swarming with enemy troops lined parts of the San Cosme causeway. Strong breastworks guarded both city gates.

When Worth's division, which was to carry the main attack through San Cosme Gate, reached the stone houses, the Mexicans opened up from behind rooftop parapets with muskets and cannons. The Monterrey veterans showed the others how to force doors and windows with pickaxes and crowbars, and to burrow from house to house through interior walls, shooting the rooftop defenders from the stairwells.

After securing the suburb and capturing two enemy batteries, Worth's men resumed their march to the San Cosme Gate, whose fortified custom house was the last hurdle to their entry into the city.

• • •

With the Palmetto Regiment in the lead, followed by Colonel Watson's Marines, General Quitman's troops marched up the Belen causeway until an enemy battery began shooting at them. Observing from the San Cosme causeway that Quitman was pinned down, Worth sent two of Colonel James Duncan's guns down a side road to Quitman's aid. Their enfilading cannon fire forced the Mexicans to abandon the battery.

Reaching Belen Gate, Quitman's division ran into a two-gun enemy battery, and cannon and musket fire from the gate and the imposing Citadel, Santa Anna's operations center. Despite heavy casualties, the Americans overran the enemy works at the gate and entered the city. It was 1:30 P.M.

• • •

Beneath the San Cosme causeway, Lieutenants Ulysses S. Grant and Raphael Semmes found themselves in the company of Captain Terrett's Marines and an Army company led by Captain Horace Brooks. Advancing "an arch at a time" toward the city gate, they flanked and fired on a barricade defended by hundreds of Mexicans, scattering them. Now, the gate itself lay before them, but the rest of Worth's division was still fighting in the suburban streets behind them.

Nonetheless, Marine Lieutenants John D. Simms and Jabez C. Rich led seven Marines against a strongpoint on the left side of the gate, as the Corps commandant's son, Lieutenant Charles Henderson, who had been wounded in the leg, attacked from the front with the rest of their tiny force—and seized the gate. For fifteen minutes, under intensive enemy fire, the band of Marines held San Cosme, until compelled to withdraw with six dead.

Observing that a nearby church belfry appeared to overlook the gate and its barricades, Grant devised an audacious plan. With the help of Brooks's soldiers, Grant dismantled a mountain howitzer, lugged the pieces across several ditches and through chest-deep water, and knocked on the church door.

To the priest who answered, Grant presented his plan to use the belfry as a firing position. When the priest politely refused to let the Americans inside, Grant explained further that the priest "might save his property by opening the door, and he certainly would save himself from becoming a prisoner. . . . He began to see his duty in the same light that I did, and opened the door, although he did not look as if it gave him special pleasure to do so." The troops trundled the gun up the narrow staircase to the belfry, and there quickly assembled it. Grant was pleased to discover that they were less than three hundred yards from San Cosme Gate. "The shots from our little gun dropped in upon the enemy and created great confusion."

When Worth's division caught up with the advance party, Worth sent for Grant, liberally praised his resourcefulness, and ordered a captain to bring a second howitzer to the belfry. Grant didn't have the heart to tell Worth that the belfry was too small to accommodate two guns. He took the captain, but not his gun, into the belfry with him.

• • •

At the gate, Worth's troops encountered the same situation that had faced them on the causeway: houses full of enemy troops, and Mexican soldiers on rooftops firing down into the street. It was "emphatically a hot place," dryly observed Lieutenant Beauregard. "We left the street," recounted Lieutenant Ralph Kirkham, "took to the houses on either side, and [with pickaxes] picked our way through from house to house. . . . With pick and crowbar, [we] worked our way."

With Grant's gun and a second gun on a nearby rooftop clearing the houses ahead of them, and soldiers and Marines firing down on the enemy from other buildings, Worth's grimy troops, led by, among others, Hill, Jackson, and George McClellan—who as generals would clash at bloody Antietam fifteen years later—burrowed their way through the houses toward the gate. The final enemy battery fell when soldiers broke into a three-story building forty yards away, dashed to the roof, and raked the gunners with musket fire. "Those who were not killed or disabled by that fire seemed dazed for an instant; but in a few moments, they precipitately retreated."

By sunset, San Cosme gate was in American hands. Worth's men sank to the ground in exhaustion. The long day's strenuous exertions had drained everyone, even the iron-willed Captain Lee. In the saddle or on his feet for fifty-six straight hours—Lee had spent the previous night positioning the batteries at Chapultepec—and bleeding from a flesh wound, Lee collapsed while delivering messages for General Scott.

Quitman's division had won the race into the city, but after his men had driven away the Belen gate defenders, they were unable to advance a step further. Santa Anna had taken personal charge of the sector. Cannon and musket fire roared down on the Americans from the Citadel and nearby buildings. Quitman's men spent the night digging in, anticipating a pitched battle in the morning.

Scott's army had brought the war into Mexico City's foyer. As midnight approached, American gunners at San Cosme Gate began bombarding central Mexico City with a 24-pounder and a ten-inch mortar.

• • •

Inside the Citadel that night, a weary, anxious Santa Anna canvassed his generals about whether the army should fight on or abandon the city to the Americans. He had lost eighteen hundred men at Chapultepec, and more in the fighting on the causeways and at the city gates. His fighting force now consisted of just five thousand infantry and four thousand cavalry. Abandon the city, Santa Anna's generals counseled.

By 2 A.M. September 14, Santa Anna, the remnants of his army, and Mexican government officials were on the road to Guadalupe Hidalgo. "The brigades marched in silence. Sadness reigned in all their hearts," wrote Mexican historian Ramon Alcarez of the retreat.

• • •

Just after 1 A.M., a delegation of municipal leaders had approached San Cosme Gate under a white flag, announcing that they wished to surrender the city. The commissioners were conducted to General Worth, who sent them with an escort to Scott's headquarters at Tacubaya.

Acting on Scott's orders, Worth's division marched into the now undefended city and took up positions on the alameda opposite the Grand Plaza and palace, where it was joined by Quitman's division. As the new day dawned, a dense crowd gathered in streets surrounding the Grand Plaza.

• • •

Colonel William Harney and his hard-bitten dragoons escorted Scott and his staff, all in full dress uniforms, to the National Palace at 9 A.M. A band played "Yankee Doodle," and Marines raised the Stars and Stripes.

Quitman assigned Colonel Watson's Marine battalion to guard the palace, which would serve as Scott's headquarters. In their shakos and crossed white belts, the Marines flushed out looters and began walking their posts in the "Halls of Montezuma," where the Aztecs had administered their empire, and where Santa Anna had administered his. According to Corps tradition, it was here that an anonymous Marine wrote the lyrics to the "Marines' Hymn" and set them to the tune of the gendarme's song of Jacques Offenbach's opera, *Genevieve de Brabant*. Corps legend has it that the "blood stripe" on the blue dress trousers of its officers and noncoms commemorates the Marine blood spilled at Chapultepec and San Cosme Gate.

• • •

Scott had accomplished the seemingly impossible. With no more than ten thousand men, he had marched 280 miles into Mexico's heartland and captured the enemy capital. Always heavily outnumbered, the American army had won every battle, while living almost entirely off the land. "History will no doubt speak of our achievement as more glorious than that of Cortes," wrote Lieutenant Daniel Hill four days after entering Mexico City.

The Duke of Wellington, who had believed that Scott was doomed when he broke free from his supply line, now pronounced Scott's campaign "unsurpassed in military annals. He is the greatest living soldier."

• • •

As the Americans occupied the National Palace, an angry murmur ran through the throngs jamming the streets around the Main Plaza. Santa Anna might have skulked out of Mexico City without making a last stand, but not all of the city's inhabitants were ready to quit the war. They had gone to bed believing that Santa Anna's troops would fight for their city, and had awakened to find themselves in the enemy's power. "The infamous and eternally accursed Santa Anna abandoned us all . . . to the mercy of the enemy, and did not leave even one sentinel to defend us," fumed the lawyer, Jose Fernando Ramirez.

The seven thousand American troops suddenly seemed puny in the midst of two hundred thousand unfriendly Mexicans.

The first gunshot came from a rooftop and hit Colonel John Garland in the leg as he stood with a group of officers. Instantly, musket fire erupted from rooftops all around the plaza.

Many Mexican National Guard soldiers—the "Polkos" whose untimely revolt had sealed Vera Cruz's downfall—had remained in Mexico City with their families when Santa Anna withdrew to Guadalupe Hidalgo. Muskets in hand, these men now poured into the streets to defend their city, joining two thousand convicts whom Santa Anna had freed and armed before leaving the city. "A most wonderful species of warfare was commenced," sardonically noted Lieutenant John James Peck. The second battle for Mexico City had begun.

• • •

It was as though the ceremony in the Grand Plaza had released a stopcock that had dammed up the Mexicans' hostility. The Americans were met by gunfire from churches, homes, convents, and from the windows, roofs, and walls of buildings everywhere; by defiant mobs in the streets; and by hurled rocks and bottles. "In all the streets which the enemy occupied, they fought with boldness and enthusiasm," wrote Alcarez, the Mexican historian. Scott's inspector general, Lieutenant Colonel Hitchcock, closed the bars and gambling parlors. Then he warned that the Americans "would destroy the city and give it up to pillage if the firing does not cease."

But when the U.S. casualty list continued to grow, eventually reaching two hundred killed and wounded, Scott cracked down hard. Artillery batteries were positioned on all the major streets, and wherever defiant crowds gathered, the gunners cleared the streets with grape and canister. Orders were issued to shoot on sight any armed civilian found outdoors. Skirmishers raided homes and buildings where insurgent snipers operated; sometimes houses were demolished by round shot. "The artillery, shaking the buildings to their foundations, spread despair and death," wrote Alcarez.

U.S. soldiers pursued the convicts and Polkos and killed "great numbers of them" shocking Mexican men who had never faced severe consequences when they participated in the nation's numerous revolutions. " 'Twas a day of bloodshed and brutality such as I trust never to see again," wrote Lieutenant Hill. When night came on September 14, bodies littered the streets.

• • •

Hitchcock warned church leaders that if they did not help stop the insurgency, the army would sack the churches. When the convicts began to loot public offices and the homes of the wealthy, the municipal government and city leaders joined clergymen in suppressing the uprising.

By September 16, the insurrection was largely spent, although on that day some of Santa Anna's lancers attempted to reenter the city. They hastily retreated when the Americans shot several of them.

The ragtag insurgency was succeeded by a sinister campaign of nocturnal murders that lasted weeks.

• • •

Named governor of Mexico City, General John Quitman reinstated municipal officials at the salaries they had been paid by Santa Anna, so that the city could function normally again. He announced harsh penalties for citizens caught carrying concealed weapons, established a military tribunal, and levied a $15,000 tax to benefit hospitals and buy new clothing for the American soldiers.

25

FRUSTRATION

"If the present opportunity be not seized at once, all chance for making a treaty at all will be lost for an indefinite period—probably forever."

—Diplomat Nicholas Trist, explaining why he chose
to ignore the Polk administration's recall

FALL 1847: WASHINGTON

President Polk had labored tirelessly, nearly to the point of collapse, since returning on July 7 from a two-week goodwill trip to New England, the sanctuary of the opposition Whigs. His mentor, Andrew Jackson, had made a similar tour to rally support at the height of the 1833 nullification crisis. Amid the nation's largest manufacturing concerns, Polk had touted the Democrats' vision of a yeoman republic, while urging New Englanders to support his war measures in a "spirit of harmony and compromise." It is arguable whether the speech-making and handshaking changed many minds, but the long journey, heavy workload, and Polk's concern for the welfare of General Winfield Scott's army somewhere deep in Mexico had exacted a toll on the president's constitution. His burdens had increased when War Secretary William Marcy suffered a breakdown in August, requiring Polk and Navy Secretary John Y. Mason to take on Marcy's duties. The horseback rides that Polk had so enjoyed in April were now only a faint memory, and as Scott's army advanced on Mexico City, Polk suffered from recurring fevers. "I am waiting with great anxiety for the next arrival from Mexico," he wrote on September 23.

Too ill to attend church the next day, Polk took to his bed, just as he had thir-teen months earlier during the Wilmot Proviso debate, another stressful period. His fever worsened, and a doctor was summoned. For six days, Polk tossed and turned in his sickbed while his doctor prescribed nostrums of dubious efficacy. The fever finally broke on October 3, but another week passed before the presi-dent was able to return to work.

• • •

With Scott's army 280 miles inland from Vera Cruz, war news was three weeks in transit to Washington. At times, the delay created problems. On September 15, the day after Scott's capture of Mexico City, Polk was learning of the victories at Contreras and Churubusco, the armistice, and the commencement of Trist's nego-tiations with the Mexican commissioners. With remarkable insight, the president predicted, "I fear the armistice was agreed to by the Mexican Commander only to gain time to re-organize his defeated army for further resistance."

When Trist's report on Mexico's counterproposals and the peace talks' failure reached the State Department, Polk, still bedbound, directed Secretary of State James Buchanan to recall Trist from Mexico. The Mexican commissioners, Buchanan wrote to Trist on October 6, "not only rejected your liberal offers, but have insulted our country by proposing terms the acceptance of which would degrade us in the eyes of the world and be justly condemned by the whole American people." The secretary of state said that while the U.S. peace proposal had been "framed in a spirit of forbear-ance and moderation," and the army had purchased its provisions and respected pri-vate property, Mexico had repaid American fairness with treachery. "Our citizens have been murdered and their dead bodies mutilated in cold blood by bands of savage and cowardly guerrillas." Come home, he told Trist.

Of course, the situation in Mexico had changed since then. When Buchanan was penning the letter recalling Trist, the armistice negotiations had already ended in failure, and Scott's army had driven Santa Anna from the heights of Chapul-tepec and the gates of Mexico City. The invaders had become conquerors. And Trist was beginning new peace talks in Mexico City.

• • •

With a remnant of his former army, Santa Anna, who had never waged a guerrilla war, decided to do so now. He lingered near Puebla in the hope of inspiring the sort of spontaneous uprising that he had once so ruthlessly crushed. Upon this slender thread hung his last hope of driving Scott's army from Mexico, and of regaining the presidency that he had been forced to resign.

Santa Anna's successor, "fat, ceremonious" Manuel de la Peña y Peña, Foreign Minister during John Slidell's failed mission and now the Supreme Court's chief judge, convened the Mexican Congress at the temporary capital in Querétaro, 125 miles north of Mexico City. One of his first actions was to order Santa Anna's court martial for his unbroken string of military defeats.

• • •

While Scott did not believe Mexico was capable of resuming the war, he did not think it would sign a peace treaty, either. "The government will find itself without resources; no army, no arsenals, no magazines, and but little revenue, internal or external. Still, such is the obstinacy, or rather infatuation, of this people, that it is very doubtful whether the new authorities will dare to sue for peace on the terms which, in the recent negotiations, were made known by our minister."

The government-in-exile at Querétaro faced the same political risks as had Jose Joaquin Herrera's government when John Slidell tried to initiate talks two years earlier. If it agreed to Trist's terms, it could be overthrown; but if it did not, the United States could resume military operations and unilaterally impose harsher terms, possibly even the annexation of all of Mexico—an "All Mexico" movement in Washington was gaining support daily. Yet, perversely, Mexico's "puros," who read the American newspaper stories about the Whigs' criticism of the war, believed delay would dampen the United States's territorial ambitions.

• • •

As too often had been the case in Mexico, the competing factions bickered and schemed, and the peace talks bogged down over the same seemingly insoluble issues—the Texas border, New Mexico, and California—that had doomed the armistice negotiations. Other Mexican officials sought British mediation, hoping to force Trist to modify his demands. The British declined and instead supplied Trist with "impartial advice" and the services of a translator.

For Mexico, the preeminent issue continued to be the Texas border, inextricably tangled up as it was with Mexican pride and honor. Trist believed that if negotiators could agree on a border, the United States would then be able to purchase California, and even New Mexico.

Possibly for this reason, Trist hinted to the Mexican peace commissioners that the United States might agree to a buffer zone between the Rio Grande and Nueces—evidently forgetting the fact that, from the Polk administration's standpoint, the border question was the war's *casus belli,* and therefore nonnegotiable.

• • •

Before Buchanan's October 6 letter recalling Trist reached Mexico City, Scott's report on the Mexico City victories arrived in Washington. Accompanying it was a letter from Trist urging a more flexible position on the Texas border question, and describing Mexico's proposal to keep Los Angeles and San Diego, while ceding only San Francisco. Polk angrily instructed Buchanan to draft a second letter to Trist, recalling and rebuking him. "He had no right to depart from his instructions, and I disapprove of his conduct in doing so," grumbled Polk. "I can never approve a Treaty, or submit one to the Senate, which would dismember the State of Texas, and Mr. Trist's suggestion, if agreed to, would have done [this] by depriving the State of the country between the Nueces and the Rio Grande."

Buchanan's October 25 letter, sent by special courier, informed Trist that Texas had already assumed jurisdiction of the Nueces–Rio Grande territory. "Considering the enterprising and energetic character of the American people, it would be impossible to expel by force the inhabitants between the Nueces and the Rio Grande from their possessions and to convert this territory into a desert for the security of the Mexican frontier." The letter closed with the words, "The President has directed me to reiterate your recall."

• • •

Scott had left Colonel Thomas Childs and four hundred men at Puebla when he marched to Mexico City in early August. Childs had had his hands full trying to stop guerrillas from attacking and murdering American travelers on the National Highway. Then, General Joaquin Rea and two thousand cavalrymen, who had begun operating in the Puebla area in late August, cut off the Americans' water supply. Guerrillas stole seven hundred U.S. mules, and Rea's cavalry ambushed the thirty-two dragoons who tried to pursue the thieves. Thirteen mutilated bodies were sent in a cart to the U.S. encampment.

In mid-September, Rea surrounded Childs's garrison and commenced a low-grade siege, launching occasional raids but no all-out attack. After Scott captured Mexico City, Santa Anna and his two thousand remaining troops joined Rea.

Together, they intended to wrest Puebla from Childs and to sever Scott's communications with Vera Cruz.

OCTOBER 9, 1847: HUAMANTLA

Informed of Childs's dire situation, General Joseph Lane, who had commanded
the Second Indiana Regiment when it ran away at Buena Vista, set out from Jalapa
with four thousand men. Santa Anna broke off the siege and marched down the
National Highway to meet Lane.

Twenty-seven miles northeast of Puebla at El Penal Pass, the Mexicans left the
National Highway and entered Huamantla. Santa Anna planned to allow Lane's
column to pass by, and then fall on the rear of his two-hundred-wagon baggage train.

Lane's scouts, however, found out that Santa Anna was in Huamantla, and
Lane led three thousand men toward the town, leaving his wagon train under a
strong guard on the National Highway.

With Lane were Captain Sam Walker and three federalized Texas Ranger companies that had been campaigning with Colonel Francis Wynkoop's mounted battalion against the guerrilla bands prowling the National Highway. Walker had
recently been imprisoned in Perote castle—also his prison after the Mier debacle
in 1842—for having accused Wynkoop of running away during a skirmish with
bandits.

• • •

Surprised by the Americans' sudden appearance outside Huamantla, Santa Anna
sent two thousand lancers to meet Lane's troops, while hastily pulling back his
artillery. In a long column, the lancers galloped out of Huamantla, drew up in a
line, and charged the Americans.

Instantly, Walker and the mounted troops burst from Lane's ranks and counterattacked. The Texans broke the lancers' formation, chased the Mexicans into
town, and rode into the middle of an intensive musket–cannon crossfire. During
the brutal, close-combat fighting, Walker beheaded a cannoneer with a swipe of
his sword before he could fire his gun. But by the time that Lane's infantrymen
caught up with Walker's dragoons, sending the Mexicans into flight, Walker lay
sprawled dead in the street, shot twice.

General Lane impetuously ordered his men to "avenge the death of the gallant
Walker . . . and take all we could lay hands on," thereby violating the canons of civilized

warfare. The soldiers pillaged and burned houses and stores, and stripped and raped women. The streets resounded with "shouts, screams, reports of fire arms and the crash of timber and glass as the troops batte[red] down the doors and windows," wrote Lieutenant William Wilkins. "Dead horses and men lay about pretty thick, while drunken soldiers, yelling and screeching, were breaking open houses or chasing some poor Mexicans who had abandoned their houses and fled for life."

The soldiers buried Walker in a secret place before returning to their camp on the National Highway, leaving behind two hundred men who were too drunk to march.

The reprehensible affair was the last major battle of the war.

• • •

On October 2, Mexico City was jolted from its peaceful early-morning slumber by a "violent slamming of the doors." Beds jumped and shook, and chandeliers trembled and swayed. "The domes and steeples of the innumerable churches and convents reeled like drunken men. . . . Water in the reservoirs was billowing to and fro, the walls around us cracking and gaping asunder." A city aqueduct broke "in 50 places."

The Mexicans, who had experienced earthquakes before, acted as though they never had. They poured into the streets in their nightclothes, shrieking, confessing their sins, and "calling on the saints for protection." From his window, Lieutenant Colonel Ethan Allen Hitchcock saw a priest on his knees in the middle of a street. In a nearby village, two thousand people prayed in the ruins of collapsed buildings to a cloud that bore an uncanny resemblance to the crucified Jesus Christ.

• • •

Within a week of Mexico City's surrender, American entrepreneurs were busy supplying Scott's soldiers with the comforts of home in new establishments, erected with lightning speed. Nearly overnight, there appeared a Union Hotel, an American Dry Goods, a St. Charles Exchange, and a Union Street Restaurant. Signs advertised "Mash and Milk at All Hours," eggnog, mince pie, a circus, theaters, and an Italian opera. Naturally, there were saloons dispensing cheap liquor. George Kendall of the New Orleans *Picayune* was impressed by the speed at which Mexico City had been "Americanized"—his use of the catchphrase possibly being the first. "Mexico is no doubt one of the best places for an American to feel proud of his nationality," observed a Pennsylvania volunteer.

While many soldiers frequented the restaurants, hotels, and saloons, at least as many devoted their spare time to visiting the Aztec pyramid at Cholula, or gathering seeds and flowers to send home in letters, or exploring the Valley of Mexico with their copies of Prescott's *Conquest,* or Frances Calderón de la Barca's *Life in Mexico.* From vendors in the streets, the soldiers bought souvenir vases, stone idols, and "sacrificial knives."

Looming in the southwest, the snow-covered volcanoes Popocatepetl and Iztaccihuatl beckoned. A party of American officers that included Lieutenants Ulysses Grant and Ralph Kirkham attempted to scale Popocatepetl, and, like Cortes, they failed to reach the summit; snowblind, they had to be led to the bottom. Donning green spectacles for their second attempt, they succeeded, overcoming altitude sickness and nosebleeds.

The soldiers patronized theatrical performances, horse races, the bullfights, and the bustling city market. Lieutenant John James Peck and other officers attended *La Somnambula,* a musical starring Carete, a diva popular in Madrid and Havana, and then held a benefit for her. Two thousand tickets were sold, and General Scott attended. A ballet troupe and a theatrical company performed nightly at the Teatro Nacional, where the orchestra played "Yankee Doodle" and "Hail Columbia." Down the street at Teatro del Progreso, a Señora Armand performed bareback stunts, which were followed by the contortions of an "India Rubberman."

It was all wonderfully exotic to the American conquerors. "If those cursed Mexicans did not shoot at one so hard, Mexico would be a delightful country to be in," a soldier observed.

• • •

Standing in the receiving line during a banquet for his officers, General Winfield Scott found himself face to face with his field artillery officer, Thomas Jackson. Deciding to have a little fun with the misanthropic lieutenant, Scott stiffly remarked, "I don't know that I shall shake hands with Mr. Jackson." Confused and embarrassed, Jackson stood blushing before the General of the Army, as everyone in the room turned to watch. Then Scott said, "If you can forgive yourself for the way in which you slaughtered those poor Mexicans with your guns, I am not sure that I can." Scott then grasped Jackson's hand and warmly shook it. He had just paid Jackson an enormous compliment.

"The army, multiplied by four, could not have entered the capital of Mexico" were it not for West Point's officers, declared Scott, raising his glass in a toast to the

Military Academy. Indeed the Mexican War had burnished the reputation of the U.S. Military Academy at West Point in its "first war." Of the 523 West Pointers who served in the war, 49 were killed, 92 were wounded, and 452 won brevet rank, the last a remarkable achievement. Generous with praise when it was due, Scott extolled "the long gray line" of West Point for training superior officers.

As Revolutionary War officers had formed the Society of the Cincinnatus to honor their wartime service, a group of Scott's officers established the Military Society of the Mexican War. Better known as the Aztec Club, the organization listed 160 members in Mexico City in late 1847. General John Quitman was the first president. (The Aztec Club survives to this day, with its four hundred members dedicated to preserving the memory of their Mexican War ancestors.)

Scott's encomiums aside, many former West Pointers were unhappy that political appointees were being promoted faster than they. They blamed the Polk administration. "What is the use of graduating at West Point and studying one's profession if we are to be rated thus by the executive?" complained Lieutenant Peck, who commanded an artillery company yet remained a lieutenant.

• • •

General Scott undoubtedly was amused and flattered when he was invited to become Mexico's dictator. Mexican leaders had discovered that the American occupation, although not ideal, was yet an improvement over the wretched turmoil of the past twenty-five years. Believing that Mexicans might learn to govern themselves if given a good example, the leaders offered Scott $1.25 million and a president's salary to assume dictatorial powers for four to six years. Scott's amusement must have turned to incredulity when the leaders revealed that their eventual goal was annexation to the United States. Scott declined.

Perhaps another motive for the proposal was to end Scott's relentless levies and seizures, which helped pay for the army's subsistence. During the occupation's first months, he collected $220,000 through government fund seizures and from so-called "in-lieu-of-pillage" donations from wealthy businessmen and landowners; licensing fees; and the sale of confiscated tobacco. Consequently, Scott was able to give a new blanket and two pairs of shoes to each soldier, to pay every wounded man $10 cash upon his discharge from the hospital, and to send $118,000 to establish an "Army Asylum" in Washington, D.C. for disabled enlisted men (today known as the Armed Forces Retirement Home). Years later, Scott asked the U.S. government for a 5 percent commission—$11,000—for raising the money. War

Secretary Jefferson Davis, perhaps because he believed that Scott had under-mined Davis's former father-in-law, Zachary Taylor, challenged the claim, and it was not paid.

• • •

At Saltillo, thousands of frustrated late-enlisted volunteers, without hope of ever seeing action, waited for the war and their enlistments to end. Zachary Taylor complained that Scott and War Secretary William Marcy "conceived I had not only done enough but quite too much; & I hardly think I will be placed in a sit-uation to accomplish anything of importance. . . ." Most of Taylor's troops felt the same way; they had enlisted to fight, not to be idle for weeks on end.

Unsurprisingly, there was trouble in the American camps. Whiskey, brandy, pulque, and mescal fueled drunken brawls and shootings. Two Virginia lieutenants dueled with muskets at thirty-five paces and were both killed. Commissary live-stock disappeared and later were found slaughtered with the meat left to rot.

Taylor and his staff punished offenders severely: stocks; flogging; marching for hours with a heavy weight; the dreaded "bucking and gagging"; and the hated "punishment horse," a high, narrow plank that a soldier might have to sit upon in discomfort and, later, in agony, for a day or more, his feet not touching the ground.

Amid this volatile mix of idle men, alcohol, and firearms, ethnicity and poli-tics sometimes supplied the spark that ignited roaring mayhem. One of the worst outbreaks occurred on a steamer near Camargo, where two companies of Georgia volunteers—one Irish Catholic and the other Protestant—brawled with pistols, muskets, sabers, knives, and fists. While trying to break up the melee, Colonel Edward D. Baker of the Fourth Illinois Volunteers was shot in the cheek and stabbed in the mouth. Baker's Illinoisans were finally compelled to open fire on the rioters, killing eight volunteers and wounding twenty more. Thomas Tennery of the Fourth Illinois reported that when he boarded the steamer the next day, he "could hear the blood scrush under the carpet from one boat's [end] to the other."

But politics and discipline, and not religion, were responsible for the so-called "Paine Mutiny," the war's only full-scale soldier insurrection. Departing from the usual practice of a regiment's soldiers electing their leaders, North Carolina's gov-ernor and General Assembly had appointed Colonel Robert T. Paine commander of the First North Carolina Infantry Regiment. This alone would not have been enough to set off even a rowdy unit like the First North Carolina, but Paine's political affiliation exacerbated matters; Paine, like the governor and most of Paine's fellow state legislators, was a Whig, while the regiment's troops were overwhelmingly Democrat. Worse, Paine was a martinet who severely punished even minor infractions. When he built a punishment horse, the trouble began.

Troops from the First Virginia Infantry Regiment and the Second Mississippi Rifles, whose encampments adjoined North Carolina's, destroyed the horse on the night of August 14, 1847, to discourage their own officers from adopting Paine's draconian measures. The next night, soldiers threw rocks at Paine's tent. Outside, he was met by a mob of cursing, threatening soldiers—Virginians, Mississippians, and a few North Carolinians—who threw rocks at him. With only his drum major by his side, Paine, armed with two pistols, ordered the men to disperse. When they did not, Paine fired into the crowd, killing one soldier and slightly wounding another. A short time later, General John Wool's regulars marched into the encampment and restored order.

The matter was far from being over. In his tent the next morning, Paine found a note, signed by nearly all of his officers, demanding his resignation. Confronted by superiors, most of the officers subsequently withdrew their names from the petition. Wool issued dishonorable discharges to two lieutenants and two privates, and an Army court of inquiry upheld the actions of Paine and Wool.

When the lieutenants, both Democrats, appealed their dismissals directly to Polk, the president restored their commissions—an instance of politics trumping Army discipline.

• • •

In Mexico City, gangs of ruffians, robbers, and disaffected former Mexican soldiers preyed on the Americans. In one night, September 26, ten U.S. soldiers were murdered. In response, Scott ordered the city's saloons to close at 6 P.M. George Kendall of the New Orleans *Picayune* ruminated that Scott's army, large enough to win the war, was too small, with six to seven thousand men, to be an effective occupation force. Kendall recommended the addition of fifty thousand troops, as withdrawal from Mexico City was out of the question, for it would be "proof positive of our inability to sustain ourselves in the heart of the Republic."

The bushwhackings were at their zenith when Colonel Jack Coffee Hays's First Texas Mounted Regiment entered Mexico City after months of pursuing guerrillas and robbers on the National Highway. It might have been true, as some Mexicans said, that the Rangers improperly grabbed Mexican women, beat up Mexican men, and shot a boy for stealing a bandanna. Whatever the reasons, a Ranger named Adam Allsens, while riding in broad daylight through a district of the city fittingly nicknamed "Cutthroat," was swarmed by robbers in the street and slashed with knives. Slumped over the pommel of his horse, Allsens somehow managed to return to the Rangers' camp, although so eviscerated that his heart could be seen beating through his ribs. He died hours later. For the rest of the day, Hays's Rangers appeared subdued over their comrade's brutal slaying. But that night, they slipped out of camp to obtain revenge.

Litters hauled the dead Mexican men to the city morgue all that night and throughout the next morning. By breakfast time, fifty-three corpses had been counted, and, by noon, more than eighty. All the victims had been shot down in the streets and left to die.

Besieged by complaints from city officials, Scott demanded an explanation from Hays. The colonel, who had not participated in the killings, defended his men. Scott took no action against the Rangers.

Days later, the Rangers clashed again with local insurgents. They killed six Mexicans who threw large rocks at them from a roof, and shot four people in a mob that stoned them. The ruthless reprisals caused a sharp decline in attacks on American soldiers. Scott, however, prudently assigned the Rangers to new duties outside Mexico City.

• • •

In the backcountry again, Hays and his Rangers were tracking guerrillas near Galaxa Pass when they flushed a thousand Mexican lancers, dispersing them. Then the Rangers picked up the trail of Santa Anna, who had vanished after Huamantla. Hays and his 350 men nearly captured him at Tehuacan, about seventy-five miles southeast of Puebla, but Santa Anna escaped, leaving behind most of his possessions. The Rangers divided up Santa Anna's uniforms, bejeweled walking canes, and other souvenirs and sent a ceremonial sword to President Polk, and the desperado general's clothing to his wife, with their compliments.

Santa Anna's army had melted away, and the Mexican government had stripped him of his generalship and announced plans to court-martial him. Now, driven from his refuge at Tehuacan, he wished only to return to exile. Mexican officials eventually permitted Santa Anna to sail to Jamaica, and he later lived in Colombia. His exile, however, was not permanent.

• • •

In February 1848, in the streets of Sequalteplan, Hays's regiment, 130 troopers from the Third U.S. Dragoons under Major William H. Polk (the president's younger brother), and a company of rifleman battled four hundred guerrillas commanded by Father Celestino Domeco de Jarauta. Capturing the town, the Americans killed and wounded 150 Mexicans and took fifty prisoners, with a loss of one dead and four wounded.

DECEMBER 1847: MEXICO CITY

Secretary of State Buchanan's two letters recalling Nicholas Trist had reached him on November 16, and Trist was now ready to leave Mexico and return to private life in the United States. Trist had read Buchanan's letters to British attaché Edward Thornton and had informed President Manuel de la Peña y Peña of his recall. Thornton and Peña y Peña together wrote Trist a letter urging him to disregard his recall and to continue negotiations; his departure would encourage Mexico's war hawks to resume the war. However, Trist intended to obey Buchanan. He had asked his wife to inform Buchanan that he would not return to the State Department, but planned to "bid adieu forever to official life. This decision is irrevocable."

In his November 27 response to Buchanan, Trist noted, without disputing its accuracy, that the reason for his dismissal appeared to be "a mere offer to refer a question to my government"—the question being the location of the Texas border. Trist advised Buchanan to appoint a new peace commissioner before Mexico's new Congress convened on January 8. In passing, he said his departure had been delayed until Scott could spare troops to escort him to Vera Cruz.

Trist appeared resigned to leaving Mexico. He had wound up his affairs and packed his bags. But in delaying his departure, Trist had unwittingly, or calculatingly —no one will ever know—opened himself to the entreaties of those who wanted him to remain. Their numbers grew steadily to include, besides Peña y Peña and Thornton, Mexican officials and British merchants who longed for peace, and even General Winfield Scott.

• • •

At the last minute, Trist decided not to leave Mexico City and to continue to negotiate. "This determination, I came to, this day at 12 o'clock," he told his wife in a letter dated December 4. "It is altogether my own." As he explained to British attaché Thornton, he now believed it imperative that a peace agreement be struck now. "If the present opportunity be not seized *at once,* all chance for making a treaty *at all* will be lost for an indefinite period—probably forever."

This conviction informed the rambling, sixty-five-page letter to Buchanan announcing that he was disobeying his recall. America desired peace, and the opportunity to obtain a treaty would be lost if it were not now pursued, Trist wrote. He cannily noted that the U.S. government was "at perfect liberty to dis-avow my proceeding, would it be deemed disadvantageous to our country." "Everything was seen upside down" by the Polk administration, alleged Trist, because it was receiving distorted information from General Gideon Pillow that had unfortunately persuaded the government to curtail negotiations.

But Trist was wrong; Pillow had not influenced the decision to end negotia-tions; it was a direct result of the Mexican counterproposal of late August, during the false armistice. However, Pillow, Polk's friend and former law partner, in fact did write letters to the president, and their backdoor correspondence portended no good for Trist but especially bode ill for Winfield Scott.

• • •

Polk was unaware of these developments as he polished his Third Annual Message to Congress. In it, for the first time, he specifically declared that California and New Mexico would be part of any peace treaty with Mexico. Forswearing any Mexican territory, as the war opponents were urging, "would be a public acknowl-edgment that our country was wrong, and that the war declared by Congress with extraordinary unanimity was unjust, and should be abandoned."

Since Polk's inauguration in 1845, California had been one of the surpassing objects of his presidency. Not only would California fulfill America's Manifest Destiny, transforming her into a continental nation, but the new territory would be a place where working men could become yeoman farmers and escape the growing wage dependency of the Eastern industrial cities.

Yet the president never alluded to this neo-Jeffersonian vision but instead framed the issue of California as a national security matter. If America relin-quished California, European powers might be tempted to claim it for themselves, Polk warned. "We might be involved in other wars more expensive and more dif-ficult than that in which we are now engaged." In this lay a kernel of truth at the end of a chain of assumptions, some of them false. As for New Mexico, it was "a frontier province, and has never been of any considerable value to Mexico," he observed dismissively, implying that it would be better off under U.S. jurisdiction. California and New Mexico "should never be surrendered to Mexico."

Since Scott's capture of Mexico City, some New York and Western Democrats had embraced the far more grandiose idea of annexing "All Mexico"—thereby establishing an American empire stretching from Canada to the Yucatan. "We must SEIZE HER MINES—hold her towns," the New York *Globe* declared, "for the good of both nations and the world at large." Because Mexico was incapable of self-government, asserted the "All Mexico" boosters, the United States should govern Mexico; her people would be grateful. The New York *Herald* fatuously observed: "Like the Sabine virgins, she [Mexico] will soon learn to love her ravisher."

But there was broad opposition to the "All Mexico" movement. Southerners blanched at the prospect of Mexico, not only becoming a free territory, but of her mixed-race inhabitants being offered U.S. citizenship. Conversely, Northern congressmen feared that it would become a *slave* territory. Others believed that the two nations were impossibly incompatible. "If we take Mexico into the Union . . . we take in her politics also," warned the *National Intelligencer.* This "bloated scheme of conquest" would backfire, the *Intelligencer* darkly predicted, with the absorption of "the spirit of her people, their narrow views, their taste for intrigue, their ignorance or disregard of the principles of individual freedom."

In his Third Message, Polk abjured any Mexican territory south of the thirty-second parallel, and within a few months, the "All Mexico" movement died a quiet death.

26

PEACE AT LAST

"Negotiated by an unauthorized agent, with an unacknowledged government; submitted by an accidental President, to a dissatisfied Senate, has, notwithstanding these objections in form, been confirmed. . . ."

—Philip Hone of New York on the peace treaty with Mexico

JANUARY 1848: WASHINGTON

Although 1848 portended peace with Mexico and the acquisition of vast new territories, President Polk faced several political crises. Characteristically, the president's response was to work harder to overcome them. Christmas Day had found him laboring on the "mass of business which I had accumulated on my table," as snow fell outside his window, his thoughts turning to his late friend and political ally Senator John Fairfield of Maine. The senator had died on Christmas Eve after undergoing knee surgery to reduce swelling. Treasury Secretary Robert Walker was recovering from his collapse in the Treasury building two weeks earlier. Balancing these reports of death and decay was news that the president's nephew and private secretary, Joseph Knox Walker, was the proud father of a newborn son.

On New Year's Day, Polk shook hands for four hours with guests attending the White House's traditional reception. Afterward, the "considerably wearied" president resumed his consultations with advisers about the latest and most pressing of the thorny problems facing him: the battle royale in Mexico City between General Scott and three of his high-ranking officers: Generals William Worth and Gideon Pillow, and Colonel James Duncan of the field artillery.

• • •

The controversy would have been dismissed as insignificant—two anonymous, unauthorized letters published in U.S. newspapers during the fall of 1847 that credited Pillow and Worth for some of the Army's recent victories—had it not involved the Army's top echelon. But because Scott had arrested the three subordinate officers, and because Worth had brought countercharges against Scott, the feud was the talk of the Army—and, when the facts became known in Washington, the talk of the capital as well.

Scott's reaction to the letters was both irrational and understandable—irrational in the sense that his touchy ego could not abide others getting credit that he believed was his due; understandable because he had long known that high-ranking officers appointed by the Polk administration, especially Generals Pillow, Franklin Pierce, and Caleb Cushing, had been sending private letters to the president and his advisers, and that Polk routinely pumped other officers for information when they returned to Washington. With good reason, Scott suspected that these reports usually did not redound to his credit. It troubled him greatly: "If I had lost the campaign it would have been difficult to heap upon me greater vexations and mortifications." Pillow's unabashed self-promotion and his close friendship with the president made him a bête noire of Scott, who described the Tennessee lawyer as "the only person I have ever known who was wholly indifferent in the choice between truth and falsehood, honesty and dishonesty; —ever as ready to attain an end by one as the other." Amid this miasma of suspicion and hostility, Scott's inspector general, Lieutenant Colonel Ethan Allen Hitchcock, had even convinced himself that Polk had helped Pillow and Worth get the letters published. "They disgust the whole army," wrote Hitchcock, yet conceded that Worth was "not yet reduced to the low level" of Pillow.

When Pillow joined Scott's army in the fall of 1846, Polk had asked his former law partner to write to him about the Mexican people and Mexico's geography, problems encountered during the campaign, "and any other information or suggestions you may think proper to make. Your letters will not of course be regarded as official. . . ." But over the following year, Pillow had seldom corresponded with the president.

And then, a week before Christmas 1847, a Pillow letter of surpassing interest reached the White House, informing the president of a matter that would prove as vexing to him as would Scott's feud with his generals. Evidently because of his deteriorating relations with Scott over the published letters, Pillow had decided on October 28 to tell Polk about Scott's and Nicholas Trist's July peace overture to

Santa Anna, sweetened by $10,000 cash and the promise of an additional $1 million when a treaty was ratified.

Pillow's account of the failed peace overture—a revelation to Polk and Secretary of State Buchanan, who had known nothing of it—landed like a firebrand in sawdust. Polk had not flinched from secretly letting Santa Anna through the U.S. blockade, or from asking Congress for $3 million in "ready money" for a peace treaty, but he now railed against Scott and Trist for acting contrary to "the national character." After Polk read Pillow's letter to his cabinet on December 18, his advisers "condemned the proceedings unqualifiedly." Three days later, Buchanan was writing in a letter to Trist of his hope that "you have not engaged in a transaction which would cover with merited disgrace all those who may have participated in it, and fix an indelible stain upon the character of our country." To Pillow, Polk wrote, "I am amazed that a proceeding so . . . calculated . . . to effect [sic] the national character, should ever have been commenced or suggested."

Polk was preoccupied with this crisis until December 30, when he received Scott's report on the arrests of Pillow, Worth, and Duncan for insubordination.

• • •

Generals Pillow and Worth epitomized the polarities found in Scott's officer corps. Pillow had risen to high rank because of his friendship with Polk and had never shed his politician's instinct for self-promotion. Regular Army officers and soldiers distrusted his judgment and derided his attempts to portray himself as a martial hero. "General Pillow has made himself the laughing-stock of the army," noted George Kendall of the New Orleans *Picayune*. "It is because [he] has the vanity to believe himself a great and most astounding military genius and the impudence to trumpet his own exploits. . . ." However, Army officers, sensible of Pillow's friendship with the president, were careful to conceal their disdain. General Zachary Taylor, who regarded Pillow as "a very small man in every respect," had even cautioned his subordinates to treat him with courtesy.

Conversely, officers respected the self-effacing Worth, a career officer who was regarded as able and brave, while sometimes impetuous. Worth had served on Scott's staff during the War of 1812 and the Black Hawk War. The men had been close friends over three decades, to the extent that Worth had named his son Winfield Scott Worth. But their friendship had recently ended. The breach had opened between them when Scott praised General Twiggs for flanking Cerro Gordo, but not Worth for his diversionary frontal assault—probably because

Pillow had botched the demonstration. Then, in Puebla, Scott had overturned Worth's proclamation sustaining existing Mexican law and had instead imposed martial law; and he had withdrawn Worth's circular to the troops warning about a possible conspiracy to poison them. Worth had indignantly demanded a court of inquiry, which returned no conclusive findings. Worth later changed his son's name to William Scott Worth.

• • •

The objectionable letters appeared in the New Orleans *Delta* under the pseudonym "Leonidas," and in the Pittsburgh *Post,* signed by "Veritas." The Leonidas letter laughably credited Pillow's "masterly military genius" for the victories at Contreras and Chapultepec, which were "unparalleled in the history of the world," surpassing even Napoleon's great triumphs. Veritas more reasonably noted that Worth and Duncan had located the route around Lake Chalco that spared the Army a battle at El Peñon. This, in fact, was true; Worth had sent Duncan to reconnoiter the lake after Scott's engineers had assayed El Peñon's daunting defenses. Following Duncan's reconnaissance, Worth had recommended marching south and west around Mexico City, and making Tacubaya the American operations base—advice that Scott had taken. While some accounts have suggested that Scott, possibly urged by his engineers, had ordered Worth to scout the Lake Chalco area, the claims made by the Veritas letter were essentially true, while the Leonidas letter's assertions were patently false.

Pillow later admitted that a Major Burns, with "strictly true" information supplied by Pillow, had written the *Delta* letter; it contained the same information that was in Pillow's highly colored, self-congratulatory after-battle report on Contreras, which Scott had ordered rewritten. While Pillow essentially was "Leonidas," Worth was not "Veritas;" it was Duncan, whose private letter to a Pittsburgh friend had been published without Duncan's permission.

After reading the Leonidas letter in the *Delta,* and the Veritas letter when it was reprinted in a Tampico newspaper, Scott angrily issued Order No. 349, prohibiting the public dissemination of unauthorized reports, or, in Scott's vernacular, "despicable self-puffings." The November 12 order identified Pillow and Worth as the culprits without actually naming them: "It requires not a little charity to believe, that the principal heroes of the scandalous letters alluded to, did not write them, or specially procure them."

With suspicion falling heavily on his commander, Duncan acknowledged that he was Veritas in a letter in the *North American,* an English-language Mexico City newspaper. Meanwhile, Worth demanded that Scott state whether he was accusing him. Scott's aide, his son-in-law, Major Henry L. Scott, slyly replied that the reference was to the letters' authors, "be they who they may." Dissatisfied, Worth, as was his right under military regulations, protested to President Polk, and complained to War Secretary William Marcy about Scott's "malice and gross injustice" toward him, behavior *"unbecoming an officer, and a gentleman."*

For presuming to write directly to Polk and Marcy, Worth was arrested for insubordinately bypassing military channels. Worth retaliated with charges against Scott. Then Pillow and Duncan were arrested for insubordination: Duncan for the Veritas letter, and Pillow for circumventing Scott to ask Marcy for a hearing. The Army of Occupation buzzed with the news.

• • •

Making up for his previously erratic correspondence with Polk, Pillow wrote the president long letters skewering Scott and Trist. "His [Scott's] hostility towards me you know, and its cause—He is as bitter towards Worth as myself and adopts this mode to gratify his malice and private hate," Pillow railed in a fourteen-page letter. "I therefore earnestly invoke the immediate interposition of the Govt. of my country to protect me against the present unlawful arrest. . . ." In Pillow's view— and he was correct in his main point, but not in casting himself as blameless— partisan politics was responsible. Duncan's "sin is that he is a Devoted Democrat, & not one of S—'s worshippers." If such abuses were not stopped, "the checks and guarantees of the Magna Carta (Constitution) [are] but a dead letter." He urged the president to recall Scott. Scott had no support and would be eviscerated by Taylor's supporters, Worth's friends, and the Whig and Democrat media, pre-dicted Pillow. "His follies, blunders & orders & outrageous conduct place him perfectly in your power—Your hands are untied—You can do as you please with him, for he is a 'dead cock in the Pot.' "

Polk had reached the same conclusion. Even before Pillow's letter reached him in January, Polk had read Scott's account of the contretemps, the objectionable let-ters themselves, and Worth's countercharge. He had concluded that Scott was entirely to blame. "This whole difficulty among the Gen'l officers of the army might have been avoided but for the folly, the vanity, and tyranny of Gen'l Scott," who was disposed to "extreme jealousy lest any other Gen'l Officer should acquire more fame in the army than himself."

No less insightfully, the president put his finger on the matter's salient point: "Without expressing any opinion upon the merits or truth of these letters, there seems to have been no necessity to make so serious an affair of them as to break up the harmony and efficiency of the army while in the enemy's country. The whole matter is most unfortunate."

War Secretary Marcy admonished Scott for prosecuting Worth for having exercised his lawful right to appeal. "The precedent will be most fatal to the essential rights of all subordinate officers."

• • •

Polk and his advisers decided that Scott must go. The president rejected a suggestion that Scott be replaced by General Taylor, because of "the trouble he had given and our dissatisfaction with him." Scott's successor would be General William O. Butler, who had fought at New Orleans in 1815 and had practiced law since then.

Scott, who had led the boldest, most successful military campaign in U.S. history, was relieved of command. Butler was instructed to convene a Court of Inquiry in the Scott–Pillow–Worth–Duncan feud at the Castle at Perote, and to release from custody Pillow, Worth, and Duncan.

• • •

The Marine Corps, which had recently proven itself as effective on land as at sea, was trying to squelch ugly allegations of cowardice in the heat of battle. While Commandant Archibald Henderson had been burnishing the Corps's reputation as an elite organization, Lieutenant John S. Devlin had accused Captain John G. Reynolds and other officers of shirking during the fighting southeast of Chapultepec, in which Devlin had been wounded, and Major Levi Twiggs killed. Evidently dissatisfied with the chain of command, Devlin had gone public with his allegations in a newspaper article. This was too much for Henderson, who court-martialed and dismissed Devlin for slandering his fellow officers.

• • •

With correspondence taking six weeks to travel between Mexico City and Washington, the Polk administration was acting on old news, while hoping that its measures would still be timely when they reached the U.S. command. They often were not. When Buchanan received a letter on January 3 from Nicholas Trist reporting that new Mexican peace commissioners had been named, Polk and his advisers did not yet know that Trist had decided to disregard his recall and continue negotiating. A day after the cabinet debated whether General Butler should assume Trist's responsibilities as well as Scott's, a report reached the White House that *Trist* had renewed negotiations. Polk angrily concluded that Trist had "become the perfect tool of Scott. He seems to have entered into all Scott's hatred of the administration, and to be lending himself to all Scott's evil purposes."

The president read with impotent fury subsequent letters confirming that Trist had disobeyed his recall. To his brother William, the dragoon major, Polk confided: "I fear he will commit some other blunder (not to use a harsher term) such as that he did commit" in discussing with Mexican commissioners the possibility of a boundary other than the Rio Grande.

Trist's defiant letter of December 6 announcing that he was remaining in Mexico reached Washington on January 15. The president sputtered: "I have never in my life felt so indignant. . . . His dispatch is arrogant, impudent, and very insulting to his Government, and even personally offensive to the President." Marcy ordered General Butler to inform Mexican officials that Trist no longer represented the U.S. government, and to bar Trist from Army headquarters. But by the time Marcy's orders reached Butler, they were hopelessly outdated.

Indeed, during January and February, the crises thudded on Polk's desk one after another, beyond all previous experience. While the president had formerly been always on the offensive, pushing his legislative agenda and prosecuting the war, he now found himself unaccustomedly troubleshooting problems of his and others' making. Yet he seldom complained about the workload. As he attended to the knotty predicaments of Trist, and Scott and his generals, Polk also monitored the court-martial of Lieutenant Colonel John C. Frémont, whose arrest by General Stephen Kearny had tainted his celebrated, albeit mysterious, role in California's conquest. In addition, Congress began demanding documents, thereby raising questions about executive privilege and the public's right to know.

• • •

The Thirtieth Congress's new Whig-majority House, elected in the fall of 1846 and seated for the first time in December 1847, wasted no time in launching inquiries into the pretexts for the war and its conduct. Helping set Congress's tough, adversarial tone was Abraham Lincoln, the freshman from Illinois's Seventh District. Three days before Christmas, Lincoln boldly challenged Polk's assertion that Mexico had shed the "blood of our citizens on our own soil." Was "the spot" where American blood was spilled really part of the United States, or had the Adams–Onis Treaty of 1819 made it Mexican territory? Lincoln wanted to know. His resolution demanded documents proving the ownership of "the particular spot on which the blood of our citizens was shed" along the Rio Grande. "Let him remember he sits where Washington sat, and so remembering, let him answer, as Washington would answer." Polk did not. Lincoln's fellow Whigs began drafting a House resolution pronouncing the war to be unconstitutional.

On January 5, 1848, the House of Representatives asked the Polk administration to hand over all the letters and documents related to Santa Anna's repatriation to Mexico in August 1846; they also wanted to see John Slidell's instructions from late 1845. The initial reaction of Polk and Secretary of State Buchanan was to refuse, because to comply "would be greatly to the prejudice of the public interests." Polk believed that there was sufficient precedent for turning down such a request, noting that George Washington in 1796 had rejected a House request for documents regarding the controversial Jay Treaty with Great Britain.

Polk and his advisers decided on January 8 that "it was my duty to refuse a compliance" with the request for Slidell's instructions, and to withhold the administration's communications with Alexander Slidell Mackenzie during his secret trip to Havana in July 1846, when Mackenzie had informed Santa Anna that he would be permitted to pass through the U.S. blockade of Mexico. "The judgment of the world would condemn [us], & . . . no Government would ever again trust us" if the Mackenzie documents were released, said Buchanan. Polk and his advisers agreed to release only the Navy Secretary's May 13, 1846 order to Commodore David Conner to permit Santa Anna to reenter Mexico.

The Polk administration quickly complied with a request that it had probably initiated in the friendly, Democrat-controlled Senate—for the correspondence between Trist and Mexican negotiators during the post-Churubusco armistice. Giving no thought to executive privilege, the president also handed over, without even being asked, his letter disapproving of Trist's invitation to the Mexicans to propose the Nueces as the U.S.–Mexican boundary; Polk was certain that the Senate would condemn Trist's actions. With the same certitude of his correctness, Polk readily complied when Whigs requested all the correspondence between the Polk administration and its generals.

The Washington *Union,* which had proclaimed the "Madness of the Whigs" in one of its headlines, accused them now of prolonging the war and, thus, aiding the enemy. "At this very moment Mexico holds out the war *exclusively* on the arguments and pretences which the opposition orators and presses among ourselves have framed for her and instructed her to employ."

• • •

Alarmed by the internal party schisms laid bare by the Wilmot Proviso, a procession of Democratic leaders urged Polk to abandon his promise to not seek a second term, and to run again in the fall. Senators Arthur Bagby of Alabama and Hopkins L. Turney of Tennessee tried to persuade the president to at least not rule out the possibility, "if the party would find it to be necessary to re-nominate" him. But Polk unequivocally declined. "I told them that my decision had been long since been made . . . and that I looked forward to the period of my retirement with sincere pleasure."

• • •

The Whig-majority House approved a resolution, by the close vote of 85–81, condemning the Mexican War as "unnecessarily and unconstitutionally begun by the President of the United States." Declared Lincoln: "Allow the President to invade a neighboring nation, whenever he shall deem it necessary to repel an invasion . . . and you allow him to make war at pleasure." Lincoln had previously characterized the remarks about the war in Polk's Third Message to Congress as "the half insane mumbling of a fever-dream. . . . His mind, tasked beyond its power, is running hither and thither, like some tortured creature, on a burning surface, finding no position, on which it can settle down, and be at ease." Lincoln's Illinois constituents took a dim view of his criticism of the war; his would-be Whig successor (Lincoln had forsworn a second term) was defeated in the fall election, and the loss was blamed on Lincoln.

The House resolution coincided with growing public dissatisfaction with the war. At an antiwar rally in Lexington, Kentucky, seventy-year-old Henry Clay, whose son had been killed at Buena Vista (three other senators also lost sons during the war: Daniel Webster of Massachusetts, John Tipton of Indiana, and Daniel Sturgeon of Pennsylvania), declared that the war was "actuated by a spirit of rapacity, and an inordinate desire for territorial aggrandizement. . . . It is Mexico that is defending her fire-sides, her castles and her altars, not we." No Mexican territory should be annexed, "to disabuse the public mind . . . of the impression . . . that the desire for such a conquest, is cherished for the purpose of propagating or extending slavery."

But after a year and three quarters of war and thousands of deaths, there was little public support for abjuring the annexation of conquered Mexican provinces.

• • •

At noon on November 2, 1847 (Polk's fifty-second birthday), Brevet Brigadier General G. M. Brooke convened the court-martial of Lieutenant Colonel John C. Frémont in the drafty old Washington armory. Brooke and eleven Army officers sat in judgment, while a captain acted as prosecutor. Frémont obtained the court's permission to be advised by civilian attorneys, who included William Carey Jones and Frémont's father-in-law, Senator Thomas Hart Benton. Nearly all the leading actors in the conquest of California were present: General Stephen Watts Kearny; Frémont; Kearny's adjutant, Captain Henry S. Turner; Commodore Robert F. Stockton; and Marine Captain Archibald Gillespie. The dashing explorer's highly anticipated trial was a welcome change from the usual Washington business of politics and war, and most of official Washington visited the spectator galleries at least once during the next three months.

Frémont was charged with mutiny, disobeying the lawful command of a superior officer, and conduct prejudicial to good order and military discipline. Acting upon Navy Secretary George Bancroft's July 1845 orders, Stockton had named Frémont military governor of California. But in 1846, General Winfield Scott and Bancroft's successor had directed *Kearny* to establish a civil government "should you conquer and take possession of California." Invoking this authority, Kearny had ordered Frémont in January 1847 to relinquish his duties to him, Frémont's superior. Frémont had replied that Stockton, not Kearny, was his commanding officer and had refused to obey Kearny's order. The stalemate had lasted until the arrival of Stockton's successor, Commodore William Branford Shubrick, who upheld Kearny.

Kearny testified that Frémont so badly wanted to be governor that he ignored the chain of command; Frémont's attorneys accused Kearny of vindictiveness. Benton complained that Kearny, knowing that he would charge Frémont at Fort Leavenworth, had thought to bring his witnesses East with him. Frémont was handicapped by Stockton being his only witness—and such a poor one that Frémont suspected that he had made a deal with Kearny.

As the trial was winding down in late January 1848, two things had become apparent to all: each of the two ranking officers in California, Stockton and Kearny, had believed that only he had authority to establish a civil government; and Frémont had been caught in the middle.

Frémont did his cause no good by badgering Kearny during cross-examination and exposing Kearny's embarrassing lapses of memory and his other shortcomings. Handsome, popular, well-connected, and more polished and articulate than the rough-hewn Kearny, whose entire career had been spent on the frontier, Frémont also profited from having his senator father-in-law and another lawyer at his elbow advising him, and his beautiful young wife, Jessie Benton Frémont, lending moral support from the gallery. Nonetheless, these advantages might not have sat well with the twelve Army trial officers—men like Kearny who had slowly advanced through the ranks after years of hard service.

On January 31, the court-martial panel found Frémont guilty of all the charges and sentenced him to be discharged from the Army. Benton would claim that it was West Point getting its revenge, when in fact just five of the trial officers were U.S. Military Academy graduates.

Moreover, while all twelve officer-judges had found Frémont guilty of all counts, six of them made an unusual recommendation—that the president grant Frémont clemency, because he had been "placed between two officers of superior rank, each claiming to command-in-chief in California."

• • •

While Polk knew and admired Frémont and had sanctioned his paramilitary adventures in California, he was determined to render a disinterested decision. He devoted up to twenty hours during the first two weeks of February to reading and rereading the trial transcript. He discussed the case with his cabinet on three occasions. On February 16, Polk announced that he would "remit the penalty and restore Lieut. Col. Frémont to duty."

But Frémont bitterly rejected the president's clemency and refused to return to military service. He led two more expeditions to the West. The first one, over the winter of 1848–1849, exposed Frémont and his men to extraordinary hardship. California's first governor became one of its first U.S. senators when California became a state in 1850.

• • •

Trist and the Mexican commissioners were making steady progress toward a peace treaty. The Mexicans were at last reconciled to a Rio Grande boundary between Mexico and the United States, and to ceding New Mexico and California, for a price. However, the amount remained a negotiable issue, as did the southern boundary of California.

While Trist had stopped trying to obtain Lower (Baja) California, and Mexico was ready to sell Upper California, Mexico claimed the boundary between the two lay north of San Diego, and Trist argued that it was south of San Diego. Alexander von Humboldt, topographical engineer Robert E. Lee, and others asserted that the boundary had always been below San Diego. The Mexicans hunted through old books and maps for evidence to the contrary. Unable to find any corroboration, the Mexican commissioners agreed to a boundary three miles south of the port of San Diego.

Mexico demanded $30 million for New Mexico and California. Trist, who had once suggested $20 million as a possible price, now refused to pay more than $15 million. The Mexican negotiators said that if they reduced their asking price, the provinces would revolt against the government.

Trist had ruined his diplomatic career by listening to Mexican officials who had urged him to continue the peace talks, recall or no. Now, faced with the possibility that it might have all been for nothing, he threatened to break off negotiations unless a treaty was signed by February 1. More ominously, General Scott began preparing to renew military operations.

The measured threats had the desired effect. On January 31, over the objections of former President Mariano Paredes y Arrillaga and other leaders, as well as radical "puros" who wanted to continue the war, the government-in-exile in Querétaro authorized the peace commissioners to accept Trist's final proposal.

The Mexican commissioners had parleyed with Trist in Mexico City, but they now insisted that the treaty not be signed under "the muzzles of American cannon," but at Guadalupe Hidalgo, a northern suburb adjoining the famous Catholic shrine.

• • •

At 6 P.M. on February 2, Trist and Mexican commissioners Luis G. Cuevas, Jose Bernardo Couto, and Miguel Atristain signed the Treaty of Guadalupe Hidalgo, ending the Mexican War.

It transferred to the United States more than five hundred thousand square miles, or nearly half of Mexico's territory—practically everything that Polk had sought. The new boundary traced the Rio Grande from the Gulf of Mexico to New Mexico's southern border at the thirty-second parallel, then ran due west before jogging north to the Gila River, following it to the Colorado River, and thence to the border between Upper and Lower California, and the Pacific Ocean.

The treaty required the United States to pay $15 million and assume responsibility for the $3.2 million in outstanding claims by U.S. citizens against Mexico. Upon the treaty's ratification by both nations, America would immediately pay Mexico $3 million cash; the balance would be disbursed in four annual installments, at 6 percent interest. It was a magnificent bargain, on the order of the 828,000-square-mile Louisiana Territory, purchased for $15 million nearly a half century earlier.

Trist sent the treaty with a cover letter to Washington by special courier, New Orleans *Delta* correspondent James D. Freanor (who signed his articles "Mustang"). Trist's letter began:

"I transmit herewith, the Treaty of peace, Friendship, Limits and Settlement signed one hour ago at the city of Guadalupe; a spot which, agreeably to the creed of this country, is the most sacred on earth, as being the scene of the miraculous appearance of the Virgin, for the purpose of declaring that Mexico was taken under her special protection."

Years later, when his anger toward the U.S. government had reached fullness, Trist professed to having felt ashamed when he signed the treaty, believing it to be unfair to Mexico. "Had my course . . . been governed by my conscience as a man and my sense of justice as an individual American, I should have yielded [to Mexico] in every instance."

• • •

In Washington, the treaty was met by frowning suspicion. Freanor delivered it on Saturday night, February 19, to Secretary of State Buchanan, who rushed with it to the White House, even though it was nine o'clock, and read it to Polk. After hearing it through once, the president coolly granted that "the terms of the Treaty are within his [Trist's] instructions which he took out in April last" and said that if it withstood closer scrutiny it "should not be rejected on account of his [Trist's] bad conduct."

Over the next two days, Polk put Trist's handiwork under the microscope but found no flaws. In his journal entries, one senses disappointment, rather than exultation that Trist had secured the very treaty that he had been sent to get. At Monday's cabinet meeting, Polk said that because Congress had recently condemned his reasons for going to war, he could not unilaterally reject the treaty but must submit it to the Senate. "If I were now to reject a Treaty made upon my own terms . . . the probability is that Congress would not grant either men or money to prosecute the war. Should this be the result, the army now in Mexico would be constantly wasting and diminishing in numbers, and I might at last be compelled to withdraw them, and thus loose [*sic*] the two provinces of New Mexico & Upper California, which were ceded to the U.S. by this Treaty."

When Buchanan objected that the United States should have obtained more territory, all the way south to "the line of the Sierra Madre," Polk lost patience with him. The president reminded Buchanan that when Congress declared war, Buchanan had opposed annexing any Mexican land, and had even wanted to publicly disavow all such designs. Buchanan replied that the twenty-one-month war's expenditures of blood and money entitled the United States to compensation. Polk didn't believe it; the real reason, he was certain, was politics. "He [Buchanan] is now a candidate for the presidency, and he does not wish to incur the displeasure of those who are in favour of the conquest of all Mexico. . . . He is an unsafe adviser."

The president sent the treaty to the Senate the next day, but the Senate was in adjournment: John Quincy Adams had collapsed at his desk in the House of Representatives and lay in a coma in the Speaker's Room.

• • •

Because Adams had become a congressman after being president and therefore had never ceased being a political player, he was never a senior statesman-confidant to subsequent presidents. In December 1845, Navy Secretary George Bancroft, at Polk's behest, had invited Adams to dinner at the White House. Adams had good-humoredly told Bancroft that before he dined with the president, Polk owed him an "explanation" for having suggested that Adams had "unwisely" ceded Texas to Spain in the 1819 Adams–Onis Treaty. When Bancroft informed Polk, the president huffed that it was "a matter of no consequence" whether Adams accepted or not, and "certainly I had no explanations to make." Adams and Polk never dined together.

But when one of Adams's granddaughters visited the White House in April 1847, Polk had pointedly treated her "with marked respect, as it was her first visit," and had personally escorted her to that evening's reception. She was the only Adams to set foot in the White House during the Polk administration.

Adams had suffered a stroke in the fall of 1846 but had recovered and resumed his duties. The stroke that felled him at his desk in the House on February 21 was massive. He clung to life in the Speaker's Room for two days. The capital's annual Washington Birthday balls and banquets were canceled.

In his eighty-first year, Adams died on February 23 in the Speaker's Room. The government suspended all business for two days, and the White House front door was draped in black crepe. Polk morbidly noted that of America's chief executives, only he, Martin Van Buren, and John Tyler now survived.

• • •

The Senate Committee of Foreign Affairs, doubting that Nicholas Trist had the authority to negotiate, much less sign, a peace treaty, sent the Treaty of Guadalupe Hidalgo to the full Senate on February 28 with a "fail" recommendation. The Senate debated it in executive session. Senators Sam Houston and Jefferson Davis wanted more territory—everything north of Tampico—while Whigs raised the issue of slavery in the new territories, as well as Trist's recall, hoping to divide the Democrats and stall ratification. But none of the divisive amendments and resolutions, including the now twice-reprised Wilmot Proviso, was approved.

The Senate ratified the treaty on March 10 by a 38–14 vote. The renowned diarist Philip Hone of New York sardonically observed that the proposed treaty, "negotiated by an unauthorized agent, with an unacknowledged government; submitted by an accidental President, to a dissatisfied Senate, has, notwithstanding these objections in form, been confirmed. . . ." Mexico's ratification was the last remaining step before the treaty could take effect.

• • •

The Senate had approved the treaty, and the Army of Occupation was poised to demobilize, but in late March the Second Missouri Mounted Regiment was marching from Santa Fe to Chihuahua. General Sterling Price had been ordered to investigate reports, either spurious or outdated, that an enemy expeditionary force was assembling at Chihuahua. Price's regiment had crushed the Taos uprising in 1847 and since then had chafed at its New Mexico peacekeeping role while other units won laurels in Mexico. Price was not going to permit this last chance for military glory to pass him by. Thus, when Chihuahua Governor Angel Trias insisted that the war had ended, Price chose not to believe him.

The dragoons tracked down some Mexican troops still in the area and chased them to Santa Cruz de Rosales, where the two sides pointlessly fought house-to-house throughout March 16. Four Americans were killed, and nineteen were wounded. Price claimed that his men killed 328 Mexicans, certainly an inflated figure.

For unnecessarily prosecuting the final action of the Mexican War, Price was reprimanded by War Secretary William Marcy for having exceeded his orders. The Second Missouri was the last unit to return home from Mexican soil.

Price's driving ambition carried him to the Missouri governorship, and then to a major general's command in the Confederate Army. As unwilling to accept that war's end as he had been in 1848, Price rode into exile in Mexico in 1865. He later returned to Missouri, where he died in 1867.

• • •

Polk selected Senator Ambrose Sevier of Arkansas to hand-carry the U.S.-approved treaty to Mexico, and to bring home a Mexico-ratified treaty. But Sevier fell ill, and the president gave the ceremonial task to Attorney General Nathan Clifford. Sevier recovered to join Clifford in Mexico City, as the Mexican Congress debated the treaty through the end of April and into May. At Querétaro on May 30, Sevier and Clifford exchanged ratified treaties with Mexican officials, and the war officially ended.

On June 12, the United States formally ended its occupation of Mexico with a quiet ceremony in Mexico City's Grand Plaza. At 6 A.M., wrote Attorney General Clifford, "the flag of the U. States was taken down from the National Palace in this city, and that of the Mexican Republic was hoisted. The customary honors were paid to both, and the ceremony passed off in perfect quiet, although the great square was thronged. The last division of the army then evacuated the place, General [William O.] Butler and Mr. [Senator Ambrose] Sevier accompany it."

JULY 4, 1848: WASHINGTON

With the same Masonic trowel used by George Washington to lay the Capitol cornerstone in 1793, Polk on this auspicious day laid the cornerstone for the Washington Monument, whose site on the Mall he and a special committee had recently selected. Begun with private funds, the monument's completion lay thirty-six years in the future, realized only after the federal government took it over.

In attendance was the largest Washington crowd since William Henry Harrison's ill-fated inauguration in 1841. The marble cornerstone, quarried near Baltimore, had traveled to the site by train and then on a wagon escorted by U.S. Marines. During the last leg of the journey, a live eagle rode on a perch atop the marble stone.

Afterward, Polk returned to the White House, where he reviewed Army troops, some of them recently returned from Mexico, that were drawn up in ranks on Pennsylvania Avenue.

Late in the afternoon, a messenger arrived at the White House with dispatches and the Mexican-ratified Treaty of Guadalupe Hidalgo. Polk immediately summoned Secretary of State Buchanan and instructed him to draft a proclamation "announcing the definitive conclusion of peace with Mexico"; he wished to sign it on "the anniversary of Independence." At 11 o'clock that night, the president signed the proclamation.

• • •

In his message announcing the end of the Mexican War, Polk observed that the war had "given the United States a national character which our country never before enjoyed," as well as two enormous Mexican provinces that "constitute of themselves a country large enough for a great empire." Without exaggeration, he declared: "Their acquisition is second only in importance to that of Louisiana in 1803."

Indeed, in just two years, the United States had achieved her "Manifest Destiny" and had almost overnight ripened into a continental empire girding North America from Atlantic to Pacific. The difficult maturation process would last many decades more, yet already America was a world power to be reckoned with.

27

AFTERWORD

"Those who served the government well in that war with Mexico fared badly with the [Polk] administration."

—Missouri Senator Thomas Hart Benton

General of the Army Winfield Scott, who had prosecuted the most audacious military campaign since the Napoleonic Wars, was relieved of his Mexico command. A Court of Inquiry convened in Mexico City from April 13 to 22 for the twofold purpose of investigating the war of words between Scott and his three court-martialed subordinates, and of getting to the bottom of the attempted "bribery" of Santa Anna in July 1847. Dozens of officers on occupational duty testified at the Mexico City hearings. The court then moved to Frederick, Maryland, pursuing Scott on his unhappy journey home. Scott withdrew his charges against Colonel James Duncan, and General William Worth withdrew his accusations against Scott, but the other charges remained.

Alternately depressed and angry, the General of the Army demurred when his soldiers and Mexican officials proposed holding ceremonies and banquets in his honor. He turned down an invitation to a reception by the Aztec Club. He declined to meet many of the visitors who came to his headquarters to bid him farewell. Scott's replacement, General William Orlando Butler, a former Kentucky congressman who was just weeks away from being named the Democrats' 1848 vice presidential candidate, was sympathetic and tried to ease the pain of Scott's ignominious departure whenever possible. One of Butler's generous actions was to retain Lieutenant Colonel Ethan Allen Hitchcock as his inspector general. The day that he left Mexico City, Scott instructed Hitchcock to distribute his wine closet to friends.

Livid over the Polk administration's treatment of Scott, Hitchcock lashed out in his diary at the "mushroom generals"—political appointees who "know nothing of the science or art of war, and who, in fact, are indebted for all the reputation they ever acquire to the science in the main body of the old regular army, which many of them pretend to despise." Although not naming him, the tirade undoubtedly was aimed at General Gideon Pillow.

Lieutenant Daniel Hill, too, denounced "the arch-scoundrel Pillow. . . . That an idiot monkey could cause the greatest Captain of the age to be disgraced upon the very theatre of his glory will not be credited by posterity. The whole Army is indignant and only the new troops have any confidence in the weak old man who now commands the victorious Army of the immortal Scott."

On May 2, 1848, Scott left Mexico on the brig *Petersburg*. Just as he had requested, there were no bands, there was no parade, and few people greeted the conqueror of Mexico when he reached New York City.

• • •

Butler dutifully expelled Nicholas Trist from Army headquarters and placed him under house arrest. When the Court of Inquiry shifted its venue to Maryland, Trist followed in its train, scornfully describing the proceedings as a "pitiable device of the pitiable being in the Presidential chair." He believed that he would be vindicated by public outrage when Americans learned of the actions by government officials, whose "own ignoble hearts" would lull them into a false sense of security.

The Court of Inquiry concluded its proceedings in Maryland on July 6 without convicting or exonerating anyone. Polk let the matter lie. Pillow, whose agitated letters to Polk had precipitated Scott's dismissal, quietly withdrew his charges against Scott.

Perhaps in retaliation over Scott's removal, Army officials in Mexico court-martialed Pillow for taking two cannons captured at Chapultepec as personal trophies. However, Pillow and his lawyers convinced the court that Pillow's subordinates had put the guns in his baggage without his knowledge. The military court acquitted Pillow.

• • •

On a warm day in July 1848, Colonel Caleb Cushing's First Massachusetts Volunteers returned to Boston. Eager to see their long-absent sons, fathers, brothers, and friends, the people thronged the streets. But when they caught sight of their loved ones, they were mortified by their tatterdemalion appearance and thinned ranks. "They were ragged, dirty, worn down by fatigue, several of them sick & half starved," John Langdon Sibley noted. "Of [Colonel] Caleb Cushing they [the soldiers] spoke in terms of unexceptional hostility," and they "hissed & whistled" when Cushing spoke at a dinner held in the regiment's honor.

A third of the Massachusetts Volunteers did not come home at all. Disease and illness, not battle wounds, were responsible for their deaths; the regiment had seen no combat. The toll was not unusual in a war that claimed seven lives from illness and disease for every man killed in action.

But Caleb Cushing's regiment was exceptional in two respects: in its vehement dislike of its wealthy lawyer commander, who had raised the regiment with his own money and then alienated his men with his harsh discipline; and in hailing from the locus of the antiwar movement, Massachusetts. It was no wonder that the soldiers' homecoming was bittersweet.

• • •

Henry David Thoreau had decamped from Walden Pond and returned to Concord, having triumphantly completed *A Week on the Concord and Merrimack Rivers.* But to his chagrin, the book was such a resounding flop that seven hundred unsold copies ended up gathering dust in his attic. His self-confidence shaken, Thoreau withheld from publication the journal of his two years and two months at Walden Pond. But *Walden* would be all the better for his many revisions before its publication in 1854.

Perhaps not the pragmatic Polk, but possibly the idealistic Thomas Jefferson would have recognized a kindred spirit in Thoreau and appreciated his relentless individualism and suspicion of government—"I heartily accept the motto, 'That government is best which governs least'; and I should like to see it acted up to more rapidly and systematically"—and his severe disapproval of industrialism's excesses: "The condition of the operatives is becoming every day more like that of the English; and it cannot be wondered at, since . . . the principal object is, not that mankind may be well and honestly clad, but, unquestionably, that the corporations may be enriched." Interestingly, the minimalist government aphorism paraphrased by Thoreau came from the expansionist editor John O'Sullivan's introduction to his *United States Magazine and Democratic Review* in 1837.

• • •

In cities where the returning soldiers were welcomed with the largest, most enthusiastic celebrations—New York, Cincinnati, Philadelphia, and Pittsburgh—relatively few believed that the war, now that it had ended well for the United States, had squandered lives and money. Most Americans believed Mexico's subjugation and the acquisition of California and New Mexico well worth the price paid.

• • •

In dollars and cents, the war was a bargain, costing $140 million ($58 million for military operations; $18 million for the treaty; and $64 million in veterans' pensions and benefits paid out beginning in 1887)—or roughly 37 cents for each of the 530,706 square miles acquired through the Treaty of Guadalupe Hidalgo. During the sixteen months between Palo Alto and the fall of Mexico City, U.S. troops had won nearly every one of the thirty skirmishes and battles, while taking forty thousand enemy prisoners (some captured multiple times), and seizing a thousand cannons.

But in human terms, the Mexican War had the highest ratio of deaths to participants of any U.S. war: 125 per thousand, nearly twice the 65 deaths per thousand troops engaged during the Civil War. Of the 116,000 Americans under arms during the war, 1,721 were killed in action or died of their wounds, 4,102 were wounded, and 11,155 died of disease, illness, accidents, or other causes. Of the volunteer units, the Mississippi Rifles, Jefferson Davis's unit, sustained the most battle deaths, 59, followed closely by South Carolina's Palmetto Regiment, with 56 killed.

Mexican battle losses have been estimated at 14,700 killed and wounded, of the estimated 82,000 serving as regular troops or guerrillas. More than a thousand civilians were killed or wounded at Monterrey, Vera Cruz, Mexico City, and Huamantla.

America's victories inspired music, plays, novels, and fashion trends. Stephen Foster composed "Santa Anna's Retreat from Buena Vista," and John Hill Hewitt, sometimes called the "Father of the American Ballad," wrote "Look Upon That Banner." Among the songs collected and sold in songbooks were "The Rio Grande Quick March," and the extravagantly titled "The Fall of Vera Cruz and Surrender of the City & Castle of St. Juan D. Ulloa." There were theatrical productions titled "The Siege of Monterey, or The Triumph of Rough and Ready," "The Battle of Buena Vista and the Bombardment of Vera Cruz," and "The Battle of Mexico, or, The Capture of the Halls of the Montezumas." And there was a fecundity of "dime novels" featuring beautiful senoritas, brave Americans, and treacherous Mexicans, including *The Bridge of Buena Vista, The Maid of Matamoros, The Secret Service Ship,* and *The Texan Ranger.*

The returning soldiers wore "immense moustachios" and casually salted their speech with Spanish words—adobe, sombrero, corral, lasso, patio, chaparral, and fandango—that were soon absorbed into the vernacular. American war leaders and Mexican battlefields became popular place names. Iowa, a new state in 1846, named counties for Polk, Taylor, Scott, Worth, Ringgold, O'Brien, Buchanan, Frémont, Butler, Buena Vista, Cerro Gordo, and Palo Alto.

• • •

The Mexican War was the exclamation point on the Roaring '40s. The Industrial Age–equipped volunteer soldiers had demonstrated the power of the American dynamo. But the factories, the penny press, the telegraph, and the expanding railroad system were only outward manifestations: the real engines were a fierce nationalism and the incredibly optimistic belief, never before shared by an entire nation, that there were no limits to what people could accomplish.

It was no accident that "progress" and "reform" entered everyday speech during the '40s. Perhaps naively, Americans believed in mankind's perfectibility through inventions, better social arrangements, behavior modification, and education, and in a native, Thoreau-esque philosophy that celebrated the individual. These bracing articles of faith would enter a hiatus during the terrible conflict that lay a dozen years ahead.

The Mexican war abounded in American "firsts": the first successful offensive war, fought almost entirely in the enemy's country; the first large-scale amphibious landing; the first occupation of an enemy capital; the battlefield debut of the U.S. field artillery; the first time that large numbers of West Point graduates led troops into combat; and the first war in which the public read about developments in reporters' dispatches, not government announcements.

The penny press enabled Americans to vicariously roam the battlefields at Monterrey, Buena Vista, Cerro Gordo, Churubusco, and Chapultepec. The correspondents' incisive accounts helped fan the embers of nationalism, largely dormant since the wars with England. Fifty years would pass before anything like it would be seen again.

Abiel Abbot Livermore, a Unitarian minister and war opponent, believed these were troubling developments. The news accounts glorified violence, she said. "The seed of future wars has thus been sown broadcast over our country, and wrong impressions have been made upon thousands of young and ductile minds which will never be effaced." Indeed, the war stories surely fired the martial ardor of many boys who would joyously don Union blue or Confederate gray in 1861.

• • •

A week before Trist and the Mexican commissioners signed the Treaty of Guadalupe Hidalgo, New Jersey mechanic James W. Marshall discovered gold while building a sawmill for John A. Sutter in California's lower Sacramento Valley. The California gold rush was on. By the end of 1849, California's hills and valleys teemed with a hundred thousand people who had come from all over the United States and abroad, hoping to strike it rich. In 1851, the "Forty-niners" mined gold worth an estimated $55 million—over $1 billion in modern currency.

California was not only America's Eldorado but also its new window on the Pacific. As they had long dreamed of doing, Northeastern businessmen utilized California's excellent harbors to expand their trade in the Far East. In the early 1850s, President Millard Fillmore's administration sent Commodore Matthew Perry to Japan to establish diplomatic and trade relations. Perry and Japanese representatives in 1854 signed the seminal Treaty of Kanagawa, opening two Japanese ports to U.S. commercial vessels.

• • •

The editor John O'Sullivan informed Polk in June 1848 that Cuban planters were plotting the overthrow of the Spanish government. The planters were upset that English bondholders were reportedly urging the English government to take over Cuba until their bonds were paid. English intervention, the planters warned, would either spark a slave revolt, or lead to the abolition of slavery in Cuba—both consequences devastating to their interests. By seizing control of the island and petitioning the United States for annexation, the planters hoped to preserve slavery in Cuba.

Wanting neither England to take over Cuba, nor a revolt whose result was doubtful, Polk laid a plan to buy Cuba from Spain for $100 million. Unfortunately, the U.S. minister to Spain was Romulus M. Saunders of North Carolina, who spoke no Spanish, and who, it was jokingly said, could barely speak English. Unaware that Spain regarded Cuba as the crown jewel of her crumbling colonial empire, Saunders bluntly asked Spain's foreign minister whether an offer would be considered. Saunders's bumbling overture went nowhere.

Then the Yucatan seceded from Mexico, and civil war erupted. Because the Yucatan and Cuba were widely regarded as the Gulf of Mexico's "lock and key," expansionists urged Polk to act, fearing that England or Spain would intervene if the United States did not. But with the Army tied up in Mexico, the president was understandably not eager to plunge the nation into a remote jungle war. He handed off the issue to Congress without a recommendation. For the same reasons as Polk, Congress took no action.

As much to deny England a toehold in Central America as to secure a potentially priceless commercial asset, the Polk administration signed a treaty with New Grenada (present-day Colombia and Panama) that included a right-of-way for a canal across the Isthmus of Panama. The Senate ratified it in June 1848.

• • •

As Polk had feared, the slavery issue damaged Democratic presidential nominee Lewis Cass's prospects in 1848. Northern "Conscience Whigs," antislavery Democrats, and the radical-reform New York Democratic faction known as the "Barnburners" formed the Free Soil Party. The new party nominated former President Martin Van Buren, and Charles Francis Adams, the son of the late John Quincy Adams. Van Buren had broken with Polk over William Marcy's appointment as War Secretary; Marcy belonged to the conservative "Hunker" Democrats, adversaries of the Barnburners.

While the Court of Inquiry had served the purpose of keeping Winfield Scott off the 1848 Whig presidential ballot, it had cleared the path for an even more formidable candidate—"Old Rough and Ready." When the Whigs met in Philadelphia in early June, they passed over Scott, who was then on trial in Maryland, and chose Zachary Taylor as their nominee. (In 1852, Scott won the Whig nomination but lost the election to Democrat Franklin Pierce. Scott was the Whig Party's last presidential nominee.) Taylor was paired with Millard Fillmore, a rising New York politician.

Some Southern Democrats, led by John C. Calhoun, deserted Cass to vote for Taylor, a fellow slaveholder. "The fact, that [Taylor] is a slaveholder, a Southern man, a cotton planter, is one of no little importance," wrote Calhoun. The Free Soilers split the Democratic vote in New York between Cass and Van Buren, enabling Taylor to capture the state's thirty-six electoral votes and win the tight race—the first U.S. election in which all citizens voted on the same day.

The war had shattered the Democratic Party coalition that had elected Polk and had divided the party along the slavery fault line. But Democrats would recover and would reclaim the White House in 1852 with Pierce, followed by James Buchanan—whose campaign would not suffer in the least from Washingtonians' long-whispered suspicion that he was homosexual. (Henry Clay enjoyed mocking Buchanan in a feminine voice, and Andrew Jackson and others had called him "Aunt Nancy.")

MARCH 1849: WASHINGTON

On March 1, the president and president-elect attended a formal White House dinner with forty high-ranking officials and their wives. Besides Polk and Zachary Taylor, the guest list included the defeated Democratic presidential candidate, Lewis Cass; the vice president-elect, Millard Fillmore; Secretary of State James Buchanan; and Senator Jefferson Davis, Taylor's former son-in-law. It was a remarkable conflation of past, present, and future, and of political allies and adversaries—four present and future U.S. presidents, and Davis, who would preside over the Confederacy a dozen years later. "Not the slightest allusion was made to any political subject," Polk observed.

The dinner was a personal victory for Taylor, who had traveled a long way, literally and figuratively, from the unhappy times in northern Mexico when he was certain that Polk and Scott were plotting his downfall—times when he "would as soon have heard of [Polk's] death, if true, as that of any other individual in the whole Union."

At this dinner, Polk was friendly and polite, but then, as before and later, he was unimpressed by "Old Rough and Ready." "Gen'l Taylor is, I have no doubt, a well meaning old man. He is, however, uneducated, exceedingly ignorant of public affairs, and, I should judge, of very ordinary capacity. He will be in the hands of others, and must rely wholly upon his Cabinet to administer the Government."

Indeed, Taylor, who would have been content to retire to his Louisiana plantation and dote on his grandchildren rather than lie down on the presidential "bed of thorns," intended to adopt just such a passive mode of governance, believing that "the president has nothing to do with making laws, he must approve or veto them . . . his business is to see them properly executed." This was the polar opposite of Polk's conviction, which he explained to Congress in his last message in December 1848, that as the people's representative in the Executive Department, his job was to recommend legislation, which Congress then either approved or rejected. "There is no appeal from their decision but to the people at the ballot box."

• • •

James Polk's final working day as president lasted until after dawn the following morning. After laboring in the White House all day on Saturday, March 3 ("I resolved to leave nothing undone"), Polk and his family moved to a hotel. Polk then rode to the Capitol for the conclusion of the congressional session. "With reluctance," he signed an act creating the Department of Interior to administer the vast new Western territories. It was difficult for him to reconcile this willful expansion of government with his Jeffersonian beliefs.

In Congress's final hours, a modified Wilmot Proviso unexpectedly surfaced—the third reincarnation of the explosive measure since David Wilmot had first introduced it in August 1846. This version required Mexico's antislavery laws to remain in force in the new territories unless Congress changed them. The emergency compelled Polk to remain at his post at the Capitol, ready to veto the bill if it passed. With Congress still in session at 4 A.M. on March 4, the exhausted president returned to his hotel to lie down. At 6 A.M., a delegation of congressmen appeared at his door with two bills—neither containing the Wilmot Proviso, which had died. Polk signed them both, his last executive act.

• • •

After Taylor's inauguration on Monday, March 5, James Polk left Washington for the last time. He and Sarah embarked on a month-long vacation trip through the South that would end in Nashville and their retirement home at Polk Place, the former residence of Polk's mentor, Felix Grundy. The trip was supposed to be relaxing, but there were many receptions, dinners, and speeches, and the weather was unseasonably hot in Virginia and the Carolinas. Polk was suffering from a painful gastrointestinal disorder when his party arrived in New Orleans, which was in the midst of a cholera epidemic. The ex-president nonetheless left New Orleans in better shape than when he had arrived. The Polks made their way by steamship up the Mississippi, Ohio, and Tennessee rivers, stopping often so that the former president could husband his strength. They reached Nashville in late April.

Weeks later, Nashville, too, was swept by cholera. Polk tried to minimize his contact with other people. In his last diary entry, on Saturday, June 2, 1849, he reported having taken a carriage ride with Sarah into the countryside, and spending the rest of the day arranging his books. The cholera, when he contracted it, struck hard. He died on June 15. The descendant of the Calvinist reformer John Knox was baptized on his deathbed into the Methodist Church.

• • •

Taylor was president for just seventeen months. On Independence Day 1850, he spent hours on the Washington Mall in the broiling Southern sun watching the holiday celebrations. All through the afternoon, he ate fruit and raw vegetables and drank copious amounts of cold water. Two days later, he was in bed, suffering from severe gastrointestinal pain. On July 8, he predicted, "In two days I shall be a dead man." He died on July 9, of what has been variously postulated to be food poisoning or a recurrence of malaria, but might have been due to drinking contaminated water from the Potomac River. Vice President Millard Fillmore became the second president-by-succession.

• • •

Unresolved issues led to new negotiations between Mexico and the United States in 1853. Mexico complained that Indians were crossing the border to raid northern Mexico settlements and demanded that the depredations end. The United States contended that the Mexican–U.S. border had been drawn from inaccurate maps and should be moved south of the Gila River in New Mexico and the future state of Arizona. And Santa Anna, once again Mexico's president, needed money once more.

America's chief negotiator, James Gadsden, railroad entrepreneur and Minister to Mexico, openly acknowledged that he wanted to build a railroad along the Gila River that would connect New Orleans and California. Secretary of State Jefferson Davis evidently viewed Gadsden's flagrant conflict of interest as an incentive to bargain well. On December 30, Mexico agreed to transfer to the United States thirty thousand square miles of Mexico borderland for $10 million. Twenty-five years later, the Southern Transcontinental Railroad was built beside the Gila River.

• • •

Because of Trist's stubborn refusal to abandon the peace talks, the United States had avoided a long, draining guerrilla war and the disastrous consequences feared by Polk if no treaty were signed: Congress's eventual refusal to finance the war, withdrawal, and the loss of California and New Mexico. But Trist paid a steep price for his courageous decision to defy his recall and complete the negotiations.

He was dismissed from the State Department, and Polk and Buchanan refused to pay his salary and expenses after November 16, the date when he had received notification of his recall.

Trist dropped out of sight; for years, he worked for a railroad, always struggling to remain solvent. In 1871, during President Ulysses S. Grant's administration, Congress voted to pay the seventy-year-old Trist back salary and accrued interest of $14,559, and Grant appointed him postmaster of Alexandria, Virginia.

Just as Nicholas Trist was arguably the most consequential U.S. negotiator since James Monroe in 1803, so was Winfield Scott the ablest U.S. military strategist since George Washington. Scott's strategic and tactical precepts dominated the Army's operations through the first years of the Civil War, when they evolved into a newer, deadlier warfare.

If Polk had been more patient, if he had trusted his peace negotiator, and if he had kept politics out of his relations with his generals, he might have rewarded, rather than punished, Trist and Scott. Their mistreatment tarnished Scott's epic march deep into the enemy heartland and Trist's signal achievement in obtaining every U.S. peace objective.

Senator Thomas Hart Benton, whose son-in-law arguably was a collateral casualty of James Polk's obsessive micromanagement, noted: "Those who served the government well in that war with Mexico fared badly with the [Polk] administration." Taylor "was quarreled with"; Scott, relieved of command; John C. Frémont, court-martialed; and Trist, "recalled and dismissed."

• • •

Nominated in 1856 as the Republican Party's first presidential candidate, Frémont lost the election to James Buchanan. Henceforth, his portion would be failure and disappointment. A major general during the Civil War, he was removed from supervision of the Department of the West in St. Louis because of poor leadership and was given command of the Union army in western Virginia. There he was out-generaled by another Mexican War alumnus, Thomas "Stonewall" Jackson. Demoted, Frémont resigned and left public life. He failed in business, and only Jessie Frémont's earnings as a writer saved them from poverty.

• • •

In 1861, the seventy-five-year-old Scott was still the General of the Army, although his weight had ballooned to more than three hundred pounds, he no longer could ride a horse, and he walked with difficulty. As the Civil War began, Scott pleaded with his favorite officer, Robert E. Lee—for whom Scott was said to have "an almost idolatrous fancy"—to lead the Army of the Potomac. But it was no use; Lee resigned his U.S. Army commission to command the army of his beloved Virginia.

Lee took to heart Scott's overarching belief in offensive warfare, as did Pierre G. T. Beauregard, James Longstreet, Jackson, and a host of other Confederate generals. The Mexican War had served as their classroom in practical tactics and strategy, as well as a laboratory in which the field artillery refined its terrible lethality.

The South's skillful generalship counterbalanced the Union's numerical superiority, until Ulysses S. Grant, another Mexican War alumnus, fitted Scott's aggressive tactics and strategies to a new, relentless warfare. Utilizing his greater numbers and resources to grind down the enemy through attrition, Grant battered Lee's army into submission in Virginia in 1864 and 1865, as another Mexican War veteran, William Tecumseh Sherman, conducted a scorched-earth campaign in Georgia and South Carolina.

While Lee was the officer Scott most admired, George P. McClellan was the one who most faithfully emulated Scott. After McClellan became commander of the Army of the Potomac in 1861, he put to good use Scott's discipline-based training methods. And, like Scott and Lee, McClellan preferred flanking movements to minimize casualties. Ambitious, politically ruthless, and surpassingly egotistical, McClellan so undermined Scott with the Lincoln administration that Scott was forced to retire. McClellan succeeded him as General of the Army.

During the Peninsular Campaign of 1862 in eastern Virginia, "Little Mac" tried to replicate Scott's Mexico City campaign by leading 110,000 superbly equipped and trained Union troops up the York Peninsula to capture Richmond. But McClellan's congenital cautiousness—President Abraham Lincoln called it "the slows"—gave Lee time to raise more troops, and Jackson time to join Lee. The offensive was a failure. After his removal from field command in 1862 for not attacking Lee as he retreated from Antietam, McClellan, as Scott had done a dozen years earlier, pursued the presidency. Nominated by the Democratic Party in 1864, McClellan was decisively defeated by Lincoln.

EPILOGUE

"Nations, like individuals, are punished for their transgressions."

—Ulysses S. Grant, suggesting that the Civil War

was punishment for the Mexican War

Mexican historians generally agree that the Mexican War had two principal causes: the annexation of Texas, and President James Polk's determination to possess California and New Mexico. American leaders never understood Texas's surpassing importance to Mexico. "The Mexican government waited for a commissioner who might restore relations and determine the Texas issue, while the North Americans considered the Texas issue settled and were only interested in buying territory," wrote the historian Josefina Zoraida Vazquez.

Mexico's chaotic political drama prevented its government from contriving an articulate diplomatic response when John Slidell attempted to open treaty talks. And after Mexico's defeat, conservatives blamed liberals, and liberals blamed conservatives. But Mexicans of all political affiliations blamed their leaders, particularly Santa Anna for his slipshod prosecution of the war. As one disillusioned politician sadly observed: "Everyone without exception behaved in such a manner that we richly deserve the scorn and derision of all cultivated peoples. We are nothing, absolutely nothing."

Many Americans believed that the war imparted a valuable lesson to the Mexicans. "The moral shock has been eminently beneficial to them," noted Navy Lieutenant Raphael Semmes. "They have been taught, anew, to admire our institutions, to wonder at our unexampled progress, and to inquire into its causes." In his Fourth Annual Message to Congress, Polk observed, with no little smugness, "Our beloved country presents a sublime moral spectacle to the world."

Far more accurate than Semmes's fatuous observations or Polk's cynical rhetoric is the lamentation attributed to General Porfirio Diaz, who decades later become Mexico's dictator: "Poor Mexico! So far from God and so close to the United States."

Indeed, the war taught Mexico to fear and distrust the United States, it shattered Mexico's pretensions to military professionalism and her national pride, and it only worsened her abiding problems. Chief among them was the power struggle between army, clergy, and landowners that had precipitated so many revolutions since Mexico threw off Spanish rule in 1821. In the aftermath of the Mexican War, the three factions were no closer to sharing power; the war in fact sharpened their differences, making it impossible for Mexico to forge a national spirit or identity.

• • •

In 1853, clergymen and merchants again turned to the exiled Santa Anna, living in New Grenada (present-day Colombia). Santa Anna made the most of his fifth presidency, adopting the title "Most Serene Highness" and staging lavish entertainments that sometimes included a procession of his mistresses. But he had no program other than to retain and enjoy his dictatorial powers. In 1855, with revolts breaking out everywhere, Santa Anna resigned. His lands were confiscated, and he returned to New Grenada.

In 1864, monarchists at last got their titular ruler: Archduke Maximilian of Austria, whose patron, Napoleon III of France, envisioned a French puppet regime reigning beside a victorious Confederate States of America. The Northern victory and U.S. diplomatic pressure on France dashed that dream, with Napoleon distancing himself from Maximilian's regime. As the monarchist government tottered in 1866, Santa Anna, his ambitions undimmed by his seventy-two years, sailed for Vera Cruz in a last attempt to regain power. Twenty years earlier, the U.S. Navy had abetted his repatriation; this time, American naval officers turned him away.

At the age of eighty and nearly blind from cataracts, Santa Anna returned to Mexico for the last time in 1874, settling in Mexico City. Few people remembered him. He died in 1876, the year that Porfirio Diaz began thirty-five years of authoritarian rule.

Diaz's iron-fisted reign, inimical to liberty though it was, yet gave Mexico the stability she had long needed to develop an industrial base, to build railways and public works, and to establish an international commerce.

• • •

Texas President Anson Jones once pronounced it "a foregone conclusion of Mr. Polk when he came into office, to have that war with Mexico." While Polk's goal never was to fight Mexico, but to resolve the Texas question and to obtain California, by ignoring Mexico's resentment over the loss of Texas, Polk doomed any hope of peacefully obtaining California. He assumed that "graduated pressure" would persuade Mexico to negotiate: after all, it had worked with England in Oregon. He sent Zachary Taylor to Corpus Christi, while William Parrott worked behind the scenes in Mexico City to stimulate interest in negotiations. Perhaps in due time, if the impatient Polk had waited for a Mexican regime amenable to negotiations, there might one day have been a treaty without war.

But in the fall of 1845, spurious reports reaching Washington suggested that England was trying to obtain California. Deciding that they could wait no longer, Polk and his advisers implemented new, provocative measures: making the success of John Slidell's diplomatic mission the arbiter of war or peace, endowing John C. Frémont and Commodore John Stockton with broad powers to uphold U.S. interests in California, and sending Taylor's army to the Rio Grande—the single action guaranteed to force Mexico either to negotiate or fight. Predictably, war resulted.

Within the narrow, logical parameters established by the Polk administration, the facts led to no other course of action.

• • •

Polk's dubious justification for the nation's first offensive war—"American blood shed on American soil"—was the first time, but not the last, that an American war had commenced on arguable grounds. Questionable pretexts would later launch the Spanish–American and Vietnam wars and the 2003 Iraq invasion: the mysterious explosion that sank the USS *Maine;* the alleged North Vietnamese gunboat attacks on the USS *Maddox* in the Gulf of Tonkin; and Iraq's purported weapons of mass destruction. Crushing Spain in ten months spared William McKinley a backlash over his war but prolonged fighting spurred challenges to the underlying causes of the wars prosecuted by Polk, Lyndon Johnson, and George W. Bush.

As did other presidents, Polk and his allies coerced support for their war agenda by accusing opponents of providing the enemy with "aid and comfort," the constitutional definition of treason. This gambit forced the opposition to walk a tightrope—authorizing war funds to demonstrate their support for the troops, while criticizing the policies that necessitated the expenditures.

But even this political cudgel can lose its capacity to cow opponents. Fortunately for Polk, Nicholas Trist, in defiance of his recall, made a treaty with Mexico before support for the war unraveled altogether. Johnson and Bush discovered that Americans grow impatient with drawn-out conflicts when they are not integral to survival, to upholding vital national interests, or to preserving the world order.

• • •

The Mexican War ended with the best outcome, from America's standpoint—a clear-cut victory and a treaty containing everything that Polk had sought. During Polk's single term, enough land for "yeoman farmers" was added—1.2 million square miles encompassing Texas, Oregon, California, and the New Mexico territory—to keep at arm's length the emerging wage economy with its concentrations of wealth and government power that Thomas Jefferson had so dreaded. All told, Jefferson and his acolytes James Monroe, Andrew Jackson, and Polk annexed a staggering 2 million square miles to the United States, 54 percent of her present 3.7 million square miles. The Mexican Cession would be America's last major annexation for more than a century.

Polk was everything that Andrew Jackson had known that he was, a devoted disciple of Jefferson who would "fearlessly carry out all his principles heretofore acted upon, neither turning to the right or to the left." Indeed, James Polk was the last Jeffersonian to occupy the White House.

• • •

In rating his predecessors, President Harry Truman placed Polk in the august company of George Washington, Thomas Jefferson, and Andrew Jackson. "He said exactly what he was going to do and he did it." At a century's remove from Polk's administration, it was not surprising that the straight-talking thirty-third president would admire the eleventh president. But this was not the case throughout the latter nineteenth century, when Polk was derogated for the Mexican War.

Only with the revival of American nationalism during the early twentieth century did Polk's reputation become commensurate with his considerable achievements. In determinedly fulfilling the continental dream of an America stretching from "sea to shining sea," Polk is deservedly ranked in the top tier of presidents. Yet his fierce devotion to the work at hand sometimes blinded him to potential problems until they metastasized. Thus, he was taken by surprise when the war reawakened the poisonous debate of "that peculiar institution," slavery, although he instantly recognized the threat posed by the Wilmot Proviso. For this, Polk shares culpability with every American leader from Washington to Lincoln in failing to avert the Civil War.

• • •

Without question, the Mexican War removed the fetters on the slavery issue and perhaps even "hastened by 20 or 30 years the question of slavery," as Massachusetts Senator Charles Sumner gloomily observed. (After delivering a venomous antislavery speech in May 1856, Sumner was bludgeoned at his Senate desk into a coma by a South Carolina congressman.)

Indeed, only expedients, stopgaps, and compromises—none sufficient beyond its day—lay between union and secession, chief among them the Compromise of 1850 and the 1854 Kansas–Nebraska Act, the latter permitting "popular sovereignty" to decide whether new Western territories would be slave or free. But the violent struggle in Kansas over this question pushed North and South into opposing camps whose increasing polarization spiraled into war preparations.

The armies of blue and gray whose six hundred thousand dead stained the Civil War's battlefields would be led by more than fifty generals who had received their baptisms-by-fire in Mexico. Among them were Union Generals Ulysses S. Grant, George B. McClellan, John C. Frémont, George G. Meade, William Tecumseh Sherman, Joseph Hooker, George H. Thomas, and Henry W. Halleck; and Confederate Generals Robert E. Lee, Joseph E. Johnston, Stonewall Jackson, Braxton Bragg, Albert Sidney Johnston, James Longstreet, A. P. Hill, and Jubal A. Early.

• • •

Ulysses S. Grant wrote that his Mexican War service gave him an "appreciation of my enemies"—former fellow officers that he faced on the battlefields of the Civil War. But in the case of one officer, Robert E. Lee, he learned a different lesson: "that he was mortal."

Grant believed that the Civil War was America's divinely ordained punishment for the "unholy" Mexican War: "Nations, like individuals, are punished for their transgressions," he wrote in his *Memoirs*. "We got our punishment in the most sanguinary and expensive war of modern times."

BIBLIOGRAPHY

30th Congress, 1st Session, Executive Document 8. "Message from the President of the United States to the Two Houses of Congress at the Commencement of the First Session of the Thirtieth Congress," with 1,360 pages of related documents. Serial Set, No. 515. Washington: Wendell and Van Benthuyson Printers, 1848.

30th Congress, 1st Session, House Executive Document 60. "Messages of the President of the United States with the Correspondence therewith communicated, between the Secretary of War and other Officers of the Government." Serial Set, No. 520. Washington: Wendell and Van Benthuyson, Printers, 1848.

Adams, Charles Francis (ed.). *Memoirs of John Quincy Adams, Comprising Portions of His Diary from 1795 to 1848.* Vol. 12. New York: AMS Press, 1970 (originally published 1874–1877).

Alcaraz, Ramon, et al. (eds.). *The Other Side: Or Notes for the History of the War Between Mexico and the United States.* New York: Burt Franklin, 1970.

American Historical Review. Vol. 11. New York: Macmillan, 1906.

Anderson, James W., James M. Denham, and Keith L. Huneycutt (eds.). "With Scott in Mexico: Letters of Captain James W. Anderson in the Mexican War, 1846–1847." In *Military History of the West,* Vol. 28, No. 1. Spring 1998.

Bailey, Thomas A. *A Diplomatic History of the American People.* New York: Appleton-Century-Crofts, 1964.

Ballentine, George. *Autobiography of an English Soldier in the United States Army.* New York: Stringer & Townsend, 1853.

Bancroft, Hubert Howe. *History of California.* Vol. 5. San Francisco: The History Company, 1886.

Barbour, Philip Norbourne, and Martha Isabella Hopkins Barbour. *Journals of the Late Brevet Major Philip Norbourne Barbour, Captain in the 3rd Regiment, United States Infantry, and his Wife, Martha Isabella Hopkins Barbour.* New York and London: G. P. Putnam's Sons, 1936.

Bauer, K. Jack. *The Mexican War, 1846–1848.* New York: Macmillan, 1974.

———. *Surfboats and Horse Marines: U.S. Naval Operations in the Mexican War, 1846–1848.* Annapolis: United States Naval Institute, 1969.

————. *Zachary Taylor: Soldier, Planter, Statesman of the old Southwest.* Baton Rouge: Louisiana State University Press, 1985.

Beauregard, P. G. T. *With Beauregard in Mexico* (T. Harry Williams, ed.). New York: DaCapo Press, 1969.

Benet, William Rose (ed.). *The Reader's Encyclopedia: An Encyclopedia of World Literature and the Arts.* New York: Thomas Y. Crowell Company, 1948.

Benjamin, Thomas, and Jesús Valasco Màrquez. "The War Between the United States and Mexico, 1846–1848." In *Myths, Misdeeds and Misunderstandings: The Roots of Conflict in U.S.–Mexican Relations.* Wilmington, DE: SR Books, 1997.

Benton, Thomas Hart. *Thirty Years' View: A History of the Working of the American Government for Thirty Years, from 1820 to 1850.* New York: D. Appleton and Company, 1856.

Bergeron, Paul H. *The Presidency of James K. Polk.* Lawrence: University Press of Kansas, 1987.

Biographical Directory of the United States Congress, 1774–1989. Washington: Government Printing Office, 1989.

Boyer, Paul S. (ed.). *The Oxford Companion to United States History.* Oxford and New York: Oxford University Press, 2001.

Brands, H. W. *Andrew Jackson: His Life and Times.* New York, London, Toronto, Sydney, and Auckland: Doubleday, 2005.

————. *Lone Star Nation: How a Ragged Army of Volunteers Won the Battle for Texas Independence—and Changed America.* New York: Doubleday, 2004.

Buchanan, James. *The Works of James Buchanan* (John Bassett Moore, ed.). Philadelphia and London: J. B. Lippincott, 1909.

Buhoup, Jonathan W. *Narrative of the Central Division, or Army of Chihuahua, Commanded by Brigadier General Wool.* Pittsburgh: M. P. Morse, 1847.

Bumgarner, John Reed. *Sarah Childress Polk: A Biography of the Remarkable First Lady.* Jefferson, NC and London: McFarland, 1995.

Byrnes, Mark E. *James K. Polk: A Biographical Companion.* Santa Barbara, Denver, and Oxford: ABC-CLIO, 2001.

Callcott, Wilfrid Hardy. *Santa Anna: The Story of an Enigma Who Once Was Mexico.* Norman: University of Oklahoma Press, 1936.

Carlinsky, Dan. "Civil Service." *Smithsonian.* February 2005.

Carruth, Gorton. *What Happened When: A Chronology of Life & Events in America.* New York: Signet, 1991.

Carson, Kit. *Kit Carson's Autobiography* (Milo Milton Quaife, ed.). Chicago: The Lakeside Press, R. R. Donnelley & Sons Co., 1935.

Caruso, A. Brooke. *The Mexican Spy Company: United States Covert Operations in Mexico, 1845–1848.* Jefferson, NC and London: McFarland, 1991.

Chaffin, Tom. *Pathfinder: John Charles Frémont and the Course of American Empire.* New York: Hill and Wang, 2002.

Chamberlain, Samuel E. *My Confession.* New York: Harper & Brothers, 1956.

Chance, Joseph E. *Jefferson Davis's Mexican War Regiment.* Jackson and London: University Press of Mississippi, 1991.

Clay, Henry. *The Papers of Henry Clay* (Melba Porter Hay and Carol Reardon, eds.). Lexington: The University Press of Kentucky, 1991.

Concise Dictionary of American Biography (2nd Ed.). New York: Charles Scribner's Sons, 1977.

The Congressional Globe. Washington: Blair & Rives, 1834–1873.

The Constitution of the United States of America. With the Declaration of Independence and the Articles of Confederation. New York: Barnes & Noble, 2002.

Cooke, Philip St. George. *The Conquest of New Mexico and California: An Historical and Personal Narrative.* New York: G. P. Putnam's Sons, 1878.

Cortés, Carlos E. (ed.). *The United States' Conquest of California.* New York: Arno Press, 1976.

Coulter, Richard, and Thomas Barclay. *Volunteers: The Mexican War Journals of Private Richard Coulter and Sergeant Thomas Barclay, Company E, Second Pennsylvania Infantry* (Allan Peskin, ed.). Kent and London: The Kent State University Press, 1991.

Crawford, Mark (ed.). *Encyclopedia of the Mexican–American War.* Santa Barbara, Denver, and Oxford: ABC-CLIO, 1999.

Cuevas, Luis Gonzaga. "The Future of Mexico." In *The View from Chapultepec: Mexican Writers on the Mexican–American War* (Cecil Robinson, ed.). Tucson: The University of Arizona Press, 1989.

Cutler, Wayne. "President Polk's New England Tour: North for Union." In *Essays on the Mexican War* (Cutler, Miguel E. Soto, John S. D. Eisenhower, and Douglas W. Richmond, eds.). College Station: Texas A&M Press, 1986.

———. "Jackson, Polk, and Johnson: Defenders of the Moral Economy." In *Tennessee Historical Quarterly,* Vol. 54, No. 3. Fall 1995.

Dana, Napoleon Jackson. *Monterrey Is Ours! The Mexican War Letters of Lieutenant Dana, 1845–1847* (Robert H. Ferrell, ed.). Lexington: The University of Kentucky Press, 1990.

Dana, Richard Henry Jr. *Two Years Before the Mast.* New York: New American Library, Signet Classics, 1964.

Davis, Jefferson. *The Papers of Jefferson Davis* (James T. McIntosh, ed.). Vol. 3. Baton Rouge and London: Louisiana State University Press, 1981.

Davis, William C. *Lone Star Rising: The Revolutionary Birth of the Texas Republic.* New York, London, Toronto, and Sydney: Free Press, 2004.

Dawson, Joseph G. III. *Doniphan's Epic March: The 1st Missouri Volunteers in the Mexican War.* Lawrence: University Press of Kansas, 1999.

DePalo, William A. Jr. *The Mexican National Army: 1822–1852.* College Station: Texas A&M University Press, 1997.

Descendants of Mexican War Veterans Web site. Zachary Taylor and Winfield Scott battle reports, www.dmwv.com.

DeVoto, Bernard. *The Year of Decision, 1846.* New York: Truman Talley, 1942.

Dickens, Charles. *American Notes.* London: Penguin, 2000.

Dilworth, Lt. Rankin. *The March to Monterrey: The Diary of Lieutenant Rankin Dilworth, U.S. Army.* El Paso: Texas Western Press, University of Texas at El Paso, 1996.

Diplomatic Correspondence of the United States, Inter-American Affairs, 1831–1860. Mexico, 1831–1848 (Mid-Year). Vol. 8, Docs. 3128-3771. William R. Manning (ed.). Washington: Carnegie Endowment for International Peace, 1937.

Doubleday, Abner. *My Life in the Old Army: The Reminiscences of Abner Doubleday* (Joseph E. Chance, ed.). Fort Worth: Texas Christian University Press, 1998.

Drabble, Margaret (ed.). *The Oxford Companion to English Literature.* Oxford and New York: Oxford University Press, 1983.

Drake, Francis S. *Dictionary of American Biography.* Boston: James R. Osgood and Company, 1876.

Dusinberre, William. *Slavemaster President: The Double Career of James Polk.* New York: Oxford University Press, 2003.

Edwards, Frank S. *A Campaign in Mexico with Colonel Doniphan.* Ann Arbor: University Microfilms, 1966.

Egan, Ferol. *Frémont: Explorer for a Restless Nation.* Garden City: Doubleday, 1977.

Eggenburger, David. *A Dictionary of Battles.* New York: Thomas Y. Crowell, 1967.

Eisenhower, John S. D. *So Far From God: The U.S. War with Mexico, 1846–1848.* New York: Random House, 1989.

Engelmann, Adolph. "The Second Illinois in the Mexican War: Mexican War letters of Adolph Engelmann, 1846–18470." In *Journal of the Illinois State Historical Society.* Vol. 26. April 1933–January 1934.

Faulk, Odie B., and Joseph A. Stout Jr. (eds.). *The Mexican War: Changing Interpretations.* Chicago: The Swallow Press, 1973.

Fischer, David Hackett. *Washington's Crossing.* New York: Oxford University Press, 2004.

Foner, Eric. "Free Labor and Nineteenth-Century Political Ideology." In *The Market Revolution in American Social, Political, and Religious Expressions, 1800–1880* (Melvyn Stokes and Stephen Conway, eds.). Charlottesville: University Press of Virginia, 1996.

Forbes, Alexander. *California: A History of Upper and Lower California from Their First Discovery to the Present Time.* London: Smith, Elder and Co. Cornhill, 1839.

Francaviglia, Richard V. "The Geographical and Cartographic Legacy of the U.S.–Mexican War." In *Dueling Eagles: Reinterpreting the U.S.–Mexican War, 1846–1848* (Richard V. Francaviglia and Douglas W. Richmond, eds.). Fort Worth: Texas Christian University Press, 2000.

Freeman, Douglas Southall. *R. E. Lee, A Biography.* Vol. 1. New York and London: Charles Scribner's Sons, 1934.

Frémont, John Charles. *The Expeditions of John Charles Frémont.* Vols. 1, 2 (Donald Jackson and Mary Lee Spence, eds.). Urbana, Chicago, and London: University of Illinois Press, 1970, 1973.

————. *Memoirs of My Life*. New York: Cooper Square Press, 2001.

Frost, J. *The Mexican War and Its Warriors*. New Haven and Philadelphia: H. Mansfield, 1848.

Funk & Wagnalls New Encyclopedia. Funk & Wagnalls, 1983.

Furnas, J. C. *The Americans: Social History of the United States, 1587–1914*. New York: G. P. Putnam's Sons, 1969.

Gallatin, Albert. *Selected Writings of Albert Gallatin* (E. James Ferguson, ed.). Indianapolis and New York: Bobbs-Merrill, 1967.

Garrison, William Lloyd. *William Lloyd Garrison and the Fight against Slavery. Selections from The Liberator* (William E. Cain, ed.). New York and Boston: Bedford Books of St. Martin's Press, 1995.

Giffen, Guy J. *California Expedition: Stevenson's Regiment of First New York Volunteers*. Oakland: Biobooks, 1951.

Gillespie, Archibald H. "Further Letters of Archibald H. Gillespie" (Richard R. Stenberg, ed.). In *California Historical Society Quarterly*, Vol. 18, 1939.

————. "Gillespie and the Conquest of California" (George Walcott Ames Jr., ed.). In *California Historical Society Quarterly*, Vol. 17, 1938.

Goetzmann, William H. *Exploration & Empire. The Explorer and the Scientist in the Winning of the American West*. New York and London: W. W. Norton, 1978.

Going, Charles Buxton. *David Wilmot, Free Soiler: A Biography of the Great Advocate of the Wilmot Proviso*. New York and London: D. Appleton, 1924.

Goodwin, Doris Kearns. *Team of Rivals: The Political Genius of Abraham Lincoln*. New York, London, Toronto, and Sydney: Simon & Schuster, 2005.

Graebner, Norman A. *Empire on the Pacific: A Study in American Continental Expansion*. Santa Barbara: ABC-CLIO, Inc., 1983.

————. *Manifest Destiny*. Indianapolis and New York: Bobbs-Merrill, 1968.

Grant, Ulysses S. *Personal Memoirs of U. S. Grant* (E. B. Long, ed.). New York: Da Capo, 1982.

Griffin, John S. "A Doctor Comes to California: The Diary of John S. Griffin, Assistant Surgeon with Kearny's Dragoons, 1846–1847." In *The United States' Conquest of California* (Carles E. Cortés, ed.). New York, 1976.

Haecker, Charles M., and Jeffrey G. Mauck. *On the Prairie of Palo Alto: Historical Archaeology of the U.S.–Mexican War Battlefield*. College Station: Texas A&M University Press, 1997.

Harlow, Neal. *California Conquered: War and Peace on the Pacific, 1846–1850*. Berkeley, Los Angeles, and London: University of California Press, 1982.

Harris, J. George. *Polk Campaign Biography*. Knoxville: Tennessee Presidents Trust, 1990. First published in installments in the *Nashville Union*, August 1–September 16, 1844.

Haynes, Sam W. *James K. Polk and the Expansionist Impulse*. New York: Longman, 2002.

Heidler, David S., and Jeanne T. Heidler (eds.). *Encyclopedia of the War of 1812*. Santa Barbara, Denver, and Oxford: ABC-CLIO, 1997.

Henry, Capt. William Seaton. *Campaign Sketches of the War with Mexico.* New York: Arno Press, 1973.

Hill, Daniel H. *A Fighter from Way Back: The Mexican War Diary of Lt. Daniel Harvey Hill, 4th Artillery, USA* (Nathaniel Cheairs Hughes Jr. and Timothy D. Johnson, eds.). Kent and London: The Kent State University Press, 2002.

Hitchcock, Ethan Allen. *Fifty Years in Camp and Field: Diary of a Major-General* (W. A. Croffut, ed.). New York and London: Knickerbocker Press, 1909.

Holman, C. Hugh. *A Handbook to Literature* (4th Ed.). Indianapolis: Bobbs-Merrill Educational, 1980.

Hughes, John Taylor. *Doniphan's Expedition.* College Station: Texas A&M University Press, 1997.

Hussey, John Adam. "The Origins of the Gillespie Mission." In *California Historical Society Quarterly,* Vol. 19, 1940.

Ingersoll, Lurton D. *The Life of Horace Greeley.* New York: Beekman, 1974.

Jackson, Andrew. *Correspondence of Andrew Jackson* (John Spencer Bassett, ed.). Washington: Carnegie Institution of Washington, 1933.

Jackson, Mary Anna. *Memoirs of Stonewall Jackson.* Louisville, KY: Prentice Press, 1895.

Jefferson, Thomas. *Notes on the State of Virginia.* New York: Penguin, 1999.

Johannsen, Robert W. *To the Halls of Montezuma: The Mexican War in American Imagination.* New York: Oxford University Press, 1985.

Johnson, Kenneth. "Nicholas Trist." In *The Mexican War: Changing Interpretations* (Odie B. Faulk and Joseph A. Stout Jr., eds.). Chicago: Swallow Press, 1973.

Johnson, Paul E. *A Shopkeeper's Millennium: Society and Revivals in Rochester, New York, 1815–1837.* New York: Hill and Wang, 1978.

Johnson, Timothy D. *Winfield Scott: The Quest for Military Glory.* Lawrence: University Press of Kansas, 1998.

Jones, Anson (ed.). *Memoranda and Official Correspondence Relating to the Republic of Texas, Its History and Annexation.* New York: Arno Press, 1973. (First published 1859).

Kendall, George Wilkins. *Dispatches from the Mexican War* (Lawrence Delbert Cross, ed.). Norman: University of Oklahoma Press, 1999.

Kirkham, Ralph W. *The Mexican War Journals and Letters of Ralph W. Kirkham* (Robert Ryal Miller, ed.). College Station: Texas A&M University Press, 1991.

Krakauer, Jon. *Under the Banner of Heaven: A Story of Violent Faith.* New York, London, Toronto, Sydney, and Auckland: Doubleday, 2003.

Kunhardt, Philip B. Jr., Philip B. Kunhardt III, and Peter W. Kunhardt. *The American President.* New York: Riverhead Books, 1999.

Langer, William L. (ed.). *An Encyclopedia of World History.* Boston: Houghton Mifflin, 1940.

Larkin, Thomas O. "California in 1846 and Its Resources as Then Known. A Report to the U.S. Government." In *The United States' Conquest of California* (Carlos E. Cortés, ed.). New York: Arno Press, 1976.

Lavender, David. *Climax at Buena Vista. The American Campaigns in Northeastern Mexico, 1846–1847.* Philadelphia and New York: J. P. Lippincott, 1966.

Leonard, Thomas M. *James K. Polk: A Clear and Unquestionable Destiny.* Wilmington, DE: SR Books, 2000.

Lincoln, Abraham. *Speeches and Writings, 1832–1858.* Library of America, 1989.

———. *Great Speeches: Abraham Lincoln.* New York: Dover, 1991.

Lowell, James Russell. *James Russell Lowell's The Biglow Papers. A Critical Edition* (Thomas Wortham, ed.). DeKalb: Northern Illinois University Press, 1977.

Magoffin, Susan Shelby. *Down the Santa Fe Trail and into Mexico* (Stella M. Drumm, ed.). New Haven, CT and London: Yale University Press, 1926.

Marszalek, John F. *Sherman: A Soldier's Passion for Order.* New York: Free Press, 1993.

Marti, Werner H. *Messenger of Destiny: The California Adventures, 1846–1847, of Archibald H. Gillespie, U.S. Marine Corps.* San Francisco: John Howell, 1960.

Maury, General Dabney Herndon. *Recollections of a Virginian in the Mexican, Indian and Civil Wars.* New York: Charles Scribner's Sons, 1894.

McAfer, Ward, and J. Cordell Robinson (eds.). *Origins of the Mexican War: A Documentary Source Book.* Salisbury, NC: Documentary Publications, 1982.

McCaffrey, James M. *Army of Manifest Destiny: The American Soldier in the Mexican War, 1846–1848.* New York and London: New York University Press, 1992.

McClellan, George B. *The Mexican War Diary of George B. McClellan* (William Starr Myers, ed.). Princeton, NJ: Princeton University Press, 1917.

McCormac, Eugene Irving. *James K. Polk: A Political Biography.* Berkeley: University of California Press, 1922.

McFeely, William S. *Grant: A Biography.* New York and London: W. W. Norton, 1981.

McPherson, James M. *Battle Cry of Freedom: The Civil War Era.* New York and Oxford: Oxford University Press, 1988.

McWhiney, Grady, and Sue McWhiney (eds.). *To Mexico with Taylor and Scott, 1845–1847.* Waltham, MA; Toronto; and London: Blaisdell, 1969.

Meade, George Gordon. *The Life and Letters of George Gordon Meade, Major-General United States Army.* Vol. 1. New York: Charles Scribner's Sons, 1913.

Merk, Frederick. "Dissent in the Mexican War." In *Dissent in Three American Wars* (Samuel Eliot Morison, Frederick Merk, and Frank Freidel, eds.). Cambridge, MA: Harvard University Press, 1970.

———. *The Monroe Doctrine and American Expansionism, 1843–1849.* New York: Alfred A. Knopf, 1968.

Metcalf, Clyde H. *A History of the United States Marine Corps.* New York: G. P. Putnam's Sons, 1939.

The Mexican Soldier 1837–1847: Military Organization, Dress, Equipment and Regulations. Mexico City: Editions Nieto-Brown-Hefter, 1958.

The Mexican War and Its Heroes. Philadelphia: J. B. Lippincott, 1858.

Miller, Roger Gene. *Winfield Scott and the Sinews of War: The Logistics of the Mexico*

City Campaign, October 1846–September 1847. Masters thesis, North Texas State University, 1976.

Millett, Alan R. Semper Fidelis: *The History of the United States Marine Corps.* New York: Free Press, 1991.

Moore, H. Judge. *Scott's Campaign in Mexico, from the Rendezvous on the Island of Lobos to the Taking of the City.* Charleston, SC: J. B. Nixon, 1849.

Morison, Samuel Eliot. *The Oxford History of the American People.* New York: New American Library, 1972.

Morris, Richard B. (ed.). *Encyclopedia of American History.* New York: Harper & Brothers, 1953.

Moskin, J. Robert. *The Marine Corps Story.* New York, St. Louis, and San Francisco: McGraw-Hill, 1977.

National Intelligencer, 1846–1847. University of Texas-Arlington Special Collections.

New York *Daily Tribune,* June 1846–May 1847. Chapel Hill: University of North Carolina, Davis Library, Microfilm.

The Norton Anthology of American Literature. New York and London: W. W. Norton, 1979.

Oates, Stephen. "Los Diablos Tejanos." In *The Mexican War: Changing Interpretations* (Odie B. Faulk and Joseph A. Stout Jr., eds.). Chicago: Swallow Press, 1973.

Oswandel, J. Jacob. *Notes of the Mexican War.* Philadelphia, 1885.

Owen, Tom. *The Taylor Anecdote Book. Anecdotes and Letters of Zachary Taylor.* New York: D. Appleton, 1848.

The Oxford Dictionary of Quotations (3rd Ed.). Oxford, New York, Toronto, and Melbourne: Oxford University Press, 1980.

Peck, Lt. John James. *The Sign of the Eagle: A View of Mexico—1830 to 1855.* San Diego: Union Tribune Publishing Co., 1970.

Philbrick, Nathaniel. *Sea of Glory: America's Voyage of Discovery, the U.S. Exploring Expedition, 1838–1842.* New York: Viking, 2003.

Pillow, Gideon, and James Polk. "Gideon Pillow–James Polk Letters," *American Historical Review.* Vol. 1. New York: MacMillan. 1906.

Pletcher, Donald M. *The Diplomacy of Annexation: Texas, Oregon and the Mexican War.* Columbia: University of Missouri Press, 1973.

Polk, James K. *Correspondence of James K. Polk* (Wayne Cutler, ed.) Knoxville: University of Tennessee Press, 1993.

————. *The Diary of James K. Polk, During His Presidency, 1845 to 1849* (Milo Milton Quaife, ed.). Chicago: A. C. McClurg, 1910.

————, *Presidential Papers Microfilm.* Washington: Library of Congress, 1964.

Ponce de Leon, Antonio. "Brazito Battle Report." In *New Mexico Historical Review,* Vol. 3, 1928.

Prescott, William Hickling. *History of the Conquest of Mexico, and History of the Conquest of Peru.* New York: Modern Library, 1936.

Price, Glenn W. *Origins of the War with Mexico: The Polk-Stockton Intrigue*. Austin: University of Texas Press, 1967.

Ramirez, Jose Fernando. *Mexico During the War with the United States*. Columbia: University of Missouri Press, 1950.

Reichstein, Andreas V. *Rise of the Lone Star: The Making of Texas*. College Station: Texas A&M University Press, 1989.

Rejon, Manuel Crescencio. "Observations on the Treaty of Guadalupe." In *The View from Chapultepec: Mexican Writers on the Mexican–American War* (Cecil Robinson, ed.). Tucson: University of Arizona Press, 1989.

Remini, Robert V. *Andrew Jackson and the Course of American Empire*. New York: Harper & Row, 1977.

Richardson, James D. (ed.). *A Compilation of the Messages and Papers of the Presidents, 1789–1897*. Vol. 4. Washington: Published by Authority of Congress, 1899.

Richardson, Rupert N., Adrian Anderson, and Ernest Wallace. *Texas: The Lone Star State* (6th Ed.). Englewood Cliffs, NJ: Prentice Hall, 1993.

Richmond, Douglas W. "A View of the Periphery: Regional Factors and Collaboration During the U.S.–Mexico Conflict, 1845–1848." In *Dueling Eagles: Reinterpreting the U.S.–Mexican War, 1846–1848* (Richard V. Francaviglia and Douglas W. Richmond, eds.). Fort Worth: Texas Christian University Press, 2000.

Ricketts, Norma Baldwin. *The Mormon Battalion: U.S. Army of the West 1846–1848*. Logan: Utah State University Press, 1996.

Ripley, R. S. *The War with Mexico*. New York: Burt Franklin, 1970. (Originally published 1848)

Rister, Carl Coke. *Robert E. Lee in Texas*. Norman: University of Oklahoma Press, 1946.

Robinson, Cecil (ed.). *The View from Chapultepec: Mexican Writers on the Mexican–American War*. Tucson: University of Arizona Press, 1989.

Robinson, Fayette. *Mexico and Her Military Chieftains: From the Revolution of Hidalgo to the Present Time*. Hartford: Silas Andrus & Sons, 1848.

Robinson, Jacob S. *A Journal of the Santa Fe Expedition under Colonel Doniphan*. Princeton, NJ: Princeton University Press, 1932.

Roth, Mitchell. "Journalism and the U.S.–Mexican War." In *Dueling Eagles: Reinterpreting the U.S.–Mexican War, 1846–1848* (Richard V. Francaviglia and Douglas W. Richmond, eds.). Fort Worth: Texas Christian University, 2000.

Ruiz, Ramón Eduardo. *The Mexican War: Was It Manifest Destiny?* New York: Holt, Rinehart and Winston, 1963.

Sampson, Harold Peck. *The Antislavery Speaking of Joshua Reed Giddings*. Carbondale: Southern Illinois University PhD dissertation, 1967.

de Santa Anna, Antonio Lopez. *The Eagle: The Autobiography of Santa Anna* (Ann Fears Crawford, ed.). Austin, TX: Pemberton Press, 1967.

Santoni, Pedro. *Mexicans at Arms: Puro Federalists and the Politics of War, 1845–1848*. Fort Worth: Texas Christian University Press, 1996.

Scheina, Robert L. *Santa Anna: A Curse Upon Mexico*. Washington: Brassey's, 2002.

Schroeder, John H. *Mr. Polk's War: American Opposition and Dissent, 1846–1848*. Madison: University of Wisconsin Press, 1973.

Scott, Winfield. *Memoirs of Lieut.-General Scott, L.L.D.* New York: Sheldon, 1864.

———— et al. *General Scott and his Staff*. Documents and private correspondence. Freeport, NY: Books for Libraries Press, 1848.

Scribner, Benjamin F. *A Campaign in Mexico*. Philadelphia: James Gihon, 1850.

Sears, Louis Martin. *John Slidell*. Durham, NC: Duke University Press, 1925.

Seigenthaler, John. *James K. Polk*. New York: Henry Holt, 2003.

Sellers, Charles. *The Market Revolution: Jacksonian America, 1815–1846*. New York and Oxford: Oxford University Press, 1991.

————. *James K. Polk: Jacksonian, 1795–1843*. Princeton, NJ: Princeton University Press, 1957.

————. *James K. Polk: Continentalist, 1843–1846*. Princeton, NJ: Princeton University Press, 1966.

Semmes, Lt. Raphael. *The Campaign of General Scott in the Valley of Mexico*. Cincinnati: Moore & Anderson, 1852.

————. *Service Afloat and Ashore During the Mexican War*. Cincinnati: William H. Moore, 1851.

Shaara, Jeff. *Gone for Soldiers*. New York: Ballantine, 2000.

Singletary, Otis A. *The Mexican War*. Chicago and London: University of Chicago Press, 1960.

Smith, Ashbel. *Reminiscences of the Texas Republic*. Austin, TX: Pemberton Press, 1967.

Smith, Franklin. *The Mexican War Journal of Captain Franklin Smith* (Joseph E. Chance, ed.). Jackson: University of Mississippi Press, 1991.

Smith, George Winston, and Charles Judah (eds.). *Chronicles of the Gringos: The U.S. Army in the Mexican War, 1846–1848. Accounts of Eyewitnesses & Combatants*. Albuquerque: University of New Mexico Press, 1968.

Smith, Gustavius Woodson. *Company "A" Corps of Engineers, U.S.A., 1846–1848, in the Mexican War* (Leonne M. Hudson, ed.). Kent and London: Kent State University Press, 2001.

Smith, Henry Nash. *Virgin Land: The American West as Symbol and Myth*. New York: Vintage, 1959.

Smith, Isaac. *Reminiscences of a Campaign in Mexico*. Indianapolis: Chapmans & Spann, 1848.

Smith, Justin H. *The Annexation of Texas*. New York: Barnes & Noble, 1941. ("Corrected Edition" of 1911 original.)

————. *The War with Mexico*. New York: Macmillan, 1919.

Sobel, Robert. *Conquest and Conscience: The 1840s*. New York: Thomas Y. Crowell, 1971.

Soto, Miguel E. "The Monarchist Conspiracy." In *Essays on the Mexican War*. College Station: Texas A&M Press, 1986.

Stephenson, George M. *The Political History of the Public Lands from 1840 to 1862.* New York: Russell & Russell, 1917.

Stevens, Isaac. *Campaigns of the Rio Grande and Mexico.* New York: D. Appleton, 1851.

Stevens, Peter F. *The Rogue's March: John Riley and the St. Patrick's Battalion.* Washington and London: Brassey's, 1999.

Strode, Hudson. *Jefferson Davis, American Patriot, 1808–1861.* New York: Harcourt, Brace, 1955.

Taylor, Zachary. *Letters of Zachary Taylor from the Battle-Fields of the Mexican War.* Rochester and New York: Kraus Reprint Co., 1908, 1970.

Tennery, Thomas D. *The Mexican War Diary of Thomas D. Tennery* (D. E. Livingston-Little, ed.). Norman: University of Oklahoma Press, 1970.

Thomas, Emory M. *Robert E. Lee.* New York and London: W. W. Norton, 1995.

Thoreau, Henry David. *The Selected Works of Thoreau.* Boston: Houghton Mifflin, 1975.

Time Almanac 2003. Boston: Time Inc. Home Entertainment, 2002.

de Tocqueville, Alexis. *Democracy in America* (J. P. Mayer and Max Lerner, eds.). New York, Evanston, and London: Harper & Row, 1966.

Turner, Henry Smith. *The Original Journals of Henry Smith Turner: With Stephen Watts Kearny to New Mexico and California, 1846–1847* (Dwight L. Clarke, ed.). Norman: University of Oklahoma Press, 1966.

Ubbelohde, Carl, Maxine Benson, and Duane A. Smith. *A Colorado History* (6th Ed.). Boulder: Pruett, 1988.

United States Magazine and Democratic Review. Microfilm, 1846–1847. Vols. 20, 21. Chapel Hill: Davis Library, University of North Carolina.

Vandiver, Frank E. *Mighty Stonewall.* New York, Toronto, and London: McGraw-Hill, 1957.

Vazquez, Josefina Zoraida. "The Colonization and Loss of Texas: A Mexican Perspective." In *Myths, Misdeeds and Misunderstandings: The Roots of Conflict in U.S.–Mexican Relations* (Jaime E. Rodriguez and Kathryn Vincent, eds.). Wilmington, DE: SR Books, 1997.

———. "Causes of the War with the United States." In *Dueling Eagles, Reinterpreting the U.S.–Mexican War, 1846–1848* (Richard V. Francaviglia and Douglas W. Richmond, eds.). Fort Worth: Texas Christian University Press, 2000.

Volo, James M., and Dorothy Deneed Volo. *The Antebellum Period.* Westport, CT, and London: Greenwood Press, 2004.

Wallace, Isabel. *Life & Letters of General W. H. L. Wallace.* Chicago: R. R. Donnelley & Sons, 1909.

Wallace, Lew. *Lew Wallace: An Autobiography.* New York and London: Harper & Brothers, 1906.

The Washington Union, Microfilm, 1846–1848. Richmond: Library of Virginia.

Watson, Henry Bulls. *The Journals of Marine 2nd Lt. Henry Bulls Watson, 1845–1848* (Charles R. Smith, ed.). Washington: History and Museums Division, Headquarters, U.S. Marine Corps, 1990.

Waugh, John C. *The Class of 1846. From West Point to Appomatox: Stonewall Jackson, George McClellan and Their Brothers.* New York: Warner Books, 1994.

Webb, Walter Prescott. *The Texas Rangers: A Century of Frontier Defense.* Austin: University of Texas Press, 1987.

Webster, Daniel. *The Private Correspondence of Daniel Webster* (Fletcher Webster, ed.). Boston: Little, Brown, 1857.

Webster, Lucien Bonaparte, and Frances Webster. *The Websters: Letters of an American Army Family in Peace and War, 1836–1853* (Van R. Baker, ed). Kent: Kent State University Press, 2000.

Weems, John Edward. *To Conquer a Peace: The War between the United States and Mexico.* Garden City: Doubleday, 1974.

Wheelan, Joseph. *Jefferson's Vendetta: The Pursuit of Aaron Burr and the Judiciary.* New York: Carroll & Graf, 2005.

Whitman, Walt. *Complete Poetry and Selected Prose* (James E. Miller Jr., ed.). Boston: Houghton Mifflin, 1959.

———. *The Gathering of the Forces: Writings while editor of the* Brooklyn Daily Eagle, *1846–1847.* New York and London: G. P. Putnam's Sons, 1920.

Whitney, David C., and Robin Vaughn Whitney. *The American Presidents.* New York: Prentice Hall, 1993.

Whittier, John Greenleaf. *The Complete Works of John Greenleaf Whittier.* New York: Sully and Kleinteich, 1892.

Wilentz, Sean. *Chants Democratic: New York City & the Rise of the American Working Class, 1788–1850.* New York: Oxford University Press, 1984.

———. *The Rise of American Democracy: Jefferson to Lincoln.* New York and London: W. W. Norton, 2005.

Wilkins, Frederick. *The Highly Irregular Irregulars: Texas Rangers in the Mexican War.* Austin, TX: Eakin, 1990.

Williams, T. Harry. *P. G. T. Beauregard, Napoleon in Gray.* Baton Rouge: Louisiana State University Press, 1955.

Winders, Richard Bruce. *Mr. Polk's Army: The American Military Experience in the Mexican War.* College Station: Texas A&M University Press, 1997.

———. " 'Will the Regiment Stand It?' The 1st North Carolina Mutinies at Buena Vista." In *Dueling Eagles: Reinterpreting the U.S.–Mexican War, 1846–1848* (Richard V. Francaviglia and Douglas W. Richmond, eds.). Fort Worth: Texas Christian University Press, 2000.

Woodward, Arthur. *The Great Western, Amazon of the Army.* San Francisco: Johnck & Seeger, 1961.

Zahler, Helen Sara. *Eastern Workingmen and National Land Policy, 1829–1862.* New York: Columbia University Press, 1941.

Zeh, Frederick. *An Immigrant Soldier in the Mexican War* (William J. Orr, ed.). College Station: Texas A&M University Press, 1995.

NOTES

PROLOGUE

xiii–xiv   "Like an actor": Bauer, *Mexican War,* p. 236; Ballentine, p. 144.

xiv   "Scott himself secretly": Scott, *Memoirs,* vol. 2, p. 414.

xiv   " 'Everyone expected to hear' ": McClellan, p. 54; G. Smith, pp. 14–15.

xiv   "Far more ebullient": Zeh, pp. 9–10; Ballentine, p. 147.

xiv   "Anchored at Sacrificios Island": Oswandel, p. 68.

xiv   "A pair of third-class": Ballentine, p. 147; Bauer, *Surfboats,* p. 80; McWhiney, p. 104.

xv   "Six days earlier": McWhiney, pp. 101–2; Alcarez, p. 180.

xv   "Aboard Commodore David Conner's": Semmes, *Service,* pp. 125–27.

xv   "Planting their black velvet": Prescott, pp. 164, 142.

xv   "A military scholar": T. Johnson, p. 28; Bauer, *Mexican War,* p. 245.

xvi   "This day was": Scott, *Memoirs,* vol. 2, p. 418; T. Johnson, pp. 40–41.

xvi   "After rendezvousing at": Oswandel, p. 64; Bauer, *Surfboats,* p. 76; Grant, p. 59; Johannsen, p. 238; Hitchcock, pp. 239–40; Bauer, *Mexican War,* p. 244; Ballentine, 149.

xvi–xvii   "Four days before": Hitchcock, p. 237; *Concise Dictionary of American Biography,* p. 194; Bauer, *Surfboats,* p. 77.

xvii   "At 5:30 P.M., a cannon": Zeh, pp. 10–11; G. Smith, pp. 15–16.

xvii–xviii   "From the line": Bauer, *Surfboats,* 81; McWhiney, p. 105.

xviii   "The Mexicans didn't": Bauer, *Mexican War,* p. 244; Coulter and Barclay, pp. 39–40; McWhiney, p. 105; Oswandel, p. 64.

xviii   "Five hours after": Bauer, *Mexican War,* p. 244; Johannsen, p. 98; Scott, p. 421; McWhiney, p. 107; Zeh, p. 11.

xviii   "From behind Vera Cruz's": Alcarez, pp. 180–83.

xix   "Polk insisted that": J. Richardson, vol. 4, pp. 437–43.

xix   "The ambush enabled Polk": J. Smith, *War with Mexico,* vol. 1, p. 195; Schroeder, p. 33.

CHAPTER 1: "THE MOLE"

1   "President-elect James K. Polk": Byrnes, p. 103; Dickens, p. 129.

2   "Exactly four years": Kunhardt, pp. 211–12.

2   "Earlier on the morning": Byrnes, p. 103.

2   "Polk and Tyler arrived": *Biographical Dictionary of Congress,* pp. 865–66; Byrnes, p. 103; Sellers, *Continentalist,* pp. 209–11.

2–3   " 'Without solicitation on' ": Harris, pp. 31–32; J. Richardson, vol. 4, pp. 373–82.

3   "Jackson's former speechwriter": Sellers, *Continentalist,* pp. 209–11.

3   "The new president": Harris, pp. 13–15; J. Richardson, vol. 4, pp. 373–82; Byrnes, p. 201.

3   "Polk said the United States' title": J. Richardson, vol. 4, pp. 373–82; Leonard, p. 88; Sellers, *Market Revolution,* p. 416.

4   " 'I am in favour' ": Polk, *Correspondence,* vol. 7, p. 107.

4   "Then, on February 28, 1845": Sellers, *Continentalist,* p. 215; Buchanan, pp. 118–19.

4   "Polk pledged to 'consummate' ": J. Richardson, vol. 4, pp. 373–82.

4–5   "When Polk finished": Sellers, *Continentalist,* p. 211.

5   "That night at the two": Ibid.

5   "Nearly a million": Volo, pp. 323–25.

5   "The telegraph, invented": Morison, vol. 2, pp. 249, 293; *Encyclopedia of American History,* p. 536.

5–6   "In 1789, three million": J. Richardson, vol. 4, pp. 375, 402; Dickens, p. 206.

6   "With just four years": Sellers, *Continentalist,* pp. 300–301; Polk, *Correspondence,* vol. 10, p. 37.

6   "Yet the president had confided": Sellers, *Continentalist,* p. 213.

6   "Polk would launch": Caruso, p. 77.

7   "Polk was born": Sellers, *Jacksonian,* pp. 5–8, 18–22, 30–39.

7–8   "A thin, undersized": Ibid., pp. 39–40; Harris, pp. 5–6.

8   "He asked his father": Sellers, *Continentalist,* pp. 41–45, 49, 54–55; Leonard, p. 6; Harris, p. 7.

8   "Polk studied law": Seigenthaler, p. 24; Sellers, *Jacksonian,* pp. 58–60.

8   "Her father, Joel": Sellers, *Jacksonian,* pp. 74–75, 93, 329, 460; Byrnes, pp. 130–31.

8   "Politics was the Polks' ": Sellers, *Jacksonian,* p. 277; Haynes, p. 78.

9   "As befitted a descendant": Sellers, *Continentalist,* p. 4; Sellers, *Jacksonian,* pp. 106–7, 355, 399; Byrnes, pp. 179–81.

9   "Polk's sober outlook": Seigenthaler, pp. 119–21.

9   ". . . so he willed himself": Leonard, p. 7.

9   "John Quincy Adams assayed": Bergeron, p. 245; Sellers, *Jacksonian,* p. 117; Adams, vol. 9, p. 64.

9   "His Jeffersonian orthodoxy": Sellers, *Jacksonian,* pp. 133, 408; Polk, *Correspondence,* vol. 10, p. 194.

9–10   " 'I would sell out the' ": Sellers, *Jacksonian,* p. 152.

10   "Polk's Jeffersonianism was": Ibid., pp. 7, 25.

10   "Soon after the Revolutionary War": Morison, vol. 2, p. 42.

10–11   "However, these battles": Wilentz, *Chants Democratic,* p. 14; Jefferson, pp. 170–71.

11–12   "In 1823, Polk": Leonard, pp. 8–9.

12   "The modest land reform": Sellers, *Jacksonian,* p. 66.

12   "Polk aided the president": *Encyclopedia of American History,* pp. 154–55; Byrnes, p. 9; Whitney, p. 73.

13   "Then, in December 1835": Dusinberre, pp. 123–24; Merk, *Monroe Doctrine,* p. x.

13   "For six weeks": Sellers, *Jacksonian,* pp. 312–16; Morison, vol. 2, pp. 278–80; Dusinberre, pp. 123–24, 159.

13   "In 1840, he failed" Sellers, *Continentalist,* p. 6; Sellers, *Jacksonian,* pp. 382, 488.

CHAPTER 2: THE DYNAMO

14   "Twenty years of Jacksonian": Leonard, pp. 1–3.

14–15   "A Harvard alumnus": Thoreau, pp. xv, 270–76; *Reader's Encyclopedia,* pp. 280–81; *Norton Anthology,* vol. 1, pp. 1510–11.

15   "On the Fourth of July": *Norton Anthology,* vol. 1, p. 1509.

15   "Thoreau employed the same": Ibid., p. 1511.

15   "Under the heading of Economy": Thoreau, p. 247.

15–16   "Thoreau's *Walden* touches": Morison, vol. 2, pp. 281, 284; DeVoto, pp. 9, 32; *Reader's Encyclopedia,* pp. 140, 399–400.

16   " 'The trumpet of reform' ": Morison, vol. 2, p. 272; Volo, p. 176.

16   "The revolutionary Hoe rotary": Volo, pp. 205–6; Johannsen, pp. 16, 176; *Norton Anthology,* vol. 1, p. 1206; *Encyclopedia of American History,* p. 706.

16–17   "Employing Horace Mann's": Morison, vol. 2, p. 272; Volo, p. 83.

17   "Beneficiaries of this new": DeVoto, pp. 215–16; *National Intelligencer,* May 14, 1846.

17   " 'The Young American' ": Graebner, *Manifest Destiny,* p. 6.

17   ". . . two U.S. steamship lines": Morison, vol. 2, p. 226.

17–18   "Travelers now preferred": Volo, p. 329; Furnas, pp. 343–48.

18   "Businessmen discussed a transcontinental": *Encyclopedia of American History,* p. 428; Graebner, *Empire,* pp. 93–95.

18   "Thoreau and the Transcendentalists": Johannsen, pp. 283–84; Tocqueville, p. 591.

18   "During his rambles": Tocqueville, pp. 508–9.

18   "Walter Scott's historical": Volo, pp. ix–x, 213–14; Johannsen, pp. 147–49, 180–82, 245–47.

18–19   "In the pages of his": Morison, vol. 2, p. 282; Graebner, *Manifest Destiny,* p. 8.

19   "The 'Little Magician' ": Morison, vol. 2, pp. 238–40.

19   "All three major": Seigenthaler, pp. 78–79.

19   "The Panic of 1837": Kunhardt, pp. 18–23; Whitney, pp. 87–88.

20   "Tyler was a lifelong": Sellers, *Continentalist,* p. 61.

20   "With far less fanfare": Ibid., pp. 51–58; Polk, *Diary,* vol. 1, p. 42n.; Leonard, p. 76.

20   "In a just-published letter": Sellers, *Continentalist,* p. 51; Brands, *Lone Star,* p. 505.

20   " 'I am quite sick really' ": Sellers, *Continentalist,* p. 61.

21   "After party leaders dismissed": Haynes, p. 59; Sellers, *Continentalist,* p. 71; Polk, *Correspondence,* vol. 7, p. 137.

21   "In Baltimore, Southern delegates": Pillow and Polk, pp. 833–43.

21   "Washington politicians were just": Sellers, *Continentalist,* p. 100.

21   "The Democrats adopted": Haynes, pp. 62–65; Sellers, *Continentalist,* pp. 90–91.

22   " 'Who is James K. Polk?' ": Sellers, *Continentalist,* pp. 100–101.

22   "Adams Huntsman, a": Ibid., p. 105.

22   "From the Hermitage": Ibid., p. 139.

22   " 'We have had one' ": Ibid., p. 140; *Norton Anthology,* vol. 1, p. 2033.

22   "The old way": Polk, *Correspondence,* vol. 8, p. xv.

22–23   "Clay's 'American System' ": Ibid., p. x; Byrnes, p. 151; Leonard, p. 24; Sellers, *Continentalist,* p. 134; Seigenthaler, p. 94.

23   "Clay believed that slavery": Seigenthaler, pp. 77–78; J. Smith, *Annexation,* p. 297.

23   "The Ithaca (N.Y.) *Chronicle*": Byrnes, p. 183.

23   " '. . . my object will be' ": Polk, *Correspondence,* vol. 8, p. 456.

23–24   " 'Polk and Dallas are' ": A. Jackson, vol. 6, pp. 329–30; Sellers, *Continentalist,* p. 157.

24   "The *Times* of London": *Congressional Globe,* January 4, 1845; Sellers, *Continentalist,* p. 157; Adams, vol. 12, p. 168.

24   "Polk and the fading Jackson": Sellers, *Continentalist,* p. 184.

CHAPTER 3: THE PACIFIC DREAM

25–26   "Scientists, artists, sailors": Philbrick, pp. 58, 332, 350–51.

26   "Both nations took credit": Morison, vol. 2, p. 142.

26   "American missionaries settled": Haynes, pp. 126–29; Byrnes, p. 150; Philbrick, pp. 259–60; Merk, *Monroe Doctrine,* p. 66.

27   "Wilkes, whose Byronic": Philbrick, pp. 264, 304.

27   " 'Great Britain was never' ": Sellers, *Continentalist,* pp. 236, 242, 358; Polk, *Correspondence,* vol. 11, p. 69, vol. 7, pp. 333, 368.

28   "Polk extended an olive branch": Polk, *Diary,* vol. 2, p. 101. At about this time, after making notes on a "very important conversation" with Secretary of State James Buchanan regarding Oregon, Polk began keeping a diary. Beginning on August 26, 1845, Polk rarely missed a day during his nearly four-year career as a diarist. His candid account—up to a thousand words a day—of daily life through forty-two months of his presidency has no counterpart. First published in the twentieth century, Polk's diary is insightful and informative, yet it was consciously written for posterity and is at times notable in its omissions. Ironically, he never transcribed the notes of the conversation with Buchanan that launched his career as a diarist.

28   "Britain spurned the overture": Polk, *Diary,* vol. 1, p. 360; Sellers, *Continentalist,* p. 385.

28   "The Royal Navy began": Haynes, p. 129; Sellers, *Continentalist,* pp. 235, 380.

28   "English diplomats in Washington": Bailey, pp. 230–35; Polk, *Diary,* vol. I, pp. 244–45.

28–29   "While Lieutenant Wilkes's three-thousand-page": Philbrick, pp. 338–40.

29   "On St. Louis's streets": Graebner, *Empire,* pp. 9–10, 13, 90.

30   "John Quincy Adams": Haynes, p. xi; Adams, vol. IV, pp. 438–39.

30   "Months later, in the": Leonard, pp. 3, 56; McCaffrey, p. 66; Polk, *Correspondence,* vol. 10, pp. 61–62; Graebner, *Empire,* pp. 123–24.

30   "In 1823, when": Merk, *Monroe Doctrine,* p. 217; Boyer, pp. 513–14.

30–31   " 'We must ever maintain' ": J. Richardson, vol. 4, pp. 385–416; McCormac, p. 690; Byrnes, p. 165.

31   "The London *Times*": Merk, *Monroe Doctrine,* p. x.

31   "While some Eastern merchants": Graebner, *Empire,* pp. 99, 225, 227–28; McCormac, p. 359; Washington *Union,* June 2, 1845.

31   "However, other New England": Pletcher, p. 523; Graebner, *Empire,* pp. 20–21.

31–32   " 'If California ever becomes' ": R. Dana, pp. 217–18; Graebner, *Empire,* p. 219; Frémont, *Expeditions,* p. 659.

32   "Dana was a poet's son": R. Dana, p. 9.

32   "Dana assayed the native": Graebner, *Empire,* pp. 53–54.

32   "The country, Dana astutely": R. Dana, pp. 75, 163; Graebner, *Empire,* pp. 47–49.

32–33   "Frémont's richly detailed": Frémont, *Expeditions,* pp. 428–29, 658–59.

33   " 'The air was filled' ": Ibid., pp. 668–69, 672.

33   "Frémont and his thirty-nine men": Ibid., pp. 426-28, 434, 722, 726, 758.

33   "Frémont's report to Colonel": Ibid., pp. xix, 426.

33   "Spain had been the first": Merk, *Monroe Doctrine*, p. 105; Forbes, pp. 79–80.

33–34   "The Spanish viceroy": Funk & Wagnalls, vol. 15, p. 36; Forbes, pp. 54–55.

34   "Father Francis Junipero": Forbes, pp. 80–94, 101–26.

34   "The missions lay": Graebner, *Empire*, pp. 43–44; Larkin, pp. 1–2.

35   "Then, in 1835, Mexican dictator": Haecker, pp. 15–16; Larkin, pp. 2, 8; R. Dana, p. 125; Leonard, p. 145; Graebner, *Empire*, p. 45.

35–36   "As decay beset": Larkin, p. 3; Graebner, *Empire*, p. 12; Caruso, p. 114; Pletcher, p. 209; Leonard, pp. 127–28; DeVoto, p. 51.

36   "Thomas O. Larkin arrived": Caruso, pp. 112–13; Larkin, p. 63; Pletcher, p. 280; *Diplomatic Correspondence*, vol. 8, pp. 735–36; Graebner, *Empire*, pp. 51–52, 69.

36–37   "Buchanan's instructions to Larkin": Buchanan, vol. 6, pp. 275–77.

37   "Larkin began quietly": Ibid.; Merk, *Monroe Doctrine*, p. 115; Larkin, p. 10.

37   ". . . Jackson in 1835 offered Mexico": Merk, *Monroe Doctrine*, pp. 106–7; Price, pp. 26–27; Pletcher, p. 210.

37–38   "In the fall of 1842": Harlow, pp. 7–9; Philbrick, pp. 32, 40; Leonard, p. 132.

38–39   "Wilson Shannon, the U.S. minister": Pletcher, pp. 420–23; Merk, *Monroe Doctrine*, pp. 114–15; Bancroft, vol. 5, pp. 209, 215–22; *Diplomatic Correspondence*, vol. 8, p. 695; Graebner, *Empire*, pp. 6–7, 81–82.

39   ". . . the province erupted in civil": *Diplomatic Correspondence*, vol. 8, pp. 698–702, 755; Bancroft, pp. 30–35, 38–39.

39–40   "(In 1842, a ranch": Furnas, pp. 373–74; J. Smith, *War with Mexico*, vol. 1, p. 319; Graebner, *Empire*, pp. 72–73.

40   "Small wonder that": Graebner, *Empire*, p. 92.

CHAPTER 4: THE LONE STAR REPUBLIC

41   "Born in 1794": Callcott, pp. 3–4, 10, 20, 30–31.

41–42   "Named governor of the Yucatan": Ibid., pp. 55, 65, 71.

42   "Elected president in 1833": Ibid., pp. 105, 107–8, 116–20.

42   "In 1536, exactly three hundred years": Encyclopedia of World History, pp. 497–98.

42   "While seeking the mouth": Ibid., p. 510; Richardson et al., pp. 1–2; Brands, *Lone Star*, pp. 21–25, 34–35.

43   "In 1820, when only": Reichstein, pp. 28–29; Brands, *Lone Star*, pp. 21, 56–68, 92–93, 106, 133–137; Wheelan, p. 270.

43   "South Texas became a thriving": Vazquez, "Colonization," pp. 50–54.

43–44   "Mexican tariffs and restrictive": Richardson et al., p. 66.

44   "In 1824, Texas and": Ibid., p. 62; Brands, *Lone Star*, pp. 152–56, 204, 219–20; Leonard, p. 83; Vazquez, "Colonization," p. 65.

44   "As Austin was being led": Brands, *Lone Star*, p. 234.

44–45   "In 1825, President John Quincy": Haynes, p. 114; Cuevas, pp. 82–84; Ruiz, p. 110; Price, p. 16; Brands, *Lone Star*, p. 197.

45   "Santa Anna's heavy-handed" W. Davis, p. 87; Vazquez, "Colonization," pp. 70-72; Brands, *Lone Star*, pp. 240–44, 248.

45–46   "A Mexican army led": Brands, *Lone Star*, pp. 261–62, 265, 273, 278, 297.

46   "When he was informed": W. Davis, p. 220; Brands, *Lone Star,* p. 309.

46   "Indeed, Santa Anna planned": Brands, *Lone Star,* p. 309; Callcott, p. 129.

46   "Houston ordered Bowie": Brands, *Lone Star,* pp. 309, 319, 323–26, 337; Richardson et al.,
             pp. 106–7.

46–47   "Santa Anna's cannons": Brands, *Lone Star,* pp. 346–47, 358–61.

47   "At daybreak on March 6": Richardson et al., p. 107.

47   "Travis was the first": W. Davis, p. 221; Brands, *Lone Star,* pp. 360, 378; Richardson et al.,
             pp. 107–8.

47   "After failing to reinforce": Brands, *Lone Star,* pp. 387–97.

48   ". . . Santa Anna marched east": Ibid., pp. 409, 420, 425–29.

48   "Texans had harshly criticized": Ibid., p. 440.

48   "Acting initially on their": Ibid., pp. 444–59.

48–49   ". . . Santa Anna consented": Haecker, p. 12; Brands, *Lone Star,* pp. 463–69, 476.

49–50   "But whatever his personal": Brands, *Lone Star,* pp. 477–78; Remini, p. 365.

50   "An ailing Stephen Austin": Brands, *Lone Star,* p. 479.

50   "The new republic led": J. Smith, *Annexation,* p. 434.

50–51   "In 1841, Texas President": Merk, *Monroe Doctrine,* pp. 10–11.

51   "Santa Anna, once more": Callcott, pp. 156–58, 179–80; Brands, *Lone Star,* pp. 492–93.

51   "A graver threat": Brands, *Lone Star,* p. 491; Richardson et al., pp. 128, 134.

51–52   "In 1844, Secretary of State": Price, pp. 38–44.

52   "In Congress, Texas annexation": Whitney, pp. 91–92; Sellers, *Continentalist,* p. 50; Leonard,
             pp. 66–69.

52   "Mexico's minister in Washington": Buchanan, vol. 6, pp. 118–19; *Diplomatic Correspon-*
             dence, vol. 8, pp. 705–9.

52   "James Buchanan, the new": Buchanan, vol. 6, pp. 118–20.

CHAPTER 5: TO MANUFACTURE A WAR

53   "In rejecting a Senate request": J. Richardson, vol. 4, p. 383.

53–54   "Another likely reason": Leonard, p. 75; Sellers, *Continentalist,* pp. 215–19.

54   "Polk and his advisers": Caruso, pp. 23–24; Price, pp. 75, 107–11.

55   "The commodore's grandfather": Fischer, pp. 164–65.

55   "Morven later served": Philbrick, p. 337; Seigenthaler, p. 75; Whitney, p. 92; Price,
             pp. 49–58; Caruso, pp. 23–24.

55–56   "In Galveston, Stockton rendezvoused": Buchanan, vol. 6, pp. 130–31; Caruso, pp. 20–22;
             J. Smith, *Annexation,* p. 455; Polk, *Diary,* vol. 1, p. 207.

56   "Stockton enlisted Sherman": Sellers, *Continentalist,* p. 222; Caruso, pp. 26–28; Price,
             pp. 119–22; Pletcher, pp. 198–99.

56   "Just whose plan": Caruso, pp. 23–24.

56   "Stockton's emissary was": Ibid., pp. 28–29; Jones, p. 48.

56–57   "The skeptical President Jones": Caruso, pp. 28–29; Jones, pp. 46–50; A. Smith, pp. 66–67.

57   "A week after Wright": Polk, *Correspondence,* vol. 9, pp. 422–28.

57   "Jones's Attorney General": Jones, pp. 467, 469.

57–58   "General Edwin Morehouse": Ibid., pp. 46–47, 50–51; Merk, *Monroe Doctrine,* pp. 30–37;
             Price, p. 125; Pletcher, p. 199; Caruso, pp. 32–34.

58-59   "The British charge d'affaires": Haynes, p. 116; Merk, *Monroe Doctrine,* pp. 30–37, 87–88; Price, pp. 135–36, 151; J. Smith, *Annexation,* pp. 457, 466; Polk, *Correspondence,* vol. 9, p. 431; Jones, pp. 46, 54; McCormac, p. 370; Caruso, pp. 28–29.

59   "While neither Polk's diary": Caruso, pp. 32–35.

59   "On June 18, 1845": Ibid., p. 33; Pletcher, p. 253.

59–60   " 'Texas may now be' ": Polk, *Correspondence,* vol. 10, pp. 108–109.

60   "Mexico angrily pronounced": *Congressional Globe,* 29th Congress, 1st Session, Appendix, pp. 865–66.

60   " 'I have opposed it for ten' ": Adams, vol. 12, p. 202.

CHAPTER 6: THE ARMY AND THE BORDER

61   "The corps was now deploying": House Executive Document 60, p. 81 [June 15, 1845 order from War Secretary William Marcy].

61–62   "Taylor, sixty-one, blunt": Bauer, *Taylor,* pp. 1–83; T. Johnson, p. 153; Scott, *Memoirs,* vol. 2, pp. 381–83; Bauer, *Mexican War,* pp. 6–7; Hitchcock, p. 196; Frost, pp. 225–35; Whitney, p. 101; Engelmann, p. 438; Chamberlain, pp. 140–41; Chance, p. 76.

62–63   "Taylor struggled with pessimism": Taylor, pp. xx, 46.

63   ". . . Colonel Ethan Allen Hitchcock": Hitchcock, p. 192.

63   "Such sentiments appear": DeVoto, p. 15; *Concise Dictionary of American Biography,* p. 439; Hitchcock, p. 236.

63   "While some officers": Hitchcock, pp. 195–96; I. Stevens, p. 111.

63–64   "The Washington *Union*": *Washington Union,* June 2, 1845; Pletcher, p. 256; Merk, *Monroe Doctrine,* p. 81.

64   "In mid-August 1845": Price, pp. 165–66; House Executive Document 60, pp. 82–84; *Diplomatic Correspondence,* vol. 8, pp. 741–42, 748; Polk, *Diary,* vol. 1, pp. 9–10.

64   "More Army units reached": Bauer, *Mexican War,* pp. 32–35; J. Smith, *War with Mexico,* vol. 1, p. 140.

65   "Hitchcock believed Texas's assertion": Hitchcock, pp. 200, 203.

65   "By sending Taylor to the Nueces": Sellers, *Continentalist,* p. 261; Bauer, *Mexican War,* pp. 19, 26; Polk, *Correspondence,* vol. 10, p. 197.

65   "But if, contrary to": Leonard, p. 185; Bauer, *Mexican War,* pp. 393–94; Pletcher, pp. 269–71, 602; Polk, *Correspondence,* vol. 10, pp. 275–76.

65   "Whigs either deliberately": McCormac, p. 377.

66   "The first known reference": Merk, "Dissent," p. 35; Merk, *Monroe Doctrine,* pp. 137–40; Bailey, p. 173.

66   "In 1836, twenty years": Haecker, p. 12; McCormac, p. 373.

66   "Nor had Presidents Jackson,": Merk, *Monroe Doctrine,* p. 141; Haynes, p. 118.

66–67   "Only when persuading Texas": Polk, *Correspondence,* vol. 9, p. 431; McCormac, pp. 408–9.

67   "Robert Greenhow, the State": Merk, *Monroe Doctrine,* pp. 144–45.

67   "When the printed map": Hitchcock, p. 198.

67–68   "He was a dentist": Caruso, pp. 43–45; Sellers, *Continentalist,* pp. 233–34; Polk, *Correspondence,* vol. 10, p. 122; Johannsen, pp. 305–6.

68   "Parrott's June 10 report": Caruso, pp. 43–45; Graebner, *Empire,* p. 108; Leonard, p. 149; *Diplomatic Correspondence,* vol. 8, p. 725.

68   "Through October 18, Parrott": Caruso, pp. 46–49; Graebner, *Empire,* p. 117.

68–69   " 'I have good reasons' ": *Diplomatic Correspondence,* vol. 8, pp. 747, 751, 760.

69   "In an editorial bearing": *Washington Union,* October 2, 1845.

69   "Then, Mexico City consul": *Diplomatic Correspondence,* vol. 8, p. 766.

69   "Polk and Buchanan chose": Buchanan, vol. 6, pp. 302–5.

69   "Before Mexico would accept": *Diplomatic Correspondence,* vol. 8, pp. 766, 768–70.

69   "They had given Slidell": Ibid., p. 763.

CHAPTER 7: THE NEGOTIATIONS THAT NEVER WERE

70   "Tall and square-jawed": Sears, pp. 8, 13, 75–77, 205; Pletcher, pp. 276–79; *Concise Dictionary of American Biography,* p. 833.

70–71   "Polk instructed Slidell": Polk, *Correspondence,* vol. 10, pp. 249–50.

71   "Slidell's response on September 25": Ibid., p. 268.

71   " 'I am exceedingly desirous' ": Ibid., pp. 362–63.

71–72   "The Polk administration's craving": Buchanan, vol. 6, pp. 294–305; *Diplomatic Correspondence,* vol. 8, pp. 172–82.

72   "A letter from Polk": Polk, *Correspondence,* vol. 10, p. 363.

72   " 'No president who performs' ": Polk, *Diary,* vol. 4, p. 261.

72   "The president paid": Bergeron, p. 230.

72–73   "When Walker took a vacation": Bumgarner, pp. 15, 66.

73   "During the first year": Polk, *Diary,* vol. 1, p. 316, vol. 2, p. 360.

73   "Besides immersing himself": Polk, *Correspondence,* vol. 9, p. 198; Polk, *Diary,* vol. I, pp. 39, 55, 352–53; Sellers, *Continentalist,* p. 45.

73–74   "The president kept a rigid": Sellers, *Continentalist,* pp. 301, 306; Bergeron, pp. 34–35; Marine Band Web site, at www.marineband.usmc.mil; Haynes, 81–85.

74   "Besides serving as her": Bumgarner, pp. 63–64, 73; Bergeron, p. 231; Byrnes, pp. 223–24.

74   "Peña y Peña reminded": *Diplomatic Correspondence,* vol. 8, pp. 788–89.

75   "The president had hoped": Dr. Wayne Cutler interview, James K. Polk Project, Tennessee Presidents Center, Knoxville, Tennessee, July 18, 2005.

75   "Refusing to acknowledge": *Diplomatic Correspondence,* vol. 8, pp. 795–99.

75   "In a letter to Secretary": Sellers, *Continentalist,* pp. 399–400.

75–76   "There is no evidence": Haynes, p. 125; Polk, *Correspondence,* vol. 10, p. 433.

76   "During twenty-five years": Winders, *Mr. Polk's Army,* p. 174; *Time Almanac* 2003, p. 120.

76–77   "The price of his return": Callcott, pp. 90, 156–59, 161, 175; C. Robinson, p. xxxviii; DeVoto, p. 3.

77   "In February 1846, Colonel": Polk, *Diary,* vol. 1, pp. 223–25, 226, 228; Caruso, pp. 63–66.

77–78   "John Slidell's diplomatic": Polk, *Correspondence,* vol. 10, p. 449.

78   "Herrera's successor was": F. Robinson, pp. 247–48; Polk, *Correspondence,* vol. 11, pp. 25, 34n., 57–58.

78   "Polk's assessment of Paredes": *Diplomatic Correspondence,* vol. 8, p. 808; Soto, pp. 66–78; Pletcher, pp. 357–58; Haynes, p. 135; Bauer, *Mexican War,* p. 26; Leonard, p. 153; DePalo, p. 94.

78–79   " 'On January 13, he ordered' ": Polk, *Correspondence,* vol. 11, pp. 57–58.

79   "After a February 17 cabinet": Polk, *Diary,* vol. 1, p. 234.

79   "On March 12, Buchanan": Buchanan, vol. 6, pp. 402–4; Polk, *Diary,* vol. 1, p. 303.

79   "But even as Buchanan": *Diplomatic Correspondence,* vol. 8, pp. 821–24, 828.

80   "On April 21, when it was": J. Smith, *War with Mexico,* vol. 1, p. 150; Polk, *Diary,* vol. 1,

pp. 183–5, 297, 319, 343, 354; Sellers, *Continentalist,* p. 195; Polk, *Diary,* vol. 3, pp. 359–60; Seigenthaler, p. 130.

CHAPTER 8: THE WAR BEGINS

81	"Cross, who had three": Meade, pp. 62, 66.
81–82	"With the U.S. Army's": Bauer, *Mexican War,* pp. 33–34.
82	"The issue had come to": Hitchcock, pp. 204–6.
82	"When the petition": Polk, *Diary,* vol. 1, pp. 284–85; Bauer, *Mexican War,* p. 35.
82–83	"The next day, April 11": Meade, pp. 62, 66; Bauer, *Mexican War,* p. 47; *Origins of Mexican War,* vol. 2, pp. 132–33.
83	"On April 21, eleven": Barbour, p. 41.
83	" After interviewing Mexican": N. Dana, pp. 49–52; Henry, p. 81.
83	"Cross's death and Ampudia's": Meade, p. 66.
83–84	"Lieutenants Stephen D. Dobbins": Meade, pp. 66–68; *Origins,* pp. 132–33.
84	"Porter's death, coming": Meade, p. 68.
84	"The orders from Washington": House Executive Document 60, p. 90; J. Smith, *War with Mexico,* vol. 1, p. 143.
84	" 'I shall lose no time' ": House Executive Document 60, p. 90; Meade, p. 28.
84	" 'I hope for a war' ": Meade, p. 48.
85	"Lieutenant Ulysses S. Grant": Grant, p. 30; Hitchcock, pp. 213, 216, 222.
85	"When the Americans reached": House Executive Document 60, pp. 123–24, 127–29.
85	"As the Army of Observation": Pletcher, p. 374; Barbour, p. 17.
85–86	"Taylor tried to arrange": Barbour, pp. 118–20.
86	"Three days later": McCormac, p. 411.
86	"Although a stranger to": Barbour, pp. 20–21; J. Smith, vol. 1, p. 146.
87	"While Taylor exuded": Ripley, vol. 1, pp. 132–35; Barbour, p. 22; Pletcher, p. 383.
87	"The Rio Grande Valley's": Meade, p. 56; P. Stevens, pp. 107–8; Scribner, p. 22.
87	"Dozens of deserters": P. Stevens, pp. 52–53; Ballentine, p. 282.
87–88	"The Mexicans in Matamoros": P. Stevens, pp. 1–3, 106.
88	"U.S. officers added": Barbour, pp. 28–31; N. Dana, pp. 40–42.
88	"Robed priests sprinkled": Smith and Judah, p. 60.
88	"Major Barbour observed": Barbour, pp. 27–28.
88–89	"When finally completed": Meade, p. 74; P. Stevens, pp. 112–13.
89	"The fort's defenses": P. Stevens, pp. 112–13; N. Dana, pp. 45–58; Meade, pp. 59–60; Haecker, pp. 83–85.
89	"General Mejia's successor": F. Robinson, pp. 258–59; Barbour, pp. 33–35.
89	"Ampudia ordered U.S. Consul": House Executive Document 60, pp. 138, 140.
90	"Taylor replied that": Ibid., p. 140; *Diplomatic Correspondence,* vol. 8, pp. 845–46.
90	"Taylor ordered the Navy": House Executive Document 60, pp. 135–40; Bauer, *Mexican War,* p. 47; *Origins,* vol. 2, pp. 127–30.
90	" 'It will . . . compel' ": *Congressional Globe,* 30th Congress, 1st Session, Appendix, p. 153.
90	"On April 23, Mexican President": J. Smith, *War with Mexico,* vol. 1, pp. 150–52; *Origins,* vol. 2, pp. 134–35; DePalo, pp. 98–99; Pletcher, p. 440.
91	"Major General Mariano Arista": Barbour, p. 37.

91   "Brigadier General Anastasio": Haecker, pp. 24–25; McCormac, pp. 413–14.

91   "Gaunt and hard-bitten": P. Stevens, pp. 109–10; Daiss, www.savannah-online.com.

91–92   "Twenty miles north": Ripley, vol. 1, pp. 107–8; Bauer, *Mexican War*, pp. 47–48; Henry, p. 82.

92   "Chipita reached Fort Texas": P. Stevens, p. 110; Bauer, *Mexican War*, p. 48; Barbour, p. 45.

92   "Expecting an attack": Prescott, p. 219; Ripley, vol. 1, p. 109.

92   "In his report": *Origins*, vol. 2, p. 137.

CHAPTER 9: "A STATE OF WAR EXISTS"

93   "On Friday, May 8": Polk, *Diary*, vol. 1, p. 382; *National Intelligencer*, May 9, 1846.

94   "Dismissed as mediocrities": *Concise Dictionary of American Biography*, pp. 636–37; Byrnes, pp. 7–8, 142–43; Sellers, *Continentalist*, p. 213; Carruth, p. 337.

94   "Polk wanted to ask": Polk, *Diary*, vol. 1, pp. 384–85; Merk, *Monroe Doctrine*, p. 159.

95   "Polk read Taylor's dispatch": Polk, *Diary*, vol. 1, pp. 386–88.

95   "The president broke his rule": Ibid., p. 387.

95   "Monday's *National Intelligencer*": *National Intelligencer*, May 11, 1846.

95–96   "Polk's message, read at noon": J. Richardson, vol. 4, pp. 437–43.

96   "To quash dissent": Merk, "Dissent," pp. 37–39; *Congressional Globe*, 29th Congress, 1st Session, pp. 791–93.

96   "Democrats drowned out": *Congressional Globe*, 29th Congress, 1st Session, pp. 794–95.

97   "Ohio Congressman Joshua": Sampson, p. 103; *Congressional Globe*, 29th Congress, 1st Session, Appendix, pp. 642–43; Sellers, *Continentalist*, p. 421.

97   "Davis, who did not": Schroeder, p. 13.

97   "Even the few squeaks": *Washington Union*, May 11 and 12, 1846.

97   "In the Senate": Schroeder, pp. 22–23.

97   "Calhoun challenged the preamble's": *Congressional Globe*, 29th Congress, 1st Session, pp. 784, 795.

97–98   "Benton recommended that": Ibid., pp. 785, 795.

98   "The Mexicans, said Texas": Ibid., pp. 795, 800.

98   "Pressured by Allen": Polk, *Diary*, vol. 1, 391–92; *Congressional Globe*, 29th Congress, 1st Session, pp. 795, 800–803; Benton, vol. 2, p. 680; Pletcher, p. 392; Schroeder, pp. 16, 24.

98–99   "Polk signed the war bill": Polk, *Diary*, vol. 1, pp. 395–96; J. Smith, *War with Mexico*, vol. 1, p. 190.

99   "Newspapers applauded Congress's": Smith and Judah, p. 11; Johannsen, p. 10; *Washington Union*, May 25, 1846; *Concise Dictionary of American Biography*, p. 663.

99   "Northern critics were murmuring": *Washington Union*, October 10, 1846; *National Intelligencer*, May 15, 1846; Jones, pp. 46–47; Hitchcock, p. 225.

100   "The London *Times* wrote": Merk, *Monroe Doctrine*, p. 163.

100   "Secretary of State Buchanan": Buchanan, vol. 6, pp. 484–85.

100–101   "In his diary that night": Polk, *Diary*, vol. 1, pp. 397–99; Sellers, *Continentalist*, pp. 421–22.

101   " 'I declared my purpose' ": Polk, *Diary*, vol. 1, pp. 437–38; vol. 2, pp. 56–57, 76; Sellers, *Continentalist*, pp. 423–24.

101–2   "At Fort Leavenworth": Polk, *Diary*, vol. 1, pp. 403, 438–439; J. Smith, *War with Mexico*, vol. 1, pp. 286–89.

CHAPTER 10: THE EXPLORER AND THE MARINE

103   "The previous evening, companions": Frémont, *Memoirs,* pp. 484–88.

103   "In just one week": Bancroft, vol. 5, p. 24; Marti, p. 36.

103   "Gillespie had sailed from": Buchanan, vol. 6, pp. 275–77.

103   "Gillespie handed Frémont" Frémont, *Memoirs,* p. 489.

103   "According to Frémont's *Memoirs*": Ibid., pp. 488–90.

103–4   "Gillespie also told": Harlow, p. 80.

105   "The Polk administration's *written*": Polk, *Diary,* vol. 3, p. 395; Bancroft, pp. 89–90.

105–6   " 'What the purpose was' ": Bancroft, p. 86 [Excerpt from committee findings].

106   "Larkin's letter, dated": *Diplomatic Correspondence,* vol. 8, pp. 735–36.

106   " 'Everything coming from California' ": Hussey, pp. 46–47.

107   "He and his advisers": Bergeron, p. 72; Pletcher, p. 282.

107–8   "Stockton was to operate": Hussey, pp. 50–51; Polk, *Diary,* vol. 1, p. 67; *Concise Dictionary of American Biography,* p. 74.

108   "The conversation then evidently": Polk, *Diary,* vol. 1, p. 71.

108   "A few days later, Gillespie": Hussey, pp. 50–51.

108   "On the evening of October 30": Bauer, *Mexican War,* p. 183; Hussey, p. 43.

108   "Gillespie had already received": Hussey, pp. 48–49; Marti, p. 7; Graebner, *Empire,* pp. 157–58. In 1833, Hooper was working for his father-in-law, William Sturgis of Bryant, Sturgis & Co. in Boston, when Richard Henry Dana Jr. signed on as a seaman on the firm's brig, Pilgrim.

108–9   "In his journal entry": Polk, *Diary,* vol. 1, p. 83; Marti, pp. 38–39.

109   "Judging by Gillespie's future": McCormac, p. 388.

109   "On the last day": Gillespie, "Further Letters," pp. 219, 225–26.

109   "On February 10": Gillespie, "Further Letters," p. 228; "Conquest," p. 125.

110   "An equally powerful British": Bancroft, pp. 199–203.

110   "Because of the detour": Gillespie, "Conquest," p. 131.

110   "Within hours of the": Bancroft, p. 63.

110   "General Jose Castro's twenty-five": Gillespie, "Conquest," pp. 136–137.

110   "Beside the campfire": Ibid., p. 271.

110   "Unknown to Gillespie": Marti, p. 34.

111   "Around midnight, Kit Carson's": Frémont, *Memoirs,* pp. 490–95; *Diplomatic Correspondence,* vol. 8, pp. 856–57.

111   " 'We kill some' ": Frémont, *Memoirs,* p. 495.

111–12   "A pale, slender man": Egan, p. 7; Chaffin, pp. 23–25.

112   "After teaching mathematics": *Concise Dictionary of American Biography,* p. 324; Egan, p. 37.

112   "With Kit Carson guiding": *Concise Dictionary of American Biography,* p. 324.

112–13   "As she did after": Frémont, *Memoirs,* pp. 414, 419–20.

113   "According to Frémont's *Memoirs*": Ibid., pp. 418–19.

113   "Benton and Polk administration": Caruso, pp. 107–8; Frémont, *Memoirs,* pp. 420–24.

113   "On June 23, 1845, Frémont": DeVoto, p. 40.

114   " 'I had before my mind' ": Frémont, *Memoirs,* p. 457.

114   "Traveling at a leisurely": Chaffin, p. 285.

114   "On March 5, a Lieutenant": Bancroft, p. 10n.

114   "Provoked by the letters' ": Frémont, *Memoirs,* pp. 458–60.

115   " 'While this was being' ": Ibid., pp. 460–64; Bancroft, pp. 12–13; *Diplomatic Correspon-
            dence,* pp. 834–36.

115   "From this aerie": Frémont, *Memoirs,* pp. 460–62.

115   "Castro announced that": Ibid., pp. 462–64.

116   "Monterey Prefect Don Manuel Castro": Ibid., pp. 500–503.

116   "Gillespie and Frémont exhorted": Smith and Judah, pp. 25, 145–47; Gillespie, "Conquest,"
            p. 271; Bancroft, p. 101; Frémont, *Memoirs,* p. 519.

116   "Castro had reportedly": Bancroft, pp. 78–80, 101.

116–17   "Frémont sent Gillespie to": Frémont, *Memoirs,* pp. 504–5, 519; Moskin, p. 62.

117   "Frémont led a preemptive": Frémont, *Memoirs,* p. 517.

117   "The settlers were disappointed": Ibid., p. 516; Bancroft, pp. 78n., 94–95, 95n.; Gillespie,
            "Conquest," p. 279.

117–18   "Informed that two hundred": Frémont, *Memoirs,* p. 522; Bancroft, pp. 105–7.

118   "Frémont appointed Merritt": Frémont, *Memoirs,* p. 509; Bancroft, pp. 109–17.

118   "Merritt and two other": Bancroft, pp. 120–21, 133–35; Frémont, *Memoirs,* p. 520.

118   "William B. Ide gave a": Larkin, pp. 63–64; Bancroft, pp. 118, 146–47; Chaffin, p. 327;
            Frémont, *Memoirs,* pp. 523–24.

119   "He could no longer sit": Chaffin, p. 330; Frémont, *Memoirs,* p. 520.

119   " 'He has made several' ": Polk, *Diary,* vol. 1, pp. 412–13.

119   "General Jose Castro increased": Bancroft, pp. 133–35, 142–44; Richmond, p. 133.

119   "Torre's division of fifty": Chaffin, p. 331.

120   "Ford's men stumbled upon": Larkin, p. 48; Gillespie, "Conquest," p. 276; Bancroft, pp. 164–68,
            170–71; Frémont, *Memoirs,* p. 525.

120   "The rebellious settlers officially": Caruso, pp. 130–31; Larkin, pp. 63–64; Bancroft,
            pp. 184–85.

121   "Commodore John Sloat's six": Bancroft, p. 254n.; *Concise Dictionary of American Biography,*
            p. 942; *Encyclopedia of the War of 1812,* p. 150.

121   "On May 17, William Parrott's": Bancroft, pp. 202–4.

121–22   "Consul Larkin came aboard": Frémont, *Memoirs,* p. 537.

122   "And then, on July 5": Ibid., pp. 540–42; Bancroft, p. 229.

122   "July 7 dawned bright": Bancroft, p. 230.

122   "At 9:30 a.m., the harbor": Ibid., p. 231.

122–23   "Met by only": Ibid.; *Diplomatic Correspondence,* vol. 8, p. 878; Bauer, *Mexican War,* p. 171.

123   "At the customs house": Bauer, *Mexican War,* pp. 170–71; Bancroft, pp. 235–36; *Diplomatic
            Correspondence,* vol. 8, pp. 877–78n.

123   "News of the Navy's": Bancroft, pp. 185, 231–32; J. Smith, *War with Mexico,* vol. 1, p. 335.

123   "When the eighty-gun HMS": Frémont, *Memoirs,* pp. 532, 542.

123–24   "U.S. and British sailors": Ibid., p. 533.

124   "Sloat reacted with dismay": Ibid., pp. 533–34.

124   "He rejected Frémont's proposal": Bancroft, p. 250.

124–25   "Sloat's June 6 letter": Caruso, p. 132; Frémont, *Memoirs,* pp. 536–37.

125   "He quietly informed Stockton": Gillespie, "Conquest," p. 277; Bancroft, pp. 253–54.

125   "The new Pacific Squadron": Pletcher, p. 436; Bauer, *Mexican War,* pp. 172–74.

CHAPTER 11: TESTING THE ENEMY

127   "But before Taylor could": Haecker, pp. 26–27.

127–8   "But rumors had reached": F. Robinson, pp. 252–53; Ripley, vol. 1, pp. 109–10; Haecker, pp. 26–27.

128   "Taylor's men were awakened": Barbour, pp. 51–52.

128   "Anxious to obtain information": Henry, p. 85; Bauer, *Mexican War,* pp. 50–52; Barbour, p. 52.

128–9   "Slightly built, slouching, and": Henry, pp. 85–89; Frost, pp. 299–301; *Mexican War and Its Heroes,* pp. 179–81; Weems, p. 126; Winders, *Mr. Polk's Army,* p. 100.

129   "Walker returned to": Henry, pp. 85–89.

129   "Scouting ahead for": Ripley, vol. 1, p. 136; Barbour, p. 53.

129   "Thus, it was almost": N. Dana, p. 45.

129–30 "While the initial bombardment": Ripley, vol. 1, pp. 112–15; N. Dana, pp. 59–62; Meade, pp. 59–60.

130   "A Mexican shell struck": N. Dana, pp. 59–62.

130   "On the fourth day": Haecker, pp. 81–83, 67; N. Dana, pp. 59–60; Meade, p. 60.

130   "On May 6": *Congressional Globe,* 29th Congress, 1st Session, Appendix [Hawkins Report], pp. 681–682; Bauer, *Mexican War,* pp. 50–52.

131   "Over six days, the enemy": *Congressional Globe,* 29th Congress, 1st Session, Appendix [Hawkins Report], pp. 681–682; Meade, p. 84; N. Dana, pp. 59–60; Ripley, vol. 1, pp. 115–116.

131   "Most Americans regarded": Haecker, p. 89 [From Edward M. Coffman's *The Old Army: A Portrait of the American Army in Peacetime, 1784–1898*], pp. 139–41.

131   "In Mexico, the U.S. troops": Smith and Judah, p. 1; Roth, p. 43; J. Smith, *War with Mexico,* vol. 1, p. 159.

131–32 "Most of the regulars": Haecker, pp. 88–89; Winders, *Mr. Polk's Army,* pp. 103–8.

132   "Yet, the logjam": Winders, *Mr. Polk's Army,* pp. 52–53.

132   "A private made $7": J. Smith, *War with Mexico,* vol. 1, pp. 191–912; Winders, *Mr. Polk's Army,* p. 122.

132   "Although woefully understrength": Winders, *Mr. Polk's Army,* p. 92; McCaffrey, pp. 38–39; Haecker, p. 66.

132–33 "During Calhoun's 1817–1825": Haecker, pp. 59–60, 14–15.

133   "Poinsett's horticultural legacy": *Concise Dictionary of American Biography,* p. 794; Haecker, pp. 14–15.

133   "Its guns, weighing sixteen hundred pounds": Lavender, pp. 227–28.

133   "In each of the Army's": Haecker, pp. 19–21, 75, 83–85.

133–34 "Field artillery officers": Mexican War and Its Heroes, pp. 174–75; Smith and Judah, p. 101.

134   "The blue-uniformed infantryman": Winders, *Mr. Polk's Army,* pp. 24, 92–99; Haecker, pp. 70–73.

134   " 'A better army, man' ": Grant, p. 84.

134–35 "About noon, dragoons that": Haecker, p. 53; *Congressional Globe,* 29th Congress, 1st Session, Appendix, p. 675; Barbour, p. 54.

135   "In his glittering dress uniform": J. Smith, vol. 1, p. 165; Smith and Judah [Report of engineer Lt. Jeremiah Mason Scarritt], p. 66.

135 ". . . standing tall in their": J. Smith, *War with Mexico*, vol. 1, p. 165.

135 "Its enlisted ranks were": Haecker, pp. 17–18.

135 "Arista's men were armed": Haecker, pp. 60–65, 85–87, 102.

136 "Taylor's twenty-three hundred men now saw": Ibid., p. 31.

136 "Both armies practiced": Ibid., pp. 31, 98–102.

136 "Major Samuel Ringgold's field": Barbour, p. 54; Smith and Judah [Lt. Scarritt report], p. 66; *Congressional Globe*, 29th Congress, 1st Session, Appendix [Gen. Taylor report], p. 675; Haecker, p. 39.

136 "The combatants then settled": Smith and Judah [Lt. Scarritt Report], p. 66.

136–37 "Ringgold's battery moved and": Barbour, pp. 54–56; Meade, pp. 79–80; *Congressional Globe*, 29th Congress, 1st Session, Appendix [Gen. Taylor report], p. 677; Haecker, pp. 35, 41–42, 99.

137 "Captain Duncan's flying artillery": Barbour, p. 56; *Congressional Globe*, 29th Congress, 1st Session, Appendix [Gen. Taylor report], p. 675; Meade, pp. 79–80.

137 "Mexican gunners cut down": *Congressional Globe*, 29th Congress, 1st Session, Appendix [Gen. Taylor report], p. 675.

137 "Torrejon's cavalry now attacked": Ibid., pp. 675–76; Bauer, *Mexican War*, pp. 54–56.

137–38 " 'It was truly a shocking sight' ": Henry, p. 95.

138 "Palo Alto's marshy grasses": *Congressional Globe*, 29th Congress, 1st Session, Appendix [Gen. Taylor report], p. 675; Haecker, pp. 50–53; Bauer, *Mexican War*, pp. 54–56; Eggenberger, p. 321; Henry, p. 95.

138 "His army had withdrawn": J. Smith, *War with Mexico*, vol. 1, pp. 170–72; Ripley, vol. 1, p. 125.

138–39 "At a war council": Ripley, vol. 1, pp. 123–24.

139 "Scouts reported that Mexican": Meade, p. 80; *Congressional Globe*, 29th Congress, 1st Session, Appendix [Gen. Taylor report], p. 676.

139 "Taylor sent forward": *Congressional Globe*, 29th Congress, 1st Session, Appendix [Gen. Taylor report], p. 677.

139 "Taylor grasped his drawn sword": *Congressional Globe*, 29th Congress, 1st Session, Appendix, pp. 676–77; Henry, p. 100.

139–40 "Colonel James McIntosh suddenly": Henry, pp. 126–27.

140 "Two-dozen men under Captain": J. Smith, *War with Mexico*, vol. 1, pp. 173–75; Barbour, p. 60.

140 " 'The pursuit now commenced' ": Barbour, p. 60.

140 "General Arista was in his tent": J. Smith, *War with Mexico*, vol. 1, pp. 173–75; Bauer, *Mexican War*, p. 62; *Congressional Globe*, 29th Congress, 1st Session, Appendix [battle reports], p. 683; Pletcher, p. 401.

140 "Throwing away their weapons": *Congressional Globe*, 29th Congress, 1st Session, Appendix [battle reports], pp. 676–77.

140–41 "Taylor's men seized all": Meade, pp. 80–81, 89; Bauer, *Mexican War*, p. 62; *Congressional Globe*, 29th Congress, 1st Session, Appendix [battle reports], pp. 677, 683.

141 "In his report, Taylor": *Congressional Globe*, 29th Congress, 1st Session, Appendix [battle reports], pp. 676–77.

141 "Arista, who had crossed": *Diplomatic Correspondence*, vol. 8, p. 855; Ripley, vol. 1, pp. 140–41.

141 "Taylor might have crushed": Barbour, p. 56; Ripley, vol. 1, pp. 138–39.

141 "Mead called it a 'perfect inability' ": J. Smith, *War with Mexico*, vol. 1, pp. 177–79; Meade, pp. 82–85; Pletcher, p. 401.

142   "The Americans devoted": Barbour, p. 61; Bauer, *Mexican War,* p. 62; Eggenberger, p. 359.

142   "The men's desire to put": Bauer, *Mexican War,* p. 81.

142   "Even while facing Arista's": J. Smith, *War with Mexico,* vol. 1, pp. 177–79.

142–43   "On May 18, Taylor's army": Barbour, pp. 64–65; Bauer, *Mexican War,* p. 82.

143   "True to Taylor's promise": Meade, pp. 85–86; Barbour, pp. 64–65; Smith and Judah, p. 73.

143   "Twenty-seven miles from": Ripley, vol. 1, p. 130; Barbour, pp. 85–86.

143   "At Sunday services": Johannsen, pp. 49–51.

143–44   "Zachary Taylor saw nothing": Taylor, p. 37.

144   "After learning of Captain": Bauer, *Mexican War,* p. 57; *Encyclopedia of the War of 1812,* p. 199; Ripley, vol. 1, pp. 150–52; McCaffrey, pp. 15–16.

144   " 'Gen'l Gaines has greatly' ": Polk, *Diary,* vol. 1, pp. 450–51.

144   "The first six companies": J. Smith, *War with Mexico,* vol. 1, p. 208; Taylor, p. 20.

144–45   "In August 1845, after reading": Bauer, *Mexican War,* pp. 19–20.

145   "On June 20, after Gaines": Polk, *Diary,* vol. 1, p. 480.

145   "Polk gathered all of the": Ibid., vol. 2, pp. 13–14.

145   "The Court of Inquiry": Ibid., p. 83; Bauer, *Mexican War,* p. 58.

146   "Polk, preternaturally attuned": Sellers, *Continentalist,* p. 438.

146   "In March, Polk had weighed": Polk, *Diary,* vol. 1, pp. 308–9.

146–7   " 'Gen'l Scott did not impress' ": Ibid., pp. 401–8.

147   "He noted peevishly that": Ibid., pp. 419–21; *Congressional Globe,* 29th Congress, 1st Session, Appendix, pp. 650–51.

147   "Scott explained to Archer": Polk, *Diary,* vol. 1, p. 414n.

147–8   "Thus, when the president read": Ibid., pp. 419–21, 424; *Congressional Globe,* 29th Congress, 1st Session, Appendix, p. 651.

148   "Scott's effusively apologetic": Polk, *Diary,* vol. 1, p. 428; *Congressional Globe,* 29th Congress, 1st Session, Appendix, p. 651.

148   "Polk had already drafted": Polk, *Diary,* vol. 1, p. 428.

148   "Because of his 'brilliant victories' ": J. Richardson, vol. 4, pp. 448–49.

148   "Congress awarded Taylor": Polk–Taylor correspondence, Library of Congress, from James K. Polk Project, University of Tennessee, May 30, July 15, 1846; Taylor, p. 20.

149   "In his superb *Memoirs*": Grant, pp. 56–57, 67, 86–87.

CHAPTER 12: A QUESTION OF "PECULIAR DELICACY"

150   "Navy Secretary George Bancroft": Caruso, pp. 67–68; *Congressional Globe,* 30th Congress, 1st Session, Appendix, p. 163.

150–51   "They looked no further": Caruso, p. 69; *Concise Dictionary of American Biography,* p. 616; Sears, pp. 20–22.

151   "Mackenzie reached Havana": *Congressional Globe,* 30th Congress, 1st Session, Appendix, p. 163; Callcott, pp. 231–38; Pletcher, pp. 443–44; Caruso, p. 68–73; Leonard, pp. 169–70.

151–52   "Thousands of people watched": Callcott, p. 269; McCormac, pp. 444–45.

152   "The gunners at the Castle": Weems, pp. 197–98; F. Robinson, p. 249; Santoni, pp. 130–131; *Diplomatic Correspondence,* vol. 8, pp. 883–84.

152   "Significantly, few ordinary": Weems, pp. 197–98; Santoni, pp. 133, 136; Callcott, p. 238.

152   "Santa Anna published": Soto, pp. 66–72; Weems, p. 198.

152–53   "He lingered for weeks": Santoni, pp. 141–44.

153   "General Santa Anna, who liked": Brands, *Lone Star,* p. 308; Santa Anna, *Autobiography,* pp. 89–91; J. Smith, *War with Mexico,* vol. 1, p. 200; Callcott, p. 221; Scheina, pp. 49–51.

153–54   "Senator Thomas Hart Benton": James Polk–William Polk letter, July 14, 1846, Library of Congress, from James K. Polk Center, University of Tennessee; Benton, vol. 2, pp. 680–81.

154   "In a July 27 letter": *Congressional Globe,* 29th Congress, 2nd Session, Appendix, p. 24; McCormac, pp. 439–40; Polk, *Diary,* vol. 2, pp. 63–65; J. Richardson, vol. 4, pp. 456–57.

154   "While Polk's congressional allies": Benton, vol. 2, pp. 681–82.

154   "In fact, a week before": J. Richardson, vol. 4, p. 457; Polk, *Diary,* vol. 2, p. 50.

155   "Presented in a confidential": Polk, *Diary,* vol. 2, pp. 70–73.

155   "When the bill was introduced": Going, pp. 94–96.

155–56   "As congressmen were leaving": Wilentz, *Rise,* pp. 595–96; *Biographical Directory of the U.S. Congress,* p. 2064; *Congressional Globe,* 29th Congress, 1st Session, pp. 1215–17.

156   "When the House reconvened": Wilentz, *Rise,* pp. 595–96; *Congressional Globe,* 29th Congress, 1st Session, p. 1217.

156   "Illuminated by candles": Going [from *New York Herald*], p. 98.

156–57   "Northern Whigs voted with": Wilentz, *Rise,* p. 599; Schroeder, p. 47–55; Dusinberre, pp. 155, 173–74; The Constitution, p. 65; Polk, *Diary,* vol. 2, p. 74.

157   "The 'mischievous & foolish' ": Polk, *Diary,* vol. 2, pp. 74–75.

157   ". . . Charles Dickens's bleak": Dickens, p. 150; Sobel, pp. 180–81; *Encyclopedia of American History,* p. 443.

157–58   "Polk, the penultimate": Dusinberre, pp. 4–6, 155; Sellers, *Jacksonian,* pp. 107–8; *Congressional Globe,* 19th Congress, 1st Session, pp. 1633–53; Price, p. 18; Merk, *Monroe Doctrine,* p. 225.

158   "An unrepentant slaveholder": Sellers, *Jacksonian,* p. 313; Leonard, pp. 28–29.

158   "During the 1844 campaign": Dusinberre, pp. 11–12, 17; Sellers, *Jacksonian,* pp. 186, 446.

158   "While he was president": Polk, *Correspondence,* vol. 10, p. 478; Polk, *Presidential Papers,* Microfilm, Reel 57, Sheets 522–23, 566–67.

158–59   "The new slaves were probably": Dusinberre, pp. 11–12, 18–19; Bumgarner, p. 61.

159   "The Two Million Dollar Bill": Going, pp. 101–5; *Congressional Globe,* 29th Congress, 1st Session, p. 1220; Polk, *Diary,* vol. 2, p. 77.

159–60   "In the same long journal": Polk, *Diary,* vol. 2, pp. 76–77.

160   " 'For the executive to accept' ": Ibid., pp. 144–46; *Diplomatic Correspondence,* vol. 8, p. 885; *Congressional Globe,* 29th Congress, 2nd Session, Appendix, pp. 24–25; *Washington Union,* October 2, 1846; Pletcher [James Polk–William Polk letter, October 2, 1846], pp. 467–68.

160   "England volunteered to": Polk, *Diary,* vol. 2, p. 129; Merk, *Monroe Doctrine,* pp. 15–19; Pletcher, p. 453.

CHAPTER 13: ZACHARY TAYLOR'S ARMY

161–62   ". . . mud-plastered 'miserable hovels' ": Hitchcock, p. 234; Tennery, p. 32.

162   "The camps were ecosystems": Smith and Judah, pp. 49–52; Tennery, p. 33; Taylor, pp. 136–37; Johannsen, pp. 89–90; McCaffrey, pp. 52–53.

162–63   "Building one's immunity": Tennery, pp. 22–23; F. Smith, p. 21.

163   "The ubiquity of illness": Chance, pp. 26–29; Dilworth, p. 101nn.; J. Smith, *War with Mexico,* vol. 1, pp. 209–10.

163   "The myriad illnesses": McCaffrey, pp. 58, 61–62; Winders, *Mr. Polk's Army,* pp. 140–44.

163 "One of the worst": Winders, *Mr. Polk's Army*, pp. 152–55.

164 "The soldiers lined the riverbank": Chance, pp. 29, 32; Dilworth, pp. 34, 101nn.; N. Dana, pp. 142, 144–45; Johannsen, pp. 169–70; J. Smith, *War with Mexico*, vol. 1, pp. 209–10.

164 "Monterrey was the sanctuary": Weems, p. 217.

164 "At Monterrey, Taylor hoped": J. Smith, *War with Mexico*, vol. 1, p. 204; Taylor, pp. 45–47.

165 "Taylor professed no interest": Taylor, pp. 32, 35.

165 "Upon conquering a province": McCormac, pp. 437–38.

165 " 'We come to overthrow' ": House Executive Document 60, p. 284.

165–66 "He summoned three bishops": Polk: *Diary*, vol. 1, pp. 408–9, 411; P. Stevens, pp. 132–36, 180–81.

166 " 'Although I did not approve' ": Taylor, p. 176.

166–67 "The Schuylkill Arsenal": Johannsen, pp. 12–14.

167 "Scarce shipping was the": Taylor, p. 13; Chance, pp. 10, 26; Dilworth, p. 39.

167 "Some regiments marched": Henry, pp. 142–43; Smith and Judah, p. 75.

167–68 "Polk, too, was exasperated": Polk, *Diary*, vol. 2, pp. 117–19, 150–51.

168 ". . . mules had been used": Ibid., pp. 118, 430–31; Grant, p. 50.

168 "Already working longer hours": Polk, *Diary*, vol. 2, pp. 154, 481–82; Haynes, pp. 160–66.

169 " 'The truth is our troops' ": Polk, *Diary*, vol. 2, pp. 481–82, 492.

169 "The more the president applied": Winders, *Mr. Polk's Army*, p. 187.

169 "The president believed": J. Richardson, vol. 4, pp. 471–98.

169 "The first volunteers were": Smith and Judah, p. 42; Archibald Yell–James Polk letter, June 8, 1846, Library of Congress, from James K. Polk Center; Johannsen, p. 11; Winders, *Mr. Polk's Army*, pp. 70–72; Tocqueville, pp. 630–32.

169–70 "Baltimore filled its quota": *Washington Union*, June 1, 1846; Johannsen, pp. 25–28.

170 "The first volunteers set out": Johannsen, pp. 26–29, 58–60.

170 "The soldiers toured": Ibid., pp. 56–57; Winders, *Mr. Polk's Army*, p. 114.

171 " 'One who has never' ": Mead, pp. 90–91; Winders, *Mr. Polk's Army*, pp. 82–83.

171 "Lieutenant Abner Doubleday, the": *Concise Dictionary of American Biography*, p. 252; Doubleday, pp. 64–65.

171 "Lieutenant Daniel Hill noted": Hill, pp. 3, 7, 9, 16.

171–72 " 'A regiment of regulars' ": Smith and Judah [Scott letter to War Secretary Marcy, January 16, 1847], p. 30.

172 "The regulars were appalled": Winders, *Mr. Polk's Army*, p. 109; Johannsen, pp. 30–31; Smith and Judah, p. 31.

172 "Among Taylor's criticisms": Winders, *Mr. Polk's Army*, p. 109.

172 "After the War of 1812": Ibid., pp. 43, 70; J. Smith, vol. 1, pp. 191–92.

172–73 "Some of the regular officers' ": Winders, *Mr. Polk's Army*, p. 37; McClellan, p. 16; Sellers, *Continentalist*, p. 438; Dr. Wayne Cutler interview, James K. Polk Center, University of Tennessee, July 19, 2005.

173 "Even Colonel Samuel Ryan Curtis": Winders, *Mr. Polk's Army*, p. 198; Johannsen, p. 39.

173 "Theatrical troupes performed": Henry, p. 244; Winders, *Mr. Polk's Army*, p. 133.

173 "Printing presses that": *Concise Dictionary of American Biography*, p. 217; Johansen, pp. 223–25.

173–74 "Around their campfires": Winders, *Mr. Polk's Army*, pp. 129, 183; Henry, pp. 120–21; McCaffrey, pp. 74–78.

174   "They read aloud": Johannsen, pp. 54, 60, 147, 150–51, 161, 245–47; Chance, p. 36; Smith and Judah, pp. 6–7.

175   " 'The country expects us' ": Taylor, p. 51.

175   "For the Monterrey expedition": Dilworth, p. 103nn.; Henry, p. 152; Chance, p. 34.

175–76   "Davis had accepted command": Whitney, p. 101; Bauer, *Taylor,* pp. 69–70; Strode, pp. 12, 18, 98–104; *Concise Dictionary of American Biography,* p. 230; *Encyclopedia of American History,* pp. 648–49.

175–76   "The Taylor expedition's scouting": Johannsen, p. 38; Wilkins, p. xx; Smith and Judah, pp. 40–41; Dilworth, p. 36.

176   "Walker's Rangers were": Wilkins, pp. 25, 33, 36–42.

176–77   "In Reynosa, Army Lieutenant": Dilworth, pp. 36–37; Bauer, *Mexican War,* p. 87; Johannsen, p. 38.

177   "On August 17"; Chance, p. 30.

177   "Two days later, the first": Weems, pp. 211–12; Chance, pp. 35–36.

CHAPTER 14: MONTERREY

179   "General Taylor and his": Bauer, *Mexican War,* pp. 90–92.

179–80   "Immediately in front of them": J. Smith, *War with Mexico,* vol. 1, pp. 232–33; Smith and Judah, pp. 78–79; Bauer, *Mexican War,* pp. 90–93.

180   "Suddenly, the fort swarmed": Barbour, p. 106; Chance, p. 37; Bauer, *Mexican War,* pp. 90–92.

180   "But the dust": Smith and Judah, pp. 77–78; Hill, p. 13.

180   "As the jagged, treeless": Johannsen, pp. 79–83; Chance, p. 36; Hill, p. 13.

181   "They prepared themselves": Dilworth, p. 61.

181   "On the last leg": Henry, p. 244; Doubleday, p. 75.

181   "Canales's regulars devoted": Smith and Judah, pp. 74–75; J. Smith, *War with Mexico,* vol. 1, pp. 235–37.

181–82   "On the outskirts": Dilworth, p. 67.

182–83   "Yet disagreements and": Mexican Soldier, plate p. 48; DePalo, p. 96; Singletary, p. 2; Haecker, pp. 92–97.

183   "Within the past year": Pletcher, pp. 441–42, 484–85; *Diplomatic Correspondence,* vol. 8, pp. 727–28, 752, 888–89.

183   "The ruling 'puro' ": *Diplomatic Correspondence,* vol. 8, pp. 801–3.

184   "Hoping to raise thirty thousand": Ibid., pp. 886–87.

184   "General Ampudia, however": DePalo, p. 104; J. Smith, *War with Mexico,* vol. 1, pp. 230–34.

184   "Described by historian Justin": J. Smith, *War with Mexico,* vol. 1, pp. 225–26; P. Stevens, pp. 137–38.

184–85   "He had fortified": Bauer, *Mexican War,* pp. 92–93; Chance, pp. 39–40; J. Smith, *War with Mexico,* vol. 1, pp. 233–34, 239–41.

185   "Mejia and Ampudia had": Chance, pp. 39–41; Bauer, *Mexican War,* pp. 92–93.

185   "East Monterrey's thoroughfares": J. Smith, *War with Mexico,* vol. 1, pp. 232–33.

185   "At the last minute, he": Ibid., pp. 234–35; DePalo, p. 104.

186   "After nightfall on September": Doubleday, pp. 79–80; Zachary Taylor, September 22, 1846 report to Adjutant General Roger Jones, from Descendants of Mexican War Veterans Web site at www.dmwv.org/mexwar/documents/docs.htm#reports.

186–87   "Beyond the range of": Doubleday, p. 80; Barbour, p. 108.

187   "Lieutenant Doubleday trained": Doubleday, pp. 80–83.

187   "Lieutenant Ulysses S. Grant": Grant, p. 59.

187–88 "But no one disputed": Grant, p. 59; Frost, pp. 239–54; *Mexican War and Its Heroes*, pp. 90–91; *Concise Dictionary of American Biography*, p. 1212; Henry, p. 219.

188   "Led by three companies": J. Smith, *War with Mexico*, vol. 1, pp. 242–43; *Mexican War and Its Heroes*, pp. 196–97; Kendall, pp. 125–26.

188–89 "About 650 U.S. infantrymen": Hill, p. 23; Kendall, pp. 130–31.

189   "Gaining the summit": Hill, p. 23; J. Smith, *War with Mexico*, vol. 1, p. 243; Kendall, pp. 130–31.

189   "At the height of Worth's": Kendall, pp. 128–29.

189   "For the past hour, since": Zachary Taylor, report to Adjutant General Roger Jones, September 22, 1846, from www.dmwv.org/mexwar/documents/docs.htm#reports; Frost, pp. 259–64; Ballentine, p. 163; Chance, p. 42; Bauer, *Mexican War*, p. 105nn.

190   "The gunners in the Black": Chance, pp. 42–43; Dilworth, pp. xxii–xxiii, 69.

190   "Lieutenant Grant, the restless": Grant, pp. 52–53.

190   "The Americans ran into grapeshot": Chance, p. 43.

190–91 "Captain Electus Backus's": Smith and Judah, p. 81; Chance, p. 43.

191   "After the bloodied": Chance, p. 44; Dilworth, p. xxiii.

191   "Three hundred yards from": Chance, pp. 44–45.

191–92 "Expecting a reciprocal": Chance, pp. 81, 188nn.; Alcarez, p. 73.

192   "Astride his charger Tartar": Chance, pp. 45–47.

192   "American soldiers crouching": Smith and Judah, p. 90.

192–93 "Grant, rated as West": Grant, pp. 54–55; *Concise Dictionary of American Biography*, p. 368.

193   "Upon receiving Colonel Garland's": Chance, pp. 48–49; J. Smith, *War with Mexico*, vol. 1, pp. 254–55.

193   "Taylor's grimy, exhausted": Henry, pp. 233–34.

194   "At a shouted command": Chance, pp. 49–50.

194–95 "In the 3 A.M. darkness": Hill, pp. 24–25; Kendall, pp. 112–14, 132–34; J. Smith, *War with Mexico*, vol. 1, pp. 246–47.

195   "Worth's shock troops": Hill, pp. 24–25; J. Smith, *War with Mexico*, vol. 1, p. 247; Smith and Judah, p. 89.

195–96 "The Mississippi Rifles": Chance, p. 51.

196   ". . . Jefferson Davis led a patrol": Chance, pp. 51–53; J. Smith, *War with Mexico*, vol. 1, p. 255; Grant, p. 55; Zachary Taylor, report to Adjutant General Roger Jones, September 23, 1846, from www.dmwv.org/mexwar/documents/docs.htm#reports.

196   "Taylor's scratch force": Chance, p. 53.

196   "At times, Taylor got too" Henry, p. 207.

196–97 "Under a flag of truce": Chance, pp. 53–54; Zachary Taylor, report to Adjutant General Roger Jones, September 25, 1846, from www.dmwv.org/mexwar/documents/docs.htm#reports.

197   "Major John Munroe set up": Chance, p. 53; Hill, p. 26; Kendall, pp. 138–39.

197   ". . . General Worth led two columns": Doubleday, pp. 92–94; Kendall, pp. 136–38.

197–98 "Texas Rangers who had fought": Smith and Judah, p. 89; Doubleday, p. 95; Kendall, pp. 136–37.

198   "Taylor's withdrawal from": J. Smith, *War with Mexico*, vol. 1, pp. 257–58.

198   "Blue-uniformed American troops": L. Webster, p. 112.

198   "Ampudia offered to withdraw": Chance, p. 53; Hill, p. 26; Zachary Taylor, report to Adjutant

General Jones, September 25, 1846, from www.dmwv.org/mexwar/documents/docs. htm#reports.

199　　" 'As the president of' ": Taylor, pp. 61–62; Zachary Taylor, report to Adjutant General Jones, September 25, 1846, from www.dmwv.org/mexwar/documents/docs.htm#reports; J. Smith, *War with Mexico*, vol. 1, p. 259.

199　　"When his conduct of": Chance, pp. 91–92.

200　　"Perhaps Ampudia's tentativeness": Bauer, *Mexican War*, pp. 99–101; Doubleday, p. 99.

201　　" 'They went out sullenly' ": Chance, p. 57; Grant, pp. 55–56.

201　　"The Americans recognized": Henry, pp. 223–24.

201　　"Monterrey residents returned": Chance, pp. 58–59.

201　　"The Americans requisitioned:" Niles' National Register, Baltimore, Maryland, January 15, 1848, at www.dmwv.org/mexwar/mwstats.htm#casualties.

201–2　　"An American circus came": Henry, p. 254; Hill, pp. 27–28; Wilkins, pp. 104–9; F. Smith, p. 21.

202　　"On October 11": Polk, *Diary*, vol. 2, pp. 181–83; McCormac, p. 449; *Washington Union*, October 12, 1846; Taylor, p. 67.

202–3　　"Upon reconsideration, however": Polk, *Diary*, vol. 2, pp. 198–200.

CHAPTER 15: THE WAR IN THE WEST

204　　"Ordered in 1827 to build": *Funk & Wagnalls*, vol. 16, p. 28; Leavenworth Web site, at garrison.leavenworth.army.mil/sites/about/history.asp; Carruth, p. 308.

205　　"From the porch of": Frost, pp. 281–83; Bauer, *Mexican War*, pp. 129–30; *Concise Dictionary of American Biography*, p. 514.

205　　"Kearny was to capture": Smith and Judah [Senator Benton letter to Col. R. Campbell, governor's aide, May 14, 1846], p. 112.

205–6　　"Traders who traveled the": J. Smith, *War with Mexico*, vol. 1, pp. 287–88; Hughes, p. 19; Smith and Judah, pp. 122, 479; Dawson, p. 44; Turner, p. 65n.

206　　"Hoping to deprive": *Congressional Globe*, 29th Congress, 2nd Session, Appendix, pp. 13–14; Dawson, pp. 57–62.

206　　"On June 23, the eve": Hughes, p. 18.

206–7　　"On May 30, two weeks": *Congressional Globe*, 29th Congress, 2nd Session, Appendix, p. 44; Smith and Judah, p. 113; Polk, *Diary*, vol. 1, pp. 438, 443.

207　　"This third army would": Polk, *Diary*, vol. 1, p. 444.

207　　"Because no major trail": Hughes, pp. 22–27; Dawson, pp. 57–61.

208　　"Men wilted in the": Edwards, p. 25; Hughes, pp. 29, 38.

208　　"In southern Kansas": Hughes, p. 30; Edwards, p. 31.

208　　"As they followed": Edwards, p. 35.

208–9　　"Built in 1833 by": Ubbelhode, pp. 38–39; Dawson, p. 63; Hughes, p. 32.

209　　"Kearny's men captured three": Hughes, p. 32; Turner, p. 66.

209　　"On August 2, the Army": Hughes, pp. 34–35; Turner, pp. 66–70.

209　　"Near Las Vegas, New Mexico": Hughes, p. 39.

209　　"Kearny, however, had no": Turner, p. 71.

209–10　　"A new alarm swept": Smith and Judah, pp. 115–19.

210　　"On August 18, fifty-two": Bauer, *Mexican War*, p. 130; Smith and Judah, pp. 122–23.

210　　"Santa Fe's surprising": Caruso, pp. 95–102; Smith and Judah, p. 119. James Magoffin was later arrested while attempting to perform the same office in Chihuahua and was imprisoned until the end of the war. His genial captors, however, permitted him to entertain them, with the consequence that Magoffin, his captors, and their guests consumed 3,392 bottles of champagne by the end of the war. The U.S. government compensated Magoffin for $37,780.96 in expenses.

210   "In his proclamation": House Executive Document 60, p. 170; Hughes, p. 43; McCormac, pp. 460–62; Polk, *Diary,* vol. 2, p. 282.

211   "In three weeks, the efficient": Dawson, pp. 83–86; Smith and Judah, p. 128.

211   "They contemptuously nicknamed": Dawson, p. 78; J. Smith, *War with Mexico,* vol. 1, p. 296; Turner, p. 74.

211   "Learning that Mexican dragoons": Edwards, p. 62.

211   "For the most part": House Executive Document 60, pp. 174–75.

212   "Kearny split his command": Turner, pp. 74–75; Dawson, p. 79; Smith and Judah, p. 126.

212   "With a small wagon train": Turner, p. 75.

212   "The Mormons' large numbers": Morison, vol. 2, pp. 307–8; *Funk & Wagnalls,* vol. 18, pp. 79–80; Dawson, pp. 9–10; DeVoto, pp. 85–86; Krakauer, pp. 103, 108–9.

212   "In 1839, the Mormon prophet": Morison, vol. 2, pp. 307–8; *Funk & Wagnalls,* vol. 18, pp. 79–80; DeVoto, pp. 79–80.

213   "As more than ten-thousand": Polk, *Diary,* vol. 1, pp. 205–6.

213   "The Mormon emissary": Brigham Young–James Polk letter, August 9, 1846, Library of Congress, from James K. Polk Center, University of Tennessee.

213   "In late June, Army": Polk, *Diary,* vol. 1, p. 445; Byrnes, pp. 139–40; Ricketts, pp. 2–3.

213–14 "With Colonel Allen unable": Ricketts, pp. 46–52.

214   "The battalion entered Santa": Ibid., pp. 62–72.

214–15 "Weeks earlier, Kearny's dragoons": Benton, vol. 2, p. 717; Carson, p. 108; Turner, pp. 79–83.

215   "The dragoons passed": Turner, pp. 85–92.

215   " 'It is *labor, labor* from' ": Ibid., pp. 93, 116.

215   "When he learned of": Cooke, pp. 77, 92; Ricketts [Cooke report to Kearny], p. 117.

215   "As the Mormons' provisions": Ricketts, pp. 94, 104, 108; Cooke, pp. 103, 140–42.

216   "Since the only enemy": Cooke, pp. 105–6, 109, 149, 176, 184; Ricketts, pp. 101, 113–15.

216–17 "Kearny impetuously threw": Turner, pp. 144–47; Marti, p. 96; Bauer, *Mexican War,* p. 187; Cooke [Kearny official report], pp. 256–58; Gillespie, "Conquest," p. 349; J. Smith, *War with Mexico,* vol. 1, pp. 341–42; Watson, p. 256.

217   "The dragoons limped": Griffin, pp. 47–48.

217–18 "Pico had received fresh": Cooke, pp. 185–94; Ricketts, pp. 72, 86.

218–19 "The 317 members of": Ricketts, pp. 169, 185–86.

219   "When Stockton had taken": Gillespie, "Conquest," pp. 348–50; J. Smith, *War with Mexico,* vol. 1, pp. 338–40.

220–21 "A grim Colonel Sterling Price": Cooke [Col. Price report to Adjutant General], pp. 112–124; Smith and Judah, pp. 128–31.

221   "On the San Gabriel River's": Cooke, p. 272.

221   "Now, pausing only": Watson, p. 270; Griffin, p. 61; Cooke [Kearny report to Adjutant General], pp. 266–267; Smith and Judah, pp. 159–162.

221   "Gaining the northern riverbank": Griffin, p. 61; Cooke, p. 267; Watson, pp. 270–72; J. Smith, *War with Mexico,* vol. 1, p. 343.

221–22   "Kearny believed that his": McCormac, pp. 474–75; Cooke, pp. 273–74; Bauer, *Mexican War,* p. 192.

222   "Colonel Flores's force": Watson, p. 276; Smith and Judah, p. 162.

222   "Among the five Americans": Cooke, p. 267; Gillespie, "Conquest," pp. 349–50.

222–23   "But where was John Frémont": Frémont, *Expeditions,* vol. 2, pp. xxxiii–xxxvi; J. Smith, *War with Mexico,* vol. 1, p. 345.

223   "Without the authority": Pletcher, p. 437; Frémont, *Expeditions,* vol. 2, pp. xxxv–xxxvi; Cooke, p. 272.

223   "Stockton did not hold": Robert Stockton–James Polk letter, August 26, 1846, Library of Congress, from James K. Polk Center, University of Tennessee; Frémont, *Expeditions,* vol. 2, p. xxxvi; Bauer, *Mexican War,* pp. 194–95; Turner, pp. 155–56.

223   "The First New York Volunteers": Giffen, p. 17; Polk, *Diary,* vol. 1, pp. 473, 481; *Congressional Globe,* 29th Congress, 2nd Session, Appendix, pp. 14, 44.

224   "Colonel Jonathan D. Stevenson": Graebner, *Empire,* pp. 156–57; Giffen, pp. 8–17; McCaffrey, pp. 48–49.

224   "Arriving in California six": Marszalek, pp. 57–61.

224   "Stockton's self-proclaimed": *Congressional Globe,* 29th Congress, 2nd Session, Appendix, pp. 46–47.

224–25   "After meeting with Kearny": Frémont, *Expeditions,* vol. 2, pp. xxxviii–xxxix; Bauer, *Mexican War,* pp. 195–96.

225   "War Secretary William Marcy": Frémont, *Expeditions,* vol. 2, p. xxxix; DeVoto, pp. 421–444; McCormac, p. 475.

225   "On August 22, 1847": McCormac, p. 475; Frémont, *Expeditions,* vol. 2, pp. xxxix–xxxil, 375, 380–81; Benton, vol. 1, pp. 715–16; Bauer, *Mexican War,* p. 368.

225   " 'If the Administration has' ": *National Intelligencer,* August 14, 1847.

CHAPTER 16: AMERICA'S XENOPHON

226   "Pacifying New Mexico's Indian": Dawson, pp. 91, 96; Hughes, p. 75.

227   "The Missouri frontier lawyer": Hughes, p. 186.

227   "Alexander Doniphan was": Dawson, pp. 1–9, 30–32; Magoffin, pp. 121–23nn.; J. Smith, *War with Mexico,* vol. 1, p. 299.

227–28   "Doniphan's mounted volunteers": Dawson, pp. 36–37.

228   "Navajo scouts shadowed": J. Robinson, pp. 58–63; Hughes, p. 94.

228   "The Missourians traded": J. Robinson, pp. 55, 46–48, 58–63.

228   "A volunteer captain described": Dawson, pp. 96–97; J. Robinson, pp. 46–48.

228–29   "The Missourians found five hundred": Dawson, pp. 98–99; Hughes, pp. 95–102.

229   "In the vanguard": Dawson, pp. 79, 106.

229   ". . . Kearny had assigned three": Dawson, pp. 103–4, 109 [From Ruxton of the Rockies, pp. 168–70].

229–30   "The volunteers knew": Edwards, pp. 76–77.

230   "The volunteers awakened in": Hughes, pp. 131–34; Edwards, p. 82.

230   "Because the Missourians": Edwards [Report of First Lt. C. H. Kribben], p. 170.

230   "A mounted Mexican officer": Hughes, pp. 131–33; Dawson, pp. 111–113; McCaffrey, p. 158.

231   "Ponce de Leon's cavalry": Hughes, pp. 132–35; Dawson, p. 114; Ponce de Leon, pp. 386–89; Edwards, p. 85; J. Robinson, pp. 66–67.

231–32   "General John E. Wool's fourteen hundred": Ripley, vol. 1, p. 150; Weems, p. 209.

232   "Only Gaines, Scott": *Concise Dictionary of American Biography,* p. 1209; *Encyclopedia of the War of 1812,* pp. 62, 562.

232   "Now sixty-two years old": J. Smith, *War with Mexico,* vol. 1, p. 269; L. Wallace, p. 163.

232   "Captain Robert E. Lee": Thomas, p. 101; Buhoup, pp. 17–18.

232–33   "Wool marched to the": Buhoup, pp. 17–19, 48; Thomas, pp. 114–16.

233   " 'The suffering for want' ": Buhoup, p. 48; Engelmann, pp. 388–89.

233   "Wool enacted strict rules": J. Smith, *War with Mexico,* vol. 1, p. 269; Bauer, *Mexican War,* p. 149; Engelmann, p. 415.

233   "At San Rosa, 105 miles": Buhoup, pp. 56–57; J. Smith, *War with Mexico,* vol. 1, p. 273; Thomas, p. 116.

234   "After three weeks in": Buhoup, p. 94.

234   "In an urgent dispatch": Buhoup, p. 97; Thomas, pp. 118–19; Smith and Judah, pp. 93–94.

234   " 'They have marched farther' ": Engelmann, pp. 419–20; J. Smith, *War with Mexico,* vol. 1, p. 275.

234–35   "Dispatches from Santa Fe": Edwards, pp. 99, 102; Dawson, pp. 131–32, 136.

235   "The Chihuahua Trail was": Dawson, pp. 133–38; J. Robinson, pp. 71–72.

235   "Winds sandblasted the": Hughes, pp. 149–50; J. Robinson, p. 73; Dawson, pp.138–40.

236   "Hundreds of Chihuahua's": Hughes, pp. 151–52, 158–60 [Col. Doniphan battle report]; Dawson, p. 144; Edwards, p. 119.

236–37   "A Mexican chaplain": Dawson, p. 145; Edwards, p. 111; Hughes, p. 160 [Col. Doniphan battle report].

237   ". . . Doniphan had commandeered": Dawson, pp. 147–48; Hughes, p. 159; *Encyclopedia of the Mexican-American War,* p. 239.

237–38   "Too late, General Garcia Conde": Edwards, pp. 112, 120; Dawson, pp. 154–55.

238   "The Mexican gunners overshot": Dawson, p. 149; Smith and Judah, p. 138.

238   "The Missourians overran": Smith and Judah, p. 138; Dawson, p. 155.

238   "Mexican lancers attacked": Dawson, p. 151; Smith and Judah, p. 138.

238   "An enemy battery": Dawson, p. 156; Hughes, p. 160; Edwards, p. 117.

238–39   "The traders' unofficial leader": Dawson, pp. 151, 157; Hughes, p. 160 [Col. Doniphan battle report].

239   "The Missourians captured": Edwards, pp. 117–18; Hughes, p. 160 [Col. Doniphan battle report].

239   "On March 2, the Army": Hughes, p. 158; Dawson, p. 163; Edwards, pp. 95–96.

239   "Initially hospitable, the Chihuahuans": Magoffin, pp. 228–29; Edwards, pp. 134–35.

240   "Doniphan banged his fist": Edwards, p. 165.

240   "They 'looked as though' ": Ibid., p. 99; J. Smith, *War with Mexico,* vol. 1, p. 313.

240   "Their exploits had been extolled": Buhoup, p. 140; Edwards, p. 99; Hughes, p. 186; Dawson, pp. 159–60.

240–41   "With mules and cattle": J. Robinson, p. 90.

241   "Near Parras, Doniphan learned": Dawson, pp. 176–78; Hughes, pp. 179–80; Smith and Judah, pp. 139–41; Richmond, pp. 140–41.

241   "New Orleans's residents": Smith and Judah, p. 31 [Nelson McClanahan–John McClanahan letter, June 19, 1847]; Dawson, p. 188.

241   "At St. Louis's grand celebration": Dawson, pp. 190–91; Hughes, pp. 186–95.

241–42   "Addressing a crowd": Dawson, pp. 191, 196–97; Hughes, p. 186.

CHAPTER 17: PLANNING A SECOND FRONT

243–44   "Before Britain and America": Sellers, *Continentalist,* pp. 310, 445–48, 487; Byrnes, pp. 104–5; Polk, *Diary,* vol. 2, pp. 26–28, 53, 63, 95.

244–45   "Polk seemingly took": Kunhardt, p. 416; Polk, *Diary,* vol. I, pp. 213, 237, 483; vol. 2, pp. 20, 106, 111, 130–31, 162–63, 216, 278–81, 328, 374; Bergeron, pp. 222–25.

245   "On September 9, the president": Polk, *Diary,* vol. 2, p. 124; Byrnes, p. 194; Philbrick, pp. 333–34.

245–46   "Because of his ill-considered": Polk, *Diary,* vol. 1, p. 418; vol. 2, pp. 16, 119, 211, 227–41.

246   "On October 17, Polk": Polk *Diary,* vol. 2, pp. 195–96; Haynes, pp. 167–71.

246   "Marcy informed Scott": Polk, *Diary,* vol. 2, pp. 198–200.

246–47   "While Scott's opinion": Ibid., p. 205.

247   "Polk's full cabinet was": Ibid., vol. 1, pp. 390–93; vol. 2, pp. 151, 222–24, 227–31, 275–76, 293; Pletcher, pp. 474–75; McCormac, pp. 470–71.

248   "During cabinet meetings": Polk, *Diary,* vol. 2, pp. 236, 300–301; Scott, *Memoirs,* vol. 2, pp. 381–83.

248   "It pained Polk": Polk, *Diary,* vol. 2, pp. 241–42.

248   "If there ever was": Ibid., p. 244.

248–49   "Taylor complained to": Ibid., p. 249.

249   "When a rumor reached him": Taylor, p. 148.

249   "The general was neither": Ibid., pp. 108–9.

249   "In November, Commodore": *Encyclopedia of the Mexican-American War,* p. 266; Bauer, *Mexican War,* p. 118; *Washington Union,* January 6, 1847 [Ann Chase letter]; Johannsen, p. 138.

250   "On December 14, Taylor": Lavender, p. 146; Chance, pp. 69–77; J. Smith, *War with Mexico,* vol. 1, pp. 360–62; Maury, p. 31.

251   "When Taylor did not": Taylor, pp. 179–82.

251   "To his son-in-law": Taylor, pp. 80, 85; Chance, p. 77; Bauer, *Taylor,* pp. 218–19.

251–52   "Taylor suspected something": *Encyclopedia of the Mexican-American War,* p. 235; Chance, pp. 76–77.

252   "At Villa Gran, he marched": Chance, p. 77.

252   ". . . 'the view of breaking me' ": Taylor, p. 89.

252   "He wrote to Scott": House Executive Document 60, pp. 1100–1102; Polk, *Diary,* vol. 2, pp. 353–59, 366; Lavender, p. 158.

253   "A New Orleans newspaper": Byrnes, pp. 185–86.

253   " 'A grosser abuse of' ": Scott, *Memoirs,* vol. 2, p. 400.

253   "A few weeks later": Singletary, p. 121.

253   "Polk, who at times": Polk, *Diary,* vol. 2, pp. 384–87; Singletary, p. 121; *Congressional Globe,* 30th Congress, 1st Session, Appendix, pp. 163–64.

253–54   "Scott now despised Polk": Price, p. 88; Scott, *Memoirs,* vol. 2, p. 380.

254   "He proudly declared": Polk, *Diary,* vol. 2, p. 236.

254   "Growing dissatisfaction with": Schroeder, p. 57; DeVoto, p. 87; Whitney, pp. 132, 516–517.

254–55   "Polk intended to recommend": Polk, *Diary,* vol. 2, pp. 259–60; J. Smith, *War with Mexico,* vol. 1, pp. 348–49.

255   "The Mexican Congress": Santoni, pp. 160–62.

255–56   "Polk devoted fully two-thirds": J. Richardson, vol. 4, pp. 471–98.

256   "Embedded in the message": Ibid.

256   "Polk's earlier proposal": Ibid.

256–57   "Finally, the president": Ibid., pp. 491–92.

257   "Whig congressmen boycotted": *Congressional Globe,* 29th Congress, 2nd Session, Appendix, p. 226.

257   "Above all, the Whigs": Merk, "Dissent," p. 56; *Washington Union,* December 17, 1846; *National Intelligencer,* December 9, 12, 1846.

CHAPTER 18: DISSENT, PATRIOTISM, AND THE PRESS

258   "Henry David Thoreau": *Norton Anthology of American Literature,* vol. 1, p. 1526.

258   " 'When a sixth of the' ": Thoreau, pp. 792, 798.

258–59   "Except for his Aunt Maria": Thoreau, pp. 772, 793; *Norton Anthology,* vol. 1, p. 1527; DeVoto, p. 213.

259   "The scholarly, deeply": Whitney, p. 56.

260   " 'No election or appointment' ": Adams, *Memoirs,* vol. 8, p. 247; Whitney, p. 61; Kunhardt, p. 171; *Encyclopedia of American History,* p. 184.

260   "Charles Francis Adams": Merk, "Dissent," pp. 48–49.

260   "The Massachusetts Legislature" Bauer, *Mexican War,* pp. 364–65.

260   "The New England Anti-Slavery": New York *Daily Tribune,* June 1, 1846; Schroeder, pp. 36–37; Pletcher, p. 458.

260–61   "Other Transcendentalists besides": Holman, p. 450; Schroeder, p. 116; *Reader's Encyclopedia,* p. 412.

261   "Theodore Parker, the minister": DeVoto, pp. 209–10; Schroeder, pp. 117–18.

261   "As American casualties": Schroeder, p. 118; Bergeron, p. 90; Garrison, pp. 34–36, 121.

261–62   "In 'Yorktown,' Whittier": Whittier, vol. 3, pp. 130–31.

262   "James Russell Lowell's satire": Lowell, pp. 52, 63, 106.

262   "The octogenarian Albert": Gallatin, pp. 467, 470, 491; Schroeder, p. 144; Johannsen, pp. 294–95.

262–63   "For all that, 'Polk's' ": J. Smith, *War with Mexico,* vol. 1, p. 124 [from New York Journal of Commerce].

263   "When Polk asserted" Ibid., p. 194.

263   " *Tanner's Traveling Map*": Johannsen, pp. 11, 114–18, 126.

263–64   "The fanciful poetic work": Ibid., p. 300.

264   "In the Brooklyn *Daily Eagle*": Schroeder, p. 33; Whitman, *Gathering,* pp. 190, 197.

264   " *'Matchless with horse'* ": Whitman, *Complete Poetry,* p. 53 [From "Song of Myself"].

264   " 'The question of extending' ": *Washington Union,* January 1, 1847.

264–65   "Even *The Harbinger*": Sellers, *Continentalist,* p. 420; DeVoto, p. 10; Schroeder, pp. 108–9.

265   "Because they were closest": Roth, pp. 103–17; Johannsen, pp. 116–19; Kendall, p. 12.

265–66   "The best known of them": Johannsen, pp. 16–19; Kendall, pp. 8–10, 15.

266   "Besides carrying the": New York *Daily Tribune,* November 1846; February, March 1847.

266–67   " 'We shall invade her' ": Pletcher, pp. 456–57; *United States Magazine* (1846), vol. 20, no. 104, pp. 100–101; New York *Daily Tribune,* May 13, December 26, and October 17, 1846; Schroeder, pp. 54–55; Johannsen, pp. 50–51; Whitman, *Gathering,* p. 122 [October 8, 1846].

267   "The *Union's* great rival": *National Intelligencer,* May 16, 1846; Pletcher, pp. 456–57; New York *Daily Tribune,* May 13, 1846; Schroeder, p. 54.

267   "Even as he marched": Hitchcock, pp. 212–14; Grant, pp. 22-23, 37, 45; Meade, vol. 1, p. 152.

268   "The professional officers": Winders, *Mr. Polk's Army,* pp. 57–59; *Concise Dictionary of American Biography,* p. 224.

268   "Taylor's unhappiness with": Taylor, pp. 28, 49, 75, 117–18.

268   "The pragmatic engineer": Thomas, p. 137.

269   "On February 6, Congress": *Congressional Globe,* 29th Congress, 2nd Session, p. 34.

CHAPTER 19: BUENA VISTA

271–72   "Arrayed in a long line": Chamberlain, pp. 111–12.

272   "For weeks, Taylor's headquarters": Lavender, pp. 166–67.

272–73   "In the remote event": Taylor, pp. 182–83.

273   "General Winfield Scott had": J. Smith, *War with Mexico,* vol. 1, p. 266; Chance, p. 78; Lavender, p. 160; Polk, *Diary,* vol. 2, p. xx.

273   "Taylor initially sent": Taylor, p. 86.

273–74   "While returning one day": Lavender, pp. 148–50; Chamberlain, p. 82.

274   "A new camp was": Lavender, pp. 150–51, 155; Taylor, p. 88.

274–75   "Thirty-five miles south": *Encyclopedia of the Mexican-American War,* pp. 159–60; Engelmann, pp. 432–34; Lavender, pp. 155–57; Chamberlain, pp. 94–97.

275   "In retribution for": Buhoup, pp. 106–12; Chamberlain, pp. 87–88; *Encyclopedia of the Mexican-American War,* p. 69.

275   "If the Mexicans offered": Taylor, pp. 83–84.

276–77   "When his 'desponding' ": New York *Daily Tribune,* March 15, 1847; Lavender, p. 163.

277   "The feverish preparations": J. Smith, *War with Mexico,* vol. 1, p. 380; Scheina, p. 54; Lavender, pp. 164–165.

277   "In addition to the infantry": Lavender, pp. 164–65; Callcott, p. 250; Eisenhower, p. 176.

277–78   "Thus, he was delighted": Wilkins, pp. 124–31, 135; Chamberlain, pp. 106–10; I. Smith, *Reminiscences,* p. 46.

278   "General Wool sought Taylor's": Chamberlain, pp. 110–11; Taylor report to War Secretary William Marcy, from www.dmwv.org/mexwar/documents/docs.htm#reports.

278–79   "As a goad to his": Lavender, p. 176; Calcott, p. 252.

279   " 'The whole country' ": Chamberlain, p. 115; Johannsen, pp. 61–62.

279–80   "At 11 A.M., Surgeon": Bauer, *Mexican War,* p. 210; Eisenhower, pp. 186–87; House Executive Document 60, p. 98.

280   "Mexican troops lunged": Lavender, pp. 184–86; J. Smith, *War with Mexico,* vol. 1, pp. 385–86.

281   "Amid reports that": Taylor report to Marcy, from www.dmwv.org/mexwar/documents/docs.htm#reports.

281   "Taylor did not know": Chance, pp. 82–83.

281–82   "Santa Anna's army": Chamberlain, pp. 118–19; Lavender, p. 188.

282   "General Santiago Blanco's": Chance, pp. 90–91; Lavender, p. 190; Chamberlain, p. 119.

282   "General Francisco Pacheco's": Chance, pp. 91–92; Engelmann, pp. 357–452.

283   "Then, in the span": Lavender, pp. 191–92; Chamberlain, p. 121; Johannsen, p. 65.

283   "Their ignominious flight": Chamberlain, pp. 121–22.

283–84   ". . . Colonel William McKee's Second": Chance, pp. 91–92; Smith and Judah, p. 8.

284   "While Pacheco was attacking": Chance, pp. 92–93; Eisenhower, p. 188.

284   "It was only 9 A.M.": Chance, pp. 92–93.

284   "At this moment of extreme": Eisenhower, p. 188; Lavender, p. 194.

284–85   "Taylor sent Colonel Davis's": Chance, pp. 95–96; Chamberlain, pp. 126–27; Taylor report to Marcy, from www.dmwv.org/mexwar/documents/docs.htm#reports; Lavender, p. 204.

285   "Their crimson shirts, white": Chamberlain, p. 122; Chance, pp. 27–28, 94–95; Lavender, p. 146.

285–86   "The new arrivals included": *Encyclopedia of the Mexican-American War,* p. 55; Scribner, pp. 65–66; Eisenhower, p. 189; Chance, pp. 94–95, 98–99; Chamberlain, p. 121; Lavender, pp. 199–204.

287   "Taylor irately ordered": Taylor report to Marcy; Henry, p. 319; Lavender, p. 206.

287–88   "Refugees excitedly told Miñón": Lavender, pp. 196–97.

288   "The First and Second Illinois": Taylor report to Marcy, from www.dmwv.org/mexwar/documents/docs.htm#reports; Lavender, pp. 207–8.

288   "Mexican troops lined": I. Wallace, p. 48.

288   "But in hand-to-hand": Chance, pp. 100–1; Chamberlain, p. 128; Henry, p. 323.

288–89   "In a race to stop": Chance, p. 107; Lavender, pp. 210–11; J. Davis, vol. 3, p. 123n. (For the next five years, Davis "suffered intensely," and he experienced occasional flare-ups of pain even forty years later.)

289   "Lancers sealed the west": I. Wallace, pp. 48–49; Buhoup, p. 126; Chance, p. 101.

289   "After lashing their tired": Haecker, p. 81; Chance, p. 210; Owen, p. 15.

289   "Just when it seemed": Chance, pp. 101–2.

289   "Santa Anna's army withdrew": Lavender, pp. 210–11; Stevens, p. 197.

290   "The exhausted Americans": Chance, pp. 104–6 [Braxton Bragg–William T. Sherman letter, March 1, 1848]; J. Smith, *War with Mexico,* vol. 1, p. 396.

291   "That night, Taylor and": Taylor report to Marcy, from www.dmwv.org/mexwar/documents/docs.htm#reports; Chance, pp. 106–7.

291   "Loud cheering erupted": I. Wallace, p. 40; *Encyclopedia of the Mexican-American War,* p. 56; Eisenhower, p. 191; Chance, p. 108; Lavender, p. 213; J. Smith, *War with Mexico,* vol. 1, p. 396.

291   "About thirteen thousand": Callcott, p. 252; Bauer, *Mexican War,* p. 217; Chance, p. 110.

292   "As the Americans prowled": Chance, pp. 108–9.

292   "Scattered everywhere, like the detritus": L. Wallace, p. 164; Scribner, pp. 65–70.

292   "Scouts reported that Santa": Chance, p. 110; Taylor report to Marcy, from www.dmwv.org/mexwar/documents/docs.htm#reports.

292–93   "When he reached Agua": J. Smith, *War with Mexico,* vol. 1, p. 398; *Diplomatic Correspondence,* vol. 8, pp. 899–900; Alcarez, p. 137.

293   "General Jose Urrea's cavalry": Chance, p. 122; Lavender, pp. 214–15.

293   "As the losses mounted": Chance, pp. 122–24; Chamberlain, p. 176.

293   "By June, the Americans": Bauer, *Mexican War,* pp. 219–20; Chance, pp. 122–24.

293–94   "While Santa Anna was": Taylor report to Marcy, from www.dmwv.org/mexwar/documents/docs.htm#reports.

294   "Zachary Taylor's name was": Johannsen, pp. 114–18.

294   "Taylor, he complained": Polk, *Diary,* vol. 2, pp. 433, 451–52; Bergeron, p. 233.

294–95   "While conceding that the": Scott, *Memoirs,* pp. 412–13.

295   "Polk refused, unconvincingly": Polk, *Diary,* vol. 2, p. 462.

295   "Taylor complained to": Taylor, pp. 97, 94–95, 182.

CHAPTER 20: THE WAR IN CONGRESS

296–97   "Hoping to stop the Wilmot": Polk, *Diary,* vol. 2, pp. 289–91, 305; *Congressional Globe,* 29th Congress, 2nd Session, p. 303.

297   " 'The movement of Mr.' ": Polk, *Diary,* vol. 2, pp. 305–6.

298   "A Democrat splinter led": Merk, "Dissent," pp. 41–42; Schroeder, pp. 5–6, 53, 65–67.

299   "Representative Garrett Davis": New York *Daily Tribune,* December 10, 1846; Polk, *Diary,* vol. 2, pp. 281, 296–97.

299   "Then, the House asked": Polk, *Diary,* vol. 2, pp. 362–63.

299   "While his family attended": Ibid., pp. 275, 293, 316–17.

299–300   "Polk's war bills languished": Ibid., pp. 275, 291.

300   "Moreover, congressional politics": Ibid., vol. 2, pp. 314, 316–17, 320, 329–30, 378; vol. 3, p. 419.

300   "Beginning on February 4": *Congressional Globe,* 29th Congress, 2nd Session, pp. 337, 344.

300   " 'The treasury and blood' ": Ibid., pp. 354–55.

300–301   "Launching a frontal assault": Ibid., p. 355.

301   "If that were true": Ibid., pp. 360, 365.

301   "Maryland Congressman William Giles": Ibid., Appendix, p. 360.

301   "Prohibiting slavery in the": *Congressional Globe,* 29th Congress, 2nd Session, pp. 351–54, 420; www.politicalgraveyard.com.

301–2   "In the Senate, Calhoun": Polk, *Diary,* vol. 2, p. 283; *Congressional Globe,* 29th Congress, 2nd Session, p. 454.

302   "Calhoun declared that": *Congressional Globe,* 29th Congress, 2nd Session, pp. 358, 554.

302   "The nearly thirty major": Register of Debates, vol. XII, part IV, pp. 4041–47; Going, p. 183; Brands, *Lone Star,* pp. 484–85; *Encyclopedia of American History,* pp. 179–80.

302–3   " 'You are rushing headlong' ": *Congressional Globe,* 29th Congress, 2nd Session, Appendix, p. 229; Schroeder, p. 124.

303   "Amid the hot words": Pletcher, pp. 460–61.

303   "Polk's congressional allies": *Congressional Globe,* 29th Congress, 2nd Session, pp. 360, 372.

303   "While careful to avouch": Ibid., pp. 397–98.

303   "Whig Congressman Luther": Ibid., Appendix, pp. 382–83.

303–4   " 'America wants no friends' ": Price, p. 93.

304   " 'The worst state of' ": *Congressional Globe,* 29th Congress, 2nd Session, p. 417.

304   "The House crossed a": Polk, *Diary,* vol. 2, p. 347; *Washington Union,* February 3, 1847; Schroeder, pp. 86–87, 125.

304   "Representative William Giles": *Congressional Globe,* 29th Congress, 2nd Session, pp. 386-87, 418.

304–5   "If America did not expand": Ibid., p. 367.

305   "But Ohio Senator Thomas": Ibid., Appendix, pp. 214–17.

305   " 'If Santa Anna, Ampudia' ": *Congressional Globe,* 29th Congress, 2nd Session, p. 392; *Washington Union,* February 9, 1847.

305   "Senators indignantly banished": *Washington Union,* February 10, 1847; Polk, *Diary,* vol. 2, p. 378.

305–6   " 'The proud bird' ": *Congressional Globe,* 29th Congress, 2nd Session, pp. 369, 390.

306   " 'If we do not get peace' ": Ibid., pp. 356–58.

306   "Whigs and dissident": Polk, *Diary,* vol. 2, p. 416.

306   "After dragging its feet": Ibid., vol. 2, pp. 372–373, 382–83.

306   "After the House added": *Congressional Globe,* 29th Congress, 2nd Session, pp. 329, 555–56, 573; Goings, p. 183; *Encyclopedia of American History,* p. 202.

306–7   ". . . a Democrat litmus test": Goings, pp. 232–33, 238–39; Polk, *Diary,* vol. 2, pp. 457–58.

307   " 'The articles in the' ": Polk, *Diary,* vol. 2, pp. 479–80.

307   "Calhoun became the nexus": Ibid., pp. 459, 470–471, 479–480.

307–8   "Santa Anna's emissary": Ibid., pp. 325–26, 331, 336–37.

308   "Mexico's response arrived": *Diplomatic Correspondence,* vol. 8, p. 896; Polk, *Diary,* vol. 2, p. 432.

CHAPTER 21: SCOTT'S EPIC MARCH BEGINS

309   "General Juan Morales's swift": Moore, pp. 11–12; Semmes, *Campaign,* p. 19; Carlinsky, pp. 27–30. Raphael Semmes one day would command the Confederate raider *Alabama,* which would seize or destroy sixty-four merchant ships and capture two thousand prisoners before being sunk by the USS *Kearsarge* in June 1864 off Cherbourg, France.

310   "Lieutenant George McClellan": Semmes, *Campaign,* p. 19; McClellan, p. 67; Moore, pp. 11–12, 14.

310   "The previous day, Commodore": Smith and Judah, p. 190; Semmes, *Service,* p. 128; *Encyclopedia of the War of 1812,* pp. 412–13; *Concise Dictionary of American Biography,* pp. 194, 777.

310   "Perry's 'mosquito fleet' ": Semmes, Service, pp. 130–31.

311   "Scott needed the Navy's": T. Johnson, p. 177.

311   " 'No duties could have' ": Semmes, *Service,* p. 76.

311   "The Mexican Navy's few": Ibid.; *Diplomatic Correspondence,* vol. 8, p. 704; Bauer, *Mexican War,* pp. 106–20.

311–12   "Lieutenant Ulysses S. Grant": Grant, p. 58; McCaffrey, p. 171.

312   " 'I am much crippled' ": Executive Document 8, p. 216–20.

312   "Before the siege began": Semmes, *Service,* pp. 107–8, 129; Executive Document 8, pp. 220–24.

312–13   ". . . Scott had polled": Scott, *Memoirs,* pp. 423–24.

313   "George Ballentine, an enlisted": Ballentine, pp. 153–54.

313   "When the northerly abated": Hitchcock, pp. 239–40; G. Smith, pp. 19–20; Scott, *Memoirs,* pp. 421–26.

313   "But their marksmanship": Hitchcock, p. 244.

313   "Lieutenant Pierre G.T. Beauregard": Ibid., p. 243.

313–14   "The dense chaparral": McCaffrey, p. 50; Maury, p. 34; Ballentine, pp. 157–61.

314   "The Guardsmen, known as": *Diplomatic Correspondence,* vol. 8, p. 899.

314–15   "After compelling Farias's": Santoni, pp. 185, 192–94; Pletcher, p. 490.

315   "But 'heavy metal' was": Semmes, *Campaign,* pp. 132–35.

315   " 'I shall never forget' ": Ibid., p. 138; Zeh, p. 20; McClellan, p. 69; Alcarez, pp. 182–88.

315   "The crashing American": T. Johnson, p. 57; Ballentine, p. 155.

316   "George Kendall of the": Kendall, p. 177; Semmes, *Campaign,* p. 138; Executive Document 8, p. 243.

316   "Mexican gunners hit": Executive Document 8, p. 242; Moore, p. 14; Semmes, *Campaign,* p. 135; Ballentine, p. 155.

316   "Inside Vera Cruz": Mexican Soldier, p. 78; Alcarez, pp. 182–88.

316   "There was a brief lull": Semmes, *Campaign,* p. 135; Alcarez, p. 188; Peck, pp. 74–75.

316–17   "At 8 A.M. on March 26": Moore, p. 16; Semmes, *Campaign,* p. 145; Peck, p. 75.

317   "Two U.S. commissioners": G. Smith, p. xvi; Semmes, *Campaign,* p. 141.

317   "The day dawned clear": McClellan, p. 73; Zeh, p. 20; Bauer, *Mexican War,* p. 252; Kendall, p. 197.

317   "The Army and Navy batteries": Smith and Judah, 194; McWhinney, pp. 120–21; Hitchcock, p. 248; Kendall, pp. 185–87.

317–18   "As Scott had hoped": Scott, *Memoirs,* p. 426; Zeh, p. 12; Bauer, *Mexican War,* p. 252; Alcarez, p. 194.

318   "On April 10, President": Polk, *Diary,* vol. 2, pp. 465, 468.

318   "Polk and the cabinet": Ibid., pp. 421, 431–39.

318–19   "Adopting a proposal": Ibid., pp. 416, 420, 422; Pletcher, p. 499.

319   "Washingtonians gathered": Johannsen, pp. 92–96, 106.

319   "The 'Little Cabinet' ": Hitchcock, p. 256; Scott, *Memoirs,* vol. 2, p. 423; Executive Document 8, p. 243.

319–20   " 'The contrast between the' ": Grant, pp. 66–67.

320   ". . . 'Old Fuss and Feathers' ": Johannsen, p. 75; Bauer, *Mexican War,* p. 73.

320–21   "Scott's experiences during the": *Encyclopedia of the War of 1812,* pp. 437–38.

321   "Never forgetting his sense": T. Johnson, pp. 27, 29–30, 44–46.

321   "At Chippewa Plain": Ibid., pp. 61–65; Eggenburger, p. 98.

321   "Nineteen days after Chippewa": T. Johnson, pp. 56–60.

321   ". . . Scott was selected to write": Ibid., pp. 74–77.

322   "In 1836, President Andrew": Ibid., pp. 112–19.

322   "Scott began his pacification": Pletcher, p. 495; Kendall, p. 193.

322–23   "In the wake of the Polkos' ": Santoni, pp. 194–96, 201–2; Callcott, pp. 258–59; McCaffrey, p. 171; McClellan, p. 82n.

323   "On April 11, General David": Smith and Judah, p. 203; Executive Document 8, p. 263.

323–24   "Captain Robert E. Lee": Freeman, vol. 1, pp. 238–41; Thomas, p. 126; Beauregard, pp. 12–13; Vandiver, p. 28; Executive Document 8, p. 263.

324   "Santa Anna's engineers": Callcott, p. 259.

324–25   "Throughout April 15 and 16": Ballentine, pp. 177–82; Hitchcock, p. 252; Callcott, p. 259.

325   "Lee led Twiggs' ": Pletcher, pp. 496–97; McClellan, pp. 74–75.

325   " 'The labor of merely climbing' ": Hitchcock, p. 252.

325   "The enemy fired down": Ballentine, p. 183; Thomas, p. 126; Executive Document 8, p. 262.

326   "The three American 24-pounders": Executive Document 8, p. 281.

326   "Lieutenant Dabney Maury": Maury, p. 36; *Concise Dictionary of American Biography,* p. 653.

326   "Harney's shock troops": Ballentine, p. 191.

327   "Shields's brigade, commanded": Frost, pp. 323–28.

327   "He was supposed to launch": Executive Document 8, pp. 258–59, 296; McClellan, pp. 81–85; I. Stevens, p. 55.

327–28   "The mangled Mexican army": Kendall, p. 215; Anderson, p. 36.

328   ". . . Captain Lee was stunned": Freeman, vol. 1, p. 245; Thomas, pp. 127–28.

328   "At a dressing station, Kendall": Kendall, p. 260.

328–29   "Wounds to the head, chest": Winders, *Mr. Polk's Army,* pp. 160–63; Haecker, p. 90; Executive Document 8, p. 263; Callcott, p. 259; Smith and Judah, pp. 349–50 [from Vera Cruz *American Eagle*]; Record Group 45, National Archives [Navy Secretary John Mason–James

Polk letter, October 27, 1846], via James K. Polk Center, University of Tennessee; McClellan, pp. 91–92.

329   "Santa Anna escaped into": Kendall, pp. 212–15; Bauer, *Mexican War,* p. 268; Owen, p. 53; Ballentine, p. 197.

329   "Santa Anna's dispirited army": Hitchcock, p. 255; McCaffrey, p. 173.

329   ". . . *El Monitor Republicano,* was": Kendall, pp. 219–20, 224.

329–30   "Twenty-five miles west of": Semmes, *Campaign,* p. 110.

330   "But General Pedro de Ampudia and": Hitchcock, p. 255; Executive Document 8, pp. 300–301; Kirkham, p. 12; Ballentine, pp. 224, 233.

330   "More fortunate than Worth's": Ballentine, pp. 204–7; Callcott, p. 3.

330   "Named for the medicinal": Smith and Judah, pp. 218, 487; Hitchcock, p. 253.

330–31   "In scrupulously following": Kendall, p. 195.

331   "Many volunteers flatly refused": Ballentine, pp. 212–13; Kirkham, p. 10.

331   "At Puebla, the aptly": Smith and Judah, pp. 226–27 [General William Worth report].

331–32   "On May 15, Worth's division": Ballentine, pp. 220–21; Kirkham, p. 19; Moore, pp. 96–98; Pletcher, p. 298; Callcott, pp. 261–62.

CHAPTER 22: PLANNING THE END GAME

333   "Lieutenant John Peck was": Peck, pp. 87–89, 98.

333   "Travelers were waylaid": Kendall, p. 237.

334   "Scott unleashed the Texas": Ballentine, p. 224; Wilkins, pp. 155, 160; Kendall, pp. 316–18.

334   "Another major problem": Bauer, *Mexican War,* p. 270; Smith and Judah, p. 222 [advertiser quote]; House Executive Document 60, p. 993; Kendall, pp. 412–13; McCaffrey, pp. 174–76; Polk, *Diary,* vol. 2, pp. 475–76.

334–35   "While the Texas Rangers": Miller, pp. 151–54.

335   "The unsatisfactory logistical": Miller, p. 119.

335   "The hero of Waterloo": P. Stevens, p. 224.

335–36   "The bandits' unremitting outrages": Hitchcock, pp. 263–64, 334–35; Smith and Judah, p. 232; Bauer, *Mexican War,* 391n.

336   "The Commissary and Quartermaster": T. Johnson, p. 195; Semmes, *Campaign,* p. 166.

336   "Built on a wooded hillside": Miller, p. 120; Ballentine, p. 231; Hitchcock, p. 257.

336–37   " 'It is certainly the most' ": Kirkham, pp. 22–23, 32–34, 38; Kendall, pp. 260-61, 275, 286; Winders, *Mr. Polk's Army,* p. 177; P. Stevens, pp. 221–22; Ballentine, p. 216.

337   "The first, written in May": Johannsen, p. 298; Hitchcock, pp. 256, 261–62.

337–38   "The American diplomat": Polk, *Diary,* vol. 2, pp. 466–67.

338   "Indeed, Trist at least": *Concise Dictionary of American Biography,* p. 1055; K. Johnson, pp. 180–81; Polk, *Correspondence,* vol. 8, pp. 418–19; Pletcher, p. 501.

338–39   "Three days after appointing": Carruth, p. 306; Polk, *Diary,* vol. 2, pp. 472–75.

339   "The instructions clearly": Polk, *Diary,* vol. 2, p. 466; *Diplomatic Correspondence,* vol. 8, pp. 201–7.

339–40   " 'I have not been more vexed' ": Polk, *Diary,* vol. 2, pp. 482–84.

340   "Polk and Buchanan also": Ibid., vol. 2, p. 476; vol. 3, p. 22; *Diplomatic Correspondence,* vol. 8, pp. 195–99; Caruso, pp. 138–44; Merk, *Monroe Doctrine,* p. 245.

340–41   "It was paradoxical": Polk, *Diary,* vol. 2, p. 476.

341–42   "Scott's angry note to Trist": *Diplomatic Correspondence,* vol. 8, pp. 902–5nn.

342   "Both men wrote accusatory": Ibid., pp. 912–13; McCormac, p. 503.

343   "Attuned to this danger": McCormac, p. 504; *Diplomatic Correspondence,* vol. 8, pp. 208, 210–12; *Washington Union,* July 22, 1847.

343   "Trist had fallen ill": McCormac, p. 509 [Gen. Scott–Gen. Smith letter, July 6, 1847, and Trist–Secretary of State Buchanan letter, July 7, 1847].

344   "But the budding peace": *Diplomatic Correspondence,* vol. 8, p. 911; Santoni, p. 203; *El Diario Oficial del Gobierno,* October 27, 1846.

344–45   "British intermediaries informed": McCormac, pp. 510–11 [Trist–Gen. Scott letter, July 16, 1847, and Scott–Trist letter, July 17]; Hitchcock, pp. 267–68.

345   "His government drafted": Callcott, pp. 264–66.

345   "Trist sent $10,000": Ibid., p. 261; Pletcher, p. 510; McCormac, p. 512.

345   " 'We are growing somewhat' ": Semmes, *Campaign,* pp. 165–66, 190.

CHAPTER 23: CLOSING IN ON THE PRIZE

347   " 'We seemed to be' ": Semmes, *Campaign,* p. 213; Prescott, pp. 503–5.

347–48   "From August 7 to 10": Semmes, *Campaign,* pp. 208–9; Kendall, p. 392; Hitchcock, p. 271.

348   "Strangely, Santa Anna": Semmes, *Campaign,* pp. 212–13.

348   "Nestled in the Cordillera": Ibid., p. 216.

348   "As in Cortes's day": Francaviglia, p. 7; Bauer, *Mexican War,* p. 287; Hitchcock, pp. 272–73; Ballentine, p. 237.

348–49   "Mexico City's foundries": Alcarez, pp. 239–42; Ramirez, p. 151.

349–50   "The 'trap' alluded to": Hitchcock, p. 273; Semmes, *Campaign,* p. 236; *Diplomatic Correspondence,* vol. 8, p. 920; Smith and Judah, pp. 236–37.

350   "General William Worth, who": Kendall, pp. 302–3.

350–51   "Worth's reconnaissance force": Semmes, *Campaign,* pp. 238–40, 258–64; Hitchcock, pp. 275–76.

351   "To meet this new threat": Gen. Scott report to War Secretary William Marcy, August 28, 1847, from Descendants of Mexican War Veterans Web site, at www.dmwv.org.

351–52   "Scott had two options": Semmes, *Campaign,* p. 265; Moore, p. 129.

352   "A second scouting party": Alcaraz, p. 269.

352   "The astute Lieutenant Semmes": Semmes, *Campaign,* p. 267.

352–53   "Traveling on foot, Lee": Moore, p. 130; Hill, p. 111.

353–54   "After Lee returned": Freeman, vol. 1, pp. 258–66; Thomas, pp. 130–33; Vandiver, p. 35.

354–55   "Days earlier, Santa Anna": Semmes, *Campaign,* pp. 272–74; Alcaraz, pp. 262, 278–79.

355   "At 3 A.M., Smith's soldiers": Semmes, *Campaign,* pp. 275–76; *Mexican Soldier,* p. 78; Hill, p. 113.

355–56   "In a mere seventeen minutes": Hitchcock, pp. 277–78; Eggenberger, p. 104; Scott report to War Secretary Marcy, August 28, 1847, from www.dmwv.org; Smith and Judah, p. 242; McCaffrey, pp. 186–87.

356   "General Valencia vanished": Alcarez, p. 281.

356   "Scott's army paused": Semmes, *Campaign,* pp. 280–83.

356–57   "The Mexican engineers": Ibid., pp. 283–84; Kendall, p. 331.

357   "Scott's six thousand men": G. Smith, p. 50; Kendall, pp. 331–32.

357–58   "Twiggs led Smith's brigade": Semmes, *Campaign,* pp. 288–89; Peck, pp. 114–15; Alcarez, pp. 282–83; Scott report to War Secretary Marcy, August 28, 1847, from www.dmwv.org; Kendall, p. 350; P. Stevens, pp. 239–42.

358   "As Worth's dense column": Alcarez, pp. 282–83; Smith and Judah, p. 246.

358   "At bayonet-point, Worth's": Semmes, *Campaign*, p. 289.

359   "His fleeing troops jammed": Scott report to War Secretary Marcy, August 28, 1847, from www.dmwv.org.

359   "Scott had won, although": Ibid.; Hitchcock, p. 479.

359   "Among the prisoners were": P. Stevens, pp. 239–42; Kendall, p. 350; Semmes, *Campaign*, p. 293.

359   "An American battle surgeon": *National Intelligencer*, November 1, 1847.

359   "After burying the dead": Semmes, *Campaign*, pp. 296–97.

360   " 'Mr. Trist . . . as well as' ": Scott report to War Secretary Marcy, August 28, 1847, from www.dmwv.org; Hitchcock, p. 284.

360   "Before Scott could send": Santoni, pp. 211–13; *National Intelligencer*, September 11, 1847 [*Diario* report, translated].

360–61 "Despair had gripped": Hitchcock, p. 286; Ramirez, pp. 152–53; *National Intelligencer*, September 11, 1847.

361   "Generals John Quitman": Hitchcock, pp. 285–87; Kendall, pp. 248, 341, 345.

361   "A packet of forty-five": Hitchcock, pp. 285–86.

CHAPTER 24: THE HALLS OF MONTEZUMA

362   "Yet, the Mexican commissioners": Alcarez, pp. 307–9; Pletcher, pp. 515–19.

362–63 "In presenting the U.S.": Callcott, p. 268.

363   "On August 27, American": Kendall, pp. 356, 358; Hitchcock, pp. 287–90.

363–64 "In Tacubaya, a pleasant": Semmes, *Campaign*, p. 315; Hitchcock, pp. 285, 287, 290; Waugh, p. 116.

364   "When they marched into": Kirkham, p. 52; *Encyclopedia of the Mexican-American War*, p. 290.

364–65 "Trist's imprudent assurance": *Diplomatic Correspondence*, vol. 8, pp. 933–34; Alcarez, pp. 319–24.

365   "Santa Anna's regrets and": Semmes, *Campaign*, pp. 303–4.

365   "On September 6, Scott": Moore, p. 152; *Diplomatic Correspondence*, vol. 8, pp. 933–34.

365–66 1042 "Santa Anna's 'explanation' ": Moore, pp. 152–54.

366   "Scott and Trist decided": *Diplomatic Correspondence*, vol. 8, p. 945; Hitchcock, pp. 292–93.

366   "At the foot of Chapultepec": Semmes, *Campaign*, pp. 319, 323.

366–67 "But Worth opposed": Alcarez, pp. 335–44; General Scott report to War Secretary William Marcy, September 11, 1847, from Descendants of Mexican War Veterans Web site at www.dmwv.org; Semmes, *Campaign*, pp. 324–27; Waugh, p. 118; Kendall, p. 374n.; *Encyclopedia of the Mexican War*, p. 109.

367–68 "H. Judge Moore": Moore, p. 160.

368   "Captain Simon Drum's battery": Scott report to War Secretary Marcy, September 11, 1847, from www.dmwv.org; Semmes, *Campaign*, pp. 327–30.

368   "There was no cannon": T. Johnson, p. 203; *Encyclopedia of the Mexican-American War*, pp. 109–10; Hitchcock, pp. 297–98; Moore, p. 160.

368–69 "As Worth's exhausted men": Kirkham, pp. 59–60; Semmes, *Campaign*, pp. 331–32.

369   "Jose Fernando Ramirez": Ramirez, pp. 153–55.

369   " 'When prosperous, he is' ": Hitchcock, pp. 299–300; Beauregard, p. 68.

369–70 "However, Lieutenant Pierre G. T.": Beauregard, pp. 68–72; Williams, p. 29.

370–71   "A prolonged artillery barrage": Scott report to War Secretary Marcy, September 18, 1847, from www.dmwv.org.

371   "Once again, Captain Lee's": Ibid.; Hill, p. 125.

371   "From morning until nightfall": Hill, p. 125; Alcarez, p. 358; Hitchcock, pp. 301–2.

371   "Captains Samuel McKenzie": Peck, pp. 127–29; Hill, p. 126.

372   "About a thousand troops": *Encyclopedia of the Mexican-American War,* pp. 74–75.

372–73   "At 8 A.M., Huger's batteries": Ballentine, pp. 260–62; Moore, p. 170; Alcarez, pp. 362–63; T. Johnson, p. 204; Semmes, *Campaign,* pp. 340–43; Frost, p. 328; Hill, p. 126; Peck, p. 130; *Encyclopedia of the Mexican-American War,* pp. 76, 201; Benjamin and Marquez, p. 99. The six Mexican cadets' remains were disinterred from the base of Chapultepec exactly one hundred years later, during the same year, 1947, that President Harry Truman memorably paid his respects during a state visit. Reburied in a nearby stone monument at the Colegia Militar, the teenagers are honored each evening during the retreat ceremony.

373–74   "The Marine Corps on this": Millett, pp. 76–77.

374   "After Twiggs's death": Moskin, p. 66; Hitchcock, p. 303; Scott report to War Secretary Marcy, September 18, 1847, from www.dmwv.org.

374–75   "On a hill near": P. Stevens, pp. 267–68; Hitchcock, p. 298; *National Intelligencer,* September 20, 1847; *Encyclopedia of the Mexican-American War,* p. 247.

375   "General Bravo Rueda": Alcarez, p. 364.

375–76   "Behind Chapultepec, on the road": M. Jackson, *Memoirs,* pp. 42–44; Vandiver, pp. 34–39; Metcalf, pp. 132–33.

376   "The battle shifted to": Scott report to War Secretary Marcy, September 18, 1847, from www.dmwv.org; Moore, p. 177.

376–77   "With the Palmetto Regiment": Moskin, p. 67; Scott report to War Secretary Marcy, September 18, 1847, from www.dmwv.org.

377   "Beneath the San Cosme": Grant, p. 155; Moskin, pp. 66–67; Metcalf, pp. 132–33.

377   "Observing that a nearby church": Grant, pp. 157–58.

377–78   "When Worth's division caught": Ibid., p. 158.

378   "At the gate, Worth's troops": Waugh, p. 123; Kirkham, p. 62.

378   "With Grant's gun and": Grant, p. 158; Waugh, p. 122; G. Smith, pp. 56–57.

378   "By sunset, San Cosme": Thomas, pp. 135–36; Scott report to War Secretary Marcy, September 18, 1847, from www.dmwv.org.

378   "Quitman's division had won": Alcarez, pp. 369–70; Semmes, *Campaign,* pp. 350–51.

378   "As midnight approached": Kendall, pp. 382–83.

379   "Inside the Citadel": Alcarez, pp. 372–73, 384; Scott report to War Secretary Marcy, September 18, 1847, from www.dmwv.org.

379   "Just after 1 A.M.": Scott report to War Secretary Marcy, September 18, 1847, from www.dmwv.org.

379   "Colonel William Harney": Hitchcock, pp. 304–6; Semmes, *Campaign,* pp. 351–52 [Gen. William Worth report]; Millett, p. 80; Moskin, pp. 67, 87.

380   " 'History will no doubt' ": Hill, p. 130; McCaffrey, p. 192.

380   " 'The infamous and eternally' ": Ramirez, p. 161.

380   "The first gunshot": Semmes, *Campaign,* pp. 352–53.

380   "Many Mexican National Guard": Scott report to War Secretary Marcy, September 18, 1847, from www.dmwv.org; Peck, p. 134.

380–81   "The Americans were met by": Scott report to Marcy, September 18, 1847, from www.dmwv.org; Peck, p. 134; Alcarez, p. 376; Hitchcock, pp. 304–6.

381–82   "But when the U.S. casualty list": Semmes, *Campaign,* pp. 353–54; Hill, pp. 128–29; Alcarez, p. 377; Hitchcock, pp. 304–6.

382   "Named governor of": Hill, p. 129.

CHAPTER 25: FRUSTRATION

382–83   "President Polk had labored": Cutler, "New England Tour," pp. 10, 29.

383–84   "His burdens had increased": Polk, *Diary,* vol. 3, pp. 180–81; Bauer, *Mexican War,* p. 367.

383   "On September 15, the day": Polk, *Diary,* vol. 3, p. 172.

383   "When Trist's report": *Diplomatic Correspondence,* vol. 8, pp. 215–16.

383–84   "He lingered near Puebla": Pletcher, p. 532.

384   " 'The government will find' ": Semmes, *Campaign,* pp. 357–58; Scott report to War Secretary Marcy, September 18, 1847, from Descendants of Mexican War Veterans Web site, at www.dmwv.com.

384   "The government-in-exile": Pletcher, p. 541; Santoni, pp. 220–22; Graebner, *Empire,* pp. 205–6.

384   "For Mexico, the preeminent": Pletcher, p. 517.

385   "Polk angrily instructed Buchanan": Polk, *Diary,* vol. 3, pp. 196–97.

385   " 'Considering the enterprising' ": *Diplomatic Correspondence,* vol. 8, pp. 217–18.

385–86   "Scott had left Colonel": *Encyclopedia of the Mexican-American War,* p. 222.

386   "Informed of Child's dire": Smith and Judah, pp. 269–70; Wilkins, pp. 115–18, 164; *Concise Dictionary of American Biography,* p. 191. After the Rio Grande battles, Sam Walker had used his considerable influence in Washington to help Samuel Colt, who had lost his six-shooter patent, to get his patent back and to obtain a contract with the U.S. government to manufacture one thousand .44-caliber six-shooters for $25 each. Known as the "Colt Patent Arm 1847," but later called the "Walker Colt," the revolver even today is considered a superior pistol.

386–87   "Surprised by the Americans' ": Wilkins, pp. 164–65; Smith and Judah, pp. 270–71; *Mexican War and Its Heroes,* p. 194.

387   "On October 2, Mexico City": Kirkham, p. 70; Kendall, pp. 400, 420; Hitchcock, pp. 307–308.

387   "Nearly overnight, there appeared": Kendall, p. 393; Johannsen, pp. 172–73.

388   "While many soldiers": Winders, *Mr. Polk's Army,* pp. 168–69; Johannsen, pp. 161–64; Kirkham, pp. 104–6.

388   "The soldiers patronized theatrical": Peck, p. 142.

388   "A ballet troupe": Kendall, pp. 409–10; Johannsen, p. 164.

388   "Standing in the receiving line": Vandiver, p. 40.

388–89   " 'The army, multiplied' ": Waugh, p. 128; Winders, *Mr. Polk's Army,* pp. 54–55; Johannsen, p. 43; Hitchcock, pp. 310–11;Thomas, p. 115; Beauregard, p. 56.

389   "Better known as the Aztec": *Encyclopedia of the Mexican-American War,* p. 30; Aztec Club Web site, at www.aztecclub.com.

389   " 'What is the use' ": Peck, p. 79.

389   "General Scott undoubtedly was": T. Johnson, pp. 209–10; Scott, *Memoirs,* vol. 2, pp. 581–82.

389–90   "During the occupation's first": Scott, *Memoirs,* vol. 2, p. 582; Ballentine, p. 269; T. Johnson, p. 218; Armed Forces Retirement Home background at www.petworthdc.net/petworth_ history_resources/soldiers_home_dcnorth.htm.

390   "Zachary Taylor complained": Bauer, *Mexican War,* p. 221; Taylor, p. 114; Winders, *Mr. Polk's Army,* pp. 136–38, 159–60; McCaffrey, p. 106; Ballentine, p. 282.

390   "One of the worst outbreaks": P. Stevens, pp. 143–44; McCaffrey, p. 72; New York *Daily Tribune,* January 28, 1847; Zeh, pp. xviii–xix; *Encyclopedia of American History,* p. 187; Tennery, pp. 18–20.

390–91   "But politics and discipline": Winders, "Will the Regiment Stand It?" pp. 68–78; Smith and Judah, pp. 425–31.

391   "In Mexico City, gangs": Kendall, pp. 396, 406–7.

391–92   "The bushwhackings were": Oates, p. xx; Webb, pp. 120–21; Wilkins, pp. 177–78.

392   "In the backcountry again": Callcott, p. 272.

393   "In February 1848": Wilkins, pp. 173–74, 181; Callcott, pp. 273–74; *Encyclopedia of the Mexican-American War,* p. 254.

393   "Secretary of State Buchanan's": McCormac, pp. 523–24; *Diplomatic Correspondence,* vol. 8, pp. 981–84.

393   "He had wound up his": Pletcher, p. 538.

393–94   " 'This determination, I came' ": McCormac, pp. 524–25.

394   "This conviction informed the": *Diplomatic Correspondence,* vol. 8, pp. 985–1019; McCormac, pp. 525–26.

394–95   "In it, for the first": *Congressional Globe,* 30th Congress, 1st Session, Appendix, pp. 1–8.

395   "Since Scott's capture of": Pletcher, p. 551; Leonard, p. 179; Schroeder, pp. 127–30; Merk, "Dissent," pp. 51–52; *National Intelligencer,* October 16, 1847.

CHAPTER 26: PEACE AT LAST

396   "Christmas Day had found him": Polk, *Diary,* vol. 3, pp. 258, 272–73.

397   "The controversy would have": Scott, *Memoirs,* vol. 2, pp. 415–17; Winders, *Mr. Polk's Army,* p. 188; Hitchcock, pp. 309, 312.

397   "When Pillow joined Scott's": Polk–Gideon Pillow letter, September 22, 1846, Library of Congress, from James K. Polk Project, University of Tennessee.

397–98   "And then, a week before": Polk–Pillow letter, December 19, 1847, Library of Congress, from James K. Polk Project; Polk, *Diary,* vol. 3, p. 251; *Diplomatic Correspondence,* vol. 8, pp. 218–19.

398   "Pillow had risen to high" Kendall, p. 427; Taylor, pp. 112–13.

398–99   "Conversely, officers respected": Singletary, pp. 134–36; Meade, p. 88.

399   "The objectionable letters": Semmes, *Campaign,* pp. 239–40, 244, 246; Graebner, *Empire,* p. 211; T. Johnson, pp. 198–99.

399–400   "Pillow later admitted": Pillow–Polk letter, December 12, 1847, Library of Congress, from James K. Polk Project; T. Johnson, pp. 210–11; Hitchcock, p. 319; Semmes, *Campaign,* pp. 251–52.

400   " 'His [Scott's] hostility' ": Pillow–Polk letter, November 24, 1847, Library of Congress, from James K. Polk Project.

400–401   " 'This whole difficulty' ": Polk, *Diary,* vol. 3, pp. 266–67, 271; Semmes, *Campaign,* p. 255.

401   "Polk and his advisers": Polk, *Diary,* vol. 3, pp. 278–83, 294–95.

401   "The Marine Corps": Millett, p. 80.

402   "Polk angrily concluded": Polk, *Diary,* vol. 3, p. 283.

402   "The president read with": Ibid., p. 320; Polk letter to Major William Polk, January 13, 1848, Library of Congress, from James K. Polk Project.

402   " 'I have never in my life' ": Polk, *Diary,* vol. 3, pp. 300–301.

402–3 "Three days before Christmas": Ibid., p. 276; Lincoln, Speeches, pp. 158–59, 168; *Congressional Globe,* 30th Congress, 1st Session, p. 64.

403 "On January 5, 1848, the House": Polk, *Diary,* vol. 3, pp. 287–88.

403 "Polk and his advisers decided": Ibid., pp. 290–92.

403 "The Polk administration quickly": Schroeder, pp. 153–54; Polk, *Diary,* vol. 3, p. 322.

403–4 "The Washington *Union*": Union article quoted in *National Intelligencer,* August 23, 1847.

404 "Alarmed by the internal": Polk, *Diary,* vol. 3, pp. 319–21.

404 "The Whig-majority House": McCormac, pp. 29–30; Siegenthaler, pp. 144–46; Lincoln, *Speeches,* pp. 168–71, 176; Goodwin, p. 122.

404 "At an antiwar rally": Kendall, p. 310; Clay, vol. 6, pp. 361–75.

405 "At noon on November 2": Frémont, *Expeditions,* vol. 2, pp. xl–xlii.

406 "Frémont did his cause no": Egan, pp. 443–61; Chaffin, pp. 375–81.

406 "He devoted up to twenty": Polk, *Diary,* vol. 3, pp. 336–38.

406 "But Frémont bitterly": Egan, pp. 462–63; Polk, *Diary,* vol. 3, pp. 336–38.

407 "While Trist had stopped": Pletcher, p. 545.

407 "Mexico demanded $30 million": McCormac, p. 537.

407 "On January 31, over": Ibid.; *Encyclopedia of the Mexican War,* p. 128.

407–8 "At 6 P.M. on February 2": Pletcher, pp. 546–49; Merk, *Monroe Doctrine,* p. 188.

408 "Trist sent the treaty": *Diplomatic Correspondence,* vol. 8, p. 1059.

408 " 'Had my course' ": Vazquez, "Causes," pp. 60–61 [from Trist papers, Southern Historical Collection, University of North Carolina, No. 2104].

408 "Freanor delivered it on": Polk, *Diary,* vol. 3, p. 345.

408–9 "In his journal entries": Ibid., pp. 348–50.

409 "The president sent the treaty": Ibid., p. 351.

409 "In December 1845, Navy": Ibid., vol. 1, pp. 128–30.

409 "But when one of Adams's": Ibid., vol. 2, pp. 493–94.

410 "In his eighty-first year": Ibid., vol. 3, pp. 350–52.

410 "The Senate Committee of": McCormac, p. 545; Graebner, *Empire,* pp. 191–92; Pletcher, pp. 562–63; Bailey, p. 263; *Concise Dictionary of American Biography,* p. 449.

410–11 "General Sterling Price had": Bauer, Mexican War, pp. 158–59; Encyclopedia of the Mexican-American War, p. 219; www.history.navy.mil; www.civilwarfamilyhistory.com.

411 "Polk selected Senator Ambrose": Pletcher, p. 563; Bauer, *Mexican War,* p. 387.

411 "On June 12, the United": *Diplomatic Correspondence,* vol. 8, p. 1088.

411–12 "With the same Masonic": Byrnes, pp. 221–22, Johannsen, pp. 3–5; Polk, *Diary,* vol. 4, p. 2.

412 "Late in the afternoon": McCormac, p. 552; Johannsen, pp. 5–6; Polk, *Diary,* vol. 4, p. 2.

412 "In his message announcing": Richardson, *Messages of the Presidents,* vol. 4, pp. 587–93.

CHAPTER 27: AFTERWORD

413 "A Court of Inquiry convened": Polk, *Diary,* vol. 3, p. 427.

413–14 "Alternately depressed and angry": Hitchcock, pp. 319–22, 328; Hill, p. 171.

414 "Butler dutifully expelled": McCormac, pp. 544–45.

414 "The Court of Inquiry concluded": Hitchcock, p. 319; Bauer, *Mexican War,* p. 374.

414–15 "On a warm day": Smith and Judah, pp. 452–53; *Encyclopedia of the Mexican-American War,* p. 91.

415   "Henry David Thoreau": Thoreau, p. 789 [from "Civil Disobedience"]; *Norton Anthology,* vol. 1, pp. 1547, 1509, 1738; Oxford Dictionary of Quotations, p. 365.

416   "In dollars and centers": Waugh, pp. 128–29; Bauer, *Mexican War,* p. 397; McCaffrey, p. 204; Winders, pp. 139–40, 147.

416   "Mexican battles losses have": *Encyclopedia of the Mexican-American War,* p. 68.

416–17   "Stephen Foster composed": Johannsen, pp. 142–43, 188, 205–6, 270, 232.

417–18   "It was no accident": Singletary, p. 3; Roth, pp. 121–22.

418   "A week before Trist": *Encyclopedia of American History,* p. 207.

418   "In the early 1850s": Ibid., p. 216.

418   "The editor John O'Sullivan": Polk *Diary,* vol. 3, pp. 476–77, 493; Merk, *Monroe Doctrine,* pp. 247–63.

419   "Then the Yucatan": Merk, *Monroe Doctrine,* pp. 207–28.

419   "As much to deny": *Encyclopedia of American History,* p. 203; Byrnes, pp. 153–54.

419   "Northern 'Conscience Whigs' ": Whitney, p. 102; Polk, *Diary,* vol. 1, pp. 104–5, 105n.; *Encyclopedia of American History,* p. 192; Schroeder, pp. 131–35, 164; Bauer, *Taylor,* pp. 215–16; Boyer, pp. 292–93; Bergeron, p. 254.

419–20   "But Democrats would recover": Johannsen, p. 309; Seigenthaler, pp. 109–10.

420   "On March 1, the president": Polk, *Diary,* vol. 4, pp. 358–59; Bumgarner, p. 101; Bauer, *Taylor,* p. 243.

420   "The dinner was a personal": Taylor, p. 118; Byrnes, p. 204.

420   " 'Gen'l Taylor is, I have no' ": Byrnes, p. 204; Polk, *Diary,* vol. 4, p. 376.

420   "Indeed, Taylor, who": Taylor, pp. 167, 134–35; Sellers, *Continentalist,* p. 325.

421   "After laboring in the": Byrnes, pp. 105–6; Polk, *Diary,* vol. 4, pp. 363–71.

421–22   "He and Sarah embarked on": Haynes, pp. 205–7; Polk, *Diary,* vol. 4, pp. 434–40.

422   "On Independence Day 1850": Taylor, pp. 134–35, 167; Bauer, *Taylor,* pp. 314–16.

422   "Unresolved issues led to": Boyer, p. 297; Bailey, p. 265; Francaviglia, pp. 14–15.

422–23   "But Trist paid a steep": Byrnes, p. 209; Merk, *Monroe Doctrine,* p. 189, Bailey p. 265.

423   " 'Those who served' ": Benton, vol. 2, p. 711.

423   "Nominated in 1856 as": Egan, pp. 462–63; *Concise Dictionary of American Biography,* pp. 324–25.

423–24   "In 1861, the seventy-five-year-old": Thomas, p. 140; Rister, p. 6; Morison, vol. 2, pp. 427–29; T. Johnson, pp. 229–33.

EPILOGUE

425   "Mexican historians generally": Rejon, p. 93; Benjamin and Marquez, p. 100; Vazquez, "Causes," pp. 42, 55.

425–26   " 'The moral shock has' ": Eisenhower, frontispiece; C. Robinson, pp. xx–xxii; Haynes, p. 194; Semmes, *Campaign,* pp. 363–64; Santoni, pp. 232–35.

426   "In 1853, clergymen": Callcott, pp. 277, 284–314; *Encyclopedia of World History,* p. 831.

427   "Texas President Anson": Jones, p. 52.

428   "In rating his predecessors": Seigenthaler, p. 103.

429   "Without question, the Mexican": Haynes, p. 199.

429   "Indeed, only expedients": Morison, vol. 2, pp. 336–38, 356–58; Boyer, p. 417; *Encyclopedia of American History,* p. 217.

429   "Ulysses S. Grant wrote": Grant, pp. 23-24, 96, 108.

INDEX

ACKNOWLEDGMENTS

I wish to thank Dr. Wayne Cutler of the James K. Polk Project at the University of Tennessee, who placed his center's resources at my disposal and shared his expertise about the Antebellum Era and James Polk. Not only was Dr. Cutler generous with his insights, he was a convivial host during my trips to Knoxville.

The Special Collections staff at the University of Texas at Arlington Library assisted me in my research when I was in Texas and supplied illustrations for this book.

The staff of the Library of Virginia in Richmond helped me find my way around the LOV's collection of Antebellum Era newspapers.

This book would not have been possible without my two "home" libraries: D. H. Hill Library at North Carolina State University in Raleigh, and Davis Library at the University of North Carolina in Chapel Hill.

Finally, I am grateful to my wife Pat for being a sounding board and ad hoc editor.

ABOUT THE AUTHOR

Joseph Wheelan, a former Associated Press reporter and editor, is the author of *Jefferson's War: America's First War on Terror, 1801–1805*, and *Jefferson's Vendetta: The Pursuit of Aaron Burr and the Judiciary*, both available from Carroll & Graf Publishers. He lives in North Carolina.